THE PROCESS OF PARENTING

THE PROCESS
OF PARENTING

SIXTH EDITION

Jane B. Brooks

Boston   Burr Ridge, IL   Dubuque, IA   Madison, WI   New York   San Francisco   St. Louis
Bangkok   Bogotá   Caracas   Kuala Lumpur   Lisbon   London   Madrid   Mexico City
Milan   Montreal   New Delhi   Santiago   Seoul   Singapore   Sydney   Taipei   Toronto

The *McGraw·Hill* Companies

Higher Education

To my grandparents and parents, and my children and their children

THE PROCESS OF PARENTING, SIXTH EDITION
Published by McGraw-Hill, a business unit of The McGraw-Hill Companies, Inc., 1221 Avenue of the Americas, New York, NY 10020. Copyright © 2004 by The McGraw-Hill Companies, Inc. All rights reserved. Previous editions © 1999, 1996, 1991, 1987, 1981 by Mayfield Publishing Company. No part of this publication may be reproduced or distributed in any form or by any means, or stored in a database or retrieval system, without the prior written consent of The McGraw-Hill Companies, Inc., including, but not limited to, any network or other electronic storage or transmission, or broadcast for distance learning.

Some ancillaries, including electronic and print components, may not be available to customers outside the United States.

1 2 3 4 5 6 7 8 9 0 DOC/DOC 0 9 8 7 6 5 4 3

Editor-in-chief: *Thalia Dorwick*
Sponsoring editor: *Jane Karpacz*
Development editor: *Cara Harvey*
Marketing manager: *Pamela Cooper*
Production services manager: *Jennifer Mills*
Production service: *Greg Hubit Bookworks*
Manuscript editor: *Molly Roth*
Art director: *Jeanne M. Schreiber*
Design manager: *Jean Mailander*
Cover designer: *Lisa Buckley*
Interior designer: *Michael Warrell*
Art manager: *Robin Mouat*
Photo researcher: *Terri Wright*
Illustrator: *Lotus Art*
Production supervisor: *Tandra Jorgensen*

The text was set in 10.5/12 Berkeley by TBH Typecast, Inc., and printed on acid-free, 45# New Era Matte by RR Donnelley, Crawfordsville.

Cover images: left, © Tony Freeman/PhotoEdit; center, © Myrleen Ferguson/PhotoEdit; right © Michael Newman/PhotoEdit

The credits for this book begin on page C-1, a continuation of the copyright page.

Library of Congress Cataloging-in-Publication Data

Brooks, Jane B.
    The process of parenting / Jane B. — 6th ed.
        p.   cm.
    Includes bibliographical references and index.
    ISBN 0-07-282669-X
    1. Parenting—United States. I. Title.
HQ755.8.B75 2003
649'.1—cd21   2003051202

www.mhhe.com

BRIEF CONTENTS

CONTENTS

CHAPTER **2**
Theories of Development and Strategies of Parenting 35

CHAPTER **3**

Cultural Influences on Parenting 67

PART TWO
Parenting at Developmental Stages

CHAPTER 7

Parenting Infants: The Years from Birth to Two 193

CHAPTER **8**

Parenting in Early Childhood: The Years from Two to Five 223

CHAPTER **9**
Parenting Elementary School Children 255

CHAPTER **10**

Parenting Early Adolescents 292

CHAPTER 11

Parenting Late Adolescents 323

CHAPTER **12**

Parenting Adults 354

PART THREE
Parenting in Varying Life Circumstances

CHAPTER 13
Parenting and Working 381

CHAPTER **14**

Parenting in Diverse Family Structures 409

CHAPTER **15**

Parenting in Times of Trauma 444

PREFACE

"For most adult humans, parenthood is still the ultimate source of the sense of meaning. For most adults, the question 'What does life mean?' is automatically answered once they have children; better yet it is no longer asked," writes the psychologist David Gutmann after testing and interviewing men and women about the impact of parenthood on their lives.[1]

Do people receive training to succeed in this important activity? No! Anyone who drives a car or cuts hair for pay must have a license or demonstrate a certain level of skill before being permitted to engage in these activities independently. But nowhere does society require systematic parenting education, which may matter most of all.

This book attempts to fill this educational gap. As with the earlier editions, the sixth edition of *The Process of Parenting* shows how parents and caregivers can translate their love and concern for children into effective parenting skills. The book strives to bring to life the child's world and concerns, so parents can better understand what their children may be thinking and feeling. The book also describes the myriad thoughts and feelings—positive and negative—that parents have so that they can better understand themselves. Finally, the book highlights the influence of the social context on both parents and children.

APPROACH OF *THE PROCESS OF PARENTING*

I have selected topics and written this book from the points of view of a parent, a clinician, a researcher, and a teacher of parenting skills. I have the firm conviction that anyone who wants to invest attention and effort in becoming a competent, caring parent can do so in his or her own way. The single prerequisite is the desire to succeed along with the willingness to invest time and energy, and the results are well worth the effort. My experience as a clinician has shown me that children face many difficult situations; with a loving, supportive caregiver, children can live life fully and happily even if temporarily engulfed by trauma.

Children are not the only ones enriched by adults' efforts to be effective parents. Helping children grow is an intense and exciting experience that brings special rewards to us as parents. Our physical stamina, agility, and speed increase as we care for infants and toddlers. Our emotional stamina grows as we deal with our own intense feelings toward our children and help children learn to express and modulate their feelings. Our intellectual skills grow as we answer young children's questions and, later, help them learn school subjects. In helping children grow, we gain for ourselves an inner vitality and richness that affects all our relationships.

ORGANIZATION

Organizing and writing the sixth edition has proven exciting and challenging. The aim has been to update and condense the material of the fifth edition and to add three new chapters, one completely new and two that expand on topics in the fifth edition. Let me describe the overall organization, noting the changes as they appear.

Like the fifth edition, the sixth edition has three parts. Part I—General Concepts, Goals, and Strategies of Parenting—includes Chapters 1–5. As in the past, Chapter 1 describes the roles and interactions of the three participants in the process of parenting—the child, the parent, and the social system—and the ways social forces shape parenting. Chapter 2, a new chapter, describes theories and strategies of parenting. This chapter presents an overall theoretical framework of systems theories and includes, along with the new additions, material that appeared in several different chapters in previous editions.

Although it incorporates selected material from the fifth edition, Chapter 3 is also largely new. Focusing on the cultural influences on parenting, it includes cultural models of parenting strategies and presents the values and distinctive influences of six major ethnic groups—Native Americans, European Americans, African Americans, Latinos, Asian Americans, and Middle Eastern Americans. The experiences of specific ethnic groups continue to appear throughout the text as they relate to the topic of discussion. For example, ethnic identity formation and prejudice are discussed in the chapters dealing with identity formation. Chapter 3 also looks at the influences of social status and of economic hardship on parenting.

Chapters 4 and 5 each detail one of the two basic tasks of parenting: (1) creating close emotional relationships and (2) shaping and modifying children's behavior.

Part II—Parenting at Developmental Stages—begins with Chapter 6 on how parents make the transition to parenthood. This chapter focuses on how the methods and timing of becoming parents influence the process of parenting. Beginning with Chapter 7, Part II describes how general concepts and basic strategies are applied to children at six different stages of development: infancy (the years from birth to two), early childhood (the years from two to five), elementary school years, early adolescence, late adolescence, and adulthood.

Chapters 7–11 deal with children from birth through the high school years. Each chapter presents updated information on children's physical, intellectual, and personal-social development during the five age periods, emphasizing ways parents can promote positive behaviors. This edition continues to pay particular attention to understanding and promoting children's emotional regulation, especially the regulation of anger and sadness.

Chapter 12, a new chapter, describes the tasks of parenting children from age eighteen onward. The main sections deal with parenting children in the transition to adulthood, parenting independent adult children, parenting dependent adult children, parenting children who move back and forth between independence and dependence, parenting dependent adults, and, finally, parenting one's own parent. Strategies used with children of younger ages are applied when appropriate.

Part III—Parenting in Varying Life Circumstances—describes how parents adapt parenting strategies to meet the challenges of everyday life—parenting and working

(Chapter 13), parenting in diverse family structures (Chapter 14), and parenting in times of trauma (Chapter 15). Chapters 13 and 14 emphasize understanding the nature of the circumstances and challenges involved in each situation and discuss how to promote effective functioning in parents and children—in combining working and parenting and in less traditional family structures, respectively. In Chapter 15, we look at different forms of trauma for children, including abuse, community violence, and the current threat of terrorism. We discuss ways to minimize the threat of trauma, ways to cope with it when it occurs, and how parents help children feel safe in a world that is sometimes unsafe.

PROBLEM SOLVING

A portion of each of the chapters in Part II deals with common problems children experience and parents must handle. Because each child is a unique individual, parents require a variety of strategies and techniques for handling problems, depending on the child and the circumstances. A problem-solving approach is presented that consists of defining the problem specifically, getting the child's point of view, making certain the problem is the child's and not the parent's, maintaining positive interactions and good times with children, considering possible actions, taking action, evaluating the results, and starting again, if necessary.

THE JOYS OF PARENTING

In addition to describing what parents do, the book describes how parents feel as they raise children. Stages of parenthood are identified, and interviews with parents provide information about what parents wish they had known about parenting before they started. The book also emphasizes the joys that parents experience. In 1948, Arthur Jersild and his colleagues at Columbia University observed that most research on parenting was focused on the problems parents experience and little attention was given to "the cheerful side of the ledger." Because this is still true today, I try in this text to redress the imbalance.

INTEGRATED COVERAGE OF PARENTING CHILDREN WITH SPECIAL NEEDS AND SUPPORTS FOR PARENTS

In previous editions of *The Process of Parenting,* the final two chapters have dealt with parenting children with special needs and supports for parents. In the sixth edition, this material has been moved into earlier chapters to present a more complete picture of parenting children at specific ages. For example, the discussion of adoption has been moved to the chapter on the transition to parenthood, and the discussion of depression has been moved to the chapter on late adolescence. Similarly, material on supports for parents has been moved to appropriate chapters—such as supports for parents of infants in the chapter on infancy.

SPECIAL FEATURES

New features of the book include, at the start of each chapter, a short outline of important topics and a brief newspaper summary highlighting a topic of contemporary interest relating to the chapter. In many chapters, there are practical questions of interest and significance to parents such as, Do the first three years of parenting count the most? What do parents do if they think their child is not developing according to the usual timetables of growth? When in conflict, should parents stay together for the sake of the children?

SUPPLEMENTAL MATERIALS

Instructor's Manual and Test Bank: Accompanying the book is an instructor's manual and test bank. Please contact McGraw-Hill for more information.

PowerWeb: Child Psychology: Accompanying new copies of the book is a passcode to access *PowerWeb: Child Psychology* at www.dushkin.com/powerweb. *PowerWeb* includes current articles, curriculum-based materials, weekly updates with assessment, informative and timely world news, Web links, research tools, student study tools, interactive exercises, and much more. If you have bought a used copy of the text, you can purchase access to *PowerWeb* at www.dushkin.com/powerweb.

ACKNOWLEDGMENTS

Writing acknowledgments is one of the pleasures of completing a book. As I read manuscript and page proofs, I am constantly reminded of all the people who have helped make this book a reality.

I wish to thank all of the clinicians and researchers who gave generously of their time not only for the interviews themselves but also to review the excerpts and clarify points: Jay Belsky, Judy Dunn, Susan Harter, Sylvia Hewlett, Barbara Keogh, Anneliese Korner, Jacqueline Lerner, Richard Lerner, James Levine, Susan McHale, Paul Mussen, Emily Visher, John Visher, Jill Waterman, Emmy Werner, and Steven Wolin.

I thank the following people for a review of the fifth edition of this book, as their comments enabled me to make more insightful revisions:

Janell L. Carroll, University of Hartford

Mufid James Hannush, Rosemont College

Melissa Kaplan-Estrin, Wayne State University

Barbara L. Mason, Utah State University

Special appreciation goes to Robert Kremers, Chief of the Department of Pediatrics of Kaiser Medical Center, for his willingness to place questionnaires about the joys of parenting in the waiting rooms. I thank the many anonymous parents who completed them there and in parenting classes. Most particularly, I express my gratitude to all those parents I interviewed about the joys of parenting and the ways they changed and grew through the experience. I gained valuable insights about the process of parenting, and their comments enliven the book immeasurably. These parents are Michelle Brown, Steve Brown, Kevin Carmack, Laura Carmack, Mark Clinton, Wendy Clinton, Judy Davis, Douglas Dobson, Linda Dobson, Jill Fernald, Otie Gould, Warren Gould, Caryn Gregg, Robert Gregg, Michael Hoyt, Henrietta Krueger, Richard Krueger, Patricia Landman, Jennifer Lillard, Kathy Malone, Chris McArtor, Robert McArtor, Charles Nathan, Jean Oakley, Paul Opsvig, Susan Opsvig, Sherry Proctor, Stewart Proctor, Robert Rosenbaum, David Schmidt, Nancy Schmidt, Moshe Talmon, Anthony Toney, Patricia Toney, Steven Tulkin, Raymond Terwilleger, Elizabeth Whitney, Julie Whitney, Kenneth Whitney, Leon Whitney, Richard Whitney, Barbara Woolmington-Smith, Craig Woolmington-Smith, and Iris Yotvat-Talmon.

My coworkers at the Kaiser Medical Center at Hayward were supportive and helpful throughout. Cynthia Seay, our medical librarian, obtained all the books and articles I requested; pediatricians and pediatric advice nurses have given helpful information about parents' concerns. I greatly appreciate the leadership at Kaiser, especially Annabel Anderson Imbert, Physician-in-Chief, and Jerome Rauch, former Chief of Psychiatry, who promote an atmosphere in which creativity flourishes.

I am extremely grateful to the staff and the freelancers at McGraw-Hill. Development editor Cara Harvey has contributed to the clarity and presentation of the topics in the book. Production editors Jen Mills and Greg Hubit have worked prodigiously to bring the manuscript to life and have been patient and understanding with corrections and revisions. I am deeply grateful to copy editor Molly Roth, who played an invaluable role not only in the copy editing but in assisting me in reducing the manuscript to a manageable length. The figures and photographs have added immeasurably to the quality of the book.

I am grateful to Paul Mussen, who, fifteen years ago, suggested that I use comments from researchers to make material more vivid for students. His concern with the social forces impinging on parenting has continued to influence my thinking.

Finally, I wish to thank my family and friends for their thoughtfulness and company. I want to thank my patients for sharing their lives and experiences with me. I hope they have learned as much about life from me as I have learned from them. Most particularly, I want to thank my children, who are now grown and live away from home. They are very much in my mind as I write, and I relive our experiences together as I explore the different developmental periods. I find that I have learned the most important truths of parenting from our interactions. I believe that when I have paid attention, they have been my best teachers.

FOREWORD

The author of this book, Jane Brooks, has had a wide variety of professional and personal experiences that qualify her as an expert in child development. She is a scholar, researcher, and writer in the discipline of child psychology; a practicing clinician working with parents and children; and a mother. Drawing on the knowledge and insights derived from this rich background of experience, she has produced a wise and balanced book that parents will find valuable in fostering the optimal development of their children—helping them to become secure, happy, competent, self-confident, moral individuals. Dr. Brooks offers guidelines that are explicitly linked to major theorists (for example, Freud, Piaget, Erikson) and findings of scientific research in child development, so that the reader is also presented with a wealth of information on physical, cognitive, social, and emotional development. Students of human development and all who work with children professionally, as well as parents, will profit greatly from reading this book.

Brooks' approach to parenting incorporates many noteworthy features. Her coverage of the fundamental tasks and issues in childrearing is comprehensive. Included are tasks shared by all parents (for example, preparing for the birth of the infant, feeding, toilet training, adjusting to nursery school or kindergarten, the adolescent's growing interest in sex) as well as special, although common, problems (such as temper tantrums, delinquency, use of drugs, and physical or mental handicaps). Critical contemporary experiences such as divorce, single parenting, and stepparenting are also treated with insight and sympathy. Brooks' suggestions for ways of dealing with these problems are reasonable, balanced, and practical; her writing is straightforward, clear, and jargon-free.

Authorities in child development generally agree that the principal theories and accumulated findings of scientific investigations are not in themselves adequate to provide a comprehensive basis for directing parents in childrearing. Given the limitations of the present state of knowledge, guidance must be based on established principles of human development *plus* the cumulative wisdom and insights of specialists who have worked systematically and successfully in child-guidance settings. Yet many, perhaps most, academically trained child psychologists pay little attention to the writing of such clinicians as Briggs, Dreikurs, Ginott, Gordon, and Spock, regarding them as unscientific "popular" psychologists. This is not true of Dr. Brooks. After careful and critical reading of their work, she concluded that, as a consequence of their vast clinical experience, these specialists have achieved some profound insights about children and have thus developed invaluable techniques for analyzing and dealing effectively with many problems that parents face. Furthermore, Brooks believes that parents themselves can successfully apply some of these techniques to resolve specific problems. Some of the experts' suggestions are therefore incorporated, with appropriate acknowledgment, where they are relevant.

The book is not doctrinaire or prescriptive, however; the author does not advise parents simply to unquestioningly adopt some "system," plan, or set of rules. On the contrary, Brooks stresses the uniqueness of each individual and family, the complex nature of parent-child relations, and the multiple determinants of problem behavior. In Brooks' view, each problem must be placed in its developmental context, and evaluated in terms of the child's level of physical, cognitive, and emotional maturity. The processes of parenting are invariably bidirectional: Parents influence children *and* children influence parents. Furthermore, families do not function in isolation; each family unit is embedded in a wider network of social systems that affect its functioning. Successful childrearing depends on parents' accepting these complexities, yet also attempting to understand themselves and their children and maintaining a problem-solving orientation.

It is a pleasure to note the pervasive optimistic, yet realistic, tone of the book. The author has recognized that promotion of children's welfare and happiness is one of the highest parental goals, and she communicates her confidence that most parents *can* achieve this. Underlying this achievement is parents' deep-seated willingness to work hard and to devote thought, time, energy, and attention to their children's development and their problems. Reading this book will increase parental understanding and thus make the difficult tasks of parenting easier.

Paul Mussen
Former Professor Emeritus of Psychology
Former Director, Institute of Human Development
University of California, Berkeley

PART

I

General Concepts, Goals, and Strategies of Parenting

1

Parenting Is a Process

In this chapter you will learn about:

- Defining **parenting** in terms of the **roles** of **child**, **parent**, and **society**
- The importance of parents to children
- The power of society to help or hinder parenting

New York Times, June 8, 2002, p. A13
California State Supreme Court
unanimously rules that parenthood is
not a matter of biology but is defined
by love and responsible caregiving.
See page 10 for details.

 Go to PowerWeb at:
www.dushkin.com/powerweb
to read articles and newsfeeds
on **parenting**, **parents**, **children**, and
other topics related to this chapter.

Parenthood transforms people. After a baby comes, parents are no longer the same individuals they were. A whole new role begins, and they start a new way of life. What does parenting really mean? How has being a parent changed in the last fifty years? How does society help or hinder parents? This chapter explores parenting as a cooperative venture among parents, their child, and society. It defines parenting, describes the roles of parents and the environment in rearing children, and focuses on how society can help both parents and children.

Four million babies are born in the United States each year.[1] The challenge for parents and society is to rear children *to attain* their full potential in adulthood. This book explores how parents do this under varying family and social conditions. By giving information on how children grow and develop and how parents' actions influence children's feelings, behavior, and growth, it aims at opening up the potential of parenthood for all adults.

WHAT IS PARENTING?

The word *parent* has several definitions—a mother, a father, one who generates new life, a guardian, a protector. Summarizing these definitions, one can say a parent is an individual who fosters all facets of a child's growth—who nourishes, protects, guides new life through the course of development.[2]

Identifying a child's parents would appear to be a simple matter. Usually, *biological parents* provide the egg and sperm to produce new life and serve as caregivers for the child as well. But this is not always the case. *Adoptive parents* become parents through action of the court. *Surrogate mothers,* most often inseminated with the father's sperm, provide the gestational womb for children they will give to that father and his wife. Parenthood by *artificial insemination* involves a woman's being impregnated through the mechanical introduction of sperm, whether that of her husband or another man.

In recent years, complex legal issues have arisen over the question of who is the parent in such cases. Does a surrogate mother have any rights to maintain a relationship with the child she bears for another couple? Does a biological father have a right to a child the mother denies is his and has given up for adoption? Can a teenage child choose to live with a nonrelated parent even when biological parents seek custody of the child? In the absence of abuse or other high risk to the child, the courts have generally favored giving a very young child to the biological parent or parents, even when the parents are not married or one parent objects to the other's having the child. Further, courts are reluctant to terminate a biological parent's contact. For example, in the Baby M case, they permit the surrogate mother to have continuing visitation with her biological child, who resides with the father and his wife.

The following excerpt from a newspaper column shows the complexity of defining a parent today in our society:

> Jaycee Louise Buzzanca is not exactly an orphan. Nor is she, if you will excuse the expression, a bastard. But the two-year-old from Orange County, California, started out her life with five parents. Now, she has none.
>
> Her story began with an infertile couple, Luanne and John Buzzanca, aka *the intended parents.* Having been on a roller coaster of fertility treatments, they set about having a child the new-fashioned way.
>
> Then there were *the genetic parents.* A sperm donor and an egg donor, anonymous and unrelated, produced Jaycee's genetic material. These two had a fateful meeting in a petri dish.

Next came *the gestational mother,* a woman whose cottage industry was growing babies. This surrogate offered up her womb for rent.

But a not-so-funny thing happened while Jaycee was still in the womb. The intended father changed his intentions. He left the intended mother. When Jaycee was born, Luanne brought her home anyway and became *the rearing mother.* But John denied any responsibility including need I add, child support, on the grounds that he wasn't the father.

The small offspring of reproductive and marital dispute was left in legal limbo.

Last week, it was revealed that a family court judge in Orange County sided with John. No, the judge said, he didn't owe child support because no, he wasn't the father. This judge went even further to say that Luanne wasn't the mother either. He called her the *"temporary custodial person."* This is how Jaycee, daughter of five, became officially a parentless child.[3]

Parenting Is a Process

In our society, we emphasize that parenting is a process that brings about an end result.[4] Parenting in general can be described as a series of actions and interactions on the part of parents to promote the development of children. Parenting is not a one-way street in which parent influences child day after day. It is a process of interaction between the two, influenced by cultural and social institutions. The interaction changes all the contributors.

Jay Belsky describes three major influences on the process of parenting: (1) the child's characteristics and individuality, (2) the parent's personal history and psychological resources, and (3) the context of stresses and supports.[5] Currently, controversy centers on the rights and responsibilities of each of the participants in this process of parenting, and our discussion will touch on these conflicting views. The description of these roles—child, parent, and society—will draw on Urie Bronfenbrenner's views regarding the ecology of development and on developmental protective and risk factors.

THE ROLE OF THE CHILD

Children bring to parenting their individual needs, gender, birth order, temperaments, and patterns of growth. These influence parents' behavior and are, in turn, influenced by parents and their larger social context.

Children's Needs

Children's immature state at birth requires that parents and society nurture children and meet their needs so they can survive. Meeting these needs reorganizes parents' lives and makes demands on society as well.

According to Bronfenbrenner and Pamela Morris, a child grows through "progressively more complex reciprocal interaction [with] persons, objects, and symbols in its immediate external environment." Further, "to be effective, the interaction must occur on a fairly regular basis over extended periods of time." A father feeding a baby and a child exploring a toy are just two examples of such interactions. The interactions must include "one or more other persons with whom the child develops a strong, mutual, irrational attachment, and who are committed to the child's development, preferably for life." The maintenance of the caregiver-child relationship depends on the attachment and involvement of a second adult "who assists, encourages, spells off, gives status to, and expresses admiration and affection for the person caring for and engaging in joint activity with the child."[6]

Bronfenbrenner and Morris believe that interactions must continue on a regular basis so activities can become more complex and stimulate further development. The child need not be biologically related to his or her parent nor live in a two-parent family, but the caregiver must have a long-term, "irrational" attachment and love for the child and receive the emotional support and respect of at least one other adult.

Children's individual qualities affect both what parents do and how much impact it has. For example, highly fussy babies demand more soothing behavior from parents than do easygoing infants; in turn, they often make parents feel ineffective by responding negatively to parents' interventions. In addition, children of differing temperaments respond in different ways to the same parental action. For instance, maternal stimulation can increase exploration and competence in less active toddlers but decrease exploration in highly active toddlers.[7]

Further, parents' perceptions of their children's individual qualities and the "goodness of fit" between the child's qualities and parents' and society's expectations and values also affect parenting.[8] For example, when parents have unrealistically high expectations of children, they see their children as functioning poorly even when objective observations indicate otherwise.[9] Or, if a child has a high activity level, she or he will fit in well with an active family but may feel out of place in a family where most members are slow-moving and quiet.

Children's Importance to Parents

We tend to think about what parents do for children, how they meet children's needs, but children meet many of parents' psychological needs as well. In surveys, two-thirds of men and women have reported that their families and love life provide the most satisfying parts of their lives.[10] Parents of all ethnic backgrounds cite the love and emotional closeness they experience with children as the most important reason for having children.[11] Further, parents talk about the special qualities of this love. Bronfenbrenner and Morris refer to an "irrational attachment."[12] Tracy Gold announced her feeling on the cover of *People* magazine: "You never imagined you could love someone this much."[13] The events of September 11, 2001, made us all more keenly aware of these strong feelings as our thoughts focused immediately on our families at that time of unprecedented national crisis.

While a large-scale study revealed that the satisfactions of parenting outweigh the problems, rearing children nonetheless places substantial demands on parents,[14] such as financial demands. According to one survey, families of limited means, with incomes of less than $38,100 per year, will spend an average of $124,800 to rear a child to age eighteen. A family of moderate means, with an income between $39,100 and $65,800 per year, will spend an average of $170,460 over the eighteen-year period, and a family with an income of more than $65,000, an average of $249,180.[15] In addition to the outlay of money, parenting may demand a loss in wages and career advancement, especially for mothers.[16]

Parenting also makes emotional demands on parents. The responsibilities of caregiving and promoting development create stress. Parents experience more daily anger than do nonparents, and their sense of well-being and life satisfaction decrease.[17] We discuss these feelings further in Chapter 4.

Children's Importance to Society

Again, we do not often think about children's vital role in our society. Children ensure that a society will continue. They maintain traditions and rituals, and they transmit societal values. In addition, they grow into economic producers who support the aging members of society as well as their own children. In a society like ours in which children represent an ever smaller percentage of the population, every child is a valued participant. As Richard Lerner, Elizabeth Sparks, and Laurie McCubbin write, "Children constitute 100 percent of the future human and social capital on which our nation must depend."[18]

THE ROLE OF THE PARENT

The parents' role is to nurture and protect children, helping them grow into competent adults. They provide direct and personalized care for children on an ongoing basis throughout development. Our society gives parents primary authority to determine children's behavior because it assumes that parents have children's best interests at heart and that children are dependent and unable to make informed decisions.[19] Parents choose where children live, what religion they will practice, which methods of discipline will be used, and what kind of education will be pursued. Society intervenes in cases of abandonment, neglect, physical harm, or potential harm to children. While there have been movements to decrease parental authority—for example, to outlaw parents' use of any physical punishment, or to give teens power to consent to medical treatments for substance abuse or pregnancy—on most issues parents still retain primary authority unless they prove inadequate or abusive in some way.

Parents bring a complex set of needs and personal qualities to their role as parent.[20] Like children, they bring their gender and their temperaments. (We talk about the effects of gender on parenting in Chapter 6.) Parents bring their past history with their own parents and a set of cultural values that shape what they do. Parents also have a richly patterned social life that includes relationships and responsibilities with a partner, extended family, and the world of work.

A Short History of Parental Roles

Until late in the nineteenth century, parents were more concerned with the physical survival of their children than with effective parenting. Because of children's precarious hold on life, parents focused on their moral state, strictly punishing any transgressions. A parent's role was guardian of the body and soul of the child.[21]

In the early twentieth century, behaviorism maintained that children were blank slates, so a parent's role was to teach children good habits through appropriate rewards and punishments. Then the 1930s and 1940s saw a welcome change from strict habit training. Freudian psychoanalysis and Arnold Gesell's observations of the healthy development of upper-middle-class children indicated that a parent's role was to understand children's needs, gratify them in socially appropriate ways, and permit the process of growth to occur as naturally as possible.

Insights from Jean Piaget and the ethologists shifted the role of parent from gratifier to facilitator of development. Piaget noted that children must act on the world in order to construct an intellectually complex view of life experience.[22] It is a parent's job to provide the experiences children need in order to develop. Similarly, the ethologists, who study human behaviors in terms of their adaptive qualities, emphasized that an organism requires environmental stimulation to develop fully.

A recent influence on limiting parents' role comes from the behavior geneticists, who study the relationship between genetic factors and people's behavior.[23] They believe that genetic makeup plays a major role in determining many personality qualities. Family environment, particularly parenting, has a limited influence on the development of children's personality and intelligence unless that environment is extreme—for example, abusive or deprived or neglectful.

All the parental role behaviors described here appear appropriate for parents today. Parents' tasks are to ensure the physical survival of the child, teach good habits, gratify needs, and stimulate all facets of development by providing enriching experiences.

Parents' Importance to Children

As just noted, parents have long been considered the most important figures in children's lives. Behavior geneticists began to question this in the early 1990s, but it was Judith Rich Harris's 1998 book, *The Nurture Assumption: Why Children Turn out the Way They Do,* that captured national attention and sparked debate on parents' importance to children.[24] This chapter discusses this important topic in detail after the description of the parenting process is complete.

Parents' Importance to Society

Parents have vital roles in our society. They provide care for children around the clock on an ongoing basis. For eighteen or more years, they feed, clothe, and pay children's expenses. With the schools, they educate children to become contributing members of society.[25] As noted, because it is difficult, if not impossible, for society to provide the level and continuity of personal care that parents happily give children, society steps in only when parents cannot fulfill their responsibilities.

VOICES OF EXPERIENCE

The Joys of Family Generations

"At her christening party, we had a tape recorder, and each guest taped a little message into the recorder. When she began to sing, she would sing into the recorder, and when her grandmother was alive, she sang the old Norwegian songs into the recorder so we have that on tape. And every year at various times, at birthdays or holidays, we would all talk into the tape recorder about what our lives had been like and what had gone on since the last time we did it. We have her singing 'Silent Night' with all the words wrong, and that has been a real thread. We have a sort of oral history, and it's a real pleasure for us." MOTHER

"Thomas Wolfe wrote *You Can't Go Home Again,* but James Agee said you do go home again in the lives of your children. It is a sort of reexperiencing what you experienced when you grew up—they're reading the same books you read, the conflicts they have are the ones you remember having with your parents, or issues that mattered to you as a child are issues for them. When you have time to reflect on them, they bring you back over and over again to issues in your own childhood that I guess you have a second opportunity to resolve. You have a different perspective on them than you did before." FATHER

"One of the interesting things was when we took our children back to Ohio. Before she could crawl, one used to scoot around on her rear end and tuck one knee under the other, and she wore out all the seats of her pants. Her great-grandmother was alive then and said, 'Oh, that is just the way her grandfather did it.' We never knew that and it was just amazing. One of our girls is so like her great-aunt who never had any children of her own and was such a lovely woman. It would have pleased her so much to see my daughter grow up. Our son looks like my father and is so much like him in every way. He has his build. My father always had a joke at dinner every night and our son has always loved jokes. As soon as he could read, he had a joke book and was always telling us jokes at dinner. Our other son looks just exactly like his father and his grandfather." MOTHER

"One of my great joys was the first time my parents came to visit us, very proudly handing my son to my father and saying, 'Here's my boy!' That was a real highlight, a great thrill. I get choked up saying it now." FATHER

"I like having my family around. For the first time in my life, I want my mother to be here. There is a basic need to have your family around you. My husband's family and cousins are here, and I have a really strong urge to have everyone around. I was not really prepared for that." MOTHER

"Being a parent has helped me to see into myself. It's very illuminating in a personal way. It brings back a lot of memories, good and bad." FATHER

A recent New Jersey case vividly demonstrated the difficulties state agencies face when they attempt to fulfill the role of caregiving parent. In January 2003, the decomposed, malnourished body of a seven-year-old boy was found in a trunk in a locked cellar, and his twin and four-year-old brothers were found chained nearby, emaciated and scarred with burns.[26] Their mother had been reported to the Division of Youth and Family Services for abuse and neglect eleven times in a ten-year period, but the agency closed the case on the family the year before. At the time, there was a report that the mother beat and burned her children, but it was not investigated because the agency could not locate the children.

The governor declared a state of emergency at the agency, and workers were ordered to investigate immediately the 280 outstanding cases of children reported as victims of abuse. Workers could not locate 110 of the possible victims.[27] A review of cases reported to the Division of Youth and Family Services in the previous five years revealed that 82 children had died or were critically injured, despite the report of abuse to the agency.[28] In Chapter 15, we discuss ways states have sought to remedy the difficulties of providing care for children when parents are not capable.

Just as society holds parents responsible for their treatment of their children, it also holds parents accountable for their children's misbehavior. Recently, a couple in Michigan were fined and ordered to pay court costs because they were judged to be lax in supervising their law-breaking sixteen-year-old son.[29]

As our society grows ever more complex, it becomes clear that parents who care for their children perform a role that society cannot easily fill.

THE ROLE OF SOCIETY

Children live in families, and families live in neighborhoods and communities in a larger society that, in turn, influences how parents carry out their tasks. Society provides values, standards of conduct, and shared views of the world. Because children are the future of society, society has a strong interest in their care and growth. Thus, it provides a set of beliefs about (1) the roles of the parent, (2) the roles of the extended family members and the community, (3) the goals of parenting, (4) approved methods of discipline, and (5) the roles of children in society.[30] Our diversified society has many cultural groups with varying beliefs on these topics. Here we focus on the general role of society; Chapter 3 explores cultural diversity.

Defining Roles

The social system defines a parent. Usually, of course, this is one or both biological parents, but in our increasingly complex society, there can be as many as five parents, as noted earlier. Further, conflicts can arise between adoptive parents and a biological parent who wishes to exert his or her right to the child. As we have seen, in the absence of abuse or other risk to the child, the courts generally favor having a young child live with a biological parent. Society, sometimes does otherwise, however. For example, the California Supreme Court recently awarded legal custody of a child to the mother's ex-boyfriend over the mother's objections that he was not the biological parent.[31] The State Appellate Court had declared that the ex-boyfriend could not be the legal father because he was not the biological father. The State Supreme Court reversed that ruling and established that the man was the legal father of the child because he had cared for the seven-year-old since birth and because no biological father had stepped forward. He was considered the constant in the child's life; without him, the child would be fatherless and homeless. The court wrote, "A man who receives a child into his home and openly holds the child as his natural child is presumed to be the natural father of the child."[32]

Society decides not only who is a child's parent, but also the basic requirements of parenting and the penalties for failure to fulfill them.[33] Because parents are expected to make most of the decisions regarding children, society imposes few, but important, requirements. Parents must see that children have immunizations before the age of five and receive an education between the ages of five and eighteen. Society also insists that parents rear law-abiding children and holds parents responsible for their children's behavior.

Society defines children's roles, as well.[34] In general, children are seen as inexperienced and dependent and are expected to follow parents' rules and requests. As society has given children, particularly teenagers, more freedom over the years—such as receiving certain medical treatments—it has also removed the protections given to children in the past. For example, children and teens are being considered responsible for legal violations and charged, sentenced, and jailed as adults. One California six-year-old who beat an infant was charged, as an adult would be, with attempted murder, a charge that was later reduced to assault and suspended until he was able to participate in his own defense.[35]

The treatment of this child stood in sharp contrast to that of two schoolchildren who had murdered a toddler in California twenty-five years earlier.[36] In that case, the children were seen as needing treatment. There was a gag order on the case, and names of the children were never made public, not even to the family of the victim. The children were sent to foster care and did not receive a criminal record.

Providing Assistance

Beyond defining roles, society steps in to support parents, providing financial assistance when parents experience difficulties. It also serves as substitute for parents when they abandon, neglect, or abuse their children. For example, the government gives parents limited financial assistance in times of economic hardship; it steps in and makes decisions about custody and living arrangements when divorcing parents cannot agree. As noted, it serves in the place of a parent when a parent is incapacitated and no other family members are available.

In addition to defining and supporting parenting, the dynamic interaction of cultural, economic, and social forces determines how families live and the challenges they confront in rearing children.

The Power of Social Forces

The Rochester Longitudinal Study illustrates the potent impact of social forces on people's lives.[37] When the environment promotes growth, individuals flourish; when the environment presents a series of challenges, individuals, particularly children, have difficulties surmounting them. The Rochester study investigated the effects of the social environment on children's intellectual and social-emotional competence from birth through adolescence. The researchers related child competence to ten environmental risk factors associated with poor outcomes for children—maternal mental illness, high maternal anxiety, rigid beliefs about development, few positive maternal interactions, minimal maternal education, unskilled parental occupation, disadvantaged minority status, single parenthood, stressful life events, and large family size. Because only a small number of men participated in the study, paternal qualities were not included in the findings.

The research yielded several important findings, which were confirmed in a subsequent study in Philadelphia. First, no one particular risk factor led to a poor outcome. Second, the accumulation of risks led to poor outcome; the more risks, the less competent the child's functioning. Children with no risks scored thirty points higher on intelligence tests than did children with eight or nine risks. Children with more risk factors had more clinical problems as well.

Third, the continuity of risk factors across childhood (a correlation of .77 between risk factor scores at ages four and thirteen) was as great as or greater than any continuity in the child's characteristics. Thus, the environment had a consistently negative or positive effect on the child. Only one child in a sample of fifty went from living in a low-risk environment (zero or one risk) at age four to a high-risk environment (four or more risks) at age thirteen, and only one child went from a high-risk environment at age four to a low-risk environment at age thirteen.

Fourth, the environment greatly limited or expanded the range of the child's competencies. The least resilient or resourceful child in a low-risk environment scored higher on measures of competence than did the most resilient and resourceful child living in a high-risk environment. "The negative effects of a disadvantaged environment seem to be more powerful contributors to child achievement at every age than the personality characteristics of the child."[38]

Fifth and finally, no single change could be made—increased income, a change in marital status from single to married—that would eliminate the risks for children. Researchers concluded that efforts to improve high-risk environments must focus on making changes in a broad constellation of factors—improving mothers' mental health, encouraging positive parent-child interactions, improving occupational status. "We can maximize the efficiency of intervention efforts when we realize that it is not being poor alone, or living in a bad neighborhood alone, or having a single parent alone that places children at risk, but rather the combination of these factors that saps the lives of families."[39]

Investigators identified protective factors that were similar for both boys and girls. These factors were related to positive changes in cognitive and social-emotional functioning in high-risk children between four and thirteen years of age.[40] Protective factors in the child, measured at age thirteen, were self-esteem, a sense of social support, and a sense of predictability about the world.

More protective factors were identified in parents' qualities. A mother's teaching style that encouraged thinking and reflection, measured when children were age four, was a protective factor. When children were age thirteen, protective factors in the mother centered on her feeling positive about herself and the child. Mothers who voiced fewer dissatisfactions, scored lower on a depression measure, and made

■ **TABLE 1-1**
EIGHT MAJOR CHANGES IN FAMILY LIFE OVER THE LAST 150 YEARS

1. Dramatic decrease in two-parent farm family

2. Decrease in family size as parents have fewer children

3. Decrease in traditional nuclear family of the 1950s with breadwinner-father and homemaker-mother

4. Decrease in residential fathers with year-round, stable, full-time employment

5. Increase in level of parents' education

6. Increase in mothers' paid employment outside the home

7. Increase in single-parent families, mostly headed by women

8. Increase in extent and severity of child poverty

Adapted from Richard M. Lerner, Elizabeth E. Sparks, and Laurie D. McCubbin, "Family Diversity and Family Policy," in *Handbook of Family Diversity,* ed. David H. Demo, Katherine R. Allen, and Mark A. Fine (New York: Oxford University Press, 2000), 382–385.

supportive rather than critical comments to children promoted children's positive development. Protective factors also included mothers' having a confidante and social support and their encouraging values of self-direction for children rather than conformity. Protective factors in the environment included fewer negative events and social support for families.

Social Forces over Time

Looking at the social forces that have shaped contemporary society helps us to understand better the social forces operating today. Table 1-1 summarizes the major changes in family life over the last 150 years. The table shows that we have moved from a country of large, extended farm families in which all members form an economic unit providing care and support for its members to smaller, nuclear families headed by one or two parents, both of whom frequently work outside the home. Although contemporary families are smaller, parents have less time with children because of work and parental separations and divorces. Because parents have many responsibilities, individuals outside the home such as day care workers, teachers, and coaches as well as community agencies participate in caring for children.

Contemporary Families

We live in an ethnically diverse society with many different sets of beliefs about family life and children. Further, we live in a society that celebrates the diversity and the distinctive values each group brings to our country. According to 2000 census data, 75 percent of the U.S. population are European Americans, 12.3 percent are African Americans, 12.5 percent are Latinos, 3.6 percent Asian Americans, 0.9 percent

American Indians/Eskimos,[41] and about 1 percent Middle Eastern Americans.[42] In 18 percent of U.S. homes, a second language is spoken; in California, that figure is 40 percent.[43] Within each of the major groups are subgroups with their own distinctive values and beliefs. See Chapter 3 for more on the cultural influences of ethnic groups.

Diverse Family Structures   The army of parents rearing children live in diverse family structures (see Figure 1-1). According to the 2000 census, 74 percent of families are married couples with one or two children, and 26 percent are single-parent families with 22 percent headed by women and 4 percent by men.[44] Single-parent families include those who have never married and those who have been divorced or widowed. About 50 percent of children growing up today will spend part of their childhood or adolescence in a single-parent family. Some families are headed by same-sex partners who have children from previous marriages, by adoption, or by artificial insemination. The need for homes for less frequently adopted children means that older adults and individuals with disabilities—individuals who would not have been approved as adoptive parents in the past—are now rearing children. Issues of diverse family structures are discussed in Chapters 6 and 14.

Employment   The vast majority of children live in families where parenting figures are employed outside the home. In married-couple families, 63 percent of mothers with children under six and 77 percent of mothers with children between six and seventeen are employed. In single-parent households headed by women, the comparable figures are 70 percent and 77 percent. Women's working boosted the

■ **F I G U R E 1 - 1**
LIVING ARRANGEMENTS OF CHILDREN UNDER AGE EIGHTEEN
IN THE UNITED STATES IN 1996

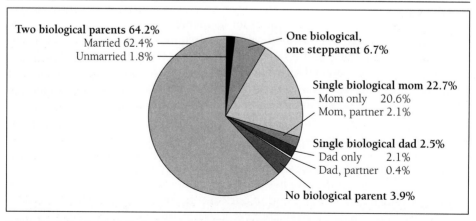

Adapted from Sandra L. Hofferth et al., "The Demography of Fathers: What Fathers Do," in *Handbook of Father Involvement,* ed. Catherine S. Tamis-LeMonda and Natasha Cabrera (Mahwah, NJ: Erlbaum, 2002), 65.

Families today are more varied than ever before—married couples with children, same-sex couples with children, single parents with children, and relatives such as grandparents raising children.

median family income to $48,950.[45] When caregivers have outside employment, extended family or day care workers take care of the children part of the day. See Chapter 13 for more on these issues.

Time Pressure   Adults, particularly parents of young children, feel rushed and starved for time. Parents who both work identify lack of time with family as the greatest source of stress in family life.[46] Time diaries over a thirty-year period indicate that Americans may feel rushed because of other factors as well as overwork.[47] Joint custody arrangements following divorce reduce the time parents have with their children as children go back and forth between biological parents and become part of a larger network of stepparents, stepsiblings, and stepgrandparents. The accelerated pace of life contributes to the feeling of pressure. Parents often must do two or more things at the same time. Further, spending about 40 percent of free time watching television takes time away from activities that give far more satisfactions. Chapter 4 presents ways of dealing with this problem.

Outside Influences   In the last two years, the most striking outside influence on families has been the threat to national security, which has engendered frequent alerts of terrorist attacks in this country as well as loved ones serving in wars in different parts of the world. Although not constant, these pressures will persist into the

foreseeable future. Terrorist alerts or threats of war, when they come, frighten children and parents who worry about children's reactions and seek ways to reassure
them. The worry about security never completely disappears but is an underlying
current of daily life. We discuss ways to deal with these problems in Chapter 15.

At a less scary level, other influences outside the family have a greater impact
than before on children because parents spend less time with them. Because parents
spend more time at work and less time with families, influences outside the family
have a greater impact on children than before. Chief among these influences is television. James Steyer, a lawyer and children's advocate, refers to it as "The Other Parent" because the average child spends forty hours per week under the influence of
values committed not to character and psychological development but to commercial success. Movies, videos, and the music industry also promote commercial values in children and adolescents. In response, Steyer has formed a group called
Families Interested in Responsible Media (FIRM) to lobby for media programs that
meet children's and families' needs.[48]

The Social Health of the Country

Mark Miringoff and Marque-Luisa Miringoff describe a Social Health Index that
provides a measure of the country's social well-being.[49] Much as economic indexes
such as the Dow Jones Industrial Average seek to describe the vitality of the economy, the Social Health Index seeks to describe how the country is faring socially.
The index is based on sixteen factors that measure longevity, health, education,
safety, employment, and wages. Changes in these measures are plotted from 1970 to
the present in order to assess improvements or failures to improve on each dimension over this period.

Changes in the Social Health Index   In their book *The Social Health of the Nation,*
the Miringoffs identify four factors that indicate improvement in social health: Life
expectancy has increased, infant mortality has decreased, poverty among people 65
or older has decreased, and the rate of high school dropouts has decreased.

Seven factors, however, indicate a decrease in social well-being in this same
period: increases in child abuse, child poverty, youth suicide, violent crime, and the
number of individuals who lack health coverage. We have seen stagnation in wages
and a large and growing gap between the earnings of those in the top 20 percent of
the population and those in the lowest 20 percent. Five factors have seen variable
performance—that is, their figures have risen and fallen over the almost thirty-year
period: teenage drug use, teenage births, alcohol-related traffic fatalities, affordable
housing, and unemployment.

Clearly, people over 65 enjoy the greatest social health with increased lifespan,
medical coverage, and low rates of poverty. Children, unfortunately, remain at greatest risk with increases in abuse, child poverty, suicide, and drug use (at times).

Figure 1-2 shows the relationship between the Index of Social Health, a combination of the sixteen factors, and the gross domestic product (GDP) from 1970 to
1998. Social health was greatest in the early 1970s and since then has dropped; it
remained relatively low even as the country prospered and had its greatest economic

■ **FIGURE 1-2**
CHANGES IN THE SOCIAL HEALTH OF THE COUNTRY

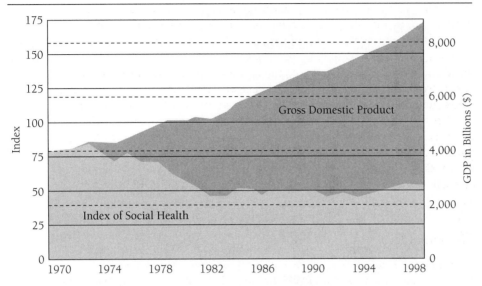

From Marque-Luisa Miringoff, "The Social Health of the Nation," *Vassar*, Winter, 2001, p. 25.

boon in the late 1990s. Because the graph reflects long-term trends, not short-term fluctuations, it is especially disturbing. Paying more attention to the indicators of social health and funding programs based on them might create greater well-being in our society.

Social Stress for Parents and Children   Developmental specialists in the fields of psychology, sociology, social work, and medicine recognize the difficult social conditions under which parents raise children today. The psychiatrist Jack Westman has edited a 2001 volume, *Parenthood in America: Undervalued, Underpaid and Under Seige*, which highlights the challenges parents face.[50] Bronfenbrenner writes of "growing chaos" in the lives of children, youth, and families.[51] James Garbarino's "Supporting Parents in a Socially Toxic Environment" makes the analogy between the environmental toxins we have had to combat and the social toxicity of the environment children and parents inhabit.[52] Like the Miringoffs, Garbarino points to poverty, abuse, and violence as sources of toxicity, but he also cites disruptions in families and an increased sense of despair. Specifically, he cites the increasing incidence of psychological problems in children as measured by responses to the Child Behavior Check List. In 1976, descriptions of children revealed that 10 percent needed psychotherapy but only about 3 percent were receiving treatment. In 1989, the comparable figures were 18 percent needing treatment and 8 percent receiving it. Another study revealed that in the 1980s, the average child in the United States reported more anxiety than did children who were psychiatric patients in the 1950s.[53] Ways to help parents and children are discussed in a later section.

INTERACTIONS AMONG CHILD, PARENT, AND SOCIETY

Figure 1-3 presents a schematic diagram summarizing the relationships of the participants in the process of parenting. It includes the activities and institutions as well as the social, cultural, and historical factors that influence these relationships. At the heart of the process are the mother and father, who are usually married to each other. They form a *parenting bond* that continues even if the *marital tie* dissolves and each marries someone else. Sometimes, a single parent has no ties to another partner.

■ **FIGURE 1-3**
THE PROCESS OF PARENTING IN A PARTICULAR HISTORICAL TIME

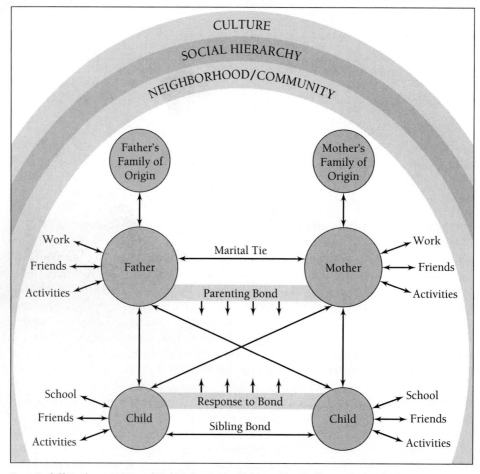

From Rudolf Dreikurs, M.D., and Vicki Soltz, R.N., *Children: The Challenge.* Copyright © 1964 by Rudolf Dreikurs, M.D. Used by permission of Dutton, a division of Penguin Group (USA) Inc.

Brothers and sisters develop what is called a *sibling bond.* When a marriage dissolves, the relationship, or bond, between siblings may provide the most continuous, steady family relationship for children who go back and forth between parents.

As shown in Figure 1-3 by the two-way arrows, parents form direct relationships with each child. They also engage in parenting behaviors to care for their child—the one-way arrows extending from the parenting bond to the children. Children respond to these behaviors in turn.

Parents are also connected to their families of origin—parents, siblings, and other relatives—who are in turn connected to them and to their children (even though the arrows from families of origin to children are not presented here).

Parents relate to work, friends, and activities in the neighborhood/community that surrounds the family. The neighborhood/community is part of a social hierarchy within a specific cultural context within a particular historical time. Thus, the family is nested in several social layers that provide support for the family, which, in essence, serves as the vital nucleus of society.

Clearly, parenting plays a central part in defining society. Now we discuss what research says about parents' role in children's lives—a question of great interest to all parents and potential parents.

HOW IMPORTANT ARE PARENTS IN CHILDREN'S LIVES? A LIVELY DEBATE

In her 1998 book, *The Nurture Assumption,* Harris provocatively states, "Parenting has been oversold. You have been led to believe that you have more influence over your child's personality than you really do."[54] She contends that parents' importance in children's growth and the formation of their adult personality is an assumption—called the *nurture assumption*—that research has not yet proven. She believes that group socialization is what prepares children for their adult lives, and thus serves as the central environmental influence in their lives. Her book has triggered critical analyses of her arguments and of socialization research, and Harris has responded to these comments. Now we shall look briefly at the main points of this debate; please see Harris's book, the articles, and the monograph listed in the footnotes for a deeper understanding of the issues.

Group Socialization As the Major Socializer of Children

As a developmental psychology textbook writer in the 1980s and early 1990s, Harris shared the beliefs of most developmental psychologists that both nature, in the form of genetic influences, and nurture, in the form of environmental influences, jointly shape children's growth and the kind of people they become. Like other psychologists, she considered parents the most important environmental influence. She believed that children's temperamental characteristics influence how parents treat them so that parenting is a two-way process.

Through continued reading, however, she became convinced that what children learn at home with parents and siblings is specific to the context of the home and is left there when children move into the larger social world. In the larger world, children learn new ways of behaving, and it is only while they are learning these new ways that they might use behaviors learned at home.[55]

Group socialization (GS) is what helps children forge the identities and the behaviors they take with them into adulthood. Children identify with peer groups they think are like themselves, and, out of loyalty to the group, they take on the behaviors of its members. Group norms socialize children to meet cultural expectations. Consistent status or position within the group develops children's long-term personality characteristics. Peers' labeling or typecasting, when positive, can contribute to confidence, assertiveness, and dominance; when negative, it can contribute to such qualities as impulsiveness and attention-seeking behavior. One-on-one peer friendships do not have a peer group's power to socialize children, because what is learned in a two-person interaction is specific to that friendship and does not generalize to the wider social world.

Harris acknowledges that she can cite only one longitudinal study to support her thesis.[56] The study showed that when adolescent boys were early physical maturers and gained high social status, they were, as adults in their thirties, confident, assertive, and dominant. In contrast, later maturing boys who had low social status were, as adult men, impulsive attention seekers. Collecting data over decades makes the study difficult to replicate.

The Importance of Genetic Influences

To support the other part of her thesis, that parents are not the most important environmental influence on children, Harris critically reviewed previous research on the effects of parenting and contends that influence attributed to parents really stems from the action of genes.[57] She claims that studies showing that children resemble their parents—bright children coming from homes with bright parents or sociable children coming from homes with sociable parents—really reflect genetic influence. She cites behavior geneticists' estimates that 50 percent of the variation in people's personality characteristics can be attributed to genetic factors. Because children inherit half their genes from each parent, their resemblance to their parent in any given behavior could well be due to genes.

Further, Harris points out that genetic factors influence the environment in which children live in three ways. First, parents' genetic qualities may lead to the creation of a certain environment that appears to foster children's behavior when it is really the genetic influence that fosters the behavior. For example, intelligent parents may provide an enriched and stimulating environment for their children. The relation between that stimulation and children's intellectual success may be due not to the stimulation, as has often been thought, but to the genes that bright people pass on to their children.

Second, children's genetically determined behaviors influence others' behavior. For example, the easygoing, adaptable baby evokes a positive response from people, and the aggressive child evokes a harsh, negative response. Third, the child's genetically-related characteristics lead the child to seek certain environmental stimulation. The intellectually bright child may go to the library often, and the athletically gifted child may pursue lessons to advance his or her skill. The child's inborn qualities stimulate the child to create an environment that advances these qualities.

Adequate Test of Parental Influence

Harris is quick to point out that while research has not proven the importance of parental influence, neither has it disproved its importance; thus it remains an assumption.[58] She believes that the ideal test of parents' impact on children's behavior is to form two groups of parents and children matched on major variables such as age, education, and income. Because both groups consist of parents and their biological children, the influence of genetic factors is controlled. Parents in the experimental group receive special parenting training, while parents in the control group do not. Then, children's behavior outside the home is assessed in objective ways. Harris doubts not that parents influence what children do *in* the home, but that they influence what the child does *outside* the home. If there were significant differences between the way children in the experimental group behave outside the home, then she would acknowledge that parents' behavior shapes what children do away from home. She has found only one study that meets the criteria, and this study showed minimal difference between the two groups.

Socialization Researchers' Response to Harris's Criticisms

Socialization researchers have taken Harris's criticisms of their research seriously and, as indicated earlier, have responded in detail to her charges. They agree with Harris that "early researchers often overstated conclusions from correlational findings; relied excessively on [a] singular, deterministic views of parental influence; and failed to attend to the potentially confounding effects of heredity."[59] They insist, nevertheless, that substantial research documents parents' influences on their children's intellectual and academic progress, their social and emotional competence, and their resistance to high-risk behaviors. These psychologists believe that while behavior geneticists' research has contributed to our understanding of the development of children's behaviors, their research strategies are problematic and their claims of parents' insignificance ignore a substantial body of sophisticated socialization research.

The Intertwining of Genetic and Environmental Influences

Just as behavior geneticists feel that socialization researchers ignore genetic influences, socialization researchers believe that behavior geneticists' research minimizes environmental influences. Socialization researchers point out that genes exist only in an environment; from the moment of conception, genetic and environmental factors affect each other. For example, during pregnancy, parents provide the environment for genetic development. While most parents' lifestyles protect intra-uterine development, mothers who expose the fetus and growing baby to alcohol and drugs can irreparably damage the genetic contributions to the child.[60] New research indicates that a prospective father's work environment and alcohol, smoking, and drug habits can affect the quality of the sperm and the coming baby as well.[61] Other intrauterine influences, such as the level of maternal stress hormones, may have subtler influence on the growing fetus. So, from the moment of conception, parents' behavior influences the growing child and can either protect or damage genetic potential.

Genetic and environmental factors are also difficult to separate in research because they are correlated. Identical twins are more alike genetically than fraternal twins, and they also receive more similar treatment. "That individuals who are more closely related genetically also have more similar shared parental environments means that observed associations between parenting and measures of child characteristics cannot be assumed to be either entirely genetic or entirely environmental in origin."[62]

Environmental Modification of Genetic Traits

Socialization researchers have criticized methods of calculating heritability—specifically, how the wide variations in heritability for a given trait depend on the samples assessed.[63] For example, samples of identical twins yielding higher estimates than do samples of adopted children.

Socialization researchers point out that behavior geneticists believe that if they identify significant genetic contributions to a behavior, the environment does not matter. Yet, environmental influence can modify even traits under strong genetic control.[64] For example, genetic factors are considered primarily responsible for height. Yet, Japanese Americans reared in this country with American diets are, on average, considerably taller than their grandparents reared in Japan, even though genetic factors determine variations in height within the group. Similarly, the IQs of adoptive children correlate highly with those of their biological mothers; however, the children have significantly higher average IQ than their mothers. Average IQ increases as the socioeconomic status of the adoptive families increases.[65] When adopted into low-status homes, the children gained an average of 8 IQ points, but when adopted into high-status homes, they gained 19 points on average. Behavior genetics research reports only that IQ was highly heritable as children tend to keep the same rank order despite the fact that the environment has led to increases in actual IQ scores. Further, behavior genetics research tells us nothing about what developmental factors contribute to the increases in IQ scores.

A Swedish adoption study shows how the environment adoptive parents provide can affect a genetic potential.[66] The study examined 862 men born out of wedlock but adopted by nonrelatives on average by eight months. Researchers classified the risk of petty criminality (nonviolent, infrequent, minor crimes, usually property offenses) for both biological and adoptive parents and noted the rate of petty criminality of the adopted men as adults. The men's risk for petty criminality varied with the risks of adoptive and biological parents. When neither biological nor adoptive parents were at risk, the men's risk of petty criminality was 3 percent; when an adoptive parent was at risk, but the biological parents were not, the men's risk was 7 percent; when a biological parent was at risk, but the adoptive parents were not, the men's risk was 12 percent; and when both the biological and adoptive parents were at risk, the men's risk was 40 percent. When a biological parent was at risk for petty criminality, the risk for the child was reduced two-thirds if that child was reared by parents not at risk. Conversely, the risk for petty criminality increased more than three times when a child at biological risk was reared by an adoptive parent at risk.

Within the more usual range of temperamental qualities, responsive parenting can modify in babies even though those qualities that are thought to be genetically determined. Jerome Kagan's longitudinal research documented that highly reactive infants showing fretful crying and much motor activity at four months were less fearful as toddlers when mothers were firm and set reasonable limits with their babies.[67] Mothers who were responsive to the child's fretting and did not set limits had toddlers who continued to be fearful. Maternal responsiveness did not have the same effects with low-reactive infants.

Greater Sophistication of Socialization Research

Socialization researchers have greater confidence in more recent studies of the influences of parenting, because they use better statistical procedures and research designs than before to control for parent-child resemblance due to genetic factors. Longitudinal studies of the effects of parents' discipline on children's behavior control for genetic influence by taking into account the child's initial level of behavior (an indication of genetic influence) and then noting how, over time, parenting methods influence that behavior.[68]

Researchers can note the effects of rearing in animal studies that manipulate the environmental experiences of animals with known genetic traits.[69] For example, both rats and monkeys differ in emotional reactivity at birth. Highly reactive animals in both species tend to be timid in exploring their environment and easily stressed. When nurturant foster mothers rear such reactive rats and monkeys, the animals grow up to be less anxious, more able to explore the environment, and more stress resistant. When highly nurturant foster mothers rear highly reactive monkeys, the monkeys not only decrease in anxiety but show many competencies. They are quick to explore their environments, and they are less distressed by weaning than are the highly reactive monkeys reared by mothers in the average range of nurturance.[70] When highly reactive foster monkeys enter group life at the age of six months, those reared by nurturant foster mothers are extremely effective leaders and rise to the top of the dominance hierarchy. They are skilled in avoiding stress and gaining support so they can deal with whatever stress exists. If female, the foster monkeys of nurturant mothers become competent mothers, whereas emotionally reactive infants reared by control mothers in the average range of nurturance show deficits with their offspring.

Studies of rhesus monkeys raised in a neonatal nursery for one month, then reared with peers from one to six months, reveal that peer-reared monkeys have normal physical and motor development and positive attachments to their peer-mates, but the peers do not seem to serve as a protective, secure base from which to venture forth.[71] When compared with mother-reared monkeys, peer-reared monkeys are more anxious in novel situations and in interactions with new peers. They are hesitant to play, their play is more immature, and they fall to the bottom of the dominance hierarchy. Their brain chemistry changes as well.

These animal studies suggest that early rearing conditions can greatly affect the behaviors of the young, for better or worse; that physiological functioning as well as behavioral development is affected; and that the changes are passed along to the next generation via parenting behaviors.[72]

Parents and Peers

Although Harris insists that peers are more important socializing forces for children than are parents, the animal studies just described outline special roles for both parents and peers. Parents provide the nurturance, protection, and security that enable offspring to venture forth confidently. Peers provide play interactions that serve to introduce all the skills necessary in adult life and allow children to practice them. Longitudinal research on the attachment relationships from birth to adulthood yields similar findings. L. Alan Sroufe writes,

> Parent and peer experiences combine to prepare the individual for adult social relationships. The capacity for close relationships is a developmental construction, taking root in early attachment relationships and being sustained throughout by supportive parents, but put into practice and elaborated in the symmetrical relationships of the world of peers.[73]

Parents As Advocates

We think of parental influence as parents' directly influencing children's behavior by teaching, modeling, encouraging, supporting, and loving their children. But parents also influence children's behavior indirectly through assembling resources and helping children draw on them to promote the child's growth.

For example, parents who have children with disabilities and who have worked to help their children develop their full potential have changed our culture's way of viewing disabilities and have greatly expanded the resources and opportunities available to children with disabilities and their parents.[74] These parents have lobbied for improvements in educational programs, living arrangements, and community respect for children so that their children can become more fully integrated into the mainstream. Parents' advocacy has resulted in fewer children living in institutions and more living with biological or adoptive families. More community living arrangements for adults with disabilities have also arisen. Parents have demanded and obtained greater educational resources, greater community integration, and expanded occupational opportunities for children.

In addition to improving society's treatment of their children, parents make special contributions to their children's daily lives. "They frequently have expectations that help to elevate the functioning of their children with disabilities in a positive version of a self-fulfilling prophecy. They think that their children can learn so they create favorable environments in which to teach them, and thus they do learn more than they would in less favorable environments."[75]

Children of outstanding achievement also benefit from parents' extra efforts and commitment. Benjamin Bloom and his coworkers studied 120 young men and women who achieved international recognition for high levels of performance in a variety of fields.[76] The researchers interviewed the individuals, their family members, and teachers and coaches to understand the process by which the children achieved such excellence.

Few of the individuals, the researchers noted, were identified as special in the beginning. A combination of individual commitment, family support, and outstanding instruction led to accomplishment. Parents sought instruction for children, scheduled practices, and provided support and encouragement, emphasizing the ethic of hard work and doing one's best. As children's skills grew, parents found more-advanced teachers and coaches and made financial and time commitments not only to provide instruction but also to attend recitals, games, and meets. In fact, the whole family's schedule sometimes changed to accommodate the child's training and performance schedule.

As children advance, parents continue their emotional and financial support. Studies of talented and world-class achievers emphasize that enormous effort on the part of many people goes into the gradual development of superior accomplishment. Clearly, whether children have special difficulties or potential talents, parental support is essential along the way.

A Study That Meets Harris's Requirements

Philip Cowan and Carolyn Cowan have carried out exactly the kind of study that Harris said would show that parents' behavior influences their children's growth and development.[77] Based on many years of work studying parents' adjustments to parenting and later to their children's transitions to school, the researchers designed intervention groups for parents of four-year-olds who were to start school within the year. Parents participating in the study were well-functioning volunteers who had not previously sought mental health services, yet their scores on measures of depression and marital stress indicated that many were experiencing stress in their daily lives.

Parent groups met two hours per week for sixteen weeks, included fathers as well as mothers, and focused on relationships in the family with an emphasis on how feelings might affect parenting and children's development. There was also a control group that received no intervention. After family members filled out checklists, they carried out a variety of tasks while their behavior was assessed in the laboratory. Tests measured children's intellectual achievements, and teachers and peers rated children's personality characteristics in kindergarten, at the end of first grade, and again in the fourth grade.

All parenting groups consisted of four couples and two mental health professionals, one male and one female. In the two-hour parent groups, members discussed five topics central to parents' and children's adjustment—"parents' sense of self, their experience of relationships with one another, with their parents, and with their children, and the life stressors and social support that they experienced."[78] In each session, parents received time to raise questions or problems. Researchers devised two forms of the parenting groups. In one group, leaders were told to focus on marital issues and parents' relationship as a couple in the open-ended discussion periods; in the other group, leaders emphasized parents' relationship with their children.

When compared with children whose parents were in the control group, children of parents in the intervention groups were more competent and effective. They had higher academic achievement, fewer behavior problems, and more positive self-concepts. Those whose parents were in groups that focused on parent-child issues had higher self-esteem in kindergarten and fewer worries and anxieties in first grade than did children whose parents were in the control group. Those whose parents were in the intervention groups emphasizing marital relationships scored higher on an achievement test in kindergarten and lower on measures of aggressive, impulsive behaviors in first grade.

So, this study met all of Harris's requirements for illustrating parents' influence. There was a control group receiving no intervention; there were groups with parenting interventions; the effects on the child's behavior were measured outside the home, with ratings not by parents but by teachers, peers, and researchers; and the influence was still observed more than two years later.

Summing Up the Debate

Harris's critical examination of parents' influence on their children's lives has sparked conferences, articles, and analyses of both behavior geneticists' and socialization research. Each side has made serious points about the importance of genetic and environmental contributions to children's behavior. As a result, socialization research is more carefully controlled to detect evidence of genetic influence, and conclusions about the effects are more carefully specified than they were in the past. We have not, however, advanced our understanding much beyond the wise conclusions of Anne Anastasi in 1958.[79] She wrote then that the important question was not how much variance in a trait is attributable to heredity and how much to the environment, but rather, how genes and the environment interact to influence the development of any given behavior. Advances in research design and attention to this basic question of how the two forces propel development will help us achieve a greater understanding of development.

Some have expressed concern about the possible negative consequences of emphasizing the genetic contributions to children's behavior to the exclusion of environmental forces. Such an emphasis may discourage parents from exerting extra effort to change their children's behavior, such as increasing school achievement or sociability. Furthermore, such an emphasis may discourage government and other agencies from funding programs that increase parenting skills as a way of changing children's behavior because "It's all in the genes." Harris never intended her ideas to have such effects, but that may remain beyond her control. As we shall see throughout the book, whatever the influence of genes, many environmental interventions are effective.

PARENTING LICENSE

Although some behavior geneticists believe parents are unimportant, David Lykken has a different view. Despite the fact that his work has demonstrated high heritability for certain traits, he nevertheless believes that parents' behavior can have such a profound influence on children's lives that parents should be *licensed* to have a child. Having studied criminal behavior and its antecedents, he is convinced that immature, impulsive parents doom a child to a life of difficulties:

> Most of the 1,400,000 men currently locked up in American prisons would have become tax-paying neighbors had they been switched in the hospital nursery and sent home with a mature, self-supporting, married couple. The parent with whom they did go home would in most instances not have been fit to adopt someone else's baby. . . . For evolutionary reasons, human beings are reluctant to interfere with the procreational rights of any person, no matter how immature, incompetent, or unsocialized he or she might be. In consequence human beings tend not to think about the rights of a child to a reasonable opportunity for life, liberty, and the pursuit of happiness.[80]

Lykken would require prospective parents to get a license, just as adults have to get a license to drive a car or operate a motorcycle. Similar to the requirements for adoptive parents, a parenting license would require proof of (1) legal age, (2) marriage, (3) employment or economic independence, and (4) no history of violent criminal behavior. If parenting courses were available, he would require a certificate of completion. Proof of marriage is required because Lykken believes the biggest risk factor for adult problems is lack of a biological father. If prospective parents are gay or lesbian and therefore do not meet the requirements, they can appeal to a family court for a license. If parents had a child without a license, the child would be removed and placed for permanent adoption. If a divorce occurred after the child was born, the child would remain with the parents.

The marriage requirement is controversial, and some psychologists such as Sandra Scarr believe it is a restriction of Constitutional rights.[81] Lykken states that if couples object to marriage, they can sign a legal contract indicating they plan to stay together for twelve years to provide stability in the child's life.

To critics of licensure, Lykken replies that no system will eliminate all problems, but he insists, "Parenthood is both a privilege and a responsibility. The privilege of parenthood would not be determined by test scores or family trees, but by behavior. . . . If you wish to have a child, all you have to do is to grow up, keep out of trouble, get a job, and get married."[82]

PRACTICAL QUESTION: WHAT ARE SOCIETY'S OBLIGATIONS TO PARENTS?

As we have seen, parents profoundly contribute to their children's growth, but so does the social system, as the Rochester Longitudinal Study documented. Here we discuss society's obligations to parents and children.

A comparison of the supportive services available to children and parents in the United States with those offered in other countries provides a broad background for understanding what options society has for supporting parents. Let us start with what the United States currently offers children and parents. The government provides to all children free public education from ages five to eighteen and to all parents a specific tax exemption for each dependent child and a tax credit for child care or preschool expenses. Further help is extended only when a child has a specific disability or the family lives below the poverty level.

By contrast, other industrialized countries offer all children free public education beginning at age three and health care. Families are given an allowance or direct cash benefit up to 5 or 10 percent of the family income per child.[83] Many countries are adding a guaranteed minimum child support payment if an absent parent does not pay. In addition, most countries require government or business employers to provide paid maternity leave for twelve weeks. In fact, the United States is one of only six countries in the world (the others are Australia, New Zealand, Lesotho, Swaziland, and Papua New Guinea) that do not provide paid maternity leave.[84] The Family and Medical Leave Act in the United States permits a parent to take twelve weeks of unpaid leave.

Not only do we fail to give financial support to children and families, but we fail to give psychological support as well. Jay Belsky and John Kelly, summarizing observations from Belsky's study of new parents, write of society's failure to acknowledge parents' contribution to society:

> As I watched our couples cope with financial concerns and with all the other challenges of the transition, I found myself deeply moved. The quiet dignity and courage of our new fathers and mothers—specially our employed mothers–was inspiring to behold. But as I watched them, I also found myself deeply troubled by how little public acknowledgment, how little public support and gratitude they and other new parents receive for their selflessness and devotion.
>
> In its better moods our society now treats the family with benign neglect; in its darker moods, as a source of parody. None of our participants complained about the lack of public support for their family building, but it affected them—in many cases by making the routine sacrifices of the transition that much harder. It is difficult to sacrifice oneself when the larger society says the overriding purpose in life is devotion to self, not devotion to others. And in a few cases it made those sacrifices too far to go. The rising divorce rate, falling school grades, widespread drug use—all ills that plague the American family today—are complex and have many sources. But I think one major source is that our society no longer honors what I witnessed every day of the Project—the quiet heroism of everyday parenting.[85]

Survey data support Belsky and Kelly's observations. A 1996 survey of 2,600 adults (nonparents and parents of European American, African American, and Hispanic backgrounds) reveals that only 12 to 17 percent describe children and adolescents as friendly and respectful.[86] A much larger percentage—30 to 50 percent—see them as wild, disorderly, disrespectful, undisciplined, and uncontrolled in public. Nonparents and parents alike blame parents for children's and teens' problems. They believe parents have children before they are ready for the responsibility, and half the respondents believe parents spoil children and fail to give them appropriate discipline. Only 22 percent of nonparents and 19 percent of parents feel it is common for parents to be good role models for children. All recognize, however, that a parent's job today is more difficult than in the past, because children face problems with drugs and alcohol, more sex and violence in the media and the world outside the home, and more gangs in school.

In 1997, concerned that parents fail to receive support from the surrounding environment, the social scientists Sylvia Hewlett and Cornel West commissioned a national survey of European American, African American, and Hispanic parents with incomes ranging from $20,000 to $100,000 to determine what parents want from government and employers.[87] They also conducted focus groups with a subset of the sample. In their sample, 86 percent of men and 73 percent of women had paid employment, with most of the men (70 percent) and fewer women (43 percent) working full-time. Twenty percent reported that they held two jobs to support the family; only 18 percent of women were stay-at-home mothers. Many parents (62 percent) reported at least some community activities with children.

The parents surveyed were also asked their opinion of what government and employers do and can do to support parents in rearing children. Only 6 percent of the sample think either government or employers were doing a great deal to help parents; 84 percent believe that government could help parents, and 76 percent think that employers could act to support parents. Further, parents believe that government can take a variety of actions to ease their financial burdens and offer services to children, such as providing health care for the 9 million children who do not already have it,[88] tripling the dependent tax exemption to $7,500, doubling the tax credit for child-care and preschool expenses to $1,000 per year, eliminating sales taxes on necessities for children (such as diapers, car seats, and school supplies), providing employers tax incentives to encourage family-friendly policies (such as part-time and flex-time hours), requiring businesses with more than twenty-five employees to give twelve weeks of paid maternity or paternity leave at times of birth or adoption, and extending school hours each day and throughout the year to better match parents' work schedules. Parents also want government to require gun makers to install safety devices to prevent firearm accidents among children. Finally, parents believe that employers can adopt policies that give parents more time with family, such as allowing parents to take two additional weeks of leave without pay each year and ensuring three days of paid leave for family needs such as school conferences or doctors' visits.

Believing that neither government nor employers are giving parents the supports they require, Hewlett and West have organized the National Parenting Association to assist in lobbying for what they want. Hewlett and West point to the success of the AARP (American Association of Retired Persons) in organizing voters and focusing the attention of government and business on the needs of older Americans. The decline in the poverty rate among people over 65 illustrates the effects of AARP lobbying that began in 1958. In 1960, the poverty rate of people over 65 was 35 percent; in 1995, the comparable figure was 11 percent, just about half the poverty rate of children. The poverty rate among children dropped from 27 percent in 1960 to a low of 14 percent in 1969 but then rose to 20 percent in 1984 and fluctuates around that number because there was no strong voting block to ensure protection of children's interests. Organizing an effective voting block would not be easy, as the proportion of parents in the electorate dropped from 55 percent in 1956 to 35 percent in 1996 because of the general aging of the population.

Still, Hewlett and West point to the success of government programs benefiting families after World War II. A Parents' Bill of Rights (Table 1-2) is based on the G.I. Bill of Rights that so effectively supported the educational and occupational advancement of parents and the housing needs of families in the 1950s. The benefits were available for all veterans and represented an investment that boosted the economic well-being of everyone.

The G.I. Bill was an expression of gratitude to men and women who performed incalculable service to their country by risking their lives in the war. Parental rights would also be an expression of gratitude to parents who perform service for their country by rearing the next generation. They spend enormous amounts of time and money to rear children who will grow into healthy, competent adults whose work and taxes will support an ever increasing older population of adults. Creating and rearing such children is indeed a great service to the country.

■ **T A B L E 1-2**
PARENTS' BILL OF RIGHTS

I. Time for Children
  A. Paid Parenting Leave—24 weeks that either parent can use in the child's first six years
  B. Family-Friendly Workplaces—tax incentives for companies offering flexible hours and home-based work
  C. A Safety Net—income support for poor parents with children under six; teen mothers would live with experienced mothers

II. Economic Security
  A. Living Wages—$7.00 per hour minimum wage and subsidies for low-wage workers
  B. Job Opportunities—programs that improve job skills
  C. Tax Relief—eliminating payroll taxes for parents; extended childcare credit
  D. Help with Housing—mortgage subsidies; rent vouchers

III. Pro-Family Electoral System
  A. Incentives to Vote
  B. Parents' Voting in Behalf of Children

IV. Pro-Family Legal Structure
  A. Stronger Marriage—tougher standards for marriage and greater obstacles to divorce
  B. Support for Fathers—paternity leave; generous visiting for noncustodial parent
  C. Adoption Assistance—benefits to people adopting children

V. Supportive External Environment
  A. Violence-Free and Drug-Free Neighborhoods
  B. Quality Schooling; Extended School Day and Year
  C. Childcare and Family Health Coverage
  D. Responsible Media
  E. Organized Voice—creation of organization to promote parents' interest

VI. Honor and Dignity
  A. Index of Parental Well-Being—measure reflecting parents' wages, time for children, affordable housing, and health care
  B. National Parents' Day
  C. Parent Privileges—education for parent who cares for child; reduced costs for certain family activities

From Sylvia Ann Hewlett and Cornel West, *The War against Parents* (Boston: Houghton Mifflin, 1998), 230–258. Copyright © 1998 by Sylvia Ann Hewlett and Cornel West. Reprinted by permission of Houghton Mifflin Company. All rights reserved.

INTERVIEW
with Sylvia Hewlett

Sylvia Ann Hewlett is chair of the National Parenting Association and, with Cornel West, coauthor of The War against Parents.

In addition to the Parents' Bill of Rights, are there other ways society can help parents?
Having a place for parents is important. There is no place for parents in our public life. That is so easy to change, and the symbolism of those changes is so powerful. It shows that we are supporting and celebrating parents' doing things with children. One of the ridiculous examples of how shortsighted our public places are is the newly designed children's center in Central Park. It is a beautiful place for the under-five crowd. It has all kinds of wonderful hands-on stuff—little story-time corners as well as the petting zoo.

But look at the fee structure going in; it is typical of many children's museums and children's parks around the country. If you are over two, you have to pay three dollars—not an insignificant amount—a parent pays seven dollars, but senior citizens get massive discounts. So what you see outside on any nice afternoon is a row of mothers having designated one mother to go in with the children because they cannot all afford to go in. If we are serious about encouraging parent-child recreational time, the first thing we have to do is make the fee structure reflect that. We should be encouraging single parents to take their children there. It is educational and absolutely something mothers should be doing with children. Yet when it is ten dollars a visit, they cannot do that. You stand there and look at the fees, and your jaw drops, because the group that does not need the subsidy in this context at all is the one that is privileged.

Another thing that makes me crazy in this city and is typical of other cities is that there is no place on buses for parents and young children and their strollers and other equipment. I take the bus across town to get one of my children at school. I go with my toddler, and there is no place to sit, no place to put the stroller. Now, buses have learned to recognize the needs of the elderly and the disabled. Right up front there are nice seats for them but no seats for pregnant mothers or parents with babies or young children. You get on a New York City bus, clutching your toddler, your equipment, and a stroller, and the first thing you do is feel apologetic about being there. The bus driver scowls at you, and no one wants to sit near you. It's a ridiculous situation, and it doesn't happen in other countries.

I also think there should be a parents' room in every school. At present there is no place to go, to hang out, to have coffee and read a little literature about developing reading skills or something. I think the whole thing about having a place for parents, an honored place in our public squares and in our schools and on our transportation system, is so critical. There is a tiny movement to create parking spaces in suburban malls for mothers with young children, but the efforts for programs like that are few and far between. That could spread like wildfire if a few communities did it. You need leadership. You need political leaders to take the issues seriously.

MAIN POINTS

Parenting is

- nourishing, protecting, and guiding new life
- providing basic resources, love, attention, and values

The process of parenting involves

- ongoing interaction among children, parents, and society
- children who have their own needs and temperaments and at the same time meet important needs of parents
- parents who have responsibilities to rear their children and meet their children's needs
- society as a powerful source of support or stress for children and parents

Contemporary families

- reflect increasing diversity in the United States
- face concerns stemming from employment trends, time pressures, outside pressures such as television, and the general social health of the country

Research in response to the nature versus nurture debate

- centers on the ways that genes and environment influence child development
- explores the importance of peers in children's development
- has become more rigorous but as yet has not settled the debate
- suggests the importance of environent *and* genes as interacting forces

Parents are

- the single most important influence and resource in a child's life
- not the only influences on children's behavior; peers, media, communities, and social events outside the family all affect children's behavior and development
- advocates who can make social changes to help children
- so influential that some suggest that parents be required to have a license to be parents
- in strong agreement that the government needs to be more financially supportive of parents and that employers need to allow parents more time with families

U.S. society

- offers parents fewer supports than are given to parents in European countries
- provides fewer benefits to children than do European nations
- may respond to parents' and children's needs only when parents organize and vote to obtain what they need

EXERCISES

1. From the year you were born, trace the social influences acting on your parents as they raised you. For example, for the 1980s, such influences might have included the high rate of women's participation in the workforce, the high rate of divorce and remarriage, the drop in skilled-labor jobs, and the instability of jobs in corporate America. Show the effects of social change on your daily life and the ways your parents cared for you—for example, if your mother's working resulted in specific day care, if divorce led to your being in two homes, if remarriage introduced more adults into your life, if violence affected your family life.

2. Based on the material in this chapter, write a job description for a parent. You may want to revise the job description as you read future chapters.

3. Suppose that parents had to obtain a license in order to have a child as David Lykken suggests. What would you require for such a license?

4. Read the newspaper for one week and cut out all the articles of interest to parents, including news and feature articles. Describe what these articles tell you about the parenting experience today. The articles might focus on solving certain kinds of behavioral problems or providing opportunities for children's optimal development (certain play or educational activities), or they might consider laws relating to parents' employment benefits or to the rights of parents and children in courts when parents divorce or must pay penalties because of children's behavior.

5. How can parents change society's negative view of them and their children?

ADDITIONAL READINGS

Borkowski, John G., Ramey, Sharon Landesman, and Bristol-Power, Marie, eds. *Parenting and the Child's World: Influences on Academic, Intellectual, and Socio-Emotional Development.* Mahwah, NJ; Erlbaum, 2002.

Harris, Judith Rich. *The Nurture Assumption: Why Children Turn out the Way They Do.* New York, Free Press, 1998.

Hewlett, Sylvia Ann, Rankin, Nancy, and West, Cornel, eds. *Taking Parenting Public.* Lanham, MD: Rowman & Littlefield, 2002.

Steyer, James P. *The Other Parent.* New York: Atria, 2002.

Westman, Jack C., ed. *Parenthood in America: Undervalued, Underpaid, and under Siege.* Madison: University of Wisconsin Press, 2001.

CHAPTER

2

Theories of Development and Strategies of Parenting

IN THE NEWS

New York Times, November 5, 2002, p. D5
In the search for understanding the origins of brain development, cultural biologists share the beliefs of Peter Huttenlocher that experience influences the wiring of the brain structure present at birth. They conclude that culture influences the wiring as well as the contents of the brain. See page 40 for details.

 Go to PowerWeb at:
www.dushkin.com/powerweb
to read articles and newsfeeds
on **learning, parenting, parents,** and other topics related to this chapter.

Providing loving care and opportunities for children to develop competence and self-esteem is a daunting responsibility. Parents looking for guidelines to do this find that there is no one theory of parenting to consult. In this chapter we look first at theories of child development and how they provide a general direction for parents. We then look at styles of parenting derived from specific research on parent-child interactions. Finally, we look at how parenting programs contribute to parents' effectiveness.

Despite the importance of parenthood to adults and society, most parents come to the experience with little preparation. Some have had nursing or teaching jobs that have given them useful knowledge and experience with children. Many have baby-sat. But few new parents learn even the most basic child-care practices until they are preparing for childbirth in the last month of pregnancy. As one well-educated father said, "I wondered how could they let him go home with us, this little package weighing seven or eight pounds. I had no idea of what to do. I kind of knew you fed him, and you cleaned him, and you kept him warm, but I didn't have any hands on experience, anything practical."

Although theories of child development usually do not provide specific direc-tions for parents, parents can gain insights from them on how to relate to children and how to help them grow. From its early origins in the late nineteenth century, developmental psychology considered the genetic and biological factors as well as the social aspects of life to be important to the development of the child.[1] Early the-ory was broad based, with roots in biology and branches extending into the social community that carried suggestions about how to improve the environments of children. Over time, theories began to focus on either inborn features of develop-ment or environmental sources of growth and change. This latter approach led to learning theorists, who emphasize that growth comes from the patterns of rewards, punishments, and stimulation from the environment. Learning theorists have pro-vided much guidance for parents. We have maturationists, such as Arnold Gesell, who emphasize that the pattern of growth lies within the child and will unfold in stages over time. Gesell's and his coworkers' books chronicling children's growth are still widely read as guides to parents' behavior with children.[2]

The most current theories, however, have returned to embrace genetic, biologi-cal, psychological, and social influences as determiners of development. They all fall under the umbrella of an overall approach called the systems view of development, which we examine first to provide a theoretical context for the individual theories. Then we take up a fuller discussion of learning theory, psychoanalytic theory, and theories of knowing the world.

SYSTEMS VIEW OF DEVELOPMENT

Currently, many psychologists endorse a systems view that integrates genetic, phys-ical, behavioral, and environmental influences on development. Gilbert Gottlieb writes,

> The systems view sees individual development as hierarchically organized into multiple levels (e.g., genes, cytoplasm, cell, organ, organ system, organism, behavior, environ-ment) that can mutually influence each other. The traffic is bidirectional, neither exclu-sively bottom-up or top-down.[3]

Figure 2-1 describes the bidirectional transactions that occur at all levels. No level of influence is more important than the others. A dynamic relationship exists among the levels, so that the effect of any given stimulus or event depends "on the rest of the system, making all factors potentially interdependent and mutually con-straining."[4] An individual's behavior, then, cannot be understood apart from its

■ **FIGURE 2-1**
A SYSTEMS VIEW OF PSYCHOBIOLOGICAL DEVELOPMENT

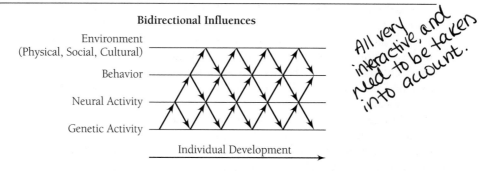

Source: Gilbert Gottlieb, Douglas Wahlsten, and Robert Lickliter, "The Significance of Biology for Human Development: A Developmental Psychological Systems View," in *Handbook of Child Psychology,* 5th ed., ed. William Damon, vol. 1: *Theoretical Models of Human Development,* ed. Richard M. Lerner (New York: Wiley, 1991), p. 241. This material is used by permission of John Wiley & Sons, Inc.

genetic and physiological underpinnings, and the individual cannot be understood apart from his or her environment.

Development occurs not as a result of any one factor, as we often think, but as a result of the dynamic interaction of these levels of influence.[5] We are familiar with the idea of a fixed, predetermined sequence that shapes behavior. For example, we learn that genetic influences shape infants' temperamental responses, which in turn elicit positive or negative responses from caregivers in the environment. There were numerous examples of this fixed sequence in the discussion of the behavior geneticists' views in Chapter 1.

In systems theory, there is no fixed, predetermined sequence of gene, neural pathways, behavior, and effect on the environment, but only a set of possibilities that depend on the interaction and feedback from the other parts of the system, including the physical and social environment.[6] The environment influences the physiological and cellular reactions in the body that, in turn, can affect the actions of genes at the cellular level. These genetic changes can then influence later behavior. For example, the effects of a parent's substance abuse on the genetic potential of the developing fetus, cited in Chapter 1, provide an example of how the environment of the organism can change genetic potential, which in turn shows up in the person's intellectual and social behavior. Further, these genetic changes can be passed on to the next generation.

In developmental theory, a given stimulus can engender many possible responses, depending on the interaction of all the different levels of influence. Conversely, there are many paths that can arrive at a given developmental outcome.[7] For example, as we shall see in Chapters 8 and 9, a child's hyperactive, impulsive, inattentive behavior can occur for many reasons. Some children have a strong family history of, and most likely a genetic predisposition to, the behavior. Some children born prematurely develop these behaviors. We know, too, that children exposed at young ages to domestic violence are at risk for neurobiological changes in brain structure and later difficulties in concentration and inattention. So, numerous paths lead to the same behavior.

Systems theory insists that while there are many possibilities in development, action at any one of these levels can restrict development.[8] Again, we are very aware that the genes place broad limitations on development, but as the results of the Rochester Longitudinal Study showed in Chapter 1,[9] and as the behavior geneticist David Lykken insists,[10] the psychosocial environment can also place severe limitations on individual growth.

Many recent advances in research tools support a systems perspective. For example, imaging techniques have shown us that much supposedly genetically determined brain development actually involves input from the environment. Beginning with conception, environmental factors such as nutrition, physical surroundings, care, and stimulation influence "how the intricate circuitry of the human is 'wired.'"[11] After birth, environmental input and stimulation establish and strengthen connections among brain cells, thus shaping the architecture of the brain. Daniel Siegel summarizes this new emphasis on the plasticity of the brain:

> An infant is born with a genetically programmed excess in neurons, and the postnatal establishment of synaptic connections is determined by both genes and experience. Genes contain the information for the general organization of the brain's structure, but experience determines which genes become expressed, how, and when. The expression of genes leads to the production of proteins that enable neuronal growth and the formation of new synapses. Experience—the activation of specific neural pathways—therefore directly shapes gene expression and leads to the maintenance, creation, and strengthening of the connections that form the neural substrate of the mind. Early in life, interpersonal relationships are a primary source of the experience that shapes how genes express themselves within the brain. . . . Experiences lead to an increased activity of neurons, which enhances the creation of new synaptic connections. This experience-dependent brain growth and differentiation is thus referred to as an "activity-dependent brain process."[12]

Evolutionary Developmental Theory

Evolutionary developmental theory is a systems theory that looks at behavior in terms of Darwin's concepts of natural selection and reproductive fitness.[13] Evolutionary psychologists believe the following:

> Genetically based variations in physical or psychological features of an individual interact with the environment, and, over many generations, these features tend to change in frequency, resulting, eventually, in species-wide traits in the population as a whole. Thus, through the process of natural selection, adaptive changes in individuals, and eventually species, arise.[14]

Adaptive behaviors that enable individuals to survive, grow to maturity, and reproduce offspring are passed along through the genes to future generations. Neither genes nor the environment dominate the process of natural selection; it is the interaction of these two forces that produces development. The inherited psychological mechanisms that have evolved over time are specific modules designed to deal with important areas of experience:

Rather than seeing the human mind as consisting of a general-purpose processing mechanism that can be applied to a wide range of problems, evolutionary psychologists typically see the mind as consisting of a set of modules, each specialized to deal with a certain type of problem. Within social psychology, domain-specific abilities have been hypothesized for attachment, hierarchical power, coalition groups, reciprocity, and mating.[15]

Darwin used the term *reproductive fitness* to refer to individuals' success in surviving, maturing, reproducing, and passing their genes on to the next generation. Contemporary evolutionary psychologists use the term *inclusive fitness* to describe individuals' success in reproducing their genes not only through producing their own offspring but also by nurturing the offspring of relatives who share a smaller percentage of genes.[16] For example, children carry 50 percent of their parents' genes. One can also pass on one's genes through nurturing younger siblings who share 50 percent of the genes and nieces and nephews who share 25 percent of the genes.

Evolutionary psychologists look at human behavior in terms of its usefulness in promoting adaptation to the environment. They describe how current patterns of life have evolved in the process of natural selection.[17] Early human beings lived in small, hunting-gathering tribes requiring organized, cooperative, social behaviors. A large brain evolved to produce the more complex social behaviors required. Such a brain meant that an infant had to be born in an immature state so that the body of the mother could accommodate the birth of the child. Being born in an immature state required a longer period of dependence on caregivers. The longer period of dependence in turn encouraged the father's ongoing protection and support of mother and child. Thus, the human family evolved.

While critics believe that evolutionary theory primarily interprets what has already happened, evolutionary psychologists believe that their views deepen our understanding of certain contemporary family patterns of behavior.[18] Evolutionary theory accounts for the willingness of parents to sacrifice their own personal needs and invest enormous energy to care for children as children carry on their genes. It also accounts for infant-parent attachment behavior, described in a later section of this chapter. In predicting that parents invest more care in biological children than in stepchildren with whom they share no genes, it provides a possible explanation for the fact that stepchildren are more likely to be physically harmed or abused than biological children as

> restraints against acting violently toward nonrelated children are much less than the restraints involved with one's genetic children. . . . We are not suggesting that the killing of stepchildren, or unrelated children in general, was once adaptive in our evolutionary past . . . rather, we argue that in high-stress situations in which violence is apt to occur, the evolved tendencies that inhibit aggression against one's biological children are not as easily activated for one's stepchildren.[19]

Critics believe that too much emphasis is placed on inborn qualities, but evolutionary psychologists respond that they believe inborn traits are influenced by interaction with environmental forces. They insist that we can change behavior patterns adaptive to a previous environment but no longer effective in contemporary life. In the past, mothers provided exclusive caregiving because only they could provide breast milk. That pattern can be altered to include fathers as equal caregivers, since breast milk can now be expressed, refrigerated, and used at a later time.

The neurobiologist Peter Huttenlocher challenges some of the beliefs of evolutionary psychologists. He agrees that inborn genetic programs may account for the development of "relatively simple, basic functions, such as the motor and primary sensory cortex,"[20] but more complex processes such as language and thought become specialized and organized on the basis of experience. The numerous examples of the plasticity of the brain "make a good case for largely environmentally regulated rather than innate cortical systems. A correlate to high plasticity of the brain is the finding that the cerebral cortex is less modular than previously thought, and that in many ways it [the cortex] acts like a multipotential distribution system."[21] For example, when young children are learning language, both hemispheres of the brain are involved, and as language becomes more refined, the areas of the brain involved become more localized. If the language is complex, the area of the brain that is activated increases to accommodate the difficulty of the task. So, the brain responds to the task at hand.

Although evolutionary theory may be incorrect about the inheritance of modules designed to deal with certain areas of experience, its focus on the adaptive aspects of human behavior can provide thought-provoking insights. It takes a look at "the big picture"[22] of human behavior, relating present behavior patterns to a past extending back thousands of years.

Developmental Contextual Theory

Richard Lerner and his coworkers have also applied the systems perspective to parenting.[23] In their view, because person and environment are fused, children and parents form a single unit. Parent-child relationships are nested in a multilayered social environment that provides the context for development. This context includes the extended family, the social networks of parent and child outside the family, institutions in the larger community (such as school and work), society, and culture. The behavior of children and parents affects the social context, and the social context makes demands and shapes the behavior of parents and children to fit social values.

In developmental contextual theory, both individuals and their social worlds are seen as active and changing entities. We tend to be aware of the changes in individuals but less aware of the changes in social institutions. For example, over time, the social organization of our society has become more accepting and supportive of single-parent households, so that children in single-parent homes may not experience the social ostracism that children in such families experienced thirty years ago. Still, the social organization has presented enormous economic challenges for these families, especially those headed by women, and these challenges have not changed with time.

Lerner and his coworkers believe that we can interpret parents' behaviors only in the light of the context acting on parents. For example, harsh parental discipline produces not just one effect but many possible effects depending on the child's age and the ethnic and social class of the family. They view the effects of most parenting behaviors as the results of interactions with other social forces.

Adaptive behavior does not depend on just the child's characteristics, or the parents' behaviors, or the demands of the social context, but on whether there is a good match or fit among these interacting forces. The term *goodness of fit* refers to the match among the child, the parent, and the social context. Highly active children who live on a farm where they work with animals before and after school and walk a mile to school may be highly valued at home because of their great energy. In school they can sit still and pay attention because so much of their out-of-class time is active. The social context of their daily life fits very well with their characteristics.

Contrast that with the situation of highly active children who live in small apartments and whose parents both work. Before and after school, they go to the babysitter's where they get little outdoor time and little exercise. Instead, they watch TV. In school they squirm in their seats and frequently get up to walk around. At home, they nag their parents to let them go out to play, but the parents are reluctant to let them be outside unsupervised. The parents are irritated by the nagging and the teacher's frequent telephone calls about their child's behavior. There is not a good fit between these children's characteristics and what the parents and teacher ask of them. Such children are often labeled as behavior problems.

Because the social context is an integral part of each child's life, Lerner has great concerns about the few supports offered to children and their parents in this country. In particular, he expresses concern that social policy does not reflect the importance of programs that provide support to both parents and children over long periods. He cites Early Head Start programs and Healthy Families in Massachusetts programs as being comprehensive, effective programs that prevent the development of children's problems.

Bioecological Theory of Development

Urie Bronfenbrenner is a systems theorist who emphasizes the ecological context of development.[24] The term *ecology* refers to the environments that human beings encounter in daily life as they grow and develop. Having initially focused attention on the environmental systems, Bronfenbrenner has recently modified his model to include internal biopsychological characteristics that shape the individual's response to the environment. In doing so, he believes that he has provided as differentiated a picture of the individual as he already had provided of the environment.

Bronfenbrenner describes the internal biopsychological characteristics as dispositions, skills, abilities, resources, and demands that the individual brings to interactions with the environment. He also distinguishes between processes and the environment. *Processes* are the daily interchanges the child has with people and objects in the environment (see Chapter 1).

The environment includes several systems. The *microsystem* is the pattern of activities and daily interactions with objects and people—parents, caregivers, teachers, coaches, peers. This is what is discussed in most chapters of the textbook—the interactions children have with other people and objects every day. The *mesosystem* consists of interactions and interrelationships between parents and other people who care for children—parents and teachers, parents and day care providers, parents and coaches (see Chapters 9 and 13).

The *exosystem* includes agencies and institutions that influence children's daily lives but do not include children as participants, such as parents' employers (see Chapter 13) and community and government agencies. For example, employers can promote or complicate parents' relationships with children by their policies on time off for children's activities or illnesses. The *macrosystem* is the broad cultural context in which mesosystems and exosystems exist—culturally shared blueprints about how things are done, such as how children are cared for. We discuss this topic throughout but in the most detail in Chapters 1 and 3.

As we noted in Chapter 1, Bronfenbrenner is quite concerned at what he calls the growing chaos in children's and parents' lives. Like Lerner and other systems theorists, he looks to programs that are committed to improving the social lives of both parents and children.

LEARNING THEORIES

Learning theories describe how organisms, including human beings, develop new responses based on experience in the world. Learning theories trace their origins to the work of Ivan Pavlov in the late nineteenth and early twentieth centuries and have been important forces in developmental psychologies for more than a hundred years.[25] They stress the role of environmental stimulation in determining behavior change and have shown less interest in what goes on inside the organism than systems theorists have shown.

Pavlov demonstrated that dogs acquired new behaviors when new signals were linked with already existing responses. Termed *classical conditioning,* such learning is especially important for understanding how new responses relate to an individual's emotional and physiological responses. In everyday life, a stimulus (i.e., trigger) is followed by a response. In Pavlov's first experiment with dogs, the sight of food caused the dog to salivate. The sight of food was called the *unconditioned stimulus,* and salivating, the *unconditioned response.* When a neutral stimulus, a buzzer, was paired many times with the sight of food, the buzzer alone came to trigger the response of salivating. The buzzer was called the *conditioned stimulus* because only after many pairings with food could it elicit the response.

We see the process of classical conditioning in everyday life when people who experience a strong emotional feeling attach that feeling to other stimuli present at the time. Later, those stimuli may trigger the emotional response. For example, a child is frightened by a barking dog who nips him playfully. The next time the child sees a barking dog, he feels frightened because he associates the barking alone with the fear that he felt when the barking dog was accompanied by the dog's nip.

Pavlov concentrated on stimuli that preceded the behavior of interest. American learning theorists concentrated on changing behavior through *operant* or *instrumental conditioning,* which involves forming new associations between stimuli and responses on the basis of positive or negative consequences following the behavior. John Watson, the founder of behaviorism, applied the theory to rearing children. Watson believed that children are blank slates who need to learn good habits. In

Psychological Care of Infant and Child, he in 1928 advised parents to have strict, consistent schedules of daily life:

> There is a sensible way of treating children. Treat them as though they were young adults. Dress them, bathe them with care and circumspection. Let your behavior always be objective and kindly firm. Never hug and kiss them, never let them sit on your lap. It you must, kiss them once on the forehead when they say good night. Shake hands with them in the morning. Give them a pat on the head if they have made an extraordinarily good job of a difficult task. Try it out. In a week's time you will find how easy it is to be perfectly objective with your child and at the same time kindly. You will be utterly ashamed of the mawkish, sentimental way you have been handling it.[26]

Although this advice now seems extreme and even absurd, it is hard to exaggerate the impact the behaviorists had, here and in England. Mothers refused to feed their children even a few minutes before the end of the prescribed four-hour period and were afraid to hold and cuddle their babies. They were told that adherence to rigid rules was necessary if their children were not to go astray later in life.

Social learning theorists believe that, in addition to learning from rewards and punishments, children learn by observing models and imitating them. In fact, imitation of a model will occur even when the child receives no reward; observation of another person's behavior is enough to stimulate imitation. Children often "do as we do and not as we say" because they have observed us and are imitating our behavior instead of our words. They are most likely to imitate models who are warm, nurturant, and powerful. In extreme circumstances, when there is no model of warmth and power to copy, children will imitate a hostile, rejecting figure.

Social learning theorists such as Albert Bandura have focused on the active nature of the learner who chooses goals to pursue, reflects on performance, and makes adaptations in behavior to achieve success. In determining learning, the learner's thoughts and interpretations of the environment are as important as environmental rewards and punishments.[27]

So learning theories emphasize primarily, though not exclusively, the environment's contribution to growth and development. Social learning theorists such as Bandura also look to the individual's thoughts and interpretations of what the environment provides as an important element in development.

PSYCHOANALYTIC THEORIES

Working at the same time as Pavlov, Sigmund Freud concentrated on the emotional development of individuals, particularly those aspects that led to psychological problems.[28] He developed a theory that encompassed healthy behavior as well. Here we can review only a very brief description of one aspect of his theory—his view of childhood development.

Freud saw psychological development as arising from individuals' impulses to gratify basic physical needs, particularly sexual needs, within the boundaries of acceptable social conventions in order to avoid criticism or punishment from important figures. In talking to patients, he noticed that he could trace many adult behaviors back to experiences in childhood, so he set about describing the significant dimensions of childhood. He divided childhood into psychosexual stages that unfolded over time from birth through adolescence. The person's progression through these stages, as he or she strove to gratify impulses, and others' reactions to these strivings shaped adult personality. Freud emphasized the importance of appropriate gratification of children's natural impulses; such views contrasted with those of Watson. The pediatrician Benjamin Spock studied psychoanalysis for six years and incorporated many of Freud's insights into his best-selling *Baby and Child Care,* first published in 1946.[29]

Alfred Adler, a Viennese psychiatrist and an early follower of Freud, was the first to break with Freud.[30] He continued psychiatric work, pursuing an interest in the healthy and positive aspects of human behavior. He believed that human beings are purposive, decision-making beings, born with an innate capacity for cooperation, a strong desire to be part of a larger social group, and a genuine interest in and concern for other people. In his theory, he claimed that this inborn capacity for finding fulfillment in social living must be developed in day-to-day life experiences. To promote optimal development, Adler described methods of childrearing and effective principles of education that would promote optimal social development.

Rudolf Dreikurs, a Chicago psychiatrist, centers his strategy on Adler's ideas and shows how they are useful in today's world. A democratic society requires childrearing techniques that will prepare individuals to live in a free society as equals with other individuals. Freedom is not the absence of rules but order imposed by the agreement of everyone concerned. Parents influence children by gaining their cooperation, using encouragement to stimulate the development of children's inner resources, and applying logical and natural consequences to change children's behavior. Dreikurs makes numerous suggestions to parents in his books *The Challenge of Parenthood*[31] and *Children: The Challenge.*[32] His views were expanded in *STEP//TEEN: Systematic Training for Effective Parenting of Teens* by Don Dinkmeyer and Gary McKay.[33] We review Dreikurs's ideas in greater detail in Chapters 4 and 5.

Erikson's Lifespan View of Development

Erik Erikson, a Freudian psychoanalyst with a strong interest in cross-cultural research and the social determiners of personality, has devised a scheme for understanding lifespan psychological development, drawing on his clinical experiences with patients, insights from his longitudinal research with healthy children, and his own cross-cultural research.[34] In addition to expanding stages of development to include adult growth, Erikson also focused much greater attention on the positive, healthy aspects of development than Freud did.

Erikson describes growth as a series of eight stages, as shown in Table 2-1. In each stage, the individual has specific physical and psychological needs. Each stage has a developmental crisis that must be met and resolved. People have positive and negative experiences in satisfying needs, and both kinds of experiences are important for optimal development. If we have only positive gratifications, we never learn how to cope with difficulties. However, for healthy growth, the balance should favor the positive side. When this occurs, a strength or virtue develops.[35]

■ **T A B L E   2-1**
ERIK ERIKSON'S EIGHT STAGES OF LIFE

Ages	Crisis	Virtue
0–1	Trust versus Mistrust	Hope
1–3	Autonomy versus Shame/Doubt	Will
3–5	Initiative versus Guilt	Purpose
5–12	Industry versus Inferiority	Competence
12–19	Identity versus Identity Diffusion	Fidelity
19–	Intimacy versus Isolation	Love
20–	Generativity versus Stagnation	Care
	Integrity versus Despair	Wisdom

Erik H. Erikson, *Childhood and Society,* 2nd ed. (New York: W. W. Norton, 1963), n. 35.

Erikson does not believe that we solve each crisis once and for all. Later experiences can change earlier resolutions, for better or for worse. For example, stress during adulthood can disrupt mature ways of coping, so that for a brief period the individual may seem immature. Positive experiences in adulthood can reverse mistrust or doubt developed in childhood.

Let us look at each of the stages in Table 2-1. In the first year of life (stage 1), when caregiving is sensitive and reliable and the balance of experience is positive, children develop a sense of trust and a feeling of hope about life. In the toddler years (stage 2), when children receive opportunities and encouragement for self-direction, they develop a sense of autonomy, the ability to act independently, and strength of will—the ability to make free choices and to act with self-control.

In the preschool years (stage 3), children acquire more skills and initiate more complex activity. When the sum of experiences is positive, they develop a sense of purpose, the ability to set and pursue goals, free of fears of failure, punishment, or criticism. In the elementary school years (stage 4), children attend school and are industrious and productive. If experiences of success and accomplishment outweigh experiences of frustration and inferiority, children develop a sense of competence, the feeling that they can apply their skills to accomplish goals.

In adolescence (stage 5), teens incorporate sexuality into their evolving sense of self and develop an identity—a sense of sameness and continuity of self. Erikson emphasizes that we incorporate social values in our individual identities. For example, we all incorporate, in our own ways, society's views of what men are, what women are, what members of our ethnic group and religion are.

Individuals need to have their identities validated and confirmed by their parents and society. If teenagers cannot integrate previous life experiences with their emerging capacities and obtain confirmation from others that they are who they think they are, role confusion results. They remain uncertain of who they are and where they are heading. When life events and family members have not been supportive, an individual may develop a negative identity. He or she may become a delinquent, a dropout, a person who feels unable to do anything positive. When the balance of the experiences falls on the positive side and a sense of identity is formed, the virtue that develops is fidelity—what Erikson describes as faithfulness and loyalty to one's choices, whether they be persons, goals, or ideals.

The first stage of adulthood (stage 6) is the establishment of intimate personal ties. Intimate relationships involve the mutuality and surrender of the self to the other person and the relationship. The ability to be close to other people leads to the virtue of love—sharing of identities between friends and partners. This is a freely chosen, active love and involves transferring the love experienced in the developing years of childhood to adult relationships actively sought by and mutually important to the two partners.

The second stage of adulthood (stage 7) is the initiation of generativity, or the creation of new life. In the past, women have most often experienced this in the family setting, in creating home and children; men have done so in their work, in creating new products and ideas. However, parenting and work now are significant activities for both sexes. The virtue that develops in this period is care—concern for and attention to what has been created, even if this requires sacrifice.

In the final stage of life (stage 8), the focus returns to the individual and the development of a sense of ego integrity. People must come to terms with their lives and be satisfied with who and what they are and what they have done. The virtue or strength that develops during this period is wisdom, a deep understanding of life that is enriched by coming to terms with the prospect of one's own death. Erikson points out that children will be able to face life if elders can face death.

Examining the ego qualities and the virtues of each stage, we can see that Erikson describes the growth of active, adaptive individuals who are independent, giving, and concerned with other people and the world around them. Erikson believed that children grow best when they experience reliable and trustworthy caregiving, opportunities for self-directed activity, and parental and social confirmation that what they make and do is valuable. In Erikson's scheme of development, parenting is important to both the child who receives it and the parent who gives it.

Lifespan Attachment Theory

Attachment is "an enduring affectional tie that unites one person to another, over time and across space."[36] In 1958, the London psychoanalyst John Bowlby, influenced by animal studies, ethological theory, and his own studies of infants, used the term *attachment* to describe the parent-infant relationship. He believed *attachment* implied positive ties that lead to healthy development, as opposed to the negative connotations of *dependency*, the term Freudians used to characterize the child's relationship with the parent. While the term *attachment* initially referred to early parent-child relationships, its use has broadened to apply to adults' relationships with their own parents and with their partners and spouses.[37] We focus first on its use in research with parents and young children and then on its use in describing adult relationships. Note that attachment studies were most frequently carried out with mothers at first but then began to include fathers as well.

INTERVIEW
with Susan Harter

Susan Harter, a professor of psychology at the University of Denver, has spent twenty years studying the development of the self and self-esteem and has written numerous articles and chapters on the subject.

You have done a great deal of research on self-esteem. More than any other quality, I would say, parents hope to help children develop self-esteem. What can they do to promote it in their children?

We have identified two broad themes that impact children's self-esteem. First, the unconditional support and positive regard of parents and others in the child's world are particularly critical during the early years. What do we mean by support? It is communicating to children that you like them as people for who or what they are.

That sounds relatively easy but is in fact extremely difficult. Most of us as parents are far more skilled at providing conditional regard or support for children even though we are unaware we are doing it. We approve of our child if he cleans up his room or shares or doesn't hit his brother. So our support is conditional on his conduct. However, it isn't perceived by children as supportive at all. Basically it specifies how the child can please the parents. That does not feel good to children.

Unconditional regard validates children as worthy people and lets them know they are appreciated for who they are, for their strengths and weaknesses. It also involves listening to them, which is very validating to children as well as adults. So many well-meaning parents, and I make the same mistake, preach at their kids because we think we have a lot to say. We think we're teaching when we are really preaching. We don't refrain from talking; we don't shut up, listen well, and take the child's point of view seriously.

With unconditional support early on, children internalize positive regard so that when they are older, they can approve of themselves, pat themselves on the back, give themselves psychological hugs—all of which contribute to high self-esteem.

Another major part of self-esteem, beginning at about age eight, is feeling competent and adequate across the various domains of life. One does not have to feel competent in every domain in order to experience high self-esteem. Rather one needs to feel competent in those domains that he or she judges to be *important*. Profiles of competence for two children in the different areas of athletic, social, and intellectual competence can look very similar, but one child can have high self-esteem while the other can have low self-esteem. They both can feel competent in the same areas and feel inadequate in the same other areas. What distinguishes the *low*-self-esteem child is the fact that areas of incompetence are very important to his or her feeling of being worthwhile; thus the child doesn't feel good about himself or herself. The *high*-self-esteem child feels the low areas are very unimportant and so still feels good about himself or herself.

Attachment is a strong psychological bond to a figure who is a source of security and emotional support. This is not the same as the more general term *bonding*.[38] Attachment refers only to that aspect of the parent-child relationship that gives the infant feelings of safety, security, and protection and provides a safe base from which to explore the world. In infancy and childhood, the relationship is asymmetrical, in that infants derive security from parents, but not vice versa. In adult relationships, attachment involves a mutual, reciprocal relationship in which partners provide security and a safe base for each other.

Most research on attachment focuses on its development and its influence on childhood behavior. Initially, attachment was measured in a laboratory situation developed by Mary Ainsworth and termed *the Strange Situation.*[39] Observers noted the quality of mother-child interactions during play and noted the child's reactions to the mother's leaving the room, a stranger's entering, and the mother's return. Attachment is first measured when an infant is twelve months old, and can be measured periodically thereafter. Childhood attachment has also been measured by drawings and an Attachment Q-Sort that observers can use with older children.

Infants and children differ not in whether attachment takes place—almost all children become attached as part of life—but the quality of attachment differs. The most common form of attachment is the secure one.[40] Securely attached infants feel happy and secure with mothers; they protest when mothers leave and are happy and seek closeness when they return. About 60 to 70 percent of U.S. samples are described as securely attached.

There are three forms of insecure attachments. About 20 percent of U.S. infants are described as having *anxious-avoidant* attachments—being unconcerned when mothers leave and uninterested in their return. About 10 to 20 percent are described as having *anxious-resistant* attachments—strong protests when mothers leave and difficulties establishing closeness on return, alternately seeking the mother and resisting closeness.

More recently, a third form of insecure attachment has been identified as *disorganized/disoriented* attachment. Babies with such attachments show unpredictable changes in their behavior with the parent. At times, they happily approach the parent as a securely attached infant would, and at other times, they avoid the parent. Thus, their behavior is considered disorganized. They are also termed disoriented because they show signs of conflict and confusion as to how to respond to the parent by "freezing" or "stilling" when they are near the parent. Such attachments occur less frequently in low-risk families (13 percent), but the percentage increases in high risk families—28 percent in multiproblem families receiving supportive services, and 82 percent in families whose members mistreat babies.[41]

Development of Attachment   By seven or eight months, babies show attachment to parents. The baby seeks out the parent, is fearful when the parent leaves, and uses the parent as a safe physical base from which to explore the world. When parents are accepting of the baby, emotionally available, sensitive to the baby's needs, and cooperative in meshing activities with the baby's tempo, a secure attachment develops. When parents are intrusive and overstimulate the child, the babies are likely to form anxious-avoidant attachments, and when parents are insensitive to babies' cues and often unavailable, babies form anxious-resistant attachments.[42]

Disorganized/disoriented attachments are found in families where a parent appears frightened or traumatized, and, as a result may appear frightening to the child. As noted, these forms of attachment are more common in multiproblem and abusive families. They are also more common in families with adolescent or depressed mothers of all incomes. Compared with adult mothers, adolescent mothers appear less attuned to babies' needs and less consistent in how they relate to them.[43] Depressed mothers are less engaged and more negative in their interactions with their babies.[44]

Stability of Attachment   Stability of attachment can be assessed in childhood, and there are now studies assessing the stability of attachment from childhood to adulthood. Stability of attachment varies with the sample. When attachment classification was first studied in the 1970s, researchers found a 70 to 80 percent rate of stability in attachment from twelve to eighteen months. In recent large-scale studies, however, the rate over that same time interval has dropped to about 50 percent.[45] Many changes in the patterns of infants' lives may account for the lower stability today. For example, many more mothers of infants work, more fathers are involved in child care, and more tensions exist because of the instability of parents' employment.

Secure attachments appear to be more stable than insecure attachments, perhaps because positive, satisfying relationships are likely to be self-perpetuating.[46] Studies of attachment classifications over an extended period yield mixed results. Two show substantial stability (about 70 percent) for the classification of security from one year to late adolescence and early adulthood,[47] and two do not.[48] Instability appears to be related to negative life events, such as divorce or loss of emotional support, that change the quality of the parent-child relationships. Conversely, one short-term study found that when mothers of infants gained experience and confidence in their effectiveness, their relationships with their children improved, and anxious-avoidant attachments at twelve months changed to secure ones at eighteen months.[49] The evidence from both the short-term and longer-term studies reveals that factors that produce changes in the emotional quality of the parent-child relationship will tend to change the quality of the attachment.

Importance of Attachment   Psychologists speculate that strong attachments to parents and fear of strangers are important because they help the infant survive.[50] Secure attachment ensures that the child will remain responsive to the parent's guidance so the parent can continue to protect the child as the child becomes more independent. Further, Thomas Bower presents another reason for the importance of attachment.[51] He believes that the baby develops a communication system with a partner, usually the mother but possibly a twin or other adult. A complex individual style of relating develops, with shared vocalizations and gestures. Without the partner, the baby feels lonely and isolated. No one pays attention in the same way, and the fear of separation develops. The baby fears no loss of food or of love, but solitude and loneliness. Bower speculates that if shared communication is the basis of separation anxiety, then such fear should decrease as the child develops speech and can communicate with others. And indeed, it does diminish as speech develops.

Psychologists believe that experiences in attachment relationships provide a framework for babies' understanding of the world.[52] From these relationships, babies build internal models of how people relate to one another. Babies develop expectations of how well others will understand and respond to them, how much influence they will have on others, and what level of satisfaction they can expect from other people.

From these relationships, babies also develop a sense of their own lovability and competence. When others respond positively to their overtures, babies feel valued and influential and anticipate similar responses from adults in new situations. When babies are ignored or rejected, they may develop a sense of unworthiness and helplessness.

When interactions make up a consistent pattern, babies acquire a sense of order and predictability in experience that, in turn, generalizes to daily activities and to the world at large. Babies develop expectations about family routines and activities, and they pattern their interest in toys and in exploration on their caregivers' emotional reactions.

The benefits of early attachments extend to the future. Securely attached one-year-olds are more curious later in childhood than are insecurely attached ones.[53] They attack a problem vigorously and persistently but accept help from others and are not aggressive. Children with insecure attachments at one year tend later to be more anxious and more likely to have tantrums when presented with problems.

Social and Cultural Influences on Attachment   When living conditions are difficult, because of either economic stress or marital tensions, the proportion of insecure attachments rises.[54] Moreover, when unusual circumstances exist, parents' sensitivity as a means of promoting secure attachments can be overridden. For example, in Israeli samples of infants, 80 percent of those infants who slept at home at night were securely attached, whereas only 48 percent of infants who slept in a communal arrangement were securely attached.[55] The two groups of infants did not differ, however, in temperament and early life events.

Cross-national comparisons of the proportions of secure/insecure attachments reveal that broad cultural influences shape the responses of infants to the laboratory situation measuring attachment and that the percentages of infants in different classifications differ from those in middle-class samples in the United States. In Germany, where early independence is strongly encouraged once babies are mobile, about 49 percent of babies show anxious-avoidant attachments, 33 percent show secure attachments, and 12 percent show anxious-resistant attachments.[56] When encouraged to spend time separated from the mother, babies show less protest at mothers' going and less clingy, dependent behavior on her return than do American babies.

In Japanese culture, where a close relationship between mother and child is encouraged and separations from the parent rarely or never occur, babies almost never demonstrate anxious-avoidant attachments but are much more likely than babies in other cultures to protest mothers' leaving and find it so stressful that they cannot adjust easily to their return. Japanese babies have about the same rate of secure attachments as U.S. babies, but anxious-avoidant attachments are rare or absent, and anxious-resistant attachments occur in about 30 percent of babies.[57]

Separation history, then, appears to affect children's responses to mothers' leaving and returning. Within U.S. culture, babies of working mothers are less likely to protest their leaving the room and less interested in their return, presumably because they have had more experience with temporary separations and adjust to them. In Japan, babies of working mothers show attachment patterns similar to those of U.S. babies, presumably because their experience of separations is similar to that of babies in this country.[58]

Attachment to Both Parents   Until recently, the mother-child bond was considered the only attachment of importance in infancy. As researchers have observed parent-child interactions and attachments more carefully, however, they have found that babies become attached to both parents. The quality of the relationship with each parent determines the attachment. Although it is possible to be securely attached to one parent and insecurely attached to the other, attachment classifications are most often the same for both parents. Yet even when attached to both parents, babies still seek comfort from mothers when they are distressed.[59]

Adult Attachments   Research has focused primarily on attachment in infancy and early childhood, but "attachment is a lifespan phenomenon."[60] The concept can be applied to couples' relationships, to parents' attachment to their own parents, to parents' ties with their adult children as parents age, and to certain close relationships with friends. Here we focus on parents' attachments to their own parents.

Most often assessed by means of an Adult Attachment Interview, in adulthood attachment is assessed as a general quality, a state of mind regarding attachment. Interviews focus on adults' current feelings concerning childhood experiences with their parents. Researchers then derive adult attachment classifications from the experiences described in the interviews and from the way the person organizes and describes the experiences.[61] Classifications are secure/autonomous, dismissing, and preoccupied. They are generally stable when repeated up to four years later.

Securely attached parents, even those who experienced traumatic events, value these early attachments and place negative childhood events in perspective so they can think about and understand the effects of these events on their life. Insecurely attached parents who also dismiss the importance of these early events and attachments minimize the influence of these events on their present life. They see themselves as independent and strong adults. Insecurely attached parents preoccupied with past events seem confused about their experiences with early attachment figures. They remain entangled in feelings of anger, helplessness, conflict, or fearfulness, and they cannot gain insight or closure regarding these early experiences.

Securely attached parents are direct and open in their dealings with others and are not inclined to misperceive situations. Toward their children, they are emotionally supportive, sensitive, and responsive, yet they can set clear and consistent limits.

Insecurely attached, dismissive parents emphasize their independence and strength in the face of parental rejection, and they remain cool and remote from their children. As they do not believe their parents mattered in their life, they do not try to help or support their children emotionally. Confident of their abilities, they have few doubts about their parenting effectiveness. They report few negative thoughts about children in difficult childrearing situations.

Insecurely attached, preoccupied parents behave in a confusing and inconsistent manner with their children. Warm and gentle at times, they become angry and forceful with children at other times. They have many negative thoughts about children in difficult childrearing situations, blaming the problems on the child's personality. Clearly, parents' views of children and their styles of relating to them stem from a general way of perceiving and relating to people based on early life experiences.

Additional studies of parents' attachment to their own parents reveal that the group of securely attached parents consists of two subgroups—those with continuous secure attachments and those with "earned security."[62] Continuously securely attached parents are those who report early positive relationships with parents and have a current secure working model of attachment. Parents with earned security are those who describe difficult early relationships and hardships with parents but who, nevertheless, can gain distance from the hard times, put those experiences in perspective, and develop a secure working model of attachment. Their childhood experiences were as difficult as those of the group of parents who have insecure attachments with their parents, and they have as many sad, depressed feelings as do insecurely attached parents. Parents with earned security, however, differ from parents with insecure attachments in that they have worked through their painful feelings from harsh childhood experiences. They are then able to develop a flexible, warm style of parenting similar to that of parents with continuous security. Even during stressful times, parents with earned-security attachments maintain warmth and positive relationships with their children. Nevertheless, even those parents who have not worked through their difficult childhood experiences are insensitive parents only when they are stressed.

Psychoanalytic theories help parents understand both the child's inner drives and needs and the important contributions they make to long-term development as the child goes about meeting these needs. Like systems theories, they attend to the inner physiological aspects of growth and the social context of development, but unlike systems theories, they focus primarily on intimate relationships. Erikson and some of the attachment theorists discuss the impact of the larger societal context, but overall they emphasize intimate bonds.

THEORIES OF KNOWING THE WORLD

Here we look at two theories of knowing about the world as they have implications for parents. Jean Piaget, the Swiss psychologist, deepened our understanding of how children's minds grow and develop when he emphasized the importance of the child's active construction of knowledge.[63] Intellectual competence is a dynamic process in which the child explores the world, takes in information, and organizes it into internal structures called *schemes*. The process of taking in and organizing information is termed *assimilation*.

As children obtain new information, they find their internal schemes inadequate and modify them to account for the new information. The process of changing internal schemes to incorporate new facts is called *accommodation*.

Intellectual growth is a constant interplay of taking in new information (assimilation) and modifying it (accommodation) to achieve balance or equilibrium between the individual's structure of the world and the world itself. *Equilibration* is the active process by which the individual achieves this effective balance.

Piaget believed that intellectual growth is not just a matter of adding more and more refined schemes. Growth also results from new ways of responding to experience and organizing it. Piaget described intellectual growth in terms of four major periods, each with its own substages (see Table 2-2, p. 54). In the first two years, the sensorimotor period, knowledge comes from perceptions and motor activity, and schemes consist of action patterns. Within this period, the infant first repeats reflexive behaviors and becomes skilled at them, then repeats simple acts for their own sake—opening and closing the hands or kicking for the fun of it. The baby's own actions are the focus of interest; babies act for the sake of the action itself, not to achieve a purpose. Then in subsequent stages in this period, the child directs attention outward to the environment, repeating acts to observe change. Gradually, the child acts to achieve a purpose, for example, to grasp a toy or reach an object.

Toward the end of the first year, babies come to understand the permanence of objects. This major occurrence is essential to the development of a coherent world. The understanding that each object has an independent existence and permanence leads to exploration of these objects and how they work. Babies also begin to imitate simple gestures such as waving goodbye and, in the second year, more-complex actions such as imitating a parent's opening a door with a key.

Beginning at eighteen months to two years, babies begin to move from immediate experience of objects, people, and whatever is present at the moment to representational thought. They begin to use language and symbolic or mental representations. Piaget illustrates mental representations with the example of his sixteen-month-old daughter who saw another toddler have a temper tantrum when he was put in a playpen. The next day, she herself, when placed in her playpen, had a similar tantrum. Clearly the child remembered the tantrum and imitated it after a period of delay. Children do not have language, so she could not have a verbal memory. Piaget suggests that children store the memory of those motor movements associated with visual images and imitate them.

Language increases from a few single words at about one year to about fifty words and two-word sentences at age two, with a leap of nine hundred words by the time the child is three and to about fourteen thousand words when the child is six. This is an average of about nine new words a day. Language development goes hand in hand with cognitive development. As children have more-complex thoughts to communicate, they require more words and longer sentences to express these thoughts.

In the preconceptual stage of the preoperational period, children's use of language and symbols becomes more complex. Dreams and nightmares increase, as does interest in symbolic play—"The two sticks will be my bow and arrow." These developments plus the beginning of drawing all indicate advances in intellectual abilities. Questions increase in the preschool years, first about the names of objects and activities, then about the nature of the world, and why routines are necessary.

Although children are curious, Piaget believes their concepts are limited because they pay attention to only a small number of characteristics, usually to sensory features. They cannot look at objects and group them into the same logical basis as do

■ TABLE 2-2
JEAN PIAGET'S PERIODS AND STAGES OF INTELLECTUAL DEVELOPMENT IN CHILDHOOD

	Ages	Behaviors
Sensorimotor period	0–2 years	Child perceives, then acts.
Reflexive stage	0–1 month	Baby practices built-in reflexes such as sucking.
Primary circular reaction stage	1–4 months	Baby repeats acts such as opening and closing hands. Baby often uses two senses at same time, e.g., seeing and hearing.
Secondary circular reaction stage	4–8 months	Baby repeats acts to see change in the environment, e.g., kicks mobile to make it go.
Coordination of secondary stage	8–12 months	Child uses responses to solve problem; e.g., child removes wrapping to get toy.
Tertiary circular reaction stage	12–18 months	Child is interested in properties of objects themselves, how they work. Can imitate more accurately.
Beginning of thought	18–24 months	Child begins to use language and symbolic mental representations.
Preoperational period	2–7 years	Child learns to represent objects, people, and perceptions with symbols (e.g., language); can reason intuitively but not with a set of verbalized principles.
Preconceptual stage	2–4 years	Child can represent mentally what is seen or heard with language; child is more imaginative in play.
Intuitive stage	4–7 years	Child can reason intuitively but pays attention to appearances of objects, e.g., believes taller, thinner glass holds more than short, fat glass.
Concrete operations period	7–11, 12 years	Child can think more logically and is not bound by appearances. Child can grasp relations between objects and easily arranges a series of sticks by length.
Formal operations period	12 through adulthood	Child thinks logically and abstractly, thinks about possible alternative situations, imagines future.

Adapted from Herbert Ginsburg and Sylvia Opper, *Piaget's Theory of Intellectual Development* (Engelwood Cliffs, N.J.: Prentice-Hall, 1969).

older children. They do not easily understand relational terms like *darker* or *lighter* unless the objects being compared are quite different.

Intellectual growth takes two leaps in the elementary school years. From four to seven (the intuitive stage), the child can figure out problems intuitively and give reasons for what he or she thinks. The reasons are based on what is seen and observed at the moment rather than on a set of verbalized principles or operations. At about age seven, the child enters the period of concrete operations.

What does Piaget mean by concrete operations? He means that children can think more logically and are not so bound by the appearance of objects. They grasp the relations among a series of objects and easily arrange a series of sticks by length with little trial and error. Their thought moves quickly from a subset of elements to the whole picture. Children can think more logically and form classes, because they have a keen interest in understanding the mechanisms or principles by which objects operate.

From age twelve to fourteen, adolescents begin to think like adults. They enter the formal operations period, during which they come to think more abstractly than before. Although children can think logically about tangible objects, not until adolescence can they reason logically about verbal propositions or hypothetical situations. In this period, adolescents can analyze problems in their heads and enumerate all possible combinations of events and take action to see what possibilities actually exist. They can think about their own thoughts and the thoughts and reactions of others. Abstract thought processes focus on concerns about justice and equality. As adolescents try to apply these concepts to their everyday lives, some become involved in social action groups or volunteer activities.

Piaget's theory emphasizes action in the development of thinking and reasoning powers. Children have natural desires to explore and learn, and their intellectual growth progresses from attention to bodily movements and action to the qualities and uses of present objects to increasing abstract reasoning about ideas and concepts. Parents are more effective when they understand that children's response to and understanding of the world sometimes differ from their own.

While Piaget emphasizes individual action and maturing capacities, the Russian psychologist Lev Vygotsky, born in the same year as Piaget, emphasizes the social aspect of intellectual growth.[64] He believes that knowledge, thought, and mental processes such as memory and attention all rest on social interactions.

Whatever children learn they first experience at the social level in a social interaction with someone and then internalize it at the individual psychological level. For example, an infant watches how an adult shakes a rattle or plays with a toy and then carries out the same action. Later, the child independently performs the activity.

Social interactions rest on the organization of the individual's culture and society. Every culture has a view of the world and the way to solve problems. Language, writing, art, and methods of problem solving all reflect this social worldview. Adults use these societal forms in interacting with children, and children internalize them.

Social interaction not only conveys societal knowledge of the world but also plays an important role in stimulating children to learn that knowledge. Vygotsky describes a unique concept called the *zone of proximal development*. There is a range of actions a child can perform alone, demonstrating a capacity that is clearly internal. This is what most of us would consider the child's level of ability. But Vygotsky points out that the child's behavior in this area can improve. When a more experienced person guides or prompts the child with questions, hints, or demonstrations, the child can respond at a more mature level not achieved when the child acts alone. So, the child has potential that emerges in social interaction. For example, a child learning how to talk may use a particular number of words spontaneously. That would be the child's verbal ability. A mother, however, might increase the number of words by prompting the child to remember what she called an item when she used it or by waiting for the child to add an action to an object he just identified, saying, "The doggie?" and waiting for "runs" or "goes bow-wow."

This zone of behavior, extending from what the child can do alone to what the child has the potential to do when guided, is the zone of proximal development. Vygotsky's interest goes beyond what the child can do to what the child's learning potential is. Teaching has the greatest impact, he believes, when it is directed to the child's potential at the high end of the zone of proximal development. The experienced person helps the child do alone what he or she can initially do only with guidance.

Like Piaget, Vygotsky believes that the child is an active learner, but he focuses on the strategies children use to become proficient and to learn more efficiently. Teaching encourages children to develop and use strategies to learn a task. For example, children can use strategies to remember material, and part of teaching involves helping them develop and use these strategies.

Language plays a significant role in mental development. Language develops from social interaction and contact and initially is a means of influencing others. Adults talk to children, influencing their reactions or behavior. Children initially guide their own behavior with external language similar to that already heard. They talk to themselves as others have and guide their behavior with their speech. Many a young toddler will say, "No, no," to herself as a way of stopping forbidden action, with varying degrees of success. As the child matures, the speech that guides behavior becomes internal or inner speech. Such inner speech becomes thought in the older child.

The theories of Piaget and Vygotsky suggest that parents' role is (1) to provide opportunities for independent exploration and action in the world and (2) to interact with children, serving as a model and guide in the world, helping them reach their potential.

The theories we have reviewed provide several insights for parents. Systems theories emphasize the integration of all levels of the individual's experiences—physiological, emotional, intellectual, social, and behavioral. As we shall see throughout the book, social-emotional experiences trigger physiological reactions, and physical experiences trigger social-emotional ones. In addition, parent and child form a unit that is nested in a tightly structured social system that affects parent and child interactions. Events in the larger society can trickle down to the child and trigger physiological and social-emotional reactions. Community violence, for example, affects children's emotional and physiological well-being.

Theories also help us understand that changes in children's behaviors come both from an unfolding of internal stages of growth (e.g., intellectual growth) as well as from environmental stimulation. Environmental stimulation includes consistently applied positive and negative consequences and parents' sensitive and responsive participation with the child in the growth process.

While systems theories pay attention to all aspects of experience, other theories concentrate on describing particular aspects of individuals' experiences. Psychoanalytic theories focus on the psychological growth that occurs in response to significant emotional relationships with others. Attachment theory focuses on the security and protection that parent-child relationships provide and describes the powerful force of attachment relationships in helping children develop many competencies. Erikson's theory describes the psychological changes that occur across the lifespan in response to a broad array of personal relationships within and outside the family.

Learning theorists emphasize the contributions of the external environment and the rewards and punishments it provides as major catalysts to growth for everyone. Piaget, too, attends to the environment, but he views it as providing an opportunity for children's exploration and active construction of knowledge. Vygotsky combines attention to relationships as catalysts for intellectual growth with attention to individuals' responses and organizing strategies for dealing with the world. So, systems theories provide a broad landscape of development, and other theories develop various aspects of this broad picture in detail.

STYLES AND STRATEGIES OF PARENTING

Psychologists' studies of socialization provide useful information. *Socialization* is the process by which adults in a society help children acquire and refine the skills and behaviors appropriate to that society.[65] As we shall see in Chapter 7, babies appear preprogrammed to respond to their caregivers and to imitate them, and parents appear preprogrammed to respond positively to babies. Thus, an atmosphere for influencing children exists from the beginning of life.

Parenting Styles

In studying how parents help children acquire approved behaviors, researchers have focused on variables like parental warmth, permissiveness, control, and democratic practices and related them to the development of a wide variety of behaviors in children, such as anxiety, fearfulness, aggressiveness, curiosity, originality, and responsibility.

Diana Baumrind's careful research on the antecedents of children's competence has led to the identification of three styles of parenting that are important in understanding children's functioning at different ages and in different ethnic groups.[66] Observing middle-class children at nursery school and at home with their parents and following them through childhood and into young adulthood, she sought the parenting behaviors related to instrumental competence—the capacity for socially responsible, independent behavior that included positive, cooperative relationships with parents and peers and purposive, achievement-oriented behavior in the world.

Authoritative parents exercise firm control over the child's behavior but also emphasize independence and individuality in the child. Although the parents have a clear notion of present and future standards of behavior for the child, they are rational, flexible, and attentive to the needs and preferences of the child. Their children are self-reliant and self-confident and explore their worlds with excitement and pleasure.

Authoritarian parents employ similar firm control but in an arbitrary, power-oriented way without regard for the child's individuality. They emphasize control without nurturance or support to achieve it. Children of authoritarian parents, relative to other groups of children, are unhappy, withdrawn, inhibited, and distrustful.

Permissive parents set few limits on the child. They are accepting of the child's impulses, granting as much freedom as possible while still maintaining physical safety. They appear cool and uninvolved. Permissive parents sometimes allow behavior that angers them, but they do not feel sufficiently comfortable with their own anger to express it. As a result, the anger builds up to unmanageable proportions. They then lash out and are likely to harm the child more than they want to. Their children are the least independent and self-controlled and could be best classified as immature.

Expanding on Baumrind's findings, Eleanor Maccoby and John Martin describe a fourth style of parenting.[67] Following a two-way classification of parents on two dimensions—warm/responsiveness and control/demandingness—their four types of parents are *authoritative* (high on warmth and high on control), *authoritarian* (low on warmth, high on control), *indulgent* (high on warmth, low on control), and *neglectful* (low on warmth, low on control). When Baumrind looked at the parenting of adolescents, she too added a type termed neglectful.

[handwritten margin note: 4 types of Parenting]

Laurence Steinberg and his coworkers have used Maccoby and Martin's classification of parents to understand adolescent competence in four areas: (1) psychological adjustment, (2) academic performance, (3) avoidance of rule-breaking behaviors like drinking, drugs, and delinquency, and (4) freedom from depression and anxiety.[68] Surveying a large multiethnic sample of European American, African American, Hispanic, and Asian American adolescents from ages fourteen to eighteen, the researchers obtained adolescents' descriptions of their parents and classified parents as authoritative, authoritarian, indulgent, and neglectful. They then looked at the relationships between parents' behaviors and teens' functioning.

Regardless of the adolescents' sex and their socioeconomic or ethnic background, authoritative parenting was related to adolescent self-confidence, competency, self-reliance, avoidance of delinquent activity, and general good mood. In European American and Hispanic families, authoritative parenting was also related to school achievement, but African American and Asian American students did not show increased school performance. Even if only one parent was authoritative and the other was not, adolescents achieved better grades than did those growing up in families with two nonauthoritative parents.[69]

Trying to determine what aspects of authoritative parenting make it so effective, Marjory Gray and Laurence Steinberg established three core dimensions: acceptance and involvement, strictness and supervision, and psychological autonomy granting.[70] *Acceptance and involvement* reflects parents' responsiveness to children's needs and individuality. *Strictness and supervision* involves parents' monitoring and supervising teens' behavior so it conforms to family rules. *Granting autonomy* involves allowing children freedom to express their individuality and contribute to family decision making.

A self-report questionnaire administered to 10,000 students, fourteen to eighteen years of age, of diverse socioeconomic and ethnic backgrounds revealed that the three dimensions of parenting have distinct effects on adolescents' adjustment. Results were similar in all four ethnic groups—European American, African American, Hispanic, and Asian American. Parents' acceptance and involvement were related to adolescents' reports of academic achievement, a positive identity, and adoption of appropriate roles. Parents' acceptance and involvement also appeared to be related to adolescents' general feeling of personal well-being. The researchers wrote, "We suspect that teens excel in most areas of their lives when they simply feel that they come from a loving home with responsive parents, regardless of whether they perceive other shortcomings in their parents."[71] Parents' strictness and supervision were related to students' developing a strong sense of self-control and discipline. Teens developed good study habits and the capacity to avoid drug use, school absence, and delinquent behaviors. Parents' granting of autonomy promoted feelings of self-confidence and competence in teens, which enabled them to act in socially appropriate ways.

The greater the parents' involvement, supervision, and autonomy granting, the more teens reported competence and psychological well-being. Medium amounts of supervision appeared most predictive of school achievement. Parents' involvement and autonomy-granting were related to lack of psychological distress and worrying. When parents were described as providing all three aspects of authoritative parenting, teens reported the most effective functioning and greatest sense of well-being. If parents provided either high involvement or autonomy, teens' internal psychological distress was reduced.

Parenting Strategies

Nancy Darling and Laurence Steinberg distinguish between parenting styles (such as authoritative, authoritarian parenting) and specific parenting strategies (such as spanking).[72] Parenting styles are broad categories that include parents' attitudes, beliefs, and ways of reasoning about their own and children's behavior. Such styles create an emotional climate in the home, influence the choice of specific parenting strategies, and moderate the effects of the more specific practices. For example, authoritative parents are more likely to use reasoning than physical punishment, though they might use spanking for a specific behavior, such as running in the street. Further, evidence suggests that spanking has no one effect—the effect depends on the context of the home in which it occurs (see Chapter 5).

Although parenting styles are strongly related to children's behavior, breaking down the broad categories into more specific beliefs or strategies has not increased the predictability of children's behavior. The core dimensions that Gray and Steinberg discussed are still very close to the original styles of parenting. The specific strategies that we look at in Chapters 4 and 5 and throughout the book are the main contributors to warmth/responsiveness and control/demandingness.

Mothers' smiles increase babies' good humor, smiling, and laughter and increase the likelihood babies will approach others in a positive, smiling way.

PRACTICAL QUESTION: ARE THE FIRST THREE YEARS THE MOST IMPORTANT FOR PARENTING?

Psychological theories emphasize the importance of early experience. In addition, the new emphasis on the plasticity of the brain has underlined this importance and attracted public attention. It sparked a 1997 White House conference, Early Childhood Development and Learning: What New Research on the Brain Tells Us about Our Youngest Children. Major magazines and newspapers featured articles on the topic, and *Newsweek* devoted a special edition to children's development in the first three years of life.[73] Political action in California, based on this new emphasis, sponsored and helped to pass a 1998 proposition allocating all cigarette tax money to programs for children under five years of age.

Some observers have drawn broad conclusions from this work and insist that if children do not receive certain kinds of stimulation in the early years, they will not develop their full potential. Such interpretations of the research have increased parents' anxieties as to whether they are providing sufficient and appropriate stimulation for their children. Research on infants' incredible capacities for observation, exploration, and learning has added to parents' anxieties about the adequacy of the stimulation they provide their infants and toddlers. Here, we look at the impact of parents' behavior with children in the first three years and address two questions: Does parenting matter more in these years? If so, what should parents be doing?

The Importance of Experience in the Early Years

Parental care in the first months of life is critical for the child's survival and well-being. Close physical contact with the mother serves to regulate the infant's hormonal levels, sleeping patterns, eating patterns, heart rate, and vagal tone.[74] (*Vagal tone* refers to the neural control of increases and decreases in the heartbeat and is considered a measure of individual differences in the expression and regulation of emotion.) In the first few weeks of life, infants who receive extra carrying and physical closeness cry less than babies who are not carried as much, and they are more visually and aurally alert.[75] When mothers are away or unavailable because of hospitalizations or trips, babies do not eat, sleep, or function physically and socially as well as they did before the mothers' absence.[76]

Parents' closeness and caring support infants' physical growth and well-being. As we saw in Chapter 1, parents' care can also help physiologically overreactive infants stabilize their responses to stimulation, thereby avoiding fearful and inhibited behavior in later childhood.[77] Effective parenting for these infants involves setting limits and enabling infants to find coping strategies when they are upset.

The complex forms of communication and interaction that are established between parent and child in the early months of life can, when supportive, promote positive moods and approaches to the world.[78] As noted earlier, children incorporate their experiences with attachment figures and form an internal model of how people relate to one another. When attachment is secure, babies can soothe themselves, explore the world more freely, and develop positive interactions with others.

Further, early positive attachments with parents may buffer the child against difficulties.[79] In a sample of poor families, children with positive attachments with mothers in the infant/toddler years showed better adaptation in the elementary school years than did those who had insecure attachments, even though both groups of children had displayed problems in the preschool years. The early positive experience may have given the children an advantage by providing early models of care and self-worth that stimulated these children to seek out similar experiences later.

In addition to promoting security, parents' behavior in the first few years of life may promote intellectual growth through childhood and adolescence. Longitudinal research following a sample of middle-class children found that parental qualities and family patterns of interaction, assessed when children were twenty-one months old, predicted intellectual growth.[80] Investigators controlled for parents' intellectual ability and found that a mother's energy, tension, and concern for the child predicted a son's intellectual level from age two to eighteen and a daughter's intellectual development from age eight to thirty. Mothers with energetic qualities were thought to do more things with their children and perhaps were more responsive to them. The study also found that a son's intellectual growth was related to the father's satisfaction with his work, and a daughter's above-average intellectual level was associated with the parents' marital compatibility and the father's interest in and closeness with his daughter. The results of the study could not determine whether the effect of the environment occurred before, during, or after the first two years of life. But the important finding is that—even with parents' intellectual ability controlled for—the family emotional milieu, as measured at twenty-one months, had predictive significance for the intellectual performance of boys and girls from early childhood into adulthood.

Just as positive experiences can predict later well-being, early negative experiences create certain consequences as well. The babies of depressed mothers show less affectionate behavior with their mothers, touching them less, and they are more likely to be angry, irritable, and poorly controlled than babies of nondepressed mothers. The negative behavior of babies of depressed mothers is associated with changes in frontal cortical brain activity as measured by EEG recordings.[81] Longitudinal follow-ups with these babies will determine the long-term significance of these early differences. Infants who experience violence have elevated hormone levels, and some researchers speculate that the chronic experience of traumatic violence may lead to hyperarousal of the sympathetic nervous system and the physiological responses related to the fight or flight response.[82]

Positive experiences in early life, nonetheless, do not guarantee healthy development throughout childhood. Secure attachments can change to insecure attachments and vice versa, and many events can intervene.

In examining this sampling of studies, we have seen that parents' positive emotional involvement is a primary influence on children's emotional and intellectual development. In their book *The Scientist in the Crib*, Alison Gopnik, Andrew Meltzoff, and Patricia Kuhl write that infants are drawn to relationships with parents. Parents, they believe, already know many of the behaviors needed to foster babies' growth:

> For babies and young children, care and teaching are inseparable. The very actions that nurture babies give them the kind of information they need. . . . The scientific research says that we should do just what we do when we are with our babies—talk, play, make funny faces, pay attention. We just need time to do it.[83]

The Modifiability of Early Experiences

As noted earlier, some observers believe that if children do not receive stimulation early in life, they will not be able to develop certain capabilities. While research indicates that there may be critical windows for the development of perceptual and motor abilities in animals, such critical windows for the development of human behaviors are few and greatly extended in time. John Bruer, reviewing the evidence concerning critical periods in the development of human behaviors, concludes,

> The odds that our children will end up with appropriately fine-tuned brains are incredibly favorable, because the stimuli the brain *expects* during critical periods are the kinds of stimuli that occur everywhere and all the time within the normal developmental environment for our species. It is only when there are severe genetic or environmental aberrations from the normal that nature's expectations are frustrated and neural development goes awry.[84]

Thus, stimulation need not occur at a specific time for an ability to develop, but the timing may make it easier to develop that ability early.

What about the modifiability of early cognitive functioning? Let us look first at language development. There appears to be a critical period that may last as long as ten years. Studies have found that a child deprived of language until age six can, with time, learn to speak with correct grammar. If the child has been deprived until age thirteen, the child can learn only a few words and no grammar.[85]

It has long been known that babies are born with the ability to make all the sounds of all the languages in the world, but that they lose that capacity over time. They become limited to the sounds of language they hear routinely. Thus, if a child learns a foreign language before the age of ten, he will unlikely speak that language with an accent; after the age of ten, however, he will tend to speak with an accent. His brain will have become hardwired to produce the sounds heard routinely.

Until recently, the inability to make the sounds of other languages easily was thought to be irreversible. Recent research, however, shows that adults can be retrained to produce sounds not found in their native language. Using a computer that slows and elongates speech sounds enabled Japanese adults to carve out new neural circuits to distinguish the English-spoken sounds *L* and *R*, which in Japanese form a single sound.[86] Natural speech alone resulted in little or no improvement in the Japanese adults' ability to make these distinctions, but the exaggerated speech of the computer, as speech might be heard in infancy, followed by gradual training toward conversational speech, produced results. So, under the right conditions, changes can occur in behavior thought to be irreversible.

When it comes to more general cognitive abilities, early intervention programs improve cognitive and social functioning in children from poor families. But what about later interventions? Three examples of later stimulation are given here.

The first example involves a junior-senior high school on Long Island that initiated a program titled Success Through Academic Readiness (STAR) for twenty-seven ninth-graders who were failing.[87] The school was one of Long Island's very poorest, and the program, funded by the nonprofit Institute for Community Development, provided money for the additional staffing of a full-time psychologist, social worker, career and college coordinator, program director, and outreach worker. These people worked together to provide a level of attention and consistency that these students lacked in everyday life. The students received two additional hours of daily activities, including workshops on peer pressure, trips to museums, and tutoring. School counselors assigned for the four-year period remained available to students. Observers attribute the success of the program to the staff's emotional involvement and the relentless encouragement and support they gave the students. Help was always available, and when students missed class, phone calls were made to the home to inquire about problems, difficulties, and plans to return to school.

Four years after the inception of the program, twenty-five of the twenty-seven students were college bound. In a comparable group of twenty-five students who did not accept the invitation to join the program, twenty-three had dropped out of school. Although the program cost $5,000 per year per pupil in addition to the

$9,380 the district spent on each pupil, the total cost of $14,380 was still less than the $16,000 per year per pupil spent in wealthier neighboring districts. One can see here that the same emotional involvement and concern that predicted intellectual growth in middle-class toddlers helped to produce academic success in this group of economically impoverished, low-achieving students.

The second example involves an army program that provided educational opportunities for recruits despite their low scores on entrance tests.[88] Follow-up of 7,000 low-scoring recruits who remained in the army found that although only 66 percent had completed high school at the time of entrance, 96 percent had completed high school at the time of follow-up twelve to seventeen years later. At entry, only 1 percent had scores above the thirty-first percentile; at the time of the follow-up, however, 27 percent had achieved this score. So, learning opportunities extended to young adults also have benefits.

The third example comes from the longitudinal study, discussed earlier, that identified family characteristics associated with intellectual growth. Following the children through adolescence into middle age and[89] comparing late adolescent IQs with IQs obtained in middle age, researchers found that the group as a whole made modest gains in verbal, performance, and overall IQ scores. Eleven percent of the sample gained more than thirteen IQ points, and 11 percent decreased six or more IQ points. The group that decreased in IQ points contained many individuals who were heavy alcohol users and people with debilitative illnesses. Those who increased in IQ points tended to be married to spouses whose IQs were ten points more than that of study members when they were adolescents. The researchers conclude that the results "encourage us to believe that means can be found to promote intellectual growth among adults, as they have for young children."[90] So parents can rest assured that their efforts and stimulation are important at every step of growth.

In Conclusion

Early experiences are significant because they shape the way the brain processes information, and they can set in motion self-perpetuating ways of responding to people and the world. There are few fixed windows of critical development unless deprivation is extreme and sustained. However, stimulation at any time in development leads to learning and accomplishment, and exciting results of new research, such as the computer-based retraining of adults' language discrimination, may help us find ways to increase individuals' development throughout life.

MAIN POINTS

The theories reviewed here
- share many features in common
- deepen parents' understanding of development
- agree in assigning environmental input a significant role in development
- focus on different aspects of development

Systems theories emphasize

- complexity within the individual and in levels of environmental organization
- the integration of all levels of experience within the individual
- that the individual and the social context form a unit
- the importance of both genetic and environmental influences on development
- adaptive behavioral qualities that evolve to promote survival
- the goodness of fit between the individual's behavior and social demands

Learning theories

- emphasize primarily the role of the environment in stimulating development
- structure learning in terms of rewards and punishments
- pay attention to the roles of imitation, modeling, and observation in learning
- are beginning to incorporate the learner's characteristics in the learning process

Psychoanalytic theories

- emphasiez the inner needs and drives individuals seek to satisfy
- focus on how intimate family ties promote development
- stress the importance of the early years of experience
- vary in their attention to the social context of the individual's experience

Theories of knowing the world emphasize

- the importance of children's unfolding abilities and active exploration of the world
- the social nature of learning about the world
- the parents' role in providing appropriate environments for exploration and learning

Parental styles

- focus on two broad dimensions of parents' behavior—warmth/responsiveness and control/demandingness
- shown in authoritative parenting (high warmth/responsiveness and high control/demandingness) are linked to many positive aspects of children's and teens' behavior
- predict children's behavior more effectively than does the use of specific strategies
- are difficult to break down into specific behaviors

In the very early years of life, sensitive, responsive parenting

- helps regulate the child's physical system
- influences ways the child's brain organizes and handles stimulation

- can set in motion for the child self-perpetuating ways of relating to the world and others
- does not predict functioning throughout childhood and adulthood

EXERCISES

1. Which of the theories of children's development seems most useful to you in understanding children's growth and how adults contribute to their development? Why?

2. Erikson's theory of lifespan development focuses on the importance of positive experiences and strengths. Review your own life in terms of the positive experiences and strengths you have developed. For example, you may have developed a love of the outdoors from camping activities with your family and feel you developed independence and a sense of responsibility to the environment.

3. How does the concept of attachment specifically help adults make sense of their experiences in life within and outside the family?

4. Do you see any situations in which either the authoritarian or permissive style of parenting might be useful? Do you think parents agree with researchers that the authoritative style is most effective?

5. As a parent (or imagining yourself as one), do you prefer to think that your children's development depends very much on what you do or did early in their lives, or do you prefer to think that what is happening currently in their lives determines their current behavior? Why?

ADDITIONAL READINGS

Bowlby, John. *A Secure Base: Parent-Child Attachment and Healthy Human Development.* New York: Basic Books, 1988.

Bruer, John T. *The Myth of the First Three Years.* New York: Free Press, 1999.

Erikson, Erik H. *Childhood and Society.* 2nd ed. New York: Norton, 1963.

Gopnik, Allison, Meltzoff, Andrew T., and Kuhl, Patricia K. *The Scientist in the Crib.* New York: Morrow, 1999.

Huttenlocher, Peter. *Neural Plasticity.* Cambridge, MA: Harvard University Press, 2002.

3

Cultural Influences on Parenting

IN THE NEWS

New York Times, March 30, 2003
America's military force of 1.4 million relies on youth, particularly minority youth, who seek opportunities for education and occupational advancement not available to them in civilian life. See page 84 for details.

Go to PowerWeb at:
www.dushkin.com/powerweb to read articles and newsfeeds on **cross-cultural issues, culture and parenting**, and other topics related to this chapter.

Culture provides a nest for all the parent-child interactions we look at throughout the book. In this chapter we look at the many ways cultural forces shape the process of parenting. In discussing the broad trends in parenting within ethnic and social groups, we also learn about the great diversity within each group. We examine how socioeconomic status provides a context for the development of all members of our society. Finally, we look at how poverty and the lack of social resources affects parenting.

Culture is the set of values, beliefs, ways of thinking, the rituals, and institutions of a group or population.[1] Culture provides ways of seeing the world and partially determines the patterns of behavior in everyday life. As we saw in Chapter 1, it is a dynamic force that responds to social, political, and economic events, and that shapes the meaning of these events for us.

In the United States, we do not have just one culture that affects us all. Americans do share a common core of beliefs and values—for example, love of freedom, belief in equal rights and equality of opportunity, desire to remedy problems and improve life, and belief in the importance of education. Yet, the way these beliefs are organized and expressed in everyday life depends on many factors such as geographic area of residence (North, South, East, or West; urban or rural), ethnic group (European Americans, African Americans, Latinos, Asian Americans, Native Americans, and Middle Eastern Americans, all with subgroups), social status within the group, religious orientation, gender, age, and personal experiences. Thus, individuals receive many cultural messages from their own groups, which organize and integrate members in unique ways. In this chapter we look at the major cultural influences that affect parents today.

The social scientists Sara Harkness and Charles Super believe that culture provides a *developmental niche* in which children develop.[2] This niche includes (1) the physical and social settings for parents and children, (2) the childrearing practices the culture recommends, and (3) the psychological characteristics valued in caregivers. So, culture shapes a broad range of parental behaviors, from the more general values parents teach to the concrete aspects of daily life such as where children eat and sleep.

We look first at two cultural models of parent-child relations. We then look briefly at the history of immigration to this country, or how the many ways contemporary ethnic groups came here. We look at the ways families in each of the major ethnic groups interpret the tasks of parenting. Finally, we look at the ways both social positioning within groups and economic hardship affect parenting.

Major social influences include racial and ethnic backgrounds. *Race* refers to "phenotypic differences that arise from genetic or biological dispositions such as skin color or hair texture."[3] *Ethnicity* refers to "an individual's membership in a group sharing a common ancestral heritage based on nationality, language, and culture. Psychological attachment to the group is also a dimension of ethnicity, referred to as 'ethnic identity.'"[4]

Race is a controversial term at present. Some scientists call it a meaningless concept because few genetic differences among races exist. Some geneticists and epidemiologists, however, want to maintain the distinction because they seek to understand and provide interventions for diseases that affect racial groups differently.[5] Geneticists identify five racial groups: (1) *sub-Saharan Africans; Caucasians,* which include Europeans, Middle Easterners, and those from the Indian continent; *Asians,* which include Chinese, Japanese, Filipinos, and peoples from Southeast Asia; *Pacific Islanders;* and *Native Americans.* In addition, mixtures of the groups occur. Many African Americans, for example, are mixtures of sub-Saharan African people and Caucasians. Many ethnic groups exist within these racial groups. For example, in the United States Caucasians include people of German, Irish, or Italian descent. Asian Americans include Hmong, Filipino, Chinese, Japanese, and others. In addition, religious groups form cultures that provide niches for development. For example, the Amish culture of northern European origin provides a distinctive way of life that affects all aspects of its members' lives. The Amish dress in the plain clothing of seventeenth century rural Europe. They do not use any electricity but adapt hydraulic power if possible. They send their elementary school children to public schools, but prefer that their adolescents not attend high school. While religions do not usually demand such a withdrawal from the main culture, many do prescribe ways of life—no alcohol, no caffeine, prayers several times a day—that differ from the American mainstream.

In this short chapter, we focus on cultural influences of ethnic groups, social status, and poverty or lack of resources on parenting. We continue to discuss ethnic differences throughout the book, as appropriate. For example, the formation of ethnic identity is discussed in Chapters 8, 9, and 10 when we consider identity formation.

CULTURAL MODELS OF PARENT-CHILD RELATIONSHIPS

Patricia Greenfield and Lalita Suzuki have surveyed differences among many ethnic groups and describe two cultural models—the independent and the interdependent models—that provide a framework for organizing and understanding what parents think matters and what they do with children.[6] Table 3-1 (p. 70) outlines these two models, which apply to many different cultural and social groups rather than any ethnic group in particular.

In the independent model, parents help children become self-sustaining, productive adults who enter into relationships with other adults by choice. The child receives nurturance to develop autonomy, competence, and a freely chosen identity that in adulthood merges with others outside the family.

In the interdependent model, parents help children grow into socially responsible adults who take their place in a strong network of social relationships, often within the family, that place obligations on the adult. Parents indulge the young child, but as children grow older, they are expected to internalize and respect the rules of parents and other authorities. Parents and relatives are respected and obeyed, and family and group needs matter more than individual ones.

Although cultural beliefs and values are deeply ingrained and often invisible, they are not fixed and unchangeable. The anthropologist Jean Briggs writes,

> The notion that meaning inheres in culture and that people receive it passively, as dough receives the cookie cutter, is rapidly being replaced by the idea that culture consists of ingredients, which people actively select, interpret, and use in various ways, as opportunities, capabilities, and experience allow.[7]

James Youniss describes a series of studies showing that immigrant parents can identify the cultural values of their new country and socialize their children to fit in while the parents maintain their more traditional beliefs.[8] Youniss reviewed studies of two groups who emigrated from Croatia to the United States. One group lived

■ **T A B L E   3-1**
CONTRASTING CULTURAL MODELS OF PARENT-CHILD RELATIONS

	Developmental Goals	
	Independence	**Interdependence**
Developmental trajectory	From dependent to independent self	From asocial to socially responsible self
Children's relations to parents	Personal choice concerning relationship to parents	Obligations to parents
Communication	Verbal emphasis	Nonverbal emphasis (empathy, observation, participation)
	Autonomous self-expression by child	Child comprehension, mother speaks for child
	Frequent parental questions to child	Frequent parental directives to child
	Frequent praise	Infrequent praise
	Child negotiation	Harmony, respect, obedience
Parenting style	Authoritative: controlling, demanding, warm, rational	Rigorous and responsible teaching, high involvement, physical closeness
Parents helping children	A matter of personal choice except under extreme need	A moral obligation under all circumstances

From Patricia M. Greenfield and Lalita K. Suzuki, "Culture and Human Development: Implications for Parenting, Education, Pediatrics, and Mental Health," in *Handbook of Child Psychology,* 5th ed., ed. William Damon, vol. 4: *Child Psychology in Practice,* ed. Irving E. Sigel and K. Ann Renninger (New York: Wiley, 1998), 1085. Reprinted by permission of John Wiley & Sons, Inc.

very much as a self-contained community, stressing their traditional values, customs, and language. The other group became assimilated into the new culture. Both groups, however, socialized their children to be more independent, questioning, and self-directed than the parents had been raised to be, thus helping their children fit into their new culture.

Cultural models influence not only what parents do in their homes but also the qualities children take with them into the larger society.[9] Children more easily adapt to the larger culture when the home culture is the same as that of the larger society. For example, problems can arise when the home culture conflicts with that of the school. U.S. teachers and schools operate on the independent model, emphasizing individual effort to achieve knowledge. Questions and expressions of opinion are encouraged and seen as signs of intellectual curiosity. Children's quiet acceptance of the teachers' statements may be interpreted as a lack of interest or a lack of intelligence. So, we need to recognize that children may live in a home culture that differs from the culture in school and the larger society.

To illustrate how culture influences parental behaviors, let us look at a study in which samples of U.S. mothers and Italian mothers of infants four to sixteen months old were interviewed and observed in their homes with their babies to determine the mothers' conceptions of development, their goals, and their practices with their infants.[10] The participants were all members of nuclear families of parents and children.

U.S. mothers' long-term goals for their children were that they develop (1) economic and emotional independence, (2) a sense of well-being and happiness that did not depend on financial success, and (3) honest and respectful interpersonal relationships. A short-term goal was to provide sufficient stimulation for the child's growth, which the mothers worried they were not providing.

Italian mothers' long-term goals focused on social relationships and physical and economic well-being. All of the Italian mothers mentioned good health, financial security, and a good family life as important. Their definition of a good family life included a spouse and children. These mothers felt much less pressure than the U.S. mothers did, because they did not feel responsible for the outcome of the child's development. Italian mothers considered all mothers adequate by virtue of being mothers and believed that children turn out as they will.

This study found that goals and attitudes determined how infants and mothers spent their days. U.S. infants spent their time in one-on-one interactions with mothers (about one-third of the time) or in isolation in their rooms, sleeping or playing with toys. Although other people came in and out of the home, they, including siblings, did not participate much in the care of the child. In Italy, infants had little direct interaction with mothers (10 percent of the time) and were almost never alone. They slept in the same room as their parents, often until the second birthday, and were regularly in the company of two or three people. For all but one infant, at least one grandparent lived nearby and visited daily.

As infants began to get around, U.S. parents babyproofed the environment and let the child crawl about; at ten months, infants spent 52 percent of observation time in crawling and exploring on the floor freely. Mothers taught infants at this age preliminary safety rules, as they felt it was important for the child to explore and accept some responsibility for safety. Mothers felt reassured that their children were developing well when they were active and curious. Italian mothers, on the other hand, believed free exploration was too dangerous—too cold, even in the summer, and involving too many hazards. Their ten-month-old infants spent about 26 percent of observation time in crawling on the floor. When it was time to walk, infants were always supported by adults who held their hands. None of the Italian mothers felt concern that their children were not more independent.

U.S. mothers placed great emphasis on establishing good sleep patterns. By four months of age, most infants slept in their own beds, often in their own rooms, though several shared a room with a sibling but none with their parents. Getting enough sleep was very important, and mothers established schedules and rituals for helping children get enough sleep, even when children resisted naptime or bedtime. In contrast, Italian mothers rarely held to any sleeping schedule, and babies often dropped off to sleep in the midst of family activity without bedtime rituals or songs. One mother had no schedule because she felt it was cruel to deprive the child of family time.

With regard to eating behaviors, however, the attitudes of the two groups of mothers were reversed. U.S. mothers felt their children could regulate their food habits. Infants ate on demand and often at different times from when the family ate, so eating was an activity involving mother and child, with the mother talking while she fed the infant. As children got older, they were encouraged to feed themselves. Italian infants, in contrast, were required to eat on four-hour schedules and to come to family meals, even if they had to be awakened to do so. Solid foods were begun at four months, and infants had to eat certain amounts. They were expected to get used to eating rituals even if they did not like them, because eating was a social activity with the family.

Overall, then, U.S. mothers put primary emphasis on independence—in play, exploration, eating, and sleeping alone at bedtime. Italian families enveloped their infants in complex social interactions, which required adaptation on the part of the babies and gave few opportunities for independence.

PATTERNS OF IMMIGRATION OF ETHNIC GROUPS TO THE UNITED STATES

The United States is a land of immigrants. Immigration formed us and continues to exert an influence on our society; in the last decade alone, 13.3 million immigrants arrived here.[11] The historian Joseph Illick writes,

> The earliest immigrants to America were the Homo sapiens who hiked across the treeless plain—now the Bering Strait—that connected Siberia to Alaska, a distance of less than 60 miles. They came during the late Ice Age (Wisconsin glaciation) when sea levels were several hundred feet lower than they are today. Twenty thousand years ago, the harsh weather conditions and limited supply dictated that only small bands of constantly mobile hunters, on the trail of mammoth, bison, reindeer, and musk ox, could survive. These were the original American Indians.[12]

They lived in tribes and nations and "achieved a substantial harmony between the local ecology and human subsistence."[13]

Thousands of years later, immigrants from England arrived in what is now Virginia and Massachusetts in 1607 and 1620, respectively.[14] In 1619, Virginians began to import slaves from the West Indies,[15] so that by 1648, the Virginia colony numbered 15,000 people, of whom 300 were African American slaves.[16] The African American population grew and by 1763 composed almost one-third of the American population of one and a half million.

German immigrants began to arrive in the seventeenth century. Between 1820 and 1870, seven and a half million immigrants came to the United States, primarily from northern and western Europe.[17] At about the same time, Chinese men came to

Children of different ethnic groups learn what is distinctive about their group and form a bicultural sense of identity that includes their ethnic group membership.

the West Coast to work in the gold mines and on the railroads, and in 1877, they constituted 17 percent of the population of San Francisco. Their families remained in China; money was sent there, and the men visited occasionally. Irritated by this growth, petitioners to Congress succeeded in gaining passage of a law in 1882 prohibiting Asian immigration.

Between 1880 and 1920 almost twenty-three and a half million immigrants arrived from southern and eastern Europe.[18] Concerned about the expanding population, Congress passed laws in the 1920s, restricting the total number of immigrants and limiting the areas from which they could come. Immigrants from the Western hemisphere were not subject to these laws. Laws in the 1960s did away with the national quotas and expanded the total number of immigrants admitted to 700,000, not including spouses and children of United States citizens. Since these laws were changed, large numbers have continued to come from Asian and Latin American countries.

Groups that come to this country experience a process of *acculturation,* defined as a process "of learning about a new culture and deciding what aspects are to be retained or sacrificed from the culture of origin."[19] Because culture is multidimensional, immigrants must attend to many new aspects of experience—language, food, customs, and social attitudes. Adaptation can be difficult.

This *process of acculturation*[20] occurs in stages. Initially, immigrants may feel relief at being here and idolize the new culture, then disillusionment may set in as the process brings frustrations and difficulties, and finally, they come to a realistic acceptance of the new country with its positive and negative features. The host country also changes as it includes groups with new cultural traditions. When people retain aspects of and attachment to their culture of origin and still feel comfortable with and attached to the customs of the new culture, they are described as having a *bicultural identity*. Today, members of ethnic groups usually have some form of bicultural identity or attachment to their culture of origin. This stands in contrast to the past, when people coming to this country were expected to give up their previous customs and become assimilated into mainstream culture, becoming "like everyone."

While many immigrants came to this country willingly, with high hopes for a better life of greater freedom and better jobs, many others came under duress. Most African Americans were brought to this country as slaves, and while small numbers earned or gained freedom, most remained slaves until emancipation in 1863. Many other immigrants left their countries in Europe, Latin America, Asia, and the Middle East involuntarily to escape political persecution.

Once here, many members of ethnic groups have sometimes experienced persecution and poor treatment at the hands of established authorities. For example, Native Americans who negotiated with the U.S. government in good faith were cheated out of land, moved about the country, forced to live on reservations, and later forced to send children to boarding schools.[21] Even after slavery was abolished, African Americans faced state laws of segregation and unequal treatment in large sections of the country until the 1950s and 1960s. During World War II, Japanese Americans were taken from their homes and their land and placed in relocation camps far from home. As a result of such poor treatment, members of ethnic groups frequently distrust established authorities.

Many members of ethnic groups have experienced *prejudice,* defined as irrational, negative thoughts, feelings, and judgments about a person because of their race, religion, or nationality.[22] *Discrimination*—unfair treatment because of race, religion, or nationality—may accompany the prejudice, but need not. Prejudice and discrimination against people because of their race is termed *racism.* Many other groups—religious as well as regional or social groups—also face prejudice and discrimination. While we often consider European Americans to have escaped such experiences, Michael Novak wrote in 1974 about the prejudice he experienced growing up as a Roman Catholic boy whose grandparents were from Slovakia. He was embarrassed by his name and his religion. "We did not feel this country belonged to us. We felt fierce pride in it, more loyalty than anyone could know. But we felt blocked at every turn."[23]

THE CULTURAL INFLUENCES OF MAJOR ETHNIC GROUPS

We now focus our attention on six main ethnic groups, roughly in order of their arrival here—Native Americans (0.9 percent of the 2000 population), European Americans (about 75.1 percent), African Americans (12.3 percent), Latinos (12.5

percent), Asian Americans (3.6 percent), and Middle Eastern Americans (between 0.5 and 1 percent of the population).[24] Each of these groups contain subgroups. Native Americans include representatives of over 500 tribes. European Americans come from all over Europe. The Latino/Latina group includes individuals from Central and South America as well as those from the Caribbean Islands. Asian Americans include people from a broad geographic area ranging from Korea and Japan in the north to China, Thailand, Cambodia, Vietnam, India, Pakistan and the Philippine Islands in the south. Middle Eastern Americans include people from Lebanon, Syria, Egypt, Iraq, Iran, Jordan, Palestine, Afghanistan, Saudi Arabia, and Kuwait. Within each subgroup, diversity exists among individuals as well because of social status, religious views, and personal experiences. Thus, any broad social trends we talk about will not apply to every person in the group or every subgroup.

We can look only briefly at the general characteristics of major ethnic groups' parenting, keeping well in mind that our knowledge about socialization in different ethnic groups is limited for a variety of reasons. First, social scientists have only recently made a concerted effort to move beyond the readily available, middle-class European American samples that form much of what is known about the development of children. Second, when they have turned greater attention to ethnic groups, they have looked frequently at groups of children at risk, so that results from a wide range of children in ethnic groups are rare.[25] Third, most studies have compared a particular ethnic group to European American samples and focused on the ways in which that group is deficient. Few studies have examined the psychological paths of development within ethnic groups, looking at factors that influence differences among subgroups belonging to the same ethnic group. Fourth, there are few studies with longitudinal samples of children of different ethnic groups, and such studies rarely draw on in-home observations of family interactions with both parents involved.[26] Such studies have yielded mostly information about development in the European American samples and need to be carried out for other ethnic groups as well. So, our understanding of socialization within ethnic groups is limited at present but expanding.

For each group, we shall look at current information about the group, a brief historical perspective, general values, contemporary families, and the socialization of children in the family. Table 3-2 (p. 76) presents demographic information on each group discussed except Middle Eastern Americans, for which the U.S. census has no data.

Native American Families

In 2000, approximately two and a half million Native Americans lived in the United States—a 25 percent increase in the population since 1990, when they numbered two million. They come from over 500 tribes, speaking more than a hundred languages. Approximately 60 percent live in urban settings; the remainder live near or on reservations.[27]

Historical Perspective   Native American history is distinctive because they were the first immigrants, as noted earlier, and they have experienced unique hardships

DEMOGRAPHIC CHARACTERISTICS OF FIVE ETHNIC GROUPS*

	Total Population	Native Americans	Whites[†] (European Americans)	African Americans	Latinos	Asian Americans
Percentage of Total Population	—	0.9%	75.1%	12.3%	12.5%	3.6%
Median Age	36	28	37	30	26	33
Education of Population over Age 25						
High School +	84%	73%	85%	78%	57%	86%
College +	26%	13%	26%	16%	11%	44%
Advanced Degree	—	—	9%	5%	3%	15%
Median Household Income[‡]	$42,228	$32,143	$44,517	$29,470	$33,565	$53,635
Families below Poverty Level[‡]	11.7%	23.5%	9.9%	22.7%	21.4%	10.2%
Children under 18 Living						
In Two-Parent Family	74%	—	78%	44%	71%	80%
In Female-Headed Household	22%	—	17%	50%	24%	13%
In Male-Headed Household	4%	—	5%	6%	5%	7%
Average Number of Children per Household						
Married Couple	1.87	—	1.93	1.99	2.14	—
Female-Headed Household	1.75	—	1.66	1.91	1.95	—
Male-Headed Household	1.50	—	—	—	—	—
Percentage of Children Born						
To Teen Mothers	12%	20%	11%	20%	16%	4%
To Single Mothers	33%	58%	27%	68%	43%	15%

*Middle Eastern Americans were not included in the table because the U.S. Census does not currently recognize them as a minority.

[†]Census category is "white"; not all are European Americans.

[‡]Figures on poverty for Native Americans are for 1999 and from www.factfinder.census.gov/servlet/ GCTTableP11. Figures on income and poverty for other categories are for 2001 and from the U.S. Census Bureau at www.census.gov.

Unless otherwise noted, all statistics are for the year 2000 and from *Statistical Abstract of the United States: 2002*, 122nd ed. (Washington, DC: U.S. Government Printing Office, 2001).

as a minority culture. They have been forcibly removed from their land. At times they have been confined to reservations. They have had their children taken off to boarding schools, with their language and cultural traditions forbidden. Such mistreatment has stopped, but only fairly recently.

Though poorly treated, Native Americans have made notable contributions to mainstream U.S. culture. The eminent historian, Samuel Eliot Morison, wrote in 1965,

> These natives first welcomed the Europeans, then fought them, and finally were subjugated by them. They gave the Europeans some of the world's most valuable agricultural products—maize, tobacco, the potato, cassava, and chocolate. They taught their conquerors hundreds of skills and so frequently mated with them that millions of people in the United States, Canada, Mexico, Central and South America have Indian blood in their veins. The Indians have so influenced, indeed so transformed, the lives of white and black men in North America that we are eager to know where they came from and how their culture developed.[28]

He concluded, "In peace as in war the Indians have had a profound effect on later comers to America. Our culture has been enriched by their contribution. Our character is very different from what it would have been if this continent had been uninhabited when the Europeans arrived."[29]

Their childrearing, described in early settlers' accounts, meets many of the criteria of effective parenting in our times. They were very child centered. European settlers were surprised at how affectionate and caring they were with infants and young children. At that time, Europeans were distant from their infants because so many died. Native Americans nursed children for about two years and kept children physically close to them. When children reached age three and were mobile, parents gave them great freedom to move about and explore the world with only minimal restriction for safety reasons. Little or no physical punishment for children existed.

Adults guided and supervised children, teaching them needed skills. Boys were reared to be hunters and warriors; girls, to be planters, gatherers, and nurturers of children. Both sexes had to be physically strong, hardy, and knowledgeable in survival skills. Parents encouraged children to develop independence, self-control, and stoicism. They also taught children to be grateful to a benevolent Spirit for giving them life and purpose.

Although the government attempted to eliminate traditional Indian culture and language, a small number of Indian tribes, such as the Hopi, managed to maintain their traditions.[30] Between 1890 and 1920, the government established boarding schools some distance from the reservations and forced Native American children to attend them for twelve years. Family members were not permitted to visit children during the school year, which dramatically reduced parental influence and socialization. Between 1920 and the 1970s, children usually attended these schools but were not forced. Not having had models of parenting behavior for much of their childhood years, many Native Americans find rearing children a great challenge.

General Values   Themes of traditional native American values include (1) strong identification with the social group and with the natural environment in which one lives, with little sense of self apart from the group and nature, (2) cooperation with the group to share the burdens of work, (3) focus on the present moment, (4) respect for the wisdom of the older generation, and (5) strong spiritual values.[31] Many Native Americans have become Christians and see little contradiction in also continuing to uphold the spiritual values of their heritage.

Contemporary Families   The Native American population of two and a half million is a young one, with 50 percent under the age of twenty-eight, in comparison with a median age of thirty-seven for the European American population. They have lower rates of high school graduation, college degrees, and advanced degrees, but the majority do graduate from high school.[32] See Table 3-2 for specific figures.

Current statistics indicate that Native American Families face many challenges (see Table 3-2). Their median family income falls below that of European Americans and Asian Americans but is about the same as that of African Americans or Latinos. They have high rates of poverty, fewer children living in two-parent families, and a high rate of babies born to unmarried mothers. They also tend to have a higher rate of alcohol abuse, though the majority of Native Americans are not substance abusers.[33]

Socialization of Children   We have less information on the socialization of children in this group than for children in the other groups, because children make up a much smaller percentage of the population. We do know, however, that Native Americans have retained their traditions of valuing children, keeping them close in the early years and giving them more independence as they grow older.

They have also continued the tradition of minimizing gender differences in socialization and respecting the contributions of both boys and girls. "Balance is an important factor in the socialization of boys and girls. The need to balance masculine and feminine characteristics, such as developing compassion in boys and strength in girls, is seen as vital to personal wholeness."[34] In tribal life, boys produce and play a creative role. Women are nurturers but also encouraged to be leaders. Thus, an individual can embody many positive traits, as seen in the description of Wilma Mankiller, the former principal chief of the Cherokee Nation: "She is all those converged together. Like all of us can be. Warrior, peacemaker, mother, father, Beloved woman, the white and the red merged together, to take our story back."[35]

Native Americans also value creativity in children, including them in ceremonial traditions as well as music, dance, and art. Some become writers, filmmakers, and artists. Many take an active part in preserving the languages and tribal traditions as they become adults.

While maintaining traditions, Native Americans also feel the pressures of contemporary life. Often, both parents must work, but sometimes extended family lives in the home and can help to care for the children. There appears to be a higher rate of child abuse in this group, perhaps because many grandparents spent years away from their parents in boarding schools and have not had models of parenting to rely on and pass on to children.[36] Community support has been important when parents cannot care for their children.

Americans of European Descent

European Americans make up about 75.1 percent of the population of 280 million. They trace their origins primarily to northern and western Europe, with Germany, Ireland, England, Italy, France, Poland, and Scotland providing the bulk of the immigrants to this country.[37]

Historical Perspective We have already reviewed their pattern of immigration to this country. Like other groups, European Americans came to this country for many different reasons—to gain political and religious freedom, to escape persecution, and to seek a better way of life. Early settlers included indentured servants who earned their passage and freedom by working for a predetermined period.

General Values We see the major values of European Americans in the New England mothers described earlier in the chapter and in the independent model of culture. This culture emphasizes the importance of the individual, of the independent self, and of striving and attaining self-generated goals.

Contemporary Families With a median age of thirty-seven, European Americans are the oldest population of all ethnic groups. They are an advantaged group, with high levels of education and income (see Table 3-2).

Families are generally stable. Seventy-eight percent of children live in two-parent families, 17 percent in mother-headed families, and 5 percent in father-headed families. Twenty-seven percent of children are born to single mothers, and 11 percent to teen mothers.

Socialization of Children Up until the last decade, most of what is known about children's socialization in the United States has been based on middle-class European American families, so here is a brief summary.[38] As we saw in the study comparing U.S. mothers with Italian mothers, European American parents emphasize giving children encouragement and freedom to explore and learn about the environment and their world. The parents' role is to provide opportunities and support for growth, but children are expected to draw on their own abilities to improve and advance. This group gives less emphasis than do other cultures on the active teaching of social skills and on emotional regulation in the family and with others.

Americans of African Descent

African Americans make up 12.3 percent of the U.S. population and until the 2000 census were the second largest ethnic group in the United States. Now, they are third, with Latinos making up 12.5 percent of the population.

Historical Perspective Most African Americans are descendants of slaves brought to this country against their will, indirectly via the West Indies or directly from West Africa, where family patterns differed from those of Europeans.[39] In comparison to

European American families, which were nuclear families organized around marital ties, West African families were organized on the basis of kinship ties, and a husband and wife usually joined a compound of extended family members on either the bride's or groom's family.[40] There were also polygamous marriages, in which a husband and his wife or wives and relatives lived together. In African families, decisions were made by the head of the family and the rest of the male members of that generation. All the adults felt responsible for all the children, who lived together as brothers and sisters rather than as half-siblings or as cousins. Loosely supervised by the adults, the older children were often responsible for the care of younger children. When they came to this country, African Americans brought this form of family life with them.

The institution of slavery shaped African American families in this country. Slaves were encouraged to marry formally or informally and to have children because children meant capital to the owner.[41] A small percentage of children were born out of wedlock, usually fathered by the owners. Slavery disrupted family life. Mothers often left their infants shortly after birth to work full-time. Other relatives and older siblings cared for the children. A theme of mutual longing of mother and infant prevailed in African American songs. The sale of one or more family members further destroyed the fabric of family life.

African Americans valued marriage, as evidenced by their rushing to have their marriages officially registered in counties where they lived after the Civil War.[42] Many searched for family members who had been sold during slavery in the hope of reuniting the family. Immediately after the Civil War, when laws and the military enforced equal rights for African Americans, African Americans made gains in education and in financial and political power. These gains were short-lived as segregation laws, often termed Jim Crow laws, were passed, enacted, and declared constitutional in the 1890s and restricted where African Americans could live, go to school, eat, and shop. Despite the fact that they had contributed to the country by fighting in all its major wars and remaining loyal to the country even when not given equal rights, they faced limitations in all areas of life.[43] For example, soldiers who fought in both World Wars came home to be treated as unequal citizens.

Not until the 1950s and 1960s did the courts declare these laws unconstitutional. From the latter parts of the nineteenth century to well into mid-twentieth century, people used vicious attacks on and lynching of African Americans to incite terror and helplessness. From 1882 to 1968, 4,743 people were lynched in this country, with 3,446 of them African American.[44] For almost thirty years, the government left lynching unpunished; the first government prosecution of lynching took place in 1919.[45] Vicious killings continued, as in 1955, when the mutilated body of Emmett Till was found. Following that period, guns predominated in the murders of African Americans, such as Martin Luther King, Jr., and Medgar Evers, for their actions in the community.

Through the days of segregation, the Great Depression, World War II, and the years following, family life continued to be strong, and three-quarters of children continued to live in two-parent families until the 1960s.[46] At that time, rapid urbanization and the disappearance of stable, unskilled employment for men led to a drop in the marriage rate but not the birthrate. That led to the increase in the number of one-parent families headed by women. This trend, first seen in African American families, has occurred to a lesser degree in other ethnic groups.

General Values   Andrew Billingsley believes that the following West African family values have survived and been incorporated in contemporary life: (1) the primary importance of blood ties over all others including marital ties, (2) a reliance on extended families rather than nuclear families, (3) the great value placed on children, (4) the importance of and respect for elders, (5) flexibility in role behaviors, (6) emphasis on balancing the needs of the individual with the needs of the family or group, and (7) the importance of obligations to other family members.[47] Reviewing research, Ross Parke and Raymond Buriel describe additional African American values that promote close families: (1) living near other family members and seeing relatives frequently, (2) including relatives and nonrelatives in the extended family and having "fictive" kin or close family friends who are called "auntie," "uncle," or "cousin," and (3) having numerous gatherings, parties, and celebrations for holidays and other special occasions.[48]

Contemporary Families   With a median age of thirty, African Americans on average are younger than European Americans and Asian Americans (see Table 3-2). Although their level of education is not that different from that of European Americans, their median household income is the lowest of all ethnic groups, and they have the highest family poverty rate.

African American families face challenges in rearing children. Sixty-eight percent of babies are born to single mothers, with 20 percent of babies born to teen mothers. African American children are more likely to live in families headed by single parents than are children in other ethnic groups, and these families experience more financial pressures and the stresses that follow from that. Fifty percent of children live in single families headed by women and 6 percent, in families headed by men. Still, 44 percent of children live in two-parent families.

Socialization of Children   African American mothers are younger, have more children, and have them more closely spaced together, compared with European American mothers.[49] These patterns of childbearing may account for the evidence that African American parents appear to make earlier demands on children to be responsible and independent.

Although their family culture is warm and supportive, research suggests that African Americans may be harsh and parent centered in their approach to childrearing. Vonnie McLoyd writes, "Evidence from a number of studies based on observations, self reports, and responses to vignettes suggests that black parents are more severe, punitive, and power assertive in the discipline of their children than white parents of similar socioeconomic status."[50] Though strict, they are not cold and rejecting in disciplining children. They, like parents in all other ethnic groups, make clear distinctions between punishment and physical abuse, and their forms of discipline do not result in higher rates of child abuse in the African American community when social class is controlled.[51]

INTERVIEW

Sherrie is a forty-eight-year-old African American woman who, at age forty-four, obtained a Master of Social Work degree and is in the process of obtaining her license as a clinical social worker. As part of her job working with children and families in an outpatient psychiatric clinic, she leads a parent-group for parents of out-of-control teens. Following her divorce, she raised her son from when he was three; at age twenty-eight, he is now a journalist.

Having worked with parents of many cultures, what do you see as the distinctive features of African American culture?
Born of adversity, African Americans are resilient. We are not as formal as Anglo Saxons. We are more like Mediterraneans. I think our culture is warm, rhythmic, sensual but not sexual. We have rich traditions that are holdovers from African culture. Our celebrations are rich. We can make a celebration out of anything. I knew my husband's family was very poor. When I went there for dinner, there was very little, but it was a celebration, and we were happy. You knew who you were, and you knew you were loved.

We are very connected to each other. We have fictive kin—anyone can be a relative. Sometimes people say, "half-brother" or "half-sister." They are brothers and sisters. I think there is respect for ancestors and elders. Always call elders "Mr." or "Mrs." No matter how old I got, I would never call them by their first name.

We are religious and call on God in a lot of ways. My great grandparents prayed every day. Church was important. There was no question. Black people went to church. There was a tradition and you knew you came from somewhere. I was always at home or at church. It gave me a sense of blessed assurance you belong. Not only are you a part of a church community, but you are a child of God. The black church organized voting rights. Martin Luther King came out of the church.

My great grandparents never talked about slavery or share cropping. They seemed almost to be ashamed of it, but I thought the shame wasn't on them, but on the people who enslaved them.

We grew up, hard-working people. There was pride in working. I knew the plant where my great grandparents were janitors. I thought it was so cool there. My grandmother was the custodian at the Mint. My mother worked at a hospital for the elderly. As long as you were honest, any work was good.

Are there parenting strategies specific to African American parents?
When you are in the dominant culture, you don't have to think about safety and the things you have to face because of your color. African Americans have to be careful in the world. I heard stories about the South, and a great-great-uncle disappeared. I had to help my son think about issues of safety without feeling afraid.

How did you do that?
I taught him to be respectful, polite, not to set himself up in a negative way. I taught him that backing down to preserve his safety was acceptable and fine, and if he wanted to

challenge something, he had to be prepared to pay a price. The world would look at him differently because he was a black male; he had to be aware of what it means to be black. There is a social reality, there is racism, but I didn't want him to be squelched. I wanted him to have dreams, to be creative. I never discouraged any of his dreams.

I felt the world did not have many expectations for a black boy. If someone asked him if he were going to grow up and be football player, I taught him to say, "I'm going to be a nuclear physicist." I gave him expectations. I would drive down Sacramento Street and show him the young men standing around on the street corner. I would ask him, "What are they doing?" He'd say, "Hanging out." I would drive up to the hills and show him the beautiful houses and ask him, "Do you want to live here?" He'd say, "Oh, yes." I'd tell him, "Well, if you hang out, you won't ever be able to live here."

In addition to teaching him about safety, I also had to help him when someone called him a name like "Nigger."

How did you do that?
I never felt there was any shame in slavery. If someone called him "Nigger," that was on them. My mom taught me, and I taught him, if someone called him "Nigger," "Shame on them. So, that's who you are. You are prejudiced." We walked away, and we didn't care.

People said, "Oh, Sherrie, you did such an excellent job with Jioni," but I had a lot of community support. None of my immediate friends had kids, so I enlisted people to help me. His godfather was my high school counselor. He bought his school clothes. I could call him and say, "Come and get him or you'll read about us in the newspaper." I had another friend at work who bought him his first baseball mitt, took him fishing and got him his first fishing pole. He also took him skiing.

The husband of my babysitter told me he was so active, a bundle of energy—get him into baseball. I got him into Little League. People liked having him around. He was curious. He had good manners, and he helped out. He went to visit the children of one of my coworkers, and she said, "How do you get him to eat his vegetables?" He cleared the table, and her kids didn't do anything.

People would give me advice. When he was defiant, my boyfriend would say, "Sherrie, give him a task and leave him alone." I wanted him to do it on my time. I learned from professionals to tell him, "You do this, and then, you will get that." We went to counseling when he was nine, because I didn't like the way I was yelling and screaming. The counselor said, "Mom, you're the boss." I had never set a bedtime. He was my friend, and we were both night people so we stayed up and read. I learned to set consistent limits.

It was the hardest job I ever did, but I never felt I did it alone. He was a child of the community.

Several factors may account for the greater harshness. First, African American families face greater economic stress, and economic difficulties, as we shall see later in this chapter, account for greater strain and conflicts in parenting. Second, African Americans are more likely to live in poor neighborhoods where there is greater violence, making it important for children to follow parents' rules unquestioningly. Third, African Americans need to follow community rules because harsh punishments in the community could follow if they do not.

This group highly values education, even though de jure (by law) and de facto (in fact) segregation has placed major obstacles in their path.[52] A recent book, Peter Irons's *Jim Crow's Children,* describes the continuing impact of segregation laws in producing unequal access to quality education for African Americans in this country.[53]

The military has proven an important institution for African Americans.[54] Desegregated in 1948, it has provided greater access to education and occupational advancement than has been available in civilian life. Though only about 12 percent of the population, African Americans represented nearly 30 percent of the armed services personnel in 1985. In 2000, they represented about 22 percent of all enlisted military personnel, and African American women represented 35 percent of women enlistees.[55] Education, equal opportunity for advancement, belonging, and safety are reasons cited for joining. One Chicago recruit described more fear on the streets of Chicago than in the Marines. "Being over in Baghdad, you've got a thousand people 100 percent behind you. Around here, who says you can't be going to McDonald's and that's it? Over there, you're part of everybody, you're with your friends and family, you're still safe."[56]

Churches are very important in the socialization of African American children. Between two-thirds and three-quarters of African Americans report they belong to a church.[57] The church was a place of freedom and self-direction during slavery, and it has remained a source of inspiration, help, and reform to improve the lives of all African Americans. For example, it served as the home of the civil rights movement in the 1960s. A recent example of the church's prosocial activity occurred in Oakland, California, where the murder rate greatly increased in 2002, with about 70 percent of victims being young African American men. Men from an organization called Black Men First, made up of African American men from churches and mosques, go into high-crime areas to engage young men involved in drugs and crime and present them with another way of life.[58] Billingsley quotes C. Eric Lincoln's description of the African American church as, "the mother of our culture, the champion of our freedom, and the hallmark of our civilization."[59]

Latino Families

Latinos, defined as U.S. citizens of Latin American descent, numbered thirty-five million in the 2000 census and are the second largest ethnic group, composing 12.5 percent of the population. About 58 percent of this group come from Mexico, 9 percent from Puerto Rico, 4 percent from Cuba, and 28 percent from all the other countries in Central and South America and the Caribbean Islands.[60]

Historical Perspective   Many Latinos are people born of the Spanish conquerors and the Native Americans who were already here. Mothers were Native Americans and relied on the teachings of that culture in rearing their children.[61]

Latinos were on this continent before the European Americans, but they were part of the Spanish empire that existed in St. Augustine, Florida, and extended across the southwest part of the United States.[62] Latinos in the area of Texas and New Mexico became citizens of this country after the territories became part of the United States following the Mexican War in 1848. In 1910, a million Mexicans fled the Revolution in their country and became citizens. Puerto Rico, too, became a part of the United States following the Spanish American War in 1898. In 1917, they gained citizenship and the possibility of coming to this country at will.

Waves of immigrants came from other countries and islands, particularly after the lessening of restrictions in 1965. Immigrants from Cuba and other Latin countries have come to escape political persecution, and some anticipate returning to their countries when there is greater freedom. Many immigrants, especially those from Mexico and other countries that are geographically close, retain strong ties to family members in their countries of origin, visit there frequently, and maintain strong attachment to their original cultures.

General Values   Because Latinos come from many countries, the group as a whole is quite varied. Nonetheless, they share many values. First, they value attachment to the family and group.[63] Like Native Americans, Latinos identify themselves with the family and see it as an extension of themselves. They feel obligated to help other family members, and they seek support, advice, and help from family members. They often live in extended family systems, with relatives coming to live for varying lengths of time. The extended family is a problem-solving unit that helps all members deal with the stresses of everyday life. Research suggests that the strong family support has positive benefits—more infants are breast-fed, and children receive more care from relatives.

Second, Latinos emphasize socially sensitive, considerate relationships with others. Children are expected to have a "proper demeanor" with others—courteous, mannerly behavior that reflects concern for their feelings. Competitiveness may be discouraged if it interferes with positive feelings within the group.

Third, respect for elders and authority is important.[64] Grandparents, for example, are looked up to and serve as models for younger children and adults. Even when children are grown and have families of their own, they must respect their parents and grandparents.

Fourth, more than 80 percent of Latino families are Roman Catholics, and their religion structures many rituals and family activities. "The cultural emphasis on respect, group harmony, and cooperation in interpersonal relations is in line with the religious themes of peace, community and self-denial."[65]

Contemporary Families   Latino families are younger and larger than those of other groups. A large number of Latinos were not born in this country, by one estimate 38 percent, and many of them have lacked educational opportunities, perhaps explaining the lower level of educational attainment in the Latino group.[66] Despite the lower educational level, their income is greater than that of African Americans who, as a group, have more education. Like Native Americans and African Americans, Latinos face challenges in rearing children. A high percentage of children are born to teen and to single mothers, and a large number live in single-parent families who have less income.

Socialization of Children   Research comparing Latino families to European American families reveal many of the same differences that the European American—Italian comparison did. Comparisons of middle-class and working-class European American and Puerto Rican mothers of toddlers show that both groups of mothers want their toddlers to develop into loving, self-controlled individuals, but the groups differ in culturally significant ways.[67] European American mothers want children to become independent, self-confident, happy children who explore the world. Puerto Rican mothers want children to have "proper demeanor"—to be quiet, attentive, and respectful of others' needs.

In these studies, European Americans stress individualism, and Puerto Ricans stress interdependent behaviors. These goals then shaped their ways of relating to their toddlers in their day-to-day interactions. Both groups of mothers showed equal physical or verbal affection with children, with the exception that Puerto Rican mothers were more affectionate during teaching tasks. Puerto Rican mothers were more likely to feed toddlers and more likely to structure their activities and to give directions for play than were European American mothers. In teaching activities, Puerto Rican mothers took an active role and were more likely than European American mothers to signal the child's attention, give commands, and give verbal affection in teaching a task. When toddlers were playing freely, Puerto Rican mothers continued to be active and gave more commands than did European American mothers.

European American mothers were more likely than Puerto Rican mothers to encourage children to feed themselves and to play while mothers watched, and European American mothers spent more time teaching toddlers to learn tasks such as coloring and playing with blocks. They more often gave suggestions rather than the directions that the Puerto Rican mothers gave toddlers.

Latino parents continue to be active and controlling as children grow older. Children absorb their parents' values. As adolescents, for example, Mexican American teens are more likely than European American teens to feel they have obligations to respect, help, and support their families.[68] Further, adolescents who have this value feel closer to their parents and siblings and have somewhat higher educational aspirations. Differences were large and consistent across socioeconomic groups within the ethnic group.

Like African American parents, Latino parents place a great emphasis on education and want their children to succeed.[69] Exactly why Latino children have performed less well, in the sense of having lower rates of high school and college graduation is not clear. Explanations fall into two main categories: (1) those that point to differences in the culture or in parenting beliefs and methods and (2) those that point to poor schools, poor preparation, and few financial resources for college.

A recent survey from the Pew Hispanic Center indicates that finances are the main reason Latino students do not finish college.[70] While poor preparation plays a role, Richard Frey, the survey's author, stated that lack of money is the main obstacle to college graduation. Latino students enroll in college, usually two-year colleges first, in higher numbers than do European American students, but they tend not to complete the four-year degree. Latinos receive less financial aid than do European American students. Because they are older students and tend to have more obligations for family support, they cannot borrow the large sums that the average student incurs by graduation—$17,000 in loans and $3,000 in credit card debt. The report concludes that increased financial aid for students already enrolled in college is an efficient way of boosting the percentage of Latino college graduates.

This problem affects not only the Latino population but society as a whole. "Over the next twenty-five years, the report said, the white working-age population will shrink by five million as baby boomers retire, while the Latino working-age population swells by eighteen million. These numbers make improved education of Latinos vitally important for the nation's workforce."[71]

Americans of Asian Descent

Asian Americans made up almost 4 percent of the population in the 2000 census. They trace their origins to more than twenty-eight different countries in Asia.[72] In this brief space, we can discuss only broad trends among the national groups, which may have their own specific emphases. In addition, diversity exists within groups, depending on how many years the family has been in this country.

Historical Perspective   Asian Americans trace their attitudes toward children to Confucian and Buddhist philosophies that transcend national borders.[73] Young children are considered to be closely attached to the spiritual world because of their greater likelihood of mortality. They are regarded as pure, innocent, and good. These beliefs encourage parents to revere and protect their young. In this culture, just as plants require physical care in the form of watering and fertilizing, as well as shaping in the form of pruning and directing growth, so children require physical care and direction.

As noted earlier, the Chinese began coming to this country in the 1840s but were later restricted. The Philippine Islands became a commonwealth of the United States in 1898 and remained so until it became an independent republic following World War II. It has contributed a large number of immigrants and continues to do so.[74]

Japanese Americans began to come to Hawaii and to this country around the turn of the twentieth century because of economic conditions in Japan. The 1924 Immigration Act ended their immigration until after World War II. Japanese Americans prospered; by 1941, 40,000 Japanese adults lived on the west coast with their 70,000 American-born children. At the beginning of World War II, most of these individuals were taken from their homes and sent to relocation camps in desert and mountain areas in the western states until the end of the war because of security concerns. Nonetheless, some Japanese Americans served with great distinction in the U.S. military. In the 1970s the government made compensation for each Japanese American incarcerated during World War II.[75]

Since the immigration laws changed in 1965, many immigrants have come from Asia, especially Southeast Asia. These people have often come to escape persecution at home or to find better economic prospects here. While Japanese Americans (41 percent), Chinese Americans (30 percent), and Filipino Americans (24 percent) were the major subgroups prior to 1970, now the most numerous groups are Chinese (24 percent), Filipino (20 percent), and Southeast Asian (14 percent).[76]

General Values   Like many other groups, Asian Americans stress the interdependence of family members. The family is the focus of life; the self exists and is defined in relation to other family members, who have obligations to be close and supportive. Well-functioning adults feel required to discuss major decisions with other family members and get their support before proceeding. Outside the family, one has obligations to country and to work.[77]

Control is a second important value.[78] Families are organized with fathers as the figures in control, and mothers subordinate to them. Mothers, however, take complete charge of children, and so from a child's point of view, mothers appear to be authorities as well. Children are obligated to respect and obey these authoritative figures.

Contemporary Families   Asian Americans exceed all groups in educational attainment and income. Families are more stable, with more children in two-parent families and far fewer children born to teen and single mothers, compared with any other group. As a result, they have one of the lowest rates of poverty.

Socialization of Children   Asian cultures believe that infants and toddlers cannot reason, making parents totally responsible for their well-being.[79] The high level of care they provide and their willingness to put the child's needs above their own reflect the responsibilities they feel toward children. They indulge young children and do all within their power to please them.

Asian American families emphasize family connectedness. Physical closeness is a way of promoting the infant's feeling of connection with family members. Mothers speak gently to young children and describe their own and others' feelings so infants can learn to empathize with how others feel.

Though children are often indulged in the early years, when they become five or six they are expected to meet the demanding standards of parents and outside authorities.[80] While Asian Americans value independence, they interpret the concept differently from European Americans, who define independence as freely expressing one's feelings and reactions and making decisions on one's own. Asian Americans view independence as expressed within the family. Children reflect their independence by becoming more able to meet family expectations.

Asian American parents exert more control than do European American parents, but it is not the cold, authoritarian control often seen in European American families.[81] Rather, it is control in the sense of teaching and governing the child in order to promote safety and growth. Parents monitor children closely and guide behavior in approved directions. When control is defined as governing the child, research finds no negative effects of control for the child. Control defined as domination, as in the European American community, affects children more negatively.

Shaming has also been considered part of many Asian cultures. Children's attention is drawn to how their behavior affects and is regarded by others. The possible negative response from others then shapes the child's behavior. A form of teaching related to shaming is termed *opportunity education*. A parent points out another child's behavior, along with its positive or negative consequences, as an example that the child can copy or avoid, depending on the circumstances.

Asian Americans value education, and parents sometimes value themselves in terms of how well their children do in school and how much education they get.[82] Parents tend to see achievement as the result of the child's intense and prolonged effort rather than being caused by innate ability. They expect children to work hard; as parents, they provide resources and tutoring as needed. As children go on in school, Asian American parents do not get as highly involved in volunteer activities as some other groups of parents do. While achievement is important, Asian American parents also value the love of learning.

We have spoken of Asian Americans as a group, but a great deal of diversity exists among them. A study comparing the parenting of Filipino American, Japanese American, and European American mothers around eating behaviors highlights differences among these groups.[83] Mothers in each group defined slightly different goals in parenting. European American mothers wanted children to become happy, independent, creative adults. Japanese American mothers wanted children to develop into achieving adults who could manage life's demands while maintaining well-ordered lives that included close contact with families. Filipino American mothers had a slightly different emphasis. They wanted children to develop into responsible citizens who are well-mannered and respectful of authority.

The groups used slightly different ways to shape their children's meal time behaviors. Both Japanese American and Filipino American mothers were more child centered in their interventions than were European American mothers. Japanese American mothers, and fathers when they participated, focused all their attention on the toddler, engaging and feeding the child, and permitting the child to stop whenever full. Filipino American mothers were also child centered, but they kept babies on their laps during family mealtimes and spoon-fed children until they ate all that the parents thought they should. European American meal times were not toddler centered but focused on older children and fathers. Toddlers ate finger foods and sought attention as they needed it, and mothers responded to their needs.

Filipino American mothers were more directive than Japanese American mothers, restricting babies' movements and insisting that babies do as the mothers requested. Japanese American mothers subtly directed children's behavior. They encouraged cooperation by making games of what the child wanted to do and gently guiding the child to do what the parent wanted. European American mothers were the least directive.

As the study reports,

> Filipino- and Japanese-American mothers were highly attentive and affectionate toward their infants, but also either overtly (Filipino-American) or subtly (Japanese-American)

controlling. Mothers conveyed the message that being a member of a tight family group involves both the warmth and attentiveness of belonging and also the obligation of conforming to adult wishes. The Caucasian-American mothers in this sample allowed more autonomy and were more relationally distant. They encouraged innovation as they focused on infants' completing their goal-directed actions—regardless of whether these disrupted the rest of the group.[84]

The groups differed in ways of relating to babies. European American mothers encouraged babies to engage others verbally—by talking and becoming part of mealtime conversations, while Japanese American mothers encouraged babies to seek contact by trying to accomplish a task and by obtaining help as needed.

Americans of Middle Eastern Descent

Middle Eastern Americans trace their origins to many different countries—Lebanon, Syria, Egypt, Palestine, Iraq, Jordan, Yemen, Saudi Arabia, Afghanistan, and Kuwait. Like all other ethnic groups, this group includes several social and religious subgroups. The majority of Middle Eastern Americans are Christians (77 percent), with Muslims making up about 23 percent.[85] Middle Eastern Americans make up a small percentage of the population, estimated at between one and three million, living in predominantly urban areas.[86] A large majority are native-born Americans, and 82 percent are citizens.[87]

Historical Perspective   Middle Eastern Americans have immigrated in several waves. The first wave, at the end of the nineteenth and early twentieth centuries, included agricultural workers from Lebanon who sought better economic conditions as the silk crop was failing. They became skilled laborers or small store owners. Christians came also to escape the Ottoman practice of making the children of Christians who did not convert to Islam serve in the military. The common bond of religion eased their transition into U.S. society. The early immigrants set up a "chain migration," in which the first member of a family established here saved money for the next member to come, so that eventually a broad network of family members was here and living close together.

The restrictive immigration laws of the 1920s halted immigration until after World War II. At that time, and continuing since then, events in the Middle East have triggered waves of immigrants, most recently of Muslims. Their social backgrounds have varied, with some being highly educated individuals who studied and remained here, and some being poor refugees from conflicts there. Those who came as students and remained did not bring other relatives here and were more likely to marry an American because they had more contact with U.S. culture than did other subgroups.

General Values   Middle Eastern Americans place great value on religion and family. More than country of origin or skin color, religion defines people. Churches and mosques are centers of social as well as spiritual life. Marriage outside one's religion is frowned on.

In secular life, the most important value is the large, extended family formed by patrilineal descent lines. Middle Eastern Americans are raised to think of family interests before their own. Blood ties matter more than marital ties, but because cousin marriages are approved in this culture, many husbands and wives are of the same patrilineal family and can live close to both families.

> Although patrilineality may include patriarchy, it entails a wider set of duties and obligations. Patrilineal rules give older generations power over younger, and men privileges over women. Yet it is necessary to mention that women have more power than Westerners conceive. Their power lies within their patrilineage, in their roles as mothers and sisters, and in their ability to influence relationships. It also lies in their potential to disrupt the social system by noncompliance with patriarchy.[88]

Obligations to family members are paramount with financial as well as psychological support expected. When families bring relatives here from their countries of origin, they find jobs for them or help them start businesses. About 40 percent of Middle Eastern Americans report they landed their first job through a relative. Middle Eastern Americans also send money to relatives in their country of origin—in one study in Canada, 50 percent of foreign-born Middle Easterners and 22 percent born in Canada sent money home regularly.[89]

Upholding family honor is quite important. In this patrilineal culture, women's sexuality is of concern both before and after marriage. Women can be beaten, banished from the family, and in rare instances killed for having sexual relations outside of marriage and bringing shame on the family.

In return for the demands made on individuals, families provide protection, feelings of security, and closeness with others.

Contemporary Families   For this small ethnic group that lacks official minority status, statistics comparable to the other groups are hard to find. Middle Eastern American families are larger than those of other groups. In one study, 38 percent of women, half of whom were ages twenty to twenty-nine, had five or more children and presumably could have more.[90] The Middle Eastern median family income for 1990 was $39,580, higher than the median U.S. family income of $35,225. The Middle Eastern American income continues to be higher than average, perhaps because women often work in family-owned stores and businesses.[91]

Middle Eastern Americans, on average, are highly educated, with 82 percent having a high school degree, 36 percent a college degree, and 15 percent an advanced degree.[92] Seventy-two percent work in managerial, professional, technical, and administrative jobs; as a result, the group has a low overall poverty level of 10 percent, comparable to that of European Americans and Asian Americans.[93]

Middle Eastern American families immigrating to this country in the last decade have values that differ greatly from those in mainstream American culture. This makes rearing children difficult in many ways. In addition, these families must deal with Americans' lack of knowledge and understanding of their traditional culture and Islam. Since September 11, 2001, such families are also dealing with the suspicion and prejudice that has followed the terrorist attack in New York by men from

Saudi Arabia. Although groups of Muslims and Christians have met to increase understanding of each other's cultures, it is not an easy time for many Americans of Middle Eastern descent.

Socialization of Children   Like all other ethnic groups, Middle Eastern Americans place a high value on children. Like many other groups, they indulge very young children. In extended families, many adults and older children look after and safeguard them.

As a patrilineal culture, they emphasize respect for elders and privileges for boys.[94] Sons are highly valued and given greater advantages and more freedom than are girls. Even though many women contribute to family businesses, gender socialization is traditional. Girls are encouraged to help at home, behave modestly in public, and spend most of their social time with family and relatives. Early marriages are encouraged and make it harder for girls to obtain advanced education.

Particular tensions between parents and teens may arise when the teens want to spend time with peers and engage in school activities. Parents expect teens to continue to participate in religious activities and visit and socialize with extended relatives, but teens in this country want to pursue their own activities. The resolution of such conflicts depends, in part, on the support teens and parents can bring to bear. If the family is an extended one in a large, Middle Eastern community, the teens will have a harder time asserting their wishes, because parents have much support for theirs. If the family has few relatives and little communal support for parents, then teens may gain greater freedom.

While boys are permitted to date before marriage, girls are not encouraged to date. In one study, 80 percent of wives never dated before marriage and another 10 percent dated very little. Permitted to work before marriage girls are encouraged to find teaching, clerical, secretarial, or other jobs where there are not a high proportion of men.

As in many other ethnic groups, second, third, and fourth generation Middle Eastern Americans are probably not so tied to the traditional ways of childrearing. However, recall that significant numbers of this ethnic group have immigrated since 1990, reflecting quite traditional orientations to families and children. Many Americans might disapprove of the Middle Eastern way of life. Yet Palestinian American women, in one survey, believed their lives were better than those of most other American women; in another, 47 percent of Muslim women "felt they were treated as well [as] or better than the average American."[95] Only 33 percent of Muslim women born in the United States shared this opinion.

The Self-Esteem of Ethnic Groups

As reported on standardized inventories, global self-esteem is considered a measure of how individuals regard themselves. Concern that prejudice and discrimination have led to both negative self-concepts and low levels of self-esteem in ethnic groups has prompted research examining the self-esteem in such groups. Research comparing the levels of self-esteem of European Americans and African Americans found that African American global self-esteem is as high or higher than that of

European Americans, despite the negative experiences many African Americans endure in this society.

Jean Twenge and Jennifer Crocker carried out a meta-analysis of studies of self-esteem to determine whether other groups also scored as high as African Americans.[96] They looked at 712 comparisons of self-esteem among African Americans, European Americans, Native Americans, Latinos, and Asian Americans and found that African Americans scored highest on standardized inventories yielding measures of global self-esteem, followed by European Americans, Latinos, Native Americans, and Asian Americans. Asian Americans scored significantly lower than the first three groups. African American and Latino scores are lower on inventories that include a subscale measure of academic self-esteem than on inventories that do not.

The rank ordering of these groups on inventories of self-esteem does not follow the pattern of negative stereotyping of the groups in this country. Surveys of the national population suggest that European Americans are viewed most favorably, then Asian Americans, then Latinos, then African Americans. (Native Americans were not included in those surveys.) Despite being the most devalued, African Americans think well of themselves and have thought well of themselves in studies over the past twenty years. Further, although Asian Americans are considered most favorably of all other groups except European Americans and have higher levels of education and income than all other ethnic groups, they report the least positive self-perceptions.

The socioeconomic status of the subjects tended to reduce the differences among the groups. High-status individuals of all groups tended to be more alike in their levels of self-esteem than do low-status individuals. In fact, high-status Latinos scored higher than their European American counterparts.

With respect to age, the differences in self-esteem among the five groups were smallest in elementary school and grew larger through high school and into the adult years. This suggests that initially, all children tend to make positive statements about themselves, but as they grow older, they become more socialized in their culture's views of what is appropriate to say about oneself. Those groups that emphasize an interdependent self had scores that decreased with age. With respect to gender, boys and men in minority groups scored lower in relation to male European Americans than girls and women did, compared with their female counterparts. The authors speculate that European American girls and women may have lower self-esteem, relative to the boys and men in their group; therefore the girls and women in other groups come closer to them.

Examining self-esteem in relation to the subjects' geographic area of residence, gender, age, and the years of data collection yielded interesting findings. The self-esteem of African Americans and Asian Americans was highest in areas where that group had greater concentrations of population. For example, African Americans' self-esteem was highest in southern states that had the greatest numbers of African Americans. This is similar to the finding that African American students at African American colleges have higher self-esteem than do African Americans at European American colleges. Also, African Americans' self-esteem showed a larger difference over other groups in those southern states where African Americans compose more than 30 percent of the population. Asian Americans living on the west coast, where there are higher concentrations of Asian Americans, reported higher self-esteem than did Asian Americans in other parts of the country.

The subjects' cohort (year of birth) and the subjects' age at the time the data were collected also related to scores on self-esteem. In 1980, about twenty years after the civil rights movement began in the United States, African American scores on global self-esteem inventories began to rise. Twenge and Crocker speculate that the emphasis on the experiences and contributions of African Americans to this country, and the civil rights movement's emphasis on group pride and self-respect, affected children who absorbed these messages in the 1960s and 1970s. As they got older, they retained the high self-esteem that the data collected after 1980 reflected. Cohort differences are found for other groups as well. The most recently born Asian Americans and Latinos differ least from European Americans. European Americans are not dropping in self-esteem, so the other groups are rising.

The authors conclude that, rather than a single factor, a variety of cultural factors explain self-esteem in different ethnic groups. First, the cultural influence of the ethnic group itself plays a role. Scores are highest for groups that have an individualistic orientation that emphasizes independence, setting personal goals, taking control to achieve these goals, valuing uniqueness, and seeking to stand out from others. European Americans and African Americans emphasize these beliefs. Having an individualistic orientation does not mean that collectivist goals have to be ignored, though they usually are in the European American group. Groups that stress an interdependent self that seeks harmony with others, not superiority to them, also are more likely to stress self-criticism and therefore score lower on measures of self-esteem. Asian American, Latino, and Native American groups emphasize the interdependent self, and these are the groups that score the lowest on the inventories.

Social factors also affect the cultural groups' beliefs. As ethnic groups reside longer in this country and are exposed to its an individualistic orientation, their self-reports begin to resemble those of European Americans. As noted, this does not mean that groups abandon their emphasis on social or group needs; cultures can retain both sets of beliefs and balance the demands of each.

Self-esteem seems to flourish when groups receive positive messages from the communities in which they live. When political and social movements emphasize a group's contributions and when groups feel support from large numbers who share their cultural orientation, then self-esteem increases. Since individuals of higher status in all groups make positive comments about themselves, we can speculate that higher education, a major marker of status, brings with it an increasing appreciation of the self.

COMMONALITIES AMONG CULTURAL THEMES

In recognizing that culture exerts powerful impact on what parents do, we should not overlook the commonalities among cultural influences in this country. All cultures place a high value on children and families, and most parents want their children to grow up to be effective adults, however they define effectiveness.

The majority of European Americans embrace the independent model of parent-child relationships. The other ethnic groups, including some sub-groups of European Americans such as Italian Americans or Greek Americans, use a more interdependent model, emphasizing respect for elders and tradition, the importance of the extended family and family obligations, early indulgence of children followed (usually) by firm expectations, and a strong reliance on spiritual values. Because older European Americans describe these values as the ones they were raised with also, we can assume that large segments of the population endorse an interdependent model. If immigration continues as it has and if ethnic groups continue to have a larger number of children, this model may come to equal or replace the more dominant independent model of today.

While ethnic groups may have special goals and concerns regarding children, parents' behavior has similar effects on children regardless of the ethnic group, family structure, social status, or gender of parents and children.[97] Parental support, monitoring children, and avoidance of harsh punishment are three aspects of parents' behavior that have been linked to children's positive growth and well-being in European American samples of parents and children. Recent analyses of national samples of parents and children that include African American and Mexican American parents as well as European American parents of all educational and financial backgrounds indicate that parental support and avoidance of harsh punishment are associated with good grades, psychological adjustment, and rule-following behaviors in boys and girls from five to eighteen in all groups. Parental monitoring was not associated with positive outcomes except for a finding that in one-parent families, monitoring was related to better grades and fewer behavior problems.

In the adolescent years, parents' acceptance and involvement were related to teens' reports of academic achievement and general feeling of well-being in four ethnic groups—European Americans, African Americans, Latinos, and Asian Americans.[98] The greater the parents' involvement, supervision, and autonomy granting, the more teens reported competence and well-being.

A finding that initially emerged in African American samples has been found in European American and Latino samples as well. Nonabusive spanking that occurs in the context of warm family relationships is not related to an increase in children's behavior problems and aggression over time from ages four to eleven.[99] Spanking in the context of little emotional support is associated with increases in problem behaviors over time in the three ethnic groups.

We have now looked at differences in parenting goals and strategies among members of different ethnic groups and looked at similarities in the effects of their strategies. As Mary Kay DeGenova wrote in *Families in Cultural Context,*

> No matter how many differences there may be, beneath the surface there are even more similarities. It is important to try to identify the similarities among various cultures. Stripping away surface differences will uncover a multiplicity of similarities: people's hopes, aspirations, desire to survive, search for love, and need for family—to name just a few. While superficially we may be dissimilar, the essence of being human is very much the same for all of us. Experience the paradox of diversity: that "we are the same but in different ways."[100]

THE INFLUENCE OF SOCIOECONOMIC STATUS

We have seen that ethnic background shapes parents' goals, strategies, and values with regard to children. Equally or more important is the influence of the family's social status within the ethnic group.

Erika Hoff, Brett Laursen, and Twila Tardif state that socioeconomic status (SES) provides a developmental niche for parent-child relations.[101] Social position partly prescribes the settings children live in, their parents' childrearing practices, and the psychological characteristics of their parents.

Three variables—parents' occupation, education, and level of income—make up SES. Because the three variables, though correlated, can vary, SES is a complicated concept. Thus, one middle-class family may have an average income, education, and occupational status, while another middle-class family of average income and occupational status may have a higher educational status. Even if the two families had different values, both would be considered middle class.

Although income at or below the poverty level affects parenting (see the next section), income above the poverty level appears less influential in shaping parenting beliefs than do education and occupational status. The influence of social status, like that of culture, is not fixed. For example, parents' occupations may change as the result of increased education, or a family may find great success in some endeavor and their income may rise sharply. Conversely, income and social status may drop as a result of unemployment. Further, parents change their ideas about parenting as a result of new information.

Summarizing the research on the influence of SES on parenting, Hoff, Laursen, and Tardif state that higher SES parents are more likely than lower SES parents to have a child-centered orientation to parenting. They seek to understand children's thoughts and feelings and to make them important partners in the process of parenting. They elicit opinions and encourage children's participation in making rules. Lower SES parents are more parent centered than are higher status parents. They see themselves as authorities and want children to comply. When children do not obey, such parents are harsh and punitive.

A second major finding is that differences in SES correlate with more differences in verbal than nonverbal interactions between parents and children. A third finding is that higher-status parents talk more to children and elicit more speech from them. They also show more responsiveness when children do speak, and they encourage the development of verbal skills by supplying more labels that describe what children see and do.

The description of such differences may sound uninteresting and unimportant, but an unusual study has documented the profound impact of these differences on young children's lives. Betty Hart and Todd Risley recorded the words spoken to and by children in their homes from the ages of one to three years.[102] Investigators visited the homes of forty-two families of professional, working-class, and welfare backgrounds for an hour each month. The children in the study were European American and African American. Results indicated no gender or racial differences in language acquisition, but they did reveal large differences based on social group.

All children in the study experienced quality interactions with their parents; all heard diverse forms of language spoken to and around them; all learned to speak by the age of three. However, the differing amounts and kinds of language heard in the homes surprised the investigators.

First, professional parents spoke about three times as much to their children as did welfare parents and about one and a half times as much as did working-class parents. Children in professional families heard about 487 utterances per hour; children in working-class families, 301; children in welfare families, 178.

The emotional tone of the conversations also reflected startling differences. In professional families, children received affirmative feedback (confirming, elaborating, and giving explicit approval for what the child said) about thirty times an hour, or every other minute. In working-class families, children received affirmative feedback fifteen times an hour, or once every four minutes. In welfare families, children received positive feedback six times an hour, or once every ten minutes. Professional parents gave prohibitions about five times an hour, and welfare parents about eleven. Children in welfare families heard twice as many negative comments as positive ones, whereas children in professional families heard primarily positive comments and rarely any negative ones.

These findings have important implications for the development of self-concept and general mood as well as for language development. Language differences in the home strongly predicted vocabulary growth and intellectual development for the next five years. The most important predictors of vocabulary and intellectual competence were the emotional tone of the feedback and the amount of linguistic diversity the child heard.

Encouragingly, the study shows that all parents have the capacity to promote language and intellectual development, because they already have the ability to speak and interact with children effectively. Of course, some parents need to increase certain kinds of behavior—namely, their verbal interactions with their children—and provide more positive feedback to them.

THE INFLUENCE OF ECONOMIC HARDSHIP

In the previous section, we looked at families with low income above the poverty level. Here we look at what happens to families when income falls below that level.

Parents who lack resources to care for their children experience increased stress in meeting the challenges of daily life. When experiencing economic hardship, parents become more irritable, depressed, and more easily frustrated.[103] Their psychological tension has a direct impact on their parenting and on their children. Such parents stimulate their children less, and they use less effective parenting practices. They do not communicate with children as openly or share power as much as they do in less stressful times. This tension affects children's schoolwork and behavior. When economic conditions improve, parenting skills improve, as does children's behavior.

In one study, the parenting behavior of parents of adolescents varied by the level of economic strain.[104] Regardless of ethnic background (European American, African American) or family structure (one-parent or two-parent), financial strain was related to parents' having greater conflict with adolescents, less involvement in their schooling, and lower school achievement. Financial strain overrode the influence of ethnic background and family structure in predicting conflict with children and children's decreasing grades.

Economic strain also has an indirect effect on children's behavior. When parents are upset and frustrated, they argue with each other and give each other less support, so parenting declines because parents are not working together.[105] When fathers remain supportive of mothers during economic hardship, mothers' parenting skills do not decrease at all.[106] Although social support from outside the family helps to reduce parents' low moods, it is support from the other parent that maintains parenting effectiveness.

Who Are the Poor?

The most common measure of poverty is the official federal index of poverty developed in the 1960s and based on pretax, cash income and the number of people in the family.[107] The index is determined by the estimated cost of food multiplied by three, as food was found in surveys to absorb about one-third of the family income. For example, the 2000 poverty threshold for two people was $11,569; for a family of three, $14,128; and for a family of four (two adults and two children), $18,104.[108]

In addition to the poverty index, a measure of duration of poverty yields important information for understanding the effects of poverty.[109] One-third of all children in the United States will be poor for least one year before they reach age eighteen, and two-thirds of those who are poor spend less than five years in poverty. Fifteen percent of poor children, however, are poor for more than ten years of childhood, and these children experience the most severe poverty, because their family cash income is half that required to exceed the poverty index.

Children, particularly the youngest, are the poorest individuals in the United States.[110] In 2001, the rate of poverty for children under eighteen was 16.3 percent.[111] Rates of poverty are higher for children in certain ethnic groups.[112] In 1999, 33 percent of African American and 30 percent of Hispanic children were living in poverty, compared with 13 percent of European American and 12 percent of Asian American children. Studies on the persistence of poverty have to be carried out over many years; those reported in the 1980s focused primarily on comparisons between African American and European American children. Ninety percent of persistently poor children are African American.[113]

Rates of poverty vary according to family structure, with children in single-parent families more likely to be poor than those in two-parent families.[114] Still, in one study, almost half the years children spent in poverty occurred when they were living with two parents. Although African American children are more likely to be living in single-parent families and are thus more at risk for poverty, living in two-parent families does not protect these children against higher rates of poverty. In one study, European American children in two-parent families averaged six months in poverty, whereas African American children in two-parent families averaged three years. In another study, European American children who spent their entire childhoods in single-parent families had the same rate of poverty as did African American children in two-parent families.[115]

Many factors influence rates of poverty. Declines in the number of children per family and increases in parental education generally decrease poverty.[116] Vonnie McLoyd points to three factors that push more children into poverty: decreases in the number of skilled jobs that can support families, increases in the number of single-parent families, and reductions in government benefits to families.[117]

The Effects of Poverty on Children's Development

Jeanne Brooks-Gunn and Greg Duncan describe the effects of poverty on various aspects of children's functioning.[118]

Birth Outcomes and Physical Health   Low birth weight (less than 2,500 grams) and infant mortality are almost twice as common among poor infants as among nonpoor infants. Further, growth stunting (being less than fifth percentile in height for one's age), often considered a measure of nutritional status, is twice as common in poor children as in nonpoor children. Lead poisoning, often related to many physical and cognitive impairments, is 3.5 times more common among poor children than among nonpoor children. Not surprisingly, poor children are less often characterized as having excellent health than are nonpoor children and more often described as having fair or poor health.

When educational programs include interventions to improve health, test scores increase.[119] For example, an assistant superintendent of schools in Chula Vista observed several years ago that the schools with the poorest academic progress were those with the greatest absenteeism for health reasons. He approached the director of the local medical clinic, who was also concerned about children's health care. Many of the children lacked health insurance and used expensive emergency room services for routine problems. Such bills went unpaid, and the clinic lost money. The school, the medical center, and the city organized a mobile medical clinic that went from school to school, providing routine care for children. The clinic was linked with a family clinic on the school grounds, and parents were helped to fill out papers for federal health benefits.

Health improved. Children attended school more regularly. In class, they were alert and attentive. Academic performance and test scores improved. Clearly, health played a major role in this change.

Cognitive, Emotional, and Behavioral Development   Table 3-3 (p. 100) reveals that poor children are more likely to experience cognitive delays and learning disabilities than are nonpoor children. The poorer the child, the greater the delay. These differences appear on ability measures as early as two years of age and persist into the elementary school years. These differences persist even when mother's age, marital status, education, and ethnicity are controlled for.

■ **TABLE 3-3**
SELECTED POPULATION-BASED INDICATORS OF WELL-BEING FOR POOR
AND NONPOOR CHILDREN IN THE UNITED STATES

Indicator	Percentage of Poor Children (unless noted)	Percentage of Nonpoor Children (unless noted)	Ratio of Poor to Nonpoor Children
Cognitive Outcomes			
Developmental delay (includes both limited and long-term developmental deficits) (0 to 17 years)	5.0	3.8	1.3
Learning disability (defined as having exceptional difficulty in learning to read, write, and do arithmetic) (3 to 17 years)	8.3	6.1	1.4
School Achievement Outcomes (5 to 17 years)			
Grade repetition (reported to have ever repeated a grade)	28.8	14.1	2.0
Ever expelled or suspended	11.9	6.1	2.0
High school dropout (percentage 16- to 24-year-olds who were not in school or did not finish high school in 1994)	21.0	9.6	2.2
Emotional or Behavioral Outcomes (3 to 17 years unless noted)			
Parent reports child has ever had an emotional or behavioral problem that lasted three months or more	16.4	12.7	1.3
Parent reports child ever being treated for an emotional problem or behavioral problem	2.5	4.5	0.6
Parent reports child has experienced one or more of a list of typical child behavioral problems in the last three months (5 to 17 years)	57.4	57.3	1.0
Other			
Female teens who had an out-of-wedlock birth	11.0	3.6	3.1
Economically inactive at age 24 (not employed or in school)	15.9	8.3	1.9
Experienced hunger (food insufficiency) at least once in past year	15.9	1.6	9.9
Reported cases of child abuse and neglect	5.4	0.8	6.8
Violent crimes (experienced by poor families and nonpoor families)	5.4	2.6	2.1
Afraid to go out (percentage of family heads in poor and nonpoor families who report they are afraid to go out in their neighborhood)	19.5	8.7	2.2

Note: This list of child outcomes reflects findings from large, nationally representative surveys that collect data on child outcomes and family income. While most data come from the 1988 National Health Interview Survey Child Health Supplement, data from other nationally representative surveys are included. The rates presented are from simple cross-tabulations. In most cases, the data do not reflect factors that might be important to child outcomes other than poverty status at the time of data collection. The ratios reflect rounding.

Jeanne Brooks-Gunn and Greg J. Duncan, "The Effects of Poverty on Children," *Future of Children 7*, no. 2 (1997): 58–59. Reprinted with permission of the David and Lucille Packard Foundation.

Poor children are twice as likely as nonpoor children to repeat a school grade or drop out of school. The duration and timing of poverty influence its effects on children's functioning. Those children who live in poverty thirteen years or longer have significantly lower scores on cognitive measures than do those who experience only short-term poverty. Poverty in the first five years of life is negatively associated with high school graduation, whereas poverty in the adolescent years is not.

Poverty is less clearly related to emotional outcomes than to physical and cognitive development. Parents of poor and nonpoor children report the same number of behavioral problems, with current poverty related to such behaviors as hyperactivity and peer problems. These differences are found even when mothers' age, education, and mental status are controlled.

In addition to facing differences in health and cognitive skills, poor children are more likely to experience hunger, abuse, and neglect. They are more likely to experience violent crimes and to be afraid to go out in their neighborhoods. As teens, they are more likely to bear a child out of wedlock.

Although Table 3-3 highlights increased stresses for poor children, compared with nonpoor children, it also suggests that poverty does not affect all areas of functioning. Most poor children perform at grade level, almost 80 percent graduate from high school, and they are no more likely than nonpoor children to have emotional problems.

Pathways Accounting for the Effects of Poverty   Greg Duncan and Jeanne Brooks-Gunn identify five ways that poverty affects children's development—health, home environment, style of parenting, parents' mental health, and neighborhood characteristics.[120] Health status is a consequence of poverty, but it also influences children's subsequent development because low birth weight is associated with learning disabilities, grade retention, and school dropout rates.

Duncan and Brooks-Gunn refute the argument that the problems of the poor result from parents' genetic endowment or their work ethic.[121] They report that siblings reared in the same family with the same parental attitudes can differ in the age and duration of poverty in their lives and thus serve to control for the effects of parental characteristics on poverty. That sibling differences in income were related to siblings' years of completed schooling suggests that income does matter even when genes and work ethic are controlled for.

With limited income, parents can afford fewer resources in the home for stimulating development—fewer toys and activities and less reading material. The lack of stimulation in the home is thought to account for up to half the effects of poverty on the IQs of five-year-old children. Parents' limited income increases anxiety and depression in parents, decreasing their parenting effectiveness. Parental stress also increases parental harshness with children, which may account for the decrease in children's school achievement.

Still, there is great diversity among poor parents.[122] While poor parents face an increased risk of depression—for example, up to 40 percent of poor mothers in a work-training program score in the clinical range of depression—a large percentage do not. While many poor parents use harsh parenting procedures, many do not. With support from family, church, and the community, parents are warmer and more supportive of children.

As we saw earlier in the Hart and Risley study, families from professional, working class, and poor parents all manifest the same behaviors—all talked to children and could be positive and encouraging. What distinguished the groups was the percentage of time that each group spent in the activity. So, poor parents have basic skills, but stress or other financial demands sap their energy. Thus, their children do not reap all the benefits they might from their parents' behavior.

Ways to Intervene

In the past, parents could find two forms of assistance—cash-transfer programs that gave money directly to poor children through Aid to Families with Dependent Children (AFDC) and programs that provided services such as Food Stamps and subsidized lunches. Food Stamps and AFDC, available to all families with a certain level of income, were termed entitlement programs. In 1996, the Personal Responsibility and Work Opportunity Reconciliation Act, more often termed the Welfare Reform Bill, eliminated the sixty-year-old guaranteed AFDC program and replaced it with block grants to states that could use the money in any way they wished to provide temporary assistance to poor families (Temporary Assistance to Needy Families or TANF). There were many requirements for receiving this money.[123] No one person could receive aid through TANF for more than five years over his or her entire life, and states were free to reduce the limit further if they wished. The law demanded work requirements that varied with the ages of the children in the family after twenty-four months of family assistance. Fifty percent of the state's welfare recipients had to be working in order for the state to continue to qualify for money at the end of five years. In addition, the law changed supplementary programs like the Food Stamp program and Supplemental Social Security Income for children.

The Welfare Reform Bill has led to a 50 percent decrease in the number of welfare cases. In 2001, median family incomes for all except the wealthy dropped or remained the same, and the number of families living in poverty increased.[124] The number of people living in severe poverty, defined as living at half the poverty level, increased by almost a million, or 7 percent. Further, many welfare families are meeting the five-year deadline, beyond which they cannot receive benefits. States such as New York have developed safety-net programs to help these individuals, but many may fall through this net.[125]

So, the success of these new interventions is difficult to assess. Many individuals found jobs but still needed economic help.[126] The number of children living in poverty decreased in the boom economic years of the late 1990s but is expected to rise as incomes drop. The fate of children in families that exhaust benefits or do not meet work requirements remains unclear. Researchers had expected that young children would feel the effects of mothers' increased work, but a recent study showed that adolescents who had less monitoring from mothers who worked had poorer school performance than did control adolescents whose mothers received welfare under the old system.[127]

Duncan and Brooks-Gunn are concerned most about the group most vulnerable to the effects of poverty–young children. These authors recommend that states consider the possibility of exempting families with very young children from time limits and other requirements. Though critics of welfare fear that this would merely encourage mothers to have children, the number of people on welfare is only weakly linked to benefits. Such benefits are available in various forms in Europe.

In addition to guaranteeing a small amount of money for the parents of young children, these authors recommend increasing service delivery programs that would target the effects of poverty. They cite programs that would improve the health and nutrition of children as well as the learning environment in the home. Improvements in health and nutrition do not necessarily occur as income increases, and by themselves, these programs offer benefits. "Since about one half of the effect of family income on tests of cognitive ability is mediated by the home environment, including learning experiences in the home, interventions might profitably focus on parenting."[128] Proven programs exist as models for such forms of intervention.

They also call for further research to compare the benefits of different kinds of programs, such as cash assistance, service delivery, and guaranteeing income to mothers of infants. They conclude,

> We have argued that increases in poverty are likely to leave developmental scars on children. And the welfare reforms will most certainly increase both the number of successful transitions from welfare to work *and* the number of severely economically disadvantaged children. Recent research suggests that economic deprivation is most harmful to a child's chances for achievement when it occurs early in the child's life. Economic logic suggests that policies aimed at preventing either economic deprivation itself or its effects are likely to constitute profitable social investments in the twenty-first century.[129]

PRACTICAL QUESTION: WHAT HAPPENS WHEN PARENT EDUCATORS AND PARENTS HAVE DIFFERENT VALUES?

Knowing that individuals within different ethnic and social groups may have particular values based on both culture and personal experiences makes us aware of the wide variety of beliefs possible about the goals and strategies of parenting. Tammy Mann, a parent educator, questions the effectiveness of parent educators when the mainstream philosophy of parenting they teach differs from the ideas and experiences of the parents whom they seek to influence.[130]

After the birth of her son, she became keenly aware of the discomfort parents can feel "when asked to abandon childrearing practices and beliefs that may be intrinsic to their very definitions of themselves."[131] In rearing her own child, she realized how she treasured the authoritarian parenting strategies of her warm and giving parents even though they did not meet the mainstream model of authoritative parenting (described in Chapter 2).

She lived in the South in a two-parent family. When she was two, the family moved to Detroit accompanied by many aunts, uncles, and cousins, so she grew up with a large extended family who had frequent gatherings. The extended family periodically returned to the South for vacations, traveling together in "caravans."

Her parents shaped and controlled children's behavior without discussions of children's preferences or ideas. Children had to obey. Such control was to help children grow into accountable and responsible adults. Her parents expected children to help in the family from an early age. They emphasized respect for elders, manners, and polite behavior to others. Her mother had a strong religious faith, and the family participated regularly in church activities. Education was very important, and both parents wanted their children to go further in school than they had.

As a parent, Mann finds herself maintaining her son's strong connections to the extended family. Though she, with her husband and son, live far from other relatives, she makes sure he visits the extended family in the summer, and all three travel to the South for family reunions. This does not substitute for the warm cocoon of the extended family she experienced as a child in Detroit, but she duplicates those childhood feelings for her son as best she can. Because religion has been so important to her and her parents, she delights in her son's spontaneous and easy reliance on prayers as a way of coping with the stress of waking up in the night alone.

She sometimes feels uncomfortable wanting to follow the values that have been such strengths for her and her brother and sisters, because they do not conform to what experts recommend. For example, she does not value independence, individual expressiveness, and achievement above all. Instead, she stresses family connectedness, responsibility to others, a strong religious faith, and educational achievement. She suspects that parents she has worked with in the past may have felt as alienated from mainstream parenting beliefs as she has, and she worries that rejecting, "aspects of who we are, in an attempt to become something else deemed 'better,' can be more destructive than practitioners sometime imagine."[132]

She believes parent educators and practitioners must first try to understand families and their values before intervening. Though the particular characteristics defining effective behaviors differ, most all parents share the common desires of wanting children to become well-functioning adults. Parents are striving to do their best as they deal with issues of nurturance and setting limits. In rearing children, parents confront their own values regarding the importance of independence, compliance, respect, and achievement. Educators must help parents find the strategies and solutions that both help their children develop and fit with parents' values and earlier experiences.

Vivien Carlson and Robin Harwood describe a four-session program to help parent educators become aware of their own cultural orientations and values with respect to parenting and then to use their increased awareness to better understand and help parents.[133] Carlson and Harwood state that many educators are surprised to discover that cultural beliefs are more than a set of beliefs endorsed by a group. Groups pass on unspoken ways of viewing the world, but individuals interpret these beliefs uniquely in terms of their own experience. Thus, educators have to pay attention to the unique beliefs, socialization goals, and values of the parents they work with. They also have to be sensitive when parents' values differ from their own.

In this program, educators learn to ask questions to discover the long-term goals parents have for children, such as independence, social relatedness, respect and deference, and individual achievement. They also learn to identify parents' expectations about milestones, such as children's feeding themselves, being toilet trained, and sleeping by themselves.

During the course of the training, participants came to realize that knowledge of group history and characteristics is valuable, but not sufficient, for culturally sensitive practice. In particular, they appreciated the training emphasis on specific questioning strategies for use in exploring cultural beliefs and values with families, with 95 percent of participants agreeing or strongly agreeing with the statement, "I will use the information about socialization goal categories and questioning strategies in my work with families."[134]

Such information enables educators to provide more effective and relevant services to parents.

MAIN POINTS

Culture provides
- ways of viewing the world
- goals and strategies for parenting
- a developmental niche for parent-child relations

The cultural models of parent-child relations include
- the independent model, stressing children's independence, initiative, and the capacity for setting and achieving goals
- the interdependent model, stressing children's becoming part of a strong social network that nourishes and supports them

Members of ethnic groups in this country
- have often experienced prejudice and rejection
- differ in values and strategies of parenting, with European Americans preferring the independent model and most other groups preferring the interdependent model
- differ in levels of self-esteem, with members of individualistic cultures reporting higher global self-esteem and members of interdependent cultures reporting lower global self-esteem
- report higher self-esteem when they feel supported and appreciated by their community
- are similar to each other in valuing children and wanting them to grow into effective adults
- appear to receive the same positive effects from supportive parenting

Parents of differing socioeconomic status have
- different views of their roles, with higher-status parents being more child centered in their approach and lower-status parents being more parent centered in their approach
- different goals and strategies, with higher-status parents valuing verbal interactions with children, eliciting and understanding feelings, and negotiating differences, and lower-status parents valuing obedience and strict discipline for noncompliance

- similar forms of interactions with children but spend different amounts of time doing them

Poor children

- are more likely to suffer birth complications, cognitive delays, abuse, and neglect than are nonpoor children
- lack income that affects the quality of their health care, home environment, and neighborhoods
- tend to experience conflict and tension because their parents face stress from financial pressure

Parent educators benefit

- from exploring their own values about parenting
- from programs that help them to pay attention to parents' goals and preferred strategies

EXERCISES

1. Everyone receives many cultural messages from the groups to which they belong, whether determined by ethnicity, religion, geographic area of residence, age, or gender. What groups most strongly influence your views of the world and your general values?

2. Look at the ethnic influences that are part of your heritage. What values of these groups have you incorporated into your own life?

3. Recall the independent and interdependent models of parent-child relations. What are the advantages of each? Which of the two is more appealing to you? Why?

4. What are your short-term and long-term goals for parenting?

5. If you were a parent educator and working with a parent with a set of values that differed greatly from yours, how would you handle it?

ADDITIONAL READINGS

DeGenova, M. K., ed. *Families in Cultural Context: Strengths and Challenges in Diversity.* Mountain View, CA: Mayfield, 1997.

Demo, D. H., Allen, K. R., and Fine, M. A., ed. *Handbook of Family Diversity.* New York: Oxford University Press, 2000.

Hart, B. and Risley, T. R. *Meaningful Differences in the Everyday Experiences of Young American Children.* Baltimore: Brookes, 1995.

Illick, J. E. *American Childhoods.* Philadelphia: University of Pennsylvania Press, 2002.

McAdoo, H. P., ed. *Black Children.* 2nd ed. Thousand Oaks, CA: Sage, 2002.

CHAPTER

4

Establishing Close Emotional Relationships with Children

IN THE NEWS

New York Times, November 5, 2002 Grandparents Are Powerful Supports for Parents and Can Even Extend the Lives of Grandchildren. See page 128 for details.

Go to PowerWeb at: www.dushkin.com/powerweb to read articles and newsfeeds on **emotion and communication, emotional development, emotions,** and other topics related to this chapter.

The first parenting task—establishing a close emotional relationship with a child— sounds easy enough. But how do parents create close ties with their children? How do they help children become contributing members of the family? To help everyone live together happily, how do parents increase closeness and manage anger and frustration? How do they reduce the stress of everyday life to maintain harmony in the family?

In the previous chapter we looked at cultural influences on parenting and saw that parents of different ethnic groups differ in their short-term and long-term goals for children and in their strategies for achieving the goals. We also saw that members of all ethnic groups seek close emotional relationships with their children and cite such relationships as their main reason for having children.[1]

In this chapter we look at how parents go about building these relationships. We start with the strategies that all groups would endorse—sensitive and attentive care, family rituals, supportive parenting—and then move on to strategies, such as promoting a democratic atmosphere or coaching children on how to manage feelings, that only subgroups of parents might endorse. Close relationships involve strong positive feelings and negative ones as well, such as anger and frustration. As such, we examine ways to manage these feelings and the everyday stresses that often give rise to them.

FOSTERING A HARMONIOUS FAMILY ATMOSPHERE

To begin, we look first at the power of positive feelings. Then we examine strategies for creating them with family members: (1) loving and sensitive care, (2) talking and telling stories, (3) practicing family rituals, (4) giving supportive parenting, (5) relying on respect and encouragement to help children grow, (6) creating a democratic atmosphere, (7) coaching children in how to manage their feelings, and (8) providing opportunities for self-expression. Parents also need support for themselves so they can maintain realistic expectations of themselves and their children.

The Power of Positive Feelings

In Chapter 2, we saw that positive attachments are powerful stimulants of competent behavior in parents and children. When parents have positive attachments to their own parents and to their partners, they also tend to have secure attachments to their children. These secure attachments promote competence in their children's behavior in a variety of areas. When people are happy with each other, they are more likely to be understanding and sympathetic.[2]

Good feelings come from one's own actions and successes as well as from relationships. Following the development of a sample of men from early adolescence to late middle life, Kirk Felsman and George Vaillant identified boyhood competence as an important forerunner of adult mental health. Boyhood competence—a summary measure of working part-time, having household chores, participating in extracurricular activities, getting school grades commensurate with one's IQ, participating in school activities, and learning to make plans—generates feelings of effectiveness. Felsman and Vaillant write, "Perhaps what is most encouraging in the collective portrait of these men's lives is their enormous capacity for recovery—evidence that the things that go right in our lives do predict future successes and the events that go wrong in our lives do not forever damn us."[3]

Studies reveal that if children simply think of some pleasant event for a short time, their performance improves and their behavior becomes more friendly, responsive, and responsible. These children resist temptation more successfully and respond to unfair treatment with fairness and generosity.[4]

Happy feelings inoculate us against the effects of negative events. Further, longitudinal research shows that how one spends leisure time, how one has fun in childhood, predicts later psychological health more than does the presence or absence of problems in childhood.[5]

Experiencing positive feelings helps family members not only enjoy life and function more effectively but also handle problems. A program designed in Holland to reinforce potential family strengths focused on eight areas of positive parent-child communication (which are listed in Table 4-1).[6]

■ **TABLE 4-1**
EIGHT FORMS OF POSITIVE PARENT-CHILD COMMUNICATION

---

1. *Naming with approval.* The parent provides a positive verbal description of what is occurring when the parent and child interact, so that the child understands the significance of the interaction.

2. *Taking turns.* All family members have an opportunity to express themselves and gain the appropriate attention from other members; no one is left out.

3. *Strengthening the weak link.* Any family member who is less interactive and assertive, whether child or adult, is encouraged to be more active.

4. *Following.* The parent makes verbal and nonverbal responses following an interaction with the child. The parent both comments on the interaction and looks at the child.

5. *Saying yes.* The parent phrases all directions to the child in terms of what the child is to do—"Carry your coat" not "Don't drag your coat on the floor."

6. *Supporting initiative.* Any initiative the child makes to learn something receives a positive response from the parent.

7. *Taking the lead.* The parent takes action and guides the child's behavior so that the child knows what is expected and that the parent is in charge.

8. *Sharing pleasant moments.* The parent takes time to enjoy the child and share in pleasurable moments.

These eight activities are broad enough to be adapted to interactions with growing children of any age, though there might be less saying yes and taking the lead with teenagers or older children than with younger ones.

Adapted from Anita Weiner, Haggai Kuppermintz, and David Guttmann, "Video Home Training (The Orion Project): A Short-Term Preventive and Treatment Intervention for Families of Young Children," *Family Process 33* (1994): 441–453.

Increasing these positive forms of communication enabled families to improve their behaviors in all areas. For three to four months, social workers in Israel went into the homes of welfare families in which parents were having difficulties with preschool children. For the first ten or twenty minutes of the weekly hour-and-a-half visit, they videotaped family interactions. At the next visit, the workers and the family members watched the tape that workers had already reviewed for positive interactions. Workers identified and reinforced one form of positive parent-child interaction at each visit. Occasionally, the workers modeled a positive interaction not yet observed in the family.

Prior to the intervention, few of the families interacted positively with their children—rarely making positive comments to children about their behaviors or sharing pleasurable times with them. The families receiving the intervention went from a mean of 1.83 on an index of positive parent-child communication at the start of the program to a mean of 8.04 at the end of the visits, and they maintained these changes six months after the program ended. The mean index of a group of control families who did not receive visits remained unchanged over a comparable period.

The intervention concentrated on positive behaviors, but an index of negative interactions—shouting at children, hitting them, and ignoring their attempts to get close—declined as well. Results included nonsignificant declines in shouting and hitting but significant declines in ignoring children's bids for closeness. When children cried or sought attention for a problem, parents were more likely to pick them up or give them some other form of attention. So, focusing on the positive increased the family closeness that was maintained over time and helped to decrease negative behavior as well.

Close Emotional Relationships

Parents begin to form a positive parental relationship when they love the child as a special person. Dorothy Briggs describes the psychological climate that enables children to feel their parents' love: "Nurturing love is tender caring—valuing a child just because he exists. It comes when you see your youngster as special and dear—even though you may not approve of all that he does."[7] Children are loved simply because they exist—no strings attached, no standards to meet. This is the "unconditional support" that Susan Harter refers to in her interview in Chapter 2 and Emmy Werner suggests in hers (see pages 112–113).

Loving attention to a child creates a close relationship in which the parent and child share experiences, understandings, and joint intentions. Shared reciprocal interactions lead to mutual understanding and a state of intersubjectivity, or shared meanings.[8] Parent and child create a relationship in which both participate; they form a unit that one cannot reduce to separate individuals.

Parents form close relationships with children of all ages in two basic ways—by providing sensitive, responsive care that meets the child's needs and by becoming an interactive social partner who shares the child's response to life's experiences. Sensitive, responsive care fosters the child's feelings of security and closeness to the parent. Sensitive care changes with the age and individual qualities of the child. Becoming a social partner who provides appropriate stimulation and shares the child's experiences and pleasures in life takes many forms, depending on the age of the child, as we discuss in subsequent chapters.

Storytelling

Telling stories draws family members close to each other. As Susan Engel writes,

> We all want to know who we are and how we came into our world. We all want to know that we were recognized, that we are singular and special. And we each learn this, in part, through the stories we are told about our beginnings. We reencounter ourselves constantly throughout life and confirm what we already know by telling, over and over again, one version or one aspect of the story of our life.[9]

Storytelling begins at birth. "Babies are surrounded by the stories parents, siblings, and friends tell one another, and to them, a captive audience. By the time children are 2 and 3 years old, they begin adding their own voices to the stories that surround them."[10] Stories initially consist of only a few words about an event—"Played house. I was baby." Observations reveal that mothers and toddlers tell about nine stories each hour.[11] In addition to telling stories to others, young children, as they play, often construct ongoing stories of what they are doing, monologues that will later develop into thoughts and daydreams. By the time children grow up and are in college, they tell as many as five to thirty-eight stories each day.

Stories serve several purposes.[12] They shape our views of ourselves, other people, and events in our lives. We often discover more about what we think, feel, or know in the course of telling someone about an experience. We gain information about the world and our culture from the narratives told each day.

Engel gives parents tips for encouraging children to participate in storytelling. Children tell stories when they feel "confidence and joyousness in telling stories,"[13] and parents give that confidence when they listen attentively, expressing interest with smiles, gasps, facial expressions, repetitions. Parents collaborate in the stories by asking open-ended questions that encourage elaboration, and they expose children to a variety of stories and poems that stimulate children's stories. "Families that are able to make sense of their experiences, pleasant or challenging, however, provide their children with a meaning-making system that can better prepare them for an unpredictable world."[14]

Family Rituals

Steven Wolin and Linda Bennett describe the positive force of family rituals in everyday life and in the long-term development of children.[15] They divide rituals into three categories: (1) *family celebrations* (Thanksgiving, Christmas), (2) *family traditions* (vacations, birthday activities), and (3) *patterned family interactions* (dinnertime, bedtime). They believe that these rituals provide a sense of rhythm and continuity to life that increases children's feelings of security and their capacity to communicate with adults.

Rituals provide stability by ensuring predictability in family life—no matter what else happens, the family eats dinner together, decorates the Christmas tree, and

INTERVIEW
with Emmy E. Werner

Emmy E. Werner is a research professor of human development at the University of California, Davis. For three decades, she and her colleagues Jessie Bierman and Fern French at the University of California, Berkeley, and Ruth Smith, a clinical psychologist on the Hawaiian island of Kauai, have conducted the Kauai Longitudinal Study, resulting in books such as Vulnerable but Invincible, The Children of Kauai, Kauai's Children Come of Age, *and* Overcoming the Odds.

From your experience of watching children at risk grow up on Kauai, what would you say parents can do to support children, to help maximize their child's potential? From your work with children at risk, what helps children survive and flourish even when faced with severe problems?

Let me say that, in our study, we studied the offspring of women whom we began to see at the end of the first trimester of pregnancy. We followed them during the pregnancy and delivery. We saw the children at ages one, two, and ten, late adolescence, and again at thirty-two and forty years. We have test scores, teachers' observations, and interview material at different times on these people. We have a group of children who were at high risk because of four or more factors. They were children who (1) experienced prenatal or perinatal complications, (2) grew up in poverty, (3) lived in a dysfunctional family with one or more problems, and (4) had a parent with alcohol or mental health problems.

You ask me to comment on parenting and what parents can do, but first I would like to urge that we redefine and extend the definition of parenting to cast a wider net and include people who provide love in the lives of children. I like to talk about *alloparenting,* the parenting of children by alternate people who are not the biological parents—they can be relatives, neighbors, siblings.

In our study of vulnerable but invincible children, we found that a major protective factor was that at least one person, perhaps a biological parent, or a grandparent, or an older sibling, accepted them unconditionally. That one person made the child feel special, very, very special. These parent figures made the child feel special through acts. They conveyed their love through deeds. They acted as models for the child. They didn't pretend the child had no handicap or problem, but what they conveyed was, "You matter to me, and you are special."

Now, another theme in our findings is that the parent figure, whoever he or she was, encouraged the child to reach out to others beyond the family—to seek out a friendly neighbor, a parent of one of their boy or girl friends, and, thus, learn about normal parenting from other families.

serves special meals on birthdays. Rituals also provide stability by linking the present family with the past and the future. Families carry on certain traditions from grandparents, and children grow up planning to carry out the same activities with their children.

The drama and excitement of rituals and traditions encourage communication among family members. Family members are more affectionate and more involved

The resilient child was temperamentally engaging. He or she encouraged interaction with others outside the home and was given the opportunity to relate to others.

I had no preconceptions about this protective factor, but what came through was that somewhere along the line, in the face of poverty, in the face of a handicap, faith has an abiding power. I'm not referring to faith in a narrow, denominational sense, but having someone in the family or outside of it who was saying, "Hey, you are having ups and downs, this will pass, you will get through this, and things will get better."

Another thing was that these children had an opportunity to care for themselves or others. They became nurturant and concerned, perhaps about a parent or a sibling. They practiced "required helpfulness."

Now, another protective factor is whether the children were able to develop a hobby that was a refuge and gave them respect among their peers. One of our study members said later, "If I had any doubts about whether I could make it, that hobby turned me around." The hobby was especially important as a buffer between the person and the chaos in the family. But it was not a hobby that isolated you from others; it nourished something you could share with other people.

As many of the children looked back, they describe how a positive relationship with a sibling was enduring and important. As adults, they commented with surprise on how supportive the relationship was and how these relationships were maintained despite great distances and despite dissimilarities in life and interests.

What did adults say they wanted to pass on to their own children?
Looking back as adults, they felt that some sort of structure in their life was very important. Even though the family life was chaotic, if a parent imposed some reasonable rules and regulations, it was helpful.

They emphasized faith as something to hang on to and make this clear to their children. As parents now they are quite achievement motivated. They graduated from high school, and some went back and got additional training. They encourage their children to do well in school.

The main theme that runs through our data is the importance of a parent figure who says "you matter" and the child's ability to create his or her own environment. The children believed they could do it, someone gave them hope, and they succeeded against the odds.

with one another at celebrations and holidays. In addition, rituals reduce the gap between parents and children, because everyone engages in the rituals as equals—everyone in the family hits the piñata at a birthday, everyone eats lots of food at Thanksgiving.

Children who grow up in alcoholic families who nevertheless maintain their family celebrations and rituals are less likely to become alcoholics themselves than are

Family rituals, such as dinners and holiday celebrations, give members feelings of security.

children who grow up with an alcoholic parent who does not maintain traditions.[16] The rituals serve as protective, positive forces at times of stress, giving children added feelings of security and closeness to others.

The family therapist William Doherty uses the term *intentional family* to refer to "one whose members create a working plan for maintaining and building family ties, and then implement the plan as best they can."[17] Without a plan, families become victims of the two drains that sap families' energy—time pressure and television.

Doherty's categorization of rituals differs from Wolin and Bennett's, as his focuses on the purpose of the ritual rather than on the form. He divides rituals into (1) *connection rituals* that promote bonding between family members (family outings, vacations),(2) *love rituals* for showing love to each member (birthdays, Mother's Day, Father's Day), and (3) *community rituals* that connect members to the larger community (weddings, religious activities).

Doherty lists seven major principles for establishing rewarding family rituals:

1. Get agreement between adults in the family.
2. Expect that cooperation from children will emerge gradually.
3. Have as much participation as possible from all family members.
4. Have clear expectations of what will happen and who will do what.
5. Reduce conflict through open communication and respect for others' feelings.
6. Protect rituals from the demands of other activities.
7. Be willing to change or modify the rituals as needed.[18]

In his book *The Intentional Family*, Doherty provides numerous examples of how families overcome the stumbling blocks of lack of time and conflicting views to establish rituals that bring closeness and a sense of meaning to all family members.

Providing Respect and Encouragement

Rudolf Dreikurs believes that children have built-in capacities to develop in healthy, effective ways.[19] Because children seek to be active and competent, a parent's main task is to provide an environment that permits this development. The child's strongest desire is to belong to a group. From infancy, the child seeks acceptance and importance within the family, but each child develops a unique path to family acceptance. The child accomplishes this task by using innate abilities and environmental forces to shape dynamic relationships with other family members.

Do parents usually help children discover their own strengths and abilities? No, says Dreikurs. Most often, parents tear down children's confidence with such comments as "I can do it for you faster" or "You are too little to set the table." Dreikurs recommends that parents use encouragement to help children develop their abilities. He defines encouragement as a "continuous process aimed at giving the child a sense of self-respect and a sense of accomplishment."[20] Encouragement is expressed by word and deed. A parent's facial expressions, tone of voice, gestures, and posture all tell children how the parent feels about them. In many different ways—cuddling, active play, gentle nurturing—a parent can communicate that children are worthwhile and capable of participating in social living.

Parents provide encouragement when they (1) encourage self-sufficiency on the child's part, (2) identify the child's positive contributions and help, and (3) teach children to ask for what they need. When parents give encouragement, they call attention to the challenge of the task—"Practicing is hard right now, but you'll really enjoy playing the piano as you get more experience."

Finally, parents encourage development when they emphasize children's gains. They show children how far they have come since starting the activity. Encouraging comments often refer to the completed task, but children soon learn that enjoyment comes from the process as well as from final success.

Handling Mistakes   In all families, children make mistakes. Dreikurs describes parents' tendencies to overemphasize the errors children make. Parents want so much for children to grow up and do well that they sometimes point out every minor mistake and continually tell children what they must do to improve. Under such a regime, children may feel they have to be perfect to be accepted. That fear can immobilize the child. As Dreikurs observes,

> We all make mistakes. Very few are disastrous. Many times we won't even know that a given action is a mistake until after it is done and we see the results! Sometimes we even have to make the mistake in order to find out that it is a mistake. *We must have the courage to be imperfect*—and to allow our children also to be imperfect. Only in this way can we function, progress, and grow. Our children will maintain their courage and learn more readily if we minimize the mistakes and direct their attention toward the positive. "What is to be done now that the mistake is made" leads to progress forward and stimulates courage. Making a mistake is not nearly as important as what we do about it afterward.[21]

When children learn a healthy attitude toward mistakes early on, they are freer to explore and act; as a result, they learn and accomplish more. A healthy attitude consists of believing that mistakes are an expected part of life; though often accidental, they do have causes and many times can be prevented. So children and parents can learn to look at mistakes carefully and find out what to do differently the next time. Mistakes are proof that the child is trying to do something but may not be quite ready to do it. Mistakes are incompletions, not failures. The child can take more time in learning the activity or practicing to achieve the goal. Though unfortunate in the sense that they take up time and sometimes cost money, mistakes are often valuable, because a child learns what is not effective. In addition, many warm family memories center on mistakes that were overcome.

Research supports Dreikurs's advice on handling mistakes and documents the power of parents' explanatory style in shaping children's way of thinking about themselves and their abilities.[22] Some children, at a very early age, show vulnerability to criticism. After receiving criticism about a single mistake, they generalize the criticism to their overall ability and feel helpless and inadequate. Vulnerable children five to six years of age who lack a clear concept of ability interpret the criticism as a comment on their goodness or badness as a person. When children feel helpless and inadequate, they give up and find improving difficult. Sensitive children are more likely than confident children to report that parents make critical comments about their mistakes. Sadly, even very young children internalize these comments and feel helpless and inadequate when they make a mistake.

Martin Seligman, who has studied the widespread effects of optimistic and pessimistic attitudes toward adversity, advises parents to teach children how to dispute global, pessimistic beliefs or interpretations of mistakes and difficulties.[23] Parents can teach children that a negative event has many causes, some beyond their control. For example, a student may get a poor grade on a test because she did not study enough, the test was unusually hard, the class has many bright students and the test was graded on a curve, the teacher came late and allowed less time for the exam, or the student was nervous and could not organize her answers as well. The student might blame herself, saying she is stupid, is going to fail the class, and will not be able to take more courses in that area. She is "latching onto the worst of all these possible causes—the most permanent, pervasive, and personal one."[24]

Parents can teach their children to dispute pessimistic interpretations with such questions as "What is the evidence for my belief?" "What are other, less destructive,

■ **T A B L E   4-2**
DEALING WITH ADVERSITY

Adversity:	My teacher, Mr. Minner, yelled at me in front of the whole class, and everybody laughed.
Belief:	He hates me and now the whole class thinks I'm a jerk.
Consequences:	I felt really sad, and I wished that I could just disappear under my desk.
Disputation:	Just because Mr. Minner yelled at me, it doesn't mean he hates me. Mr. Minner yells at just about everybody, and he told our class we were his favorite class. I guess I was goofing around a little, so I don't blame him for getting mad. Everyone in the class, everyone except for maybe Linda but she's a goody-goody, but everyone else has been yelled at by Mr. Minner at least once, so I doubt they think I'm a jerk.
Energization:	I still feel a little sad about being yelled at, but not nearly as much, and I don't feel like disappearing under my desk anymore.

Martin E. P. Seligman, *Learned Optimism* (New York: Pocket Books, 1990), 241.

ways to look at this?" "What is the usefulness of this belief?" Seligman advises, "Focus on the changeable (not enough time spent studying), the specific (this particular exam was uncharacteristically hard), and the nonpersonal (the professor graded unfairly) causes."[25] Then parents and children can generate alternative explanations and future actions. Seligman calls his method the ABCDE—Adversity, Belief (usually negative), Consequences (usually negative), Disputation, Energization—method. This method is illustrated in Table 4-2.

Coaching Children to Manage Emotions

A study by John Gottman and his associates indicates that when parents coach their five-year-old children in how to deal with feelings, the children function better physically and psychologically when they are eight years old. They perform better academically and are socially more competent with peers. They are physically healthier as well, perhaps because coaching helps children modulate their emotional reactions, which modulation, in turn, helps their physiological system function better.[26] Coaching involves listening to children's feelings, accepting and validating them, using I-messages regarding one's own feelings, and helping children solve problems while maintaining acceptable limits concerning the expression of feelings. (We discuss each of these later in this chapter.)

The Gottman study also finds that parents differ in their attitudes and thoughts about how important feelings are in life. Some parents have a heightened awareness of their own and their children's feelings and a strong conviction that feelings are a central part of life. Feelings signal that change is required. Anger serves to initiate action in frustrating situations, and sadness slows a person down to have time to cope with loss. These parents feel comfortable with their feelings, and they consider that a major parental task is to help their children live happily with their own emotional reactions. They do this by coaching children to label their reactions, validating the importance of their feelings whatever they might be, and teaching their children strategies for expressing the feelings appropriately. Feelings do not frighten these parents. Rather, parents see such feelings as opportunities to become closer to their children through sharing the strong reactions and teaching ways to handle them.

Other parents feel uncomfortable with feelings and seek one of three ways to handle the discomfort.[27] *Dismissive* parents minimize the importance of feelings, making light of or ignoring them because they believe the feelings may make matters worse. *Disapproving* parents criticize, judge, and punish children for the expression of feelings. These parents usually disapprove of only a subgroup of feelings such as anger and sadness or just those feelings that arise under certain conditions such as a "minor event." Children of dismissive and disapproving parents have a hard time trusting their own judgment. By learning that their feelings are wrong, they come to believe there is something basically wrong with *them* for having the feelings. Because they have little experience in acknowledging and dealing with their feelings, they often have difficulty controlling them and solving problems. Finally, *laissez-faire* parents accept all feelings and often comfort the child when the child experiences a negative emotional reaction, but they do little to teach or guide the child in how to express feelings appropriately. These parents seem to believe that expressing the feelings in any form—whether appropriate or inappropriate—will take care of the problem. Their children do not learn to cope with feelings constructively and have difficulty concentrating and learning in school and in making friends.

So, the three types of response—ignoring or criticizing feelings so they occur as little as possible and accepting all expressions of feeling without providing guidance for expression—lead to similar kinds of problems for children, such as the inability to regulate feelings and to feel comfortable with themselves and others. Coaching children not only helps them deal better with their feelings and with social and cognitive endeavors; it also frequently brings parents and children closer together because parents feel they really understand their children.

On the basis of their research, Gottman and his colleagues describe five key steps in emotion coaching:[28]

Step 1: Parents recognize when they are having a feeling, what that feeling is, and when others are having feelings.

Step 2: Parents consider feelings as opportunities for intimacy or teaching. When the child is upset, happy, or excited, parents see this as an opportunity to be close to the child and to teach the child how to express feelings appropriately.

Step 3: Parents listen empathically and validate the child's feelings. They use active listening skills and validate what the child feels without trying to argue the child out of the feeling (see "Active Listening," following).

Step 4: Parents help the child verbally label the feeling. The child may be confused about what he or she is feeling. Labeling the feeling is identifying the feeling, giving the child a word for the strong emotion; it is not telling the child how to feel. Labeling a feeling while the child is experiencing it appears to have a soothing effect on the child's nervous system. Labeling feelings also helps a child see that he or she can have two feelings at the same time.

Step 5: Parents set limits while helping the child solve the problem. Parents limit the way feelings are expressed; they do not, however, limit the child's having the feeling itself. Anger, for example, is acceptable, but hitting a sibling is not. Parents help the child think of possible actions to express feelings and ways to achieve his or her goals in the situation.

Several additional strategies help parents implement these five steps. First, parents should avoid criticism, sarcasm, mockery, or humiliation when they talk to children about feelings. The importance of this advice cannot be overemphasized. In one study, parents' negative reactions (minimizing, becoming distressed, assigning punishment) in response to children's emotional reactions predicted poor emotional regulation and poor social functioning in children two to six years later.[29] No doubt the children's poor emotional regulation intensified parents' negative responses. Still, parents' negative reactions predicted children's problem behaviors six to eight years later even when effects of early problem behavior and emotional regulation were controlled for.

Second, in emotion coaching, parents use scaffolding and praise in teaching. *Scaffolding* is giving basic information or other assistance to help the child begin problem solving. Parents also give specific positive feedback to the child at the beginning and then let the child take over and handle the situation.

Third, parents focus on the child's agenda, not on their own. If a child is upset while the parent is paying bills, the parent puts away the checks and focuses on the child. Parents' use of these steps and strategies enables children to feel comfortable with their emotions and to find appropriate means of expressing them.

Active Listening   *Active listening* is Thomas Gordon's term for what parents do when they reflect their children's feelings.[30] Parents listen to children's statements, pay careful attention to the feelings expressed, and then frame a response similar to the child's statement. If a child says she feels too dumb to learn a school subject, the parent might feed back that she feels she is not smart enough. Here is one of Gordon's examples of active listening:

> CHILD: I don't want to go to Bobby's birthday party tomorrow.
> PARENT: Sounds like you and Bobby have had a problem maybe.
> CHILD: I hate him, that's what. He's not fair.
> PARENT: You really hate him because you feel he's been unfair somehow.
> CHILD: Yeah. He never plays what I want to play.[31]

If the parent's response is accurate, the child confirms the feedback with a positive response. If the parent's interpretation is wrong, the child indicates that and can correct the misinterpretation by expanding on his feelings. The parent can continue active listening to understand what is happening to the child.

Active listening has many advantages. First, it helps children express feelings in a direct, effective way. As feelings are expressed and parents accept them, children feel understood and learn that they are like everyone else.[32]

Second, as feelings are expressed, parents and children together learn that the obvious problem is not necessarily the real or basic problem. Like the rest of us, children use defenses and sometimes start by blaming a friend, a parent, or circumstances for what they are feeling. As parents focus on the feelings, children gradually come to identify the underlying problem and discover what they can do about it.

Third, listening to children's feelings is sometimes all that is needed to resolve the problem. Often when we are upset, sad, or angry, we simply want to express the feeling and have someone respond, "It is really painful when a friend walks off with someone else and leaves you behind." The response validates the feeling as being justified and important, and frequently that is all we want.

What must parents do to become active listeners? First, Gordon warns parents not to attempt active listening when they are hurried or when they are preoccupied. Active listening requires persistence, patience, and a strong commitment to attend to both the child's words and accompanying behavioral clues. Furthermore, there are times when active listening is not appropriate. If a child asks for information, give the information. If a child does not want to talk about his feelings, respect the child's privacy and do not probe. Similarly, if active listening and the dialogue have gone as far as the child is willing to go, then a parent needs to recognize that it is time to stop.

One of the mothers in Haim Ginott's parenting group raised the question of reflecting back feelings of great sadness over a loss.[33] Is this wise? Does it help children? Ginott responded that parents must learn that suffering can strengthen a child's character. When a child is sad in response to a real loss, a parent need only empathize, "You are sad. I understand." The child learns that the parent is a person who understands and sympathizes.

I-Messages   As we have seen, when a parent is angry, frustrated, or irritated with a child, the parent can communicate his or her feelings constructively with an I-message rather than nagging, yelling, or criticizing. The I-message contains three parts: (1) a clear statement of how the parent feels, (2) a statement of the behavior that has caused the parent to feel that way, and (3) a statement describing why the behavior is upsetting to the parent. For example, a parent frustrated with a teenager's messy room might say, "I feel upset and frustrated when I look at your messy room, because the family works hard to make the house look clean and neat and your room spoils our efforts."

Parents need to spend time analyzing their feelings and becoming more aware of exactly how they feel. Gordon points out that, often, when a parent communicates anger at a child, the parent may actually be feeling disappointment, fear, frustration, or hurt. When a child comes home an hour late, the parent may launch into a tirade. The worry that grew into fear during the hour of waiting is transformed into relief that the child is safe, and that relief is then translated into angry words intended to prevent a recurrence of this disturbing behavior. The parent who has learned to use accurate I-messages is less likely to misplace anger and to use a child as a scapegoat.

What should a parent do if a child pays no attention to I-messages? First, be sure the child can pay attention to the I-message. Do not try to communicate feelings when the child is rushing out of the house or is already deeply immersed in some other activity. If an I-message is then ignored, send another, more forceful message, in a firm tone of voice.

Sometimes, a child responds to an I-message with an I-message. For example, when a parent expresses distress because the lawn is not mowed, the daughter may reply that she feels annoyed because mowing interferes with her after-school activities. At that point, the parent must "shift gears," as Gordon puts it, and reflect back the child's frustration by using active listening.

I-messages have several benefits. First, when parents use I-messages, they begin to take their own needs seriously. This process benefits all family relationships because parents feel freer—more themselves—in all areas of life. Second, children learn about the parents' reaction, which they may not have understood until the I-message. Third, children have an opportunity to solve problems in response to I-messages. Even toddlers and preschoolers have ideas, not only for themselves but also for others. Siblings often have good ideas about what might be bothering another child in the family. They think of things that might have escaped the attention of parents.

I-messages can convey appreciation—"I feel pleased when you help me with the dishes because then we have time to go to the store for your school supplies." I-messages are also useful in heading off problems and in helping children see that their parents have needs, too. These messages, termed *preventive I-messages*, express parents' future wants or needs and give children an opportunity to respond positively. For example, if a parent says, "I need quiet so I can drive the car," the child learns what to do to be helpful.

Although closeness is enjoyable for and helpful to children, some parents do not feel good about themselves or some of their own qualities, causing them to wonder if their children might not be better off remaining distant from them. They fear that their children will pick up their bad qualities. Research on close and nonclose relationships among adolescents and their parents reveals that children who feel close to their parents are less likely to take on the parents' negative qualities than are children who feel distant. Parents' negative behaviors are a more potent influence on children when parents and children are not close.[34] Thus, even when parents have many self-doubts and self-criticism, closeness with them and all their failings is still a positive experience for their children.

Providing Opportunities for Self-Expression

Family relationships are most harmonious when both children and parents have outlets for expressing feelings. Activities such as daily physical exercise, drawing, modeling clay, painting, and cooking all serve as outlets to drain off tensions and irritations and provide individuals with additional sources of pleasure and feelings of competence. Wise parents provide children with a variety of outlets so that they develop many skills. Research indicates that childhood leisure activities, especially a wide variety—such as painting, reading, and participating in athletics—are more predictive of psychological health in adulthood than are the child's own personality characteristics. These activities promote self-confidence and self-esteem, which increase psychological health.[35]

IDENTIFYING AND DEALING WITH NEGATIVE FEELINGS

Active listening and I-messages help parents and children deal with negative feelings once they are aroused. But preventing stress is a major way to decrease negative feelings. To do this, we need to identify sources of stress in everyday life. Strategies to minimize hassles and negative feelings in the family include (1) creating family time, (2) developing a support system, (3) maintaining realistic expectations, and (4) learning ways to manage negative feelings.

Sources of Negative Feelings

Emotional extremes in parents, such as violent anger or clinical depression, affect children's behavior. Negative moods in the course of daily life—such as those caused by limited free time and the overall challenges of parenting—can also adversely affect parents' interactions with children and children's behavior.

Lack of Time   As noted in Chapter 1, parents identify the lack of time with family as the greatest source of stress in family life.[36] Studies of time diaries over a thirty-year period and survey data on time use yield provocative findings. John Robinson and Geoffrey Godbey, summarizing their extensive work in *Time for Life,* point out that, according to time diaries recorded by participants, adults overestimate the number of hours they work.[37] They also underestimate the amount of free time they have, defined as that time not spent in essential activities such as work, self-care, and family and household activities.

Robinson and Godbey argue that of the 168 hours available each week, about 68 go to sleeping and necessary self-care such as eating and grooming. Of the 100 remaining hours, about 53, on average, go to working and direct family care, about 7 to discretionary self-care, and about 40 to free time. Parents of young children have less free time than do adults in other age groups—about 30 hours per week, occurring mostly on weekends—but they still have about an hour more free time than was available to parents in 1965. According to the reserachers, single parents have considerably less time with their children—about 3 hours less per week—so their children lose time with them and daily time with the absent parent in the case of divorce.

Many would argue with these conclusions, but Robinson and Godbey's data and analysis of others' data do point to the fact that people may have more free time than they realize and that feelings of "time-famine" have other causes. Robinson and Godbey believe that Americans feel rushed not because of extra work but because of the accelerated pace of life. They write,

> Speed and brevity are more widely admired, whether in serving food, in the length of magazine articles, or in conversation. As the pace of life has speeded up, there has been a natural tendency to assume that other time elements have been reshaped as well. Primary among these assumptions is the notion that hours of work (duration) are increasing and that those who feel most rushed must work the longest hours.[38]

Feelings of lack of time may also come from the fact that Americans spend about 40 percent of their free time in an activity that gives them less satisfaction than most other leisure activities—namely, watching television. Thus, they do not take the time they have for more satisfying social activities and pursuits with family and friends. We discuss ways to decrease the stress of lack of time later in this chapter.

Interestingly, studies of time diaries reveal that children have increasingly less time for activities and conversations with parents.[39] A University of Michigan study found that in 1981, children had about 63 hours per week for discretionary activities—free time when they were not eating, sleeping, in school, or engaged in self-care. In 1997, they had only 51 hours, a 16 percent decline in free time. Time in school increased from 21 hours per week to 29 hours per week, and time spent in self-care and getting ready to go places increased as well. Time spent talking to parents, however, decreased 100 percent. In addition, parents and children have less time with each other, because about 50 percent of children experience divorce, and many go back and forth between two households and thus see less of each parent. So, time pressures exist for both parents and children.

Everyday Negative Moods   Minor daily hassles at work or with children contribute to parents' negative moods, which in turn affect parenting and children's behavior. Negative moods bias what parents recall about children's past behaviors, shape parents' interpretations of current behavior, and cause parents to discipline children more harshly.[40]

Hassles do not have to be intense or prolonged. In one study, even a briefly induced negative mood reduced mothers' positive comments and verbal interactions with their children during play and laboratory tasks.[41] In another study, being distracted by a simple task involving anagrams resulted in parents' being less positive, more irritable, and more critical of and interfering with their preschoolers.[42]

The hassles that generally trigger a negative mood stem from the daily challenges of parenting rather than major difficulties with children.[43] Hassles fall into two broad categories: (1) the effort required to rear children—continually cleaning up messes, changing family plans, running errands to meet children's needs—and (2) the challenge of dealing with irritating behaviors such as whining, sibling fights, and constant demands.

Parents' personality characteristics, their coping styles, and the amount of support available to them can intensify or decrease stress.[44] Outgoing, sociable, optimistic parents are less likely to respond to hassles with negative moods. Parents who use avoidant coping styles, who wish stress would go away so they wouldn't

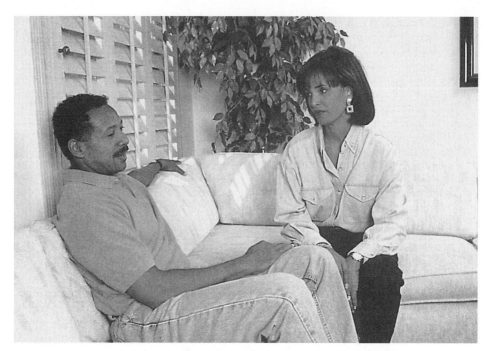

When parents achieve a fair compromise to conflict, children feel minimal stress.

have to deal with it, experience increased stress. Parents who use positive reappraisal of the situation, who feel they are learning from the situation and becoming more skilled, experience decreased stress and retain their self-confidence.

Everyday Anger   Many researchers have documented that when children are exposed to different forms of anger, they respond with emotional arousal that triggers changes in heart rate and blood pressure,[45] as well as the production of hormones.[46] Whether the angry interaction is actually observed or only heard from another room, or whether only angry silence is observed, young children react in a variety of ways.

A majority of children show signs of anger, concern, sadness, and general distress that can disrupt play, lead to increased aggressiveness, or result in attempts to end the conflict or comfort the participant.[47] Almost half of children primarily feel distress with a strong desire to end the fight. Slightly over a third of children are ambivalent, revealing both high emotional arousal and upset but at the same time reporting that they are happy. A small percentage (15 percent) give no response. The ambivalent child is the one who becomes more aggressive in behavior.

Not surprisingly, then, children exposed to parents' fighting at home have strong physiological and social reactions to anger.[48] They tend to comfort the mother if she is involved in an angry exchange in a laboratory setting. With their friends, they characteristically play at a less involved level, and when anger occurs, they find it very hard to handle.

Children become particularly upset when arguments center on child-related issues or when parents imply children are to blame for the argument.[49] If parents reassure them that they are not to blame, children are less distressed. When children feel conflict is their fault, they are likely to intervene to try to stop it. Even children as young as four believe they can reduce parental anger, and, in part, they are right.[50] Parents say they are more likely to stop fighting when children aged four to six intervene. Older children believe there is less they can do to stop parents from fighting—and they are right, because parents pay less attention to their pleas.

Does this mean that parents should never fight or disagree in front of children? No. Conflict is a natural part of life when people live close together, and children may need to observe how conflicts are settled in order to learn these skills themselves. In their work, Mark Cummings and his associates discovered that children who viewed angry adults who found a compromise to a situation had emotional reactions that were indistinguishable from their responses when viewing friendly interactions.[51] They had the most negative reactions to continued fighting and the "silent treatment." Their responses to submissions or changes in the topic indicated that they did not consider the situation resolved. So, what matters most to children is whether adults achieve a fair compromise that settles conflicts after they erupt.

Even when there is no particular distress, family members, both parents and children aged five to fifteen, see themselves as major causes of angry feelings in others.[52] Family members believe they are major sources of angry feelings in others. Children accurately perceive that they cause mothers' anger; mothers' diaries confirm that children's noncompliance and demandingness cause their anger.

Mothers, however, do not realize that they are the major source of children's anger. Mothers believe that children's anger comes from events outside the home and that happiness comes from within the home, but children report the opposite. They see their happiness coming from friends and personal accomplishments, and irritations and anger from the family.

In short, all family members see anger as very much a part of family life. Children appear the most accurate in seeing their behavior as a major cause of family anger—though on any given occasion they can be mistaken—and the family routines and demands as the main source of their own irritations.

Creating Family Time

Because parents experience stress from lack of time, what can they do to feel less pressured and create more family time? Robinson and Godbey make several suggestions.[53] First, they suggest that parents might feel less pressured if they realized that their feelings of time-famine, although genuine, are not related to the actual number of free-time hours available to them. Free time is available in small chunks during the week and larger ones during the weekend, but parents must plan carefully to make good use of it. "Free time requires commitment, imagination, reflection, and discipline if we are to use it wisely."[54]

Second, they advise parents to spend free time in activities that give them satisfaction. Television, as noted earlier, absorbs 40 percent of people's free time, despite the fact American adults do not rate it as satisfying as most other activities they engage in and list it as the first activity they would give up in a time crunch. What is the charm of television? "As an activity, television viewing requires no advance planning, costs next to nothing, requires no physical effort, seldom shocks or surprises, and can be done in the comfort of one's own home—with pizza only a telephone call away."[55]

Third, Robinson and Godbey voice their concern for what they term *time-deepening activities*—that is, doing two or more things at the same time to maximize one's use of time. They believe that this contributes to people's feeling stressed and rushed. They describe a friend who wrecked the car while talking on the car phone as the audiotape was playing and the friend ate lunch from a McDonald's bag. Eating dinner while listening to the television and reading the newspaper is another example of such time-deepening activities that may only add to feeling rushed.

Instead of time-saving efforts, Robinson and Godbey recommend cultivating time-savoring skills in order to appreciate

> the simpler delights of life as they are occurring: the taste of good food, the presence of good company, and the delights of fun and silliness. To be happier and wiser, it is easier to increase appreciation levels more than efficiency levels. Only by appreciating more can we hope to have a sustainable society. While efficiency, at least as envisioned in American society, always starts with wanting more, appreciating may start both with valuing more what is already here and with wanting less.[56]

The authors believe that Americans may have begun to slow down. The percentage saying they had less free time than they did five years earlier dropped from 54 percent in 1991 to 45 percent in 1994/1995. The proportion saying they had about the right amount of free time increased from 35 percent in 1993 to 42 percent in 1995. Although it is unlikely that parents of young children fall in this group, parents can begin to chronicle what they do and how they can shift to do more truly satisfying activities with family members and others.

Developing a Support System

When parents receive support from friends, relatives, and each other, they experience less stress and fewer negative moods. The support may come from organized parenting groups such as those attended by the couples in Carolyn Pape Cowan and Philip Cowan's study.[57] Those groups, which each included both husbands and wives, met over a long period and were shown to decrease couples' stress.

Grandparents As Supports   As psychologists turn their attention to important people outside the child's nuclear family, they look to grandparents, who exert influence in direct and indirect ways.[58] Grandparents influence grandchildren directly when they serve as caregivers, playmates, and family historians who pass on information that solidifies a sense of generational continuity. They are a direct influence when they act as mentors to their grandchildren and when they negotiate between parent and child. They influence grandchildren indirectly when they provide both psychological and material support to parents, who then have more resources for parenting.

When parents describe their own feelings and what causes them, children learn to be more sympathetic and understanding toward others.

Because minority families interact more with extended family members, more information on the role of grandparents in such families is available than for other families. For example, in 1984, 31 percent of African American children lived in extended families with one or both parents.[59] The extended family often includes one or both grandparents. Grandmothers help families nurture and care for children in a less structured, more spontaneous way than is possible when only two generations are present. The grandparents' role depends on whether one or both parents live in the home. For example, grandmothers are less involved in parenting when both parents are present.[60]

In general, contacts between grandparents and grandchildren vary, depending on the age, health, and proximity of the grandparents.[61] Grandparents typically see their grandchildren once or a few times a month. Although a few studies suggest that only a small percentage of grandparents enjoy close, satisfying relationships with their grandchildren, many other studies indicate that young adults generally feel close to grandparents (averaging 4 on a 5-point scale of emotional closeness) and that "the grandchild–grandparent bond continues with surprising strength into adulthood."[62]

Geographic proximity is the most important predictor of the nature of the relationship.[63] When grandparents live close by, contact naturally increases. When grandparents are young and healthy enough to share activities, grandchildren feel close because of the shared fun. At the same time, when grandparents are older and in poorer health, grandchildren feel close because they can help them.

Gender plays a role in such relationships. Grandmothers are more likely to be involved with grandchildren than are grandfathers, and they appear to play a powerful role in children's well-being.[64] Anthropological research presented at an international conference on grandmothers indicates that the involvement of grandmothers and older female kin enhance the lives of their grandchildren.[65] In one study, the presence of the maternal grandmother increased childhood survival at age six to 96 percent; the survival figure for homes without grandmothers was 83 percent. The presence of the paternal grandmother did not change the childhood survival rates.

Evolutionary psychologists argue that maternal grandmothers provide more care and resources for grandchildren because they are absolutely certain that they have a genetic connection to the grandchild through their daughter. The survival of grandchildren means that their genes will survive. Maternal grandfathers and paternal grandparents cannot be as certain of the genetic connection, because a woman could bear a child not genetically related to them if she were unfaithful to her spouse. As a result, they have less motivation to nourish and support grandchildren.

Other psychologists point to psychological reasons for the greater impact of maternal grandmothers. Women may find the greatest support in help from their own mothers, who have long histories of providing loving care for them. When mothers feel cared for, they and their offspring fare better.

Other research indicates that some types of support given by maternal and paternal grandparents differ little.[66] A 1996 survey of Germans over age 65 found that, on average, they gave 9 percent of their pensions to children and grandchildren regardless of whether they were families of sons or daughters.

When grandchildren are very young, they see grandparents as sources of treats and gifts. When grandchildren are in elementary school, they look to grandparents to share fun activities with them, and in early adolescence, they also take pleasure in sharing a variety of activities with them. Grandchildren often see grandparents as more patient and understanding than their parents, and contemporary grandparents try to live up to this expectation.[67] They seek to be supportive to grandchildren rather than intrusive and critical. A grandparent can become particularly close at times of family change and serve as confidant and advocate for the child who could become lost in the chaos of events (see Chapter 14).

Maintaining Realistic Expectations

We all approach new experiences with expectations. Expectations are built from what authorities tell us and what we and other people we know have actually experienced. If expectations are realistic, they can help us prepare for an event, function at our best, and elicit the most positive results for all involved.

Realistic expectations prevent the stress that results when our experience differs vastly from what we expected. Violated expectations lead to self-questioning and self-doubt. For example, for new parents, violated expectations are associated with lowered energy and lack of confidence as a parent.[68]

Parents' expectations also play a role in defining a hassle. For example, parents who grew up with siblings and have a realistic view of how much arguing siblings do are less stressed when their own children squabble. Having realistic expectations of children based on an understanding of their individual qualities and needs prevents parents from feeling stress, because children do not perform as the books say they should or as the parents did as children.[69] Parents develop realistic expectations from reading, from observing their own and other children, from talking to other parents and sharing problems with them, and from their own experiences as a parent.

Managing Negative Feelings

Because anger, stress, frustration, and guilt are all part of rearing children, parents need to find their own strategies for controlling the expression of these feelings. When these feelings lead to criticism, nagging, yelling, and hitting, both parents and children suffer. Children are hurt and discouraged; parents feel guilty and inadequate.

Nancy Samalin, who runs parent groups on dealing with anger, suggests that families compile lists of acceptable and unacceptable ways for parents and children to express anger.[70] Acceptable ways include such actions as crying, going for a walk, and yelling, "I'm mad." Unacceptable ways include destroying property, hitting, spitting, and swearing.

Of course, I-messages are the most direct way to express anger, but sometimes people want physical outlets such as work or exercise. Table 4-3 lists a variety of ways to deal with anger.

To parents who feel guilty about or frustrated with the mistakes they have made, Jane Nelson, using Dreikurs's guidelines, suggests following a three-step program: (1) recognize the mistake, (2) reconcile with the child by apologizing, and (3) resolve the problem with a mutually agreed-on solution.[71] Nelson advises parents to view mistakes as opportunities for learning. Seeing mistakes in that way reduces parents' self-criticism and their resistance to recognizing them. Apologizing is a behavior children can emulate when they have made a mistake. It also enables parents to experience children's quickness to forgive.

Dreikurs emphasizes that, like children, parents must develop the courage to be imperfect. He writes,

> The importance of courage in parents cannot be overemphasized. Whenever you feel dismayed or find yourselves thinking, "My gosh, I did it all wrong," be quick to recognize this symptom of your own discouragement; turn your attention to an academic and impersonal consideration of what can be done to make matters better. When you try a new technique and it works, be glad. When you fall back into old habits, don't reproach yourself. You need to constantly reinforce your own courage, and to do so, you need the "courage to be imperfect." Recall to your mind the times that you have succeeded, and try again. Dwelling on your mistakes saps your courage. Remember, one cannot build on weakness—only on strength. Admit humbly that you are bound to make mistakes and acknowledge them without a sense of loss in your personal value. This will do much to

■ **TABLE 4-3**
EIGHT WAYS TO DEAL WITH PARENTAL ANGER

1. Exit or wait—taking time out is a way of maintaining and modeling self-control.

2. Make "I," not "you," statements to help the child understand your point of view.

3. Stay in the present—avoid talking about the past or future.

4. Avoid physical force and threats.

5. Be brief and to the point.

6. Put it in writing—a note or letter is a way of expressing your feelings in a way that the other person can understand.

7. Focus on the essential—ask yourself whether what you are arguing about is really important and worth the energy involved.

8. Restore good feelings—calmly talk over what happened or give hugs or other indications that the fight is over.

Adapted from Nancy Samalin with Catherine Whitney, *Love and Anger: The Parental Dilemma* (New York: Penguin Books, 1992).

keep your own courage up. Above all, remember that we are not working for perfection, but only for improvement. Watch for the little improvements, and when you find them relax and have faith in your ability to improve further.[72]

PRACTICAL QUESTION:
HOW DO CHILDREN DEFINE THE GOOD PARENT?

Thus far we have looked at close relationships from the point of view of how a parent promotes them. Let us look at the qualities children of different ages say they want in the "good parent" or "good mother."

Preschoolers interviewed about the qualities of a good and a bad mommy and daddy suggest that good parents are physically affectionate and nurturant, especially in providing food for children. In addition, good parents like to play games with their children and read to them, and they discipline them—that is, they keep children from doing things they should not, but they do not spank them or slap them in the face. Bad parents have the opposite qualities. They do not hug or kiss, do not fix food, do not play games. They hit and do not let children go outside. Bad parents are also described as irresponsible—they go through red lights, throw chairs at people, and do not read the newspaper.[76]

As children grow older, they continue to value physical nurturing and affection, but they also appreciate qualities reflecting psychological nurturing. Mothers' good qualities include "understanding feelings and moods," "being there when I need her," and "sticking up for me." Children continue to emphasize the limit-setting behaviors in a good mother—"She makes us eat fruit and vegetables," "She yells at me when I need it"—but they want their mother to consider their needs and wishes in setting the rules. Older children still enjoy mutual recreational time—playing, joking, building things together. Finally, as children get older, they appreciate the teaching activities of the good mother.[76]

When early adolescents and their parents talked in a group about their definitions of a good parent, they agreed on several qualities.[77] Early adolescents' definitions touched on three main themes—attention to the child's feelings and individuality, spending time together, and parents' self-control. For early teens, the good parent is one who "listens," "respects you for who you are," "gives you a hug when you are sad." These teens emphasized spending time together, going places together, and having a parent who "knows when to be silly, not always serious." They saw the good parent as one who "manages their temper," "doesn't bark at you," "knows when to stop talking," and "tells you what they want you to do before you have to do it."

The parents of these teens focused first on qualities of responsibility. A good parent is one who "is a good role model," "teaches the child how to behave," and who is "consistent," "committed to being a good parent," and "firm but loving." They, too, focused on the good parent's self-control—"has patience," "manages their temper," is "nonreactive to bad behavior," and "never says 'I told you so.'" Although they focused less on the child's feelings and on time spent together, they did mention the importance of "listening" and "having a good time together."

In sum, children's descriptions of the good parent point to three main areas—being a sensitive caregiver, a social partner, and a person with self-control.

INCREASING THE JOYS OF PARENTING

The challenges, hassles, and frustrations of parenting often obscure the real joys in rearing children. Yet the joys are what compensate for, and at times completely eliminate, all the negative feelings. Despite their importance, little has been written about the joys of parenting. In a remarkable study fifty years ago, Arthur Jersild and his colleagues interviewed 544 parents about the joys and problems of childrearing. They introduce the book with the following comments:

> There has been relatively little systematic study of the cheerful side of the ledger of childrearing. Studies of characteristics that bring headaches to a parent have not been matched by surveys of characteristics that warm a parent's heart. . . . The fact that the emphasis has been so much on the negative side is perhaps no more than one should expect. Behavior that is disturbing to the parent or to others usually calls for action or for a solution of some sort, and as such it also attracts the research worker. On the other hand, what is pleasant can be enjoyed without further ado.[73]

Parents have many opportunities to be happy and to enjoy their children. In the interviews, parents reported 18,121 satisfactions, far more than the 7,654 problems described. The most common joys are easy to guess: the child's special qualities as a person, companionship and affection, parents' feelings of satisfaction in helping another person grow, and pleasure in watching the child's growth. What is not so easy to guess is that parents' joys, reported in Jersild's study and in this author's interviews with parents, relate to the everyday experiences and interactions—that are readily available to all parents—not to outstanding achievements alone.

To experience this pleasure, parents need not be interacting with children at the time. Parents can enjoy watching children in their daily lives—having fun with a playmate or a grandparent or exerting effort to accomplish a goal. Even disciplining a child can bring satisfaction in doing the right thing for the child. A father describes such a feeling:

> Another great joy is like painting a good picture or taking a good jump shot. It's doing something that is just right for your kids. It just hits the target. It might be, after reprimanding him and sending him to his room, going up and talking to him, telling him you love him and to come downstairs now. Just knowing how good a thing that is, how appropriate it is. It may be buying the fishing rod for a child that he desperately wanted. It is the pleasure of pleasing someone you care about and pleasing him on the basis of personal knowledge you have about him.

Jersild and his coworkers were wrong, however, in claiming that these pleasures can be enjoyed without further ado. Parental action is required to savor the daily joys often lost in the rush of life. Enjoying everyday interactions requires two rare commodities—parents' time and attention. Consider an out-of-town visitor's remark to a resident that she thought the town's greenery was really beautiful. The resident replied, "Oh, I never really notice it." That is what often happens with parents and children—the special and pleasurable qualities are overlooked. As Robinson and Godbey point out, savoring experiences brings richness to lives. When people do this, they receive the rewards Jersild and his colleagues describe in concluding their study. About parenthood, they write, "Perhaps no other circumstance in life offers so many challenges to an individual's powers, so great an array of opportunities for appreciation, such a varied emotional and intellectual stimulation."[74]

MAIN POINTS

Positive feelings

- help people be more understanding and sympathetic
- contribute to later psychological health when experienced in childhood through competencies and satisfactions
- improves parent-child relationships when parents pay attention to them in their interactions with children

Close emotional ties rest on the parent's love for the child

- as a unique person
- as expressed in sensitive daily care and in becoming a social partner
- in the sharing of feelings and thoughts

Storytelling
- begins at birth and helps children discover who they are
- reinforces close relationships as parents and children share experiences

Family rituals
- provide stability by ensuring predictability in family life
- encourage communication among family members
- link family members with the past and the future
- serve as a protective factor in times of difficulty

Emotion coaching
- involves listening to children's feelings and expressing one's own
- is avoided by parents who are dismissive, disapproving, or laissez-faire
- involves five steps of identifying, labeling, and validating feelings and helping the child find appropriate ways to express them

Close relationships grow when parents
- encourage the child and give the child a sense of self-respect and accomplishment by allowing as much independence as possible
- avoid criticism that discourages the child and instead help the child deal with mistakes
- teach children to communicate their needs

Disruptive negative feelings include
- stress from lack of time with family members
- daily hassles
- family anger

When adults express unresolved anger in the presence of a child, the anger
- produces feelings of sadness, anger, and guilt in the child
- makes it hard for the child to learn to express his or her own anger—some children become overly passive and others overly aggressive
- makes the child assume blame for the anger and feel responsible for fixing the situation
- has minimal impact when parents resolve conflict fairly

Strategies for dealing with negative feelings include
- creating family time
- developing a support system
- maintaining realistic expectations
- learning to deal with negative feelings

The joys of parenting
- arise from everyday experiences
- are often overlooked by parents

Children see the good parent as
- a sensitive caregiver
- a social partner
- a person with self-control

EXERCISES

1. Imagine a time when you were a child and felt very close to one of your parents (if you like, you can do the exercise for each of your parents), and describe your parent's behavior with you. What qualities of your parent created the closeness? Share these qualities with class members. Is there a common core? If you do this exercise with each of your parents, note gender differences. Have your mother and father at times shown different qualities of closeness with you? Have your classmates experienced differences in their mothers' and fathers' behavior toward sons and daughters?

2. Imagine a time when you were a child and felt distant from one of your parents (again, you can do this for each of your parents), and describe your parent's behavior with you. What qualities of your parent created the distance? Again, share these qualities with class members and find the common core. Are these qualities the opposite of qualities that lead to closeness, or do they represent a variety of dimensions? Do the qualities you discovered in Exercises 1 and 2 support what clinicians and researchers say is important?

3. Take turns practicing active listening with a classmate. Have a partner active-listen as you describe one or several of the following situations, and then you active-listen as your partner does the same: (a) Describe a time when you were upset as a child. (b) Describe negative feelings in a recent exchange. (c) Describe scenes you have witnessed between parents and children in stores or restaurants. (d) Follow the directions your instructor hands out for what one child in a problem situation might say.

4. With a classmate, practice sending I-messages. Again, choose from a variety of situations: (a) Recall a situation when a parent was angry at you when you were growing up and describe I-messages your parent might have sent. (b) Recall a recent disagreement with a friend or instructor and give appropriate I-messages. (c) Describe public parent-child confrontations you have witnessed and devise appropriate I-messages for the parents. (d) Devise I-messages for problem situations presented by your instructor.

5. Think back to the family rituals from your childhood. Which ones were most meaningful to you? The most enjoyable? Which ones do you want to pass on to your children? Which ones do you not want to pass on to your children? Is there a common theme to those you liked and disliked?

ADDITIONAL READINGS

Doherty, William J. *The Intentional Family*. New York: Avon, 1997.

Engel, Susan. *The Stories Children Tell*. New York: Freeman, 1999.

Gottman, John M., and DeClaire, Joan. *The Heart of Parenting: Raising an Emotionally Intelligent Child*. New York: Simon & Schuster, 1997.

Robinson, John P., and Godbey, Geoffrey. *Time for Life*. University Park: Pennsylvania State University Press, 1997.

Seligman, Martin E. P. *The Optimistc Child*. New York: Houghton Mifflin, 1995.

CHAPTER

5

Shaping and Modifying Children's Behavior

IN THE NEWS

San Francisco Chronicle, June 26, 2002
Columbia University psychologist warns parents that use of physical punishment puts children at long-term risk for developing negative behaviors like aggression. See page 146 for details.

 Go to PowerWeb at:
www.dushkin.com/
powerweb to read articles
and newsfeeds on **learning**, **discipline**, **parenting**, and other topics related to this chapter.

Helping a child learn appropriate behaviors and values requires years of parental effort. Modifying a child's behavior with fair and firm limits challenges parents. Deciding what is "fair" is no simple task. What realistic expectations can parents have for a particular child of a particular age? What behaviors are appropriate? Getting the child to meet such expectations can be even more difficult. How do parents effectively communicate their expectations and limits? What if expectations are clear but the child fails to meet them? To establish firm boundaries, parents must enforce limits by using appropriate problem-solving techniques to modify behavior.

Children do not naturally do all the things parents want them to do. When children are infants, crying and whining and fussing are their only means of drawing attention to what they need—food, a dry diaper, a burp, a hug. Their crying brings caregivers who satisfy their needs, thus reinforcing the crying. As children's skills increase, they develop more positive means to get what they want—asking, gaining cooperation from others, doing it themselves. Their parents' task is to encourage new behaviors to replace the coercive (forcing or pressuring) ones so natural to the infant.[1] In this chapter, we look at the many steps parents take to do this. We also focus on parenting strategies for children of different temperaments and different genders.

THE LEARNING PROCESS

As we saw in Chapter 3, parents have many different goals in helping their children become members of their social group. They want children to learn specific behaviors (staying out of the street, making requests with polite language), and they want children to learn values and morals (being kind to others, avoiding physical or psychological harm to others).[2] These values can vary according to the particular social group of the parents. Whatever their goals, parents take many actions to encourage children to adopt approved behaviors. *Socialization* refers to the process by which adults in a society help children acquire and refine the skills to meet the demands of the social group.

Children learn in several ways. As we have seen, they learn by observing models and imitating them. Models can include parents, siblings, or playmates. Children tend to imitate models who are warm, nurturant, and powerful. When such models are unavailable, children will imitate a cold, rejecting model.

Children also learn by the consequences of their actions. A reward or positive consequence increases the chance an action will occur again. Rewards may be pleasurable internal feelings that are not observable. Often, rewards are external—getting attention, earning privileges, achieving a goal. When behavior leads to no reward or a negative consequence, then the behavior is less likely to occur than is a positively reinforced action. Consequences are most effective when they immediately and consistently follow the behavior.

When parents use low-power strategies such as reasoning and helping children understand the consequences of their actions, their children are more likely to internalize parents' rules and values than are children of parents who use high-power strategies such as threatening and spanking.[3] Low-pressure strategies also enable children to learn the procedures and behavioral scripts of everyday life. Children can then more easily think through the outcomes of different actions; they can run through a mental simulation of what will happen and make appropriate choices. As a result, children increase their understanding of their own behavior and others' reactions to them.[4]

When they show children how to be helpful in stores, parents are structuring the situation to prevent problems.

In contrast, when parents use high-power strategies, children may conform quickly, but they are less likely to internalize the rules and more likely to follow them only as long as a powerful external authority is present. Further, they are likely to become angry and resistant to high-power strategies.

A new focus in learning emphasizes learning as a collaborative process.[5] Instead of looking at learning as a process in which children acquire information from experts and gradually approach competence, this approach emphasizes the dynamic process in which individuals gain new behaviors and understandings in the course of adjusting to ongoing events and people. Learning occurs not in the acquisition of bits of knowledge but in the changing nature of the child's participation in activities.

The collaborative process of learning emphasizes that the child actively initiates learning, as seen in many of Jean Piaget's observations of children and, more recently, in an observational study of toddlers who initiated 82 percent of the interactions with a caregiver.[6] Parents provide support for learning, structuring the learning environment, engaging the child's interest and effort, tailoring the task to the child's level of ability, and providing support and guidance as the child learns the task. In many ways, the parent is a supportive coach who helps the child learn in the zone of proximal development, which we discussed in Chapter 2.

PROMOTING LEARNING

Helping children learn socially approved behaviors and values is a two-pronged process: (1) parents send a clear, direct message to the child of what they want, its importance to the parents, and the expectations the child will comply with the request and (2) children accept the message, consider the request fair, and fulfill it without feeling a loss of autonomy or self-respect.[7] Parents take many steps to encourage children's cooperation with their requests. They establish a collaborative atmosphere, set realistic expectations of the child, structure the environment so the child can easily do what is asked, provide encouragement and support, and actively teach the child what is to be done.

Establishing a Collaborative Atmosphere

Gerald Patterson and Philip Fisher consider children's compliance or increasing willingness to follow parental requests to be the result of a process that begins in the earliest years of life and occurs over time.[8] Parents create an atmosphere of *receptive compliance,* defined as a "generalized willingness to cooperate with (or perhaps, to 'exchange compliances with') a partner."[9] Sensitive parents, responsive to their children's needs, form secure attachments to their children; they therefore create early in life a climate in which children are willing to comply because their parents attend to their needs and wishes. The children act out of their commitment to the relationship with their parents. Throughout the learning process, parents give children the encouragement and support needed to persevere in the often frustrating learning process.

In addition to creating and maintaining a warm collaborative relationship, parents can use certain parenting strategies to promote compliance. Such strategies include paying positive attention to children, spending time with them, encouraging skill development, monitoring children's activities, and engaging in problem solving when difficulties arise.[10] These proactive behaviors, described as positive responsive parenting, are more powerful in preventing children's noncompliance than are consistent rewards and punishments. For example, Charles Martinez and Marion Forgatch followed 238 divorcing mothers and their first-grade sons for two and a half years and found that when mothers learned principles of positive responsive parenting, their sons' noncompliance remained low, while the noncompliance rates increased for sons whose mothers received no interventions.[11]

Setting Realistic Expectations

Parents establish realistic expectations based on the child's age and temperament and the family's needs and values. Throughout the book, we discuss how parenting changes with the age of the child. In a later section of this chapter, we examine how a child's temperament shapes parenting. The family's needs and values influence what parents expect. For example, when both parents are employed outside the home, finishing chores before school becomes important. If the family lives on a busy street, emphasis may be placed on safety rules. Social and cultural values, as noted in Chapter 3 and discussed throughout the book, also shape many expectations about behaviors, such as independence, sociability, and respect for elders.

Helping Children Meet Expectations

Having established realistic expectations, parents help children meet them in several ways. First, they structure the child's physical environment. Parenting is easier when the family house can be arranged to meet children's needs, with play space available outdoors and furniture, rugs, and decorations selected with an active family in mind. Locking up dangerous substances, having locks on drawers containing knives, clearly marking sliding glass doors—all these changes minimize the opportunities for children to harm themselves and help children lead safe, healthy lives. Figure 5.1 presents additional suggestions for childproofing a house.

Second, parents help children meet parental expectations by establishing a regular daily routine. A regular routine makes a habit of certain behaviors that children learn to do automatically. For example, doing chores routinely increases children's general helpfulness, while doing chores sporadically does not.[12] In addition, most of us function better with a regular routine of eating, sleeping, and exercising. Here again, however, children's individual tempos must be taken into account. For example, some children are slow to wake from sleep and so need more time in the morning to get started. Other children need more time to wind down at night, so their bedtime routines may have to be started earlier than usual.

Third, parents help children meet expectations by monitoring children's behavior and stimulation. They schedule their children's activities in such a way that their children do not become overly tired or overly excited. For example, parents do not take a preschool child shopping all morning and then send the child off to a birthday party in the afternoon.

Fourth, parents prepare children for difficult situations or changes in routine. They may calmly rehearse a visit to the dentist, letting the child practice with a doll or stuffed animal, so the child will be much less likely to feel overwhelmed when the real event occurs. Parents can use rehearsal to prepare children for other changes in routine, such as a vacation or a change in day care.

Paying Attention to Positive Behaviors

As noted earlier, when behaviors result in a positive consequence, the behavior tends to occur again. Positive consequences can include internal pleasurable feelings. Children run and jump because it is fun. They draw and build because these activities are pleasurable. Parents have to do little to promote these behaviors.

Many times, though, parents provide the positive consequences that ensure that a particular behavior will continue. Rewards or external positive consequences fall into two broad categories—*social rewards* of attention, smiles, and approval and *material rewards* of special gifts or purchases or special privileges and activities, such as an outing or having a friend over. Learning theorists encourage parents' use of social rewards, as they bring families closer together and create an atmosphere of trust.

■ **FIGURE 5-1**
CHILDPROOFING THE HOUSE

Bedroom

1. Install devices that prevent windows from opening and child from getting out or falling out.
2. Cover electrical outlets.
3. Inspect toys for broken and jagged edges.

Bathroom

1. Keep safety caps on all bottles.
2. Keep medicines, aspirin, rubbing alcohol in locked cabinets.
3. Adjust water heater so water is not scalding hot.
4. Use rubber mats in bath and shower.
5. Keep bathmat next to tub and shower.
6. Do not allow young child alone in bath.

Living Room

1. Cover electrical outlets.
2. Check safety of plants.
3. Put rubber-backed pad under small scatter rugs.
4. Pad sharp edges of tables.
5. Have screen for fireplace.

Have lock for door.

Stairs

1. With young child, block off tops and bottoms of stairs.
2. If necessary, mark top and bottom steps.

Kitchen

1. Keep vomit-inducing syrup on hand.
2. Store soaps, cleaners, all poisonous chemicals in locked cabinet.
3. Have guard around burners or use back burners on stove so child cannot pull contents onto self.
4. Unplug all appliances when not in use.
5. Store sharp knives in safe place.
6. Store matches out of child's reach.

Dining Room

1. Cover electrical outlets.

Garage-Workroom

1. Keep tools out of child's reach.
2. Keep poisons locked up.
3. Store paints and other toxic materials out of child's reach.
4. Store nails and screws in safe place.

General

1. Install smoke alarms in house.
2. Have fire extinguishers.
3. Plan fire escape routes.
4. Keep poison control, fire, police department numbers by telephone.

Adapted from *Working Mother,* October 1985.

Attention is the most positive consequence for children and often for adults as well. Parents are advised, then, to pay positive attention to the many ways in which their children change and conform their behavior to meet parents' requests. In the rush of everyday life, parents tend to rush from one problem behavior to another and pay attention only when the child's behavior needs modifying. Thus the child hears only what requires changing and rarely hears appreciation for his or her positive actions. Parents are more successful when they attend to the positive more often than they make requests for change.

Teaching Acceptable New Behaviors

Sometimes positive attention alone cannot establish appropriate behaviors. Parents must actively teach children what they want them to do. The most effective way to teach children is to have parents model the desired behavior. Because children may not spontaneously do what parents want them to do, parents show the child what they want done. They move very young children through the necessary steps, verbalizing each step as they go—"This is how you put on your shirt." Parents can break the task into separate units and describe what is being done while the child does it. Parents offer encouragement and praise after each step. After the child has thoroughly learned the behavior, only occasional praise is needed.

In some situations, the child cannot carry out the behaviors the parents want to reward, so the parents must *shape* the child's existing behavior. For example, suppose a mother wants her five-year-old to begin making his bed, but he does not know how. The first step for the mother is to decide what behaviors come closest to the specific behavior she wants the child to learn, such as pulling up the sheets and bedspread. She then rewards these behaviors. As the behaviors increase in frequency, she demands a higher level of performance—such as tucking in the sheets and smoothing the bedspread—before giving the reward.

Shaping behavior is also a useful approach with schoolchildren with poor report cards. Parents can reward the highest passing grade on the first report card. They can then contract with children for rewards if there are specific improvements on the next report card. Because grading periods are usually six weeks long, parents may reward good test performance during that period or contract to give small regular rewards for teachers' weekly reports of acceptable work.

ESTABLISHING AND ENFORCING RULES FOR APPROPRIATE BEHAVIOR

Theoretically, one can raise children using only rewards and ignoring all misbehavior, which subsequently becomes extinguished for lack of reward. In everyday life, however, parents usually must deal more directly with behavior that violates rules. When the child actively does something not approved, parents have two tasks before them: (1) stating limits effectively and then (2) enforcing them.

Stating Limits Effectively

Children are more likely to follow rules that are clearly, specifically, and firmly stated, than vaguely worded or implied rules. "I want you to play outside for a while" is more effective than "Be good this afternoon." If possible, parents should phrase the rule in a positive form, also stating its purpose: "Carry your coat so it stays clean," not, "Don't drag your coat on the floor." Children respond well when rules are phrased in an impersonal way. "Bedtime is at eight" is more likely to result in compliance than "You have to go to bed now."

When possible, parents should give children options—"You can have hot or cold cereal." Having choices gives children some control over what is happening. Parents can also give options when they prepare for changes in behavior. For example, they might say, "In five more swings, it is time to leave the park." This gives children a chance to get ready to follow the rule.

Parents are most effective when they prioritize rules. Health and safety rules are most important—stay out of the street, always let us know where you are. Next are what might be called rules that ease social living—rules that make being together easier. This category includes rules against destroying other people's property and rules of general consideration such as being helpful with chores or being quiet when others are sleeping. Third in priority come conventional rules—how to use a napkin and silverware. Even young preschoolers are more impressed with the importance of kindness to others than with social conventions.[13] Last on the list are rules governing behaviors that involve the child's choice—what clothes to wear, what games to play, and so on. Unless a safety issue is involved, parents need not expend enormous energies getting children to do things just as they would like them to in these areas of individual preferences.

Enforcing Limits

When rules have been stated clearly but children do not follow them, parents need to enforce them. Before acting, however, parents must do two things. First, they must ask themselves whether their children continue to break the rule because, in some subtle way, parents are rewarding the rule-breaking behavior. Parents sometimes tell children to stop running or to stop teasing but then undermine themselves with a chuckle and a shake of the head to indicate that the child has a lot of spirit and that they admire that spirit. So the child continues.

Second, parents must be sure they are in general agreement about enforcing the rules. If parents disagree strongly on enforcing rules, they should negotiate the differences with mutual problem-solving techniques. If parents frequently disagree, they may want to delay setting the consequence for a particular behavior until they can talk with each other, because children view such parental conflicts as justification to do what they want to do.

Parents have many options in enforcing limits, as the following sections explore.

Mutual Problem Solving   Using Thomas Gordon's mutual problem-solving technique is a useful first step for enforcing limits.[14] Employing this approach, parents identify the rule breaking as a problem to them, a problem they want children to help them solve so that children, too, will be satisfied with the outcome. Parents solicit their children's opinions and work together to find a win-win solution agreeable to all concerned. For example, when children are consistently late for dinner or do not come to the table when called, parents present this as a problem they all must solve. The underlying assumption is that the family's working together can find an alternative that satisfies everyone. There are six steps to the problem-solving process: (1) defining the problem, (2) generating possible solutions, (3) evaluating possible solutions, (4) deciding on the best solution, (5) implementing the decision, and (6) doing a follow-up evaluation.

When an agreed-on solution is not followed, parents must send a strong I-message of disappointment and surprise as soon as possible. Perhaps the child can be helped to keep the agreement. Or perhaps another problem-solving session is needed. Gordon advises against the use of penalties to enforce agreements. Parents should assume children will cooperate instead of starting with a negative expectation expressed in the threat of punishment. Children frequently respond well to trust.

Just as parents want children to perform certain behaviors, so children want to attain certain objects, activities, and privileges. Using the behavioral system of *contracting*, parents offer desired rewards in exchange for the performance of certain activities. For example, if a child does his chores (making his bed, clearing the table) without reminders, he earns an extra fifteen minutes of time for playing. Likewise, an older child may be given use of the family car on the weekends if she maintains acceptable school grades and arrives home at the prescribed times.

Natural and Logical Consequences   The terms *natural consequences* and *logical consequences*[15] are used jointly and interchangeably but have slightly different meanings. Natural consequences are the direct result of a physical act. For example, if you do not eat dinner, you experience hunger. If you stay up late, you become tired. Logical consequences are events that follow a social act. For example, if you lie, other people will not believe you. If you misuse the family car, your parents will not trust you with it. Natural and logical consequences are directly related to the act itself and are not usually imposed by others. Exceptions exist, however. A natural consequence of running out into a busy street is being hit by a car. To prevent such a consequence, parents generally use a logical consequence. If a child starts toward the street, the child may be restricted to playing in the house.

Logical consequences differ from punishment in several ways. Logical consequences are directly related to what the child has done—if children do not put their clothes in the laundry, they will have no clean clothes. A punishment may have no logical relationship to what the child has done—a spanking is not the direct result of being late for a meal but is the result of the parent's authority. The method of logical consequences does not place moral blame or pass moral judgment on the child. The child has made a mistake and pays the price. The parent stands by as an adviser rather than a judge.

Punishments   If the preceding methods do not work, parents use punishments. Punishment means giving a behavior a negative consequence to decrease the likelihood of its recurrence. There are six general principles for using punishments:

1. Intervene early. Do not let the situation get out of control. As soon as the rule is violated, begin to take action.

2. Stay as calm and objective as possible. Sometimes, parents' upset and frustration are rewarding to the child. Parents' emotions can also distract the child from thinking about the rule violation.

3. State the rule that was violated. State it simply and do not argue about it.

When children have angry outbursts, parents must stay as calm as possible so they can deal effectively with the children's behavior.

4. Use a *mild* negative consequence. A mild consequence has the advantage that the child often devalues the activity itself and seems more likely to resist temptation and follow the rule in the future.

5. Use negative consequences consistently. Misbehaviors continue when they are sometimes punished and sometimes not.

6. Reinforce positive social behaviors as they occur afterward; parents do not want children to receive more punishments than rewards.

Punishments require varying degrees of effort on the parents' part. The following punishments range from mild to severe. First, *ignoring* might seem the easiest punishment in that the parent simply pays no attention to what the child says or does. It requires effort, however, because the parent must keep a neutral facial expression, look away, move away from the child, and give no verbal response or attention to what the child says or does. Ignoring is best for behaviors that are not harmful to anyone. For example, children's whining, sulking, or pouting can be ignored.

A second punishment is *social disapproval*. Parents express in a few words, spoken in a firm voice with a disapproving facial expression, that they do not like the behavior. When children continue disapproved behavior, parents can institute a consequence—removing a privilege, using the time-out strategy, or imposing extra work. When families have contracts, children agree to carry out specified chores or behaviors in exchange for privileges. When certain behaviors do not occur, children lose privileges.

Finally, *time out* is a method best reserved for aggressive, destructive, or dangerous behaviors. It serves to stop the disapproved behavior and to give the child a chance to cool off and think about the rule violation. The time-out method has many variations. The child can be requested to sit in a chair in the corner, but many children get up. If the child is required to face the corner, parents can keep a young child in the corner for the stated time. With older children, parents may want to add the rule that if the child does not comply with time out for one parent during the day, making the presence of both parents necessary, then the child will spend twice the amount of time in time out. The time need not be long. For young children, the number of minutes in time out should equal the number of years in age.

It is best to have only two or three behaviors requiring time out at any one time. Otherwise, a child may spend a great deal of time in the corner for too many different things. Further, both parents and all caregivers need to agree on the two or three things that will lead to time out so the child receives punishment consistently.

When children get older and have many toys and recreational pleasures in their rooms, such as stereos and computers, restriction to their room is not an effective punishment. For these children, it is better to substitute extra work or chores that have a constructive outcome such as cleaning the garage or devoting time to a community activity.

Ineffective Forms of Discipline   A review of over three hundred studies[16] identifies four kinds of problems in disciplining children: (1) inconsistent discipline, referring to inconsistency both on the part of one parent and between two parents; (2) irritable, harsh, explosive discipline (frequent hitting and threatening); (3) low supervision and low involvement on the part of the parent with the child; and (4) inflexible, rigid discipline (use of a single form of discipline for all transgressions regardless of seriousness). All four forms of ineffective discipline are related to aggressive, rule-breaking behavior from children that frequently leads to social difficulties with peers.

The Use of Physical Punishment

In June 2002, the psychologist Elizabeth Gershoff warned parents that although they gained children's immediate compliance when they used corporal punishment, they risked long-term psychological harm to children.[17] Yet over 90 percent of parents report that they have used physical punishment at one time or another.[18] Are all children therefore at risk? Here we examine the many factors that can help parents answer this question.

Definition of Levels of Physical Discipline   First, we must distinguish among forms of physical discipline. Physical punishment is often divided into two categories: (1) mild physical punishment, defined as a slap or two with the flat of the hand on the buttocks or extremities without causing any physical injury to the child and normatively used with young children between ages two and six, and (2) abuse, including beating, kicking, and punching that results in injury to the child.[19]

In spite of these categories, researchers face many difficulties in classifying parents with regard to their use of physical punishment.[20] First, as self-reporters of such use, parents may not be accurate. Second, parents are often asked only whether and how often they spank within a specified period of time, such as the preceding week. Some parents who rarely spank but did that week may be identified as using physical punishment in the same category with others who rely more heavily on spanking. Also, a frequent user of physical punishment who did not happen to use physical means that week would be classified as a nonuser. Although researchers think that these errors cancel each other out, they do not know for sure. Third, parents are rarely asked how severely they spank their child, so whether the physical punishment is mild, harsh, or abusive remains unclear.

Prevalence and Frequency of Physical Punishment   Keeping in mind all the difficulties of identifying those who use different levels of physical punishment, let us look at the prevalence and frequency of spanking. When asked whether they have ever spanked their child, between 70 percent and 94 percent of parents say they have.[21] While spanking has decreased over the past three decades, still the vast majority have spanked a child.[22] In two large-scale studies, about two-thirds of parents of preschoolers aged three to five had spanked their child in the previous week, with an average of one to three spankings, depending on the sample and subgroup.[23]

In a telephone survey, caregivers for 60 percent of children reported that they used physical punishment and minor physical violence (pushing, grabbing, shoving, and slapping), and 10 percent reported one or more instances of physical abuse or severe violence, consisting of kicking, biting, or hitting with a fist.[24]

In a 1993 survey of middle-class families, 83 percent of parents reported using physical punishment.[25] Although most spanked a few times a month or less at mild to moderate intensity, researchers were concerned that about a third of the parents were reported by their children (who were interviewed separately from their parents) to use objects to hit them, and many said this occurred in about half the punishments. About 17 percent of children said they were hit a few times a week, and 4 percent said they were hit daily.

Spanking starts early in life. About 50 percent of parents report that they had spanked their child of under a year of age one or more times in the preceding week.[26] Spanking increases in the years from two to five, when between 60 and 65 percent of parents report having spanked a child. Beginning at age five, spanking decreases, so only about one-third of parents report having spanked their child in the previous week; by ages nine or ten, that number drops to about 20 percent. Parents also report giving preschoolers, on average, more spankings per week (three) than they give older children (two).[27]

Characteristics of Parents Who Use Physical Punishment   Parents who are young, single, and under financial stress are more likely to spank than are older, married parents who have financial resources.[28] Still, as noted, 83 percent of middle-class parents in one study and 94 percent of middle-class parents in another used physical punishment.[29]

Mothers are more likely to use physical means of discipline than are fathers, perhaps because they do more of the daily child care.[30] African American parents are more likely to use physical punishment than are European American or Latino parents.[31] People who live in rural areas and in the southern part of the United States are more likely to use physical means of discipline than are parents in urban areas and the northern part of the United States.[32] Parents who identify themselves as religiously conservative report more frequent physical punishment than do those who do not identify themselves as religious conservatives,[33] and Catholics report less spanking than do Protestants.[34] Physical discipline is more likely, then, when parents are under stress or when they hold more traditional or conservative values.

Characteristics of Children Who Receive Physical Punishment   As noted, preschool children are more likely to receive physical punishment than are elementary and high school students. Boys are more likely to be spanked than girls—in one study, 67 percent of boys received spankings, compared with 57 percent of girls.[35] Children described as having difficult temperaments and being noncompliant received more spankings than did other children. Spankings also occurred more frequently in families in which parents and children argued and in which parents had fewer supports.

Reasons Given for Spanking   Seventy percent of parents nominated by teachers-of-the-year as outstanding parents reported spanking and gave such reasons as the need to get children's attention in the face of a dangerous act.[37] A middle-class sample of parents gave a variety of reasons for spanking: "Nonphysical punishment is not effective." "Children learn better from punishment than rewards." "Young children don't understand reasoning." "Physical punishment builds character and prepares children for the outside world, which can be cruel if children have not learned the consequences of their behavior." A common reason was "It worked for me when I was growing up."[38]

Parents in this study were most likely to use spanking and hitting when children were out of control, disobedient, or disrespectful. Four factors related to parents' use of physical punishment: (1) parents' belief in its usefulness, (2) parents' own experience with it as a child, (3) an authoritarian style of parenting, and (4) children's problems of aggressiveness and acting out. Although 93 percent justified its use, 85 percent of those who used it said they would rather not. They felt they were angry when they did it and that it upset the children; they wished they had alternatives. Even though most children in the sample were hit infrequently and at low levels, all children reported that physical punishment hurt and made them angry and upset. Nonetheless, although the children did not like it, they felt parents had a right to use physical punishment. Children in other surveys have also reported they believe parents have that right.[39]

Of concern to the researchers was the fact that parents continued its use despite their discomfort with it and its doubtful value. Parents seemed to rely on it as a continuation of their own childhood experience of physical punishment rather than to institute change and learn new methods. The investigators were concerned that the children in the sample would continue the practice for the same reason.

Effects of Physical Punishment There is no doubt that physical abuse is related to many difficulties for children (see Chapter 15). Here we focus on the effects of mild to moderate physical discipline. As just noted, both parents and children feel angry and upset at the use of physical discipline. Children tend not to learn from it, so it seems more effective to find other ways to deal with problems. Experts agree that parents will have the best results in modifying children's behavior if they first use mild negative consequences along with reasoning.

Diana Baumrind believes that the effects of a spanking, which she defines as a slap or two with the flat of the hand on the buttocks or the extremities, depends on the context of the parent-child relationship.[40] Much research supports this position. The most recent study involved data collected from 1,990 children over a six-year period as part of the National Longitudinal Survey of Youth. It included a sizable number of African American and Latino parents as well as European American parents.[41]

In this study, mothers were categorized into three groups—no spanking in the last week, spanking once in the last week, and spanking more than once in the last week—when their children were four years of age and at two-year intervals over the next six years. When children were four, there was no relationship between the use and frequency of spanking and the child's behavior problems. Some children with few behavioral problems received many spankings, and some children with many behavioral difficulties received no spankings.

Being spanked, however, increased behavioral difficulties over time. While the behavior problems of all children increased from age four to ten, those whose mothers continued to spank had more behavior problems than did those who had not been spanked, unless moderating influences were present. When parents increased their spanking in these years, the increase in problems was greater than when spanking decreased or stayed the same. The findings were the same for all groups, so the effects of spanking did not differ as a result of ethnicity.

Children's mothers were also described in terms of their emotional warmth and supportiveness. Children with warm and supportive mothers had fewer behavior problems. Further, as the authors concluded,

> Although spanking can have a negative impact on children's socioemotional functioning over time, this effect is moderated by the emotional context in which such spanking occurs. When spanking occurs in the context of strong overall emotional support for the child, it does not appear to contribute to a significant increase in behavior problems.[42]

This finding was consistent in all three ethnic groups. It suggests that when physical punishment is accompanied by warmth and reasoning, children interpret the punishment as a caring parent's response to misbehavior and not as rejection.

An extensive review of studies from 1974 to 1995 on the effects of nonabusive or customary physical punishment supports Baumrind's contention that the effects of spanking depend on the parent's overall relationship with the child.[43] The review of 35 studies found that with abusive discipline excluded, nonabusive spanking led to a decrease in noncompliant behaviors. Physical punishment was associated with no detrimental effects when it was not severe, when it did not involve any implement, when it was used less than weekly, when it was used with young children two to six and possibly with children seven to twelve, when it was accompanied by reasoning, when it was used as a backup to other strategies, and when parents were not violent with other family members. Parents had the best results when they were positively involved with children, were acting in terms of children's needs rather than their own motivations, did not arouse fear in children, provided consistent discipline, did not use verbal put-downs, and changed their main discipline to grounding as children grew older.

On the other hand, Gershoff's review of 88 studies of corporal punishment shows that physical punishment is related to children's rapid compliance with parents' requests but also to long-term negative outcomes in several areas of functioning.[44] Children who received physical discipline were more likely to be aggressive, antisocial, and delinquent and less likely to have self-confidence, good relationships with parents, and an internal sense of moral values. Gershoff makes several suggestions for improving studies of the effects of physical punishment and discusses the variables that would give us a better understanding of the process involved for both parents and children when parents use physical punishment.

How can these studies have produced such contradictory findings? A careful examination of Gershoff's methodology reveals flaws that would favor negative outcomes. For example, she included studies with physical punishment of teenagers, and she included studies of abusive levels of physical punishment. When Diana Baumrind, Robert Larzelere, and Philip Cowan reanalyzed the studies using only mild punishment, they found only one study concerning children eighteen months to six years that indicated a very small effect size for increased aggression as a result of physical punishment.[45] However, other measures of discipline in this age period resulted in even greater increases in aggression. They wrote,

> Because the effect sizes linking CP [corporal punishment] to detrimental outcomes in young children are often smaller than those linking other forms of punishment to such outcomes, we might conclude that parents should refrain from all forms of punishment because all punishment harms young children.[46]

We can conclude that parents who have positive, warm relationships with their children and use reasoning and mild physical punishment with young children from ages eighteen months to about five years, do not appear to be placing these children at risk of long-term harm. Physical punishment in the absence of a warm relationship appears to contribute to an increase in children's behavior problems. Beyond age five, parents are well-advised to find other disciplinary strategies.

Patterson and Fisher point out that because physical punishment reinforces a vicious cycle, it may be difficult to discontinue.[47] When children do not comply, parents argue and then use physical discipline. When children comply, parents see that such discipline "works" and are therefore encouraged to use it again. Sometimes, during arguments, parents threaten physical punishment but do not carry it out because of children's protests. Thus, children are encouraged to protest loudly in the next encounter. In this way, parents and children train each other to escalate to a maximal level of protests and punishments. The researchers believe that the parenting strategy of physical punishment reflects both the parents' and the children's behavior, and stopping the parent's physical punishment would not necessarily stop the negative cycle.

Several European countries have banned parents' use of physical discipline. Should the United States do so as well? Because of the potential for abuse and because physical punishment is related to aggressiveness among children and to a more violent society, the social scientist Murray Straus wishes to ban physical punishment in schools and at home.[48] He cites statistics from a national, representative sample of children revealing that the more corporal punishment a child receives in middle childhood and early adolescence, the greater the probability of the child's being a delinquent. In another longitudinal study of delinquency, those boys who experienced corporal punishment were more likely later to be convicted of a crime. Straus recognizes that not all physical punishment results in adult criminality, but he says that even if spanking increases adult violence by 10 percent, it is worth eliminating to decrease violence by that amount.

Other social scientists such as Baumrind believe that research does not support a blanket injunction against spanking.[49] As we have seen, when a parent uses spanking in the context of a warm parent-child relationship and uses reasoning as well, then there are "no documented harmful long-term effects."[50] Further, she points out that in Sweden, where physical punishment was outlawed at home and at school in 1979, both parental physical abuse of children and violent acts by teenagers increased.

All social scientists, whether they accept the use of mild physical punishment or wish to ban it, emphasize the importance of the steps described in Chapter 4 and earlier in this chapter to encourage approved behaviors through teaching and positive rewards. Discouraging the use of physical punishment, while a useful first step, does not automatically put in place the strategies of supportive parenting described earlier. The pediatrician Robert Chamberlin, for example, identifies the use of physical punishment as just one risk factor related to poor outcome for children. Because the accumulation of risk factors is what causes the most damage, he believes that communities and professionals need to join with parents to promote the "affectionate and cognitively stimulating types of parenting behavior that appear more directly related to positive developmental outcomes rather than focus on whether or not parents use physical punishment."[51] Baumrind also cautions professionals,

It should be the concern of professionals who work with parents to respectfully offer them alternative disciplinary strategies, using carefully evaluated intervention programs, rather than to condemn parents for using methods consonant with their own, but not with the counselor's, beliefs and values. Parents who choose to use punishment often seek guidance in using it efficaciously. Efficacious punishment is contingent upon the child's misbehavior, as well as upon the parents' responding in a prompt, rational, nonexplosive manner and with knowledge and consideration of the child's developmental level and temperament.[52]

HOW A CHILD'S TEMPERAMENT INFLUENCES PARENTING STRATEGIES

In Chapter 1, we discussed the effects of genetic contributions to parenting. A major way that genes are thought to influence parent-child relationships is through a child's temperament. *Temperament* is defined as "constitutionally based individual differences in emotional, motor, and attentional reactivity and self-regulation."[53] The specific neurophysiological processes thought to underlie temperament are not yet known. Differences in temperament among newborns appear hours after birth in such behaviors as the amount of crying, ability to soothe oneself and be soothed by a caregiver,[54] and enjoyment at being hugged and cuddled.[55]

Although investigators differ on the specific dimensions of temperament, a thorough review of studies indicates six basic aspects of temperament: (1) *fearful distress,* emphasizing the baby's fearfulness and poor adaptability to new situations; (2) *irritable distress,* emphasizing fussiness, irritability, and distress at limitations; (3) *positive affect,* including laughing, smiling, and approaching objects and stimuli; (4) *activity level;* (5) *attention span,* or persistence; and (6) *rhythmicity,* or predictability of behaviors.[56]

To what degree do these differences persist? Some children showing certain temperamental qualities early on do not continue to show them later, but others do. For example, vigorous neonatal movements in the nursery were related to high activity levels at ages four and eight,[57] and activity level at twelve months predicted activity level and extroverted behavior at six and seven years.[58] High physiological reactivity (as measured in high motor activity and crying) to novel stimuli at four months was related to inhibition in behavior in the toddler years, which, in turn, was related to being less outgoing and expressive in early adolescence.[59]

Although early crying and fussiness did not endure, irritability at seven months tended to last for the next year or two. Difficult temperament measured at six months (which included negative affect, lack of rhythmicity, and persistence in behavior) predicted difficult temperament at thirteen and twenty-four months and behavior problems at age three.[60] Stability from infancy to ages seven and eight has been found for such qualities as approachability and sociability, rhythmicity, irritability, persistence, cooperativeness and manageability, and inflexibility.[61] Impulsivity at age three has been linked to measures of impulsivity, danger seeking, and aggression at age eighteen.[62]

Research shows that temperament influences parenting, but in an inconsistent way.[63] For example, difficult temperament stimulates greater parental involvement and attention in some mothers, who later become frustrated and uninvolved, and brings about in other mothers a negative and uninvolved approach from the start.

Early high reactivity stimulates in some mothers a soothing and solicitous approach but in other mothers a firm insistence that the infants learn to soothe themselves.[64] However, no studies show that a positive, sociable baby stimulates a negative reaction in parents.[65]

Temperament also influences how children respond to parents' disapproval and how easily they can regulate their feelings and their behavior. Furthermore, parents' behavior in establishing rules and shaping behavior has different outcomes, depending on the child's temperament. For example, infants' emotional regulatory ability appears to be the forerunner of behavior control in toddlerhood.[66] One study found that five-month-old infants who could regulate their emotions in response to frustration could by age two and a half conform to parents' requests. Experiencing frustration in infancy may be essential to developing regulatory skills. If infants do not experience frustration, perhaps because of general low reactivity, they might not experience sufficient emotional arousal to develop and practice regulatory skills.

Other research suggests that toddlers who are relatively reactive and responsive to others' behavior, who are relatively fearful and quick to feel bad at their own wrongdoing, respond well to gentle discipline; so, parents need to do little to help these children internalize the rules.[67] Relatively fearless toddlers who have little reaction to their own wrongdoing do not benefit from gentle low-power techniques, nor do they benefit from high-power strategies that arouse their anger. Instead, they learn rules most easily when parents establish a positive, initially cooperative partnership based on a secure attachment. More securely attached, fearless children comply with what the mother wants because of the relationship, not the specific disciplinary techniques she uses.

How much can parents influence temperamental qualities? Research shows that sensitive parenting can help children overcome early temperamental difficulties.[68] Sensitive, responsive caregiving can help irritable babies, who are more likely to have insecure attachments, develop positive attachments to parents. Early limit-setting can help highly reactive infants learn self-soothing strategies and become less inhibited as toddlers.[69] Clearly, no one set of interventions will help all children. Rather, parents should be sensitive, flexible caregivers who target their behaviors to provide a "good fit" with their child's temperamental qualities. Sybil Escalona uses the term *effective experience* to describe what parents provide each child—the kind of experience that helps the child develop optimally.[70]

For more on temperament, see the interview with Jacqueline and Richard Lerner (pages 154–155).

PRACTICAL QUESTION:
HOW DO PARENTS SELECT INDIVIDUALLY
APPROPRIATE STRATEGIES IN REARING CHILDREN?

Joan Grusec states, "Effective parenting consists of constant appraisal and flexible behavior in the face of constantly changing features of children and situations. Parents must be aware of the characteristics of their children and how their children will react, and willing and able to tailor their actions accordingly."[71] Parental

INTERVIEW
with Jacqueline Lerner and Richard Lerner

Richard Lerner holds the Anita L. Brennan Professor of Education position at Boston College, and Jacqueline V. Lerner is a professor of education at Boston College.

Parents are interested in temperament and what this means for them as parents. What happens if they have a baby with a difficult temperament that is hard for them to deal with? Is this fixed? Will they have to keep coping with it?

R. Lerner: We don't believe temperament necessarily is fixed. We believe that temperament is a behavioral style and can, and typically does, show variation across a person's life. We're interested in the meaning of temperament for the person and the family in daily life.

J. Lerner: Although we know temperament is present at birth, we don't say that it is exclusively constitutionally derived. Temperament interacts with the environment. We find children who do seem to stay fairly difficult and children who stay fairly easy. Most children change, even from year to year. Given this, we can't possibly believe that temperament ever becomes fixed unless what happens in the family becomes fixed.

R. Lerner: What we are concerned with are individual differences. They are identifiable at birth, but they change, we believe, in relation to the child's living situation. We find that what one parent might call difficult is well below the threshold of another parent's level of tolerance for difficulty. What some people find easy, others find quite annoying.

In fact, you can find in our case studies examples of how difficult children ended up developing in a particular context that reinterpreted their difficulty as artistic creativity. One girl picked up a musical instrument at age thirteen or fourteen and began playing. She had a gift for that. Prior to that, she had a difficult relation with her father, who found her temperamental style totally abhorrent to him. As soon as she had this emerging talent, he said, "Oh, my daughter is an artist. This is an artistic temperament." They reinterpreted the first thirteen years of their relationship, believing they had always been close.

We believe the importance of temperament lies in what we call "goodness of fit" between the child's qualities and what the environment demands. The child brings characteristics to the parent-child relationship, but parents have to understand what they bring and how they create the meaning of the child's individuality by their own temperaments and their demands, attitudes, and evaluations. Moreover, I think parents should understand that both they and the child have many other influences on them—friends, work, or school.

When you think about the fit with the environment, how do you think about the environment; what is it?

R. Lerner: We have divided demands from the environment into three broad categories: the physical characteristics of the setting, the behavioral characteristics of the environment, and the behavioral and psychological characteristics of the other important people in the child's life.

J. Lerner: The setting has physical characteristics, and the people have behavioral characteristics and demands, attitudes, and values.

R. Lerner: Parents need to understand the demands of the context (the living situation) they present to the child by means of their own values and behavioral style. Even the features of the physical environment the parents provide can affect the child's fit with the context. Parents need to understand there are numerous features of the context; because of the child's individuality, a better or lesser fit will emerge. For example, if your child has a low threshold of reactivity and a high intensity of reactions, you don't want to put that child's bedroom next to a busy street. If you have a choice, you'll put that child's bedroom in the back of the house or won't let the child study in any part of the house where he or she will get distracted.

A poor fit also occurs if you have a child who is very arrhythmic and you demand regularity, not necessarily as a verbal demand but perhaps in the way you schedule your life. You begin to prepare breakfast every morning at 8:00, the bagel comes out at 8:05 and disappears at 8:15, and some days the child makes it and some days not. The parents have to see how they may be doing things that create poorness of fit. It's not just their verbal demands but also their behavioral demands and the physical setup of the house.

J. Lerner: Some parents don't see what they are reinforcing and what they are teaching their child through their demands. There has to be consistency between the demands and the reinforcements. Sometimes you don't want to be too flexible. I learned this the hard way. My nine-year-old tells me about what I have done in the past. "But when I did this last week, it was okay and now it isn't."

In actively trying to get the child to behave or in trying to change a temperamental quality, parents need to focus themselves on what behaviors they want reinforced and what ones they don't. They need to be perceptive on both ends of the response—the demands they are setting up and what they are actually reinforcing. If you know a child is irregular in eating in the morning and you want to change the pattern because you know he'll get cranky and won't learn well if he doesn't have a full stomach, be consistent. "You don't walk out the door unless you have had at least three bites of cereal and a glass of juice." But if you let it go one morning, you can expect the child to say, "Well, yesterday you didn't make me do that."

From your research, do you see potential supports for children as they are growing up?

R. Lerner: More and more children experience alternative-care settings, and this has to become a major support. The socialization of the child is moving out of the family more and more, and we are charging the schools with more of the socialization duties. Throughout infancy and childhood, the alternative caregiving setting is the day care, the preschool, and, obviously, the school. These settings have to be evaluated in terms of enhancing the child's fit and the ability to meet the demands of the context.

sensitivity and responsiveness to children's needs is important, but so is the capacity to shape behavior.

As we have seen in earlier chapters, many social factors besides the parents themselves influence their choice of strategies. Parents' social and ethnic backgrounds, their financial resources, the social support they receive from partners and family, and characteristics of the child such as age, sex, and temperament all affect these choices.[72] Even so, parents often wish they had a single solution to each kind of problem they encounter in childrearing—one way to handle temper tantrums, one way to deal with teenagers' rebelliousness. Unfortunately, there is no one formula that all parents can use to raise all children. Each child, as well as each parent, is a unique individual.

When parents have difficulties, a seven-step problem-solving approach seems most useful. The approach allows parents to choose *interventions* (actions to change a problem behavior, such as holding a mutual problem-solving session or setting up a reward system) that take into account the child's age and temperament and the family's social values and living circumstances. It also enables parents to encourage the qualities that they and their ethnic group value. Here are the seven steps:

1. Spend pleasurable time daily with the child.
2. Specifically identify any problem; observe when and how often it occurs.
3. Question yourself on the reality of the problem.
4. Get the child's point of view.
5. Carry out an intervention.
6. Evaluate the results of the intervention.
7. Start over again if necessary.

How do parents select interventions? Most use a combination of the techniques described earlier in this chapter to enforce limits, but parents develop beliefs about the effectiveness of low-power, authoritative methods as opposed to high-power, authoritarian methods.[73] Often, parents react in terms of these beliefs.[74] As noted in Chapter 4, however, a parent's affect is perhaps a more important determiner of the choice. When parents are under stress, angry, or upset, they tend to assert power. This is true of depressed mothers as well. According to one study, even though many such mothers believed in the importance of low-power techniques, their resentment of the child and the parenting role—not their beliefs—determined the choice of their parenting behaviors.[75]

The complexity of using childrearing strategies increases when we realize that children may not be learning by the strategy parents are using. In a perceptive and humorous article, Jane Loevinger illustrates this problem with the example of a five-year-old who hits his younger brother.[76] The parent who punishes the older child with a spanking may actually be teaching that child that it is permissible to use physical aggression to obtain one's ends. On the other hand, the parent who uses reason and logic in dealing with the older boy may find that the child, seeing that no punishment follows hitting, will keep doing it.

So why use a strategy at all? Why not just do whatever comes to mind at the time? Because, says Loevinger, those children who have the most difficulties growing up and functioning are raised by parents who are impulsive, self-centered, and unable to follow a set of guidelines. "The chief value of a parental theory," writes Loevinger, "may well be in providing a model for the child of curbing one's own impulses out of regard for the future welfare of another."[77]

When we combine the problem-solving approach with the parental qualities and behaviors all strategies advise—modeling desired traits, respecting the child's and parents' own needs, having confidence that the child can learn what is necessary, and sharing problems and solutions in family meetings—then parents can effectively foster the growth and development of their children. Each individual has a unique potential to discover and develop. Arnold Gesell and Frances Ilg state it well:

> When asked to give the very shortest definition of life, Claude Bernard, a great physiologist, answered, "Life is creation." A newborn baby is the consummate product of such creation. And he in turn is endowed with capacities for continuing creation. These capacities are expressed not only in the growth of his physique, but in the simultaneous growth of a psychological self. From the sheer standpoint of creation this psychological self must be regarded as his masterpiece. It will take a lifetime to finish, and in the first ten years he will need a great deal of help, but it will be his own product.[78]

Parents have the privilege of serving as guide and resource as their child creates a unique "psychological self."

MAIN POINTS

Parents set the stage for learning by
- establishing a collaborative relationship
- developing realistic expectations of the child
- helping children meet expectations
- rewarding approved behaviors consistently
- setting limits with clear, positive statements of what they want

To enforce rules, parents can
- use mutual problem solving
- let natural or logical consequences of the act teach the child
- use punishments to decrease the disapproved behavior

Nonabusive spanking as a punishment
- is used by most parents at one time or another but most often by young parents under stress
- may or may not have detrimental effects, depending on the context of the parent-child relationship
- is best supplanted by other forms of negative consequence

Ineffective forms of discipline include

- inconsistent discipline
- harsh, explosive discipline
- low supervision of the child
- rigid, inflexible discipline

Temperament

- is the individual's constitutionally based way of responding to the world
- influences the usefulness of parenting strategies

The advantages of the seven-step problem-solving approach are that

- parents can take into account the child's individuality
- parents can retain their own goals and values for their children's behavior

EXERCISES

1. Write a description of the disciplinary techniques your parents used with you in your elementary and high school years. How would you characterize your parents' methods and your response to them?

2. Choose some behavior you want to improve on—for example, regular exercise—and work out a reward system to encourage that behavior. Chart the frequency of the desired behavior before and during the reward period. If time permits, observe the frequency for a week after you stop the reward system. Share your experiences with classmates. What kinds of rewards have most successfully helped you and other students improve your behavior?

3. Choose some behavior you want to eliminate. Chart the occurrence of the behavior before any intervention. Then, choose a negative consequence that will occur after every repetition of the undesired behavior. If you wish, choose to reward the opposite of the undesired behavior at the same time. Then monitor the occurrence of the undesired behavior. If time permits, observe the frequency of the behaviors after you have stopped the consequences. For example, you may decide you want to stop procrastinating going to the library. Decide that every time you postpone going to the library for five minutes or longer, you will have to stay at the library an extra thirty minutes. If you go to the library on time, permit yourself to leave ten minutes early.

4. Observe parents and children together at a playground, in the grocery store, or at another public place. Select pairs of children of approximately the same age and contrast how their parents treat them. Do the parents show similar behavior? What theories of learning do they appear to be using? What parental behaviors seem effective with the children? Observing each child for five minutes, time how often the parent intervenes to maintain or change the child's behavior.

5. Select a friend's behavior that you wish to change. For example, you might decide to change a friend's habit of being late for meetings or of not calling when she says she will. Devise a system of rewards or a system of positive/negative consequences to change the behavior. Carry out your plan for five weeks and note the change.

ADDITIONAL READINGS

Dinkmeyer, Don, and McKay, Gary D. *The Parent's Handbook.* Circle Pines, MN: American Guidance Service, 1989.

Gordon, Thomas. *Teaching Children Self-Discipiline.* New York: Times Books, 1989.

Kurcinka, Mary. *Raising Your Spirited Child.* New York: Harper Perennial, 1992.

Nelson, Jane. *Positive Discipline.* New York: Ballantine Books, 1987.

Severe, Sal. *How to Behave So Your Children Will, Too!* New York: Viking Penguin, 2000.

Parenting at Developmental Stages

6

Becoming Parents

IN THE NEWS

San Francisco Chronicle, July 4, 2002
Prospective parents may be able to wait before seeking fertility treatments. See page 171 for details.

 Go to PowerWeb at: www.dushkin.com/ powerweb to read articles and newsfeeds on **parents, pregnancy, reproduction,** and other topics related to this chapter.

Why do people want to have children? How do they go about deciding to have children? Does it matter if you have children when you are younger or older? Does how you become a parent matter? How do parents adjust to the changes after a baby arrives?

This chapter describes how people become parents. It talks about what they hope to experience with their children and how they decide when they are uncertain. It looks at how parents' relationships change as they incorporate a baby into their lives.

Each individual who becomes a parent does so within unique circumstances. Some plan enthusiastically; others become parents without deciding to do so. Factors including the parent's age, career and social status, economic situation, extended family, and community support system make the process of anticipating, having, and raising a child special for each.

REASONS FOR HAVING CHILDREN

In Chapter 1, we saw that children meet parents' basic needs for having close emotional relationships with others and give parents the satisfaction of helping them grow and develop.[1] Table 6-1 lists seven major reasons men and women, parents and nonparents alike, give for having children. In general, these reasons are listed in similar order in different ethnic groups, with the exception that African Americans, rural residents, and people with less education are more likely than other groups to view children as providing economic utility and security in old age.[2]

Reasons for not having children center on three broad factors—restrictions (loss of freedom, loss of time available for other activities, increase in workload), negative feelings evoked by children (worries concerning children's health and well-being, difficulties of discipline, disappointments in children or in self as a parent), and concerns about the child being poorly cared for. Research suggests that prospective parents, while aware of the costs, plan children on the basis of the positive experiences they anticipate rather than limiting the number because of the difficulties.[3]

Although only about 10 to 15 percent of adolescent mothers plan their pregnancies, their decision to continue the pregnancy is related to their values for having children.[4] In a study of how adolescent mothers rank order the value of children,

---

■ **T A B L E   6-1**
PARENTS' REASONS FOR WANTING CHILDREN

---

1. Love and satisfying, close relationship with others

2. Stimulation and excitement of watching children grow

3. Means of self-development—becoming more responsible, more sensitive, more skilled in relationships

4. Way of achieving adult status—parenthood is "proof" of being mature

5. Sense of creativity and achievement in helping child grow

6. Expression of moral, religious belief

7. Utility—belief that children will care for parents when parents are older

---

Adapted from Lois Wladis Hoffman and Jean Denby Manis, "The Value of Children in the United States: A New Approach to the Study of Fertility," *Journal of Marriage and the Family* 41 (1979): 583–596.

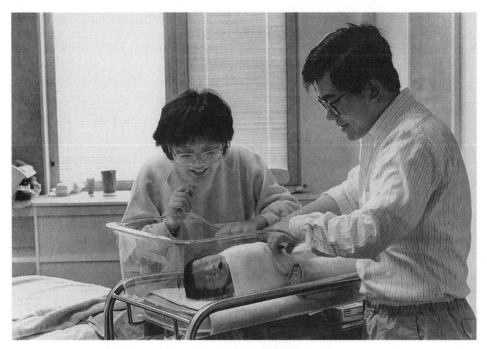

Becoming a parent gives meaning and purpose to life.

Gerald Michaels found that their ordering of values for having children is similar to that of adults.[5] Adolescent mothers are more likely to see children as a source of power and influence and less likely as a measure of adult status; still, like adults, adolescent mothers want children because they see children as sources of love, fun, stimulation, and achievement.

Adolescent mothers are more likely to view children positively when these mothers have few ways to get needs met.[6] For example, adolescent mothers who did not work or who did not feel very independent or self-sufficient were likely to have a high desire for children. These feelings, combined with the example of their own mothers, who also had children early, increased the value they placed on children. Viewing children positively, however, was related only weakly to subsequent parenting.

THE DECISION TO PARENT

Today, girls and women can become parents from early adolescence into their sixties—a fifty-year span—and boys and men can become fathers from adolescence through life. Physical ability, however, is not the only requirement for parenthood. The social characteristics, education and employment, enable parents to support a child. Parents' psychological characteristics are important as well. Reviewing research, Christoph Heinicke identifies three qualities that provide "an optimal parenting environment": feelings of self-esteem; the capacity for positive mutuality in relationships, especially with the partner; and the capacity for flexible problem solving.[7]

There is no magical age at which one is ready to become a parent. Although age is an indicator of one's ability to become pregnant and take on the parental role, the way one decides to become a parent reflects one's problem-solving skills and psychological maturity.

About two-thirds of children are actively planned.[8] Let us look at decision making in different groups of parents.

Married Couples

When couples become parents, the most important factor in understanding their decision and its effects is whether the partners agree on the decision. Carolyn Cowan and Philip Cowan identified four decision-making patterns.[9] *Planners* (52 percent) discussed the question and made a definite decision to have or not have a child. *Acceptance of fate* couples (14 percent of those expecting) had unplanned pregnancies that they accepted either quietly or, in many cases, enthusiastically. *Ambivalent* couples (about 26 percent) expressed both positive and negative feelings about being parents, with one parent leaning in one direction and the other parent leaning in the other direction. *Yes-No couples*, (about 10 percent) were in marked conflict about having or not having a child.

The couples' decision-making process regarding pregnancy was related to their problem-solving skills in other areas. Yes-No couples were less effective in solving everyday problems, just as they were less effective in deciding about the pregnancy. The decision-making process regarding pregnancy was also related to marital satisfaction over time. When couples plan the decision, regardless of whether they do or do not have a child, their marital satisfaction remains high following the birth or an equivalent time period. Couples who accept an unplanned pregnancy have a drop in marital satisfaction, but their initial level is so high that they are still as satisfied as the parents who plan the decision.

Marital dissatisfaction was most marked among couples who are ambivalent or in conflict but still have a baby. Ambivalent couples were not as high as the other couples in their initial satisfaction levels, and these levels dropped when they had a baby. Ambivalent couples who did not have a child retained a high satisfaction level. The Yes-No couples had the least satisfaction. Of nine Yes-No couples who had a child, seven had divorced by the time the child entered kindergarten. In all seven cases, the husband did not want a child. The two women who did not want to have children seemed better able to adjust, and their marriages continued.

Unmarried Parents

In 2000, one-third of births were to unmarried mothers.[10] Parents who have never been married form a heterogeneous group. Research has focused primarily on unmarried mothers, who include (1) young and older women who marry after the birth of the child, (2) young and older women who do not marry after the birth of a child, (3) women who adopt a child, and (4) women who have a child by assisted reproductive technology (ART, described later in detail). In addition, some unmarried lesbian and gay couples choose to have children by adoption or by ART, and some single fathers adopt or have a child by ART. We know much less about these groups than about unmarried women.

Many factors account for the increase of births to unmarried women.[11] They include the decreasing earning power of potential husbands and fathers; the general postponement of marriage and the increase in the divorce rate, both of which leave a greater number of women in their later childbearing years without a husband but with a desire for a child; the greater number of women with established incomes; and the public assistance available to single women. Data reveal that unmarried mothers as a group have few economic advantages. Further, government assistance is currently shrinking, thus reducing economic supports for unmarried mothers even more.

People think of unmarried mothers as being teenagers, but two-thirds of births to unmarried mothers are to women in their twenties and thirties, many of whom had their first child as an unmarried teenager.[12] Of women born in the 1960s, 70 percent of those who had their first birth outside marriage had all their children outside marriage. Births to unmarried women are more likely for women of lower socio-economic status, for women growing up in mother-only families, and for women in disadvantaged neighborhoods, in metropolitan areas, and in areas outside the South.

People tend to think that the typical unmarried woman having a child alone is an economically advantaged, professional woman like Murphy Brown, but statistics indicate the average unmarried woman is in her thirties whose living conditions resemble those of teenage mothers. Although almost half of such mothers worked 500 hours in the year prior to the birth of the child, about half were on welfare and not economically self-sufficient prior to the birth.[13]

Let us now look at the decision-making process in the different types of unmarried parents.

Unmarried Heterosexual Couples   About 40 percent of babies born to unmarried women are born to women living with the baby's father.[14] Though these unions are more unstable than marriages, research shows that within five years, 60 percent of such parents will marry, 12 percent will continue to live together, and 28 percent will separate. About 45 percent of children of these couples are planned, and having a child increases the rate of marriage.[15]

These couples have less education and lower earnings than do married couples but higher education and greater earnings than do single mothers. Compared with married couples, cohabiting men and women have more egalitarian attitudes toward gender and share the workload at home and responsibilities for earnings more equally.[16] Because relationships in stable cohabiting couples are much like those in married couples, it seems likely that they decide to have children in similar ways, though there is no research on this yet.

Lesbian and Gay Unmarried Couples   Three or four decades ago, most lesbian and gay parents were parents from a heterosexual marriage that had ended in divorce. They maintained relationships with their children when they formed same-sex partnerships.

More recently, through adoption or with the aid of assisted reproductive technology, lesbian and gay partners can choose to become parents.[17] Like heterosexual couples, lesbian and gay parents consider whether they have the economic resources and psychological readiness to provide care. In addition, they have to plan strategies for dealing with negative reactions and prejudice against their sexual orientation.

Though research in this area is limited, as many as 50 percent of gay men would like to become fathers.[18] Men who became fathers through adoption or surrogacy had higher self-esteem and fewer negative attitudes about homosexuality than did men who were not fathers. The group of nonfathers could be divided into those who wanted to be fathers and those who did not want to be fathers. These two groups did not differ in self-esteem or attitude about homosexuality.

To become parents, lesbian and gay couples need information about available resources on adoption or assisted reproductive technology. They also must consider the legal aspects of parenthood when one parent is the biological parent and the other is not and may therefore have no legally recognized bond to the child. These issues are best handled prior to the child's arrival.

Adolescent Single Parents   Recent longitudinal research concerning the early development of adolescents who become parents in the United States[19] and New Zealand[20] suggest that adolescent pregnancy occurs as a result of an accumulation of risks occurring over an extended period.

These risks fall into four categories: the adolescent mother's social background, early family relationships, individual personality characteristics, and peer relationships.[21] The social backgrounds of adolescents who become teen parents contain many risk factors such as being the child of an adolescent mother, living in a single-parent home with a parent who has little education, living in poverty, and living in a community with a high level of poverty and welfare assistance.

The family relationships of adolescent parents often embody change and conflict. Their parents are less involved and less affectionate than parents of teens who do not have teen pregnancies, and they provide less monitoring as well. With parental supervision, teens headed in the direction of deviant behavior tend to stay involved in school and avoid pregnancy.[22]

Children's characteristics are also related to later teen pregnancy. Following a sample of low-income children, researchers found that eight-year-old girls who were described by peers as aggressive or aggressive and withdrawn were more likely to be teen mothers than were those girls who were low or average on aggression and withdrawal.[23] In addition, the prospective mothers were more likely to have school and conduct problems in elementary and high school and were more likely to drop out.

Early maturation and high rates of sexual activity increase girls' chances of becoming pregnant as teens.[24] Girls with these risk factors have more gynecological problems and sexually transmitted diseases. They have also experienced more sexual abuse in childhood or early adolescence; in one study, 65 percent had been sexually abused—61 percent by several perpetrators.[25] Studies comparing adolescent mothers with teens who did not have babies have found that adolescent mothers are less independent, less certain of themselves, and less trusting of others.[26] They have a diffuse sense of identity and greater susceptibility to depression.

Teen mothers tend to have peer problems at early ages. Because of their aggressiveness, they are often rejected by the other children. As adolescents, they often have deviant friends who engage in rule breaking and high-risk behaviors.[27]

Most studies of adolescent parents have focused on mothers, because the fathers of their babies, in about 50 percent of cases, are in their twenties or older.[28] More recent work, though, has followed samples of boys to determine the characteristics of those who become adolescent fathers. In many instances, they share the qualities of the mothers.[29] They are from low-income families in which parents often have problems with antisocial behavior. Their parents use ineffective disciplinary techniques and do not monitor the boys well. By early adolescence, these boys begin to engage in deviant, rule-breaking activities. They also have little academic success. Another study identified similar risk factors—lower socioeconomic status, poor school performance, early sexual activity, and drug use—but concluded that the accumulation of risks, not any one of them, was most predictive of adolescent fatherhood.[30]

Once pregnant, adolescent mothers have to decide whether to continue the pregnancy. About half decide to terminate it. Those most likely to make such a decision come from middle-class families; they feel support from family and friends for their decision.[31] Adolescent mothers who release a child for adoption—in one study, 4 percent—come from small, financially stable families. They have had academic success and see other alternatives for themselves. They have positive views of adoption and believe their mothers support their decisions.[32]

Adolescent boys and girls come to parenthood having experienced multiple negative experiences over time. We can view teen pregnancy as the outcome of an accumulation of many risk factors. Teen pregnancy itself triggers a host of difficult experiences, which the next section details. The prepregnancy qualities of teen mothers and the resulting stresses that adolescent parenthood brings combine to make the development of their children difficult.

Single Mothers   An increasing number of women are making the conscious choice to have a child alone.[33] About half the women in general surveys say they would consider having a child alone if they did not have a child with a partner by the time they reached their late thirties or early forties. Strong desires for a child along with the feeling that they have lost the opportunity to do this under the ideal circumstances of marriage to a loved partner spur women to consider this option.

We do not know the precise stages single mothers go through in making their decision to have a child. Merle Bombardieri, a social worker who holds workshops and counsels prospective single mothers, believes that a third of the women later decide not to have a child.[34] She believes that feelings of loss may cause the desire for a child, and she encourages women to discover and mourn any unresolved grief. When the loss is mourned, the desire for a child may well decrease.

A national organization, Single Mothers by Choice (SMC), holds sessions for prospective mothers and urges them to consider a variety of issues: their ability to support a child financially, to mesh family life and work, to face rearing a child on their own, and to provide a loving home for a child in the absence of a father.[35] Like Bombardieri, the group also urges women to mourn the loss of the ideal pregnancy prior to conception. One study in the 1970s indicated that single women are most likely to become parents when they can build a support system that enables them to combine work with rearing children.[36]

Coerced Parenting

While most parents accept unplanned children by the time of the birth, some parents undertake parenting because they are not permitted to have an abortion. What happens to their children? Unwanted children have a more difficult time.[37] In one study, children whose mothers had twice requested abortions to terminate the pregnancy had significantly more problems and less enjoyment in life than did children whose parents wanted them.[38] In elementary school, the unwanted children had fewer friends, more behavior problems, and poorer school performance even though they had equal intelligence. In adolescence, the differences between the two groups widened, and in young adulthood, individuals unwanted before birth were less happy with their jobs and their marriages. They had more conflict with coworkers and supervisors and less satisfaction with friends. They were discouraged about themselves and their lives, but many took the positive step of getting help for their problems.

Clearly, the decision to have a child and the reasons for doing so affect children and parents for years to come. For any kind of parent, being able to plan a pregnancy and have loving support in doing so gives their children the best start in life.

THE TIMING OF PREGNANCY

Among other decisions, prospective parents must consider how their age will affect their child—biologically, psychologically, and socially. As we have seen, teen pregnancy carries with it certain risks for both children and parents. Here we explore the timing of pregnancy in greater detail, focusing on both younger and older parents.

Age and Pregnancy

A mother's age influences the biological aspects of conception, the pregnancy, and delivery. For example, being either very young or over thirty-five is related to increased difficulties.

Adolescent Mothers   Although teenage mothers experience few difficulties becoming pregnant, they suffer more pregnancy complications and have babies with problems more often than do mothers in their twenties or early thirties. Prematurity and low birth weight, which increase the likelihood of cerebral palsy, mental retardation, and epilepsy in babies, occur most often in the babies of teenage mothers.

Two explanations have been given. One is the physiological immaturity of the mother and the other is the mother's psychosocial circumstances, such as having a less healthy lifestyle and poorer access to prenatal care. Although prenatal care improves the outcome, age still appears to be a factor.[39]

Biological risk depends somewhat on the ethnic background of the mothers. Whereas early childbearing age is related to greater risk in European American mothers, later childbearing (from ages eighteen to thirty-four) is related to greater risk in African American mothers, perhaps because their health declines as they get older.[40]

Older Mothers   The age of first-time mothers has been increasing. In the past, women over thirty-five having babies were usually having the last of their children; now, many mothers are having their first. In 2000, approximately 630,000 babies were born to women over thirty-five, and 20 percent of the babies were born to first-time mothers.[41] Factors that account for the growing number of older first-time mothers include feminism, a general postponement of childbearing, the large number of baby boomers in childbearing age, advances in contraception, better health among women, advances in reproductive technologies, and better obstetrical care.

Women over thirty-five more often have difficulties with conception of a first pregnancy. Spontaneous abortions increase from 25 percent at age thirty-five to 50 percent at forty-five,[42] and mothers over thirty-five have greater percentage of genetic abnormalities in the fetus, so screening for such abnormalities are routine for them. Like teenage mothers, older mothers have a greater likelihood of pregnancy complications such as diabetes and low birth weight babies, but these can be treated as they can be with younger women.

Assisted Reproductive Technology (ART)   Prospective parents, especially when older, can turn to special interventions when facing infertility. While infertility has traditionally been defined as the failure to conceive after a year of unprotected sex, a recent international study of fertility in 782 couples suggests that 91 percent of couples will conceive by the end of the second year of trying to conceive.[43] Couples, the investigators suggest, should not rush into fertility treatments after the first year of trying unless there is a specific reason to suspect infertility—for example, the woman has very irregular periods or either prospective parent has had a sexually transmitted disease.

Regardless of age, couples with no specific reason for failure to conceive will usually do so within two years. Women between 35 to 39 years of age had a 91 percent chance of conceiving if their partners were also under 40, but that rate dropped to 84 percent with partners over 40. This information contrasts with recent suggestions that women's fertility begins to decline in their late twenties, and men's, in their late thirties.

Interventions available to help infertile couples range from intrauterine insemination using father's sperm to surgery and the highly complex methods of assisted reproductive technologies.[44] The interventions can result in a child that is genetically related to both parents (when the parents' eggs and sperm are used), to one parent (when either the egg or the sperm is used), or to neither parent (when both donor egg and sperm are used).

Initially, ART takes the form of supporting natural processes by insemination and by chemically stimulating the ovaries to produce more eggs. In a more advanced method, the egg can be fertilized in a petri dish and then implanted in the uterus. This technique is used for women who have a blocked fallopian tube. More advanced techniques include introcytoplasmic sperm injection (ICSI), or injecting a sperm directly into the egg and then transferring the fertilized egg into the uterus. This has enabled many infertile men to become fathers.

Donor assistance takes several forms. There are sperm and egg donations and, more recently, embryo donations. Further, a surrogate mother (or birth mother) may offer to carry the fertilized embryo to term for the mother. The surrogate may also, but not necessarily, donate an egg for fertilization.

Sperm donations were the first form of donation, and have traditionally remained anonymous. For several decades, sperm banks provided healthy sperm that could be matched with the characteristics of the prospective parents. More recently, banks have asked donors whether they would be willing to be contacted when the child reaches age eighteen. Since the early 1980s, egg donations have also been available, through clinics. Because medications are used to stimulate and remove the eggs, egg donation is a more complicated procedure than is sperm donation. Perhaps for that reason, egg donors tend to be friends or relatives of the parents rather than anonymous donors, and they may well sustain an ongoing relationship with the parents.

Assisted reproductive technology and donor assistance were originally used to help couples, but these procedures have also enabled single women and lesbian and gay couples to have children. They can also help single men become parents of a child to whom they are genetically related.

Age and Parenting

Having children during adolescence presents many risks to parenting as well as pregnancy. Postponing parenthood until the twenties confers benefits on both parents and children.

Adolescent Mothers   Girls who become teenage mothers encounter more problems with fewer resources for meeting them than does the average parent. Birth to a teenage mother becomes one factor in a chain of events that predict long-term difficulties.[45]

As noted, babies of adolescent mothers are born with more problems than are those born to older mothers, and teenage mothers are less psychologically mature than are their age-mates and less effective in parenting. Compared with older mothers, they are less able to provide stable living arrangements, so their children experience more moves and changes in caretakers and male support figures.[46] Single parenthood increases the risk of poverty, but adolescent single motherhood confers an additional disadvantage to mother and child.[47] The exact reasons are not known, but lower educational attainment and the smaller likelihood of entering a stable, supportive marriage are two important factors. Ethnic origin also makes a difference. One study found that delaying parenthood to age twenty-five resulted in economic gain for European American women but not for African American women.[48]

Further studies found that African American mothers receive more support from family and friends than do Hispanic mothers.[49]

It is not surprising, then, that children of adolescent mothers are at greater risk for problems in development even if they are later-born children of teenage mothers. They are more likely to suffer from illnesses and to be seen in emergency rooms, even when families have medical coverage.[50] Infants and toddlers of teenage mothers do not differ from children of older mothers in cognitive measures; however, by the time they reach preschool age, differences begin to emerge and continue into the elementary school years, when they face a greater likelihood of academic difficulties, school failure, and behavior problems.[51] Teens of adolescent mothers are more likely than others to become teen parents (in one study, 40 percent of girls and 21 percent of boys); still, the majority of children of teenage mothers do not themselves become teen parents. Even when they delay childbearing, however, they are not as competent and well adjusted in early adulthood as are the children of those mothers who delayed pregnancy until their twenties.[52]

Although adolescent mothers and their children have many problems, diversity of outcome is a striking finding of many studies. Table 6-2 lists the protective factors that increase success for these mothers, along with risk factors that impede

■ **TABLE 6-2**
RISK AND PROTECTIVE FACTORS FOR CHILDREN OF ADOLESCENT MOTHERS

Risk Factors

1. Living in poverty with attendant problems of frequent residence changes, living in high-crime and high-violence areas, and experiencing changes in caretakers and male support

2. Birth complications: prematurity, low birth weight

3. Poor parenting from mothers

4. Behavior and school problems

5. Less social support from relatives and friends

Protective Factors

1. Being a boy

2. Having an easy, adaptable temperament

3. Having intelligence and problem-solving skills that lead to better coping

4. Mother continuing her education

5. Mother limiting number of subsequent children

6. Mother entering a stable marriage

7. Mother having high self-esteem

Adapted from Joy D. Osofsky, Della M. Hann, and Claire Peebles, "Adolescent Parenthood: Risks and Opportunities for Mothers and Infants," in *Handbook of Infant Mental Health,* ed. Charles H. Zeanah, Jr. (New York: Guilford Press, 1993), 106–119.

success. Indeed, many adolescent mothers in the United States and New Zealand[53] overcome their problems. Not surprisingly,

> The invidious stereotype of the adolescent childbearer underestimates young mothers' chances of recovery. . . . Ironically, part of the handicap of being a teenage mother may come from a widespread perception that failure is virtually inevitable—a belief that may become a self-fulfilling prophecy.[54]

Parents over Thirty-five   Although older mothers face difficulties in conception, they have many advantages as parents. Compared with younger mothers, they have more education, higher-status jobs, and, as a result, greater incomes with more money available to spend on their children.[55] Further, older parents tend to be in more stable marriages and to be more attentive and sensitive parents. Yet older parents' work and community responsibilities make incorporating an unpredictable, time-consuming young child into their lives more difficult. (Table 6-3 lists some suggestions for older parents.)

HOW THE WAY OF BECOMING A PARENT AFFECTS PARENTING

In the past there were two ways an adult could become a parent—marry and conceive and bear a child with a partner or marry and adopt a child with a partner. Assisted reproductive technologies and changes in adoption policies now offer adults other ways to become parents. What do the changes mean for the process of

■ **T A B L E   6-3**
GUIDELINES FOR OLDER PARENTS

1. Be open with children about your age and reasons for postponing children. Lying and avoiding the issue cause children to feel shame or embarrassment about your age.

2. Make a special effort to understand your children's world, as it may seem very different from the one in which you grew up.

3. Connect your children to extended family members. If this is not possible, provide an extended support network of friends who serve as uncles, aunts, grandparents.

4. Stay physically fit and energetic so you can share physical activities such as hiking and camping with your children. If you cannot participate, then see that children join friends and other adults in these activities.

5. Most important, balance the time you spend on work and nonfamily commitments with your family's needs so your children feel they are an important part of your life.

Adapted from Andrew Yarrow, *Latecomers* (New York: Free Press, 1991).

parenting? Are parents who naturally conceive and bear biological children warmer and more effective than parents who use ART to conceive and bear children who may be genetically related to only one parent? Are parents who adopt children genetically unrelated to them less attached and less caring than parents of genetically related children, as research with stepparents and stepchildren might suggest? Does the experience of infertility leave parents with feelings of insecurity and low self-esteem that make parenting more difficult? This section looks at the influence of the means of becoming parents on the process of parenting itself.

Adoption and Parenting

Like many aspects of parenting, adoption has undergone many changes in the last two or three decades.[56] Between 2 and 4 percent of children in the United States are adopted, about half are adopted by biological relatives and other kin such as step-parents, and about half by adults not biologically related to them. This section focuses on those children adopted by people not related to them.

Changes in the Nature of Adoption   Historically, adopted children tended to be the offspring of single women and were adopted shortly after birth by a married couple. In the latter part of the twentieth century, fewer babies were available for adoption because abortions decreased births to single women, and more single women kept their babies because single parents had become more accepted.

Parents wanting to adopt a child looked to other sources for children. They looked at transracial adoptions within the United States (discouraged in the 1970s and 1980s but less so in the 1990s); they considered adopting children with special needs, defined as older children or children with special physical or emotional needs. Adopting parents also began to look to orphanages in Europe, Latin America, and Asia. The number of visas issued for immigrant orphans rose from 8,000 in 1989 to 19,000 in 2001.[57] Asia and Latin America are the areas from which adopted children most often come today.

Adults previously excluded from adoption—older, single, gay or lesbian, disabled, or poor adults—are now approved for adoption.[58] Preliminary research indicates that these adoptive parents experience great satisfaction in their roles as parents and have good placement outcomes. Children adopted by single parents do as well as those adopted by young couples, even though single people tend to adopt more difficult children. In addition, legislation has enabled foster parents to adopt children in their care.

In the past, adopting parents had limited or no information or contact with biological or birth parents. In recent times, however, adoptive and birth parents have been allowed access to greater information about and more contact with each other. In some instances, the birth mother selects the adopting parents and maintains ongoing contact with the child and the family; the adopted child is sometimes included in the birth mother's family and activities. More-open adoption has helped remove the element of secrecy from the adoption process. *All* his or her parents can know what is happening to the child, and the child can know them all as well.

This greater openness about adoption, along with greater awareness of the adoption process as a result of the adoption of children from other countries, has improved people's perceptions of adoption and adoptive parents. Some companies offer parental leave for adoption. Celebrities talk about their own experiences as adopting parents or adopted children, and children from other countries talk about their two cultures of origin. Children are now less likely to be teased and made to feel different because they are adopted.

All these changes have enabled more parents to adopt more children in a better atmosphere than before. We deal with the special issues of adoption as they arise in the course of development—for example, the transition to parenting later in this chapter, telling children about adoption in Chapter 8, and forming positive identities in Chapters 8, 9, 10, and 11.

Transracial and International Adoptions   Studies of children adopted in the United States and growing up with parents of different ethnic backgrounds than themselves find that many children function well, but some report identity confusion.[59] This is greatly reduced when parents provide experiences that enable children to develop a positive racial identity, as parents adopting children from other countries are required to do.

When parents adopt children from other countries, they must meet all the criteria for adoption in that country as well as those of the state in which they live. Currently the Hague Convention on International Adoption is seeking an internationally agreed-on set of criteria to safeguard children's rights.

A major concern of parents centers on the emotional trauma children may have experienced in orphanages or other settings prior to adoption and the effects of such trauma on attachment and later psychological development.[60] Research shows that the longer the children have spent in institutional care, the more likely children will have intellectual and emotional problems; nonetheless, with major support from parents and professional help, such children improve substantially over time.

In families with transracial or international adoption, parents' forming a new family ethnic identity eases adjustment.[61] Parents become knowledgeable about any special problems children may face and serve as advocates for them. Most important, they provide experiences that connect not just the child, but the whole family, to the child's group of origin. This may mean learning a new language or new customs, celebrating new holidays, or living in new areas where there are more families of the child's origins. Such a child needs models of the culture and opportunities to have friends of his or her group of origin. Currently, organizations form tours to countries where children were adopted, in order to acquaint children with the geographical regions and, in some instances, with birth families, though this is rare because no records usually exist.

Parenting Behaviors of Adopting Parents   Many adopting parents come to parenthood with sadness at not having a biological child and anxiety from the intense scrutiny they have undergone to determine their suitability as parents. One can imagine their feeling self-conscious and uncertain in their parenting behaviors.

However, a study comparing the parenting strategies of parents who adopted a child at birth, parents who relied on donor insemination and ART, and parents who conceived a child naturally found few differences among the parenting behaviors of the three groups.[62] When children were between four and eight, adopting mothers did not differ from mothers of naturally conceived children in warmth, sensitivity, or attachment to their children. Mothers using donor insemination and ART were warmer and more involved than were the other two groups. Teachers and psychiatric evaluation judged children in the three groups as functioning equally well, with no problems.

When their children were twelve, the adopting parents continued to have warmth and control similar to that of parents of naturally conceived children. Again, psychiatric evaluation and teachers' assessments indicated that children, too, continued to function well in all three groups, with no significant differences among them. Mothers of adopted children, however, described their children as having fewer peer problems than children in the other groups but more conduct problems of rule-breaking and aggressiveness. A more objective assessment did not present such a picture. Thus, the parenting behaviors of parents who adopted a child at birth seem quite similar to those of parents who have naturally conceived a child.

In nonclinical samples of children in the community, research has found little difference in the behaviors of infants and toddlers of adopting and nonadopting parents. In contrast to the study mentioned earlier, other studies of elementary school children have found that teachers rate adoptive children as less socially, emotionally, and academically mature as peers.[63] These differences in the behaviors of the two groups continue into adolescence.

Studies of adult functioning of adopted children reveal that by early and middle adulthood, adoptees resemble adults reared in biological families.[64] In a study comparing adult adoptees with friends, the two groups were similar with respect to life satisfaction, purpose in life, intimacy, and substance use.[65] The adopted adults, however, reported lower self-esteem than did friends, though the difference of 1.5 points was small, and greater depression. More of the adopted sample (30 percent) fell in the clinical range of depression than did the sample of friends (19 percent), but 70 percent of the adopted adults fell within the normal range when the figure for the average sample was 80–85 percent. A factor in the findings was the greater variability among the adopted sample, in part related to whether the adult was seeking his or her biological family. Adopted adults seeking their biological families reported lower self-esteem and greater depression than did other adopted adults. Still, all adopted adults expressed insecurity about adult attachments. They formed relationships with peers but expressed greater discomfort in the relationships than did their friends.

David Brodzinsky and Ellen Pinderhughes caution that focusing on the problems of adopted children obscures the real benefits of adoption for children.[66] Recall from Chapter 1 that the biological children of parents at risk for petty criminality adopted early in life and reared by adopted parents not at risk for petty criminality had less than one-third the risk of these behaviors in adulthood as did children reared by their at-risk biological parents.[67]

INTERVIEW
with Steve and Michelle

Steve and Michelle, already the parents of a four-year-old boy, had twins, a boy and a girl, with the help of a gestational surrogate mother. They were delighted to be interviewed about their experiences doing this. Their son had been age three and Michelle had been eight and a half months pregnant with a girl when the placenta ruptured, after which they lost the baby, and the operation to save her life eliminated the possibility of her carrying another child.

Steve: We were devastated, and had grief counseling that gradually transitioned into counseling about how to have another child. We explored adoption and went to seminars about adopting children from China, South America, and we also explored surrogacy. We went to two different agencies and had interviews, and decided to try surrogacy, and if that was unworkable, then adoption.

Michelle: We chose an agency in which all the women in charge—the owner, the lawyer who drew up the contract—had children by surrogate parenting. It was a very carefully run place. All the surrogate mothers, and their husbands—most were married—had to be screened psychologically. The surrogate mothers had to have given birth to at least one child and had a smooth pregnancy and delivery. They were paid to do it, but if money were the primary goal, then they could not be surrogate mothers. They could not have big debts either. We also were screened for psychological stability.

Steve: We almost balked about the way the owner wanted to choose the mother, but we went along with it. We could look at a book of surrogate mothers and pick a few we definitely liked, and a few we did not want, but the owner would make the final match for the first interview. If we didn't think the person would work, she would choose someone else. The reason she did this was so prospective parents would not be interviewing a number of people trying to decide on a person. When we questioned her about this method, she said, "Trust me," and she hit a home run. She picked Anisa. We all had dinner together—the owner and her husband, Michelle and I, and Anisa and her husband. It was a social occasion, and there was almost no discussion of surrogacy.

Anisa was charming, and she was a dream surrogate. She was from a Seventh Day Adventist family so she was a vegetarian, only occasionally had any caffeine, and she had a healthy lifestyle. Also, she was a billing clerk in an obstetrics and gynecology office of a husband and wife team so she had constant access to a medical support network. The woman M.D. was her best friend, and she took a great interest in the pregnancy, too.

Most surrogates are picky about the couple they do this for, and most want a "virgin" couple. They want to bring the first child into the world for a childless couple, to provide them something they could not have otherwise. We already had a child, but Anisa wanted to help us have a sibling for our son. She has been very close to her sister, and she wanted to provide that kind of relationship for our son. After the dinner, we all felt positive about going ahead, so we had a meeting to settle the parameters of the relationship. We had to decide how many times to try, how many babies she would carry. The cost of one child would be $15,000, with an additional charge of $5,000 for twins. We knew we would be happy with twins as twins run in the family, and Anisa agreed, but we all left any more than that for later discussion.

We also had to decide what kind of relationship we would have afterwards. All of us wanted an ongoing relationship. She is an important person in our lives. We see her a few times a year, and every holiday she sends the children gifts, and we always send her flowers or gifts at holidays.

Michelle: We had to go through the process of in vitro fertilization. I had to take fertility drugs to stimulate the ovulation of eggs, but I had done that with our son. Anisa had to take drugs to suppress her cycle so it matched mine, and she had to take drugs so that she could be receptive after my eggs were harvested, fertilized, and ready for the transfer to Anisa. If there are too many embryos that are surviving after the transfer, you have to decide what to do. Three embryos were seen on the first ultrasound, but a week later, there were only two so we were very happy with twins.

During the pregnancy, I talked regularly on the phone with Anisa. She lives about 200 miles from here. I would call and see how things were going. I never had any worry about her taking care of herself as she worked in a medical atmosphere and knew how important diet and sleep were. Sometimes I'd tell her, "Oh, go out and get a new maternity outfit." Her husband was such a low-key guy. I don't know that a lot of guys would go along with her carrying someone else's children. He was an unsung hero. We never worried she would want to keep the children. She had two girls, and the babies were always referred to as "Michelle's babies," and she was carrying them because I could not.

Steve: The labor and delivery were very smooth. About a month before, she had to go to the hospital for a day, but she carried the twins to eight and a half months. She was in the delivery room, our parents were there, our aunt, Anisa's parents were there, and her husband. We drove down, and David, our son was with us, but he had been exposed to chicken pox and could not go into the maternity ward. So, someone was always with him.

Michelle: With David, I had a painful labor of fifty hours, but Anisa was sitting in the labor room, calm, with an occasional "Ooh." Then the doctor said, "You're ready," and she hadn't moaned or screamed or anything. She was completely calm and casual, like it was nothing. It was so amazing to me how easy it was for her. That first night Anisa and I spent the night with the twins in the hospital. The next morning I went to the motel and got a nap and David and Steve were at the hospital. When I went back, the doctor said, "Everything is perfect. Do you want to take the babies home?" Anisa's daughters came and saw the babies, and we took pictures.

Steve: It was an emotional time for everyone. Anisa was happy because it was so successful. It was a risk to offer someone that. We were thrilled to have the twins, and they slept all the way home.

Michelle: We were on an emotional high for a year because it was such an amazing thing, and we wanted everyone to know about it. And there is more use of surrogacy than you would think. Once you begin to talk about it, you find that many people have been involved. I was talking to someone at work who was visiting here, and he made the comment, "Ever since my wife did surrogacy for a neighbor," and went on to describe something. Friends offered to be surrogate mothers, but we decided to get an objective third party.

How do the twins, now five, understand Anisa's role?

Steve: The counselor told us that young children understand helping, and we told them that Mommy made the babies, but she needed help to get them to birth—her tummy could not carry them so Anisa helped us and carried the twins to birth.

Other studies comparing adopted children with children who were reared by parents who had considered giving them up or were ambivalent about keeping them found that adopted children functioned better.[68] Adopted children also functioned better than children living in institutions or long-term foster care, and better than children living in poverty.

Adoption clearly provides benefits to children, even though children will have to deal with whatever mysteries exist about biological parents or have a more complex path to identity formation, as we shall see in later chapters.

ART and Parenting

Recall that children born through assisted reproductive technology may be genetically related to one, both, or neither of their parents. Major studies carried out primarily in Europe found that whether parents rely on in vitro fertilization or donor sperm, their parenting behaviors resemble those of parents who naturally conceived their children.[69] Even though parents have experienced numerous anxieties about having children and numerous medical procedures, these difficulties do not detract from their parenting. In fact, when compared with parents who naturally conceived children, mothers in donor insemination families were described as warmer, more sensitive, and more responsive when children were in early elementary school and again at age twelve. Children in these families thought their mothers were as warm as other mothers. Interviewers described fathers in donor insemination families as more detached in matters of discipline when children were twelve, but mothers and children did not perceive any differences in these fathers' behaviors. Teachers' ratings and psychiatric assessment of the records revealed that the children in all these groups were equally competent and as socially skilled as children reared by parents who had had no difficulties in conceiving.

At present, not much research on children conceived through egg donations exists.[70] Research that has included families with anonymous egg donors indicates no difficulties in parenting. We lack results on families in which egg donors are known to families.

Legal and ethical issues have arisen in this area. Should the fertilized embryos of mother and father be implanted in the mother after the parents divorce? Should frozen sperm or eggs be used after divorce to create children? Should models advertise and sell eggs? Should clinics help women in their sixties become pregnant, although they might not live long enough to raise the child?

A paramount issue is whether children of donor conception have the right to know this fact and learn about their biological origins.[71] At this point, few are told. While secrecy during childhood seems to have no effect on the child's functioning and well-being, adults who learn they have other biological parents often grow angry. They feel deceived about their roots and motivated to find the donor.

The American Fertility Society recommends telling children about their origins. In England, the law permits children to request nonidentifying information about the donor at age eighteen, and in Sweden, individuals conceived by donor eggs or donor sperm have the right to identifying information at age eighteen and can contact the donor if they wish. In the United States, the tendency in the past has been not to tell children, and records have been destroyed, but currently there is a move to adopt the policies of Sweden. The Sperm Bank of California, for example, already requests permission from donors to give children identifying information when they are eighteen, and 80 percent of donors have agreed. The first children have recently reached eighteen, so we shall soon see how this works out.[72]

The desire for greater openness is supported by studies of open adoption (adoptions in which the birth parents continue to have contact with the child and the adopting parents) that reveal that a lack of secrecy and a better understanding of one's biological parents have improved the adjustment of adoptive children.[73] The situation of children of donor eggs and donor sperm is not exactly comparable to that of adopted children, as a biological parent did not "give them up" but instead helped create them for their rearing parents. Still, knowing about a donor and the fact that one can have contact with this person later in life may eliminate the anger and the feeling of a missing biological connection that some adults of donor sperm or donor eggs feel.

So, these studies indicate that genetic ties between parent and child are not necessary for satisfying, committed parenting and the effective functioning of children. In addition, the feelings of loss that parents experience when they cannot conceive a biological child do not interfere with later satisfying and effective parenting. Indeed, these parents appear more committed, more emotionally involved with and appreciative of their children, perhaps because they have had a more difficult time becoming parents. As one mother said, "Every night I stand in each of my children's rooms for a few minutes, watching them sleep, and recall the terrible childless years. I came so close to never having them. I am humbled by, and deeply thankful for, the miracle of my children."[74]

TRANSITION AND ADJUSTMENT TO PARENTHOOD

The arrival of a baby changes every aspect of married life, from finances to sex life, sleeping habits, and social life. Although many first-time parents report that nothing could have adequately prepared them for the experience, knowing what to expect can still help parents cope.

Parents' Preparenting Personal Characteristics

There tends to be continuity between parents' preparenting characteristics and their relationships with their own infants, which, in turn, affect the infant's subsequent development. The kinds of early experiences that promote effective parenting in men and women include those that promote adaptiveness, autonomy, and flexibility in both parents.[75] When parents feel secure and competent as individuals and worthy of care themselves, they tend to be responsive, caring parents. For example, according to research, pregnant women who had positive relationships with their parents envisioned themselves as confident mothers; later, they interacted with

INTERVIEW
with James Levine

James Levine is the director of the Fatherhood Project at the Families and Work Institute. He served as a principal consultant to Vice Present Al Gore in drafting the federal initiative on fatherhood, created by executive order in 1995.

As a result of your work regarding fathering, do you think that, on average, fathers bring special qualities to parenting?

That's a difficult question in the field. Do they bring something different, and if they do, is this culturally or biologically determined? I think what fathers bring that is different centers on two dimensions. First, there is a fair amount of research that fathers' interactive style with young children is different from mothers'. With young children, they have a more rough-and-tumble style. On average, dads whoop it up with little kids. They chase them, throw them up in the air, roll around with them. Ross Parke has a theory that this type of interaction has some relationship to how children relate to the social world outside the family.

The second dimension I think is really important is father is a man and knows what it is like to be a man in this society, what it takes. While my wife and I can guide our children in terms of basic values, there are some ways I can talk to my son about what the world expects of him and what it has felt like to me to be a man in this society, what the expectations are of men and women. I also share that perspective with my daughter. So my wife and I bring a different storehouse of experience to parenting, different ways of being in the world based on the way the world expects us to play roles as men and women.

What are the best ways to get men involved in parenting?

There are several issues. I think the absolute key is the couple's expectations of what the father's role will be. If the mom doesn't expect the dad to be involved, and the dad doesn't expect to be involved, that's a prescription for noninvolvement. If Mom doesn't expect Dad to be involved and Dad might want to be involved, he won't be involved. The mother is the gatekeeper in the relationship. Many women say they want husbands to be involved, but in effect, they want them to be involved as a sort of mom's subordinate or assistant. Mom's the manager, telling Dad how to be involved as opposed to assuming Dad will be involved and will learn the skills to be a father. It is important for mothers to back off and be in the background, and let fathers be with children.

So, one key to involvement is the couple's dynamics. I don't mean to blame Mom, but there is a system here—men and women as a system—and one starts here in terms of making a supportive system for fathers' involvement.

Then let's look at men in terms of men and the system outside the couple. All the research we've done shows that men today define success on two dimensions—being a good provider and, equally important, having good relationships with children. So if you look at the values men bring to parenthood, there are generally agreed-on desires to have close relationships with their children. But, aside from the couple relationship, there are two obstacles. Men sometimes feel incompetent as to how to do this; they need skills. And, second, their work sucks them up in spite of their best intentions to give time to relationships with children. They spend a lot of time working, not to avoid forming relationships with children but as a way of caring for children.

A key to change is changing the cultural clues men get about being fathers. Looking at this from an ecological and systems point of view, we can ask, "What are the cues that men get about parenting across the life cycle?" The expectations others have about them have a lot to do with shaping their behavior. For example, prenatally if men get expectations from the health care system that they are expected to be at prenatal visits, they will be there. Mostly, however, they get the message they have no role during the pregnancy. Yet, research has shown that one of the best predictors of good prenatal care for the mother is whether the partner is involved with prenatal care.

We have found in our work with low-income men that when men understand how vital their role is even before the child is born, they can change their level of involvement. Knowing how important their role is with their babies increases the motivation of low-income men to be involved.

So at the time of birth and afterwards, if the pediatrician sends messages that he or she wants both parents at visits—"I need to know both of the baby's parents. I want to see you both, not just the mother"—that message shapes the father's behavior. Same thing at preschools or day care. They can also send messages that they want both parents, not just mothers, to be involved.

So it is the expectations that are embedded in daily interactions that are the real keys to fathers' involvement. If you look at the face-to-face interactions with maternity nurses and pediatricians, embedded in dialogues with doctors, health care providers, and teachers are messages about expected involvement. If more messages expect fathers to be involved and daily interactions offer support for fathers' involvement, fathers will be involved.

To give a specific example, West Virginia wanted to increase the rate at which fathers established paternity of children born to single mothers, and the question was how to do that. One could think about a big public-information campaign with messages to encourage involvement, but the key was the maternity nurse, who had the most influence on both the young man and the young woman. The father would come and look at the baby, and if the nurse assumed he was some bad guy and chased him away, if she did not invite him in to be involved with the baby, he would disengage and disappear. They increased the rate of paternity establishment by increasing the dialogue with fathers and also by changing what the nurse said to mothers. The nurse told mothers it is important for children to be involved with their fathers even if mothers decide not to marry the fathers. In two years, the rate of establishing paternity went from 15 percent to 60 percent of fathers who claimed paternity of babies born to single mothers.

The overall message to fathers was we want you here, we want you to establish paternity and be fathers to your children. Changing expectations encoded in daily interactions are the important elements in increasing fathers' involvement with their children.

their babies in such a way that the babies grew more competent in social and motor skills.[76] Also, as we saw in Chapter 2, parents who had a continuing positive attachment with their own parents tended to be responsive caregivers with their own children.[77]

The Power of a Positive Marital Relationship

Throughout this book, we shall see that a positive marital relationship sustains both parents as they care for their children. Further, a positive marriage is related to children's healthy growth.

When mothers and fathers feel support from each other, their competence as parents increases and interaction with the baby becomes more effective. Father-infant interactions and fathers' competence, particularly, are related to feeling support from mothers (see the interview with James Levine). Even basic activities are influenced by the quality of the marriage. Mothers experience fewer feeding difficulties when their husbands are supportive and view them positively, whereas marital distress is related to inept feeding by the mother.[78]

Intimate emotional spousal support is related also to parents' satisfaction with themselves in the parental role and with the baby. When parents are happy with each other, they smile at the baby more and play with the baby. Babies profit from this atmosphere of positive regard, growing more alert and gaining more motor skills. Conversely, a conflicted marital relationship decreases both partners' ability to function effectively as parents, which in turn affects their children.[79] We discuss this in greater detail in a later chapter.

Just as positive attachment to one's own parents promotes effective behavior with infants, so it promotes secure attachment to one's marital partner.[80] However, an imperfect relationship exists between early childhood experience and attachment to the partner, and frequently one partner can influence the behavior of the other partner in the direction of becoming more secure. Philip Cowan and Carolyn Cowan found that when a person who had an insecure attachment to his or her parents in childhood married someone with a secure history, the insecure partner took on the parenting style of the more secure partner and became calmer, warmer, and more positive. This is most likely to happen when an insecure mother is married to a secure father. An insecure father is less likely to pattern himself after his wife.[81]

What constitutes a positive marital relationship? One contributor to marital satisfaction is related to parents' agreement on role arrangements.[82] It does not matter whether couples are traditional or egalitarian in their division of tasks; satisfaction increases when couples have similar ideologies.

A second contributor to marital satisfaction is a couple's ability to communicate with each other—to express thoughts, feelings, and needs in ways each partner can hear and respond to. Communication does not have to be verbal. A look, a gesture, a touch, or an action can communicate support, agreement, or the need for further conversation.

Parents who focus on what is good about the situation or the action of the other person, who avoid negative criticism and angry exchanges, feel less stress and create less stress for each other. These parents discuss different points of view and express themselves forcefully, but they stay focused on how they can make needed changes and improve the situation, and they avoid assigning blame for problems.

Changes the Baby Brings

A great deal goes on during the early months. Parents are highly involved in the nurturing stage of parenthood,[83] caring for the child, and accepting their new role as parents. They worry, "Am I doing okay?" "Am I the kind of parent I want to be?" Gradually, parents incorporate other parts of their lives—work, extended family, friends—into their caretaking activities.

Parents may find it difficult, however, to give each other the support that is so crucial in coping during this period. A significant number of new mothers report specific problems, including (1) tiredness and exhaustion; (2) loss of sleep, especially in the first two months; (3) concern about ignoring husband's needs; (4) feeling inadequate as a mother; (5) inability to keep up with housework; and (6) feeling tied down.[84] Mothers did not anticipate the many changes that would occur in their lives when their babies arrived, in part because they did not realize how much work is involved in caring for an infant. Fathers had a similar ordering of complaints: (1) loss of sleep for up to six weeks; (2) need to adjust to new responsibilities and routines; (3) disruption of daily routines; (4) ignorance of the amount of work the baby requires; and (5) financial worries (62 percent of the wives were employed prior to the child's arrival and only 12 percent afterward). Husbands make such comments as "My wife has less time for me" and "Getting used to being tied down is hard."

The new father may see the infant as a threat to his relationship with his wife and to their lifestyle. Concern about the amount of time, money, and freedom the baby will surely consume can obscure the joy he expects—and is expected—to feel. No more candlelit dinners, or even impromptu decisions to go to a movie or to make love, not for a while. The father has not had the physical experience of carrying the baby for nine months, nor is he as likely to be as involved as the mother in the care of the newborn. For a while, at least, the needs of the baby will come before the wishes of the husband—and those needs will be frequent and unpredictable, delaying meals and interrupting sleep. Almost all fathers and mothers, however, find that emotional attachment to their babies grows and deepens if they are patient and caring.

Dimensions Underlying the Transition

Two longitudinal studies—one carried out by Carolyn Pape Cowan and Philip Cowan[85] and the other by Jay Belsky[86]—have yielded remarkably similar findings on the basic dimensions underlying the adjustment process. First, a major determiner of the ease of the adjustment process is parents' ability to balance their needs for autonomy and self-care with the need to be close to other people, particularly their spouse and child. Parents who balance concerns for "me" and for "you" and create an "us" relationship that has priority over individual needs face an easier transition. They put aside immediate wants in order to help their partner, because

■ **TABLE 6-4**
DIMENSIONS UNDERLYING THE TRANSITION TO PARENTHOOD

1. Capacity to balance individuality and mutuality

2. Communication skills of both parents

3. Attitude (positive/negative) in confronting situations and people

4. Expectations about what the baby will bring

5. Ability to devise sharing of workload that is compatible with couple's beliefs/ideologies concerning appropriate behavior for men and women

6. Ability to come to terms with patterns of behavior learned in family of origin

7. Ability to manage conflict effectively

Adapted from Jay Belsky and John Kelly, *The Transition to Parenthood* (New York: Delacorte, 1994); Carolyn Pape Cowan and Philip Cowan, *When Partners Become Parents* (New York: Basic Books, 1992).

that improves their relationship. A husband may put aside his desire to go visiting as a family, because his wife is tired and needs to rest, and he wants them both to feel good about the outing. Or a wife may not ask her husband to skip his evening jog to help with the baby, because she feels he needs to unwind from work, and she wants a relaxed family atmosphere when he is with the baby.

Other dimensions are listed in Table 6-4. Those parents most at risk for difficulties are unrealistic about the changes a baby will bring, have negative views of their partner and their marriage, and are pessimistic about solving problems. They take no action to arrive at mutually satisfying solutions to their difficulties.

Both Belsky and the Cowans agree that transitions vary by gender. Although men and women have many common experiences—both find the baby irresistible, both worry about bills and the increased work, and both feel better about themselves as a result of parenthood—they experience the transition in different ways. For one, the experience is much more physical for women than for men. Because women have a biological connection with the child during the pregnancy, labor, and delivery, the child is a greater reality to them, and many maintain the intimate physical connection with the child by breast-feeding. Men experience the pregnancy and the early months after birth from a greater distance and often feel left out. Lacking the close physical connection with the child, fathers often need more time to form a strong attachment with the baby.

In most instances, couples navigate the transition well, not because they have fewer or less serious problems than the couples who experience difficulties, but because they have developed effective ways to cope with changes and resolve conflicts.

These domains were identified through studies of couples, but they apply to the transitions of single parents as well. Single parents have to form a supportive network of individuals who can help. Whether their support group is made up of friends or family, single parents have to share with these individuals their expectations and feelings; they must all find ways to divide the workload, manage conflict, and avoid negative outbursts.

Transition for Parents Who Adopt or Who Have Premature Children

In addition to the usual stresses of the birth of a baby, parents who adopt or have premature children face additional challenges. Unlike most parents, who have nine months of preparation for parenthood, parents who adopt or have premature births are often plunged into parenthood in unpredictable ways. Adopting parents may have waited months or even years for a child when suddenly the child arrives with little warning, perhaps ill or stressed at all the changes. Workplaces may be unaccommodating, and friends may ask many questions. Adopting parents may also worry that the birth mother will change her mind.

Fortunately, adopting parents have buffers. These parents tend to be older, with all the advantages of older parents described earlier in this chapter. Compared with younger parents, they are more settled in their work, have greater financial resources, have been married longer, and have developed better coping skills.

Parents of premature children may have little or much to manage. If children are only a few weeks premature, parents may have no problems. If a child is born at twenty-four or twenty-six weeks after conception, however, the child might stay in the hospital for an extended period of time. His or her parents must consider whether the child will survive and whether long-term problems will develop. They also face the ongoing stress of dealing with hospital and medical personnel and the changing medical status of their child. Further, when the child comes home, they may need to make many changes to address the special needs of their child.[87]

Parents of premature children are advised to interact with them and to take over as much care of their children as possible in the hospital.[88] Touching, talking to babies, and carrying them in pouches or slings increases the well-being of both parents and their premature babies (see Chapter 7 for more).

In these special circumstances, all the ways listed for couples to ease the transition to parenthood are important. Support from friends or from new friends dealing with similar situations, clear communication between parents and between parents and professional workers are especially essential.

PRACTICAL QUESTION: WHAT CHANGES CAN PARENTS ANTICIPATE FOR THEMSELVES?

Parents continually develop new behaviors as they rear their children and as they deal with their frustrations as parents. So, it is not surprising that creating these new responses leads to permanent changes in parents themselves. Yet, there has been relatively little research on parents' changes as a result of parenting.

Ellen Galinsky, a consultant and lecturer on child development, found herself changing after her children were born. Curious about the meaning of her feelings, she consulted books and research reports to see what other parents were describing. Finding little to inform her, she began forming groups of parents of young children. She then interviewed 228 parents with different experiences of parenthood—married, divorced, step-, foster, and adoptive parents. These parents did not represent a random sampling but were a broad cross-section of the population.

Galinsky has divided parenthood into six stages in which parents focus their emotional and intellectual energy on the task of that period.[89] These stages differ from most in that a parent can be in more than one stage at a time with children of different ages. The first stage, occurring in pregnancy, she terms the *image-making* stage. It is a time when parents prepare for changes in themselves and in their relationships to others. The second, *nurturing,* stage goes from birth to the time when the child starts to say "no," about eighteen to twenty-four months. As parents become attached to the new baby, they arrange their lives to be caregivers, balancing their own and their child's needs and setting priorities. The third, *authority,* stage lasts from the time the child is two to four or five. Parents become rule givers and enforcers as they learn that love for children goes hand in hand with structure and order. From the child's preschool years through adolescence, parents are in the *interpretive* stage. Children are more skilled and independent, and parents establish a way of life for them, interpret outside authorities such as teachers, and teach values and morals. In brief, they teach children what life is all about.

When their children are adolescents, parents enter the *interdependent* stage. They form new relationships with children, and, though they are still authorities, their power becomes shared with children in ways it was not in past years. In the sixth stage, *departure,* parents evaluate themselves as their children prepare to leave home. They see where they have succeeded and where they might have acted differently.

Galinsky summarizes her views of how parenthood changes adults:

> Taking care of a small, dependent, growing person is transforming, because it brings us in touch with our baser side, it exposes our vulnerabilities as well as our nobility. We lose our sense of self, only to find it and have it change again and again. We learn to nurture and care. We struggle through defining our own rules and our own brand of being an authority. We figure out how we want to interpret the wider world, and we learn to interact with all those who affect our children. When our children are teenagers, we redefine our relationships, and then we launch them into life.
>
> Often our fantasies are laid bare, our dreams are in a constant tug of war with realities. And perhaps we grow. In the end, we have learned more about ourselves, about the cycles of life, and humanity itself. Most parents describe themselves as more responsible, more accepting, more generous than before they had children.[90]

SUPPORT FOR PARENTS

Various kinds of support can help parents adjust to parenting. When parents successfully meet the demands of their new roles, they feel competent and effective. These feelings of self-efficacy can continue, influencing ongoing parenting in beneficial ways. Family and friends provide informal sources of support as well as information, advice, and direct help in the form of shopping, cleaning, and cooking so parents can get some rest. Other, more formal sources of support consist of classes support groups.

Classes

Most couples are referred to classes at hospitals or in the community prior to the arrival of the baby. Even programs given in hospitals at the time of the birth can provide information that increases parents' competence in caring for their babies. Such information focuses on babies' states and their repertoire of behaviors, the ways they send signals to parents, and how parents learn to understand and respond to the signals. Especially helpful are tips on when to "engage" with babies (when they are fed and alert), when to "disengage" (when babies turn away, fall into a drowsy state), how to feed infants, and how to deal with crying.[91]

A recent study found that brief behavioral training can be useful for both parents and infants.[92] First-time parents attending childbirth classes were routinely assigned to one of two groups. During pregnancy, one group received four sessions of behavioral training in helping their newborn develop healthy sleep patterns. The control group had equal discussion time with instructors but no behavioral training. When infants were six to nine weeks old, investigators collected six measures of sleep patterns over several weeks. Infants of trained parents had longer sleep episodes, fewer night awakenings, and fewer night feedings. Trained parents experienced less difficulty with their babies and felt more competent and confident in managing babies' sleep patterns. In contrast, nontrained parents reported a greater number of hassles in caring for their infants.

Support Groups

The Cowans have found that couples groups were very helpful to new parents.[93] Six groups of four couples each met weekly for six months, beginning in the last trimester of the pregnancy. These groups, led by husband-wife pairs, provided ongoing support for parents. The groups also told fathers that they were essential participants in the parenting process. Table 6-5 lists some suggestions for making the transition to parenting less stressful.

Couples discussed the stresses of adjusting to parenting and found reassurance in learning that others have similar problems. The couples discussed activities or attitudes that reduced stress and that produced well-being and closeness between parents. The Cowans found that all the couples who were in the six-month groups at the time of the birth were still together when the child was three years old, whereas 15 percent of couples who had not been in the groups were divorced. When children were five years old, the divorce rate was the same for the two groups.

When parents conceive a child and bring him or her into the world, they embark on possibly the most life-changing experience of their lives. Whether well or poorly planned, the child elicits new behaviors from parents and at the same time brings a host of new pleasures to them. When parents can work together with each other or

■ **TABLE 6-5**
RECOMMENDATIONS TO COUPLES FOR EASING
THE TRANSITION TO PARENTHOOD

1. Share expectations.

2. Give yourselves regular checkups on how each is doing.

3. Make time to talk to each other.

4. Negotiate an agenda of important issues; if one partner thinks there is a problem, there is.

5. Adopt an experimental attitude; see how solutions work and make modifications as necessary.

6. Don't ignore sex and intimacy.

7. Line up support for the early stages after the birth.

8. Talk with a friend or coworker.

9. Find the delicate balance between meeting your needs and the baby's needs; children grow best when parents maintain a strong positive relationship.

Adapted from Carolyn Pape Cowan and Philip Cowan, *When Partners Become Parents* (New York: Basic Books, 1992).

with supportive friends and relatives, when they communicate expectations, experiences, and feelings as they care for the baby, the baby brings parents and friends and relatives closer together to share life experiences in a more intense, meaningful way than previously known. Babies demand a great deal, but they give much in return.

MAIN POINTS

People's reasons for wanting children include
- love, affection, and stimulation
- creative outlet, proof of adulthood, and sense of achievement
- proof of moral behavior and economic utility

The decision to be a parent involves
- assessing parental readiness in terms of time and psychological resources
- couples' planning children and resolving differences
- single adults' planning children
- accepting a child if unplanned
- resolving ambivalence so the child is wanted, not rejected

Changes in adoption policies and assisted reproductive technologies

- mean that people who would have been childless in the past can now have children
- raise questions about children's rights to know their biological roots

Timing of children

- depends on the psychological qualities of parents rather than their age
- affects a child's later adjustment—if parents are not mature, a child may develop later problems, as happens with children of adolescent mothers
- has resulted in negative stereotypes of teenage mothers and positive views of older ones

The means of becoming parents

- has little effect on parenting strategies
- has no documented effect on children's functioning and competence

Babies bring

- new routines and responsibilities
- great pleasures
- a special appreciation in parents who experienced infertility

Dimensions underlying a parent's transition to parenthood include

- balancing individuality and mutuality
- communication skills
- positive attitudes
- agreed-on division of labor
- parents coming to terms with their own childhood experiences

Parents experience greater ease in the transition when they

- maintain intimate bonds with their partner or a supportive friend or relative
- share expectations, feelings, and workload with partners
- line up support from friends and relatives
- adopt an experimental attitude toward solutions—trying them and seeing if they work

EXERCISES

1. Think about why and when you want children. List factors influencing your decision—school, health, financial, and work considerations of yourself and your partner. What are your positive reasons for having children? What supports will you need? Do you think it will be as hard for you to be a parent as it was for your parents?

2. Describe your expectations of parenthood. What changes will it require of you? Do you think your expectations are realistic? Describe the activities that you do now that might prepare you for being a parent—taking a course in parenting, learning to solve conflicts in a positive way, practicing communication skills with friends, learning about children and their needs. Are there other things you could be doing?

3. Plan out the support system you would organize for yourself and your partner if you were having a baby in three months. Whom would you include? How involved would your relatives be? How much extra expense would such a system create?

4. Imagine you are a fifteen-year-old girl who becomes pregnant and wants to keep her child. Investigate the resources in your community that would enable you to keep the child, remain in school, get a job. Visit the programs or day care center where your child would be cared for. Are the services adequate?

5. Imagine you and your partner required donor insemination or egg donors. Investigate the resources in your area and the requirements for people using them.

ADDITIONAL READINGS

Belsky, Jay, and Kelly, John. *The Transition to Parenthood*. New York: Delacorte, 1994.

Cowan, Carolyn Pape, and Cowan, Philip. *When Partners Become Parents*. New York: Basic Books, 1992.

Furstenberg, Frank F., Brooks-Gunn, J., and Morgan, S. Philip. *Adolescent Mothers in Later Life*. New York: Cambridge University Press, 1987.

Pertman, Adam. *Adoption Nation*. New York: Basic Books, 2000.

Yarrow, Andrew. *Latecomers: Children of Parents over 35*. New York: Free Press, 1991.

CHAPTER

7

Parenting Infants:
The Years from Birth to Two

CHAPTER TOPICS

In this chapter you will learn about:

- Parenting the newborn
- Development in the first two years
- Parent-child relationships
- Parenting strategies to maintain an optimal arousal level and promote self-regulation
- Support for parents

IN THE NEWS

New York Times, December 19, 2002
In 2001, the number of babies born prematurely (before thirty-seven weeks gestation) rose to a twenty-year high of 12 percent. This may result from an increase in multiple births caused by fertility drugs. See page 216 for details.

 Go to PowerWeb at:
www.dushkin.com/powerweb
to read articles and newsfeeds
on **infancy, infant development, toddlers,** and other topics related to this chapter.

What are babies like? How do they respond to the world? How do they relate to parents and shape what parents do? How do parents encourage babies' development and competence? What strategies do parents use if babies are born prematurely? Who and what support parents in their important roles as caregivers of the next generation?

When babies come into the world, they must depend completely on adults for their survival. Rudimentary reflexes, such as sucking and grasping, enable babies to adapt to their new world, but they rely on caregivers to provide the food, warmth, and soothing that they need to grow in their new environment. This chapter describes the parent-child interactions that promote growth and competence in the first two years of life.

THE NEWBORN

During the first three months, babies' body rhythms and states are not organized. Their irregular systems gradually settle into a more organized pattern, usually by six months.[1]

After birth the average baby sleeps about eighteen hours a day, waking every three or four hours to eat. However, some babies sleep up to twenty-two hours, and some as little as ten hours. Sleep is of two kinds. Infants spend about 50 percent of their sleep time in active, *REM sleep* (rapid eye movement sleep, sometimes termed *dreaming sleep*), and 50 percent in *non-REM quiet sleep* (when the body is relaxed and still). Over time, the percentage of REM sleep decreases, so that by age two, only 35 percent of sleep is of this kind. Over the first six to twelve months, sleep becomes organized into a longer period of eight to twelve hours at night, with two naps during the day, totaling about sixteen hours per twenty-four-hour day, on average.

Babies also cry and appear distressed some of the time. They show great individual differences in crying, however. In one study of newborn nurseries, babies cried from one to eleven minutes per hour. The average daily total per baby was about two hours of crying. Hunger and wet diapers were significant causes, but the largest single category of causes was "unknown." The crying may have expressed a social need for cuddling, warmth, or rhythmic motion.[2]

Infants' crying increases to about three hours per day at six weeks and tends to be concentrated in the late afternoon or evening hours.[3] Crying decreases to an average of one hour a day at three months. Though hunger seems to be the predominant cause, "unknown" remains the second-highest category for this age.

Early Social Reactions

Babies come into the world preprogrammed to respond to human beings.[4] They see most clearly at a distance of 8 to 10 inches, the average distance of a parent's face from the baby when being held. Babies show an early preference for objects that in any way resemble a human face—even a circle with a dot or two for "eyes." They hear best in the range of the human voice. Infants a few hours old respond to the cry of another newborn and then often cry themselves. Babies also move in rhythm to human speech.

Newborns are observant. When less than a week old, they can imitate an adult's facial expression of sticking out a tongue, fluttering the eyelids, or opening and closing the mouth.[5] This suggests that a newborn has a rudimentary sense of self as a human being capable of imitating a person and has the motor control to do it.

VOICES OF EXPERIENCE

What I Wish I Had Known about the First Two Years

"I remember when we brought him home from the hospital, and we had him on the changing table for a minute, and I realized, 'I don't know how to keep the engine running.' I wondered how could they let him go home with us, this little package weighing seven or eight pounds. I had no idea of what to do. I kind of knew you fed him, and you cleaned him and kept him warm; but I didn't have any hands-on experience, anything practical. In a way I would have liked them to watch me for a day or two in the hospital while I change him to make sure I knew how to do it. It's kind of like giving me a car without seeing whether I could drive it around the block." FATHER

"I wish we had known a little more about establishing her first habits about sleeping. The way you set it up in the beginning is the way it is going to be. Having enough sleep is so important. We went too long before we decided to let her cry for five minutes. Then she got into good sleep habits." FATHER

"I wish I had known how it would change things between me and my husband. The baby comes first, and by the time the day is over and he is in bed, we have two hours together, but I just want to curl up and take care of myself." MOTHER

"I wish I had known about how much time babies take. It is like he needs twenty-four-hour attention. For an older parent who is used to having his own life and is very set in his ways, it is hard to make the changes and still have some time for your own life." FATHER

"She had this periodic crying at night in the beginning, and you are caught in the raging hormones and somehow I thought if I just read Dr. Spock again or if I read more, I'd understand it better. And we joked about reading the same paragraph in the book over and over. We needed reassurance it would end, and at three months it ended. That was the hardest part." MOTHER

"Someone said when you have a child, it's like two appointment books—his appointment book and yours. And first you do everything in the kid's appointment book; and then when you're done, you do everything in the kid's appointment book again. I wish I had known they weren't joking. I knew that it would be a challenge, and in some ways I wish I had known more. But in other ways I think if I had really known exactly how hard it would be sometimes, I might have been more reluctant or waited longer, and that I would really have regretted—not doing it." FATHER

"I wasn't prepared for all the decisions. Is it okay if he does this or not? He's trying to do something; shall I step in so he doesn't hurt himself or shall I let him go? It's making all those choices, making sure what I feel." MOTHER

"I wish I had known what to do about climbing. He climbs all over everything. I have the living room stripped bare, but I wonder if this is the right thing." MOTHER

"I wish I had known how much time they needed between one and two. They are mobile, but they are clueless about judgment. I think it was one of the most difficult times. Even though she did not get into a lot of trouble, sticking her finger in the light sockets, still she takes a lot of time and watching, so the transition to two was great." MOTHER

Early Parent-Child Relationships

In addition to feeding babies, keeping them warm, and seeing that they sleep, parents soothe babies and regulate their physical system. A major way to do this is through physical contact with the infant.[6] As noted in Chapter 2, physical contact with mothers regulates infants' hormonal levels, sleeping and eating patterns, and heart rate. Increased physical contact, such as mothers' using Snugglies to carry newborns, also promotes mothers' sensitivity and responsiveness to their babies and contributes to secure attachments between infants and mothers.

Infant-directed speech and music provides another way to soothe and regulate babies' arousal state.[7] In recent research with premature babies in neonatal intensive care units, playing lullabies for brief periods during the day reduced babies' stress by masking hospital noises. With less stress, babies' sucking rates, weight gain, and oxygen saturation increased, and they left the hospital more quickly. Music therapists' or mothers' singing or talking directly to babies reduced stress more effectively than did recorded music.

Shortly after birth, full-term babies also respond to the lyrical qualities of mothers' speech directed to them and to the rhythms of human conversation, as well as songs sung directly to them.[8] Music seems to promote not only an optimal level of arousal but social communication and closeness as well.

In their early interactions, parents shape infants' emotional reactions, encouraging positive moods and smiling and discouraging negative moods with phrases such as, "Don't cry" or "Don't fret."[9] Babies respond to parents' emotional reactions and pattern their own after what they see parents do. Infants as young as ten weeks old mirror mothers' emotional expressions; they respond with joy and interest to mothers' happy faces, with anger and a form of fear to mothers' angry faces, and with sadness to mothers' sad faces.[10] Babies pattern their moods after mothers' moods on a more ongoing basis as well. Over time, mothers' positive expressions are related to increases in babies' smiling and laughter.[11]

As the infant's system settles down in the first two to three months of life, parents begin to engage their baby in a social dialogue during face-to-face interactions.[12] Sensitive parents adjust their behavior to the rhythm and tempo of the baby, looking for periods of alertness and readiness to respond. In face-to-face interactions, parents wait for their baby to look at them before they talk, tickle, or play games. Babies as young as three months old develop expectations about how interactions proceed, and they become distressed if these expectations are not met. For example, when a parent of a three-month-old adopts a still, impassive facial expression, the baby responds negatively and often tries to elicit the anticipated reaction by smiling or vocalizing.[13] If this does not work, the baby turns away. Similarly, if a parent arrives when the baby is distressed over a routine such as a diaper change and does not attempt to soothe the child, the baby protests.

Influencing the behavior of others who respond in return establishes babies as social partners with parents. At the same time, parents recognize babies' increasing role as active participants who have individual preferences and unique behavioral preferences. As partners, parents and babies interact and adjust to each other; they create mutual understanding and *intersubjectivity,* or a shared state of meaning.[14] In the state of shared meaning, the baby uses the parent as a *social reference* for responding to experience. For example, babies will not play with a toy if the mother has looked at the toy with disgust.[15]

Babies' temperaments and emotional reactivity influence the social dialogue between parent and child. When babies adjust well to change and are easily soothed when upset, parents can regulate the babies' environments and conditions reliably and consistently. However, when babies are fretful, easily upset by change, and difficult to soothe, parents find it harder to provide this consistent regulation, and both partners in the dialogue become frustrated.

DEVELOPMENT IN THE FIRST TWO YEARS OF LIFE

Observers have identified three periods of major reorganization in babies' development over the first two years of life.[16] They occur at about three months, seven to nine months, and eighteen to twenty months and are related to neural changes that enable babies to become more efficient learners and more effective social partners. In this section we discuss babies' physical, intellectual, language and emotional development, as well as development of self, at these stages.

Physical Development

On average, the baby grows from about 21 inches at birth to about 33 inches at the end of two years, and birth weight increases to about 29 pounds. Growth, however, involves more than an increase in size and weight; it includes increasing organization of behavior as well.

As just noted at about three months, changes occur in the nervous system. Increased myelination of nerves in cortical and subcortical neural pathways and an increase in the number of neurons improve the child's sensory abilities and bring greater stability and control of behavior. The nervous system appears more integrated. Babies seem to settle down, with greater organization of bodily functioning. Voluntary, coordinated behaviors replace reflexes as the latter gradually disappear. Babies are more awake during the day and at night drop into a quiet sleep before dreaming.

Eight months brings changes in physical development that underlie several changes in behavior. Increased myelination of neurons occurs in the motor area, in areas of the brain controlling coordination of movement, and in areas responsible for organization of behavior. At about this same time, most babies develop the capacity to sit alone. Next comes control of the trunk, which leads to creeping and crawling. Babies now can move rapidly in all directions. Finally, walking replaces crawling sometime between ten and eighteen months.

Locomotion enormously affects babies' exploratory and social behavior.[17] When babies crawl and move around their environment, they can look at, touch, and manipulate objects. Exploration triggers new social reactions to babies. When infants reach out for objects, mothers often begin to name what they are touching and to describe features of the objects, and so babies' language increases. Because babies can now initiate interactions with others more easily, locomotion also brings social changes. Crawling babies often get close to adults, crawl in their laps, and smile and vocalize more at them.

After the first year, motor abilities become more fine-tuned. Walking and running become automatic; reaching and grasping, more refined. This increase in skills enables toddlers to explore the environment more carefully than before.

Intellectual Development

Physical and intellectual development are closely intertwined in the early months and years. To learn about the world, the child must be able to come in contact with it by getting around, exploring objects, and seeing how they work.

As noted in Chapter 2, Jean Piaget believes that, in the first two years of life, the child is in the sensorimotor period of development, in which perceptions and motor activity are the sources of knowledge.[18] Infants gradually move from interests in their own bodies and actions to interest in actions involving people and objects in the environment. Toward the end of the first year, they begin to imitate others in simple actions, such as waving bye-bye. Imitation becomes more sophisticated in the second year. At about eighteen to twenty-four months, toddlers develop representational thought that leads to greater language development and more complex responses to the environment. L. S. Vygotsky, too, emphasizes the importance of language for intellectual development. Children guide their behavior with words that, with age, become inner speech that becomes thought.[19]

Parents' main role in their children's intellectual development is to provide a stimulating environment children can explore, the freedom to act and learn, and models that guide children and help them reach their full potential.

Language Development

Lois Bloom believes that language enables people to express their intentions (their thoughts, feelings, and desires) to achieve intersubjectivity with others important to them.[20] In her view, the child's drive for expression is what motivates language development. Because language involves the communication of thoughts and feelings important to people, language is closely intertwined with social, emotional, and cognitive development.

The earliest forms of communication are infants' emotional reactions—their smiles, frowns, cries. Parents who read these signals can, for example, distinguish a cry of anger from one of pain or hunger. Gradually, babies develop cooing, then babbling and the repetition of syllables as in *ma-ma* or *da-da-da*. Parents and infants develop a social dialogue. Even before they have words, babies capture adults' attention, take turns, and communicate when they babble and coo with adults. Their sounds have inflections that express happiness, requests, commands, and questions. A single word like *mama* can be a question, an order, an endearment, or a request.

Children's first words pertain to objects, people, and experiences important to them. Words describe what their feelings are about. They also usually refer to events in the present. With advances in cognitive development, words refer to past and future experiences as well.[21]

From the beginning, children use words to explain feelings, but they do not label their feelings until about age two. By the beginning of the third year, toddlers talk about positive feelings such as being happy, having a good time, feeling good, and being proud. They talk about negative emotions as well—being sad, scared, or angry. They talk about uncomfortable physical states—being hungry, hot, cold, sleepy, and in pain.[22] Aware of others' feelings as well, toddlers develop ideas about what actions cause feelings and what actions change feelings. Here are some comments from twenty-eight-month-olds: "I give a big hug, Baby be happy." "I'm hurting your feelings 'cause I mean to you." Toddlers also learn that one person's feelings can stimulate another person's actions. "I cry. Lady pick me up." "I scared of the shark. Close my eyes."[23]

Cognitive development in the second year provides children with more-complex thoughts to communicate. Thus, Bloom believes, the two-word sentence emerges to enable children to communicate their intentions and reactions to the world.[24]

Emotional Development

Emotional reactions are a central part of babies' lives; even in the earliest months, infants have a range of facial expressions that change every seven to nine seconds.[25] Infants also have characteristic emotional responses, such as joy or irritability, some of which persist over time.

As noted earlier, mothers begin to guide and shape babies' emotional reactions in the first three months of life. Mothers of boys appear more responsive to them than to daughters and match their sons' behaviors more often as well.[26]

Babies respond to others' emotional reactions and pattern their own after what they observe. They not only pattern their moods after parents' reactions but also modify their behavior on the basis of adults' emotional reactions. Confronting what appears to be a visual cliff, ten-month-old babies look to mothers' facial expressions for guidance. When mothers smile, babies continue to crawl, but when mothers look fearful, they stop.[27] As we have seen, when mothers look at toys in a disgusted manner, babies refuse to play with them.[28]

By the end of the first year, babies express interest, surprise, joy, sadness, anger, fear, and disgust.[29] In the second year, feelings become refined and stronger in all areas.

Self-Regard Toddlers gain a clearer sense of themselves as individuals. They enjoy their activities and take pleasure in their accomplishments. Unconcerned with others' reactions, they do not appear to make value judgments about their own actions.[30] Children have a beginning sense of standards, as seen in their looking for recognition when they have done something well, turning away when they have not succeeded, and showing distress and making repairs when they have broken something, even accidentally. Still, their main response is one of delight in what they do.[31]

Empathy Toddlers go beyond the infant's crying at others' distress—they take action.[32] They touch, cuddle, and rub the injured party or try to bring the child something he or she would like. Many go through a process of referring the pain to themselves. If a mother bumps her arm, the child rubs the mother's elbow and then his own. Compassionate action follows self-referencing behavior. Investigators suggest that true kindness may depend on the ability to relate others' distress to one's own.

Toddlers do not express as much concern when they are the cause of distress. They intervene to help or remedy the situation, but they do not feel guilty for causing the problem. Toddlers' concern is most frequently directed to family members, particularly to mothers, who receive much of their toddlers' comforting and helping.

Anger   Parents want most to understand children's anger. Florence Goodenough found that many factors influence the occurrence of anger.[33] Outbursts peak in the second year and are most likely to occur when children are hungry or tired (just before meals and at bedtime) or when they are ill. Thus, when reserves are down for physical reasons, tempers flare. Outbursts are usually short-lived—most last less than five minutes—and, with young children under two, the aftereffects are minimal. With increasing age, children tend to sulk and to hold on to their angry feelings. From one to two years, the immediate causes of anger seem to be conflict with authority, difficulties over the establishment of habits (eating, baths, bedtime), and problems with social relationships (wanting more attention, wanting a possession someone else has).

In the study, parents of the children who had the fewest outbursts were consistent, used a daily schedule as a means to an end, and had a tolerant, positive home atmosphere. They established consistent and fair rules. With realistic expectations that children would be independent, curious, and stubborn, they anticipated problems and found ways to prevent them. These parents tried to help children conform by preparing them for changes in activities. They announced mealtimes or bathtimes in advance so children had ten minutes or so to get ready. In these homes, parents focused on the individuality of the child. When a real conflict arose, however, they were firm.[34]

Parents of children with many outbursts were inconsistent and unpredictable, basing decisions on their own wants rather than the child's needs. These parents tended to ignore children's needs until a problem forced them to respond. In some of these families, parents imposed a routine regardless of the child's activity of the moment and forced the child to act quickly in terms of their own desire. Criticism and disapproval characterized the home atmosphere.

In short, when children are tired, hungry, or sick, they tend to respond with anger. Parental behaviors that reinforce attachment—acceptance, sensitivity to children's needs, and cooperativeness—minimize temper outbursts.

Ways to Handle Negative Feelings   Toddlers have several ways to handle negative feelings. They use words to express their feelings and to get feedback from parents about how to manage them.[35] They enlist parents' and caregivers' help in resolving the negative feelings and different situations they cannot handle. They call or pull parents to whatever they want fixed. Toddlers also use objects to handle negative feelings. They frequently use transitional objects like stuffed animals, blankets, pieces of cloth, or dolls to provide comfort in times of distress. The use of such objects peaks in the middle of the second year, when as many as 30 to 60 percent of children have them.[36]

Happiness and Affection   Toddlers feel joy in learning and the free use of their abilities. While they most enjoy pursuing their own goals, they also enjoy meeting adults' expectations. In one laboratory study, toddlers played in a mildly interested way with toys, but when adults asked them to do easy, interesting tasks, such as arranging the toys in a certain way, the toddlers did so quickly and enthusiastically.[37] Later, when allowed to play freely with no adult involved, they happily repeated the tasks. The researchers concluded that toddlers derive great pleasure from matching their actions to the words of another, and the pleasure of accomplishing a goal is a powerful motive for their obeying commands.

Affection also increases in this period. Toddlers pat, stroke, and kiss their parents, particularly mothers. They are also affectionate to animals and younger children.

Development of the Self

Integrating current research and theory, Susan Harter describes how the self begins to evolve in the first years of life.[38] From birth to four months, the infant gradually establishes predictable, satisfying patterns of eating, sleeping, quieting, and arousal. In responding to caregivers and reacting to the surrounding world, the infant develops a rudimentary organization and integration of the perceptual and sensorimotor systems and gains a first sense of self and others.

In the period from four to ten months, the infant becomes more differentiated from the caregiver in social interplay and begins to develop an interpersonal self. As this period progresses, infants form attachments to caregivers, thus experiencing an increasing connectedness to others. At the same time, infants act on the world in more complex ways and begin to get a sense of their own ability to affect objects— make a mobile move, shake a rattle. Caregivers who react positively to babies' bids for attention increase babies' sense of control over events. The regularity and consistency of babies' feelings in response to others' behaviors—for example, delight from tickles and being thrown in the air—or in sharing emotional states with others help babies develop a sense of themselves and what they can expect in interactions with others.

From ten to fifteen months, babies become increasingly differentiated from caregivers and find a greater sense of themselves as agents who make things happen. Though attached to parents, they move off, using parents as secure bases for exploration in the world.

From fifteen to eighteen months, a "me-self" develops. Toddlers begin to internalize how others respond to them—that is, they start to react to themselves as others do. Children at this age recognize themselves in a mirror, identify photographs of themselves, and respond strongly to others' responses to them.

From eighteen to thirty months, toddlers develop a greater understanding of what influences others to act; as a result, they gain a greater sense of the separation between the self and others. Developing language enables toddlers to describe themselves and what they do. By age two, they use pronouns such as *I, me,* and *mine,* and they describe their physical appearance and actions—"I run," "I play,"

"I have brown hair." Besides reflecting a growing self-awareness, describing looks and actions also actually increases self-awareness.

Development of Self-Regulation

As we have seen, self-control begins to develop in the earliest days of life.[39] In the first three months of life, infants regulate arousal states of wake and sleep and the amount of stimulation they get. They also soothe themselves.

From three to nine months, infants modulate sensory and motor activities. Although they possess no conscious self-control yet, they do use motor skills to gain parental attention and social interaction. As they reach out, form intentions, and develop a rudimentary sense of self, their capacity for control begins to emerge.

From nine to eighteen months, infants show awareness of social or task demands and begin to comply with their parents' requests. As infants act, investigate, and explore, their sense of conscious awareness begins to appear. These trends continue in the second year.

Researchers observing year-old babies' obedience to their mothers' commands in the home found that babies obey their mothers' commands when the mothers accept and are sensitive to babies' needs.[40] Mothers who establish harmonious relationships with their babies, who respect them as separate individuals and tailor daily routines to harmonize with the children's needs, have babies who are affectionate and independent, able to play alone, and (even at one year) able to follow their mothers' requests. Thus, at this early age, a system of mutual cooperation between mother and child is established and maintained as each acts to meet the requests of the other.

Although children first show control by following the requests of others, they soon begin to inhibit their activities on their own volition.[41] For example, a toddler of fifteen or sixteen months may reach for an object, shake her head, and say, "No, no." Toddlers are most successful in avoiding forbidden activities when they direct their attention away from these objects or activities—looking elsewhere, playing with their hands, finding an acceptable substitute toy. A substantial number of two-year-olds can wait, alone, as long as four minutes before receiving permission to touch.[42]

THE PROCESS OF ATTACHMENT

In Chapter 2, we described attachment as an enduring tie that binds the child to the parent, who is a source of security for the child. We also saw that secure attachments promote a variety of positive behaviors. How do parents establish such a bond?

An analysis of sixty-six studies on infants' attachments to mothers (as mothers were the focus of most studies) found that *sensitivity,* defined as the ability to perceive the infant's signals accurately and respond appropriately and promptly to the child's needs, was a major but not the only contributor to the infant's secure attachment.[43] *Mutuality* (positive harmony and mutuality in relationship), *synchronicity* (coordinated social interactions), and *positive attitude* (emotional expressiveness, acceptance, and delight in the child) all contributed to the formation of secure attachments. So, when parents are sensitive, responsive, warm, accepting, and attentive to the rhythms of the child's behavior and individuality, they create a state of mutual understanding that fosters a secure parent-child attachment.

As children become toddlers, parents maintain a state of mutual understanding through continuing sensitivity and availability as a secure base for exploration. In this state of mutual understanding, parents go on to teach and guide children, balancing support and guidance with increasing independence for the child. The effective parent observes the child's level of interaction in a situation and stays, in a sense, one step ahead. When the child confronts a new barrier, the parent steps in to give just the amount of help that enables the child to solve the problem and move on. This form of guidance is termed *scaffolding,* or balancing the child's weakness (see Chapter 4).[44]

Research shows that mothers and fathers relate differently to infants in terms of both quantity of time spent and the kinds of activities engaged in with infants.[45] Data collected in the 1980s and 1990s showed that even though many mothers had jobs, they spent more time with children. In these studies, fathers spent, on average, only 40 percent as much time with children as mothers did.[46]

Data collected from a national representative sample in 1997 reveals that fathers in intact families now spend more time with children.[47] On weekdays, fathers of infants spent 60 percent as much time as mothers in activities and in being available for activities with infants, but on weekends, they spent 80 percent as much time. Fathers do proportionately less caregiving than mothers, but they spend exactly the same amount of time in social activities. In addition to caregiving, play, and social activities, fathers also do household activities and teach children.

Though they show different amounts of involvement, mothers and fathers are equally competent as caregivers.[48] Fathers can be as sensitive as mothers in their interactions with infants, reading and responding accurately to babies' cues. Babies drink as much milk in fathers' care as in mothers'. Mothers are more likely to hold babies in caregiving activities and to verbalize than are fathers. In fact, the mother's role has been described as providing a "holding environment" for infants as they regulate their system and develop increasing skills in interactions with people and objects in the environment.[49]

Fathers are more attentive visually and playful in physically active ways than are mothers.[50] Fathers are most likely to be highly involved in caregiving and playing when the marital relationship is satisfying and their wives are relaxed and outgoing. Both fathers and mothers give mostly care and physical affection in the first three months, when babies are settling in. As babies become less fussy and more alert at three months, both parents become more stimulating and reactive.[51]

TASKS AND CONCERNS FOR PARENTS OF INFANTS

Marc Bornstein describes four main tasks for the parents of infants:[52]

- Nurturant caregiving: providing food, protection, warmth, and affection

---

VOICES OF EXPERIENCE

The Joys of Parenting Children in the First Two Years

"I love babies. There is something about that bond between mother and baby. I love the way they look and smell and the way they hunker up to your neck. To me it's a magic time. I didn't like to baby-sit particularly growing up, and I wasn't wild about other people's babies, but there was something about having my own; I just love it. And every one, we used to wonder, how are we going to love another as much as the one before; and that is ridiculous, because you love every one." MOTHER

"There is joy in just watching her change, seeing her individualize. From the beginning it seemed she had her own personality—we see that this is not just a little blob of protoplasm here; this is a little individual already from the beginning. She has always had a real specialness about her. It was exciting to see her change." FATHER

"I think it's wonderful to have a baby in the house, to hear the baby laugh, sitting in the high chair, banging spoons, all the fun things babies do. They seem to me to light up a household. When there's a baby here, a lot of the aggravations in the household somehow disappear. Everyone looks at the baby, plays with the baby, and even if people are in a bad mood, they just light up when the baby comes in the room. I think there is something magical about having a baby in the house." MOTHER

"There is the excitement of baby talk becoming real words." MOTHER

"I enjoy that she directs me more than I could sense. Before, there was a 'yes' or 'no' response, but now there is more back and forth. If I dress her, she shows me she wants to sit or stand—'Do it this way' is what she seems to say. Before, she was tired or not tired, hungry or not hungry, okay or not okay. Now there is much more variation." FATHER

- Material caregiving: providing and organizing the babies' world with inanimate objects, stimulation, and opportunities for exploration

- Social caregiving: engaging and interacting with infants—hugging, soothing, comforting, vocalizing, playing

- Didactic caregiving: stimulating infants' interest in and understanding of the world outside the parent-child relationship by introducing objects, interpreting the surrounding world, and giving information

T. Berry Brazelton and Stanley Greenspan add that experiences must be tailored to the individual characteristics of the child and that both parents and children require a community that supports parents' efforts and children's growth.[53]

We look here at two main tasks of parenting: (1) establishing an optimal state of arousal for infants and (2) promoting infants' self-regulation.

"I've heard of this, and it's true; it's rediscovering the child in yourself. Sometimes, it's the joy that he and I hop around the couch like two frogs on our hands and knees. Or we're in the bathtub pretending we are submarines and alligators. Sometimes he likes to ride around on my shoulders, and I run and make noises like an airplane or a bird. And I am not just doing it for him, but we are doing it together, playing together." FATHER

"I was just blown away by the way he tries to help other children. From a very young age, he has done this. Now, when a little girl he sees every day cries, he takes her one toy after another and says, 'This is? This is?' meaning, 'Is this what you want?' until he gets her to stop crying by giving her something she wants. He's very people oriented, very affectionate, and seems so secure." MOTHER

"Watching her grow, seeing her grow, seeing the different stages, I just take pleasure in everything she does now, because I know she will be on to a new stage soon." MOTHER

"As he gets older, I relate more, play more. He is more of a joy. Some of the joys are so unexpected. I would stop myself and open up and think, 'Oh, this is my son, he's so joyful. He's smiling for no particular reason.' I am not that joyful, but he's joyful for no reason. He reminds me of joy." FATHER

"It's the first time in my life, I know what the term 'unconditional love' means. The wonder of this little girl and nature! I have never experienced anything like that. It is 'Yes,' without any 'Buts.'" FATHER

"When I was ten years old, my school had a program in which we spent a few hours a week with babies and toddlers. I will never forget the eyes of the babies. They were so clear and trusting. I felt good every time I looked in their eyes." PROSPECTIVE FATHER

Establishing an Optimal Level of Arousal

Reducing time spent in crying and establishing healthy sleep patterns promote a state of arousal that enables babies to respond to people and to the world around them. We saw in Chapter 3 that parents achieve these ends in ways that vary by culture. The interdependent model of parenting emphasizes close physical contact and a close relationship between parent and child, and the independent model emphasizes the child's growing independence and interest in the world.[54]

Although parents in the United States most often rely on the independent model of caregiving, emphasis on behaviors characteristic of the interdependent model has grown. Many U.S. mothers are following recommendations of the medical community to breast-feed babies for at least a year, and more parents are using Snugglies and slings to carry their children, as do parents in other parts of the world. So, let us look at which strategies work best to reduce crying and promote healthy sleep patterns.

Crying   As noted, crying increases at about six weeks and decreases at about three months of age. A thorough study of crying in the first year of life found that babies had as many crying episodes at the end of the year as at the beginning, but they spent much less time in each episode.[55] Each mother tended to be consistent in how much she ignored her baby's crying; however, the group showed a wide variation in this regard. For example, one mother ignored only 4 percent of the cries, while another ignored 97 percent. Although each mother's behavior was consistent from quarter to quarter, the crying of each baby was not consistent until the last two quarters.

In the first quarter, there was no relationship between the baby's crying and the mother's behavior. In the second quarter, a trend appeared that became significant in the third and fourth quarters. Those mothers who responded immediately to the cries of the baby had babies who cried less. Conversely, ignoring a baby's cries seemed to increase the amount of crying, measured by frequency and duration. Those mothers who responded most at the beginning of the year had less to respond to at the end of the year.

What strategy is most effective in terminating crying? Picking up and holding the baby stopped the crying 80 percent of the time. Feeding, which involves physical contact, was almost as effective. The least effective method was to stand at a distance and talk to the child.

In reviewing ways of providing comfort to crying babies, Judy Dunn found that caregivers around the world soothe by "rocking, patting, cuddling, swaddling, giving suck on breast or pacifier."[56] Effective techniques provide a background of continuous or rhythmic—as opposed to variable—sensations for the child. For example, constant temperatures, continuous sounds, and rhythmic rocking at a steady rate reduce the amount of time the infant cries. Effective soothing techniques also reduce the amount of stimulation the baby receives from his or her own movements. Thus, holding and swaddling reduce sensations from the child's flailing arms and legs and thus decrease crying.

Monitoring the crying of the babies from three to twelve weeks, investigators found that supplemental carrying in a Snuggly for three extra hours per day eliminated the peak of crying that usually occurs at six weeks, reduced crying overall, and modified the daily pattern of the crying so there was less in the evening hours. Equally important, babies who were carried more were more content and more visually and aurally alert. Supplemental carrying provides all the kinds of stimulation that we know soothe babies—rhythmic, repetitive movement with postural changes. Close physical contact also enables mothers to understand and respond to their infants better.

Another recent suggestion for soothing crying babies takes a different approach. In his clinical and research training, William Sammons has observed many different kinds of babies and gradually developed the belief that babies have the ability to calm themselves, given the opportunity to develop this skill.[58] Babies suck on fingers, wrists, or arms; get into a certain body position; or focus on certain visual forms such as walls, objects, or light to soothe themselves. In his pediatric practice, Sammons has encouraged parents to engage in a mutual partnership with babies so that the infants can find their own ways to calm themselves.

Parents can combine these two latest solutions to the crying problem by increasing the amount of carrying they do and, at the same time, letting the infants find ways to calm themselves when they do cry and fuss without an identifiable cause.

Sleep   Changes are occurring in the ways parents establish sleep patterns. In most parts of the world, infants sleep with a parent (co-sleeping), and most toddlers and older children sleep with or near a parent. Surveys reveal that in the United States, infants in middle-class families sleep alone or in bassinets or cribs near a parent, and by six months of age, most sleep in their own rooms.[59] In families of lower social status, however, a significant number of babies co-sleep with parents—in one sample, 80 percent of African American infants and 23 percent of European American infants slept with their parent or parents.[60] And now a growing number of middle- to upper-class parents are sleeping with their babies, perhaps to make breast-feeding easier at night, to reduce babies' crying, or to stay connected with the child at night.

As we noted in Chapter 3, babies' sleep is a matter of great importance to American parents. There are two general approaches to helping babies sleep. The first and more traditional one in the United States was put forth by Richard Ferber in 1985[61] and by Athleen Godfrey and Anne Kilgore in 1998.[62] According to this approach, as babies mature, most learn to put themselves back to sleep at night. So, babies need to develop habits of going to sleep that they can duplicate in the middle of the night to put themselves back to sleep. If they develop the habit of falling asleep while nursing or being rocked, they will be unable to duplicate those conditions in the middle of the night and will cry. The parents' job is to develop a regular routine that soothes the child, who is then put in the crib to fall asleep alone. Parents respond to crying with verbal soothing but no picking up. Parents then increase the length of time each night before providing the soothing, and the child's crying gradually decreases. When mothers in other countries are told of this method, however, they consider it abusive or neglectful to leave the child alone to sleep.[63] The other approach to helping babies sleep is that followed by the rest of the world—namely, having babies sleep with mothers or both parents. The babies may fall asleep near the parents or in the parents' bed, but they sleep most of the night with the parents.

Controversy attends the wisdom of co-sleeping. A recent report identified over 800 deaths associated with co-sleeping over the past eight years, either because of the parent's rolling over on the child or the child's being wedged between the mattress and the wall or the headboard.[64] The counterargument is that many more babies die of sudden infant death syndrome (SIDS) when sleeping alone, and that by co-sleeping, a nearby parent could perhaps detect breathing difficulties before death. Moreover, when babies co-sleep with mothers, they nurse more, and breast-feeding is thought to be protective against SIDS. Thus, environmental factors that promote breast-feeding are thought to reduce infant vulnerability to SIDS.[65] Those parents who want to co-sleep are advised to use an attachment to their bed where the child can sleep without risk of rollover or being wedged.[66]

Although many consider Ferber to be a staunch supporter of sleeping alone, he stated in a recent interview that his children slept in the same bed with him and his wife and had to be trained to sleep in their own beds.[67] In general, his feeling is that children can sleep with or without parents. "What's really important is that the parents work out what they want to do."

James McKenna, a biological anthropologist and the director of the Mother-Baby Behavioral Sleep Laboratory at Notre Dame, believes that co-sleeping regulates the infant's physiological system. "Biologically and psychologically, infants, children, and their parents are designed to sleep close."[68] He acknowledges that there are no systematic studies of the relationship of sleeping arrangements to children's developing personality characteristics, but studies are beginning to produce evidence of the benefits of co-sleeping. For example, one study described co-sleeping children as less fearful and better behaved than children who slept alone. A study of adults who, as children, co-slept with their parents suggested the adults had a feeling of satisfaction with life. They came from Hispanic and African American families in New York and Chicago. The study, however, found no simple outcome of co-sleeping; rather, co-sleeping as a child was seen as part of a relationship embedded in a cultural and social system related to adult characteristics.

In contemporary society, co-sleeping is one facet of a larger system of *attachment parenting,* which incorporates many aspects of the interdependent model of caregiving. The pediatrician William Sears encourages parents to accept their babies' dependency needs and meet them appropriately. He describes the five Bs of attachment parenting in infancy: (1) bonding with the infant at birth, (2) breast-feeding, (3) bed sharing (co-sleeping), (4) baby wearing (carrying the baby in a Snuggly or a sling), and (5) belief in the baby's cry as an important signal. The five Bs keep baby and parents physically connected so parents can learn who their child is and be able to respond in a sensitive, caring way.[69]

Sears raised his own children this way and has been counseling parents for twenty-seven years about attachment parenting. The number of attachment-parenting advocates is on the increase, perhaps because as more mothers work outside the home, they want to find ways to stay connected to their infants and young children. Advocates of attachment parenting believe it (1) simplifies life (parents have no bottles, cribs, or strollers to manage), (2) increases parents' sensitivity and responsiveness as they get to know their babies better, (3) promotes gentle discipline because children's natural tendencies to independence and self-control are allowed to develop slowly and gradually over time, and (4) focuses on the family's needs, not just the needs of parent or infant.[70]

> With attachment parenting, parents and children find their needs in cooperation with one another, thus creating a family-centered lifestyle. A key benefit of this responsive style of caregiving is that both parents and children feel that they are getting their "cup filled" as some parents say. Children feel whole and secure, while parents feel more relaxed and confident.[71]

Attachment parenting does not require that a caregiver be at home full-time, and there is much advice on how to combine attachment parenting and working. Parents are advised to create a community of caregivers who share the parents' values and will behave in the same way toward the baby when the parents are not there. Such caregivers would give breast milk the mothers have pumped, carry the children during the day, and respond quickly and attentively to children's cries.

Parents do many things to encourage children's compliance; they persuade children and guide them in what to do.

Advocates believe that "experienced attachment parents who have seen their children through early childhood and beyond describe this gentle nurturing style as a completely fulfilling way of life."[72] Research evidence certainly supports elements of attachment parenting—the importance of sensitive, responsive care and the decrease in crying that comes from increased early carrying—but it is not clear that co-sleeping and prolonged carrying of the child are beneficial, nor is it clear that immediate gratification of desires is essential or wise for all babies. Recall that soothed fearful and inhibited children maintained those behaviors when firm support to learn self-soothing appeared more useful in helping them overcome the behaviors (see Chapter 1).

Promoting Self-Regulation

In children's first eight or nine months of life, parents nourish and give physical care to babies, meet their needs, and help them regulate their functioning. Babies cooperate in the care, but parents are the more active partners, relying on their own sensitivity to understand what babies want. Now we turn to a task that parents find challenging and demanding—helping children develop the ability to control their own behavior.

Encouraging Compliance   Toward the end of the first year, babies' increasing motor and cognitive skills enable them to plan and carry out actions that do not meet parents' approval, so even in the first year, parents begin guiding and modifying children's behavior. Babies also have the capacity to comply with simple requests. The way parents go about shaping children's behavior to meet standards establishes behavioral patterns that children use in interactions with others.

In the second year of life, toddlers gain increasing control of their behavior. The goal is not simple compliance with rules but autonomy, or *self-regulation*—the capacity to monitor and control behavior flexibly and adaptively even when an adult is not present.[73] Self-regulation is achieved by age three to four.

Parents take many actions to encourage children's cooperation with parental requests. First, they create an atmosphere of receptive compliance, described in Chapter 5.[74] When parents have secure attachments to children and are sensitive and responsive to their needs, they create a climate in which children are more likely to comply. Noncompliance is low, but when it occurs, parents use reasoning and explanations—low-power techniques—that result in a sharing of power. Sharing power with children has a strong impact because it communicates essential respect for the child as a person.[75]

In addition to creating an atmosphere for receptive compliance, parents often take preventive action to head off conflicts before they arise. Parents divert children's attention from tempting but forbidden activities by suggesting interesting substitutes. For example, in grocery stores, they suggest that children pick out items or they make a game of identifying products or colors or items to prevent whining for candy.[76]

Establishing Rules   Parents generally introduce rules that dovetail with the toddler's increasing abilities;[77] Table 7-1 lists sample behavior standards. A detailed study of mothers' rules and toddlers' compliance reveals that the major rules at thirteen months center on safety for the child, for other people (no hitting, kicking, or biting), and for possessions. At about eighteen months, the rules expand to include behavior during meals, requests to inhibit behavior and delay activity, and early self-care. At about twenty-four months, more is expected in terms of polite behavior and helping with family chores (putting toys away). By thirty-six months, children are expected to do more self-care, such as dressing oneself.[78]

Children's compliance with safety rules is high and increases with age. The time and involvement required for promoting all areas of self-regulation are enormous, and parents of two-year-olds intervene eight to ten times per hour to gain compliance. Such parents need a great deal of energy and support.[79]

PARENTS WHO FACE SPECIAL DIFFICULTIES

Which parents have the most difficulty in parenting infants and young children? In this section we look at (1) the special difficulties adolescent, depressed, and substance-abusing parents face as they rear their young children and (2) ways to help these parents.

■ **TABLE 7-1**
SPECIFIC BEHAVIOR STANDARDS, BY CATEGORY

Category	Category Items
Child safety	Not touching things that are dangerous Not climbing on furniture Not going into the street
Protection of personal property	Keeping away from prohibited objects Not tearing up books Not getting into prohibited drawers or rooms Not coloring on walls or furniture
Respect for others	Not taking toys away from other children Not being too rough with other children
Food and mealtime routines	Not playing with food Not leaving table in the middle of a meal Not spilling drinks, juice
Delay	Waiting when Mom is on the telephone Not interrupting others' conversations Waiting for a meal
Manners	Saying "please" Saying "thank you"
Self-care	Dressing oneself Asking to use the toilet Washing up when requested Brushing teeth when requested Going to bed when requested
Family routines	Helping with chores when requested Putting toys away Keeping room neat

J. Heidi Gralinski and Claire B. Kopp, "Everyday Rules for Behavior: Mothers' Requests to Young Children," *Developmental Psychology* 29 (1993): 576–584. Copyright © 1993 by the American Psychological Association. Reprinted with permission.

Adolescent Parents

Adolescent Mothers   Adolescent mothers' psychological immaturity creates difficulty in caregiving. Although they can be as warm as older mothers, adolescent mothers view their infants as more difficult, and they are less realistic in their expectations of children.[80] They foster premature independence in their infants, pushing them to hold their bottles, sit up too early, and scramble for toys before they can get them; however, as infants become toddlers, these mothers reverse their behavior and become overly controlling, not letting toddlers explore freely or have choices in activities.[81] Adolescent mothers also fail to provide a stimulating home environment conducive to learning, and they offer less verbal stimulation.[82]

Children of adolescent mothers face a greater likelihood of academic difficulties, school failure, and behavioral problems.[83] Factors that promote positive development include the mothers' improved circumstances. If a mother goes off welfare between her child's preschool and adolescent years, she reduces the risk of her child's being retained a grade. When a male figure is present, adolescent offspring have fewer behavioral problems than those with no such figure.

Although these findings come largely from studies of African American teenage mothers, work with other samples in the United States and New Zealand yields similar findings.[84] Samples with a broader representation of poor adolescent mothers of African American, Hispanic, and European American backgrounds find similar difficulties in the maturity level of all the mothers and in their abilities to translate their love for their children into supportive, nurturing care.[85] Diversity of outcome, with some mothers making heroic efforts to raise their children under very difficult circumstances, characterizes the samples.

Many teen mothers have had to face early sexual abuse. These young girls feel helpless, unprotected, inferior, and unworthy of care; as a result, they fail to develop self-protection skills and are vulnerable to predatory or uncaring men. Further, they carry these feelings and difficulties into their role as parent and often cannot protect their own children from sexual abuse. In Chapter 15, we explore the effects of sexual abuse in greater detail.

Most findings about teen mothers cut across all ethnic groups. However, African American adolescent mothers receive more support from family and friends and are less strict than are Hispanic mothers.[86]

Although they undoubtedly face many problems, adolescent mothers are often committed to their children, and many raise them successfully. Unfortunately, we pay less attention to the successes than to the failures. For example, 75 percent of teen mothers studied in Baltimore were employed and not involved with social services, yet we focus on the 25 percent who received services.[87]

Adolescent Fathers   Discussions of adolescent parenthood have focused primarily on the mother, in part because 50 percent of fathers are older and are not teenagers. Although they are typically less involved with their children than are older fathers, adolescent fathers are often not completely absent. About 25 percent of adolescent fathers live with their infants, and a national survey suggests that about 57 percent visit weekly in the first two years of life. The percentage of those visiting drops as the children grow older—40 percent when the child is between two and four and a half, 27 percent when the child is four and a half to seven, and 22 percent when the child is over seven.[88]

African American fathers are more likely to be involved than are European American and Hispanic fathers. Only 12 percent of African American fathers have no contact with their children, whereas 30 percent of European American fathers and 37 percent of Hispanic fathers have no contact.[89]

Adolescent fathers are more likely to be involved when other people in the environment support their involvement. (See the interview in Chapter 6 with James Levine.) When adolescent fathers do remain involved, however, they use many directives and negative comments, as do the mothers. Adolescent fathers were observed in one study while solving problems and tasks with their children. The fathers offered strategies for completing the tasks, but they also gave many commands and made many negative comments as the children worked on the tasks. The fathers' negative ways of relating to their children encouraged negativity and resistance in their children, thus creating a vicious cycle. Researchers concluded, "Through their fathers' early entry into parenting and their parents' lack of resources and use of negative control, these children may be shaped, like their parents before them, into the next generation of antisocial children."[90]

Help for Teenage Mothers and Fathers   Two kinds of programs attack the problems of teenage pregnancies: (1) those that postpone the birth of the first child by means of effective education and birth control and (2) those that help parents once they have had children. Both programs emphasize effective birth control while encouraging teens to develop a sense of confidence about their ability to make and carry out future goals for themselves.[91] Teen mothers also benefit from programs that help them sustain positive relationships with their children and their families.

There are also programs to encourage active parenting for adolescent fathers. In Cleveland, for example, Charles Ballard founded a private National Institute for Responsible Fatherhood and Family Development.[92] He raised money to support a small staff and formed the Teen Father Program. Fathers in his program have three requirements: They must (1) legitimize the child, (2) be in school or a general education development (GED) program, and (3) have a job. With the exception of the first requirement, these are the same actions that mothers are encouraged to take. This program has been extended to young mothers and grandparents, with the aim of strengthening the entire family. Now it is expanding to other cities, and Ballard believes there are applications to other social groups as well. "The problem is not exclusive to African-Americans and to poor people. A lot of men who have children in their homes—doctors, lawyers, politicians—are not taking care of their kids. When fathers get closer with their children, communities will become safer for all of us."[93]

Depressed Parents

Studies of depressed parents have focused on mothers, as they are the ones who interact most frequently with their babies.[94] As a group, depressed mothers look at their infants less often, touch them less often, have fewer positive facial expressions, and vocalize with infants less often than do nondepressed mothers. They are also less affectionate and play less with their babies. They see their babies in a more negative light than do nondepressed mothers. In addition, depressed mothers rate themselves more positively than others see them.

Depressed mothers' affect seems contagious, because babies of depressed mothers are fussier, more irritable, and less active than are babies of nondepressed mothers.

Further, babies of depressed mothers show these behaviors with adult nondepressed strangers, who, in turn, respond with negative affect, setting up a vicious cycle. Depression in babies is observed at birth. They have higher sensory thresholds and therefore need more stimulation to respond. They already show flat affect and low activity levels. They also have some of the same physiological characteristics that distinguish their depressed mothers from nondepressed mothers, such as elevated levels of norepinephrine and cortisol, which contribute to irritability. Moreover, by three months of age, they have EEGs that show right frontal activation similar to their mothers'.

Babies of mothers who are successfully treated for depression show no long-term adverse effects of their infant experience. Preschool children of mothers who continue to be depressed, however, show the same physiological characteristics as earlier. Further, depressed mothers continue to report having more behavior problems with their children than nondepressed mothers report with their children.

Because the effects of mothers' depression on infants' behavior are reversible, interventions to help depressed mothers and their infants are essential. Effective interventions are directed to the mother and the child and their patterns of interaction.[95] In addition to the usual psychiatric treatments of medication and psychotherapy, interventions to alter mothers' mood include massage therapy and relaxation therapy, which have been found to lower mothers' scores on measures of anxiety and depression. Further, music therapy sessions, during which mothers listen to their preferred music, appear to temporarily reduce right frontal EEG activation.

Massage therapy—provided by mothers and professional therapists—can also help infants of depressed mothers. It reduces infants' fussiness, improves their sleeping patterns, increases their ability to soothe themselves, increases their activity level, and results in more positive patterns of interaction with mothers. In one study, just rubbing an infant's legs while the child gazed at the still face of the mother reduced the infant's distress. In another study, an adult's rubbing the infant's legs while smiling and cooing increased the infant's eye contact more than did smiling and cooing alone.

Coaching also improved the interaction between mothers and children. Withdrawn, depressed mothers were encouraged to keep their infants' attention. When mothers played more games and had more positive facial expressions, their babies responded with more activity and more positive moods. Depressed mothers who were intrusive and overstimulating were thought to be more effective when they imitated their infants' behavior. Imitating babies seemed to slow mothers' responses, enabling them to react more appropriately to their infants.

Interventions that seek to change depressed mothers' lifestyles have also helped decrease depression. Becoming more active and returning to school or work improves mothers' interactions with their babies; they are less negative than depressed mothers who remain at home. In one study, mothers who were encouraged to return to school where infants were cared for in a center improved in mood and positive interactions with their infants. While there, infants received optimal stimulation and regulation of moods for significant periods of time during the day and related to their mothers better.

Substance-Abusing Parents

Although systematic research has not yet detailed the specific ways in which substance abuse affects parent-child interactions, we can make general observations on how parents' substance abuse affects children. It is difficult, however, to disentangle the effects of the substance abuse itself from the effects of the preexisting psychological and social problems of the parents and the poor living conditions that often accompany substance abuse once the child is born.

Substance abuse is associated with pregnancy and birth complications. Compared with nonabusers, pregnant women who abuse substances are less likely to be in good health and less likely to seek prenatal care, compounding potential problems with pregnancy and delivery. Their babies may be born prematurely and be small for their gestational age. Substance abuse during pregnancy affects children's prenatal development directly and can lead to fetal damage and to ongoing health problems after birth.[96]

Infants born to heroin and morphine addicts are themselves addicted, further complicating the process of nurturing these children. Preliminary research indicates that these children are more likely to have impairments in arousal, activity level, attention modulation, and motor and cognitive development. The kind and severity of impairment depends on the type, amount, and timing of the substance abuse during pregnancy.[97]

Fetal alcohol syndrome (FAS) exemplifies the kind of damage a substance, even a legal one, can do. FAS is a congenital condition acquired by some children of alcoholic mothers. These babies are stunted in growth and development and are hyperactive. Their faces are often deformed, with asymmetrical features, low-set eyes, and small ears, and their intellectual growth is retarded. Worst of all, the damage is not reversible. When FAS was first identified, experts believed that a steady, daily consumption of 3 to 6 ounces of alcohol by the mother was necessary to produce abnormalities. More recent research suggests that smaller doses have been related to such problems as low birth weight, sucking difficulties, and developmental delays.

Observational studies of substance-abusing mothers and their infants indicate that these mothers are more negative and are at times more withdrawn but at other times more interfering and directive than are non-substance-abusing mothers.[98] They have difficulty being sensitive, responsive, caregivers. Insecure attachments are more likely between substance-abusing mothers and their infants and toddlers than between non-substance-abusing mothers and their children. Similarly, alcoholic fathers are more negative in interactions with their one-year-olds and more directive than fathers who have few or no alcoholic problems.[99]

Parents' substance abuse can not only produce long-lasting physical and intellectual impairments in children but also put them at risk for other problems.[100] Parents who abuse substances are more prone to violence—toward both adults and children. They are more likely to physically or sexually abuse, neglect, or abandon their children. Even if their behavior is not that extreme, they have more angry arguments in their families; high levels of anger, as noted in Chapter 4, are damaging to children.

Programs to help parents eliminate substance abuse must pay attention to the needs of the children of these parents as well.[101] First, drug-exposed infants with vulnerability to stress may be especially affected by parents' chaotic living arrangements. Effort must be directed to helping these parents establish stable and nonviolent households. Second, because their arousal and regulatory systems are altered, these children need help on a continuing basis. They experience difficulties as they enter group situations and the demanding environment of school. More information is needed on the medications and educational interventions that would help such children. Third, psychological assistance must be available to parents and children on an ongoing basis to help them cope with a variety of everyday problems that their circumstances compound. Children of substance-abusing parents face an increased risk of developing mood problems as well as substance-abuse problems. Mental health professionals, however, must be aware of the complicated interactions of biological, genetic, and environmental factors in order to break "the continued cycle of substance use, poverty, and environmental chaos that so often tracks the lives of so many children from substance-using homes."[102]

Non-substance-abusing adults who grew up in a home where a parent was a substance abuser tend to have difficulties as a parent. Philip Cowan and Carolyn Cowan report that, to their surprise, 20 percent of the parents in their study of couples becoming parents grew up with an alcoholic parent. Although none reported current problems with alcohol, "on *every* index of adjustment to parenthood—symptoms of depression, self-esteem, parenting stress, role dissatisfaction, and decline in satisfaction with marriage—men and women whose parents had abused alcohol had significantly greater difficulty."[103]

Even more distressing was the generational legacy of the children (the grandchildren of the alcoholics) in their study. Parents saw their preschoolers as less successful, though objective measures suggested that these children functioned as well as others. "This suggests that parents who grow up with troubled and ineffective parenting develop unrealistic expectations of what they can expect of their children, and as a result, have difficulty seeing their children's behavior in a positive light."[104] (In Chapter 15, we look at how parents have dealt with growing up in abusive homes.)

PRACTICAL QUESTION: HOW DO PARENTS MANAGE WHEN CHILDREN ARE BORN PREMATURELY?

A news article reported that, in 2001, one of every eight children was born prematurely, defined as less than thirty-seven weeks gestation, and one in twelve was born "dangerously little."[105] This is the highest rate of premature births in the twenty years of record keeping. The cause is thought to be the increasing use of fertility drugs, which tend to produce multiple births, which are in turn more likely to be delivered prematurely.

The term *premature* covers a wide variety of newborns—from the child born at thirty-five weeks gestation who weighs five pounds and can go home in a few days

INTERVIEW
with Anneliese Korner

Anneliese F. Korner is a professor of psychiatry and the behavioral sciences research at Stanford University School of Medicine. She has studied infant development for the last forty years and in the last seven has collected data and developed a test, the Neurobehavioral Assessment of the Pre-term Infant. This test assesses a premature baby's progress in the early weeks of life.

You have done research with infants, particularly premature infants, for many years. What would you say are the important things for parents to do that will be helpful for their premature child?

To hang in there! One of the things that many, many studies have shown, not mine because I do not follow the infants beyond the hospital, is that when preemies go home, they usually are not as rewarding to parents, in the sense that they get easily disorganized with too much stimulation, and they are not as responsive as full-term babies. Particularly if a mother has already had a full-term baby, she will find that the preemie whom she is bringing home, who may have been very sick, may not give her the rewards that a full-term would. Sometimes parents begin to feel rejected, and a vicious cycle is set up. The less the baby responds, the more the mother tries; she overstimulates the child further, and the baby turns away even more. It takes sometimes as much as five to eight months for a baby to become more responsive; by that time many parents have become rather discouraged. It is exactly at that time when they really should be responding to the baby. One can't blame them because they have had this history of trying so hard and not getting anywhere and feeling discouraged. Kathy Barnard, for example, has said this is when parents need help. They are turned off, unrewarded, and the baby really needs them at that age, so parents need encouragement to get reinvolved.

Can a parent spoil a child with a lot of picking up?

Certainly not in the early months. In the early months, the parents are a shield for the baby, and certainly if the baby is very uncomfortable, restless, or is crying, the idea of picking him up also gives him the feeling of being able to have an effect on people. He's not spinning his wheels; he's trying to communicate, and he is successful. One hears less about spoiling babies these days.

One of the most important things for a relationship is to enjoy each other. It is infinitely more important than pushing a child to achieve. In other words, there is so much richness in the parent's responding with joy to what a baby does and in the normal give-and-take that is part of the early relationships that the interchange is a rich source of stimulation and gratification for both participants. A mother is an infinitely complicated stimulus for a baby. Enjoying the child, being reciprocal, just being there, is what it is all about.

to the low birth weight babies weighing between three pounds, five ounces and five pounds, eight ounces, and the very low birth weight babies weighing less than three pounds, five ounces. The outcomes for premature births depend on the degree of prematurity, medical problems at birth, and health status of the child in the course of early development.[106]

In the previous chapter, we discussed the experiences of most parents at birth and in the hospital; here, we discuss the special challenges caregivers face when they have had a premature baby. For example, caregivers need to remember that, in at least the first two years of life, the child's age should be measured from the time of the due date, not the actual date of birth.

Premature babies lack the special "baby" features that draw adults to them—the big heads, broad cheeks, flattened nose, and large eyes.[107] They may make little noise initially, because they may lack the strength to cry; when they do cry, their cries differ from those of healthy babies and are quite arousing. Parents also miss the pleasure of babies' smiles, because smiles appear approximately six weeks after the due date and therefore can occur months after the premature baby is born.

In addition, parenting a "preemie" is more demanding, both physically and emotionally.[108] Because preterm babies left the protective womb early, their systems are not ready for the level of stimulation they have encountered in the world, especially the world of the intensive care unit. They may be unresponsive much of the time or they may react intensely to stimuli full-term babies can absorb. So, parents have a very narrow range of behaviors that will be intense enough to stimulate but not overwhelm the baby. Thus, clinicians have described the premature baby as "more work and less fun" than full-term babies.[109]

Both mothers and fathers naturally adapt their behaviors to meet preterm babies' needs. Compared with other parents, they are more active in holding and touching babies, directing their attention. They may appear to be overstimulating as they try to compensate for their child's special needs. Over time, preterm babies come to resemble full-term babies in their development, but mothers of preterm babies may use different strategies to achieve these ends. For example, they may hold babies more to encourage mutual gaze and responsiveness, because preterm babies respond with more gazing when being held. Despite all the differences in early experiences and early parent-child interactions, preterm babies are as securely attached to parents at twelve and eighteen months as are full-term babies.[110]

Looking at preterm infants' cognitive development over time and the supports that facilitate it emphasizes the powerful effect of the mother's attitude on the baby's growth. Attitudes that mothers of full-term babies had about themselves, their babies, and their husbands were only moderately related to their babies' growth, but in the preterm sample, mothers' attitudes were very strongly related to the baby's progress.[111] When mothers in this sample felt that their role was important and that they were doing a good job, and when they felt positively about the baby, their husband, and life in general, their babies developed well. Parents' responsiveness and social stimulation are related to children's academic and social success through young adulthood.[112]

Parents of premature babies need to understand their strong and important role and the child's capacity for healthy growth, for our culture seems to hold subtle negative beliefs about preterms. When mothers were told an unfamiliar six-month-old baby was premature, they were more likely to rate the child as smaller, less cute, and less likable, even when the child was actually full term.[113] In brief interactions, they touched the child less and offered a more immature toy for play. What is startling is that the babies' behavior changed with these women, and they became less active.

College students watching videos of the interactions could tell immediately whether the child was described as full-term or preterm.

This negative view of premature babies may not affect the parents directly, because they are influenced by their daily contact with the child. Such stereotypes, however, may influence friends and relatives of the parents, who in turn affect the parents.[114] Mothers who do well tend to adopt and nurture an optimistic attitude about the long-term outcome for the child. Professional support that discusses possible difficulties and coping strategies is at times disruptive for these mothers, although such help is useful to women who feel under stress with their infants.[115]

Because preemie babies start life with special problems, parental overprotectiveness is not unusual in the first several months, as the child grows and becomes stronger. If overprotectiveness persists after the first year or exceeds what the pediatrician considers reasonable, however, parents have developed a problem. Parents must learn to grit their teeth and let their initially vulnerable babies take a few tumbles and some hurts. Giving children freedom to grow also gives parents free time to spend with each other. Sometimes they may choose to get a baby-sitter and go out. This is important. As we have discussed in Chapter 6, parents must make time to nourish the marital relationship if they are to develop a close, satisfying family life.

Many programs help mothers of preterm babies in the first three years of life. Multifaceted interventions working with mothers and children at home and in centers over a three-year period increase cognitive and behavioral functioning more effectively than do programs giving only medical care and routine services for parents.[116] Although differences in children's behavior resulting from participation in these programs disappear at ages five and eight, it is clear that added services can promote preterm babies' development and would likely continue to do so if programs were extended into the preschool and elementary school years.

Of course, all parents face certain transitions as they raise their children. The next two sections discuss the main stages of such transitions and the types of programs that can help parents through them.

PARENTS' EXPERIENCES IN FACING TRANSITIONS

As we saw in Chapter 6, when parents move from the image-making stage of pregnancy to the nurturing stage of infancy,[117] they must adjust the images they created of their anticipated baby and of themselves as parents to the reality of their infant and their actual skill in caring for the baby. When expectations have been unrealistic, adjustments are painful. At the end of Chapter 6, suggestions for easing the transition to parenthood emphasized parents' need for support and self-care while they focus on meeting infants' needs for physical care and nurturing.

Parents of toddlers face another transition—to Galinsky's authority stage (see Chapter 6). This lasts from the child's second to fourth or fifth year. In dealing with their own feelings about having power, setting rules, and enforcing them, parents have to decide what is reasonable when children mobilize all their energy to oppose them and gain their way. In the nurturing stage, parents were primarily concerned with meeting babies' needs and coordinating their own with caregiving activities.

Usually, the appropriate child-care behavior was clear—the baby had to be fed, changed, bathed, and put to bed. Although judgment was required in deciding about letting the child cry or timing sleep patterns, still the desired aim was clear.

In the authority stage, parents must develop clear rules and have the confidence not only to enforce them but also to deal with the tantrums that follow. Parents require self-assurance so they can act calmly and neutrally when they meet with opposition from their children.

SUPPORT FOR PARENTS

Parents have undertaken the most demanding and time-consuming job of their lives. However, they receive only the support and education that families provide on an informal basis and professionals offer in pregnancy and birth classes. In our contemporary society with fewer intact families, and more working grandmothers, the vast majority of parents need more help. The middle-class couples in the Cowans' study described in Chapter 6 benefited from an ongoing parents' group. Many new parents with resources find that "doulas" or pregnancy and childbirth companions provide vital help and information. They sensitize parents to their children's needs and to effective responses.[118]

Many programs are available for parents who face special challenges or have few resources. We saw a sampling of these in the discussion of teen and depressed parents and parents of premature children. Some of these intervention programs may help both low- and high-risk parents become more effective caregivers.[119] In as few as six hours of training,[120] parents might learn enough about responding to their infants to make a difference in their children's sociability, emotional regulation, and severity of attachment to the mother. Although some of the programs are intensive and expensive in terms of time and level of professional help, many, such as those advocating the use of Snugglies, those giving information in hospitals, and those sponsoring parenting groups, are highly effective without being costly. One extensive review of such programs found that short-term interventions had greater success than did longer programs.[121]

The Yale Child Study Center has organized a broad array of programs for parents and their children from birth to the early school-age years.[122] These interdisciplinary programs serve as models for presenting services that can benefit all families. They offer parent groups and professional consultations on parenting. Home visit interventions help parents attend to the physical and emotional needs of children. Special services exist for groups with particular problems, such as parents with a history of infant loss.

All these programs enable parents to learn effective responses for their particular child and contribute to parents' feelings of competency and to parental self-efficacy, defined as the belief that one can perform appropriate parental behaviors and influence the child's development.[123] Parental self-efficacy is positively related to parents' satisfaction in the parenting role and to the quality of care parents give children. It also serves as a buffer against stressful factors in the social environment and in the child's development. When difficulties arise, parents believe their behaviors make a difference, and they act. As we saw with the parents of premature children, their actions trigger a self-fulfilling prophecy. Parents who thought their actions were important were socially stimulating and responsive, and their behaviors predicted later academic and social success for their children.

MAIN POINTS

In the first two years, infants

- gain control over their bodies and learn to sit alone, stand, walk, and run
- take a lively interest in the world around them, reaching out to grasp and explore objects and the world
- develop language gradually from cooing, babbling in the early months, to words at one year and the two-word sentence by age two
- develop a wide range of emotional reactions so that, at the end of the first year, they express anger, fear, joy, pleasure, curiosity, and surprise, and by the end of the second year, they show more affection, more eagerness to please, greater resistance to parents' directives, and great delight in their accomplishments

Successful Parents

- are nurturant, material, social, and didactic caregivers
- are available, attentive, sensitive partners who synchronize their behavior with the child's individual needs
- soothe babies and help them regulate their physiological states
- form enduring attachments with their children
- stimulate development when they play and converse with children
- interact with infants in different ways, with mothers holding babies more and doing more caregiving and fathers being more playful and physically stimulating

Parents regulate children's behavior effectively when they

- establish an atmosphere of mutual understanding
- act to prevent problems
- introduce safety rules before other rules
- use low-power techniques such as reasoning and explanation when noncompliance occurs

Parents likely to have trouble establishing secure attachments with infants

- have a negative, critical approach to children because they are teens, are depressed, or abuse substances
- have difficulty effectively timing responses to children, either withdrawing or overstimulating them
- can be helped with interventions that provide education, opportunities for the parent to get to know the child, and support

Preterm babies
- make special physical and psychological demands on parents
- have a narrow range of optimal stimulation that is neither over- nor under-stimulating
- receive long-term benefits from parents' attention and stimulation

As they incorporate infants into family life, parents
- often do not anticipate the stress produced by the number of changes needed
- seek support from each other and their social network
- experience many joys

EXERCISES

1. Recalling the father's comment on page 195 that he knew so little about babies that he should not have been permitted to take one home from the hospital, work in small groups to devise an exam for new parents. Compare suggestions among the different groups.

2. Go to a toy store and spend an imaginary $150 on toys for an infant or toddler. Justify your choices.

3. Go to a supermarket or a park on a weekend and observe parents and infants or parents and toddlers. Note how the children respond to the environment around them, to parents, and to passersby. Try to find children about the same age to see how individual differences among children determine responses to the same environment. Observe parenting behaviors and describe their effects on the children.

4. Go to local hospitals and agencies to determine what kinds of instruction or hands-on training is given to parents to provide safe environments for infants and toddlers.

5. Interview mothers or fathers about how much time they spend with their infants and toddlers each day. What is the family schedule? Who does what? What do they most enjoy doing with their young child? What do they see as the greatest joys and stresses of having children?

ADDITIONAL READINGS

Bing, Elizabeth, and Colman, Libby. *Laughter and Tears: The Emotional Lives of New Mothers*. New York: Holt, 1997.

Brazelton, T. Berry, and Greenspan, Stanley I. *The Irreducible Needs of Children*. Cambridge, MA: Perseus, 2000.

Cassidy, Anne. *Parents Who Think Too Much*. New York: Dell, 1998.

Levine, James, with Pitt, Edward W. *New Expectations: Community Strategies for Responsible Fatherhood*. New York: Families and Work Institute, 1995.

Saarni, Carolyn. *The Development of Emotional Competence*. New York: Guilford, 1999.

8

Parenting in Early Childhood: The Years from Two to Five

CHAPTER TOPICS	IN THE NEWS

CHAPTER TOPICS

In this chapter you will learn about:

- Children's development

- Relationships with parents, siblings, and peers

- Parents' strategies for managing sleep, aggression, and withdrawal

- Dealing with developmental delays

- Parents' experiences and supports

IN THE NEWS

USA Weekend, November 15–17, 2002
Between 10 and 30 percent of children suffer sleep deprivation. Lack of sleep is related to problems with health, learning, and activity level. See page 238 for details.

 Go to PowerWeb at: www.dushkin.com/powerweb to read articles and newsfeeds on **child development, high-risk children, socialization,** and other topics related to this chapter.

How does parenting change as children's skills and competence increase? Does parenting become easier as children talk more, take care of themselves more, and undertake more projects? How do parents support children's growing sense of self and self-control? How do parents help children relate to peers and others outside the home? Where do parents get support as they raise their children?

The years from two to five are exciting. By age two, children have learned the basic skills of walking and talking. They have gained a sense of personal identity and a greater understanding of others' needs and feelings. In the years from two to five, they develop all these skills further. Their thinking becomes more complex, allowing them to reflect on their behavior. They consider others' wishes and regulate their response to them. As many parents can attest, they act in positive ways to help others. They have greater self-control and relate to people and the world around them in more-complex ways.

PHYSICAL DEVELOPMENT

Between ages two and five, children grow more slowly than before. However, they grow rapidly enough—from about 34 inches and 29 pounds at age two to 42 inches and 42 to 45 pounds at age five. The brains of these children are active and primed for learning. Compared with an adult brain, the brain of a three-year-old has twice as many synapses (connections) among brain cells and is two and a half times more active, requiring more glucose and having more neurotransmitters (chemicals that facilitate the transmission of information from one cell to another). When young children reach puberty, they will begin to get rid of old, little-needed connections in a process called *pruning*, and the number of synaptic connections is reduced to that found in adult brains.[1] Brain development helps the child control voluntary movements and increases alertness and memory, which in turn underlie observable advances in motor, cognitive, and personal-social functioning.

INTELLECTUAL DEVELOPMENT

Greater motor coordination enables children at this age to interact with objects in the environment in more-complex ways than was possible at a younger age. Increased attention span allows the child to pursue activities for a longer time, and increased memory enables her to recall more-detailed sequences.

Thinking becomes more complex. Children can distinguish real events from imagined ones and from dreams and nightmares.[2] Their understanding of people increases.[3] Toddlers understand that others' desires determine their actions, but preschoolers go beyond this and see that others' thoughts often determine both feelings and actions. For example, children learn that when a parent believes they pushed a younger sibling by accident, his or her feelings and responses differ greatly from those of a parent who thinks he or she pushed the sibling on purpose.

LANGUAGE DEVELOPMENT

Children progress from having about 50 words at nineteen months to having 10,000 words at age six, in the first grade, learning an average of 5.5 words per day.[4] The length of sentences grows from 2 words at age two to complex sentences of several words, with clauses.

VOICES OF EXPERIENCE

What I Wish I Had Known
about the Years from Two to Five

"I wish I'd known how to react when they lied. You know kids lie, but it hurts me terribly. It was a very painful experience even though I know I did it." MOTHER

"I wish I had known how much frustration comes just because kids are kids and you have to be tolerant. They don't have the attention span for some things. They might want to do something with you, but they can only do it for about fifteen minutes. You have to go places prepared with all his things or with things to keep him entertained. In the car on a trip, we have a lot of things for him to do. When you plan ahead, you can still be spontaneous at times. You learn that if you are prepared, things really don't have to be a hassle." FATHER

"Everything. I wish I'd known more about communication, how to talk to your children, and the most effective way to help them grow with a strong ego, a good sense of self. We were raised with a lot of 'Do this and don't do that,' a lot of demanding and dictatorial things as opposed to trying to solicit participation in the process of decision making, trying to get in touch with your child's feelings so you really do understand how they feel about things. That's really hard to learn, and I don't know how you can learn it without the experience of actually having the child. But I'm continually learning how to understand her feelings about things." MOTHER

"I think it is incredible that we don't teach anything about being a parent. I have to learn it as I go along, because I want things to be different for them than they were for me growing up. I can't use my own experiences as a guide." FATHER

"I wish I had known how to handle them so they could be spontaneous and feel good about the things they did. How to be spontaneous with them is one of the hardest things for me." FATHER

"I wish I had known how to handle things like believing in Santa Claus. I didn't know whether to encourage it or not or when to tell her there was none. She learned gradually, I think, but she doesn't want to tell her little brother yet." MOTHER

" wasn't prepared for all the decisions. Is it okay if he does this or not? He's trying to do something; shall I step in so he doesn't hurt himself or shall I let him go? It's making all those choices, making sure what I feel." MOTHER

"There is anxiety, a feeling of vulnerability I have never felt before. If he gets sick, what are we going to do? If he has a little sickness, we just hope the doctor is doing the right thing. We went through a great deal in the past few weeks choosing a nursery school for him, and we hope we have done the right thing, but is this the one for him?" FATHER

"I wish we had—because he is our first child—more of a sense of the norms. What is okay versus what is a problem and what is really bad? Is this normal, is this just kids being kids? He pushed someone at school three times; is this par for the course or is this a problem? We don't know when we are reacting and when we are overreacting." FATHER

Parents influence children's acquisition of language, as we saw in discussing social-class differences and language in Chapter 2, but Lois Bloom believes that the child initiates conversations and learns not only language from parents' responses but also social rules, others' expectations of them, and general guidelines for solving social problems.[5]

EMOTIONAL DEVELOPMENT

Preschoolers' understanding of and expression of feelings grow in breadth and complexity. Preschoolers become increasingly accurate in understanding the connections between feelings and the events and social interactions that produce them. Though they at first believe that feelings are temporary, by the end of the preschool period, they recognize that feelings can persist and are influenced by what one thinks.[6]

Children can accurately identify what triggers emotions, especially when there is a social cause for the feelings. In one study, preschoolers agreed 91 percent of the time with adults in giving reasons for other preschoolers' feelings as they occurred in the course of everyday activity.[7] Preschoolers were most accurate in understanding anger and distress and less accurate in regarding happy and sad reactions.

Even so, because differences exist between preschoolers' and adults' understanding of feelings, parents often do not understand their children's reactions. Preschoolers evaluate events by their outcomes. If wrongdoers successfully achieve their ends, the preschooler assumes that they feel good about that. The preschooler may know an act is wrong but not necessarily feel wrong or bad for doing it.[8] Children of this age are particularly happy to evade punishment while still getting what they want.[9] However, they are highly sensitive to punishment, feeling angry or sad whether the punishment is deserved or not.

Preschoolers' most common form of emotional upset is crying, which accounts for 74 percent of the disruptions at home.[10] Anger represents about 23 percent of these incidents. Parent-child interactions account for 71 percent of the upsets, with sibling conflicts accounting for only 13 percent and peer conflicts for 6 percent of the distress.

Parents' usual response to the distress is not to comfort but to give the child a practical, problem-solving response so that the child can deal with the situation. When parents encourage children to take action with problems, children are better able to plan and are more effective in social activities and other areas.

By age three, children judge their behaviors by internal standards and show pride and pleasure when they meet their standards and are upset and ashamed when they do not.[11] They hide their feelings of disappointment and guilt,[12] with girls more likely than boys to hide the negative feelings.[13]

Anger

As just noted, children continue to battle with parents about daily routines, and peers become a source of frustration as well. Increasing age reduces the outbursts of undirected physical energy and increases purposeful activity to achieve goals. The most competent children handle anger in direct ways that reduce further conflict

The relationships among siblings are emotional, intense, affectionate—and sometimes aggressive. How well siblings get along is partly determined by the parent-child relationship.

and maintain social relationships. Boys express their feelings and take no action; girls assert themselves to obtain their wishes.[14]

When children were exposed to strangers' arguing in the next room, three emotional styles of responding to anger were identified.[15] Concerned emotional responders (46 percent of children) showed negative feelings of upset during the episode and later said they felt sad and wanted to leave when they heard anger. Unresponsive children, who showed no emotional reaction, were only a small percentage of the group (15 percent). They were least likely to respond to aggressiveness in play with friends. Ambivalent responders (35 percent) showed both positive and negative feelings during the anger episode. They were upset, but later said they were happy during the episode. These children were most likely to become physically aggressive in play following the anger episode and were most responsive to aggressiveness in peers. Their behavior accounted for almost all the increased aggressiveness in play following the episode of anger. If these children had been able to handle their ambivalent feelings, they might have had no need to be aggressive.

Fear

Fears are a natural part of life as children grow up. In the early years of infancy, fears of noise, loss of support, and strangers are most evident, but these anxieties gradually fade. In the preschool years, children experience fears of animals, the dark, harm from imaginary creatures, and natural disasters such as fires and storms. Anxiety and fear in response to unfamiliar people and strange situations may result from temperamental qualities. Some individuals demonstrate marked physiological excitability when confronted with the unfamiliar.[16] Such excitability is identified in infancy and manifests itself in inhibited, avoidant behavior that persists through the toddler and preschool years.[17] As the child becomes familiar with the person or place in question, fear of the unknown sometimes dissipates. Still, many inhibited children play less freely with peers at home and in alternative care settings. They have difficulty in taking turns and in engaging in fantasy play. As we saw in Chapter 1, by not rewarding the overreactivity and by providing structure for their child, parents can help the child overcome these reactions.

Realistic concerns about dangers such as falling out of a tree and hurting oneself can motivate the child to be cautious when appropriate. Intense fears, however, can prevent the child from exploring the world and interacting with other people. Research suggests further that intense fears at this time have a long-term impact: Preschool boys who experienced intense fears of bodily harm were, as adults, anxious about sexuality, uninvolved with traditional masculine activities, and concerned with intellectual performance.[18]

Empathy

Children's ability to respond sensitively to others' needs increases as they grow. Preschoolers appear more able than toddlers to adopt the perspective of the other person and respond to him or her. Because preschoolers are better able to understand the sources of emotional reactions, their strategies for helping go more directly to the source of the problem. When another child is angry, they are likely to give some material thing to the child or share with him or her.[19] When another child is sad or distressed, they are more likely to do something positive for the child, playing with or comforting the child.

Sharing and giving with friends occurs most frequently in an atmosphere of comfort and optimism. Best friends continue to share when happy, appreciative responses follow. When sharing does not occur but the friend remains happy and smiling, the conflict does not escalate, and sharing resumes.[20]

What qualities in parents stimulate empathy in young children? Children who are kind and helpful in response to the suffering of others have mothers who are warm, caring individuals concerned with the well-being of others. These mothers expect children to control aggression, and when they do not, the mothers show disappointment—"Children are not for hitting," "Stop! You're hurting him." Mothers of empathetic children model kindness, but they go beyond that to teach children how to do what is expected. They maintain high standards and continue a warm, caring relationship with children.[21]

Children also learn empathy from books and stories that have moral themes. Fairy tales, universal favorites of children, present models of kind, caring behavior that triumphs, often after many tribulations, over evil and cruelty.

DEVELOPMENT OF THE SELF

In early childhood, children continue to define themselves in terms of their physical characteristics and their actions. While they continue to use concrete descriptions, they are beginning to organize their self-perceptions and see themselves in more general though dichotomous terms such as good or bad, smart or dumb.[22] Most children continue to focus on their positive qualities and see themselves as "all good," but preschoolers who have experienced abuse are more likely than other children to consider themselves as bad.

Children are beginning to evaluate their behavior, as noted earlier, but still they are optimistic in approaching new tasks.[23] They believe that when they want something, they will be able to achieve it, and they ignore any failures on their way. The reason is not cognitive immaturity, for they can pay attention to others' failures and make realistic predictions about their chances for success. When success matters, they believe they will be able to exert whatever effort is necessary to achieve their ends. As we shall see in later chapters, such optimism is an aid to accomplishment rather than an obstacle to it.

Gender Identity

Babies are born into a gender-typed world. In the days prior to routine ultrasounds during pregnancy, the baby's sex was usually the first fact known about a baby after birth. Today, however, the fetus's sex is often the first fact known during the pregnancy. Once delivered, babies enter an environment in which gender shapes the furniture, colors, clothing, and toys available for the child. Parents often select dolls and pink bedding and clothing for girls and sports equipment, vehicles, and blue clothing for boys.[24] Adults perceive babies identified as boys as tough and sturdy and the same babies identified as girls as frail and sweet.[25]

An important part of one's self concept is *gender identity,* defined as an individual's personal experience of what it means to be a boy or girl, man or woman.[26] Physical, social, and psychological factors contribute to gender differentiation. Physical factors include genes, which, in turn, trigger hormones that lead to the development of internal and external sexual characteristics and also influence behavior.[27] Societies and their subcultures transmit beliefs about what is appropriate for boys and girls through prescriptions of childrearing, and parents contribute their influence as well. Gender identity, however, "is not simply something imposed on children; at all points of development, children are actively constructing for themselves what it means to be female or male."[28]

From infancy, the child begins to evolve a sense gender differences.[29] At seven months, infants respond differently to the voices of men and women; by nine months, they respond differently to men's and women's faces. By one year, infants can link men's voices with men's faces and women's voices with women's faces. In this way they begin to develop a sense of gender categories.

Perhaps without realizing it, parents begin gender-typing behavior by responding in emotionally positive ways to the child's appropriate gender-stereotyped activities and choices.[30] For example, they often encourage boys to manipulate objects and explore the world and discourage them from expressing feelings and asking for help. Parents encourage girls to ask for help and to help with tasks. Through parents' emotional responses, children learn the appropriate gender labels and begin to develop a gender schema.

A *gender schema* is an organized body of knowledge of what it means to be a boy or girl. By age two, toddlers have learned to label men, women, boys, and girls and have begun to associate gender labels with objects, activities, tasks, and roles. Twenty-five-month-old boys, for example, are more likely to recall and imitate gender-related activities like shaving a teddy bear than an activity associated with women—namely, diapering a teddy.[31] Toddlers also indicate awareness of gender-appropriate toys and activities. In the preschool years, they take pride in playing with gender-appropriate toys and feel self-critical when they do not.

Between two and two and a half, children identify their own gender and proudly announce, "I am a boy" or "I am a girl."[32] They gradually learn that gender is stable across time—they will always be male or female. They also learn that gender persists in different situations—a girl remains a girl whether she has short or long hair, wears pants or a dress, drives a truck or takes care of a baby. Children learn first about their own gender, and then about the other. Generally, girls have greater gender knowledge than do boys, but they are less tied to stereotyped play than are boys. Because children appear most prone to gender stereotyping while they are in the process of learning, stereotyped activity tends to peak in the preschool years.

By age three, boys and girls agree on the roles for boys and girls, men and women. They also see that both sexes have a common core of positive qualities.[33] Both boys and girls are strong, kind, unafraid, messy, dirty, smart, and quiet. They hold positive beliefs about their own sex, valuing the qualities associated with being a boy or a girl.

Up to about eighteen months of age, boys and girls show no differences in such behaviors as aggressiveness, toy play, large motor activity, and communication attempts, all of which exhibit gender differences in the next year.[34] Beginning at age two, boys prefer active pursuits and building activities, and girls prefer arts and crafts and reading. In the third year, boys and girls begin to play in same-gender groups, and this continues into the school years.

On average, boys tend to be more active and aggressive than girls. Girls are found to be more helpful and sometimes more fearful. Caroline Zahn-Waxler refers to the gender issues in problem behaviors as the problems of the warriors and the worriers.[35] We discuss parents' behavior in encouraging gender differences in children's behavior in a later section.

Ethnic Identity

Ethnic identity begins to be laid down in the preschool years, when children first learn to identify themselves as members of an ethnic group. They initially use skin color as a marker. In one study, African American and Native American preschoolers could correctly identify pictures of their racial groups, but when shown dolls, they preferred and identified with white dolls. Although these same children measured high in self-esteem, researchers speculated that their preference for white dolls showed they knew that white figures are preferred and, feeling good about themselves, chose white dolls.[36]

As they proceed through these early years and on into school, children gradually learn what is distinctive about their own ethnic group. Ethnic identity becomes more firmly established by age seven, when children of different groups realize they cannot change their ethnic identities.[37] We discuss ethnic identity formation in greater detail in Chapters 9 and 10.

DEVELOPMENT OF SELF-REGULATION

A two-year-old cannot wait or delay action well and is less flexible in adapting behavior to the social situation than is a three-year-old.[38] Even though children understand routines and rules, any strong stimulus can tempt them to forbidden behavior—a two year old, for example, may run into the street to pursue a prized ball.

Overall compliance appears to increase up to thirty months; after that, children increasingly can comply without help from parents. Still, by age four, parents remind or guide about 40 percent of the time.[39]

Although resistance to parents' requests continues for years, children of different ages adopt varying strategies for expressing their resistance.[40] Initially, toddlers rely on direct, often angry, defiance and passive noncompliance. These methods decrease somewhat with age as toddlers develop more skill in bargaining and negotiating. Despite a change in resistant strategies as the child ages, children's general choice of behavior tends to remain stable. Those children who use the most unskilled forms of resistance as toddlers use the most unskilled forms as five-year-olds. Those who use simple refusal and negotiating as toddlers are most likely to use bargaining at age five.

Children often adopt similar methods in resisting parents and in influencing them to get their own way. Children who use outright defiance to resist parents use forceful methods such as demanding and whining to get what they want. Children who resist by bargaining and negotiating use persuasion to influence parents.

Defiance occurs most frequently when parents use high-power strategies such as commands, criticisms, threats, and physical punishments to control children's behavior. Suggestions and guidance in the form of explaining, persuading, directing, and verbally assisting the child to do what is wanted all increase compliance. Giving feedback about difficulties is also helpful.[41] Verbal methods make requests clear to the child. When children understand what is wanted, compliance is high; noncompliance occurs most frequently when requests are not understood.[42]

Positive feelings increase children's compliance. In one study, mothers were trained to play with children for ten to fifteen minutes per day for a week in a nondirective, responsive manner—following the child's lead, when possible being a partner in the play, avoiding comments and questions.[43] In the laboratory, the children had more positive moods after playing in this way with mothers than did children whose mothers received no special play instructions.

In another part of the same study, when children were instructed to recall a happy, positive mood for fifteen seconds, they were more compliant in picking up blocks than were children who were instructed to recall a negative mood such as anger or fear for fifteen seconds. Although we cannot conclude from this study that responsive play leads directly to compliance—as the differences in positive mood between the two groups of children were not significant after a week of play—we can say that responsive play leads to pleasurable feelings and that a pleasurable, good mood leads to compliance.

SOCIAL DEVELOPMENT

Social development in preschoolers involves interactions with parents, siblings, and peers. Here we look at all three in turn.

Parent-Child Relationships

As children grow, verbal interactions play an increasingly important role in parents' interventions to promote close relationships and to help children learn to regulate their behavior.

Ross Parke and Raymond Buriel believe that parents meet role expectations and socialize children in three ways: (1) as an interactive partner with the child, (2) as a direct instructor, and (3) as a provider of activities and opportunities that stimulate children's growth.[44] These three ways involve direct and indirect socialization. Parents directly model and teach children such behaviors as kindness, consideration, and emotional regulation. Parents also provide an indirect influence when they encourage children's interests and activities. Let us look at parents' activities in terms of these three roles.

Attachment   Parents are interactive partners, providing sensitive, involved flexible parenting to maintain the attachment that supports children's sense of security and their trusting relationships with other people. While attachment quality in the first two years influences preschool attachment, preschoolers' present circumstances and the quality of the current relationship are what most influence preschoolers' sense of security and social adaptation.[45]

Socializing Gender Roles   Socializing boys' and girls' gender roles illustrates Parke and Buriel's three forms of parental influence. First, parents model gender behaviors in their direct interactions with children.[46] Mothers carry out more caregiving activities and are more nurturant in everyday activities; fathers are often more direct and assertive. These behaviors occur in casual interactions as well as in caretaking activities. In an observational study of parents' and preschoolers' play together, mothers were more affiliative and supportive in playing with trucks than were fathers, who were more assertive and direct than mothers. These differences were seen in European American and Latino parents and in parents of multiethnic backgrounds.[47]

As interactive partners, parents may stimulate gender-stereotyped behavior indirectly when they respond to boys and girls differently. While mothers and fathers treat boys and girls alike in many ways—they are equally attached to sons and daughters and use authoritative strategies with both[48]—they also reveal subtle differences in how they respond to boys and girls.[49] For example, mothers are more responsive to irritable infant sons than daughters; they talk more to daughters than to sons and use more supportive speech. Such differences in behavior may indirectly reinforce the gender-related behaviors of assertiveness in boys and verbal skills in girls.

Second, as educators, parents teach children directly about gender-appropriate behaviors. When given a truck to play with, one little girl commented, "My mommy would want me to play with this, but I don't want to."[50] So such teaching does not always succeed.

Third, and most important, parents teach children gender-appropriate behavior through their encouragement of different activities and interests.[51] Until recently, boys were encouraged to be more active in sports than were girls, and such activities were thought to build boys' skills in teamwork and cooperation. When girls were highly active like boys, they received more negative responses from adults. Today, both boys and girls receive more encouragement for physical activity.

Children receive similar socialization from peers and teachers in school. As noted earlier, peers beyond the age of two or three spend their playtime in same-gender groups, and their interactions there may have a strong influence on gender-related behaviors.

Parents' Stimulation of Children's Competence   Parents provide homes, objects, activities, and interactions that facilitate growth in competent functioning in all areas. Using data from the National Longitudinal Survey of Youth (NLSY), a national sample of families in which ethnic groups were oversampled to obtain data on these groups, Robert Bradley and his coworkers described the homes and daily routines of children from birth to age fourteen in four ethnic groups (European American, African American, Latino, and Asian American).[52] They noted the poverty and nonpoverty status of the family as well.

The findings reveal great diversity in the home environments and activities that parents provide for children. The overriding influence on home environment is poverty status. Regardless of ethnic group, poverty reduced not only the physical objects like books, tape recorders, and musical instruments available to children, but also—and more profoundly—the quality of parent-child interactions in *all* ethnic groups at *all* ages. For example, poor children were less likely to be hugged and kissed, less likely to be spoken to, and more likely to be spanked than were nonpoor children. Poverty status affected 88 percent of the variables used to describe the homes.

Parents vary stimulation depending on their children's age. Parents are more likely to kiss and hug infants than older children. They are more likely to respond to the attention bids of preschoolers than children of other ages. Younger children are less likely to be taken places like museums than are children over six.

Stimulation of learning in the family as measured by such things as the number of books available for children; access to tape recorders, musical instruments, lessons, and sports activities; and encouragement of hobbies predicted motor and social competence, language development, and academic achievement of children in three ethnic groups—European Americans, African Americans, and Latinos.[53] (Asian Americans were not included, because their numbers were too few for statistical purposes.) These results were found for almost all age groups and for poor and nonpoor children alike.

Interestingly, learning stimulation was related to a greater number of children's problem behaviors from early childhood to adolescence in the three ethnic groups, as reported by mothers. Possibly, mothers who stimulate learning are quick to note and report children's problem behaviors as they would like to change those behaviors. Also, the pressure to learn may produce stress for children, causing them to act out.

In addition to providing books and activities that stimulate learning and competence, parents also stimulate growth when they play with children. In these years, parents engage in two forms of play—interactional play and object play.[54] Initially, parents structure and facilitate the play, but they give children an ever larger role. In the preschool years, children become the primary initiators and directors. Interactional play includes the rough and tumble play that fathers and children enjoy. Families in the United States engage in such play more than do families in other countries. It peaks when children are one to four, and for boys is related to social competence and popularity with peers in the preschool years. Such play, however, is related to abrasive peer relationships for girls. Interactional and object play involve more verbal interactions and more symbolic pretend play as children grow older. In pretend play, children learn the routines of every day life; as in earlier years, parents emphasize turn-taking and other kinds of reciprocity.

Both forms of play help children develop emotional, social, verbal, and intellectual skills. For example, for children between twenty-one months and four years of age, symbolic play with mothers predicted social skills at five and a half years.

Processes of Mutual Responsiveness and of Coercion   In previous chapters, we described the importance of *reciprocity*, mutually rewarding interactions between parent and child, which plays a fundamental role in socializing the child and helping the child to internalize the family's values and standards of behavior. Studies of mothers and their children between ages two and five indicate that a system of reciprocity consists of two primary components: (1) cooperation between mother and child and (2) positive emotional tone in the mother-child interactions.[55]

Claire Kopp, who has extensively studied the development of self-regulation, emphasizes the important role of love for parents. She writes,

> Where does self-control come from? It comes from a desire to be part of a social order, a desire to have love and affection. Children do not follow rules because they think the rules are wonderful. Children are not like that. They want love and affection, and they see that by following the rules, they get love and positive reinforcement. I am concerned about children being in a situation where they are not rewarded for following the rules, where they are not given reasons for rules, and where they do not get techniques or strategies that help them develop cognitive understanding of the rules.[56]

Gerald Patterson describes the kind of process Kopp worries about.[57] He details a process of coercion that begins early in life and has consequences for the parent-child relationship and the child's behavior over time. This process is almost the mirror image of mutual reward and illustrates what happens when parents are negative and give few or no positive reinforcement for following the rules.

Like mutual responsiveness, the process of coercion begins with the interactions between mother/caregiver and infant. Either partner can start the process, and both keep it going. Typically, the infant is irritable and fussy, and the mother, for whatever reasons, is negative and unpredictable in her response. That increases the infant's irritability. The infant comes to see the world as an unrewarding, unsupportive, and unpredictable place. Or the mother may be depressed and pay little attention to the infant, who then becomes irritable and negative and triggers further negativity on mother's part.

The infant develops into a noncompliant, negative toddler who fails to follow rules. Crying, fussing, and whining give way to hitting, kicking, and breaking things to force parents to do what the toddler wants. Parents also escalate the negative exchanges with spanking. Each partner's negative response intensifies the other's response. As the cycle goes on, other family members such as siblings and grandparents become involved. The noncompliant toddler becomes the impulsive, defiant preschooler and early elementary school student; in school, aggression includes bullying, lying, and stealing.

Patterson and his coworkers have taught parents to use consistent, positive rewards to modify children's behavior. They believe that parents' use of a supportive, consistent, and positive reinforcement program creates the sensitive, caring relationship between parent and child that attachment theorists advocate. Though they believe that the temperamental qualities of parent and child affect the interactions between the two, they also believe that behavioral interventions can and do modify parents' and children's behavior. Consistent use of negative consequences, such as ignoring, loss of privileges, and time-outs, can reduce the noncompliant behaviors that occur even in the best of parent-child relationships. Like systems theorists, they also identify contextual factors, such as low income and parental divorce, that can intensify the coercive process. A two-year longitudinal study of boys from ages one to three documents the gradual development of this coercive process.[58]

Clearly, coercion can arise in any family, especially when children become preschoolers and gain new skills for noncompliance. The benefits of mutual rewards, however, can last well beyond these years.

Cultural Influences on Parenting   As described in Chapter 3, different cultures emphasize different goals in parenting. Those following the interdependent model want preschoolers to learn to value close and harmonious family relationships and to take their appropriate place in the traditional social hierarchy. A larger number of parents follow the independent model, emphasizing the goals of autonomy and self-direction.[59]

Besides uncovering differences in goals, research has revealed differences in how parents communicate and teach children.[60] Parents following the independent model most often use verbal instructions to influence their preschoolers, who are moving away from them physically. They use verbal praise to encourage approved behaviors and teach verbal self-expression as a means of encouraging curiosity and thinking. Such teaching and encouragement help children in a culture where verbal instruction is such a central part of schooling and education.

Parents stressing the interdependent model rely on empathy and the close parent-child bond to teach the child; they give little verbal instruction, because the child knows through empathy what the parent wants the child to do.[61] Children's learning occurs in an apprenticeship role, in which the child is close to the parent or teacher and gradually takes on the adult's behaviors. Verbal instruction consists of short directives with little encouragement for self-expression.

Relationships with Siblings

Because siblings are usually born within a few years of each other, many young children must deal with the introduction of another child into the family. Parents want their children to love and care for each other. The question is, How do parents promote positive relationships within the family?

Although most firstborn children get upset and often misbehave after a sibling's birth, particularly when the mother is interacting with the baby, the vast majority (82 percent) of two- to four-year-old firstborns have positive feelings about being a brother or sister. At the end of the first year, 63 percent reported wanting another sibling.[62]

Parents use various strategies to integrate a new child into the family.[63] In some families, fathers attend to the needs of the firstborn and mothers care for the newborn; in others, the father takes on more household tasks, leaving the mother time to care for both children; and in still others, both parents do all tasks. When parents are warm and responsive with both children and have secure attachments to each child, the children tend to get along with each other. When parents have a positive relationship with each other, less sibling conflict usually arises. Conversely, when parents have more conflict with each other or when parents use physical punishment with children, sibling conflicts increase.

When parents maintain high standards for behavior and have warm and caring relationships with their children, they help young children adopt kind and helpful behavior in response to others' suffering.[64] Parents not only model kindness but also teach children how to do what is expected. For instance, parents expect children to control aggression, and they show disappointment if children do not. They make clear but nonangry comments such as, "Children are not for hitting" or "Stop, you are hurting him."

INTERVIEW
with Judy Dunn

Judy Dunn is a professor at the Institute of Psychiatry in London.

What are the most important ways to help children have satisfying relationships with brothers and sisters?
It is reassuring for parents to learn how common it is for brothers and sisters not to get on. They fight a great deal. The main variable is the children's personality. This child is one way and that child is another, and they don't get along. They don't have any choice about living together, and so it's easy to see why they don't get on. It is such a "No holds barred" relationship. There are no inhibitions, and both boys and girls can be very aggressive.

It is reassuring for parents to know that fights occur not just in their family. No one really knows what goes on in other families, and so you think it is just in your own. But children can fight a lot and still end up with a close relationship.

When there is the birth of a new sibling, keep the level of attention and affection as high as possible for the firstborn. I think it's almost impossible to give too much attention to the first child at this time.

Also, keep their life as similar as possible [to the way it was before the arrival of the new baby]. Routine things matter a lot to little children. They like predictability. The mother structures their whole world, so that after a baby comes, they can be upset just by any changes Mother makes in their routine.

In middle childhood, there is a strong association between sibling fights and feelings that the other child is favored by the parent or parents. It is important to be aware how early and how sensitive children are to what goes on between parents and children. It is never too early for parents to think about the effects of what they are doing on the other child. So always be aware of how sensitive children are and avoid favoritism.

Though many older siblings feel that mothers favor younger siblings,[65] longitudinal studies of mothers' behavior with their two children when each is one or two, reveal that mothers are quite consistent in the amount of affection and verbal responsiveness they direct to each child at that age.[66] Because their behavior toward each child changes as the child grows, one can see a difference in how they treat the two when the two are different ages. Mothers are, however, less consistent in their ways of controlling different children at a given age, probably because they have learned from experience.

Peer Relationships

Two-year-olds play with peers, taking turns and sharing. They form stable relationships that can last beyond a year, and such friendships are important emotional attachments that enable them to adapt more easily to changes at preschool or day care.[67]

Preschoolers engage in more cooperative play and in more fantasy play than do toddlers.[68] They like friends who share their activities, and they want to have fun with minimum friction, so they dislike those who disrupt play.[69] While friends have as many fights as do casual acquaintances, friends handle them differently, disengaging and finding a solution that gives each partner something equal, whereas casual acquaintances fight until someone wins.[70] The majority of encounters are friendly—in one study, 81 percent—and children return friendly overtures, preferring playmates who reach out to others.[71]

Even in early childhood, some children are more socially skilled than others, as they are outgoing and able to regulate their emotional reactions in peer interactions.[72] Secure attachments to parents help children feel trusting and confident in social relationships, whereas insecure attachments increase children's feelings that others are rejecting and neglectful.[73] Parents' monitoring of young children's social interactions and guiding children to join in and play with others also increase social skills.

TASKS AND CONCERNS OF PARENTS

Parents of children aged two to five face new tasks as well as old. Parenting in this age period includes the following:

- Being a sensitive, responsive caregiver who provides feelings of security to the child
- Balancing acceptance of the child's individuality with control of his or her behavior
- Providing stimulating experiences with toys and people
- Helping children face challenges so they feel successful
- Serving as coach to foster the child's increasing competence in self-control and social relationships
- Helping the child to conform to rules outside the home
- Providing companionship and play

The years from two to five can bring frustration for parents and children in the daily routines of sleeping, eating, and so forth. Problems at home can lead to trouble for the child at school or at day care. This section emphasizes ways to help children maintain self-regulation through getting optimal amounts of sleep, managing temper outbursts and high activity, and reducing sibling rivalries, aggressiveness, and social inhibition.

Sleeping

A USA Weekend article begins, "In an on-the-go nation that prides itself on 'getting by' on very little sleep, children are the latest victims of this cultural disinclination toward rest."[74] While experts do not understand the precise role of sleep in promoting growth and development, they do know that lack of sleep can affect the immune system and growth as well as learning and behavior. Sleep enables people to process and store the day's events and improves the efficiency of learning. Infants, who are constantly learning, sleep longer and more deeply and have more dream periods than do older children (see Chapter 7). When children do not get enough sleep, their hyperactivity increases, and they are more likely to be diagnosed as hyperactive.

Sleep problems, as measured by parent report, are high in the preschool years and decrease with age.[75] Still, there is modest stability in problems across time and, even at this young age, sleep problems are related to emotional and behavioral problems and to high activity, so it is important for parents to ensure that children get sufficient sleep. Between eighteen months and three years, children usually need between eleven and thirteen hours per night, and from four to twelve, about ten hours per night.[76] Between 10 and 30 percent of children are thought to be sleep deprived.

Because everyone goes to bed together, parents who practice co-sleeping may have few difficulties getting children to go and to stay there. Still, many parents who co-sleep do not want to go to bed as early as their children, so they may have trouble getting children to bed.

Parents promote good sleep habits by establishing a regular, enjoyable, nighttime ritual that prepares the child for going to bed. It may include a bath, songs, stories, and a brief massage to relax the child. The activities should be restful and relaxing and not stimulating.

Children have to learn to fall asleep in ways they can duplicate in the middle of the night when they awake as we all do. Older infants, toddlers, and preschoolers often develop sleep routines that they cannot duplicate on their own. When they wake up in the night and cannot go back to sleep, they cry, wanting comfort, or, if older, they crawl into their parents' bed for the rest of the night. Parents can change children's sleep associations, if they feel the change is important. Children will be very uncomfortable in the beginning but will gradually learn new associations.

Richard Ferber describes a gradual method for changing sleep routines.[77] He pays attention to the child's feelings and needs for security, at the same time setting limits in ways that shape the child's behavior. Parents should start his method only when they have the time and commitment to carry it out for several nights. Because it means that they will also go without sleep in the beginning, they should start on a weekend or at time with few stresses. First, parents must be sure children fall asleep alone in their rooms at night and at nap time without the presence of a parent. The main thrust of the program is to let the child cry for increasingly long periods before going in briefly to reassure the child he or she is not being abandoned. Parents can speak to the child for a minute or two and pat the child but must leave again within two to three minutes, while the child is still awake. Parents enter *not* to stop the crying or get the child to sleep, but only to reassure the child there is no abandonment. If the child continues to cry for ten minutes, parents return, reassure the child again, and leave. If the child is still crying at the end of fifteen minutes, parents repeat the intervention. After that, parents go in every fifteen minutes if the child is still crying. Any awakenings in the middle of the night are treated in exactly the same way. The same procedure is followed at nap times, but a child who is still crying at the end of an hour is allowed to get up. On subsequent nights, five minutes is added to each interval so that the first entry on the second night occurs after ten minutes of crying, the second after fifteen minutes, and all other entries after twenty minutes. By the end of seven days, parents wait for thirty-five minutes of crying before making the first entry, forty minutes for the second, and forty-five minutes for still other occurrences. Nap intervals are treated the same as the night ones for that day, with the child always allowed to get up after an hour of crying.

Note that Ferber's approach takes account of the child's feelings and provides emotional support to the child at the time of change. It also uses behavioral principles to shape the child's behavior. Parents must be consistent in their use of this method and willing to lose their own sleep to help children learn what many accept as healthy sleep habits. Daytime caregivers must follow the same rules.

Many children in the preschool years develop fears about sleeping at night. They are afraid to go to bed, afraid of monsters and eerie creatures coming. Offering a possible explanation for such fears, Ferber says that as children get into bed and begin to relax, they have less control of their thoughts. As their minds run free, children may feel out of control. Even children who are confident and assertive in the daytime can experience night fears. Parents can practice active listening to understand the child's concerns. Ferber writes,

> So, your child does not need protection from monsters, she needs a better understanding of her own feelings and urges. She needs to know that nothing bad will happen if she soils, has a temper tantrum, or feels anger toward her brother or sister. At these times, she can be most reassured if she knows that you are in complete control of yourself and of her and that you can and will protect her and keep her safe. If you can convince her that you will do this, then she will be able to relax. Your calm, firm, and loving assurance will do more to dispel the goblins than will searches under the bed.[78]

Sometimes children will awake in the night crying and upset from scary dreams. If they have had a nightmare, they will be awake and can often tell parents about the dream. Though these dreams occur at night, they are related to the conflicts, feelings, and stresses of the day. Nightmares are a part of growing up. They peak at about the time children enter school and again at ages nine through eleven. A child waking up from a nightmare is afraid and needs reassurance rather than logical arguments. A parent can remain with the child until he or she falls back to sleep, or perhaps can lie down with the child, but it is best not to make the latter practice a habit.

If nightmares occur frequently, parents can begin to examine what in the child's daylight hours is causing the trouble. There may be an adjustment to a new brother or sister, or a change to a new preschool group. Helping the child cope with stress during the day is the surest way to prevent nightmares.

It is important not to confuse nightmares with night terrors. In both cases the child awakes in the night, appearing very frightened. The causes for these two behaviors, however, differ. Nightmares are scary dreams that occur during light REM sleep, and they result in full awakening, often with the child's having some memory of the dream. The child will call and want comfort. Night terrors, however, occur during a partial awakening after a very deep state of sleep. They take place during the first few hours of sleep at night—about one and a half to three or four hours after the child goes to sleep—just as he is entering a light state of sleep. The child is not fully awake when he calls or cries. The cry may sound like a scream, and so the parents assume the child has had a nightmare. In this case, however, if a parent tries to hold the child, he pushes the parent away; comforting does not help. The child may drop back to sleep automatically and have no memory of the night terror the next day.

For nightmares, reassurance and comfort are the effective parental response. For night terrors, parents should not attempt to wake the child or offer comfort. They should avoid interacting with the child unless she requests it and let her fall back to sleep. If they believe it was a night terror, they should not make too much of it with the child, who may be frightened to hear how terrified and out of control she felt. Night terrors disappear as children get older.

Temper Tantrums

Temper tantrums are common responses to parents' requests. Recalling Florence Goodenough's study on anger from Chapter 7, let us examine what Haim Ginott, Thomas Gordon, Rudolph Dreikurs, and the behaviorists suggest about parental management of children's temper tantrums. Ginott recommends accepting all angry feelings but directing children's behavior into acceptable channels. Parents can do this verbally by saying, "People are not for hitting; pillows are for hitting" or "Scribble on the paper, not on the wall." Neither parent nor child is permitted to hit. If verbal statements do not end the tantrums, parents take action, even in public. Mothers have reported stopping the car until the fighting stopped in the back seat, or returning home if a child has a tantrum in a store.[79] These methods require time, but the mothers report success and say they felt better as a result of taking action.

Gordon suggests finding substitute activities to head off trouble. If no jumping is permitted on the sofa, parents can allow children to jump on pillows on the floor. Once anger surfaces, Gordon suggests that parents listen actively and provide feedback about the frustration and irritation the child feels—sometimes children need nothing more than acceptance of what they are feeling.

Gordon recommends mutual problem solving to find a solution agreeable to both parent and child.[80] Even when a compromise is not possible and a child is still upset, active listening may be useful. He cites the example of a child who could not go swimming because he had a cold. When the child's mother commented that it was hard for him to wait until the next day, he calmed down.

Dreikurs recommends many of the techniques that Goodenough found were used by parents whose children had few tantrums. In establishing routines, Dreikurs suggests being flexible with children, concerned with their needs and interests, but firm in enforcing the routines.[81] When tantrums occur, parents are urged to ignore them and leave the room. Ignoring a child is appropriate in public as well as at home.

The behaviorists use a similar method of ignoring. John Krumboltz and Helen Krumboltz tell of a little boy who learned that if he cried and had a tantrum, his parents would pick him up instead of paying attention to the new baby.[82] When

VOICES OF EXPERIENCE

The Joys of Parenting Children Ages Two to Five

"When she was four she was the only girl on an all-boy soccer team. Her mother thought she was signing her up for a coed team, but she was the only girl, and she enjoyed it and liked it even though she is not a natural athlete. She watched and learned and got good at it, and we got a lot of joy out of watching her." FATHER

"Well, every night we have a bedtime ritual of telling a story and singing to her. This is probably beyond the time she needs it, but we need it." MOTHER

"He's very inventive, and it's fun for both of us when he tells stories or figures out ways to communicate something he's learned or heard. When his mother had morning sickness, he heard the baby was in her tummy so he figured out the baby is making the morning sickness, pushing the food out." FATHER

"It's fun to get home in the evening; he comes running out and jumps up, which is really fun. It's a wonderful greeting." FATHER

"One of the delights that comes up is reading him stories, telling him the adventure of John Muir, at the four-year-old level. We were talking about places to go, and I said, 'Maybe we could go visit the home of John Muir.' He said, 'Oh, great, then I could go up there and have a cup of tea.' And I remembered I had told him a story about Muir's having tea in a blizzard, and he remembered that. He put that together, and it came out of nowhere. It knocked me over that he remembered that image." FATHER

"I enjoy her because I can talk to her; we have these wonderful conversations, and she can tell me about something that happened to her today at school that was really neat for her, and I just love to hear about it." MOTHER

"It's fun to hear him looking forward to doing things with us. He'll ask how many days until Saturday or Sunday because on those days I wait for him to get up before I have breakfast. Usually I'm up and gone before he gets up. He likes to come out and get up in my lap and share my breakfast, and it's a ritual. He looks forward to that and counts the days." FATHER

they realized that their actions were creating the tantrums, they agreed to ignore the outbursts. When the boy learned that he gained nothing by banging his head and demanding what he wanted, the tantrums stopped. The behaviorists insist that parents must be firm and consistent. Otherwise, tantrums will continue, and each time children will hold out longer because they have learned that they can win by outlasting the parents.

Stanley Turecki and Leslie Tonner distinguish between the manipulative tantrum and the temperamental tantrum.[83] Some children use tantrums to manipulate the parents into getting them what they want. In the case of a manipulative outburst, Turecki recommends firm refusal to give in. Distracting the child, ignoring the outburst, and sending the child to his or her room are all techniques for handling that kind of tantrum.

"She's really affectionate, always has been, but now out of nowhere, she'll tell you she loves you. She likes to do things with you, and when you give her special attention, one on one, she really likes it. We play games—Candy Land or Cinderella—or just one of us goes with her to the supermarket or to the park. We read stories every night and do some talking. Sometimes I put a record on and we dance." FATHER

"The joy comes from the things we do as a family, the three of us—going to see Santa Claus together or to see miniature trains and take a ride. Early in the morning we have a ritual. When he gets up early, he has a bottle of milk and gets in bed with us; the lights are out, and we are lying in bed, and he tells us his dreams and we watch the light outside and see the trees and see the sun come up. We do that in the morning, and it is a quiet joy." FATHER

"The things that children do, you know they understand, but they haven't got the words to say what they want, so they tell you in the other things they do. They let you know they understand. It is so exciting to see her grow, and say, 'Yes, Daddy.' At thirty-one months, they are so smart, they comprehend so much; but they cannot convey it in words. You see it in their actions." FATHER

"The time I like best with her is hanging out together, and she loves doing projects with me. She likes to help me with a project when I am working in the garage, and I'll show her how to use tools, and it's a special time with Dad." FATHER

"One night at dinner, he was watching his little sister who's one, and he said, 'Do you think when she gets to be a big girl she'll remember what she did as a baby?'" MOTHER

"I like going for a walk with her, and we went skipping rocks at the reservoir. I was going to show her how to skip rocks because she had never seen that before. Of course, she wanted to try it, and I didn't think she was old enough to do it. I had found the best skipping rock; it was just perfect. I was going to hold her hand and do it with her. She said, 'No, I want to do it myself.' I thought, it is more important to just let it go. So I said, 'Here let me show you how.' So I showed her, and she said, 'No, I can do it.' She threw it and it skipped three times! The first time she ever threw one! She wanted to stay till she did it again, and we did a little; but it will be a while before she does that again, I think." FATHER

In the more intense temperamental tantrum, children seem out of control. Some aspect of their temperament has been violated, and they are reacting to that. For example, the poorly adaptable child who is compelled suddenly to switch activities may have an outburst, or a child sensitive to material may do so when he or she has to wear a wool sweater. In these instances, Turecki advises a calm and sympathetic approach; parents can reflect the child's feelings of irritation or upset: "I know you don't like this, but it will be okay." Parents can then put their arms around the child, if permitted, or just stay near the child. No long discussion of what is upsetting the child takes place unless the child wants to talk. If the situation can be corrected, it should be. For example, if the wool sweater feels scratchy, let the child remove it and wear a soft sweatshirt. This is not giving in, but just correcting a mistake. All parents can do then is wait out the tantrum.

Throughout a display of the temperamental tantrum, parents convey the attitude that they will help the child deal with this situation. Though parents change their minds when good reasons are presented, they are generally consistent in waiting out the tantrum and insisting on behavior change when necessary.

Sibling Rivalry

When a younger sibling is born, the older child feels jealousy and anger, as well as caring, warmth, and protectiveness. As children grow and become mobile and verbal, new kinds of problems arise.

In applying Ginott's principles to sibling rivalry, Adele Faber and Elaine Mazlish suggest that parents consider themselves negotiators in these situations.[84] They can recognize that each child's feelings are unique and justified and can accept the feelings without necessarily approving them. As long as neither child is in danger, parents need not feel they must settle the differences. A parent can always interrupt and say, "Hitting doesn't solve problems." If that fails to stop physical aggression, parents can step in and calmly separate the children.

Gordon advocates the use of active listening. This enables children to express their feelings and grants them freedom to resolve differences. When children listen actively to each other, a climate is created in which children can work out their own problems. One mother whose children were four, six, and eight found that the children, including the four-year-old, devised rules that decreased fighting and name calling. The children were upset by verbal insults and decided they would try to send I-messages. If the situation became too heated, they would go to their rooms to cool off.

Dreikurs considers sibling rivalry in detail. He believes that parents can reduce the jealousy among children by making it clear to all that each child in the family is loved for his or her individual qualities and that it is not important whether one child does something better than another. Parents love each child, but a child's trust of that love can be diminished when parents use one sibling's behavior to humiliate another child—"Why can't you be more like Jimmy—he ate everything on his plate."

When siblings bicker or fight, Dreikurs recommends treating all children the same. They are all sent to their rooms if play becomes noisy. If one child complains about another, parents can react so that children feel a responsibility to live in peace. Parents can point out that a child who acts up today may only be trying to retaliate for an incident that happened yesterday. Misbehavior involves all children in the family, and they can learn to take care of each other. Cooperation can be fostered by taking children on family expeditions and having all the children play together. When they see that life is more fun when they cooperate and get along with each other, children learn to settle their differences.

Behaviorists also suggest that parents withdraw from the sibling fights and reward cooperation as a way to increase positive interactions. Children blossom when they hear praise for their good points. Once a fight breaks out, however, parents are encouraged to say as little as possible and to offer a reward for good behavior.

All these techniques are important. Parents must decide which ones will work best in a particular situation: helping children become aware of each other's feelings, increasing verbal communication, ignoring fights or administering punishments while making sure to reward positive interactions.

High Activity Levels

As the brain develops from birth to age three, a child's motor activity increases. From age three to nine, as the brain matures, the child's attention span increases, focusing improves, and motor activity decreases. The inability to inhibit motor behavior is, perhaps, the biggest single behavior problem in boys and often is identified as a problem in the preschool years. The child may always have been active, but when a great interest in activity continues after full learning is achieved in the toddler period and is accompanied by such other qualities as excessive restlessness, short attention span, and demanding behavior that permits no delay in gratification, problems arise. A child who experiences these problems is not necessarily hyperactive. Children with high levels of activity still within the normal range are perceived negatively by preschool teachers, parents, and peers.[85] They are restless, fidgety, poorly controlled, and impulsive. They do not respond well to limits and are often seen as uncooperative and disobedient. With peers, they are outgoing and self-assertive, aggressive, competitive, and dominant. Children described this way at ages three and four are viewed similarly at ages seven and seven and a half.

Both mothers and fathers of highly active children often possess qualities similar to those of their children.[86] They tend to be directive, intrusive, and rather authoritarian with children. They engage in power struggles and competition with their children.

What can parents do? First, parents must get out of the vicious negative cycle that has been created. They must begin to spend some positive time with their children, enjoying them.

At the same time, parents establish structure and daily routines in which the child takes an active role and puts to constructive use the high energy level that might otherwise be disruptive. The structure need not be rigid, but a general schedule of many daily activities will help a child. If, for example, the child has a simple breakfast that he or she can help fix—cereal, juice, toast—confidence and independence are encouraged, energy is consumed, and structure is accepted.

Donald Meichenbaum and Joseph Goodman have found that impulsive children can be taught to guide their behavior and achieve greater control by using a form of self-instruction.[87] Parents show the child what they want done and at the same time talk about what they are doing. The child then acts and talks out loud to describe the actions—"First I take off my pajamas, then I hang them up, then I put on my shirt and pants."

The behaviorists Robert Eimers and Robert Aitchison advise parents to be alert and consistent in providing rewards for positive behaviors.[88] Highly active children often feel rewarded by the attention they receive for misdeeds. "Try to catch the child being good," they suggest, and give rewards of praise and social approval. These seem to be more important than material rewards to active children.

To increase attention span, Eimers and Aitchison recommend helping children with puzzles and other games that require concentration. They urge parents to

INTERVIEW
with Paul Mussen

The late Paul H. Mussen was a professor of psychology at the University of California, Berkeley. A former director of the Institute of Human Development on the Berkeley campus, he coauthored many books, including The Roots of Prosocial Behavior in Children *with Nancy Eisenberg in 1989. He is also an editor of* The Handbook of Child Psychology, 1983 *edition.*

Parents are very interested in moral development. What can they do to promote this in their children?

With my bias, modeling is of primary importance. It is *the* single most important thing parents can do. Parents create a nurturant environment in which the child wants to imitate the parents' behavior and the parents behave in an altruistic way so that there is an identification with the parents. Parents also can try to get the child to participate when they are doing something for someone else.

Then parents use empathy-eliciting disciplinary procedures in which they make the child aware that he or she has hurt someone. In the early years with toddlers, it is a disciplinary technique that involves showing clearly and emphatically that you disapprove, but at the same time making clear that someone else was harmed by what the child has done—"You pulled her hair. Don't ever do that again. You really hurt her."

In general, I think the disciplinary practices are very important. Studies show the empathy-eliciting techniques—so-called induction and reasoning as opposed to power-assertion (spanking and threatening)—are important because they focus not on punishing the child but on pointing up the consequences of what is done. So, first eliciting empathy, then later reasoning with the child are important.

Rewarding altruistic behavior when it occurs is important. The research evidence here is not as strong as one might like, but it does suggest this.

Discussing moral issues at home is critical both from the point of view of moral thinking and from the point of view of moral behavior. Older studies showed that the model's behavior was the critical thing, not what the model said. More recent studies show that verbal responses can be helpful also. You are giving the child some codes or

praise the child for completion of the task rather than for correctness. Poorly coordinated active children benefit from opportunities to develop physical skills. Games that involve running, balancing, and gymnastic movements are helpful. Drawing and playing with Legos or other construction toys also facilitate the development of fine motor coordination.

Aggression

Temper outbursts and hyperactivity reflect anger, lack of control, and noncompliance, but they do not necessarily involve aggression.[89] *Aggression* is out-of-control

rules that the child can then apply later on when various situations arise. So the discussion and what, for lack of a better word, we used to call preaching—in effect, discussing problems, making principled statements—can be helpful.

Giving children assignments of responsibilities fairly early at the child's level is also useful. For example, in the schools, a young fifth-grader can help a second-grader, and at home, older siblings can help younger siblings. Having chores and assigning tasks in such a way that children get satisfaction from accepting responsibility is important.

Those are the important disciplinary techniques—modeling, a nurturant milieu so the child identifies with the modeling, reasoning, discussing rules and principles so the child can use them later, rewarding positive behavior when it occurs, and giving opportunities for satisfaction from accepting responsibility.

What are the things parents should avoid doing?
One thing to avoid is behaving immorally themselves. Another is being inconsistent—occasionally not reacting to misbehavior that harms someone else and at other times punishing it and at still other times rewarding it. Inconsistent patterns of reaction should be avoided. Also be very alert in terms of inconsistency with respect to what the parent says and what the parent does.

In general, I feel that power-assertive techniques (like spanking) should be avoided because they produce the wrong orientation. They give the impression that authority can do whatever it wants and the rest of us just have to go along. They result in less independent moral judgment, and they make the point that aggression can be a successful means of getting what you want.

Avoid underestimating children's understanding, because I think they are a lot more sensitive to these issues than we might think. And I don't think they should be babied or patronized when you are handling something. Let them be involved in making decisions. Assume that they can understand when you are trying to use inductive techniques. Parents sometimes feel they have to play down to children, and I don't think that's true.

behavior that is destructive and hurts others or their possessions. Concerned at their preschooler's aggression, some parents respond with anger and impulsive behavior. In their frustration, they try to force the child to change through power-assertive strategies that prove to be ineffective. They do not, however, take consistent, ongoing action to change the child's behavior, because they consider it a temporary phase the child is going through. This is the coercive family process described by Patterson.[90]

His research, however, suggests many actions parents can take to decrease aggressive behavior, even aggression that has developed over a length of time. First, parents must control their own angry responses to their children. These responses present a negative model of response to frustration that children copy. Their anger also creates an atmosphere of high emotional arousal that keeps children from taking in what parents are trying to teach.

Second, parents need to use a consistent set of positive rewards for nonaggressive behaviors and negative consequences like time-outs for aggression to teach children control.

Third, parents teach children specific social skills and skills of emotional control, as described in Chapter 4. Research indicates that aggressive and disruptive preschoolers retain strong interests in and concerns for others and want to get along. These concerns decrease as disruptive children get into elementary school.[91] At this earlier age, then, parents can rely on children's desire for good relationships with others to teach the positive skills necessary to get along with them. In teaching nonaggression, such parents have to take a more active role than they might wish. Research shows that parents of aggressive children expect that they can issue directives and commands, and children's social behaviors will change. As we have seen, however, it is not that simple.

From beginning to end, parents must become more positive in their view of their child and in the emotional tone of their interactions. Parents often reject the aggressive child as Patterson described, but children need parents' positive regard and the feeling of being special to them.

Social Withdrawal and Inhibition

Like aggressive behaviors, social withdrawal and inhibition may have many origins—in the temperamental qualities of child and parent, attachment experiences, parenting techniques, and contextual factors.[92] As described in Chapters 1 and 7, physiological reactivity and arousal in infancy are related to fearful and inhibited behavior in toddlers. Children who have anxious and insecure attachments to mothers at one year are more likely to be inhibited toddlers who become more withdrawn as they get older. When parents are critical and use authoritarian, high-power strategies to control children's behaviors, their preschoolers tend to be fearful and inhibited. Parental and family qualities such as maternal depression and economic stress can reduce parents' effectiveness, leading to withdrawal and inhibition in their children.

Even though withdrawal causes significant problems for children, parents are generally more concerned about aggressiveness. Parents of withdrawn children are often surprised and puzzled at their children's behavior, often feeling embarrassed and guilty about it. Believing that shyness is an inborn quality, they tend to use high-power, directive strategies with children to change the behavior. These usually do not work. Such parents can, however, take many positive actions that resemble the effective strategies parents of aggressive children use.

First, they can express a positive attitude toward their child as a person. Parents of withdrawn children tend to be negative in their comments about them, expressing the view that parents have to step in and help children function, but this is not a helpful attitude.

Second, they can be supportive in teaching social skills and encouraging play with others. At the same time, they have to stand back and permit the child to act independently. In their zeal to help their physiologically reactive child, they may have become overprotective, too worried about an upsetting interaction, and therefore too controlling. The child does not have a chance to learn that he or she can succeed independently.

Third, parents have to look at their own behaviors. Do they model a fearful, inhibited approach to new situations and people? Do their own problems interfere with their ability to be positive and to support their child? If so, they need to try to change themselves as part of their attempt to help their children.

PRACTICAL QUESTION: HOW CAN PARENTS HELP WHEN CHILDREN HAVE DISABILITIES OR DEVELOPMENTAL DELAYS?

These early years involve rapid development in children's skills and abilities. Some children show clear signs at birth that they will have developmental delays. Perhaps a genetic disorder or birth difficulties have resulted in significant problems for the child. Sometimes, however, the delay is identified later, when the child fails to develop certain skills. For example, a language disorder may show up in the second or third year of life when the child does not learn to talk at the same rate as other children. More pervasive developmental delays in language and the capacity for social relationships with others may also become identified over time.

How can parents help such children psychologically? As soon as disabilities or delays are detected, parents must seek professional consultation if not already provided. Research indicates that, for most disabilities and delays, the earlier the diagnosis and intervention, the greater the child's progress. Because of individual differences in children's rates of growth, accurate diagnosis is sometimes complicated. If delays or disabilities are mild, telling a significant delay from slow growth within the average range can be difficult. In any case, professional consultation is essential and provides directions for parents.

Parents must first obtain all appropriate services for children and arrange the family routines to include them. This can be a full-time job. Once this is done, these parents' tasks are the same as those of other parents—to provide feelings of acceptance, appreciation, and security through sensitive, responsive interactions with the child and to support the child's own motivation to grow and function effectively.

A child's disability or delay affects all family members.[93] Mothers and fathers confront experiences they never anticipated. Their lives include many professionals and numerous activities that come on top of all the usual childrearing tasks. Yet, the family and family support are the most valuable aids in helping children achieve their maximal potential. This book cannot detail the many physical, cognitive, language, and social disabilities and delays that occur or the many therapies for them.

Here we focus on parents' care and the family's emotional atmosphere as engines for development.

Linda Gilkerson and Frances Stott write,

> Children who have a congenital disability may experience disability as an inherent part of their body and self. Like other aspects of the child, the disability contributes to a sense of identity and is in need of acceptance, appreciation, and affirmation. . . . Infants initially develop unimpeded by an awareness of their disability. However, the moment with the most potential for emotional trauma comes not when the child realizes that he or she is different but when the child discovers that the differences are perceived by society as inferior.[94]

As the child grows and develops, the disability takes on different meanings. At all ages, parents must convey that the child's worth lies in being who she or he is, not in becoming "normal" or like others. The authors review the "fix-it model of disability" in which the child's value lies in working hard and making progress to become "normal." According to one therapist, children with disabilities must come to see themselves as both intact and disabled at the same time, and to do this they require their families' love and acceptance. Supportive relationships within the family help children develop a sense of themselves as willing, purposive individuals who can act.

A ten-year longitudinal study of children with motor and other disabilities and delays supports the importance of family emotional atmosphere and parents' sensitive and responsive caretaking.[95] The child's disability predicted growth in intellectual, social, and adaptive skills over this period. Beyond the disability, however, personal characteristics of the child and the family predicted progress in development. Children's ability to regulate feelings and behavior and express them appropriately, as rated by teachers, and children's ability to remain motivated to learn predicted progress. Sensitive and responsive mother-child interactions predicted growth in social and communication skills.

Parents' stress was related to the extent of the disability and to their child's level of stress as reflected in behavior problems. When children did not develop behavior problems, mothers' stress remained stable and low over the period. Social support and good problem solving skills reduced parents' stress.

Early intervention programs for children from birth to age three generally include psychological services for the entire family. When these programs are delivered in school at age three, however, family members are usually no longer included, and the emotional functioning of all family members is often ignored. From the results of the longitudinal study, one can see that reducing parents' stress and children's emotional problems would aid development and would be worthwhile additions to such programs.

PARENTS' EXPERIENCES IN FACING TRANSITIONS

In these years, parents continue in what Ellen Galinsky terms the *authority stage*. Many parents, bogged down in battle with their young children, find themselves doing and saying things they vowed they never would—the very words they hated to hear from their own parents when they were children. Parents are shaken and upset as their ideal images of themselves as parents collide with the reality of rearing children.

Parents' images of themselves undergo revision in light of the way they actually behave. Because it involves change, this can be a painful process. Parents must change either their ideal image or their behavior to come closer to living up to their own standards. Their images of children change as well. Parents discover that children are not always nice, loving, cooperative, and affectionate. Children can be extremely aggressive—breaking things, hitting parents, pulling their hair.

One father described how he coped with these feelings by revising the kind of parent he wanted to be and by finding new ways to relate to children so that he met the images he wanted to keep of himself as a parent:

> Stanley and his wife have one son, eighteen months old. Stanley is a doctor. "In my family, growing up, when someone got angry at someone, they'd stop loving them—which made me feel abandoned as a child. . . .
>
> "When my son gets angry, the easiest thing for me to do would be the same—walk out and slam the door.
>
> "I tell him that even though I've said no, I still love him. I hold him while he's having a temper tantrum, and I tell him it's okay for him to be angry with me.
>
> "Being able to do this is recent, new, and learned, and it's hard work. In the past, I couldn't see beyond my own feelings. What I've now learned is that I have to see past them.
>
> "Another thing I've learned is that if I've gotten angry at my son or if I've done something that I feel I shouldn't have, I'm not the Loch Ness monster or the worst person in the world. I learned the reparability of a mistake."[97]

Parents must also deal with each other as authorities. Both parents' agreeing on how and when to enforce rules is wonderful, but this frequently does not happen. One parent is often stricter or less consistent; one may dislike any physical punishment, but the other may believe it is the only technique to handle serious rule breaking. Communicating with each other, finding ways to handle differences, matters for all parents. They may, for instance, agree to back each other up on all occasions. Other times, they may agree to discuss in private any serious misgivings they have about the other's discipline; then the original rule setter can revise the rule. Still other times, one parent may decide to let the other handle discipline completely. This is a less desirable solution because it means one parent is withdrawn from interaction with the child. Parents need to find ways to resolve differences so they support each other in childrearing. Mutual support is the most important source of strength in parenting.

Single parents and employed parents must work with other authorities, such as day care providers or relatives who provide major care, to develop consistent ways of handling discipline. Again, communicating with other caregivers helps provide consistent solutions to problems. When authorities do not agree, children become confused and are less able to meet expectations.

As parents become aware of their personal feelings about being an authority and learn to deal with them, they can put these misgivings aside and deal more neutrally with rule enforcement. As with handling infancy, a range of preparation such as gaining information from books, groups, parenting courses, and other parents helps parents handle the demands of conflicting feelings in the authority stage.

SUPPORT FOR PARENTS

Recall from Chapters 1 and 6 the parents' support groups that Philip and Carolyn Cowan organized to help parents cope with the transition to parenting and then with the transition to the child's being in school.[98] The parents were middle-class couples who were not seeking clinical services, but when asked, reported stress in coping with change and meeting all their responsibilities to each other and to their children. These weekly programs lasting many months gave parents opportunities to talk over feelings and responses, hear other people's solutions to problems, and generally become more sensitive and aware of their thoughts, feelings, and actions. Parents' participation in the groups when children were about to start school was related to better functioning of the children in kindergarten and first grade.

Such groups help parents develop realistic expectations for their children and themselves. As one parent stated, in these early years, one is not exactly sure of what the limits or expectations should be, and these groups can provide information, discuss what the range of individual differences are, and which strategies work with various children. Parents can then more easily manage problems and enjoy the time with their children.

MAIN POINTS

As their motor, cognitive, language, and social skills increase, toddlers and preschoolers

- develop a greater sense of self and independence
- take pleasure and delight in their new accomplishments
- express new emotions of pride, embarrassment, and shame
- refuse to do what parents want if it conflicts with their own goals
- gradually learn control of their behavior through internalizing rules and standards

As their independence grows, children also develop closer relationships with others, and they

- become more physically affectionate with family, friends, and pets
- become more concerned about others
- are kinder and try to resolve angry interactions

- take delight in complying with some adult requests and meeting a standard of behavior
- are more likely to follow parents' requests than not

As they develop a greater sense of individuality, toddlers develop a sense of gender identity that

- is proudly announced at about two to two-and-a-half years
- initially is based on parents' positive and negative emotional responses to gender-appropriate activities
- organizes activities so that boys manipulate objects and explore the world more and girls express feelings, ask for help, and give help more

Parents whose children function well and have secure attachments

- are available, attentive, and sensitive to the child's individual needs
- grant the child as much independence as possible within safety limits
- provide models of kind, caring, controlled behavior
- talk with the child to explain reasons for what is done, to understand the child's view of what is happening, and to let the child express himself or herself
- play with the child to increase the child's positive mood and desire to cooperate in routines and activities

Parents regulate children's behavior effectively when they

- establish a process of mutual reward
- act to prevent problems
- avoid coercive reciprocity
- introduce rules that dovetail with the child's abilities
- use low-power techniques such as reasoning and explanation when noncompliance occurs
- work together so children get a set of consistent limits
- do not abuse their power

Problems discussed center on

- sleep
- sibling rivalry
- handling temper tantrums and high activity levels
- dealing with aggression and withdrawal
- helping children with disabilities feel accepted

Joys include the child's

- delight in increasing skills and personal achievements
- helping behaviors
- greater communicativeness

EXERCISES

1. Interview two couples who have preschoolers. Ask them about their children's daily routines and their worries and pleasures regarding their children. What are the sources of stress and support for the parents? Are the stresses and supports similar in the two families?

2. In groups, recall early experiences of gender learning. (a) Did the teachings deal with activities, appearances, feelings? (b) Who was teaching you about gender-appropriate behavior—parents, siblings, peers, relatives, teachers? (c) Were you more likely to accept the teachings of adults or of peers? Make a group list of the kinds of experiences members had. (d) Are similar experiences occurring today?

3. In groups, recall early experiences with siblings. Was there much fighting? Did parents teach children how to get along? Did parents punish children for not getting along? What seems to make for the best relationships with siblings? What roles do siblings play in your lives as you get older?

4. Watch Saturday morning television programs for children and decide how much time and what specific programs you, if you were parents, would permit your toddler and preschooler to watch. Justify your choices.

5. Interview three preschoolers about their joys in life. What do they like best to do? Do they get to do it as much as they want? How can parents make their lives happier? Are their requests reasonable? Do you think parents are aware of what makes their children happy?

ADDITIONAL READINGS

Eisenberg, Nancy. *The Caring Child.* Cambridge, MA: Harvard University Press, 1992.

Golombok, Susan, and Fivush, Robin. *Gender Development.* New York: Cambridge University Press, 1994.

Gottman, John. *Raising an Emotionally Intelligent Child.* New York: Simon & Schuster, 1994.

Greenspan, Stanley I., and Wiedner, Serena. *The Child with Special Needs.* Reading, MA: Addison-Wesley, 1998.

Murphy, Tim, and Oberlin, Loriann Hoff. *The Angry Child.* New York: Three Rivers Press, 2001.

CHAPTER

9

Parenting Elementary School Children

CHAPTER TOPICS	IN THE NEWS
In this chapter you will learn about:	*San Francisco Chronicle,* December 12, 2002
▨ Children's development	Suvrey reveals alarming number of California children are physically unfit and overweight, raising fears of unprecedented risk for chronic disease later; legislators urged to enforce physical education programs in schools. See page 256 for details.
▨ Social relationships with parents, siblings, and peers	
▨ Main parenting tasks	
▨ Ways parents promote healthy lifestyles, emotional control, school success, social skills	
▨ Ways parents help children with common school difficulties	

 Go to PowerWeb at: www.dushkin.com/powerweb to read articles and newsfeeds on **education, physical development, socialization,** and other topics related to this chapter.

The first day of school launches a child on a sea of opportunity to increase his or her competence. Stress accompanies the greater independence. How does a child manage in this expanded world away from the protection of the family? Parents' roles change dramatically as they encourage independence and continue to guide the child's behavior but also take on the task of interpreting the outside influences the child confronts. How do parents foster the child's development at school? How do they promote reliable habits and self-regulation? How do they help children deal with upsetting experiences and disappointments that lie beyond parental control?

The years from five to eleven are a time of expansion for children. They have learned the routines of living—eating, dressing, toileting—and can take care of many of their own needs. They express themselves easily. Their world enlarges as they go off to school, meet new friends, and adjust to more demanding tasks. While they grow in competence, stress increases in their lives as well. Because they now compare themselves with others and against external standards, they worry about their competence in many areas and feel vulnerable to embarrassment and feelings of inadequacy. Parents play a powerful role in helping children cope with these new demands.

PHYSICAL DEVELOPMENT

From ages five to ten, girls and boys have approximately the same height, weight, and general physical measurements. At five they are about 42 inches tall and weigh about 40 to 45 pounds. By age ten, they stand at about 52 inches and weigh about 75 to 80 pounds. In the elementary school years, children's coordination is well developed. They ride bikes, skate, swim, play team sports, draw, and play musical instruments. Nearly all the basic skills in the area of gross (running, skipping) and fine (cutting with scissors, drawing) motor coordination are laid down by age seven, and further development consists of refining these skills.

Because of lack of physical activity and increasing obesity, children today are not as physically fit as children in the past. In 2001, 77 percent of California's 5th-, 7th-, and 9th-graders failed six aerobic strength and body fat tests, and performance levels decreased with age.[1] The entire state reflected these findings. Even in wealthy Marin county, 18 percent of children were overweight and almost 28 percent were unfit. Such percentages were generally highest in urban and poorer areas of the state. Public health officials are concerned that children face long-term health problems from the twin problems of overweight and lack of physical fitness. Developmental problems could also occur, in that children's motor and physical skills may be affected.

INTELLECTUAL DEVELOPMENT

Three major cognitive changes occur in the elementary school years.[2] First, children learn to reason generally. At about age seven, children become less focused on their own perceptions and more involved in the objective properties of what they observe. They organize their perceptions and reason about a broader range of objects and situations. Because they also more easily adopt the other person's point of view, they understand other people and their reactions better. At the end of this age period, around ten to twelve, thinking becomes more abstract and more closely resembles adults' ways of reasoning.

Second, children at this age organize tasks and function more independently than before. They observe their own behavior and their thinking processes as well as set

VOICES OF EXPERIENCE

What I Wish I Had Known
about the Elementary School Years

"I wish I'd known how much you need to be an advocate for your child with the school. When we grew up, our parents put us in public school and that was it. Now, you have a lot more options, and the public schools aren't always great; so you realize how active you need to be in order to ensure a good education for your children." MOTHER

"The main thing, I think, is how important temperament is. My daughter was in one school that was very noncompetitive; that's a wonderful philosophy, but it wasn't right for her. She is very competitive, and in that atmosphere she did not do as well. So with the second child, we are going to be more careful to see that there is a good fit between her temperament and what she is doing." FATHER

"I was surprised that even though the children are older, they take as much time as when they were younger; but you spend the time in different ways. I thought when they started school, I would have a little more time. Instead of giving them baths at night and rocking them, I supervise homework and argue about taking baths. Knowing that things were going to take as much time would have made me less impatient in the beginning, and I would have planned better." MOTHER

"I learned that especially from five to eight, say, children are not as competent as they look. They really can't do a lot of things that on the surface you think they can. They have language, and they look like they're reasoning, and they look like their motor skills are okay. So you say, 'When you get up in the morning, I want you to make your cereal,' and they can't do it consistently. And so because we didn't know that with the first child, I think we made excessive demands on her, which led to her being a little harsher on herself. Now with the second one, if she can't tie her shoes by herself today, even though she could two weeks ago, we're more likely to say, 'Okay,' instead of, 'Well, you can tie your shoes; go ahead and do it.' If you give them a little help, it doesn't mean you are making babies of them; it means they have room to take it from there." FATHER

"I wish I'd known more about their abilities and work readiness. My daughter had some special needs in school. In preschool, she did well, although I could see there were immaturities in her drawings and writing, but she got lots of happy faces. I was misled by the positive comments they always wanted to make to her, and I thought she was doing better than she was. When she got to school, it came as quite a shock that she was having problems. With my son, I have been more on top, and I ask more questions about how he is really doing, because I want to get any special needs he has addressed. My advice to any parent is that, if at all possible, volunteer in your child's school. I gave up half a day's pay, and in my financial situation that was a real hardship. It is very, very important to keep a handle on not just what is happening educationally, but also who the peers are and what is going on." MOTHER

and pursue their own goals. Third, they acquire knowledge in an organized learning environment—school—that sets standards by which they and others evaluate their performance.

SCHOOL

School is a major organizing force in parents' and children's lives. School provides opportunities for learning, but it also places demands and stress on both parents and children. School occupies five to six hours of children's day throughout much of the year, and it determines their evening activities as well. Children must function in large groups of initially unknown children and adults. They also must meet standards of behavior and achievement.

Before discussing what parents can do to help children succeed, let us see why school success matters.[3] First, it gives children academic skills that will help them function effectively throughout life. Second, school success in the early elementary school years appears to serve as a protective factor against the development of high-risk behaviors in adolescence—delinquency, substance abuse, teen sexuality, and violence. Third, competence in school activities is related to social acceptance and social competence, which in turn reinforce academic success.

Influences within the Home

Jacquelynne Eccles, Allan Wigfield, and Ulrich Schiefele list four parental factors that contribute to children's motivation and outcomes in school—parents' social characteristics, their general beliefs and behaviors, their specific beliefs about their child, and their specific behaviors.[4]

Parents' Social Characteristics   Parents' education, income, marital status, and number of children, as well as neighborhood characteristics, determine the resources available to parents to encourage their children's achievement at school. Nonetheless, a parent's limited resources need not determine what happens with children. Ben Carson, an internationally recognized African American pediatric neurosurgeon at Johns Hopkins University, describes how his mother—married at thirteen years of age to a man who, she later learned, had another family—raised her two sons.[5] She worked as a domestic, sometimes holding two or three jobs to make ends meet. When Ben was in the fifth grade, he was at the bottom of his class and nicknamed "Dummy." Very concerned, his mother insisted the two boys turn off the television. She required that they read two books per week from the Detroit Public Library and give her a written report on each book. The boys did not know for some years that she could not read the reports.

Ben read books about animals, plants, and rocks. Later that year, he was the only student in his class able to identify a particular rock. He suddenly realized, "The reason you knew the answer was because you were reading those books. What if you read books about all your subjects—science, math, history, geography, social studies? Couldn't you then know more than all those students who tease you and call you a dummy?"[6] Within a year and a half, he went from the bottom of his class to the top. With relatively few external resources, his mother took action that promoted her son's success.

Parents' General Beliefs and Behaviors   Parents' general beliefs and behaviors create an emotional climate in the home that influences children's achievement. By forming secure attachments with their children, balancing independence and structure, and providing appropriate adult models for learning, parents help their children develop competence and motivation to achieve.

Parents' general beliefs about gender-appropriate behaviors shape what they provide for their sons and daughters. For example, they tend to provide boys with manipulative toys that develop spatial abilities. They are less likely to enroll daughters in computer programs and competitive athletics, and they are more likely to direct sons toward gifted programs. These behaviors in turn influence their children's achievement.

Cultural values about the sources of achievement influence what parents expect of children and themselves. In the United states, European American parents view the child's innate ability as the main determiner of achievement. They consider it their role to give children emotional support in schoolwork. Failure is seen as a sign of limited ability. Asian American parents, however, believe hard work and effort determine success. They take an active role in seeing that their child exerts the necessary work and effort to achieve high standards. Failures are seen as remediable with increased effort.

Parents' Beliefs about their Child   Parents' beliefs about a child's skills and abilities and reasons for success shape children's achievement. Parents can encourage or discourage academic work by saying a child has ability or, conversely, has no skill at a task. They can soften a failure by identifying it as remediable through further work.

Parents' expectations regarding school achievement predict children's academic success more accurately than do the child's ability scores.[7]

Parents' Specific Behaviors   As noted in the previous chapter, parents' stimulation through books and activities predicts achievement. Providing stimulating toys and opportunities for exploration; reading to children; encouraging conversation, verbal expression, and curiosity; providing lessons and activities that develop children's skills—all contribute to children's academic success. Further, although we do not often think of emotional regulation as an important skill for school success,[8] it is essential if children are to deal with the frustrations of learning new material and getting along with others.

Parents also organize the home and the daily routine so the child has a time and place to do schoolwork. Parents also spend time giving spelling words and listening to reading.

Parents play an active role in helping children learn basic skills.

Influences within the School

The staff's expectations of students, the organization of the school, the cohesiveness of the staff, the staff's sensitivity to students' needs, and the staff's recognition of performance do appear important for student achievement. Further, teachers' skills in managing conflict can reduce or increase children's behavior problems, such as aggressiveness.[9]

Children develop strong attachments to teachers and their schools when children are actively involved in the learning process and have opportunities and rewards for developing competencies. Effective teachers, like effective parents, have clear, fair, and realistic expectations of students.[10] Teachers emphasize mastery-based learning in a cooperative atmosphere in which students teach each other.

Influences within Students

Children who have personal maturity when they enter school adjust relatively easily.[11] Children who enter school with friends or who have a stable group of friends outside school also adjust relatively easily.[12]

Most children start school with positive beliefs about their abilities and capacities to learn. Children in first grade believe all children can learn and that all they need is effort—those who do best have worked the hardest.[13] Another group of children react strongly to failure and criticism.[14] When they fail a task or receive criticism, they feel bad, blame themselves and see themselves as bad people who deserve punishment, even at young ages. They feel unworthy and inadequate, helpless to change the situation. Such children see failure as a sign they lack some innate quality. Because they believe that no amount of effort or hard work will lead to achievement, they abandon any attempts to improve. They avoid challenging tasks and give up at the first sign of difficulty. In contrast, children who persist see criticism or failure as signs to look for a different solution or ways to improve some aspect of their work. They feel good about what they have done and anticipate that others will appreciate their efforts as well.

Some training programs give children strategies for goal setting and interpreting failure in different ways, as well as encouraging these children to enjoy the process of learning rather than focusing on the achievements of learning. Such programs reduce feelings of helplessness.[15] We talk about this further in a later section.

Children from certain cultural backgrounds may feel at a loss to achieve in what seems a strange environment.[16] They may be used to working in cooperative ways, focusing on the effects of objects on people, learning from traditions, and obeying standards. The school atmosphere of competition, objective knowledge gained from reference books, and questioning teachers may require adjustment.

Despite such cultural differences, children of different ethnic groups enjoy school, feel good about themselves and their achievements, and expect to do well in the future. They work hard and are self-disciplined.[17]

EMOTIONAL DEVELOPMENT

Elementary school children understand their feelings better than preschoolers do and realize that feelings depend, in part, on what led up to the event and how the event is interpreted.[18] For example, at ages six and seven, children are pleased with their success whether it comes from luck or effort. When they are nine and ten, children feel proud only if they believe their effort produced the success.

Children are most likely to express their inner feelings when they are alone or with another when they believe that person will respond in a positive, understanding way.[19] Unfortunately, as children—particularly boys—grow older, they anticipate a less positive response from others, even from parents. Thus, older boys are much less likely to express their feelings than are girls or younger boys.

Common Feelings of Schoolchildren

Elementary school children experience many common feelings, which parents can help them handle. Children's ability to regulate their emotions appears related to temperamental qualities,[20] but parents' understanding helps guide them toward achieving self-control.

INTERVIEW
with Barbara Keogh

Barbara K. Keogh is professor emeritus of educational psychology at the University of California, Los Angeles. Her research interests include the role of children's temperament in children's adjustment to school.

For many parents with children in the elementary school years, issues concerning school are quite important—how to get children ready for school on time, how to help them behave in school, how to get them to do schoolwork. You have done a great deal of research on children's temperament and school, and I think temperament plays a role in many children's adjustment.

It intrigued me when I started work in this area, a long time ago, that most of the work with temperament had been done with interactions in families, and yet when you think of the number of interactions that teachers have with children per hour, per day, in a classroom and add that up over the school year, temperament is an enormous potential influence.

When we began our research, we found that teachers have a very clear picture of what teachable children are like. One of the very important contributors to teachability is the stylistic variables or temperament variables that characterize children. Some children are easy to teach. They settle down better, they are not as active, they are not as intense, their mood is good, they adapt well, they like novelty, they are curious. All those things make teachers think, "Gee, I am a great teacher," when they have a whole classroom full of children with those characteristics.

So we are really operating on the assumption that children's experiences in school are influenced by individual variations in temperament. We have tried to document and understand the kind of impact these variations have on the teachers. We have used the concept of "goodness of fit" in a loose way.

I am convinced, and this is not a new idea, that teachers do not operate at random. They make decisions based on how they attribute the reasons for the behavior. They may think that active, distractible children are mischievous and need to be restricted and punished, and that children who are very slow to warm up or are withdrawn are lazy and uninterested. When we work with teachers and make them aware of temperamental characteristics, we get a very consistent response: "Oh, I never thought of that." Making teachers sensitive to temperament variations helps them reframe the child's behavior, and it makes the behavior much less upsetting to teachers.

It also carries planning implications. If you know a youngster is very distractible, very active, and very intense, then you can predict that every time you have a long wait in line, there's going to be a problem with him. It's predictable.

Empathy   Because children's awareness of others' feelings increases in elementary school, they are better helpers and are more likely to offer social strategies rather than material ones to change distress when they see it in other people, for example, suggesting playing with a friend rather than giving a toy.[21] Children are

When teachers begin to think of the individual variations on a temperamental rather than motivational basis, they begin to manipulate the environment more effectively. Temperament helps teachers reframe the problem behavior so it is not viewed as purposeful. This is true for both temperamentally "difficult" and "slow to warm up" children.

Another example I like is that most of the youngsters in an elementary class are delighted by novelty. The teacher says, "Oh, we are going to have a wonderful surprise today. At ten o'clock the fire department is coming." Most of the kids are excited. There will be a few "slow to warm up" youngsters who will say, "But at ten o'clock we are supposed to do our reading." They are upset because the usual routine is not followed. The teacher thinks, "What's the matter with that child? Why isn't he interested?" The child has a need for routine and a tendency to withdraw from newness or change. These children can profit from advance preparation. If they know a day in advance, they get a little forewarning.

Do you have any advice for parents as to how to help their children adjust to school?
Certainly parents have to be advocates for their child. That is absolutely necessary even if it means being confrontational, which is often not too productive. But certainly parents need to be aware when their child is unhappy at school, when their child is having problems, and address the problem with school people.

It has to be recognized that when we are working on a ratio of twenty-five youngsters to one teacher, there are going to be good matches and poor matches in any class. In no sense does that demean the quality of the teacher or the nature of the child. But there are differences in style, and some styles match better than others.

One thing parents can do is to provide teachers with some recognition that their child might not be a good match for this classroom. It helps the teacher to know that the parents are aware of that. So they can direct their mutual efforts to modify the class so the demands are more reasonable, or they can give the child extra help in modifying his or her behavior so it is more compatible with what is going on in that class.

Do you feel that most teachers are willing to change?
Yes, I do. We have worked with a lot of teachers in our research, and I think it helps them to think of ways that they can structure the situation so it is more compatible with the student without loss of educational goals. Yes, we have found teachers to be very open, and they were able to relate what we were saying to different children they have known: "Oh, yes, that's like Joey."

most likely to help others when they feel happy, competent, and effective themselves. They are also most likely to help if they like the person and that person has helped them in the past. So, positive feelings about oneself and others lead to generosity at this age.[22]

Aggressiveness   Aggression decreases during this period, but consistent individual differences emerge and tend to persist over time. Further, aggressive children often have problems such as poor peer relations and difficulty in acquiring academic skills. See the section on peer relationships for more on aggression.

Fearfulness   With age, children grow less fearful. Many of the fears of the pre-school period—of animals, of the dark—decrease. Some specific ones remain, how-ever—fear of snakes, of storms. These fears appear related to temperamental qualities involving general timidity. Up to age five, fears are equally prevalent in boys and girls, but beginning with the school-age years, sex differences increase. Fears and phobias are more prevalent in girls at all ages.

Loneliness   For a long time, social scientists thought that children could not expe-rience loneliness prior to adolescence, when they became more separate from the family. Recent research, however, finds that five- and six-year-old children have con-ceptions of loneliness as clear as those of adults.[23] They describe feelings of being sad and alone, having no one to play with. The remedy, they report, is to find a playmate. Older elementary school children give even more poignant descriptions of loneliness—"feeling unneeded," "like you're the only one on the moon," "always in the dark," "like you have no one that really likes you and you're all alone."

Extreme loneliness is related to lack of friends, shy and submissive behavior, and a tendency to attribute social failure to one's own internal inadequacies. Such lone-liness, in turn, prevents the child from interacting with others and intensifies the problem.

Unhappiness   In one study, parents and teachers described 10 to 12 percent of a representative sample of ten-year-olds as often appearing miserable, unhappy, tear-ful, or distressed.[24] The children themselves reported similar depressive feelings. Boys and girls were equally as likely to report such feelings.

Children around the world, regardless of sex or socioeconomic status, agree with each other on what is upsetting even more than do adults and children within the same culture.[25] The loss of a parent is the most devastating occurrence, and the birth of a sibling the least upsetting. Parental fights are highly stressful. Children reveal their sensitivity in their distress at embarrassing situations—wetting their pants, being caught in a theft, being ridiculed in class. Although many students like school, it also causes them anxiety, frustration, and unhappiness, with many chil-dren worrying about grades, being retained, and making mistakes. Adults may be surprised at children's sensitivity to embarrassing situations and their concern about school. The data emphasize that children can have a perspective on life that is quite different from that of their parents and often not immediately apparent to parents.

Daily journals of elementary school students in the United States reveal that boys are more likely to cite external situations and demands such as school, chores, inter-ruptions, and environmental factors as sources of stress.[26] Girls report disappoint-ments with self and others and failure to live up to responsibilities as sources of stress in their lives.

Coping with Stress

In facing stress, children adapt in many ways. First, they use their own resources and the tools their parents give them. Second, they turn to trusted people for further support and guidance.

Strategies   Children are most likely to strike at the roots of the difficulty when the problem stems from peers or school, where they feel they have more control. Children tend to use distraction strategies to adjust to situations they cannot control, such as doctors' visits.[27] Children also tend to use enjoyable activities to buffer themselves from stress. Athletics, being at home with families, and special treats of food or surprises all help children to deal with stressors.[28]

Supportive People   When dealing with stressful or negative situations, children often seek others to help them. Children "perceive mothers as being the best multipurpose social provider available, in contrast to friends and teachers, who are relatively specialized in their social value."[29] Friends provide companionship and emotional support second only to parents. Teachers provide information but little companionship. Fathers are excellent providers of information, but are generally less available for direct help. Figure 9-1 (page 266) illustrates where children of different ages and ethnic groups seek support.[30] Until early adolescence, parents and extended family provide the primary sources of support. Extended family are more important for African American and Hispanic children than for European Americans.

DEVELOPMENT OF THE SELF

In elementary school, children become capable of integrating behaviors and forming a more balanced view of themselves that takes into account both positive and negative qualities.[31] They are no longer limited to thinking of themselves in extreme terms—instead of smart or dumb, they think of themselves as smart at some things and not so smart in others.

Children also begin to evaluate their behavior in comparison to their peers. In the early grades, comparisons may be overt and direct—"I can finish the work faster than you"—but as children grow older, comparisons become subtler and less direct—"I have more friends than the other girls in my class."

We discussed in Chapter 6 that adopted children view themselves and their adoptive status in different terms as their thinking becomes more complex during this period.[32] Children become more curious about their biological origins and what led parents to give them up. They also begin to experience the loss of their biological family. "It is the experience of loss that ultimately leads to a sense of ambivalence about being adopted, as well as the emergence of adoption adjustment problems."[33]

Parents must provide a supportive family atmosphere and acknowledge that the child's experience of himself or herself is different from that of most children

■ **FIGURE 9-1**
CONVOYS OF SUPPORT BY AGE AND ETHNICITY

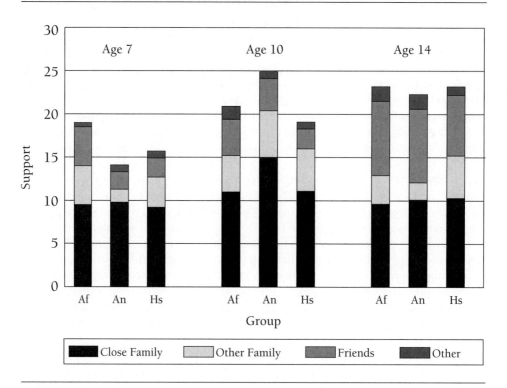

Af = African American, An = Anglo (European) American, Hs = Hispanic

Mary J. Levitt, Nathalie Guacci-Franco, and Jerome L. Levitt, "Convoys of Social Support in Childhood and Early Adolescence: Structure and Function," *Developmental Psychology* 29 (1993), p. 815. Copyright © 1993 American Psychological Association. Reprinted with permission.

because the child comes from two families. On the other hand, parents must not overemphasize this difference. Ongoing communication of the child's feelings can help parents understand the child's experiences and feelings and permit the child to hear the parents' points of view.

Gender Identity

Psychologists used to think that gender development was largely completed in the preschool years. Studies of older children, however, reveal that gender identity continues to develop over a long time; in fact, it never truly ends.[34]

Children in elementary school reason about the constancy of gender identity in more advanced ways than before.[35] Preschoolers comprehend the stability of gender over time, and many comprehend the stability across situations. In the elementary school years, though, fewer children explain the constancy in terms of gender norms and external appearances, such as clothing, than do younger children. Further, an increasing number of children explain gender constancy in unchangeable, operational terms such as physical characteristics—"I have a penis"—or concepts such as "God made me a girl." Although one might expect that a greater realization of the constancy of gender identity would lead to more gender-stereotyped interests and behaviors, children in these years, particularly girls, are more flexible in their preferences for activities, chores, and future occupations than they were as preschoolers, and this flexibility increases with age.

Children develop a set of attitudes about what is gender appropriate, and, as noted in the previous chapter, these gender-appropriate schema motivate children to engage in gender-appropriate activities. At the same time, however, personal experiences and interests shape children's views of what is gender appropriate for them as individuals.[36] Children show greater flexibility with regard to psychological traits than to activities or occupations of the opposite gender. Those children who do endorse activities and occupations usually associated with the opposite gender do so because they believe these activities and occupations are appropriate for both genders.

The most flexible and tolerant children come from families where parents and same-sex siblings are flexible in their activities. Same-sex peers also play an important role in promoting flexibility and tolerance.

Ethnic Identity

Children learn about their own ethnic identities in a process similar to that involved in gender identity.[37] First, children learn to identify their ethnic group (label themselves white, African American, Hispanic). This occurs in the preschool years for European American and African American children, and a little later on for other groups such as Asian Americans. Children then learn what is distinctive about their own ethnic group. Children of all groups can do this by about age seven. Finally, again at about age seven, children learn ethnic consistency and constancy and realize they cannot change their ethnic identity. In this period, children learn what it means to be part of their culture. By age ten, they know their identity and prefer their own group.

While children learn about their ethnic identity from parents and the culture around them, they also learn about their ethnic identity indirectly from their daily activities, just as they learn about gender identity.

Collected in 1997, mothers' daily diaries of children's activities reveal significant ethnic differences in everyday routines that reflect the distinctive values of each group.[38] Compared with African American, Latino, and Asian American children, European American children spend more time playing, more time in sports activities, and less time studying. They spend more time reading than do African American and Latino children but less time than do Asian American children. This pattern of active, social pursuits fits well with European American mothers' beliefs that studying and academic skills are less important than the development of social skills and general cognitive skill.

African American children differ from the other three groups in spending more time in church and church activities; Latino children enjoy more household and family activities; Asian American children spend more time in educational activities. These patterns of behavior reflect the values of each ethnic group.

Children not only learn what it means to be part of their group, but they also come to prefer their own group, seeing it quite positively and viewing other groups less favorably. Studies indicate that in-group favoritism develops first in children by about age five.[39] Children initially prefer their own group without looking at the out-group negatively. Attitudes toward out-groups develop gradually in the early elementary school years. Out-group prejudice appears least likely to develop when children attend a multiethnic school where they have interactions with children of different groups and when they can describe negative qualities about the in-group. Children's ability to recognize negative qualities about their own group seems to enable them to see the positive qualities in other groups. Nevertheless, even when out-group attitudes are not negative, in-group favoritism is so great that out-group children suffer in comparison.

Self-Esteem

Susan Harter has carried out extensive research on self-development and self-esteem. Global feelings of self-worth are related to two independent factors: (1) one's feelings of competence in domains of importance and (2) the amount of social support one receives from others. Those highest in self-worth feel good about the abilities they value and also feel that others support and accept them. Those lowest in global self-worth feel they lack competence in domains deemed important and report that they receive little social support. Harter notes that no amount of social support can directly counteract one's perception of incompetence; conversely, no amount of competence can completely overcome feelings of lack of social support. So, to increase self-esteem, one has to increase both social support and feelings of competence in valued domains.

In Harter's studies, high-self-esteem children aged three to seven had two qualities—confidence in approaching situations and resilience when frustrated or upset.[41] These are also the qualities of children securely attached to their caregivers. Parental support, then, is a more important determinant of early self-esteem than is competence per se. In later childhood, both support and feelings of competence are important in determining self-worth.

The areas of competence that contribute most to feelings of self-worth are physical appearance and social acceptance by others—namely, parents and peers. Surprisingly, physical appearance and social support continue to be salient across the lifespan for individuals from eight to fifty-five years of age. Elementary school children also evaluate themselves in terms of their scholastic and athletic competence and their conduct.

Though self-esteem depends on the early positive regard given by parents and caregivers, this regard does not fix it for life. Levels of self-esteem can increase over time as individuals become more competent in areas of importance to them or as they receive increased support from others. Self-esteem decreases under the reverse conditions.

Times of change and transition, such as entrance into kindergarten, can trigger changes in self-esteem. New skills to develop, new reference groups for comparison, and new social groups for support provide the stimulus for change. Children maintain self-esteem most successfully when they join or create positive social support or when they increase in other areas of competence.

Recall from Chapter 3 that elementary school children of different ethnic groups resemble each other in self-esteem.[42] As they begin to take on culturally valued behaviors, self-esteem scores diverge, depending on the culture's values. When cultural values stress individualism, expressiveness, and self-assertion, then self-esteem scores stay high as they do in African American and European American groups. When cultural values emphasize respect for tradition, interdependence with others, and critical self-evaluation, then self-esteem scores drop, as they do in Latino and Asian American groups.

In sum, self-esteem arises in elementary school children in much the same way as in adults. Factors such as social support, competence, and cultural values affect self-esteem at this age.

DEVELOPMENT OF SELF-REGULATION

Elementary school children distinguish between guilt (feeling you did something naughty, feeling very sorry, wanting to make amends, fearing others will not like you) and shame (feeling afraid of being laughed at, feeling embarrassed, wanting to run away).[43] Guilt comes when children feel they have broken a moral rule, whereas shame is related to both moral and social blunders.

By about age eight, children become more self-critical, and their self-esteem is related to their ability to control verbal and physical aggression and other negative emotions. They feel ashamed when they violate a rule, and they take pride in being able to regulate their behavior and do what is approved. This is a good reason for parents to help children meet approved standards. Children do not feel good about themselves when they engage in behaviors they know others their age do not do.[44]

Table 9-1 (page 270) lists the parental behaviors associated with children's self-regulation and prosocial behavior. Self-control and caring emerge from mutually responsive interactions with parents, from direct teaching and guidance from parents, and from parents' modeling of caring behaviors.

Children begin to reason about social interactions at early ages and, even in the preschool years, distinguish between moral rules, which concern issues of harm and justice for others, and social rules, which are conventions people agree on.[45] They consider hurting others to be more serious than breaking social conventions.

In the early elementary school years, reasoning about moral and conventional behavior becomes more complex, and children take into account the context of an event. They look at social situations and distinguish certain behaviors as matters of personal choice, other behaviors as matters of social convention, and still others as moral issues. For example, it is morally wrong to deprive a person of a basic right

■ **T A B L E   9-1**
PARENTAL QUALITIES ASSOCIATED WITH CHILDREN'S SELF-REGULATION
AND PROSOCIAL BEHAVIOR

1. Being warm and supportive with children

2. Developing mutually responsive relationships with children

3. Helping children understand others' feelings and the effects of their behaviors
   on others

4. Using reasoning and persuasion to gain children's compliance with rules

5. Including children in family decision making

6. Helping children develop an internal code of rules for behavior

7. Modeling caring and concern for others

Adapted from Nancy Eisenberg and Carlos Valiente, "Parenting and Children's Prosocial and Moral
Development," in *Handbook of Parenting*, 2nd ed., ed. Marc H. Bornstein, vol. 5: *Practical Issues in
Parenting* (Mahwah, NJ: Erlbaum, 2002), 111–142.

such as access to schooling because of race or gender, but a person has the right of
personal choice to choose friends even if someone of another race or gender is not
included.[46] Children consider it wrong to violate a moral rule even if an authoritative adult tells them to do it. For example, it is wrong to keep on fighting even if an
adult tells you to do so.[47]

SOCIAL DEVELOPMENT

In this period, children begin to spend more time away from home. While parents
and home remain the center of life activities, friends begin to claim more of children's time.

Parent-Child Relationships

Parents spend half as much time with elementary school children and give them less
physical affection, compared with preschoolers. Even so, parents enjoy parenting as
much as in earlier years, and they report as much caring and regard for children as
earlier.[48]

Parents Role in Positive Behaviors   Parents' acceptance of, involvement in, and
sensitivity to children's needs continue as major forces in helping children become
responsible, competent, happy individuals. Parents are still the number-one figures
for schoolchildren, whose greatest fear is of losing their parents.

   If problems occur, parents' actions can help improve behavior. In one study, when
parents modeled appropriate social behaviors and gave positive reinforcement for
skillful social behaviors or made extra efforts so children could be with peers, then
children who experienced social rejection gained in social skills and friendships.[49]

Children's cognitive and social-emotional competence increased for a sample of high- and low-risk children assessed at ages four and thirteen.[50] Mothers who valued children's thinking for themselves and not conforming to others had high-risk children who gained in cognitive status. For both high-risk and low-risk children, mothers' lack of depression and lack of criticism and dissatisfaction were related to children's increase in social-emotional competence. Mothers' positive statements were also related to high-risk children's growth in social-emotional competence.

Parents' Role in Negative Behaviors   Parents' behaviors contribute not only to success but to negative outcomes as well. Mothers' harsh discipline, rated by interviewers and spouses and reflected in parents' statements of choice of discipline methods, predicted children's aggressive, impulsive behavior problems at school from kindergarten through grade four.[51] Even when the initial level of problem behavior was controlled, harsh discipline—seen in yelling, threatening, pushing, and spanking—predicted increases in aggressive behaviors over the four years. These relationships are not explainable solely on genetic grounds, that is, by aggressive parents passing on these traits to children and then having to use harsh discipline. A study of adoptive parents and children found that genetic factors play a role, however, in that children at risk for aggressive behaviors (based on the behaviors shown by their biological parents) tended to evoke negative parenting, which in turn increased aggressive behavior.[52] Even so, many children who were not at risk for aggressive behavior developed aggressive behaviors when parents used harsh discipline. Thus, genetic risk is not necessary to developing aggressive behaviors when parents use harsh discipline.

Parents' Changing Roles   Because parents no longer have exclusive control of children, they tend to permit children to make decisions that the parents monitor, supervise, and approve. This coregulation or sharing of control with children serves as a bridge to the preadolescent and adolescent years when children will assume more control.[53]

Conflicts between parents and children center on children's interpersonal behavior with others (their fighting, teasing), children's personality characteristics (their irritability, stubbornness), and parents' regulating activities, like rules about TV watching, chores, bedtime, and curfews.[54] Parents tend to justify their point of view in terms of conventionality, practicality, and health issues. Children tend to listen to parents' rules that prevent harm and psychological damage to others. Children report that they have more conflicts with fathers than mothers. Rather than physical punishment, effective discipline involves removal of privileges.

Mothers' and Fathers' Roles   In the elementary school period, mothers and fathers continue to relate to children in different ways.[55] Mothers take major responsibility for managing family tasks—scheduling homework and baths, for example. Mothers are both more directive with children and more positive in their reactions to them.

Fathers, though more generally neutral in affect, continue to engage in more physical play and give more affection to both boys and girls. When fathers have high-status jobs, they have less time to spend with their children, and so low job salience is related to men's playfulness and caregiving.[56] Men are most likely to be involved as fathers when mothers do not take on all the caregiving and managing. Nevertheless, the more skillful the mothers are with children, the more skillful fathers become. Both parents are similar in being more demanding of boys than of girls and more disapproving of boys' misbehavior.[57]

Though mothers and fathers have different roles, children see them as having many qualities in common.[58] Both parents are described as loving, happy, honest, responsible, self-confident individuals. Fathers are more interested in learning and creativity than are mothers, and mothers are more concerned about others' feelings than are fathers. Children describe themselves less positively than they describe their parents but still see many similarities with them. They are loving, happy, and interested in learning and creativity, but they are far below parents in self-confidence, cooperativeness, responsibility, and honesty. Children described "having good family relationships" as the most important family goal of mothers and themselves, but feel fathers' most valued goals are "educational/vocational."

When parents make demands on the child, social responsibility increases in boys, self-assertiveness in girls. Diana Baumrind suggests that parents actively encourage characteristics outside the usual gender stereotypes. Unless they exert a specific effort to encourage a broader range of characteristics, the natural tendencies for both mothers and fathers is to encourage assertiveness in boys and cooperation and a more dependent role in girls.[59]

Socializers of Ethnic Identity   Parents play an important role in the formation of their children's ethnic identity. School-age children reason more logically and better understand parents' statements. Because they spend more time outside of parents' direct control, they are more likely to experience prejudice or, at least, confusion at the different values other people hold.

Parents serve as a buffer between children and the larger society, interpreting social experiences for their children and helping them deal with them. To socialize children with regard to racial and ethnic issues, parents first teach children (1) their own cultural values, (2) the values of the majority culture, and (3) the realities of being a member of their own group in the majority culture and how people cope with the realities.[60] Successful socialization goes beyond this to teach pride in one's ethnic group and the importance of one's own self-development.

We focus here on how African American parents socialize children, because more research is available on this group; other groups may experience a similar process.[61] African American parents think that teaching about their racial identity is important but is not *the* most important information to pass on to children. To parents, being African American means children should learn how to deal with prejudice, feel pride and self-respect, learn the value of a good education, and recognize that their fair and moral behavior is not always reciprocated.

Many African American parents do not discuss ethnic issues with their children. In a national sample, over one-third of parents reported making no statements, and few of the two-thirds who reported making a statement touched on more than one area. Which parents are most likely to talk to their children? Older, married parents who live in racially mixed neighborhoods with a sizable white population are most

■ **T A B L E   9-2**
SOCIALIZATION MESSAGES AFRICAN AMERICAN
PARENTS IMPART TO CHILDREN*

Message	% Parents
Achieving and working hard: *"Work hard and get a good education."*	22
Racial pride: *"Be proud of being black."*	17
Themes of black heritage: *"Taught what happened in the past and how people coped."*	9
Focus on intergroup relations: *Summary category of many responses—accommodate whites, use collective action to help blacks*	9
Presence of racial restrictions and barriers: *"Blacks don't have the opportunities whites have."*	8
Good citizenship: *"Be honest, fair."*	7
Recognition and acceptance of racial background: *"Realize you are black."*	7
Fundamental equality of blacks and whites: *"Recognize all races as equal."*	6
Maintenance of a positive self-image: *"Instruct children to stay away from whites."*	5 3†

*Information from the National Survey of Black Americans, a representative national sample of 2,107 men and women. Statements tabulated from the answers to two questions: "In raising children, have you told them things to help them know what it is to be black?" and "What are the most important things you have said?"

†Remaining categories of 1 or 2 percent include a variety of responses having to do with emphasizing religious principles, discussing personal traits, and stressing general self-acceptance.

From Michael C. Thornton, Linda M. Chatters, Robert Joseph Taylor, and Walter R. Allen, "Sociodemographic and Environmental Correlates of Racial Socialization by Black Parents," *Child Development* 61 (1990): 401–409.

likely to talk to children. Mothers are more likely to socialize children than are fathers. Parents living in the Northeast tend to discuss racial matters, perhaps because, as in mixed neighborhoods, there is more contact among races.

Table 9-2 summarizes socialization messages that African American parents share with their children. Only about 22 percent teach racial pride and a positive self-image, yet this is the area parents are most uniquely fitted to address. Both majority and minority children evaluate themselves the way others close to them do, and so what parents convey strongly affects the children's self-esteem. Because a minority child may get inaccurate and negative messages from other children, the media, and authority figures such as coaches or teachers, it is even more important for minority parents to encourage a positive self-image and racial pride. When parents emphasize awareness of social restrictions and barriers but at the same time encourage self-development and ethnic pride and help children develop strategies for dealing with barriers, children are happy, high in self-esteem, and successful in school.[62]

Relationships with Siblings

Siblings frequently spend more time with each other than they do with parents.[63] Their relationships improve in the elementary school years and become more enjoyable. The degree of satisfaction depends on the emotional climate in the family, because sibling relationships tend to mirror the ways parents treat each other and the ways they relate to children.[64] When parents are responsive to children and treat them fairly, then siblings have good relationships.

Conversely, when mothers and fathers are angry with each other, they are more hostile with their children, who, in turn, show anger at their siblings and their peers.[65] Children's behavior may be disruptive for a variety of reasons. They may model parents' fighting with siblings and peers or they may be so upset and irritable that they lack emotional control and become angry. They may even blame themselves for the marital conflict. Because conflict in sibling relationships during these years predict a child's level of anxiety, depression, and acting out in early adolescence, improving these relationships when tension arises is important.[66]

While most research on sibling relationships has been carried out on European American families, research with rural African American families has yielded similar results.[67] When parents have good relationships with each other and positive relationships with their children, the older siblings develop good emotional control and are supportive and caring with younger siblings. Even though these parents work long hours and have financial pressures, when parents are caring with them, the older children also show care with younger siblings.

Peer Relationships

In the elementary school years, children have more contact with peers, spending about 30 percent or more of their time with them in a wide variety of settings—school, sports, and interest groups—with less adult supervision than before. As in the preschool years, children are attracted to peers whose interests are similar to theirs.[68] They continue to prefer positive interactions and to work problems out so that everyone's needs are met. Relationships grow when children can express thoughts and feelings clearly.

In these years, children begin to compare their social behaviors with those of peers.[69] Some children are identified as popular and sought after as friends. These children are socially skilled and enter new activities or relationships in quiet ways, not drawing attention to themselves. Friendly, cooperative, sensitive to others' needs, and helpful, they rarely interfere with others' actions or plans.

Aggressive Children   Some children are rejected. This occurs mostly when they show aggressive behavior, which takes many forms. Children may physically hit or hurt others, or they may be verbally assaultive—taunting, teasing, humiliating others. This type of aggression is overt, noticeable, and more characteristic of boys than of girls.[70] Another form of aggression, termed *relational aggression,* is more subtle, not easily detectable, and more characteristic of girls. It consists of acts designed to deprive children of friends—spreading untrue rumors about a target child, organizing other children to reject the target child, refusing to be a friend unless the target child does favors. These behaviors are considered aggressive because they are meant to hurt or damage another child.

In one study, about 27 percent of boys were described as aggressive, and of those boys 93 percent were overtly aggressive.[71] About 22 percent of girls were described as aggressive, and of those girls 95 percent were engaged in relational aggression. Only about one-quarter of aggressive children used both forms to hurt children; most relied on one or the other. Note that when relational aggression is assessed, girls are almost equal to boys in aggressive behavior.

Because both forms of aggressive behavior lead to peer rejection, ongoing social problems, feelings of loneliness, and low self-esteem, interventions are important so children can gain acceptance and avoid the problems of adolescence and adulthood associated with aggressiveness in childhood.[72]

Bullying   Bullying occurs when an aggressive child targets a single child or a small group and, though unprovoked, pursues the child(ren) and uses force in an unemotional way, divorced from conflict or disagreement. About two-thirds of aggressive children are overt bullies, and 10 to 15 percent of all children are victims of overt bullying.[73] As noted earlier, almost all aggressive girls engage in relational aggression, and about 8 percent of all girls are victims of relational aggression.[74] Victims of both forms of bullying share certain characteristics. They tend to be quiet, inhibited children with low self-esteem. They are sometimes physically weaker. A small subgroup of victims are impulsive, disruptive children who invite negative reactions from others. Victims accept the aggression, withdrawing or responding with immature behavior such as crying, thus rewarding the bully's behavior. As victims continue to experience bullying, their self-esteem decreases further, and over time they become depressed and develop behavior problems at home and at school.[75] When followed up in young adulthood, victims have as many social skills as young adults who were not bullied, but bullying has left its mark. Former victims are prone to feelings of depression and low self-esteem.

Research on ways to combat bullying indicate that those children who have confidence in their social skills and resist bullying with self-assertion are able to end the victimization, even if they are initially inhibited or physically weaker children.[76] They need not be physically aggressive, but they do not tolerate the attacks. Parents can help children combat bullying by enrolling children in social skills programs that teach and rehearse self-assertion. Victimization requires intervention to help both the victim and the bully, as both suffer in the present and the future. Unfortunately, bullying rarely fades away on its own.

TASKS AND CONCERNS OF PARENTS

Because elementary school children spend more time out of parents' direct care, parenting tasks include new activities as well as previous caregiving behaviors. In this age period, parenting tasks include the following:

- Being attentive, available, and responsive and modeling desired behavior
- Structuring the home and daily routines so children have healthy lifestyles
- Monitoring and guiding children's behavior from a distance
- Encouraging new skills, new activities, and growing interest in friends
- Participating in children's activities outside the home in supportive way (room parent, den leader)
- Serving as an interpreter of children's experiences in the larger social world
- Serving as children's advocate with authorities outside the home
- Maintaining family rituals
- Sharing leisure activities and fun

As parents learn how to manage these tasks, they and their children face many concerns specific to this age. School is clearly a source of worry to children. Schoolwork is also a source of concern to parents, who pay great attention to promoting children's success in school. Other issues faced include isolation, aggression, lying and stealing, sibling rivalry, chores, and television watching.

Promoting Healthy Lifestyles

When their children were infants, parents of school-age children may have thought that when their children could sleep through the night, feed themselves, and follow simple routines and rules, they would be finished dealing with issues of eating and sleeping. As we have seen, however, healthy sleep, eating, and exercise habits continue to affect children's physical well-being, and children do not establish and maintain them without parents' help. Poor sleep and poor eating habits are related to school inattentiveness and restlessness, which interfere with being able to concentrate and learn new material.

As we saw in Chapter 8, parents establish and monitor their children's sleep habits early on. This continues through the elementary years. Because each child is unique, parents have to determine the proper amount of sleep for their child and maintain bedtimes so the child gets it.

A recent study indicates that adding an hour's sleep each night to children's existing schedule improves memory and reaction times on cognitive tests; the increase is the equivalent of two years of chronological age on these tests.[77]

Parents have no control over what children eat when they are away from home, but they do control the food available at home. Parents can buy primarily healthy foods and model healthy eating habits. If potato chips and soda are at hand, children will consume them or beg to do so. If parents do not provide such snacks, children are less likely to argue for them.

Serving healthy meals and having positive conversations during meals encourage children to enjoy eating and to eat a reasonable amount of food. While it can be difficult to plan and organize family meals with the television off, the effort is worth it.

Building regular exercise times into daily routines is difficult when both parents work, but predinner calisthenics for all family members or post-dinner walks in good weather may work. Knowing how important exercise is can alert parents to opportunities at school or in the neighborhood for children, and perhaps the whole family, to exercise.

Daily family routines and rituals organized around sleeping and eating not only lead to better physical condition of all family members, but also increase the psychological well-being of family members (see Chapter 4). A review of fifty years of research on family routines and rituals finds that routines draw family members together and improve relationships.[78]

Helping Children Regulate Feelings

Pediatricians report a growing number of children aged five to fifteen with psychological problems requiring help.[79] Research comparing the responses of pediatricians in 1979 with responses in 1996 finds that in 1979, 6.8 percent of children were identified in routine office visits as having psychological problems requiring help, and in 1996, the comparable figure was 18.7 percent. The largest increases were in attention deficit hyperactivity problems, which went from 1.4 percent of children seen in the 1979 survey to 8.5 percent in 1996, and in emotional problems, which went from 0.2 percent in 1979 to 3.2 percent in 1996.

Chapter 4 talks about coaching children to identify their own and others' feelings and to deal with them in acceptable ways. Here we focus on two common feelings—anger and discouragement—because they can be so easily aroused as part of the school experience yet must be controlled.

Anger   Tim Murphy, a psychologist and recently elected Congressman, has described a program for parents to help their out-of-control children. In describing the angry child, he makes several important points. He defines *anger* in broad terms: a feeling of displeasure, as a result of a perceived injury, and a desire to retaliate against the source of the injury. This definition reflects what many parents see in the angry child.

He describes four stages of anger: the buildup, the spark, the explosion, and the aftermath. He also describes what he terms *microbursts* of anger—the sudden, brief outbursts that end almost as soon as they start. He urges parents to attend to these microbursts. Because the child is not extremely upset, parents can often use the episodes to help the child develop a better understanding of feelings and better problem-solving skills.

Murphy describes several important characteristics of the angry child. First, rather than distinguishing sadness, disappointment, and frustration, the angry child turns all negative experiences into anger. Second, the angry child sees the source of the difficulty as someone else's deliberate action against him or her. Frustration is seen as caused not by uncontrollable events or family needs or even the child's difficulty in accomplishing something but by the parent, particularly the mother. Third, and most important, angry children are not clear thinkers or effective problem solvers. Prone to negative self-talk that immobilizes them, they cannot figure out how to make things better. Sadly, they often equate anger with power and feelings of self-esteem.

According to Murphy, the meaning of anger is in part related to family patterns of interaction. In the hurried, busy family, anger is a sign of stress. In the troubled family dealing with problems of addiction, loss, parents' psychological problems, and marital discord, anger is a sign of pain. In the angry family, anger serves as sign of power. In the indulging family, anger is a sign of desire. Indulging parents have led children to believe they should have what they want. Because they do not set many clear guidelines and do not reinforce the guidelines they do have, the child learns to persist as long and as angrily as necessary to win each battle.

Drawing on many of the anger-management strategies discussed in Chapters 4 and 5, Murphy describes positive parenting in terms of six healthy attitudes. Some of these resemble how Rudolf Dreikurs approaches the handling of children's mistakes (see Chapter 4):

1. Teach the child to be independent.
2. Emphasize the process of accomplishing the task, not just the end product.
3. Keep the childlike perspective alive in you so you can better understand and empathize with your child.
4. Choose what you say carefully; words of criticism can remain in a child's memory forever.
5. Learn to laugh at some of the difficulties and avoid taking them so seriously.
6. "Parent peacefully in an angry world;" teach the positive behaviors that will avoid the problems—for example, teach a child tolerance before the child becomes prejudiced; coach feeling expression before a child becomes angry.

Gerald Patterson's program also deals with children's angry outbursts (see Chapter 8).[81] It focuses on paying positive attention to children's behavior, engaging in fun activities, and then consistently rewarding behaviors with positive and negative consequences as necessary.

Discouragement   In these years of rapidly developing skills, meeting new friends, and learning in formal settings in comparison with others, discouragement is a common feeling, especially for the more cautious, less confident child. Martin Seligman offers a program quite useful for parents. (See Chapter 4 as well.)

Martin Seligman has documented the nature of pessimistic attitudes that lead to discouragement and withdrawal from challenging tasks. Pessimistic individuals consider difficulty a sign of a pervasive, permanent problem that is one's personal fault and is unchangeable.[82] Pessimistic children see a poor math grade as the result of their own stupidity and inability to do math. They sometimes avoid studying because they are discouraged and feel they are no good at the subject.

As outlined in Chapter 4, parents can supply new interpretations of the problem. Perhaps the child did not study enough, perhaps the child needs extra tutoring. Parents can encourage their children to look for solutions to problems and to exert effort to achieve them, as most problems will improve with such efforts from the child. Parents also must avoid critical personal comments, such as "You never learn at school—you just fool around," which can sap children's confidence. See Chapter 4 for further suggestions.

Promoting Positive Social Relationships

Parents play an important role in helping children develop effective social skills.

Helping the Shy Child   Shy children hesitate to approach others, are often uncertain of what to say to others, and are uncertain how to join games. They worry about rejection. Philip Zimbardo and Shirley Radl offer many suggestions for the parent of the shy child. These measures focus on increasing the child's expressiveness (smiling, talking more), interactions with others (starting conversations), and opportunities for social contact.[83] All these actions are designed to increase self-esteem, confidence, and socially outgoing behavior. This behavior, along with coaching about group interactions, minimizes the likelihood of a child's being bullied and enables the child to deal more effectively with bullies.

Behaviorists coach children in effective ways of interacting and provide opportunities to practice (1) participating in group activities (getting started, paying attention to the game), (2) cooperating in play (sharing, taking turns), (3) communicating with the peer (talking or listening), and (4) validating and supporting the peer (giving attention and help). The benefits are found to persist a year.[84]

Several factors are related to improvement in children's social status.[85] Children who got involved in extracurricular activities improved in social status. Whether it was the development of new skills, the opportunities for making new friends, or increased confidence and self-esteem that led to improved social status is not known. Children who took some responsibility for peer difficulties and whose parents believed good social skills were important, modeled them, and gave appropriate rewards for skillful actions also improved in status. Boys who felt self-confident and socially skilled improved their status as well.

Helping the Aggressive Child   A major form of intervention for aggressive children is to help them develop positive social skills. Much like group programs for shy children, behavioral programs for aggressive children focus on positive behaviors. These programs encourage cooperation, offer positive techniques to support peers, develop verbal skills to make requests and suggestions, teach positive techniques for anger management (as outlined in the preceding section), and provide opportunities for children to rehearse the skills that increase social competence

---

VOICES OF EXPERIENCE

The Joys of Parenting
Elementary School Children

"He's nine, and for the last several months, maybe because I'm the dad, he's come and said, 'Now there's this girl who's written me a note, what do I do?' Or, 'I have an interest here, how do I act?' I never heard any of this from my daughters. Then he says, 'What were you doing in the third grade? How did you deal with this when you were in the third grade?'" FATHER

"Being able to see life through their eyes is fun, sharing the way they see things, the questions they ask." MOTHER

"They are very loving kids. They'll give me a kiss good night and say, 'I'll love you forever.' That's a tradition." FATHER

"It was fun to see him learn to read. First, he knew the letters and then he read a little, and by the end of the year, he could read a lot." MOTHER

"I like watching them when they don't know I'm watching. They're playing or taking something apart. That's when you see how well you've transferred your values to them." FATHER

"It's fun to see the children join in with other kids. They went with their cousins to a July 4th celebration. They got right into a game with children they didn't know." MOTHER

---

and peer acceptance. In follow-up studies, children who attended such programs achieved greater peer acceptance and reduced their aggressive responses.

Helping the Bully   Dan Olweus has studied bullying extensively in Norway and developed a school-based program to decrease it. This program requires the involvement and commitment of school administrators, teachers, parents, and students. Adults create, at school and at home, an environment in which children experience warm, positive attention and firm limits against negative behaviors. Negative behaviors receive consistent, nonhostile, nonphysical consequences, and monitoring occurs in and out of school.

Interventions occur at the school, class, and individual level and include the formation of a coordinating group, meetings with staff and parents, better supervision during recess, class rules against bullying, and class meetings. At the individual level, parents, teachers, and students meet to discuss specific incidents and to develop strategies to handle them. Emphasis is on developing effective forms of communication and positive behaviors in all students, not just in bullies or victims.

Evaluated by 2,500 students and their teachers, the intervention program was found to reduce bullying by 50 percent and decrease other antisocial acts as well.

"She wrote poems in school this year. It's amazing. She's quiet, and yet when you see the poems, you realize how much goes on in her head, how observant she is." FATHER

"I like seeing how important family is to them. They enjoy seeing their cousins, they like family to visit." MOTHER

"I'm a kid again. I get to do everything I liked to do all over again." FATHER

"It's fun when she says, 'Mommy, smile at me, make me laugh.'" MOTHER

"I enjoy watching their relationship grow. They are nineteen months apart. They play together a lot. She said to me, 'Sometimes, he's fun to play with and I love him, but sometimes he's a rascal.' They do a lot of imaginary play." MOTHER

"Every night we have a talking time just before he goes to bed, either he and his Dad or he and I. He's a real deep thinker, and he likes to get advice or get a response, and he just needs that verbal connection. So a few years ago when he was five, he was talking about being afraid of death and that he might not be married and he might not have children and that would be the worst. I can hear parts of what he might hear at church or other places like school, and he takes it all very seriously; when it collides, he wants to know what the answer is. They are always things we don't know the answer to, either." MOTHER

"I can say as a father of two girls between five and ten that to be a father to girls is delightful. It's nice being looked on as a combination of God and Robert Redford. They have a little glow in their eyes when they look at Dad, and it's great. The younger one said, 'When I'm ticklish, you know why? Because I love you so much.'" FATHER

Moreover, bullying away from the school did not increase. Students expressed greater satisfaction with their schoolwork, and their social relationships with children increased. The benefits were in some instances more marked after two years than after one year.

In all areas of social difficulties—shyness, aggressiveness, victimization—taking action to learn social skills, to engage in activities that increase confidence, and to assert oneself when attacked help children improve their social status. Parents play an important role here—to ensure that children have opportunities to increase their social competence and to ensure that the school atmosphere is a safe place for all children.

Partnership of Families and Schools

In the past, people looked on the school as having a separate social entity that carried the primary responsibility for educating children. Parents played a secondary role—raising funds, volunteering in the school, and enriching the curriculum with their input and values. Recently, a partnership model for families and schools has been advanced.[87] Acknowledging the powerful impact of parents' involvement and encouragement on children's educational progress, the partnership model seeks to forge a strong link between parents and the schools. This model rests on six major kinds of involvement:

1. Parents provide a home that allows children to (a) be healthy and attend school, (b) be calm and confident enough to pay attention in class and do their work, (c) receive encouragement to perform well, and (d) have home settings that support doing homework and educational projects. Schools provide families with information on effective parenting and school-related issues; they sometimes also provide supportive programs or workshops.

2. Schools communicate and keep parents informed of school matters and students' progress and behavior. This includes notices on students' current performance, any difficulties that arise, and any noteworthy behaviors of students, as well as information on school programs, school needs, and opportunities for parental involvement in projects. Effective communication also involves channels for parents' input on programs.

3. Parents, children, and other community members contribute their own special skills to promote children's education, as in cleaning, painting, and giving cultural information of interest.

4. Teachers help parents monitor and help children learn at home. Schools make educational goals and curricula available, show parents how to assist their children, and even give joint assignments that parents and student carry out together.

5. Parents participate in school organizations and in formal or informal groups that advise educators on school priorities, school improvement programs, and parents' and students' perceptions of problems in the school environment.

6. Finally, parents and schools work with business organizations, local government agencies, and volunteer groups to form partnerships that support school programs.

Lying and Stealing

When parents create a supportive atmosphere in which children can talk about mistakes and misdeeds, and when they offer encouragement rather than criticism, lying and stealing are reduced. Still, almost every child has told a lie at one time or another, and all parents have concerns about lying and stealing because trust in others is such an important part of close relationships.

Parents are wise to express their feelings of concern about dishonesty, accept matter-of-factly that the child has lied or stolen, and problem-solve with the child ways to be more truthful and honest. If a child lies about school work, they should find out if there are special problems at school. If a child brags about false exploits, they do well to focus on why he or she needs to do this to feel good. Parents express their belief that their child wants to be honest, and as partners, they need to figure out how to bring this about. Mutual problem-solving, as discussed in Chapter 5, is very useful. In this process, the parent becomes an ally and a resource, not an accuser and a judge. The child learns that one can get help when in trouble and that one need not be perfect to be loved.

Managing Television

"Television and other media occupy more time than any other activity except sleeping."[88] A nationally representative, 1999 survey of 3,000 children's media use, defined broadly to include television, videos, video games, CD players, tape players, computers, and books, revealed that, on average, children spent about five and a half hours per day using media at home. Since children sometimes used two media at once, with the total time for media averaging six and a half hours per day. There were ethnic differences, with African American children averaging seven hours and fifty minutes per day and Latino children averaging seven hours and five minutes.[89]

Media use has not been shown to develop skills. It is primarily a solitary activity; only a majority of young children watch television with a parent. Although video and computer games can be played with someone else, they are most often played alone. The use of media does not lead to clear-cut skills, with the exceptions of reading, which develops reading skills and is related to academic progress, and educational television, which increases knowledge.

We know most about the use and effects of television, as little research has examined the impact of new technologies such as computers and the Internet.[90] As such, this section focuses on television. Television affects viewers powerfully. For example, year-old infants reacted to actresses' emotional preferences for toys just as they copied a mother's emotional responses to toys. They avoided the toys when the actress reacted negatively to them and played with the ones for which the actress expressed positive feeling.[91]

The exact impact of television depends on the characteristics of the viewer, the amount of viewing time, the general family and social circumstances, and, most important, the content of the programs. Educators have been concerned that television decreases cognitive skills and academic achievement, yet the effects of television depend on the nature of the programs watched. When children watch educational programs, they can acquire literacy and number skills and increase their knowledge of science and history. Although important for children in all income groups, educational programs especially serve children whose families have limited educational resources. Still, children's heavy viewing is related to difficulties in impulse control, task persistence, and the ability to delay gratification.[92]

Television viewing is inversely related to social background. Families with more education and more income watch less television, perhaps because they have income to pursue other activities.[93] When social status is controlled, European Americans watch less television than do African Americans or Hispanics. Hispanics watch significant amounts, perhaps as a way to improve their English and better understand U.S. culture.

Television viewing needs to be considered in light of family and social contact. Children's viewing is related to how much parents watch, the television habits of older and younger siblings, preschool attendance, and the mother's work schedule.[94] Families socialize young children's television use early on; by the age of three or four, a child's patterns are established.

Television, in turn, affects family life. Studies have found that when they are not watching television, family members talk more to each other and engage in more stimulating activities.[95] When they are watching television, family members are in close physical proximity and are more relaxed. Interestingly, adolescents who watch television with their families report feeling better during time spent with their friends.

The Effects of Television Violence

> Perhaps no greater cultural influence on children's aggressive development can be found than the effects of viewing violence on television. Laboratory studies over the past quarter-century demonstrate that viewing televised aggressive models leads immediately to increased aggressive behavior, whether assessed by "Bobo" dolls or toward peer. . . . The effect is fairly linear: the more a child watches TV violence, the more aggressive that child becomes.[96]

Repeated viewing of violent television programs has even greater effects over time. In one study, boys' preference for aggressive programs at age eight predicted aggression and seriousness of criminal arrests at age thirty, even when social class, parenting, intelligence, and initial aggression at age eight were controlled for. Reviews of the most carefully controlled studies

> indicate that the effects of TV violence are robust and account for about 10 percent of the variance in child aggression, which approximately equals the magnitude of effect of cigarette smoking on lung cancer. This finding appears to be one of the most rigorously tested and robust effects in all of developmental psychology.[97]

Children are more influenced by television violence than are adults, perhaps because they attend to the dramatic effects of the programs and have less understanding of the moral significance of the behaviors they see. In addition, they are more likely than adults to believe that television violence is real. Educational programs to decrease aggressive behavior in frequent viewers of television violence help children understand that the violence is staged and not real. These educational efforts show children how television fools them and how violence is not useful in settling everyday problems. Children actively participate in passing this information on to other children by giving talks or making videos to show how television fooled them. Follow-up studies of such programs find that fewer participants are identified as aggressive than are children who did not participate in the intervention.

Studies also show that a simple approach can reduce aggression.[98] Turning off the television and reducing time spent with violent videotapes and video games reduced children's aggression on school playgrounds. Students who participated in a program to reduce television and videotape and video game use showed a 50 percent reduction in verbal aggression on the playground. Reducing media use also reduced children's obesity.

Helping Children Use Television Effectively   Parents' example is the most significant way to influence children's television use.[99] Parents provide a model of how to use television for education, discussion, and relaxation. In addition, children also view parents' television choices; so, from the beginning, the content of parents' selections influences their children. Second, parents can monitor the amount of time children watch and encourage educational programs. Third, parents can watch programs with their children and make television viewing a social occasion by discussing the content of what they see. Fourth, parents can take community action. They can lobby television stations to follow the guidelines of the Television Violence Act of 1990 and the Children's Educational Television Act of 1990. Finally, parents can lobby schools to teach critical-viewing skills. Schools in Canada and Europe have organized media literacy training for all students, and some require students to pass a media literacy test.

Aimee Dorr, Beth Rabin, and Sandra Irlen suggest that, in addition to these direct interventions, parents organize the household and children's activities around other interests and pursuits.[100] They believe that emphasizing other activities may be a more successful way to curb television use than regulating the amount of time children watch. They also recommend that parents become active socializers of their children by promoting core values that children internalize and rely on to counteract the messages that television provides.

PRACTICAL QUESTION: WHAT CAN PARENTS DO WHEN SCHOOL AND PSYCHOLOGICAL DIFFICULTIES INTERFERE WITH SCHOOL ACHIEVEMENT?

Children may forget homework or resist doing it because it is hard. They may be anxious and have few friends at school. Such problems frustrate children and parents and require action, but they usually do not interfere with school performance and achievement. Sometimes, however, children's school difficulties are so marked that they prevent learning and successful school performance, and they require parents' and teachers' actions to remedy the situation. For example, forgetfulness on a daily basis may be part of a larger picture of general inattention, hyperactivity, and impulsivity, the core symptoms of Attention Deficit Hyperactivity Disorder (ADHD). Or children may have learning disabilities involving difficulties regarding reading, writing, or carrying out actions in the correct sequence.

These problems may not have appeared at home, and they may not be immediately apparent at school. A child may seem a little slow in "settling down" at school or a little slow in learning and printing letters, but parents and teachers may initially consider the child able to attend or do the work. When difficulties persist over time and result in lowered performance or failure to learn material, parents and teachers together must consider what to do. Space does not permit detailed discussions of attention deficit hyperactivity disorder, learning disabilities, or the great variety of emotional disorders that interfere with achievement, but a general plan for dealing with these kinds of problems is described.

School difficulties require accurate diagnosis as the first step in the process of remedying them. Learning disabilities and ADHD are common sources of problems, but they are not easy to separate, because the two significantly overlap. School study teams and school psychologists observe and test children and provide vital information in identifying sources of the problems. If difficulties do not fall into certain categories or meet certain criteria of delays, schools might not do assessments, in which case parents have to seek assessments privately. If they cannot afford such services, which can be quite expensive, parents can seek help from agencies or local colleges that provide services on a sliding-scale basis.

When specific difficulties are identified, then parents, teachers, and children meet to plan how to remedy them. It is important to involve children in the process, as they need to understand specifically what they need to change, and they may have good ideas about how to produce change. In encouraging new behaviors and skills, parents and teachers identify the specific positive behaviors they want from children. Sometimes, thinking that children know what to do, adults give general directions: "Be good in school today" or "Get your work done." Instead, they need to be specific: "When I give you a work sheet, stay in your seat until you finish it, and then you can bring it to my desk." "When you write, use a finger's width between each word." "Go slowly so you read each word."

The level of work expected must be tailored to children's abilities. When children are performing below grade level, tutoring and special assignments are required so that children are able and motivated to practice and increase their levels of performance. If assignments are too difficult at the age-appropriate level but are expected nonetheless, then children will grow discouraged and resist doing them. Levels of work difficulty can change as children learn basic skills. As with other kinds of school problems, daily contracts can be made with children regarding their behavior and the amount and kind of work they must complete to earn privileges.

Emotional problems such as extreme anxiety or depression can also decrease school performance and are usually addressed in consultation with mental health professionals. Clinicians can provide parents and schools with realistic expectations and work demands for children and help parents and teachers make plans to control the effects of the emotional reactions. They can suggest school interventions and modify them, depending on their level of effectiveness.

Serious problems at school impact family life as well. Children might hate and resist schoolwork. They might insist they cannot do the work, so parents must be sure they can. Once parents know that the work is appropriate, they must provide an atmosphere of encouragement that motivates children to strive for improvement. Parents must be sure that children continue to get all the help and support they need at school and at home.

At the same time that parents help children deal with difficulties, parents also identify children's strengths, inside and outside of school, and help children gain pleasure and satisfaction from them to balance the effort and frustration required by problem areas. For example, sports of different kinds can channel the energy and frustration of athletic children, and artistic activities such as music or drawing provide important outlets for creative children. As children progress through school, they have greater opportunities for choice in subjects, and parents can help them select courses that draw on their abilities.

Siblings may use school difficulties as a means of teasing or for comparisons that enable them to feel better about themselves and their skills. Parents must stop such behavior and teach family members that all children have their own special strengths, and everyone has one or more areas in which they must strive for improvement. Parents can express empathy for children who must spend long hours, year after year, in an atmosphere and activity that brings frustration.

Having daily fun with family members, perhaps after dinner, relaxes everyone and increases good feelings that sustain effort and motivation for the work. School difficulty is not easy for parents, children, or school personnel, but working together as a team, focusing on solutions, helps everyone feel better and leads to greater success.

PARENTS' EXPERIENCES IN FACING TRANSITIONS

Children's entrance into school marks a new stage in parenthood. Children spend more time away from their parents in school and with peers. They are absorbing new information and are exposed to new values. Ellen Galinsky describes this parental stage as the *interpretive stage*.[101] Parents share facts and information about the world, teach values, and guide children's behavior in certain directions. They decide how they will handle the child's greater independence and involvement with people who may not share similar values.

At this point, parents have a more realistic view of themselves as parents than before and a greater understanding of their children as individuals. Parents have been through the sleepless nights and crying of infancy, the temper tantrums of the toddler, and the instruction of their children in basic routines and habits. They have a sense of how they and their child will react in any given situation. Though some carry a negative view of themselves as parents, most have developed a sense of their strengths and difficulties and a confidence that, by and large, they and their children are okay. Children, however, leave the parents' control and enter a structured environment with rules and regulations. Children are evaluated in terms of their ability to control their behavior and learn skills that will help them as adults. For the first time, external standards and grades compare children with each other. Parents must deal with, and help their children deal with, these external evaluations, which may differ from those parents have formed at home.

For parents, bridging the gap between the way they treat their children and the way their children are treated by teachers, group leaders, and peers may be a constant struggle. Parents develop strategies for dealing with teachers, doctors, and principals who do not see the child as they do. An attitude that stresses cooperation among adults seems most effective. When parents share their knowledge about their child, when they seek to understand the child's behaviors that demand change, they can form a coalition with adults outside the home to produce a positive experience for their child.

In the process of explaining the world and people's behavior, parents refine their beliefs and values, discarding some and adding others. Children often prompt changes when they discover inconsistencies and hypocrisies in what parents say. If lying is bad, why do parents tell relatives they are busy when they are not? If parents care about the world and want to make it a safer place, why are they not doing something to make it safe? In the process of answering these questions, parents grow as well as children.

SUPPORT FOR PARENTS

There are many forms of support for parents of elementary school children. Parents work together with teachers and school personnel in Parent Teacher Associations or local organizations to provide the most effective schools possible. Specialized parent support groups also offer valuable information and resources. For example, Children and Adults with Attention Deficit Disorders (CHADD) provides support for families dealing with ADHD; the Orton Dyslexia Society helps with problems of reading; the Learning Disabilities Association of America, with learning disabilities. In addition, local and state organizations can be helpful.

Parent training programs also provide support. Extensive and effective programs to decrease children's aggressiveness and improve social behavior have been devised at the Oregon Social Learning Center. Patterson and his colleagues have worked with married parents, divorced single parents, foster parents, and parent-teacher partnerships to establish structure as well as positive and consistent rewards to help children learn to control aggressive behavior and develop prosocial behaviors at home and at school. These programs have found success and are being refined and expanded.

These are secular forms of support. At all age levels, parents and children find moral support and strength from religious activities as well. This source of support becomes important at this stage, because children begin to explore moral and ethical issues and are exposed to more ideas about these issues than before. Religious participation provides opportunities for discussing moral principles and applying them to everyday life.

Parents involved in religion can easily include their children. When parents have no affiliation, Joan Beck recommends that parents develop an individual belief system that they share with children as they grow.[102] The process of developing an agreed-on source of spiritual or secular meaning in life can enrich the entire family.

Religious faith also contributes to feelings of confidence and security. In their study of resilient children who overcame the difficulties of growing up in troubled families, Emmy Werner and Ruth Smith point to the importance of faith:

> A potent protective factor among high-risk individuals who grew into successful adulthood was a faith that life made sense, that the odds could be overcome. This faith was tied to active involvement in church activities, whether Buddhist, Catholic, mainstream Protestant, or fundamentalist.[103]

Children's conception of God adds security to life by providing fallible parents with a backup expert who helps them.

"God is my parents' parent and mine, too," said one girl.[104]

MAIN POINTS

As children's competence increases, by the end of this period they have
- acquired all the basic skills in gross and fine motor coordination
- developed more logical thinking abilities so that they can grasp the relations between objects
- learned greater understanding of their own and others' emotional reactions
- gained greater control of their aggressiveness and become less fearful
- learned to remedy situations they control and adjust to situations others control
- come to value themselves for their physical, intellectual, and social competence, developing an overall sense of self-worth

Schools
- are the main socializing force outside the family
- create stress in children's lives because children worry about making mistakes, being ridiculed, and failing
- promote a strong bond with children by encouraging active participation in learning and activities
- promote learning when they provide a calm, controlled environment and when teachers are gentle disciplinarians with high expectations for students
- often do not reward the values of ethnic groups that emphasize cooperation and sharing among its members
- are highly valued by many ethnic group members who wish their children to spend more time there, do more homework, and have more proficiency tests
- provide opportunities for social experiences

With peers, children
- interact in an egalitarian, give-and-take fashion
- prefer those who are outgoing and supportive of other children
- interact more effectively when parents have been affectionate, warm, and accepting with them and less effectively when there is stress in the family
- can improve relationships when they learn new skills

Parenting tasks in this period include
- monitoring and guiding children from a distance as children move into new activities on their own
- interacting in a warm, accepting, yet firm manner when children are present

- strengthening children's abilities to monitor their own behavior and develop new skills
- structuring the home environment so the child can meet school responsibilities
- serving as an advocate for the child in activities outside the home—for example, with schools, with sports teams, in organized activities
- providing opportunities for children to develop new skills and positive identities
- becoming active in school and community organizations to provide positive environments for children

Children's television viewing

- can reinforce negative social stereotypes and takes time from growth-enhancing activities
- yields benefits such as giving information, changing attitudes, and creating positive feelings, when parents regulate and monitor its use
- is strongly related to aggression when children watch violent programs

In Galinsky's interpretive stage, parents

- have achieved greater understanding of themselves as parents and of their children
- develop strategies for helping children cope with new authorities such as teachers and coaches

Problems discussed center on

- helping children meet school responsibilities
- helping children regulate anger and discouragement
- dealing with social problems such as social isolation, aggression, and bullying
- changing rule breaking behavior such as lying

Parents' joys include

- observing increasing motor, cognitive, and social skills in children
- reexperiencing their own childhood pleasure through their child's experience

EXERCISES

1. Break into small groups of four or five. Take turns recalling (a) how your parents prepared you for school, (b) how you felt the first days you can remember, (c) what your early experiences were, and (d) how confident or shaky you felt about your abilities. Then identify ways parents and teachers could have helped more. Share your group's experiences with the class and come up with recommendations for parents and teachers.

2. In small groups, take turns recalling the pleasurable events you experienced during the years from five to ten. Then come up with a class list of twenty common pleasurable events for that period.

3. Take the list of twenty pleasurable events developed in Exercise 2 and rate each event on a scale of 1 to 7, with 1 being least pleasurable and 7 being most pleasurable, as you would have when you were a child of nine or ten. What are the most pleasurable events? How do parents contribute to them?

4. In small groups, recall the fears you had as a child from five to ten. How could parents or teachers have helped you cope with those fears?

5. In small groups, discuss major activities that built sources of self-esteem in this period. Were these athletic activities? group activities like Scouts or Brownies? school activities? Come up with recommendations for parents as to the kinds of activities children find the most confidence building.

ADDITIONAL READINGS

Armstrong, Thomas. *Awakening Your Child's Natural Genius*. Los Angeles: Jeremy T. Tarcher, 1991.

Levine, Mel. *A Mind at a Time*. New York: Simon & Schuster, 2002.

Murphy, Tim, and Oberlin, Loriann. *The Angry Child*. New York: Three Rivers Press, 2001.

Seligman, Martin E. P. *The Optimistic Child*. New York: Houghton Mifflin, 1995.

Steyer, James. *The Other Parent*. New York: Atria, 2002.

CHAPTER

10

Parenting Early Adolescents

CHAPTER TOPICS

In this chapter you will learn about:

- Early adolescent development
- Relationships with parents, siblings, and peers
- Parents' tasks and concerns regarding early adolescence
- Encouraging communication, problem-solving skills, initiative, school success, and peer relationships
- Meeting boys' and girls' special needs

IN THE NEWS

San Francisco Chronicle, June 18, 2002
A poll of 750 teens aged twelve to seventeen finds that 33 percent feel pressured to buy advertised products and 10 percent of twelve- and thirteen-year-olds nag fifty or more times for products, with 55 percent of all teens saying they can get parents to give in. See page 313 for details.

 Go to PowerWeb at: www.dushkin.com/powerweb to read articles and newsfeeds on **emotion and communication, identity development, parenting,** and other topics related to this chapter.

Parents encounter many challenges during the time their children experience the physical and psychological changes that launch them into adulthood. Changes in physical form, in ways of thinking, in time spent away from parents, in school settings, and in the importance of peers all demand adaptation from both parents and teenagers. In the midst of this change, parents must support early adolescents as they search for their own identity. How do parents maintain close relationships while teenagers are becoming more independent? How do parents of different ethnic groups help their teenagers deal with the specific problems youth confront while establishing their identity? How do parents grant autonomy while continuing to monitor their children's behavior? How do teenagers balance parents' demands with pressure from peers?

The early adolescent years of eleven to fifteen include many changes and transitions for children. Leaving the childhood years of stable growth, children experience all the stresses of rapid physical growth, a changing hormonal system, and physical development that results in sexual and reproductive maturity. Thinking matures as well; as a result, they may think about situations and feelings in new ways. Most early adolescents enter the more demanding and less supportive environment of middle or junior high school. Peer relations take on a new importance and provide both great pleasure and stress.

Throughout such change, early teenagers seek a stable sense of identity—who they are, what goals they will pursue. They question parents' authority and argue their own points of view. Parents have to find ways to encourage independence and self-esteem, helping children become more competent; yet parents must continue to monitor the teenagers' behavior and not permit so much freedom that children get into trouble they cannot handle. Though taxing for parents, this is an exciting time to watch children blossom as they take their first steps out of childhood into a new life.

PHYSICAL DEVELOPMENT

Adolescence begins with biological change. From five to ten, boys and girls have about the same height, weight, and general body configuration. The physical changes of puberty, the age at which sexual reproduction is possible, begin at about eight or nine and extend to the end of the second decade.[1] The brain triggers endocrine organs to release hormones that affect children's growth and secondary sexual characteristics (breasts, body and facial hair), resulting in reproductive maturity.

For girls, these changes take place from about age eight to seventeen; for boys, on average, from eleven to twenty. Because the hormonal changes occur before any outward indications of puberty, parents do not know at first that puberty has begun. While the age at which the changes take place and the rapidity of the growth vary from child to child, the sequence of these changes remains consistent. Maturational timing also appears stable across ethnic groups with adequate nutrition.[2]

Sexual maturation accompanies the growth spurt. As mentioned, hormonal stimulation of the sex glands begins first in girls. Then, at about age nine or ten, downy, light pubic hair appears and is most often the first sign of sexual maturity. Changes in the breasts occur at the same time. In the next year, the sex organs themselves grow—the uterus, vagina, labia, and clitoris. Pubic hair continues to grow, and vaginal secretions appear. By the time *menarche* or menstruation begins at about age twelve and a half, the breast is well formed, and pubic and body hair are well developed. When girls first menstruate, they do not ovulate—send an egg to the uterus—with each period. Thus, conception is improbable though not impossible, in the period immediately following the onset of menstruation.

Boys' hormonal secretions from the sex glands first begin at about age eleven and a half, but the first visible sign of impending puberty is growth of the testes and the

---

VOICES OF EXPERIENCE

What I Wish I Had Known about Early Adolescence

"They seem to get caught up in fads in junior high. They do certain things to the max to be part of the crowd. I wish I'd known how to handle that. At what point are these fads okay, because it's important to identify with your peer group, and at what point do you say no? If they are really dangerous, then it's easy; but with a lot of them, it's a gray area, and I wish I'd known what to do better." FATHER

"I wish I had realized that she needed more structure and control. Because she had always been a good student and done her work, I thought I could trust her to manage the school tasks without my checking. But she lost interest in school, and I learned only very gradually that I had to be more of a monitor with her work than I had been in the past." MOTHER

"I wish I had known more about mood swings. When the girls became thirteen, they each got moody for a while, and I stopped taking it personally. I just relaxed. The youngest one said, 'Do I have to go through that? Can't I just skip that?' Sure enough, when she became thirteen, she was moody too." MOTHER

"I wish I'd known how to help the boys get along a little better. They have real fights at times, and while they have a lot of fun together and help each other out, I wish I knew how to cut down on the fighting." FATHER

"I wish I knew what to expect. They are all so different, and they don't necessarily do what the books say. Sometimes, I'm waiting for a stage; now I'm waiting for adolescent rebellion, and there is none." MOTHER

"I wish I had known about their indecisiveness. He wants to do this; no, he doesn't. He gets pressure from peers and from what we think is right, and sometimes he goes back and forth. I am more patient about that now." MOTHER

"I wish I had known that if we had dealt with some behaviors when they were younger, we would not have had a problem from eleven to fourteen. He was always a little stubborn and hardheaded, wanting to do what he wanted. But right now, I wish we had done something about the stubbornness because it is a problem. He does not take responsibility, and it gets him into trouble at school. Looking back it has always been a problem, but we did not deal with it." MOTHER

---

scrotum, the baglike structure that holds the testes. Pubic hair may appear as well. About a year later, as the physical growth spurt starts, the penis grows as well. Body and facial hair appear about two years after the pubic hair. Genetic factors determine how much body hair there will be.

Boys' voices change later in puberty. The larynx or Adam's apple grows significantly, and vocal cords double in length, making the voice lower. It takes many months, in some cases a year or two, for boys to regain control of their voices.

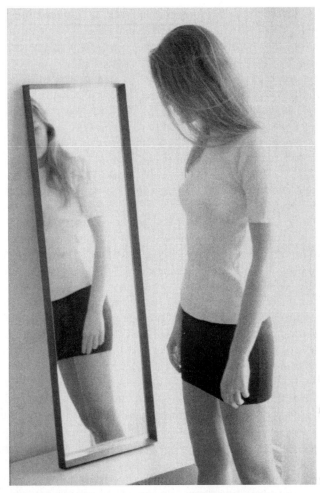

Changes in physical form, in ways of thinking, in time spent with peers, and in school away from parents demand adaptation from parents and early adolescents.

Psychological Reactions to Growth and Development

Physical qualities play an important role in how children evaluate themselves. Of the things adolescents like least about themselves, they cite physical characteristics most. Areas of concern include skin problems, height, weight, and overall figure. Early adolescents are most dissatisfied with their bodies, whereas older adolescents feel better about their bodies, and college students feel best of all. With time, adolescents adjust to all the changes that have taken place and eventually feel good about themselves.

The timing of puberty is related to psychosocial events that precede it and follow it. Family conditions affect the timing of puberty. For example, mothers with a history of mood disorders have a greater likelihood of family stress, and when biological fathers are absent, these factors together predict early timing of girls' puberty.[3] In addition, mothers with a history of mood disorders who also experience stress from relationships with boyfriends or second husbands are more likely to have daughters with early puberty. When mothers' primary romantic involvement was with biological fathers, no relationship existed between stress and early puberty. So, family stress from different sources is related to early menarche for girls. Stresses related to early puberty for boys have not been identified.

Puberty triggers the beginning of a gender difference in moods. Prior to puberty, boys and girls are equally likely to get depressed, but following pubertal changes, girls show significantly more depressive symptoms.[4] The difference is small but significant at ages thirteen and fourteen, and it increases to a larger difference in adulthood.

Pubertal changes at age ten to fourteen are associated with increases in family conflict. Several factors may play a role in the increase.[5] Hormonal changes leading to greater irritability and to negative emotionality may intensify conflict. With all the physical changes, children may assume that they are now mature and demand more freedom than parents feel is appropriate.

The timing of the changes matters. Early-maturing girls have greater difficulties than later-maturing girls.[6] They experience more conflicts with parents, perhaps because they want more freedom, and they are out of synch with their age-mates—both girls and boys—because their bodies and interests are more advanced. They sometimes lose interest in school and classmates, preferring older friends.[7]

In a sample followed from seventh through twelfth grades, early-maturing girls, defined as starting to menstruate before eleven and a half, were more likely to experience ongoing depression than were later-menstruating girls and the boys in the sample.[8] Other research indicates they are also more prone to substance use.[9]

Early maturing boys have an advantage because of increased height, weight, and muscular strength, which are valued in athletics.[10] These boys tend to be popular, outgoing, happy, and self-confident. Peers consider late-maturing boys childish because of their physical appearance. Because they cannot get attention in more approved ways, late maturers may seek it through restless, immature behavior such as clowning.

Information and preparation about puberty and all the changes it brings help reduce anxiety and worry. Many parents, however, feel uncomfortable talking to their children on this subject. Children, too, feel uncomfortable asking questions. Over half of adolescents feel they cannot talk to their parents about sexual matters, and over half feel they do not get the information they want in sex education courses—either the teacher is too embarrassed or the information is not presented.[11]

INTELLECTUAL DEVELOPMENT

Jean Piaget describes the years from twelve to fourteen as the period when adolescents begin to think like adults.[12] They enter the *formal operations period,* during which they come to think more abstractly than previously. Although children can reason logically when confronted with tangible objects and change during the period of concrete operations, Piaget believes they still cannot reason logically about verbal propositions or hypothetical situations. In this period, adolescents can freely speculate and arrive at solutions without having the objects or people directly at hand; that is, they can analyze a problem in their heads. Further, they can enumerate all possible combinations of events and take action to see what possibilities actually exist.

Their increased capacity for abstract thought enables adolescents to think about their own thoughts. They become introspective, analyzing themselves and their reactions. They are also able to think about other people's reactions and anticipate them. They think of the future, imagining what they might be doing as adults, what might be happening in the world. They can think of ideal situations or solutions and become impatient with the present because it does not meet the ideal they have pictured. Their introspection, concern about the future, idealism, and impatience with the present all affect parent-child relationships, as we shall see. Adolescents also begin to think more complexly about other people and their actions. They see people more realistically and may cease to idolize their parents.

SCHOOL

Many early adolescents make transitions to middle or junior high school in this period.[13] These school settings do not meet the psychological needs of their students, and academic achievement and interest in school decrease. Research shows increases in test anxiety and learned helplessness in response to failure. Both truancy and dropping out increase.

Today's schools are larger than before and organized so that teachers know students less well, but they are also more demanding. Larger schools with less individual attention require a level of responsibility and self-direction that many early adolescents do not have. As a result, students face what Jacquelynne Eccles and colleagues call a "mismatch" between the developmental needs of early adolescents and the opportunities offered in the school environment.[14] The pressures from school affect girls and boys of all ethnic groups in similar ways.

Parental involvement is a major determiner of positive or negative school outcome in all ethnic groups and in economically disadvantaged conditions.[15] When parents are involved and set positive expectations for children, early adolescents have more positive views of their own abilities, become engaged in schoolwork and school activities, and have better attendance and grades.[16] Parents provide a context of beliefs that shape the child's self-system, which in turn motivates action that has a positive outcome.

When parents fail to counteract students' natural discouragement with school changes and stress, students develop negative beliefs about their own abilities and self-worth, fail to attend and to do the work, and receive poor grades.[17] In even the poorest and least advantaged economic situations, parents' involvement and optimism about children's abilities enable students to achieve academic competence. Parents' actions help students to develop increased capacity for self-regulation, which then leads to achievement.[18]

For early adolescents, schools that support competence continue to have the same qualities as effective elementary schools.[19] When students view teachers as academically and emotionally supportive, then they experience less stress and less alienation at school; conversely, when they view teachers as unfair or biased, students' stress increases. When schools encourage students to focus on effort, self-improvement, and task mastery, rather than competition, students feel increased motivation and well-being. Students' needs for autonomy are met when schools encourage choice whenever possible—such as in choice of seating and work partners—and emphasize active participation in learning.

EMOTIONAL DEVELOPMENT

Reed Larson and Maryse Richards gathered extensive data on the experiences and daily lives of children aged nine to fifteen years and their parents.[20] In addition to a core sample of fifty-five Midwestern, European American, working- or middle-class families of mother, father, and early adolescent as well as other siblings, Larson and Richards also sampled 483 early adolescents. In their research, they gave electronic pagers to parents and their children and to children in the larger sample. They systematically beeped them eight times a day for seven days—all family members were beeped at the same time even if they were not together. At the end of the week, they also interviewed the participants about the week. From the 24,000 "snapshots" of daily life—7,000 from family members and 18,000 from children in the larger sample—Larson and Richards constructed a portrait of the daily emotional lives of young adolescents and their families. This section draws on this study in describing the emotional experiences and parent-child relationships of this age period.

Emotional life becomes more intense and complex during adolescence. Elementary school children rarely experience two different feelings at the same time; they rarely worry about the future or brood about others' reactions to them.[21] They live in the present, and when a difficult situation passes, they cease to think about it. So, they are more likely than early adolescents to describe themselves as very happy.

Although early adolescents' overall mood resembles that of their parents, they tend to have more emotional variability—more highs and more lows—than do their parents.[22] Part of their emotional variability stems from their heightened self-consciousness and concerns about how they appear to others. In one study, about a quarter of normal fourteen-year-olds reported feelings of being looked at, laughed at, or talked about.[23] David Elkind believes that the early adolescent "is continually constructing or reacting to an imaginary audience."[24]

Despite all the physical, social, and psychological changes of adolescence, as well as the heightened sensitivity, two-thirds of early teens report low to medium stress. The one-third who report high levels appear to be dealing with additional stress from such family events as marital arguing and divorce.[25]

Larson reports concern, however, that 27 percent of early teens reported boredom when beeped, much of the time at school and in study activities.[26] Honor students report boredom as often as do acting-out early teens. Early adolescents,

Larson writes, "Communicate an ennui of being trapped in the present, waiting for someone to prove to them that life is worth living."[27] He believes that positive development requires that teens develop initiative, defined as a feeling of internal motivation to engage in challenging, effortful activities that are pursued over an extended period of time. Later in this chapter, we discuss how parents promote this quality in children.

Depressed and negative moods also increase over the early adolescent years. Although the increase seems slight for the majority of young teens, 10 to 20 percent of parents say their children have experienced some depressed mood—sad, unhappy feelings—in the past six months, and 20 to 40 percent of early adolescents report the same.[28] Depressed mood increases from age thirteen to fifteen, peaks at seventeen to eighteen, and then drops to adult levels. As noted, girls are more likely than boys to report depressed mood, particularly early-maturing girls. We take up depression in greater detail later in Chapter 11.

Positive experiences can serve as a buffer against the effects of stress. Such experiences provide an "arena of comfort" in which early teens can escape stress, relax, and feel good.[29] When early adolescents from various ethnic backgrounds were asked about their sources of support, all pointed to the importance of close family relationships.[30] Friends are very important as well.

DEVELOPMENT OF THE SELF

Early adolescents now think more abstractly than before, and they describe themselves in terms of more general traits.[31] Though they may think of themselves as stupid because of poor grades and low creativity, they do not yet integrate this negative quality into their overall picture of themselves. The negative and positive qualities remain isolated as separate traits. This separation may serve as a psychological buffer so the negative traits from one sphere do not influence the overall view of the self.

In this period of change, adolescents begin to explore who they are, what they believe, what they want. They are in the process of forming what Erik Erikson calls a *sense of identity,* a sense of a differentiated and distinct self that is the real inner "me."[32]

The process of achieving a sense of identity occurs gradually over several years. Adolescents explore new experiences and ideas, form new friendships, and make a commitment to values, goals, and behavior. This can cause conflict and crisis as the choices get worked out. On the other hand, some adolescents choose traditional values without even considering for themselves what they want to do with their lives. They face no crisis or conflict, because they do not want to deal with issues. James Marcia terms commitment without exploration *identity foreclosure* to indicate that possibilities have been closed off prematurely.[33]

A different path is taken by adolescents who experience a *moratorium,* or an exploration without commitment. This is essentially a crisis about what they want to do. They have ideas they explore, but they have not yet made a commitment to act.

Finally, some adolescents experience *identity diffusion* in which they can make no choices at all. They drift without direction.

One study found that adolescent boys who rank high in identity exploration come from families in which they can express their own opinions yet receive support from parents even when they disagree with them.[34] Boys are encouraged to be both independent and connected to family members. Adolescent girls who rate high in identity exploration come from families in which they are challenged and receive little support from parents who are contentious with each other. Girls may need this slightly abrasive atmosphere in order to pursue a heightened sense of individuality rather than follow the path of intensifying social relationships. However, these girls do feel connected to at least one parent.

Personal Identity and Reference Group Identity

William Cross describes two aspects of identity or self-concept; *personal identity* (PI), which includes such factors as self-esteem and general personality traits, and *reference group orientation* (RGO), which includes group identity, group awareness, and group attitudes (see Figure 10-1).[35] He discusses RGO primarily in terms of racial identity, to explain why people of the same ethnic group with equal commitments to that group may have very different attitudes about ethnic identity—that is, they have very different RGOs.

He states that RGO may be prominent in some groups and not in others—for example, some European Americans think of themselves only as Americans whereas others have a strong ethnic identity as Italian Americans or Irish Americans. Cross shows the usefulness of these concepts in understanding gender identity. Two women might be similar with regard to self-esteem and self-worth, but one may have a strong RGO as a feminist and interpret much of her experience in the light of that group identity, while another woman might not.

Gender Identity

In these early adolescent years, gender identity intensifies, with boys taking on a more masculine attitude and girls becoming more egalitarian regarding sex roles.[36] Although both sexes are aware of gender-appropriate activities, gender flexibility, in terms of self-choices for activities, and tolerance of others' gender choices continue to grow.[37]

Ethnic Identity

Achieving a sense of identity is a more complicated task for minority than for majority youth. They have two cultures to explore, understand, and integrate in their quest for identity. They begin with a diffused view of their ethnic background. They talk to parents, family friends, and other adults about ethnic issues. They read books and share experiences with friends. Aware of prejudice, they think about its effects on their work and life goals. In the eighth grade, about a third of African American students are actively involved in this exploration. By age fifteen, about

■ **F I G U R E 10-1**
SCHEMATIC OF TWO-FACTOR THEORY OF BLACK IDENTITY

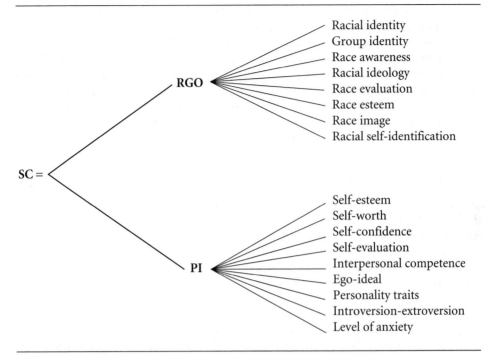

Racial identity
Group identity
Race awareness
Racial ideology
Race evaluation
Race esteem
Race image
Racial self-identification

RGO

SC =

PI

Self-esteem
Self-worth
Self-confidence
Self-evaluation
Interpersonal competence
Ego-ideal
Personality traits
Introversion-extroversion
Level of anxiety

Note: Self-concept (SC) = personal identity (PI) + reference group orientation (RGO)

From William E. Cross, Jr., "A Two Factor Theory of Black Identity," in *Children's Ethnic Socialization,* ed. Jean S. Phinney and Mary Jane Rotheram (Beverly Hills, CA: 1987), Figure 6.1, p. 122. Copyright © 1987 Sage Publications, Inc. Reprinted by permission of Sage Publications.

half of such students are actively exploring their cultural roots and traditions, and an additional one-fourth have already achieved a sense of identity.[38]

Two difficulties arise.[39] First, many parents do not talk with their children about their cultural background, and they do not share their own experiences in the majority culture. Perhaps because they do not want to burden their children with experiences that no longer occur or perhaps because they are uncomfortable with issues of culture and race, many parents remain silent and offer no models. As such, children have to seek information elsewhere and cannot consciously pattern themselves after their parents.

Second, such adolescents have to explore and integrate two cultures. Integrating one set of cultural traditions with the realities of everyday life is difficult enough. With two cultures that sometimes conflict with each other, the task becomes quite complicated.

Which values does one select? Children and adolescents ideally should be permitted a bicultural identification that includes both cultures. Youth of ethnic backgrounds who combine, for example, the emphasis on cooperation and sharing found in many ethnic cultures with the assertive independence of the majority culture are effective in a wider range of situations than are those attached to just one set of values. Because peers or family may pressure the adolescent to adopt only the traditional cultural values, a bicultural orientation is not easy to achieve.

The process of achieving identity is even more difficult when the ethnic culture is devalued and adolescents experience negative stereotyping. Youth may then refuse to explore their ethnic roots and may seek a foreclosed identity. Evidence suggests that this happened more frequently among minority than majority adolescents.[40] Some adolescents internalize the negative images, feel deficient and worthless, and develop what Erikson calls a *negative identity*. Currently, more minority youth develop a positive cultural identity and feel high self-esteem, compared with adolescents in past years. A positive ethnic identity enables youth to replace tension and defensiveness with self-confidence about the future.

DEVELOPMENT OF SELF-REGULATION

In this time of change, adolescents develop ways of handling impulses, which they will continue to use as they grow older. Longitudinal studies of early adolescents that have followed them into adulthood through their thirties and forties find adult impulse control is well predicted from behavior during this period.[41]

Jack Block has looked at family characteristics associated with under- and overcontrol.[42] He found that poorly controlled men and women come from families who, in their early adolescent years, did not give children models of effective control. The parents were not able to put aside their own concerns and interests and provide the necessary consistency in discipline. They did not reward and punish children's behavior in a logical way that teaches children how to control themselves. Instead, they used discipline only when they themselves were extremely angry. The child, fearful and panicked by the rage, could not absorb the lesson and thus never received the teaching necessary to achieve good control of impulses.

Overcontrol in men seems to come from having authoritarian and highly controlling parents. The dominant mother who sets high standards and arouses guilt to punish the child for misdeeds is a powerful figure in establishing overcontrol. Fathers in these families withdraw from the parenting role and support their wives' domination. Together, the parents so overcontrol the son that he remains fearful of impulse expression, even of pleasure, as an adult. The average girl is so well controlled that Block found it difficult to isolate any one group of overcontrolled girls to study the qualities of the family.

Although enduring modes of impulse control appear by the early adolescent years, not every impulsive act forebodes a future of impulsivity. Even the most responsible, dependable young teenager will engage in forbidden acts—partly to test the limits, partly to savor the experience, partly to impress friends. Such acts include drinking, smoking, driving the car without permission, and cutting school. How to distinguish an isolated forbidden act from a more serious problem with impulse control is a skill parents must develop.

SOCIAL DEVELOPMENT

Parent-Child Relationships

Young adolescents spend about half as much time with parents as they did in the elementary school years.[43] Parent and child are alone as often, but family activities at home and with relatives decreases.

Parent-Child Conflict   In the early adolescent years, any time with parents may well be spent in arguments. As noted earlier, parent-child conflicts increase and provide stress to children, though parents appear less aware of them.

This disparity between children's and parents' impressions exemplifies the divergent realities that can exist in families and that Larsen and Richards consider as the source of difficulties at this age. "Once we go inside family life we find that it is an illusion to talk about 'the family,' as though it were a single entity. The family is the meeting ground of multiple realities."[44] The authors believe that parents' and offsprings' inability to understand and deal with their different realities create problems for all family members.

In their sample, fathers worked hard and viewed time at home as leisure. They brought home their work stress, which affected all family members. Mothers, whether employed or not, felt they should be able to create a harmonious home atmosphere; when frustrated, they sought pleasure in activities outside the home. When parents were available and responsive, adolescents' negative feelings decreased.

Parents and children agree that mundane, routine behaviors cause the most conflicts. Schoolwork and grades become a more frequent topic as early adolescents move into junior high school. As they move into high school, chores become a focus and remain a major topic during later adolescence.[45]

Though they understand parents' insistence on following conventions, young adolescents simply do not agree with them. Early adolescents insist that many of these issues should be matters under their personal control. Though aware of their children's point of view, parents usually do not accept it as valid. Early adolescents do, however, recognize certain moral issues that they will not challenge—for example, hitting others, not sharing.

Parents and children agree that most of the time conflicts end because children follow parents' wishes. In only 18 percent of conflicts do parents follow children's requests, and joint discussion and decisions settle just 13 percent of the disagreements. So although there are conflicts, children acquiesce.[46] The basic relationship between parents and children remains solid.

Mothers, however, bear the burden of the increasing disagreements,[47] perhaps because they are more involved than fathers in routine household management and scheduling. It also may be that mothers are more emotionally reactive with adolescents, so both boys and girls argue with them more. When fathers are present as a third party in disagreements, boys are more respectful and mother-son relations improve. Father-adolescent relations are more open and interactive when mothers are not present as a third party.[48] Mothers seem to dominate the relationship, and fathers withdraw.

INTERVIEW
with Anne Petersen

Anne C. Petersen is Senior Vice President at W. K. Kellogg Foundation in Battle Creek, Michigan. Her research interests center on adolescence; with John Janeway Conger, she is the author of Adolescence and Youth: Psychological Development in a Changing World.

What do parents of adolescents need to know?

The societal view of adolescents is negative. I collect cartoons, and they portray an extreme view of adolescents as having hormone attacks, being difficult, impossible.

This belief in our country that adolescents are difficult and want to be independent is one of the biggest pitfalls for parents. We know that, though adolescents want to be autonomous, they need parents. We know that young adolescents are argumentative, sometimes obnoxious. Parents throw in the towel and that is the worst thing they can do. Adolescents need to know that parental support is there. There have been historical changes in the family, increasing the possibility for kids to be independent with cars and to have more time away from home; all these changes have exacerbated the trend toward independence and separation. Too much freedom is detrimental to adolescents' development.

Parents need to know that when you ask adolescents, especially young adolescents, who is most important to them, they say the parents, even if the parents are reporting conflict. We find, then, that parents are less positive about their adolescents than their adolescents are about them. Adolescents' off-putting behavior—telling parents to get lost because the adolescents are mature—is not really the message they want to send. They are asking for a little more space; they are asking for help in becoming autonomous and interdependent rather than independent.

Research shows that conflicts are about little things, not big things. The conflicts are not about values, but largely about doing dishes, taking out the garbage. They are a way of relieving tensions. Parents ought to be a safe source for venting tensions. If they cease to be a safe source, then young adolescents are really lost; they have no one.

Parents sometimes believe that they need to be their child's buddy, but that's not true. They need to be parents. They need to provide unconditional love, firm guidelines, and strong expectations.

Puberty and all the change that accompanies it is a difficult time for boys and girls, especially when they have to change schools. It seems to work slightly differently for boys than for girls. In general, boys seem less influenced by what is going on with par-

When parents insist on retaining power and control and refuse to give children opportunities to share decision making, children become highly peer oriented.[49] They seem to seek egalitarian relationships and mutuality with peers because they are denied these experiences with parents. When parents monitor the behavior of early adolescents but permit them input in making decisions, the adolescents are better adjusted.

Parents may find themselves especially upset when their children argue with them, because it violates their expectations of compliance and communicativeness. While the conflicts at this age do increase, children usually acquiesce to parent's

ents, but basic support is pretty important. If parental support is not there, it is very bad for girls. Those girls who have a lot of family conflict or lack support are the ones who become the most depressed.

How would you say your own research has influenced the way you rear your children?
I think it has changed a lot of things. That my daughter rebelled was a big shock. I remember vividly the day she refused to do something. There was no door banging, but she said she would not do something I had just assumed she would do. I immediately had the stereotypic reaction, "'Oh my heavens, what is going on here?" All of a sudden I realized that this was what I had been talking about for a long time. Knowing all the data, why should I be surprised that my kid goes through this too?

It helped a lot to know what could be effective in dealing with this. We had a family conference. What she was saying was, "How about taking my needs into account?" She was upset that we just assumed she would be a part of some activity. It is enlightening to realize that we don't treat an adult, a colleague, or a friend like that. It makes sense to change your behavior toward young adolescents. Well, we worked it out. There are still occasional lapses of communication, and that's where the problems really are. Somebody assumes that somebody else is going to do something, and there is either a conflict of schedules or wishes. But at least saying, "Yes, you are right, you ought to have an increasing role in family decision making" and have a forum within which to do it made a lot of difference to her. She did not have to explode. She could put her two cents in.

When there is a good reason, we change our plans to meet her needs. It is important for us to show that we do not need to be controlling things, that we do respect her views, that she does have a voice. I am sure if you were to ask both our children, they would say they do not have as much say as they would like. That is because we still do believe that we are the parents and there are some things that we need to decide.

We believe that it is important to let them see how we are thinking about things and to understand decision-making processes. So, we talk in the family about money and about vacation plans, and we really try to include them—not just out of respect for them to increasingly become a part, but also to let them see how we think about things so they have the benefit of knowing how adults make decisions. That seems to work pretty well.

requests, as we have seen. Only about 10 percent of families face serious relationship problems during adolescence, and these difficulties often precede the age period.[50] The more usual arguing reflects not dysfunction but rather the many changes parents and children are undergoing.

Harmonious Parent-Child Relations   When parents use an authoritative style of parenting—being accepting, responding sensitively to needs while still maintaining reasonable limits—teens show effective, responsible behavior.[51] Sensitive acceptance and responsiveness promote self-esteem and social connectedness; firm standards promote self-control. Parents must also be flexible and willing to modify their practices, as their child receives growing responsibility for decision making. Recall that in Chapter 9 we talked about parents' monitoring children from a distance. As they move into early adolescence, children receive even greater opportunities for decision making under parents' decreasing supervision. The art lies in knowing when to keep control of children's behavior and when to relinquish it.

Monitoring   Research shows that parental monitoring is related to children's effective functioning. As such, parents are advised to monitor children. Hakan Stattin and Margaret Kerr, however, urge a new interpretation of the findings.[52] They point out that monitoring is frequently measured by parents' report of knowledge of their children's activities and friends rather than parents' tracking and observing children's activities. Stattin and Kerr find that parents have such knowledge because children tell them what they are doing. Thus, Stattin and Kerr believe, measures of monitoring may actually measure good communication, trust, and family closeness rather than direct monitoring. When monitoring is measured by parents' control of children's activities, it appears unrelated to children's positive behaviors, even though in the same research parental knowledge predicts effective functioning. So, creating close family ties, trust, and good communication appears more important than close surveillance and tracking.

Creating Mutually Responsive Dialogues with Early Adolescents   Parents' ability to engage children in conversation and mutual problem solving is critical for family functioning during these years. What promotes parents' skills in talking to children? Mothers of fifteen-year-old girls were coached for two one-and-a-half-hour sessions to listen more, ask open-ended questions, encourage children to talk, and avoid lecturing.[53] Mothers practiced role playing and applied the skills to discussing issues of sexuality and AIDS with their daughters. Mothers who were coached spoke less, asked more open-ended questions, and were less judgmental than were uncoached mothers. Teens of mothers who were coached did not talk more than teens of mothers who were not coached, but the former did feel more comfortable in talking to mothers about sexuality, and they did report more discussion about birth control than did the other teens.

When parenting strategies were assessed and related to twelve-year-olds' problem-solving skills over a two-year period, researchers found that when parents were negative and harsh in parenting, early adolescents were negative and resistant in problem-solving sessions.[54] Early adolescents who were positive and skilled problem solvers could not change parents' harsh strategies. Supportive and nurturant parents who persisted in positive parenting, even when dealing with resistant and negative teens, helped children become more flexible, effective problem solvers. When parents avoided engaging in teens' negative overtures, teens' behavior eventually changed.

Promoting Ethnic Identity   Parents continue to serve as models and sources of information about ethnic cultures and ethnic identity. Table 10-1 presents ways parents can encourage positive ethnic identity. Controversy has arisen about whether

■ **TABLE 10-1**
METHODS TO ENHANCE IDENTITY FORMATION
OF ETHNIC MINORITY YOUTH

1. Methods should be proposed to keep minority youth in school and academically oriented, since lack of education increases the risk of poverty and disadvantage.

2. Efforts are required to heighten health consciousness, because poor health interferes with identity processes. The physical health of many minority youth lags behind that of majority youth.

3. Importance of social networks should be affirmed. As they socialize children, churches and extended families are important resources for minority families.

4. Methods should be proposed to support parents as cultural transmitters. Many ethnic group parents do not discuss their distinctive values and experiences, and such parents must receive support as they begin to do this.

5. Proposals are needed to offer a media-focused, cultural emphasis that affirms positive group identity for all youth to combat negative stereotyping.

6. Methods are needed to promote teaching of native languages and cultures, particularly for Native Americans at risk of losing their cultural heritage. Creativity is required to encourage biculturalism while preserving cultural traditions.

7. Programs are required for the special training of teachers so that they will be sensitive to cultural traditions, communicative patterns, and sometimes the language of minority students.

8. Child-rearing support by way of teaching parenting skills is required to promote parents' sense of ethnic pride and enhance the home-school partnership.

9. Improved training is required for mental health workers serving ethnic minority populations.

Adapted from Margaret Beale Spencer and Carol Markstrom-Adams, "Identity Processes among Racial and Ethnic Minority Children in America," *Child Development* 61 (1990): 305–306.

parents are wise to teach children that difficulties and failures are due to society's prejudice against them. Research suggests that such messages may be related to children's social withdrawal and peer conflict rather than self-esteem.[55] Research with fourteen- to sixteen-year-old African Americans indicates that both children's racial identity and their self-concept appear strong and positive when parents teach recognition of African American achievements, proactive strategies for dealing with the racism that African Americans encounter, and responsibility to the community as a whole.[56]

Taking Time   David Elkind has described the stress children experience when parents press them to grow up and take on adult characteristics. He writes that parents

---

VOICES OF EXPERIENCE

The Joys of Parenting Early Adolescents

"Seeing him care for younger children and babies is a great pleasure. He's a great nurturer with small children. He has endless patience." MOTHER

"He is a talented athlete, and his soccer team got to a championship game. He scored the winning goal, and when he took off with the ball down the field, I was very proud of him. It was a unique feeling of being proud that someone I had helped to create was doing that. He had felt a lot of pressure in the game, so to see how incredibly pleased he was gave me great joy." FATHER

"I enjoy the fact that she is very independent and makes up her own mind about things. She is not caught up in fads or with cliques, and I can trust her not to follow other people's ideas. The down side of that is that she resists some of my ideas as well." MOTHER

"I enjoy her sense of humor. She jokes about everyday events, and I laugh a lot around her." MOTHER

"I like that he does things I did, like play the trumpet. He started at the same age I did and since he took it up, it has rekindled my interest and I started practicing again. This last weekend, we played together. He also brings new interests too. Because he likes sailing I have started that and really like it." FATHER

"She is in that dreamy preteen state where she writes things. She wrote a poem about the difference between being alone and loneliness. She has a real appreciation of time on her own and how nice being alone can be. I like that because I had that at her age." MOTHER

"It's nice just being able to help them, feeling good because they are being helped out and benefited." FATHER

---

who experience extreme pressure in their own lives want their children to grow up quickly, eliminating that source of stress.[57] Children are pressured to achieve, to take on more chores and responsibilities, without too much participation on the parents' part. The push to turn children quickly into adults can be very detrimental at this age, however, because many early adolescents seem to like the greater freedom but cannot handle it yet. Elkind regrets this pressure on children, because it robs them of the childhood they need to grow, learn, and develop fully.

Family Events Both parents and children respond to the distress they see in those close to them.[58] When a family member develops psychological symptoms as a result of life events, and daily hassles in the home increase, then other family members are affected. When family members can deal with their individual problems without developing symptoms or becoming overly stressed, then other family members are not drawn in and upset. It is not the occurrence of a major life event that disrupts the family; it is how the individual involved copes with it.

"It's nice to see her being able to analyze situations with friends or with her teachers and come to conclusions. She said about one of her teachers, 'Well, she gets excited and she never follows through with what she says, so you know you don't have to take her seriously.'" MOTHER

"I really enjoy being in the Scouts with the boys. Once a month we go on a camping weekend, and I really look forward to that." FATHER

"I was so impressed and pleased that after the earthquake, he and a friend decided to go door to door and offer to sell drawings they made of Teenage Mutant Ninja Turtles. He raised $150 that he gave for earthquake relief. I was very proud that he thought this up all by himself." FATHER

"I was very happy one day when I found this note she left on my desk. It said, 'Hello!!! Have a happy day! Don't worry about home, everyone's fine! Do your work the very best you can. But most important, have a fruitful life!!!' I saved that note because it made me feel so good." MOTHER

"He enjoys life. He has a sense of humor. He's like a butterfly enjoying everything; eventually he'll settle in." MOTHER

"He's very sensitive, and his cousins two years older than he is ask his advice about boys. They may not take it, but they ask him even though he's younger." FATHER

"It's very rewarding to see them in their school activities. My daughter sings in the school chorus, and I enjoy that, and my son is in school plays." FATHER

"I am very pleased that she is less moody now than she used to be. We used to refer to her lows as 'Puddles of Frustration,' but she has got past that now." MOTHER

"Well, they have their friends over, and we have Ping-Pong, pool, cards, and we stressed having these things available. I enjoy playing all these games with them." FATHER

Happy family times are important, because they provide a reservoir of good feeling that sustains all family members through times of conflict and crisis. Family life focuses so heavily on routine chores that outings often provide the best means for members to share fun. Family card games, mealtime rituals, and watching certain TV programs together can also provide a sense of sharing and solidarity that adolescents report as highly meaningful to them. Making time for fun and games in a busy schedule may save time in the long run as conflicts and arguing decrease.

Relationships with Siblings

As in previous age periods, young adolescents show a great deal of ambivalence toward siblings. Ninety-seven percent of a large group of teens say they sometimes, or usually, do like their brothers and sisters, and only 3 percent say they do not like them. However, they rank brothers and sisters as one of their biggest problems, more of a problem than parents or peers.[59]

What do siblings do that is so upsetting? Primarily, they invade the early adolescent's privacy. They go into their rooms, take their possessions, try to be part of their activities. A second major complaint is that younger brothers and sisters get privileges older ones did not get at that age. Adolescents feel their brothers and sisters are getting away with something. Teasing is a third source of complaint. Sometimes teasing is not meant to be cruel but is a way of having a kind of conversation. A fourth reason for resentment is that parents favor another child. Sometimes early teens feel that older siblings get more respect and trust, and younger ones get more attention. Sibling conflict may be fueled by tensions from other areas. For example, if a teen has had a hard day with teachers and a fight with friends, she cannot come home and yell at her parents, but she can yell at a bratty brother or sister who made a face at her.[60]

Siblings can become close during these years for the same reasons that peers are close—they can understand the emotional ups and downs, the problems that early adolescents are feeling, in ways that parents may not. They may become allies in asking parents for privileges or rule changes. Sibling relationships usually improve as older siblings become more independent and no longer compete for parental attention or resources.

Peer Relationships

Young adolescents report fewer close friends than do elementary school children, but they gain more support from these relationships than do younger children (see Figure 9-1 in the previous chapter).[61] Friends have equal status, and they often understand what the other is experiencing in ways parents cannot.

In these years, children form cliques, small groups of five to nine members who choose each other as friends.[62] The most common activities are hanging out, talking, walking around school, talking on the phone, watching TV, and playing physical games. Girls spend more time than boys talking and shopping, and boys more time than girls playing contact sports. Group activities serve several purposes: They provide sociability and a sense of belonging, promote exploration of the self and achievements, and provide opportunities for learning and instruction. Hanging around and talking promote closer social relationships, whereas competitive games promote achievements and greater understanding of the self. Both kinds of activities contribute to psychological growth and give children the kinds of experiences they need to form a stable sense of identity.

In the beginning of early adolescence, teens spend most of their time in same-sex groups.[63] Girls spend only about an hour a week in the presence of a boy, and boys spend even less time in the presence of a girl. However, in the seventh and eighth grades, children spend four to six hours a week thinking about the opposite sex, but only about an average of one-half to one-and-one-third hours actually with them. As teens move through high school, they spend more time with the opposite sex.

Parents worry that their children will rely on peers for advice and guidance. As in earlier years, though, children usually pick friends who are like themselves and reflect their parents' values. Parents can relax a little when they read this conclusion of psychologists: "Although the influence of peer groups and friendships increases across adolescence, parents retain their primary influence over major decisions regarding life values, goals, and future decisions."[64]

TASKS AND CONCERNS OF PARENTS

Parents' tasks expand as they become not only caregivers and interpreters of the social world but also models for an increasing number of behaviors in the world outside the home. Parenting tasks include the following:

- Continuing to be the single most important influence in the child's life
- Being sensitive to the child's needs and open to discussion of the child's viewpoint
- Modeling self-controlled, responsible daily behavior in all areas of life and in discussions with children
- Monitoring children's activities and behavior
- Communicating information and values on important but difficult-to-discuss topics such as sexuality, substance use, and discrimination
- Making time, being available for conversation when the child is ready to talk
- Giving children more decision-making power
- Providing support as children undergo many physical changes and social challenges, so home is an understanding place
- Sharing pleasurable time

This section describes how parents use active listening skills and behavioral methods to work effectively with young adolescents. It also emphasizes parenting strategies that help children develop initiative and problem-solving skills so they can resolve intense feelings and engage in activities and peer relations that bring good feelings.

Communicating with the Noncommunicative Early Adolescent

Noncommunication is a common problem for parents, though children do not see it this way. Parents complain that children come home, go to their rooms, and shut the door. When they emerge for meals or snacks, they say little, answering any question with only a word or two. They do not talk about what they are doing, thinking, or feeling. Children do not seem unhappy, but parents feel they do not know them anymore. Parents may feel hurt when children say little to them but talk for hours on the phone to their friends.

Parents can interact with children to promote conversation. Don Dinkmeyer and Gary McKay advise three strategies: (1) comment on nonverbal behavior, (2) ask for comments, and (3) be a model of conversing.[65] For example, parents can try commenting on facial expressions or body language: "Looks like you had a good day today," or "You look happy." Teens may not follow up with any comments, but parents have made an effort.

Parents can ask for comments: "How's school going?" or "What are you and Jenny doing tonight?" If the child answers with one word or two, parents should drop the conversation and wait for another time. Parents can remain good models of communication by talking about their own day, friends, and plans.

Once teens begin to talk, parents can listen and communicate their feelings. If parents jump in with criticism, judgments of the child or others, blame, or sarcasm, children clam up. Reflecting the teenagers' feelings helps teens to continue to talk. If teens talk about problems they are trying to work out and want to discuss them, parents can ask open-ended questions and listen.

There are many "don'ts" to the process of encouraging conversation. Don't force the child to reveal her feelings. Don't give advice once the teen has begun to talk. Don't rush to find the solution. Don't hurry to answer questions; delaying an answer can stimulate thinking. Adele Faber and Elaine Mazlish give the example of a girl who asked her mother, "Why don't we ever go to any place good on vacation like Bermuda or Florida?"

The mother answered, "Why don't we?"

The girl replied, "I know, I know. Because it's too expensive. . . . Well, at least can we go to the zoo?"[66]

Faber and Mazlish describe useful techniques when teens begin to talk about discouragement or frustration. They suggest showing respect for the child's struggle with comments like "That can be hard," It's not easy," or "Sometimes it helps when . . ." then giving a piece of information: "It helps, when you're rushed, to concentrate on the most important item." Teens are free to use the information or not. Parents have to watch their tone of voice so the information does not sound like advice.

Faber and Mazlish also present interesting alternatives to saying "no." Because teens are sensitive to control and may not like to ask if they often hear "no" in response, having other ways to respond is useful and will encourage greater talkativeness. Suppose a teen wants his mother to take him to the store at 5:30 while she is cooking dinner. Instead of giving a flat "no," she can say, "I'll take you after dinner." If she cannot do it, she can say, "I'd like to be able to help you out, but I have to get dinner on the table and get to that meeting at 7:00." A parent can leave out the "no" and just give information. For example, if a teen asks for an extra, expensive piece of clothing, the parent can say, "The budget just won't take it this month." If there are ways the teen can get the item, the parent can pass that information on: "If you want that as a birthday present at the end of the month, that would be fine."

All strategies recommend fostering self-esteem and autonomy by focusing on the positive things teens do. When children feel good about themselves, they talk more. Dinkmeyer and McKay describe how parents use encouragement to foster self-esteem at times of frustration. Encouragement focuses on effort, improvement, and interest and is reflected in phrases like "You really worked hard on that" or "I can see a lot of progress" or "You were really a big help to your brother in cleaning his room." Though using all these different strategies does not guarantee a talkative teenager in the home, it does increase the likelihood of conversation.

Encouraging Problem-Solving Skills

In this age period, parents confront children's resistance on many issues. As the newspaper blurb at the beginning of the chapter indicated, teens nag and demand what parents are unwilling or unable to provide. Further, teens refuse to do what parents consider reasonable, such as clean their rooms. In Chapter 5, we examined mutual problem-solving sessions with children to resolve conflicts within the home. Now we discuss how parents can help children apply these strategies not only to impulsive disagreements at home but also to relationships with peers and others at school.

Problem solving requires the child to define the problem, become aware of his or her feelings and others' feelings and reactions, generate solutions to the problem, choose a solution and carry it out, then evaluate the results, starting over if necessary. Problem solving requires that parents remain calm so that children have opportunities to think and develop their skills. Parents can ask open-ended questions and encourage the child to continue to think of solutions.

Myrna Shure has developed "I Can Problem Solve" programs to teach children from four to thirteen to learn to find their own solutions to the problems that bother them.[67] Combining many of the communication skills discussed in this chapter and in Chapter 4 with an emphasis on having children think of alternative actions, these programs help parents avoid highly emotional battles that interfere with good communication and effective solutions.

To solve problems, Shure believes, children must (1) understand others' feelings and underlying motivations, (2) generate new solutions to the problem, (3) anticipate the consequences of each potential solution, and (4) plan behaviors in advance to avoid potential problems. Shure recommends working on only one or two of these skills at a time. Because they are often locked into their own thoughts and feelings of the moment and have trouble seeing different options for action, early adolescents need special help with all of the steps.

Parents are supportive, refusing to dictate or force solutions, but if the problem involves them, they send I-messages that express their needs and concerns. Shure recommends doing this with questions such as "How will the other person feel or react?" "What will happen if you do that?" "What is your plan?" "How will that work?" If children have no answers, parents do not push but instead let children figure the problem out, provided no danger is involved. Where parents have concerns about safety or the necessity of solving the problem now, they engage in mutual problem-solving, as described in Chapter 5.

Shure's method helps early adolescents develop the independence and ability to plan that are so necessary for children of this age. Developing initiative has similar aims.

Promoting Initiative

Based on his research with early adolescents and their families, Larson believes that, for positive development in these years, early adolescents must develop initiative, which "consists of the ability to be motivated from within to direct attention and effort toward a challenging goal."[68] An important quality in itself, initiative also serves as the foundation for important qualities such as creativity and leadership. Teens, however, experience effort and challenge in activities in which they lack interest, such as school work, and they lack effort and challenge in activities that interest them, such as activities with friends. The task is to find activities that both interest and challenge teens.

Larson believes that structured voluntary activities, pursued over time, do just this. The experience of setting goals, organizing activities (often in collaboration with peers), and accomplishing goals leads to the development of independence, decision-making skills, and self-control. These, then, carry over to other activities. For example, participation in voluntary activities in grade ten predicted increase in grade point average in grades ten to twelve. Participants in outdoor adventure programs gained in assertiveness, locus of control, and independence. Furthermore, positive changes continued for as long as two years after the program.

Larson speculates that voluntary activities, broadly structured by adults but with direct responsibility given to children for organizing and carrying out the activities, "provided an environment of possibilities for planful action, for initiative."[69] Children develop a language and way of thinking that gives them a sense of agency, of being able to accomplish what they set out to. "Children and adolescents come alive in these activities, they become active agents in ways that rarely happen in other parts of their lives."[70]

Voluntary school activities draw on the problem-solving skills that Shure encourages. Adult leaders in the activities raise open-ended questions that prompt teens to analyze and think through the consequences of actions. They are supportive and nonjudgmental. Research shows that when Little League coaches adopt an encouraging attitude, give information on how to improve, provide positive reinforcement for effort as well as for accomplishments, and stress fun and self-improvement rather than winning, players report more enjoyment in playing and greater self-esteem, and they are more likely to sign up for the team the next year than are players whose coaches are not so supportive.[71] Interestingly, positive coaches learned these skills in one three-hour session, and the techniques had the biggest effects on boys with low self-esteem.

Promoting Positive Peer Relationships

Peer acceptance involves both a cognitive understanding of others and oneself and appropriate peer behavior.[72] When children have difficulties—either being too inhibited or too aggressive—problems may exist in how they view people as well as how they behave. Aggressive children, for example, are quick to see others' negative behavior as intentional and therefore worthy of retaliation.[73] Part of the way to help such children is to encourage them to examine their interpretations of others' be-

Parents model appropriate behaviors for teenagers—exercising, not smoking, not drinking excessively.

havior and adopt more benign views of others' intentions. When they view negative behavior as accidental, children reduce their aggression. Similarly, shy, inhibited children should be encouraged to review their positive traits and identify the positive contributions they can make to social activities. Peer acceptance requires outgoing behavior that shows respect for others and oneself by listening to others, being open and friendly, having a positive attitude, initiating interactions, and avoiding aggressive, negative behaviors.[74]

Philip Zimbardo and Shirley Radl make several suggestions specifically geared for ages twelve to seventeen.[75] Because appearance matters so much to adolescents, Zimbardo and Radl suggest working from the outside in, concentrating first on appearance so that teenagers look as good as possible from their point of view. Skin problems should be attended to immediately. Parents must consult a dermatologist if skin problems cause any distress for teens. Weight, too, can be a problem. They recommend first seeing a pediatrician who can discuss weight and the means to achieve ideal weight. Parents then should have suitable foods available and serve as models of good eating patterns. Teeth sometimes need attention. Because many children and adults now wear braces, they are not the source of embarrassment they once were.

Grooming and clothes also aid appearance. Most early adolescents will take lengthy showers and shampoo their hair daily. When it comes to clothing, parents should allow the teen to follow the current fashion as far as the budget allows. When clothes are more expensive than parents can afford, possible solutions include buying, for example, one or two pairs of expensive pants rather than four or five cheaper ones. Or teens can earn money to make up the difference between what the parents can afford and what the clothes cost.

At home, parents can do all the things that increase children's sense of security and self-worth. Respecting privacy, treating the child with respect, keeping lines of communication open, giving responsibility, giving appropriate praise, not prying into the child's thoughts and feelings, and having rules and structure—these all contribute to a sense of security that enables the child to reach out to others in these sensitive years.

Handling School Problems

Experts are divided on the handling of school problems. Some give all the responsibility to the early adolescent to handle the problem; others encourage the parent to take an active role.

Haim Ginott cites the example of a thirteen-year-old boy who brought home a note from the teacher about his poor behavior.[76] His mother said, "You must have felt terrible to have to bring home a note like that." He agreed he did. His mother wrote the school that she was sure he would handle the problem. (In the past she would have yelled and screamed.) The next day, she met with the principal, but her son had already begun to improve his behavior. However, it is rarely that easy.

Thomas Gordon, as well as Dinkmeyer and McKay, considers that the child has the problem, an issue he or she must deal with. A parent can be a model of effective work habits and can be interested in the child's feelings about school, but essentially schoolwork is up to the child.

Not so with the behaviorists. Robert Eimers and Robert Aitchison describe recommendations to help an eleven-year-old boy who was failing school.[77] Testing revealed he was bright and had no special learning problem. He simply misbehaved in class and did not do homework. Eimers and Aitchison described the problem as the boy's not getting sufficient rewards for doing work. Parents found a suitable place to work, in the dining room, and the boy was given a choice of rewards for spending specified amounts of time on his homework. Initially, the amount of time he put in was brief, but gradually it was increased so that he could obtain the reward.

To improve his classroom behavior, the boy received points for working predetermined amounts of time at his desk. When he clowned in class, he was put in a brief time out. The teacher also praised the boy for on-task behavior. We can see here that parents and teachers can do many things to change school behavior—organizing the environment, giving praise and rewards for appropriate behavior, and punishing for inappropriate behavior.

Research suggests that parents should take an active role in dealing with school problems. Given the age of early adolescents, mutual problem-solving sessions and sending strong I-statements of concern might be appropriate tactics. If these do not lead to an effective plan for change, then parents can try the behavioral system. If children fall behind in school because they are not doing the work, they can find it very hard to catch up when they finally decide to take action. For this reason, the behaviorists' approach has merit.

■ **T A B L E 10-2**
TEN STEPS FOR HELPING CHILDREN DEVELOP THEIR ABILITIES

1. Understand children's special skills and areas of difficulties
2. Provide appropriate levels of stimulation that neither bore nor overwhelm children
3. Teach children that their biggest limitations are the ones they place on themselves and what they can do
4. Help children learn to ask questions and seek answers
5. Help children identify what really interests and motivates them
6. Encourage children to take sensible risks even though there is no guarantee of success
7. Help children take responsibility for their behaviors—both positive and negative
8. Teach children to tolerate and deal with frustration, delay, and uncertainty
9. Help children understand other people's feelings and points of view
10. Remember that, in helping children realize their abilities, what counts is not financial resources, but the way you interact with children and the kinds of experiences children have in everyday life

Adapted from Wendy M. Williams and Robert J. Sternberg, "How Parents Can Maximize Children's Cognitive Abilities," in *Handbook of Parenting,* 2nd ed., ed. Marc H. Bornstein, vol. 5: *Practical Issues in Parenting* (Mahwah, NJ: Erlbaum, 2002), 169–194.

Parents clearly have many ways to help young adolescents deal with various issues. Table 10-2 reflects many of the strategies this section has discussed.

PRACTICAL QUESTION: WHAT SPECIAL NEEDS DO ADOLESCENT GIRLS AND BOYS HAVE?

Girls

Mary Pipher, who has worked closely with adolescent girls, believes that, in the teenage years, girls lose their sense of themselves as individuals and become overfocused on the needs, feelings, and approval of other people. Girls have to develop "identities based on talents or interests, rather than appearance, popularity or sexuality. They need good habits for coping with stress, self-nurturing skills and a sense of purpose and perspective."[78] She believes that homes that offer both protection and challenges help girls find and sustain a sense of identity.

Parents need to listen to daughters and encourage independent thought and rational decision-making skills and to encourage friendships with boys and girls and a wide variety of activities that build skills in many areas—artistic, athletic, intellectual, and social. As a therapist, Pipher teaches adolescent girls to separate thinking from feeling and to combine these two aspects of experience in making decisions. She also teaches girls to manage pain in a positive way.

> All the craziness in the world comes from people trying to escape suffering. All mixed-up behavior comes from unprocessed pain. I teach girls to sit with their pain, to listen to it for messages about their lives, to acknowledge and describe it rather than run from it.[79]

She also encourages altruism to counter the self-absorption that is characteristic of adolescence. Helping others leads to good feelings and to greater maturity.

Boys

The clinical psychologist William Pollack believes that boys are socialized from childhood to conform to what he calls the Boys Code.[80] This code requires boys (1) to be strong, tough, and independent, even when they may feel shaky and in need of support; (2) to be aggressive, daring, and energetic; (3) to achieve status and power; and (4) to avoid the expression of tender feelings, such as warmth and empathy. He believes that boys are forced to separate from parents too early and that, if they protest, they are ridiculed and shamed. He writes,

> I believe that boys, feeling ashamed of their vulnerability, mask their emotions and ultimately their true selves. This unnecessary disconnection—from family and then from self—causes many boys to feel alone, helpless, and fearful. . . . Over time, his sensitivity is submerged almost without thinking, until he loses touch with it himself. And so a boy has been "hardened," just as society thinks he should be.[81]

Pollack advises parents to get behind the masks that boys develop by (1) becoming aware of signs that sons are hiding their feelings, (2) talking to sons about feelings and listening to what they say, (3) accepting sons' emotional schedules for revealing feelings (boys may be slower than girls), (4) connecting with sons through joint activities that can bring parents and sons closer together, and (5) sharing their own growing-up experiences with their sons. He calls for the development of "a New Boy code that respects what today's boys and men are about—one that will be based on honesty rather than fear, communication rather than repression, connection rather than disconnection."[82] Boys need to stay connected to those who love and support them and encourage them to express all their feelings. "They need to be convinced, above all, that both their strengths and their vulnerabilities are good, that all sides of them will be celebrated, that we'll love them through and through for being just the boys they really are."[83]

So, parents need to help both boys and girls find and express their own true selves. This means staying more closely connected to sons than in the past and encouraging more independence of thought and action in girls than in the past.

PARENTS' EXPERIENCES IN FACING TRANSITIONS

Many parents report that they do not feel ready to have teenage children. The childhood years have gone so fast, it seems too soon to have a daughter with a mature figure and sons with bulging muscles and low voices. Parents also find their children's sexual maturity disconcerting. They are surprised to see sons with *Playboy* magazines and hear girls talking about the sexual attractiveness of boys.

Their adolescents' mood swings and desires for greater freedom throw parents back to some of the same conflicts of the toddler and preschool years. The elementary school years were stable because parents could talk and reason with children, but now they are back to dealing with screaming, crying, moody creatures who sometimes act young but at the same time want more freedom. Parents may feel that they themselves have grown and matured as parents, able to handle crises, only to find themselves back at square one, yelling and feeling uncontrolled with their children.

Though it is difficult to give up certain images of themselves and their children, parents must do so. Children are no longer children; they are physically and sexually mature. They are not psychologically mature, however, so they still need the guidance parents can give. Parents often have to give up images of themselves as the perfect parent of an adolescent. They recall their own adolescence, the ways their parents handled them, and in many cases they want to improve on that. Sometimes they find they are not doing as well as they want and have to step back and see where they went off track.

As they mature, early adolescents gain the physical glow and psychological vitality that comes from feeling the world is a magical place. At the same time, parents are marching to or through middle age. It is hard to live with offspring who present a physical contrast to how parents themselves feel. Further, the world is opening up to adolescents just as some parents feel it is weighing them down. Parents have heavy responsibilities, often taking care of aging parents as well as growing children. Parents feel they have little time and money at their own disposal, yet they live with young people who seem to have a great deal of both.

Thus, parents have to be careful not to let resentment of the freedom and excitement of their teenagers get in the way of being effective parents. As parents develop reasonable expectations of the amount of freedom and responsibilities their children are to have, they must be careful not to overrestrict or overcriticize out of envy.

To highlight the greater freedom and control children have, Ellen Galinsky calls this the *interdependent stage* of parenting.[84] Parents have several years to work through these issues before their children are launched. When parents can become more separate from their children—can be available to help them grow yet not stifle them in the process—then parents' and children's relationships take on a new richness.

SUPPORT FOR PARENTS

Parents often feel overwhelmed by cultural forces that do not support their efforts to rear children well. For example, the media bombard teens with messages about sexuality that conform to few families' values. William Damon has developed the Youth Charter program to combat cultural forces that make rearing children more difficult.[85] Parents can initiate this program to organize teachers, clergy, police, and others who care about children to develop community practices and standards that promote children's healthy development. Parents' childrearing efforts serve as a bridge to connect children to community activities at school, with peers, and in the neighborhood. Communities have to be organized to support parents' goals.

Damon outlines a way of organizing concerned adults to identify children's specific needs and work together to find ways to meet them. Standards and expectations are drawn up for children and for the community so that parents and concerned citizens and youth can control teen drinking, vandalism, and early pregnancy and build a community more supportive of children and families. Damon writes,

> Beneath the sense of isolation that has divided our communities, we all share a deep well of concern for the younger generation. If we can find a way to tap into that well, child rearing can become the secure and fulfilling joy that it should be, rather than the risky and nerve-wracking challenge that it has become for too many parents.[86]

MAIN POINTS

In early adolescence, sexual development

- begins and takes years to complete
- triggers psychological reactions in young people
- is related to increases in family conflicts

Early adolescents

- begin to think more abstractly and analyze themselves and other people
- find the transition to junior high difficult because the school environment is a mismatch with early adolescent needs
- worry about conflicts with parents, friends, and school authorities
- experience stress when many changes occur at the same time
- are more involved than previously in peer relationships and cliques

Sense of identity

- depends on exploring a variety of alternatives and making a commitment to values, goals, and behavior
- can be foreclosed if teens make a commitment without exploring their options
- is not achieved when early adolescents experience a moratorium, or explore without making a commitment
- is achieved in a complicated way by those youth who must integrate two cultures and deal with prejudice

Peers

- are sought as primary attachment figures when parents are uninterested and give little guidance
- are sought for different kinds of relationships by boys and girls—with girls wanting to talk and express their feelings and boys wanting to engage in group activities with little self-revelation

In this period, parents

- continue to be accepting, sensitive caregivers
- provide role models of ethical, principled behavior and provide accurate information on topics such as sexual behavior and substance abuse
- monitor children's activities and behavior
- give more decision-making power to adolescents
- add to children's stress when they cannot deal with problems in their own lives

Problems discussed center on

- developing problem-solving skills
- controlling emotional reactions and dealing with social difficulties
- failures in communication
- the special needs of girls and boys

Joys include

- observing accomplishments in physical, artistic, and intellectual endeavors
- feeling good because the parent has helped the child in a specific way
- observing the child's capacity to take responsibility for self
- emotional closeness

EXERCISES

1. See the videos or DVDs of three movies such as *Boyz N the Hood, To Sleep with Anger, Avalon,* or *Parenthood.* Compare parenthood in the majority culture with that in different ethnic groups. What are the roles of grandparents and parents in each culture? How do adults socialize the young to be part of their culture?

2. In small groups, take a survey of students' school experience in the years when they were eleven to fifteen. What size was the school and what grades were included? Have each student rate that school experience from 1, very dissatisfied, to 7, very satisfied. Tabulate the average ratings for each kind of school setting and note whether students were happier when older students were included.

3. Break into small groups and have students list the kinds of experiences that increased their self-esteem in early adolescent years. With input from the whole class, write suggestions for parents who want to increase the self-esteem of their early teenagers.

4. Divide into pairs. In the first exercise, have one partner take the role of a parent who wants to talk to his or her early adolescent about appropriate sexual behavior for the teenager, while the other partner takes the role of the teen who wants more freedom. Then reverse roles, and have the second "parent" try to convey values about appropriate uses of substances in adolescent years to the second "teen." In doing this, practice active listening and sending I-messages.

5. Discuss with other students the importance of peers in their early adolescent years. Did you experience peer pressure? Did parents let you spend time with your friends? What do you think are reasonable rules with regard to time spent with peers? At what age do you think dating should begin? Why that age?

ADDITIONAL READINGS

Damon, William. *The Youth Charter: How Communities Can Work Together to Raise Standards for All Our Children.* New York: Free Press, 1997.

Elkind, David. *The Hurried Child.* Cambridge, MA: Perseus Books, 2001.

Larson, Reed, and Richards, Maryse H. *Divergent Realities: The Emotional Lives of Mothers, Fathers, and Adolescents.* New York: Basic Books, 1994.

Pipher, Mary. *Reviving Ophelia.* New York: Ballantine, 1994.

Pollack, William. *Real Boys.* New York: Holt, 1998.

Shure, Myrna B., with Israeloff, Roberta. *Raising a Thinking Preteen.* New York: Holt, 2000.

C H A P T E R

11

Parenting Late Adolescents

IN THE NEWS

New York Times, December 24, 2002
Jane Brody describes the warning signs that teens are suffering from more than moodiness; they are depressed. See page 350 for details.

 Go to PowerWeb at:
www.dushkin.com/powerweb
to read articles and newsfeeds
on **child development, health, peers,**
and other topics related to this chapter.

How do late adolescents use their parents and families as a secure base when they venture farther away from home in activities, schooling, and jobs? How do late adolescents use their new ways of thinking and reasoning to deal with the powerful challenges of greater freedom? How do they stay safe when so many risks abound? In this chapter, we look at how parents give information and support to benefit their children while they themselves are changing.

Late adolescents have matured physically and sexually. They have adjusted to bodies with new silhouettes and new capacities. Having accommodated themselves to many changes, late adolescents are ready to look to the future. They begin to envision careers, future lifestyles, and romantic relationships. At the same time, they balance pleasure with work at school or in jobs.

Parents, too, are adjusting to their children's many changes. As adolescents make choices, parents stand by to provide information and to help if problems develop. Parents in this stage sense their child's impending departure from home and what life may be like for them as older adults.

PHYSICAL DEVELOPMENT

As the physical changes of maturation near completion, adolescents must integrate them. They must learn to practice healthy behaviors, such as eating a good diet, exercising, and avoiding risky behaviors such as smoking, drinking, using illegal substances, and engaging in high-risk sexual activity. Psychosocial factors are intimately related to physical health: The leading causes of death in these years, accounting for 75 percent of deaths among adolescents, are accidents, suicide, and homicide—all potentially preventable.[1]

Health Concerns

In the high school years, girls rate their physical health as less good than that of boys their age and that of girls ten to fourteen.[2] They appear accurate in their self-assessments, as high school girls exercise less and diet more. Girls are more likely than boys to make physicians' visits and be hospitalized, primarily because of reproductive health needs. While boys give themselves a better health rating than girls give themselves, boys are twice as likely to die because they are more often involved in motor vehicle accidents.

A socioeconomically mixed group of 1,400 teens listed their health concerns as follows: acne, obesity, menstruation, headaches, sexuality, sexually transmitted diseases, substance use, "nervousness," and dental problems.[3] Concerns are similar in samples of European Americans, African Americans, and Hispanics. In large measure, these are the same concerns that adults have for teens' health.

Both boys and girls have concerns about engaging in high-risk behaviors. Because these behaviors are the main source of mortality for teens, such concerns are realistic. Figure 11-1 presents questionnaire data gathered from 3,000 high school students in 1996 and 1997.[4] More worrisome figures about alcohol use indicate that in a large-scale study of high school seniors in the class of 1992, one out of three boys and one out of five girls indicated that they had consumed five or more drinks in a row in the past two weeks.[5] Dangerous in itself, such behavior is also related to both injuries and deaths from motor vehicle accidents.

High-risk behaviors are related to current mood and life experiences. For example, girls who have depressive symptoms are twice as likely as those with no or few depressive symptoms to smoke, drink, or take drugs, and three times as likely to

■ FIGURE 11-1
RISKY BEHAVIORS: SMOKING, DRINKING, USING DRUGS;
OLDER GIRLS AND BOYS REPORT SIMILAR RATES

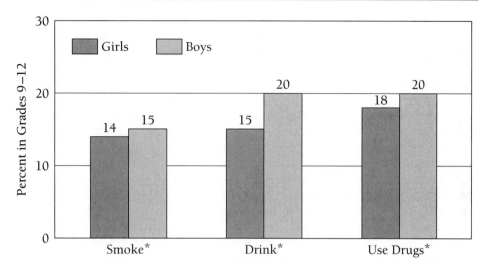

*Smoke = Smoked several cigarettes or a pack or more in the past week
Drink = Drink at least once a month or once a week
Use Drugs = Used illegal drugs in the past month

Cathy Schoen et al., *The Commonwealth Fund Survey of the Health of Adolescent Girls* (New York: Commonwealth Fund, p. 25. Reprinted with permission from The Commonwealth Fund.

have eating disorders.[6] Girls who have been physically or sexually abused or forced to have sex on dates are at risk in the same ways.

Adolescent Sexual Activity

Before they become sexual with a partner, adolescents engage in self-stimulating sexual activities like fantasizing and masturbation. These may occur separately or together—fantasies are used by half the teens who masturbate. Masturbation, which often begins between age twelve and fourteen for boys and girls, is the most common form of orgasm in both sexes in the adolescent years.[7]

Heterosexual activity usually proceeds from kissing to petting above the waist to petting below the waist, and then to intercourse.[8] Figures vary for the exact percentages of adolescents experiencing sexual intercourse. The most recent figures indicate that in 1993, about 50 percent of high school seniors had engaged in intercourse.[9]

Boys are more sexually active than are girls. In one study, almost 30 percent of boys reported intercourse by age sixteen, but only 13 percent of girls.[10] At age eighteen, the comparable figures are 64 percent of boys and 44 percent of girls. Ethnic groups vary. African American boys and girls tend to be more advanced than European Americans and Hispanics. For example, by age seventeen, 92 percent of African American boys report having had intercourse, while only 50 percent of Hispanics and 43 percent of European Americans make similar reports. By age seventeen, 40 percent of African American girls report having had intercourse, compared with 25 percent of European American and 24 percent of Hispanic girls.

Among sexually active teenagers, intercourse may occur infrequently and with a limited number of partners.[11] According to one survey, most teens had intercourse again with the first partner, but the relationships were not long-lived. The typical teen had zero to one partner with whom they had sex, usually less than a couple of times a month. About two-thirds of adolescents in one study experienced their first intercourse in the homes of parents or friends. Their partners were most often people they knew well—a steady date or close friend.

Many mothers underestimate their teens' sexual activity; though 58 percent of teens fourteen to seventeen report sexual activity, only 34 percent report that their children are engaged in sexual activity.[12] Though very responsive to perceived parental values, teens often misperceive the strength of the mother's disapproval of sexual activity, in part because they share little conversation about sex.

It is important for parents to recognize that children need to hear parents' personal views expressed, that they do not automatically know what matters to parents. When they do know, many are willing to conform. Half of adolescents who do not have sexual relations say that the main reason they do not is that they fear their parents would find out about it.[13]

Though teens want to avoid pregnancy and sexually transmitted diseases,[14] rates of contraceptive use are very low in the early adolescent years—in one study 23 percent of girls under fifteen used contraceptives within the month of first intercourse but 42 percent delayed use for the first year. In contrast, among older adolescent girls, 50 percent used contraception at first intercourse.[15] Forty-eight percent of boys age twelve to fourteen used condoms at first intercourse, compared with 60 percent of those fifteen to nineteen years old.[16]

The condom is the most popular birth control method reported by unmarried teen girls, of all ethnic groups, when they first have sex.[17] Hispanic teenagers are less likely than other groups to use contraceptives, perhaps because many are recent immigrants who have language difficulties, limited access to health care, and a cultural tradition of not preventing pregnancy.

Sexually transmitted diseases (STDs) are a major risk for adolescents because of early age of intercourse and a lack of regular contraceptive use. Next to homosexual men and prostitutes, adolescent girls have the highest rates for any age group of gonorrhea, cytomegalovirus, and pelvic inflammatory disease. Now they face the added specter of AIDS (acquired immunodeficiency disease syndrome).[18]

Because of the disease's long incubation period, the precise risk that AIDS presents to teenagers is not known. Many people coming down with it in their twenties presumably contracted it as teenagers. However, adolescents may be at high risk, because the number of teen cases is increasing and because teens often do not use contraceptives. Unprotected sex with drug-using individuals is a major form of transmission in the heterosexual population. Further, teens are more susceptible than adults to all STDs, so they may be more vulnerable to AIDS as well.[19]

VOICES OF EXPERIENCE

What I Wish I Had Known about Late Adolescence

"I wish that I had got my children involved in more family activities. When they were mostly through adolescence, I heard a talk by a child psychiatrist who said that often when teenagers say they don't want to do something with the family, at times you have to insist because they do go along and enjoy the event. I wish I had known that sooner, because I accepted their first 'No,' when I perhaps should have pushed more."
MOTHER

"This may begin earlier, but it goes through adolescence. I had always heard they look for their own independence, their own things to participate in, but until you really experience it with your own, it's hard to deal with it. When you read about independence, it sounds like it's carefully planned out. When it actually happens, all of a sudden they want to do something that they have never done before and which you firmly believe they have no idea how to do. It can be driving for the first time or suddenly announcing they want to go somewhere with friends. I knew it was going to happen, but exactly how to handle it myself and handle it with them so they got a chance to do something new without it being dangerous has been a challenge to me."   FATHER

"I wish that I had known that I had to listen more to them in order to understand what they were experiencing. I sort of assumed that I knew what adolescence was about from my own experience, but things had a different meaning to them. What was important to me was not that important to them, and I wish I had realized that in the beginning."   MOTHER

"I wish I knew how to raise children in adolescence when you have traditional values and many of the people around you do not. It's very hard to do here in California compared to the South, where we came from. There, everyone reinforces the same values, and it is a lot easier for parents."   MOTHER

"I wish I had known to be more attentive, to really listen, because kids have a lot of worthwhile things to say and you come to find out they hold a lot of your viewpoints."   FATHER

"I wish I had known it was important to spend time with the children individually. We did things as a family, but the children are so different, and I think I would have understood them better if I had spent time with them alone."   MOTHER

INTELLECTUAL DEVELOPMENT

Late adolescents' thinking advances and becomes more abstract than before. Teenagers can keep in mind several dimensions of a problem, generate more options for action, and evaluate more facts. They think in relative rather than absolute terms.

Though revealed in laboratory research studies, adolescent abstract reasoning capacities are not always seen in the decisions adolescents make in their everyday lives. For example, driver training improves the knowledge and driving skills of sixteen- to eighteen-year-olds, but increased knowledge and skill have not reduced the number of teenage driving accidents. So, teenagers have knowledge but do not necessarily have the maturity to put it to use in day-to-day actions. Applying abstract thought depends on social and emotional factors as well.[20]

Karen Bartsch focuses on another factor that affects children's and adolescents' knowledge and thinking: their individual theories about the material at hand.[21] Increasing knowledge is not accomplished by just feeding new facts into a receptive learner. First, one must dispel inaccurate theories and then present new facts when the person is receptive and ready to absorb the information. For example, as long as some teenagers hold the false belief that they can get pregnant only if they want a child, they will not take in contraceptive information, because they believe it is not relevant to them. It does not fit with their idea of how one gets pregnant. In discussing factual information with teens, parents are wise to get the teen's beliefs or underlying assumptions out in the open before presenting new facts.

SCHOOL

The transition to high school brings problems similar to those experienced in the transition to junior high school.[22] High schools are larger and more impersonal than junior high schools. The increased bureaucratic structure reduces interactions between students and teachers, so that teachers cannot easily become mentors.

In adolescence, peers play a more important role in scholastic achievements than they have in earlier years.[23] Because young teens want to gain peer acceptance, they are vulnerable to their friends' views of them. If new friends devalue academic achievement, adolescents may shift away from academic pursuits to concentrate on social activities or sports.

Parents' practices affect students' achievement. Students who describe their parents as authoritative perform well in school and are actively engaged in school activities. Students who report their parents as authoritarian or permissive have the lowest grades.[24]

Students' achievement is related also to how they feel about themselves and their abilities. Underachievement in high school, defined as getting grades significantly below what would be expected on the basis of students' ability tests, occurs in all socioeconomic and ethnic groups.[25] Compared with students of the same ability who achieved grades appropriate to their ability, underachieving boys and girls had lower opinions of their abilities, lower feelings of competence, less involvement in academic and extracurricular activities, lower educational and occupational aspirations, and more involvement in heterosexual relationships. Additionally, underachieving girls had fewer friends and less family support for their occupational desires and tended to be the youngest children.

To prevent dropping out, school interventions must occur early in students' careers so that their frustration and low self-esteem do not accumulate. Students do not drop out at the first hint of trouble; they usually have had difficulties for a long time and see little hope of reversing the process. Early interventions can enable them in some small measure to experience success and pleasure at school.

WORKING

In the school year 1998–1999, 62 percent of boys and 57 percent of girls held jobs.[26] While there have been concerns that working decreases school grades and educational motivation, the effects of working depend primarily on the nature of the job. When teens work long hours in stressful environments with little adult supervision, the likelihood of negative effects increases.[27] Employment in a favorable work environment where teens can gain skills and get to know people, however, can promote understanding of people and give experience in the responsibilities of work.[28]

EMOTIONAL DEVELOPMENT

Teens' feelings about themselves and their lives tend to remain the same from early to late adolescence.[29] Those who were happy in the first year of high school are happy as juniors. They show more stability in their feelings about friends and school, however, than they do in their feelings about family and solitude. Feelings about family tend to improve—52 percent say they are happier with family as juniors, 12 percent say less happy, and 36 percent report no change. This greater happiness appears to derive from late adolescents' broader perspective. They interpret experiences in a new light and as a result become more accepting both of family and of solitude.

Stressful life events include family loss such as the death of a parent; relationship loss such as the loss of boyfriend or girlfriend; physical problems such as having acne, needing to wear glasses or braces, or being overweight; and school problems such as failing one or more subjects or going to a new school.[30] The more stresses a middle-class teen experiences, the more likely he or she is to develop problems like depression, alcohol use, or delinquent acting out. Family support helps girls under high stress avoid difficulties. For boys under stress, the support of friends rather than family helps to reduce problem behaviors to a slight degree.

Inner city youth who experience stress cope best with negative life events when they have high self-esteem and are socially expressive with peers.[31] While they may report more anxiety than do teens with low stress, these adolescents get good grades and relate well to others despite the stress in their lives.

Adolescents who reported many negative events not only felt depressed but also experienced poor physical health following the events. Hormonal changes may also play a role in depressed mode or aggressiveness.[32] As we have seen, positive events can serve as protection against the effects of negative events when they do occur.

A sense of self-efficacy, or belief in one's abilities to take decisive action, plays a more important role in adolescence than before. Teens make many choices, some of which will have long-term implications.[33] Beliefs in their abilities to face challenges improve adolescents' emotional well-being and protect against depression at this vulnerable time. Thus, belief in one's abilities plus support from parents and peers are major deterrents to low mood. (We shall discuss depressive symptoms in greater detail later in the chapter.)

DEVELOPMENT OF THE SELF

Mid-adolescents speak of the many different "me's"—the self with my mother, the self with my father, the self with my best friend, the self with my boyfriend.[34] Seeing their behavior change with circumstances intensifies mid-adolescents' concerns about "the real me." They feel they express their true selves when they discuss their inner thoughts, feelings, and reactions to events; they express false selves when they put on an act and say what they do not mean. Teens report acting falsely (1) to make a good impression, (2) to experiment with different selves, and (3) to avoid others' low opinions of them. When they believe they have parents' support, adolescents can voice their opinions and express their true selves. The higher the level of support, the more adolescents can express themselves and the higher their self-esteem.

In late adolescence, teens come to terms with contradictory qualities by finding a more general abstraction that explains the contradiction. For example, they explain changes in mood—cheerfulness with friends and discouragement with parents—by describing themselves as moody. They also come to accept the contradictions as normal—"It's normal to be different ways with different people." As they observe their changing behaviors, late adolescents note the situations in which they show the traits they value and in which they feel support, and they come to seek out these situations.

Gender Identity

Differences   Differences in gender identity at this age appear mainly in the content of the identity, not in the process by which identity is formed. In the past, boys' identity has been linked with independence and achievement at work and girls' identity with close relationships with others. Boys have been socialized to get ahead and girls to get along.[35] These traits are expressed in their self-descriptions. Boys see themselves as more daring, rebellious, and playful in life than girls and, at the same time, more logical, curious, and calm. Girls see themselves as more attuned to people than are boys (more sympathetic, social, considerate, and affectionate) and more emotionally reactive (more worrisome, more easily upset, more needing of approval).[36]

Gay/Lesbian Identity   In adolescence, a small percentage of teens identify themselves as gay, lesbian, or bisexual.[37] For boys, the mean age of awareness of same-gender attraction is thirteen, with self-description as "homosexual" occurring between fourteen and twenty-one. For lesbians, the average age of awareness is sixteen, with self-description occurring around twenty-one years of age.

Society's negative view of homosexuality and lesbianism creates pressure and self-doubt in adolescents attracted to same-sex partners. In one study, adolescents reported strong negative reactions from parents (43 percent) and friends (41 percent) on revealing their same-sex preference. They reported discrimination by peers (37 percent), verbal abuse (55 percent), and physical assault (30 percent).[38] Because such discrimination and rejection create additional psychological problems, it is not surprising that gay adolescents are two to three times more likely to attempt suicide than are other adolescents and may make up as much as 30 percent of all completed youth suicides.[39]

In spite of others' negative views, many homosexual and lesbian adolescents evolve a positive self-concept of themselves as lovable, respectable, competent individuals. As with ethnic minority youth, support from family and others may be especially critical in forming a positive self-concept and combating the social disapproval they may encounter.

Ethnic Identity

By late adolescence, most teens have achieved a sense of ethnic identity. Ethnic identity and high self-esteem are mutually related. High self-esteem promotes exploration of ethnic identity, and ethnic identity promotes a sense of self-esteem.[40]

Studies of African American and Mexican American adolescents in schools where they were the major groups and had positive status found that all students formed a positive ethnic identity, but they differed in the degree to which they valued and identified with the broader American culture.[41] *Blended bicultural* students positively identified with both the majority and their own ethnic group. For example, they saw themselves as African and American and saw no conflict between the identities. *Alternating bicultural* students identified with the majority culture when at school or at other places but primarily identified with their own ethnic group. A third, smaller group were termed *separated* students, as they did not identify at all with the majority culture, which they felt rejected and devalued them. Among African American students, slightly over half were classified as blended biculturals, about a quarter as alternating biculturals, and 17 percent as separated. Among Mexican American students, about one-third were classified as blended biculturals, almost two-thirds as alternating biculturals, and only 2 percent as separated.

Although a positive identification with both cultures is thought to be important for personal adjustment, the three groups of students did not differ on measures of self-concept, academic grades, and level of anxiety. Thus, there appear to be three pathways to integrating the experience of having two cultures, and the pathways all seem equally related to measures of effectiveness.

DEVELOPMENT OF SELF-REGULATION

Because of new capacities for abstract thought and the ability to see more options, adolescents can attain higher levels of moral reasoning. They have internalized the rules. At the same time they can better understand others' points of view, so they can reason in a more sympathetic way, emphasizing general reciprocity between people.[42]

A major task of this age period is to engage in healthy behaviors and avoid high-risk activities such as smoking, drinking, drugs, and early sexual intercourse. Parents' support and monitoring contribute to teens' development of internal restraint or the internalization of standards that, in turn, guide their behavior onto positive paths.[43] In the next section we deal in detail with the parents' role. Here, we shall focus on adolescents' qualities that enable them to pursue healthy activities.

Adolescents' positive orientation to school and their intolerance of harmful behaviors such as physical aggression, stealing, and property damage predict avoidance of problem behaviors such as drinking, drugs, and precocious sexual intercourse for both boys and girls in three different ethnic groups.[44] Low self-esteem, low expectations of success, and having friends who model problem behaviors all predict adolescents' engagement in these disapproved behaviors.

Other individual qualities predicting drug use include a large time commitment to part-time work, higher income, and more evening recreational time.[45] Drug use tends to be lower among those with religious commitments. Further, a significant number of adolescents give up drugs such as marijuana and cocaine as more accurate information on their harmful effects becomes available.

While parents and social scientists have long worried about the negative influence of peers, less attention is paid to the positive influence of a high-achieving, competent friend who may shift a teen's behavior in a more positive direction. In the next section, we examine peer relationships more closely.

SOCIAL DEVELOPMENT

Parent-Child Relationships

Although parents see less of their adolescents, the dimensions of parenting that predict competence in the preschool years continue to predict adolescent competence reflected in self-reliant, independent behavior and in the capacity for meaningful relationships with others. Parental *commitment* along with the balance between *demandingness* (establishing rules, monitoring compliance, and enforcing rules), and *responsiveness* (being supportive of the child and paying attention to the child's needs and interests).[46] How parents relate to children during adolescence is more important in determining adolescent competence than are earlier parenting techniques.

Parenting Styles   Diana Baumrind describes six different parenting patterns and relates them to the child's drug use. *Authoritative* parents have strong commitments to children and balance demands with responsiveness to children's needs: "Unlike any other pattern, authoritative upbringing *consistently* generated competence and deterred problem behavior in both boys and girls, at *all* stages."[47] *Democratic* parents who are strongly committed to children and highly responsive to their needs are only average in demandingness. Their children are highly competent as well but are freer to explore drugs.

Nonauthoritarian-Directive parents who emphasize conventional control and value conformity have children with the least drug use, but this is accomplished by strict obedience to rules so that children are conforming and dependent on adult approval. *Authoritarian-Directive* parents are even more restrictive and less supportive and have less competent children. Parents of both types are moderately committed to their children.

Unengaged parents are neither demanding nor responsive, nor are they committed to children. They either actively reject or neglect parenting responsibilities. Free of adult authority, children from these families have little direction and are described as immature. These adolescents have had problems dating back to the preschool years, and they lack competence in many areas of adolescent functioning. *Good Enough* parents are about average on the different dimensions, and their children are about average in competence.

Although Baumrind's sample was relatively small, primarily white, and middle class, her family classifications applied equally to a large, ethnically diverse sample of 4,100 adolescents between the ages of fourteen and eighteen who were followed for two years.[48] Regardless of the adolescent's sex and socioeconomic or ethnic background, authoritative parenting was related to adolescent self-confidence, competency, self-reliance, avoidance of delinquent activity, and general good mood. In European American and Hispanic families, authoritative parenting was also related to school achievement, but African American and Asian American students did not show increased school performance. "In no cases were adolescents from nonauthoritative homes better off than those reared in authoritative families."[49] Even if only one parent is authoritative and the other is not, their adolescents achieve better grades than do those who grew up with two nonauthoritative parents.[50]

Authoritative parenting is also related to adolescent personality and peer group membership in European American students who seek out crowds who reinforce academic achievement and school involvement. These students receive the same message about values and behavior from parents and peers.

Among minority youth, no relationship exists between authoritative parenting and peer group membership. This appears to result from ethnic minority members' not having equal access to all peer groups. For example, an Asian American may be excluded from the "jocks" or the "druggies," and an African American may be excluded from the "brains" (see the section on peers).

Authoritative parenting exerts an even greater influence when the teenager's friends' parents also rely on authoritative parenting. Friends tend to be more competent, and such peers help to maintain high levels of adjustment.

Neglectful or unengaged parenting is consistently associated with low competence, psychological distress, and acting out. Adolescents from indulgent and authoritarian homes fall somewhere between those from authoritative and those from neglectful homes.

Serving As Consultants   A parent serves as a reliable resource and consultant for children in areas of importance not only by providing factual information and values, as described in Chapter 10, but also by helping teens develop the confidence to carry out effective behaviors. I can illustrate this in the area of sexual behavior. In addition to giving information about reproduction and the consequences of early sexual activity, parents promote the postponement of sexual activity by encouraging teens to have interests and activities that absorb their time and attention and give them satisfaction.[51]

Late teens may spend more time in their bedrooms than in any other setting in the home. Parents are expected to respect the teen's privacy, including phone conversations, mail, and personal effects, but they are also expected to include them in leisure activities and family events.

Parents also help adolescents develop the social skills to withstand pressure for sexual activity and to insist on safe-sex practices when they are sexually active. Further, parents provide supervision and, as far as possible, do not permit teens to be in situations that can lead to spontaneous sexual activity. For example, because first intercourse most often happens at home, parents should not go away for the weekend and leave teenagers alone at home.[52]

Parents serve as consultants in a similar way when teenagers enter the world of work.[53] They provide information about the pros and cons of different jobs and possible occupations children can consider, and they help children develop interpersonal skills to pursue vocational goals.

Encouraging Autonomy   Although conflicts about everyday issues continue, late teens accept and respect their parents' conventional views on situations and thus please their parents. Teens do not necessarily give in, but parents are more likely to grant their requests now, perhaps because teens seem to understand their reasoning.[54]

When adolescents struggle less over power with their parents, they become more self-governing and independent without giving up warm family relationships. Parents and adolescents then form a partnership directed toward establishing such autonomy.[55] When attachment is secure, parents and teens can regulate emotional responses and engage in problem-solving behaviors with relatively little anger and frustration.[56] With secure attachments, both parents and teens can discuss differences and arrive at compromises. Anger appears to motivate securely attached family members to overcome differences and restore harmony. When the attachment is secure, a balance exists between the needs of the individual and the needs of the relationship.

Relationships with Siblings

Sibling relationships improve in later adolescence, compared with those same relationships in the elementary school years and early adolescence.[57] Relationships become more egalitarian and less intense. Egalitarian relationships may occur in the context of either support or growing distance.

The standing in the family constellation partly determines the perception of the relationship. Older adolescent siblings are less likely to dominate younger siblings than before, but they also report less companionship and affection than younger siblings want. Younger siblings look up to older ones and report less conflict than older siblings report. Even though adolescents and other family members spend less time together, the attachment among siblings remains moderately strong.

Peer Relationships

In the United States in a typical week, high school students spend twice as much time with peers as with parents.[58] Relationships with same-sex and opposite-sex peers provide adolescents with similar forms of support that differ from those given by parents. Adolescents report that their relationships with friends provide intimacy, companionship, and understanding, whereas relationships with parents provide affection, instrumental help, and a sense of reliability in relationships.[59]

Three changes occur in peer relationships in these years.[60] First, peer interactions are generally unsupervised by adults. Second, they are more likely to include larger numbers of peers who form crowds. Finally, peers gravitate to members of the opposite sex.

In adolescence, intimacy increases because friendships involve more self-disclosure, expression of feelings, and support for friends as needed.[61] Friends are expected to tell each other their honest opinions and to express satisfactions and dissatisfactions with the other person. Friends also have to learn to resolve conflicts as they arise. So, friendships promote the development of social skills that, in turn, enrich friendships. Intimacy in friendships is related to adolescents' sociability, self-esteem, and overall interpersonal competence.

Adolescents feel quite loyal to their friends—in continuing friendships despite parents' disapproval and in not revealing details of the relationships to others. Although overall 56 percent would report that a friend was considering suicide, far fewer (17–20 percent) would break a confidence about drugs and alcohol, and almost none (6 percent) would reveal that a friend was shoplifting.[62]

Peer groups that form in adolescence are larger than the cliques of the early adolescent years. Bradford Brown refers to these as *crowds*.[63] As noted in Chapter 10, cliques form out of mutual choice. Crowds, though, are based on judgments of personal characteristics, and a person must be invited to join. Through time we have seen slight shifts in the kinds of crowds that exist, but generally studies find groups of "jocks" (athletes), "brains," popular kids, "druggies" or delinquents, and "nerds."

Parents' behavior indirectly influences the kinds of group friendships adolescent children form.[64] Members of four groups—"brains," popular crowd, "jocks," and "druggies"—described their parents' child-rearing practices. When parents stress achievement and monitor children closely, children tend to get high grades and belong to the "brains" group. When parents fail to monitor and do not encourage joint decision making, children tend to become part of the popular crowd and/or may be exposed to the drug crowd. Peer group norms are most likely to reinforce those behaviors that parenting strategies have encouraged.

Different ethnic groups were more likely to belong to certain groups. European-American students tended to be part of the popular crowd or the druggies. Asian Americans were more likely to belong to the "brains," and African Americans were more likely to belong to the "jocks."

Dating

By the time teens graduate from high school, most, though not all, have dated.[65] Dating gives practice in developing feelings of trust and enjoyment with the opposite sex and provides the basis for later romantic attachments. Because there are almost no studies of same-sex dating, we discuss only heterosexual dating here.

The social process of dating begins in earlier years when same-sex friendships give practice in establishing egalitarian, cooperative, supportive relationships with age-mates. In junior high school years, opposite-sex friendships increase and give early adolescents greater understanding and ease with the opposite sex. Dating and, eventually, romantic relationships develop from opposite-sex friendships and peer contacts in large-group, social activities.[66]

Although most mid-adolescents have had one dating experience, most teens are not dating at any one time. A study of middle-class, European American adolescents indicates that dating relationships are casual, short-lived, and intense.[67] When dating, teens see and talk to each other on the phone almost every day, but the relationships last, on average, four months. Dating usually occurs in public settings, and movies, hanging out, and parties are common dating activities. In late adolescence, couple-only dating increases and occurs in more private settings.

Eighty-five percent of girls and 88 percent of boys report that positive personality traits are the primary reason for dating a person, with physical attraction being the second, though less prominent reason, reported by 46 percent of girls and 68 percent of boys. Intimacy, support, and companionship are major satisfactions in dating.

Negative aspects of the relationship are also similar for boys and girls, with both disliking the level of commitment involved or some negative qualities of the person.[68]

While parent-child attachments have been considered major determiners of the quality of dating and romantic relationships, recent work indicates that the quality of dating relationships are more closely related to the quality of peer friendships.[69] When asked to describe attachment, care received, and affiliation in relationships with parents, friends, and romantic partners, adolescents' perceptions of their relationships with romantic partners was related to their perceptions of their relationships with friends, but unrelated to their perceptions of relationships with parents. The quality of peer friendships appears to play a pivotal role in the development of romantic relationships. Parents influence the quality of friendships, and the nature of the friendships in turn affects dating and romantic relationships.

TASKS AND CONCERNS OF PARENTS

In this age period, parents remain caregivers but also grant their teens greater autonomy. Parenting tasks include these:

- Continuing their commitment to children by monitoring and enforcing rules while supporting and accepting their children's individuality
- Being an available, responsive caregiver
- Serving as a model of responsible behavior
- Communicating information and values in an atmosphere of open discussion
- Serving as a consultant to children as they make important decisions
- Allowing children to separate in an atmosphere of acceptance
- Sharing enjoyable times together

The problems encountered during adolescence relate to physical and emotional functioning, social behavior, and family interactions. We now discuss how parents help their children deal with these problems.

Promoting Healthy Behaviors

Starting from the birth of their child, parents have been concerned about the child's health and safety. They have provided a healthy diet and opportunities for exercise, taken the child for vaccinations and medical and dental checkups, and done all they can to achieve this primary goal of parenting. In adolescence, parents' concerns about health and safety issues increase, as three of five deaths in the second decade of life are related to social factors such as unintentional injuries, homicides, and suicides.[70] Parents, however, lack the power to take direct action to ensure children's well-being; they must rely on teens' ability to avoid high-risk behaviors. So, adolescence is a time of worry and limited responses. Nonetheless, parents can rely on information and awareness as their most effective deterrents of high-risk behavior in teens.

Parents' Healthy Behaviors   As parents seek to promote teens' healthy behaviors and discourage high-risk ones, they need to turn first to their own behaviors. When parents promote good nutrition, exercise, good dental care, and abstinence from smoking, and when they use reasoning and grant children autonomy, their children have good health.[71]

On the negative side, when parents use substances such as alcohol, cigarettes, and marijuana, children are likely to adopt these behaviors as well, especially if there is a good relationship between parent and child.[72] In two other longitudinal studies following children from the preschool years to young adulthood, substance abusers came from families in which parents abused substances as well.[73] Recognizing the long-standing nature of the serious substance abuser's problems and their need for extensive help is important.

So, a first step for parents in promoting adolescents' healthy behaviors is to adopt such behaviors themselves. Then, parents must reinforce the children's behaviors that protect against risks.

Protective Factors   Protective factors in the family, the individual child, and the social environment can increase the likelihood of healthy behaviors and reduce the likelihood of high-risk ones. In a national sample of 12,000 high school students, adolescents who said their parents cared about them and spent time with them in joint activities reported fewer high-risk behaviors.[74] Parents' supervision and granting of autonomy have also been found to predict fewer health problems and adolescents' avoidance of drug use, with parents' supervision of teens' behavior being the single most powerful predictor of drug avoidance.[75] These findings occur in other studies as well; both parents' involvement and interest in their teens predict avoidance of smoking, drinking, and drug use. So, parents' involvement, interest, supervision, and granting of psychological autonomy are primary protective factors in avoiding high-risk behaviors.[76] There is also evidence that parents' expectations about socially acceptable behavior in other arenas such as school serve as protective factors.[77] Parents can provide these protective family factors.

Adolescents' personal qualities also serve as protective factors. Teens with a positive orientation to school, a commitment to socially approved activities and avoidance of deviancy, and good relationships with adults avoid problem behaviors.[78]

Social influences such as peer groups, school atmosphere, and religious affiliation also serve as protective factors against high-risk behaviors. Of the 88 percent of high school students who reported an affiliation with a religion, those who said religion and prayer were important to them reported a later age of first sexual intercourse and were less likely to use substances of any kind.[79]

To deal effectively with potential high-risk behaviors, parents must be aware of what their child is doing and feeling in order to both provide information and monitor behavior effectively. In the next few sections, we focus on eating problems, early sexual activity, and drinking.

Promoting Healthy Eating   A minority of adolescents develop problems in eating that result in obesity (gross overweight), *anorexia nervosa* (severe underweight), or *bulimia nervosa* (binge eating following by self-induced vomiting or purging with laxatives). In contrast to obesity and anorexia, which are observable because they change physical appearance, bulimia may be difficult to detect, because the bulimic frequently maintains average weight.

These three eating problems are not entirely distinct from each other.[80] Anorexics and bulimics may, at one point, have been obese, or they may become obese as they grow older. It is difficult to know the exact numbers of adolescents suffering from these eating disorders. Though anorexia and bulimia are rare, they do appear to be increasing. These two disorders are more commonly seen in girls than boys, most probably because physical attractiveness, defined as thinness, is so valued for girls in U.S. society.

Although the three eating problems have different outcomes in terms of physical appearance, they share several features in common. Each condition can be caused by a variety of factors: hereditary factors play a role in weight gain; physical factors such as metabolism or feedback control mechanisms may be related to anorexia nervosa; family patterns of eating and interacting influence eating behavior. Though physical and biological factors play a role, psychological and social factors contribute the most to these disorders.

In the case of obesity, families may equate love with food; adolescents may then use food to buffer them in times of disappointment. In the case of all three eating disorders, problems in identity formation may underlie the behavior. Teenagers who have found it difficult to establish separate identities for themselves as worthwhile, valued individuals may overeat, starve, or purge themselves. Anorexics often succeed in many areas but do not feel competent and independent, even though others believe they are. Underlying concerns about sexuality and interactions with opposite-sex peers can spur eating problems that prevent appropriate dating and sexual behavior because the child's appearance is so deviant.

Eating problems in turn create difficulties. People with eating disorders often feel self-conscious, depressed, and discouraged about their pattern of eating. Bulimics often fear being discovered in their purging, while anorexics fear their weight loss will be noted. Not only do psychological problems result, but serious medical conditions can follow as well. Bulimia can lead to metabolic changes, electrolyte imbalances, ulcers, and bowel problems. Severe overweight can result in heart and blood pressure problems and diabetes. Anorexia can result in electrolyte imbalances, malnutrition, cessation of menstruation, and heart problems. Anorexics have twelve times the risk of dying as do nonanorexics.[81]

Besides obtaining medical and psychological help for their child, parents can take many specific actions to ensure recovery. The nutritionist Marcia Herrin[82] believes that parents can help their children with eating disorders when (1) they move beyond anger and blame and focus on the problem at hand—namely, the eating habits; (2) both parents and the relatives involved in feeding children agree on the plan and present a united front; (3) parents form a collaborative alliance with the child to change the eating behaviors, though parents remain in charge; (4) parents expect refusals and resistance and do not take them personally; (5) parents remain flexible; and (6) parents fight the problem, not the child. Parents can also promote secure attachments with children, responding in positive and caring ways. Finally, parents should not let the eating disorder dominate their view of the child or their

VOICES OF EXPERIENCE

The Joys of Parenting Late Adolescents

"I think it's really fun to watch them grow up and mature. It's fun to see them discover things about themselves and their lives. The older ones have boyfriends, and I'm seeing them interact with the boyfriends." MOTHER

"Sometimes the kids have friends over, and they all start to talk about things. It's nice to see them get along with their siblings as well as their friends. It gives you a good feeling to see them enjoying themselves." FATHER

"I felt very pleased when my son at sixteen could get a summer job in the city and commute and be responsible for getting there and doing a good job." MOTHER

"I like it when they sit around and reminisce about the things they or the family have done in the past. They all sit around the table and talk about an outing or a trip we took, saying 'Remember this?' It's always interesting what they remember. This last summer we took a long sight-seeing trip, and what stands out in their minds about it is funny. They remember Filene's basement in Boston or a chicken ranch where we stopped to see friends. One father took the Scouts on a ski trip. They got stuck in the snow on the highway for hours, and the car almost slid off the road. He said, 'Never again.' I said, 'Don't you realize that because of those things, the boys will probably remember that trip forever? You have given them wonderful memories.'" MOTHER

"I really enjoy her happiness. She always sees the positive side to a situation. Things might bother her from time to time, but she has a good perspective on things." FATHER

"I really like to see them taking responsibility. Yesterday they had a school holiday, and I was donating some time at an open house fundraiser. They got all dressed up and came along and helped too. The older one coaches a soccer team of four-year-olds, and the younger is a patrol leader in the Scouts, so they both have responsibility for children. They complain sometimes that it's hard to get the little kids' attention to show them things, but I think they like it." MOTHER

own activities. By taking care of themselves and engaging in activities that give them pleasure, while making sure their child does things that he or she enjoys, they provide effective daily support.

Promoting Later Sexual Activity   As noted earlier, about 50 percent of ninth-through twelfth-graders indicate they have had sexual intercourse. Teens are most likely to delay sexual activity when parents express and explain their disapproval of it and when students have interests and success at school.[83] When religious values and commitments support abstinence, teens are also likely to delay sexual activity. Teens under stress from early physiological changes, work pressures, or attraction to same-sex peers are more likely to engage in sexual activity.[84]

"I enjoy that she is following in the family tradition of rowing. I rowed in college, and my brothers did, my father and grandfather did, and she saw a city team and signed up. She does it all on her own and has made a nice group of friends through it." FATHER

"I can't believe that she has had her first boyfriend and it worked out so well. They met at a competition, and he lives some distance away, so they talk on the phone. He has a friend who lives here, and he comes for a visit sometimes and does lots of things with the family. We all like him, and it is nice for her to have a boyfriend like that." MOTHER

"The joys are seeing them go from a totally disorganized state to a partially motivated, organized state. You can see their adult characteristics emerging." FATHER

"I enjoy seeing my daughter develop musical ability, seeing her progression from beginning flute to an accomplished player who performs, and seeing how much pleasure she takes in her accomplishment." MOTHER

"It really gives me a lot of pleasure to see the two of them help each other. They seem to have respect for each other. She is the brain and helps him with school, and he helps her too at times." FATHER

"I enjoy his maturity. He's so responsible. He tests us, but when we're firm, he accepts that. I'm real proud of him because he looks at the consequences of what he does." FATHER

"I enjoy his honesty and the relationship he has with his friends. He is real open with his feelings, and his friends look up to him. He's a leader." MOTHER

"He's not prejudiced. His best friends are of different ethnic groups. People trust him and like him because he's real concerned about people." FATHER

"I feel really pleased about the way the boys get along together. There is rivalry, but there is a lot of love. The older one takes the younger one under his wing, and the younger one looks up to him." FATHER

In a sample of 12,000 seventh- through twelfth-graders, about 20 percent of girls reported having gotten pregnant. Girls who did not get pregnant reported that they shared more activities with their parents and viewed their parents as disapproving of contraceptive use. They themselves recognized the many negative consequences of pregnancy and were more likely to use effective contraception at their first and most recent intercourse.[85]

Having expressed their values and shared information with their children, parents must minimize the possibility of early sexual activity by monitoring and supervising their children's time spent alone with the opposite sex. The most frequent place for first intercourse is the home of the parent or a friend. If pregnancy occurs, parents must get professional help. There are no easy answers, and parents and teens must work together to find solutions they can live with. Supportive communication with teens and medical and religious professionals can aid families in working out solutions that meet their needs.

Discouraging Alcohol Use   Although parents often are more concerned about their children's use of marijuana and other drugs, alcohol is the substance most frequently used. In 1994, alcohol was implicated in 29 percent of motor vehicle deaths of fifteen- to seventeen-year-olds and 44 percent of deaths of eighteen- to twenty-year-olds.[86]

Awareness of teens' alcohol use is essential for parents' effective management of this high-risk behavior, yet in one study, only about a third of mothers and fathers whose children reported regular alcohol use said it was possible that their child used alcohol.[87] Seventy-one percent of mothers and 69 percent of fathers were unaware that their children drank. Over 50 percent of mothers and fathers were aware that their children's friends drank, however. Parents seemed to be saying, "Other teens drink, but not my kid."

When aware, parents can take action. Minimizing household access to alcohol reduces the risk of teens' drinking. When teens are connected to parents and family members and when parents are active and available participants at home, the risk of frequent alcohol use among teens drops.[88] Teens are more likely to use alcohol when they have low self-esteem, earn low grades, work more than 20 hours per week, and experience or act on same-sex attractions. Religious beliefs and prayer also serve as protective factors.

Should problems arise, parents must seek help. Miller Newton's experience with his son provides an illuminating example. Newton served as the executive director of the state association of alcohol treatment in Florida, and his wife was a supervising counselor at a treatment agency. Both parents were knowledgeable about the use of at least one drug. Their two older children, nineteen and twenty, were both happy and competent people. The first time their fifteen-year-old son Mark came home drunk, the family rallied around him, gave him information about alcoholism in the family, and began to monitor his behavior more closely. He was a bright, curious boy with many interests and a passion for healthy living, so the family was unprepared for the next drunk episode, two months later. Mark was violent, threatening his father and brother. At that time he admitted he was using pot as well.

Close family supervision followed, and Mark was allowed to go to only certain places and had to be home at certain times. His parents said that if there were recurrences, Mark would go into a treatment program. When a fight erupted a few months later, the parents found evidence of much drug use. Mark entered a residential treatment program and has been free of drugs for several years.

In their book, Beth Polson and Miller Newton outline actions parents can take to promote a healthy, drug-free adolescence.[89] They insist that how families live day by day is the most important factor. Parents need to be involved family members who know what their children are doing and who their friends are. Then, they must make clear to adolescents that theirs is a drug-free family in which there is (1) no use of illegal drugs or misuse of any legal drugs or prescriptions, (2) no routine use of alcohol by parents, (3) no intoxication by adults, (4) no alcohol use by underage children, and (5) no use of drugs to lose weight, sleep, relax, or wake up. Every family member agrees to this contract. If a child is found to be using drugs, parents call the parents of all the child's friends to discuss ways of promoting organized student activities.

The family follows a similar plan for drug use. Casual drug use or experimentation are related to teen competence in many areas, as two longitudinal studies show,[90] but when parents have concerns about drug use, the child is taken to some additional form of counseling that deals with the child and the family. Because family members can help drug-oriented children, family counseling is important in addition to any individual therapy prescribed. As in many other areas, the family joins with other families to provide support and actions to promote a healthier, safer adolescence.

The Newtons' experiences make solving the substance abuse problem appear direct and straightforward—identify the problem and get the child into treatment. However, many families go through months and years of turmoil in dealing with their child's substance abuse.[91] Either because parents fail to recognize the seriousness of the problem or because teens refuse to enter and comply with treatment programs, parents and children can become entangled in a series of hostile arguments, threats, and chaotic scenes leading to teens' running away or police interventions.

Parents get help dealing with their own feelings of fear, anger, shame, and guilt concerning their child's substance abuse. They learn they did not cause nor can they cure the problem. Their child benefits from their support and encouragement.

Promoting Adolescents' Capacity for Emotional Regulation

In the adolescent years, boys are at high risk for poorly controlled aggressive behavior and girls are at risk for depression.

The Importance of Parents' Examples   The way parents handle their feelings impacts children's development and management of aggressive and depressed feelings. First, parents' handling of feelings serves as a model to children as to how or how not to regulate feelings. Second, the level of emotional arousal in the home, resulting in part from parents' handling of feelings and conflict with each other, may promote or interfere with teens' ability to manage their feelings.

Helping Children Control Aggressive Feelings   James Garbarino, an internationally recognized expert on the impact of violence on children, became concerned about the epidemic of youth killings, often in inner cities, and determined to discover the causes to help parents and society prevent them. Between 1996 and 1998, he interviewed young murderers and summarized his conclusions in *Lost Boys: Why Our Sons Turn Violent and How We Can Save Them*.[92] He compared his own early temperamental qualities to those of the boys who eventually killed and described all the supports and resources he had in gaining control over his early feelings.

> I myself was a difficult infant and toddler—cranky, troublesome, willful, and aggressive. At two I was found standing on the wall of the balcony outside our sixth-floor apartment

and talking to the cats in the courtyard. When my mother ordered me in, I refused. That same year, I ran away from home one night and was found wandering the streets in my pajamas. When I was three, the neighbors routinely came to my mother to complain that I was beating up their six- and seven-year-old children. When I was six I would stand at the top of the monkey bars on the playground, let go with my hands and challenge other children to try to shake me off.[93]

Garbarino describes himself as being impulsive and subject to sudden inner rages. At age twelve, he cruised the neighborhood on his bike, wondering what it would be like to commit the perfect crime, perhaps a murder. By later adolescence, however, he was president of the student council and editor of the yearbook. In 1964, the Lions Club of his city sent him to Washington, D.C., as a model youth.

Garbarino attributes his success to the tremendous help and support he received from his two loving parents, a safe neighborhood, and demanding schools.

My mother devoted her every minute to me, literally "taming" me as one would a wolf pup. My father was there for me, a positive force in my life. When I started elementary school, I was assigned to strong and effective teachers in the early grades who took charge of me and the rest of their students and made sure we behaved in a civilized manner.[94]

Although he lacked inner controls, Garbarino lived in a world

filled with people who cared for me, with opportunities to become involved with positive activities at school and in the community, and with cultural messages of stability and moral responsibility. And I believed in God. In other words, while I was still living with a stormy sea inside, I was solidly anchored.[95]

In *Lost Boys*, Garbarino contrasts his own early experiences against the accumulation of stresses that many young murderers confront in their childhoods—the lack of connection with parenting figures, the lack of caregivers' positive regard and reasonable limit setting, and stresses such as poverty, physical and sexual abuse, and family or community violence. As noted in Chapter 1, not any one stress but rather the accumulation of stresses is what leads to difficulties.

Garbarino believes that successful programs for violent boys provide (1) a safe, secure environment at home or in a community facility with people who can offer the support and positive daily messages that children require to learn to conform to adult standards, (2) techniques for promoting social skills and overall psychological development, and (3) discussions focused on moral reasoning and responsibility. Such programs have to be ongoing and continuous so children haveopportunities to learn positive social skills and emotional regulation, which take years to develop.

The average aggressive adolescent boy with conduct problems does not murder someone or go to jail; still, aggressive, rule-breaking boys do continue to have problems through adolescence and into adulthood.[96] They are more apt to abuse substances, to drop out of school, to find getting and keeping a job difficult, and to have driving infractions. Further, they tend to date girls who are also aggressive and to start families early. "It is hard to overemphasize the importance of childhood conduct problems for adjustment failures in young adulthood for males. These failures are pervasive and severe, and the consequences for the young man, his intimate partners, and the children whom he fathers are profound."[97]

What do researchers recommend? As noted in earlier chapters, attentive, fair, supportive, consistent parenting helps boys learn new behaviors to replace the forcing, irritating, negative behaviors learned at home. Social skills programs with age-mates also decrease the aggressive, disruptive behaviors that drive others away.

A third kind of intervention focuses on helping boys learn emotional regulation. In one study, aggressive boys who were emotionally volatile—irritating, disruptive, and inattentive to others—had far more problems with peers than did boys who were only aggressive.[98] Adolescents are willing to accept the teen who is only aggressive and seeks what he wants. They reject, however, the aggressive boy who fails to pay attention to others and interferes with others' activities. Thus, this boy must learn to control overreactivity and attend to others' needs. Anger management and communication skills programs can help here.

A longitudinal study of rule-breaking boys noted that about 45 percent of boys with aggressive problems also had symptoms of depression that were likely to persist into adulthood.[99] The boys who were both angry and depressed were at risk for more severe problems in adulthood than were boys who were either angry or depressed. Thus, help must deal with both sets of problems for a large number of aggressive, rule-breaking boys.

Helping Children Manage Feelings of Depression   Depression varies along a spectrum. At the one end are depressed moods—feeling down, being unhappy over an upsetting event such as failing a test or fighting with a friend.[100] The feelings may last a brief or an extended time.

In some cases, depression is a normal response to a loss—the death of a parent, the divorce of parents, the loss of an important pet, moving to a new location.[101] Children may show signs of depression off and on for months following the event, depending on the severity of the loss. Gradually this depression will lift. Adolescence brings mood changes, and many boys and girls are occasionally blue. These temporary moods do not involve the global retreat from other people and decline in schoolwork that clinical depression does.

Depression can be accompanied by angry, rebellious, acting-out behavior that masks the underlying condition. Some children who are serious discipline problems in school and become involved in drugs, alcohol, and risk-taking behavior are depressed. They lack self-esteem and feel helpless about themselves and helpless to change.[102]

The most serious end of the spectrum, clinical depression, involves depressed mood and loss of interest or pleasure in usual pursuits. The depressed person may feel blue, down in the dumps, hopeless, or helpless in dealing with the mood. Disturbances in sleep, eating, and activity patterns may or may not accompany the mood. Sometimes people awake early in the morning and cannot return to sleep. Their appetite decreases, but some may eat compulsively and gain weight. Their energy level drops, and they move more slowly and accomplish less than they did formerly. Sometimes clinical depression is accompanied by loss of concentration and poor memory, so school performance may drop. Because they feel less interested and withdraw, depressed children may have fewer friends. These are the main markers of

INTERVIEW
with Susan Harter

Susan Harter is a professor of psychology at the University of Denver and has carried out extensive studies on self-esteem. This interview is continued from Chapter 2.

Self-esteem seems very important because it gives the person a kind of confidence to try many new activities. How important is it to have self-esteem?

Self-esteem has powerful implications for mood. The correlation between how much you like yourself as a person and your self-reported mood on a scale from cheerful to depressed is typically about .80.

Low self-esteem is invariably accompanied by depressive affect. We have extended these findings in developing a model that helps us understand suicidal thinking in teenagers. We included Beck's concept of hopelessness and have measured specific hopelessnesses corresponding to the support and self-concept domains. We ask, "How hopeless are you about getting peer support, parent support, about ever looking the way you want in terms of appearance?" "How hopeless are you about your scholastic ability?" There are various separate domains.

The worst consequences occur if you feel inadequate in an area in which support is important and feel hopeless about ever turning that area around. Moreover, if you don't have support and feel there is nothing you can ever do to get that support, this feeds into a depression composite of low self-esteem, low mood, plus general hopelessness. Thus, the worst case scenario is the feeling that I am not getting support from people whose approval is important, I am not feeling confident in areas in which success is valued, I am hopeless about ever turning things around, I don't like myself as a person, I feel depressed, and my future looks bleak. That, in turn, causes kids to think of suicide as a solution to their problems, as an escape from painful self-perceptions leading to depression.

There is another scenario that may also lead to suicidal thinking, namely, the teen who has done extremely well in all these areas. Then they experience their first failure, for example, scholastically (they get their first B), athletically (they feel they are responsible for a key loss), or socially (they don't get invited to a major party). As a result, they consider suicide as a solution to their humiliation. These teens seem so puzzling, but we think that conditional support plays a role here. We saw kids whose support scores were reasonable, but when we interviewed them, they would say, "Well, my parent only cares about me if I make the varsity team or if I get all As" or whatever the formula is for that family. So conditionality of support is important.

I think it is important to point out that the reason people are spending so much energy and money on studying self-esteem is that low self-esteem has so many consequences, such as depressed mood, lack of energy to get up and do age-appropriate tasks and be productive, and, for some, thoughts of suicide. Most parents want their children to be happy, and self-esteem is an important pathway to happiness and the ability to function in today's world.

clinical depression.[103] They may also have thoughts or plans to hurt themselves or, less often, someone else.

Studies suggest that between 10 to 15 percent of children and adolescents show some signs of depression.[104] Because this occurs less before puberty, the majority of young people showing depression are teenagers. In any given year, 8.3 percent of adolescents show signs of depression, about 50 percent higher than the adult rate of 5.3 in a given year.[105] Twenty percent of teenagers report having experienced a major depression that was not treated. As noted in the previous chapter, before puberty, boys and girls are equally likely to be depressed, but after puberty, the rate for girls doubles.

Many factors are thought to cause depressive states, including biological factors. For example, a family history of depression in parents and close relatives indicates greater susceptibility to the disorder.[106] Life events such as divorce, family mistreatment resulting in abuse or neglect, and failures to learn healthy emotional expression in family settings can contribute to depression.[107]

Nevertheless, no one kind of circumstance produces depression. Some depressed children come from disorganized families that have experienced multiple stresses. Some depressed children lack friends and do poorly in school, but, as stated earlier, other depressed children are highly successful and seem to have many friends and enjoy much success.

As a result of any combination of factors, children can become depressed and develop the hopeless feeling that they are confronted with an unresolvable problem that will continue. They blame themselves as incompetent, inadequate, and unworthy in some way.[108]

Prior to puberty, suicide attempts are rare, but after puberty, the rate of suicide attempts skyrockets. Recent data from the Centers for Disease Control indicate that annually, 19 percent or 3 million teenagers had suicidal thoughts, 2 million made plans to carry it out, and 400,000 made suicide attempts that received medical attention.[109] Many attempts go undetected as teens may hide cuts or throw up pills or sleep them off, without telling anyone. Known figures reveal an average of more than a thousand attempts each day, every day of the year. About 2,500 teens kill themselves, and approximately 5,000 in the age range of 15 to 24 years. More girls attempt suicide, but more boys die.[110]

When parents notice the signs of depression mentioned earlier in this section, they should seek qualified professional help. At the present time, there are several forms of help for depression.[111] Family therapy, individual therapy, and group therapy aimed at helping the child change negative self-evaluations are useful. Medications are often used as well. Medications are sometimes prescribed, but they require careful management. Research continues on the most effective combinations of treatments for teenagers.[112] If parents are uncertain whether their concerns about their child are justified, they can always consult a therapist by themselves to determine the severity of the depression and the need to bring the child in.

Once help has been obtained for the child and the family, parents can listen and accept all the child's feelings about being depressed. Many parents, eager to see their children feel better, try to argue the child out of the depression, pointing out all the reasons the child should not be depressed—"These are the best years of your life. Enjoy them." Trying to argue someone out of depression, however, can make the individual even more depressed. He or she comes to believe that the other person is right: "I must be really weird for feeling this way."

Further, some parents minimize the importance of talk about suicide, believing that those who talk about it do not do it or that they simply want attention. Parents should never consider such talk only an attention getter. Even attention getting can be fatal, as those attempting to get attention sometimes kill themselves by mistake.

In addition to getting professional help, parents can help depressed children in several ways. First, they can help children with negative thinking, as outlined in Chapter 4. Parents can encourage problem solving when difficulties arise and express confidence that children will find acceptable solutions to problems. Programs that help prevent depressive symptoms in at-risk children are described in Martin Seligman's *The Optimistic Child*.[113]

Parents can also follow Harter's suggestions to boost children's self-exteem.

> We can intervene to improve self-esteem, by helping the individual to become more competent in areas in which he/she has aspirations, or by aiding the individual to discount the importance of domains in which high levels of success are unlikely. Self-esteem can also be improved by intervening to provide more opportunities for support and approval from significant others. Such interventions should not only enhance the individual's self-esteem, but prevent the more insidious cycles that involve hopelessness, depression, and associated suicidal thoughts and gestures that may serve as the ultimate path of escape.[114]

Promoting Positive Peer Relationships

Previous chapters' suggestions for promoting positive peer relations may apply to teens' problems as well. For example, parents can foster positive peer relationships by promoting teens' ability to regulate their feelings and resolve conflicts positively. Helping children develop communication skills and ways to manage anger so it does not spill out in uncontrolled ways with peers enables teens to have fewer conflicts and to resolve the ones they have in positive ways.

In the teen years, the quality of parent-child relationships influences the teens' orientation to peers.[115] When teens feel they have good relationships with parents and feel that parents allow them a growing role in decision making, teens are better adjusted, less likely to report extreme orientations toward peers, and less likely to seek peers' advice than are teens who feel that parents retain power and control. This latter group of teens seek the egalitarian relationship and mutuality they do not feel with parents. Relationships between fathers and teens are especially predictive of peer relationships, perhaps because fathers and children engage in many recreational activities, and skills learned there transfer to relationships with peers.[116]

Promoting School Success

Teenagers cut classes; they ignore homework assignments; they fail to complete courses; they pick courses that will not prepare them for what they say they want to do; they drop out of school. All strategists advise parents to move cautiously. Schoolwork and college and vocational choices are areas in which the children make choices. Parents, however, can serve as helpful consultants. They can place responsibility on children, question the source of the problem, seek remedies, and support children's coping techniques by reminding them of earlier successes. They can also communicate their feelings about the seriousness of the situation and the importance of dealing with it. This approach takes more time than does criticism or advice on how to improve.

When adolescents are achieving below their ability levels, studies have found two general approaches helpful.[117] The behavioral technique of regularly monitoring schoolwork by means of a progress report and giving positive consequences such as privileges and rewards helps students raise their performance level. A second strategy is a comprehensive approach to increase teens' study skills, their academic skills (by means of tutoring), and their social skills so they feel more at ease at school. Parents' involvement and use of consequences is also key to such a program. Addressing academic problems alone through tutoring or private therapy has not been as helpful as multifaceted approaches.

Fitzhugh Dodson cites an example of how parents can serve as consultants in helping children with courses of study. He received the following letter:

> My son is sixteen and he just despises the academic aspects of school (and 90 percent of it is academic). The only things he likes are wood shop, metal shop, auto mechanics, and P.E. He does poorly in all of his academic subjects. But he is very good with his hands. He loves to take his car apart and work on it, and he's terrific when it comes to fixing our TV set or tinkering with radios or CBs. But college is coming up soon, and I don't know what to do.[118]

Dodson advises getting information on community colleges or trade schools nearby, as the son seems to be suited for a skilled trade. He also says to show the young man the variety of skilled trades and how to get training in one that appeals to him. Dodson concludes with this comment: "Some parents have a snobbish resistance to the idea of their son or daughter learning a skilled trade instead of going to an academic college. I think this is a mistake. Better a good auto mechanic, happy at his job, than an unhappy and inept teacher or insurance salesman."[119]

PRACTICAL QUESTION: HOW CAN PARENTS TELL WHETHER THEIR TEEN HAS A SIGNIFICANT PROBLEM?

Even when teens are doing well, parents worry. All parents know of an outgoing, academically successful, seemingly happy teen who suddenly took a handful of pills or who almost died of alcohol intoxication. Anxious parents want to know the signs of a serious problem. Generally, changes or decreases in teens' level of functioning at school, at home, and at work can indicate one or more of several possible problems.

Marcia Herrin outlines the early warning signs of an eating disorder: obvious increases and decreases in weight; a sudden and intense interest in diets, nutrition, and nonfat foods; skipping meals; drinking only noncaloric drinks; a frantic pace of exercise or athletic activity; discomfort around eating and meals; preoccupation with physical appearance; low self-esteem; and depression.[120] These behaviors have more meaning collectively than individually. A professional can help evaluate parents' concerns.

Harold Koplewicz helps parents identify depressed teens.[121] He describes the "moody" teen who has lost a boyfriend and is down for days or weeks but recovers and continues her activities and her relationships with friends and family.

> But if the sadness persists—if [she] has become a different person, if she's lost her sense of humor, if her sleeping and eating habits are disturbed, and if she's becoming socially isolated and is suddenly having trouble keeping up with school-work—it may be that the breakup was the triggering event of an underlying depression that needs to be treated.[122]

In addition to such classical signs of depression, Jane Brody points to tiredness, boredom, irritability, temper outbursts, sudden threats to leave home, physical symptoms such as headaches or stomachaches, and anxiety.[123]

Substance abuse may be harder to detect until it becomes a serious problem, because teens often engage in such behavior away from home with peers, and parents can only detect the consequences of it—coming home drunk, a ticket for driving under the influence, loss of interest in school, cutting, a drop in grades, a new group of friends, anger and irritability at parents, a decrease in responsible behaviors such as chores, and increasing difficulties with others at school or at work.[124] Changes in eating and sleeping and an increased number of physical complaints may accompany drug use as well.

All these problems share many of the same warning signs. With the help of school and professionals, parents can get the best assessment of what is happening to their child and the form of treatment needed.

As parents identify and seek treatment for their children's problems, they often learn that they themselves have the problem but have not recognized or accepted it. Parents of depressed teens may discover, for example, that they themselves have suffered from depression. Parents of a substance-abusing teen may realize that they are problem drinkers. Parents of children with eating disorders may see they have a problem in this area as well. As parents seek treatment for teens, the whole family benefits.

PARENTS' EXPERIENCES IN FACING TRANSITIONS

To understand how parents react and adapt to the changes and turmoil of their children's adolescence, Laurence Steinberg observed 204 families for three years.[125] He found six aspects of a child's adolescent behavior that trigger parents' emotional reactions: puberty and its associated physical changes, maturing sexuality, dating, increasing independence, emotional detachment, and increasing de-idealization of the parent.

Parents with the following risk factors were most likely to experience difficulty: (1) being the same sex as the child making the transition, (2) being divorced or remarried (especially true for women), (3) having fewer sources of satisfaction outside the parental role, and (4) having a negative view of adolescence. Protective factors that eased parents' adjustments to their teens' adolescence were having satisfying jobs, outside interests, and happy marriages. The positive supports buffered parents so that, in times of difficulty with children, they had other sources of satisfaction and self-esteem.

Steinberg found that about 40 percent of parents experienced difficulties, 40 percent responded to children's changes but were not personally affected, and 20 percent enjoyed the greater freedom as their children became more independent. Based on his research, Steinberg makes the following suggestions to parents for handling this stage of family development: (1) have genuine and satisfying interests outside of being a parent, (2) do not disengage from the child emotionally, (3) try to adopt a positive outlook about what adolescence is and how the child is changing, and (4) do not be afraid to discuss feelings with mates, friends, or a professional counselor.

SUPPORT FOR PARENTS

Numerous national and local organizations can supply parents with information and resources as well as direct them to professionals in the area. For example, Eating Disorder Awareness and Prevention serves parents in Seattle; Depression and Related Affective Disorders Association helps them in Washington, D. C. Al-Anon and other anonymous family groups are available nationally and locally for families dealing with alcohol and drug problems.

ToughLove is an organization started by parents to help themselves and other parents cope with rebellious, out-of-control adolescents. Parents form support groups with other parents and develop communication with agencies and individuals to promote community responses to truancy, drug abuse, running away, and vandalism. Parents seek real consequences for this behavior so adolescents will learn to avoid the disapproved behaviors.

The founders of ToughLove, Phyllis and David York, are professionals who had difficulty with their impulsive, acting-out adolescents.[126] They found it hard to set firm, fair limits that they could enforce. Meeting and talking with other parents gave them feelings of support as they set limits and carried them out. In fact, when parents in the group find limit setting difficult, other parents will meet with the family or the teenager and back up the rules. Others offer to go to court hearings or other official meetings. By providing many sets of adults to help parents help children, the group becomes a community effort to establish and maintain a safe environment for all children.

MAIN POINTS

In this period, late adolescents

- reach sexual maturity
- engage in sexual activity, and many have their first sexual intercourse
- think more abstractly and can generate more options and possibilities

- get excited at school when permitted active participation in discussing or organizing experiments
- are stable in their feelings about friends and school but become more positive in their feelings about their parents
- are likely to become depressed or develop problems such as alcohol abuse if stress is high
- work in large numbers and can gain skills if the work environment is favorable

When late adolescents consider themselves, they

- describe themselves in psychological terms and, through introspection, begin to see patterns in their behavior
- need support from family and community
- reveal gender differences in their self-descriptions, with boys seeing themselves as both more daring, logical, and calm than girls, and girls seeing themselves as more attuned to people and more emotionally reactive than boys

Peers

- are major sources of support and companionship and are sought out in times of trouble
- having dating relationships that are often intense but short-lived
- want dating partners with positive psychological qualities and physical attractiveness

Parents

- continue their commitment to children by monitoring, supervising, and enforcing rules, yet at the same time supporting and accepting children's individuality
- serve as consultants and provide factual information on topics of importance to teens
- share more power in decision making with teens so that teens can be more self-governing in the context of warm family relationships and so they can separate with a sense of well-being

Parents' reactions to their children's growth

- stimulate their own growth, as parents often rediscover and rework feelings and conflicts from their childhoods
- often stimulate parents to find new possibilities in their own lives
- may bring parents closer to each other

Problems discussed center on

- eating problems
- substance use/abuse
- aggression

- school problems
- depression
- peer relationships

Joys include

- observing increasing social maturity and closeness with friends
- enjoying greater personal freedom
- seeing altruistic behavior
- watching adult traits emerge

EXERCISES

1. Break into small groups; discuss how parents can help their teenagers resist peer pressure to have sexual relations before they are ready.

2. Interview parents about their experience during adolescence: Did they grow up in a city or smaller town? How much freedom were they allowed? What were the rules for them? What stresses did adolescents at that time face? Whom did they go to for support? How did their parents discipline them? Return to class and break into small groups; discuss the ways that parents' experiences differ from those of adolescents of today and report to the class on four major differences.

3. In small groups, describe the most effective discipline techniques parents used with you and write ten suggestions for parents of adolescents.

4. Turn in three ways you reduced stress as an adolescent; compile a class list of ten ways to reduce stress at that age.

5. In small groups, discuss ways that adolescent boys and girls can share experiences so they can come to understand how life experiences can differ and what the stresses are for each gender. Share ideas with the whole class.

ADDITIONAL READINGS

Babbit, Nikki. *Adolescent Drug and Alcohol Abuse: How to Spot It, Stop It, and Get Help for Your Family.* Sebastopol, CA: O'Reilly, 2000.

Herrin, Marcia, and Matsumoto, Nancy. *The Parent's Guide to Childhood Eating Disorders.* New York: Holt, 2002.

Riera, Michael. *Uncommon Sense for Parents with Teenagers.* Berkeley, CA: Celestial Arts, 1995.

Steinberg, Laurence, and Levine, Ann. *You and Your Adolescent.* New York: HarperCollins, 1990.

Steinberg, Laurence, with Steinberg, Wendy. *Crossing Paths: How Your Child's Adolescence Triggers Your Own Crisis.* New York: Simon & Schuster, 1994.

12

Parenting Adults

IN THE NEWS

Parade Magazine, May 12, 2002
Gail Sheehy describes the satisfactions she has gained and the lessons she has learned from becoming a grandmother. See pages 365–367 for details.

 Go to PowerWeb at: www.dushkin.com/powerweb to read articles and newsfeeds on **aging, human development, parenting,** and other topics related to this chapter.

As all parents know, parenting is a lifelong endeavor. It continues well beyond the years the child lives at home until, finally, as the parent becomes old, the child becomes the parent to the parent. In this chapter, we look at how parents and children relate to each other as they grow older together.

A 1999 survey of Americans reveals that 91 percent consider family relationships extremely important, and another 9 percent report them to be somewhat important.[1] In the previous six chapters we have described ways to maximize the potential of these relationships from the child's conception to the child's arrival at the threshold of adulthood. We now turn our attention to ways parents can nourish these relationships when children are adults.

CRITERIA FOR ADULTHOOD

There is no single event to mark the arrival at adulthood, the way puberty marks the beginning of sexual maturity. The legal system typically defines anyone under eighteen as a child, and everyone over eighteen, an adult.[2] Adolescents can achieve adult status prior to age eighteen if they marry, have a child, enter the military, or petition the court to become emancipated minors who show proof they can support themselves financially and psychologically.

Social scientists sometimes look to educational completion and establishment in an occupation as criteria of adulthood.[3] Yet professional people often face many years of postgraduate education and training but consider themselves adults long before they have completed this training in their late twenties or early thirties. Conversely, many adolescents who have completed their educations and have a job consider themselves adults. A sample of college students listed eight factors for determining their independence from parents: self-governance, emotional detachment, financial independence, separate residence, disengagement, school affiliation, starting a family, and graduation from school.[4]

In reviewing all the criteria for adulthood, these basic criteria emerge—the ability to be financially and psychologically self-sustaining and to take on the responsibilities of adulthood such as parenthood and work.

We continue this chapter by examining some theoretical perspectives on parent-child relationships in the adult years. Because social and economic forces shape parenting in these years as they do in the childhood years, we look at the influence of historical time on parent-child relationships, as well as the diversity of family forms in these years. Then, we examine parent-child relationships in particular contexts—parenting in the transition to adulthood, parenting independent adult children, parenting dependent adult children, parenting children who move back and forth between independence and dependence, and, finally, parenting the parent. Much is written on parenting the parent, but much less on parent-child relationships in adulthood.

Theoretical Perspectives

After describing important dimensions of childhood growth, Erik Erikson focused attention on adult development in his 1950 book, *Childhood and Society*, discussed in Chapter 2.[5] A major factor influencing growth in the adult years is the caregiving role adults take on. Generating new life meets basic human needs to create and guide the next generation. Mature individuals need to be needed, and caring for children meets that need. Erikson primarily discussed parents in relation to their children in childhood; he did not, however, detail parent-child relationships when both were adults.

John Bowlby's concept of attachment can serve to help us understand parent-child relationships in adulthood. He wrote, "Whilst especially evident during childhood, attachment behavior is held to characterize human beings from the cradle to the grave"[6] and "Availability of the attachment figure is the set-goal of the attachment system in older children and adults."[7]

To Bowlby, availability means three things—open communication with, physical accessibility of, and help as needed from the attachment figure.[8] For adults, the attachment figure may only be potentially physically available and the forms of help may differ from those in childhood, but the attachment figure still remains a source of security and protection, as in childhood. As we shall see, communication, physical proximity and contact, and mutual exchange of help are aspects of adult parent-child relationships, and so can be seen as continuations of the attachment process begun in childhood.

Life-course theory points to the importance of historical time as an influence on parent-child relationships. Glen Elder writes, "Lives are lived interdependently and . . . social and historical influences are experienced through this network of shared relationships."[9] Social and economic events present successive generations with particular challenges. We shall now discuss these forces and their influence on relationships between parents and children in adulthood.

THE INFLUENCE OF HISTORICAL TIME ON ADULT PARENT-CHILD RELATIONSHIPS

In Chapter 1, we described the social and cultural forces influencing parenting in contemporary society. Many of these forces affect the parenting of adult as well as young children.

In describing changes in the structure and function of families in the last century, Vern Bengtson points to four major forms of family life: the extended farm family, the nuclear family, the diverse family, and the multigenerational family.[10] The late nineteenth and early twentieth century saw a shift from the extended farm family that was a productive economic unit and social institution to the traditional nuclear family of parents and children. At the time, Ernest Burgess noted the change and identified the new functions of the nuclear family. According to Bengtson, Burgess saw that "urbanization, increased individualism and secularism, and the emancipation of women had transformed the family from a social institution based on law and custom to one based on companionship and love."[11] The nuclear family was a "unity of individuals" interacting with each other. The function of the family was to socialize children and meet the emotional needs of its members.

The traditional nuclear family was considered the primary form of family life for much of the twentieth century, but in the 1970s, social and economic changes resulted in the decline in the number of such families. Women's entrance into the workforce in greater numbers and the dissolution of families through divorce led some social scientists to worry about the decline of family influence. Others argued that economic and social changes were leading to new and diverse forms of family life. Change from a domestic to a global capitalist economy required more than one wage earner to support a family. Because increasing secularism permitted greater acceptance of divorce and of childbearing outside of marriage, the number of single-parent families grew.

Recently, an unpredictable economic future and increasing costs of housing and child care have resulted in greater financial instability for young adults. The greater number of single-parent families with reduced income also accounts for the rise in economic difficulties for young adults. While some fear that young families do not have the material and emotional resources children require, Bengtson believes that increasingly close ties across more than two generations can provide the resources families need. He considers this the fourth shift in family life, following the shift from the farm family to the traditional nuclear family to diverse family structures that rely on two generations to sustain youth. Now we see diverse family structures relying on multigenerational support for children. "For many Americans, multigenerational bonds are becoming more important than nuclear ties for well-being and support over the course of their lives."[12]

Demographic changes in the population have made this shift possible. In the last 100 years, the lengthening of the lifespan has extended the period for shared relationships between older adults and their children and grandchildren. In 1900, the average life expectancy was 49 years for women and 46.4 years for men; today, the average is 79.4 years for women and 73.6 for men.[13] Thus, there are now thirty more years for adult children to relate to their parents and for grandparents and great-grandparents to be involved with children. In this same period, the average number of children has dropped—from 4.1 in 1900 to 1.9 in 1990.

These figures mean that the proportion of children in our society has decreased. Although the age structure of the population in 1900 resembled a pyramid, with many young people at the base and fewer older individuals at the top, it now resembles a beanpole, according to Bengtson, with equal proportions of people at all ages. Thus, adults of many ages are available to nourish the small number of children. So, despite parents' decreased availability because of work, divorce, and decreased resources, grandparents and great-grandparents step in and meet children's emotional needs for closeness. Referred to as "latent kin networks" or the "family national guard," they "muster up and march out when an emergency arises regarding younger generation members' well-being."[14]

Bengtson cites data from the Longitudinal Study of Generations collected on four generations of working and middle-class families from 1971 to 1997. These indicate that, despite changes in family structure, adolescents and youth feel as much solidarity with mothers and fathers in 1997 as their parents did with their parents in 1971.[15]

Figure 12-1 (page 358) compares the early life experiences of Generation 3 (termed Baby Boomers) with the life experiences of their children, Generation 4 (termed Gen Xers), including feelings of solidarity with mothers and fathers. Baby boomers grew up in families with more siblings, with fathers' and mothers' having less education, with mothers' more likely to be full-time homemakers, and with fewer divorces than their Generation X children. Yet the family solidarity scores of baby boomers in 1971 were very similar to the scores of their children in 1997.

■ **FIGURE 12-1**
HISTORICAL CHANGES IN FAMILY STRUCTURE AND PARENTAL ATTRIBUTES:
"GENERATION X" COMPARED WITH THEIR BABY-BOOMER PARENTS
AT THE SAME AGE

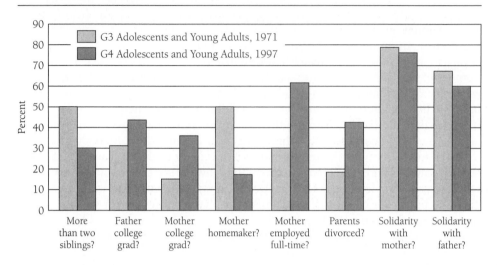

Vern L. Bengtson, "Beyond the Nuclear Family: The Increasing Importance of Multigenerational Bonds,"
Journal of Marriage and the Family 63 (2001): 11. Reprinted with permission.

Bengtson concludes that despite all the changes in family forms, children still feel solidarity with parents and maintain similar values with regard to achievement as well. Maternal employment has not changed self-esteem or values, with the exception that in 1997, Gen X young women had higher occupational aspirations than did either their mothers or Gen X young men.

Data from a multinational study of young adults' subjective well-being support Bengtson's view that multigenerational help can compensate for the difficulties children experience when nuclear families are under stress.[16] In a large multicultural study on the relationship between divorce and young adults' feelings of life satisfaction and positive mood, researchers found that children of divorced parents in collectivist cultures, which receive more support from extended family members as well as the community, feel greater life satisfaction and more positive moods as adults than do the children of divorced parents living in individualistic cultures where families have fewer resources.

DIVERSE FAMILY FORMS

Bengtson and his colleagues have used the concept of intergenerational solidarity to describe the behavioral and emotional ties among family members who have been

■ **T A B L E 12-1**
CONSTRUCTING A TYPOLOGY OF INTERGENERATIONAL RELATIONSHIPS
USING FIVE SOLIDARITY VARIABLES

Types of Relationships	Affect (Close)	Consensus (Agree)	Structure (Proximity)	Association (Contact)	Gives Help	Receives Help
Tight-knit	+	+	+	+	+	+
Sociable	+	+	+	+	–	–
Intimate but distant	+	+	–	–	–	–
Obligatory	–	–	+	+	(+)	(+)
Detached	–	–	–	–	–	–

Vern L. Bengtson, "Beyond the Nuclear Family: The Increasing Importance of Multigenerational Bonds," *Journal of Marriage and the Family* 63 (2001): 9. Reprinted with permission.

followed in the Longitudinal Study of Generations.[17] Bengtson has developed a typology of families differing in various levels of intimacy, closeness, and contact.

Table 12-1 presents five family types based on the patterns of responses on six dimensions of parent-child interactions. In a large nationally representative sample, Bengtson and his colleagues found that 25 percent of the sample were categorized as tight-knit, 25 percent were sociable, 17 percent were detached, 16 percent were intimate but distant, and 16 percent were obligatory types. No one type stands out as the most common.

Women were found to be most likely to be closely attached and tight-knit with the next generation, with only 5 percent in the detached category. Men were most likely to have sociable and obligatory kinds of relationships with children.

Income, age, and gender of children did not affect the distribution of the types. There were ethnic differences, however. European Americans were more likely than African Americans and Latinos to have obligatory relationships with mothers, and more likely than African Americans to have detached relationships. This supports other research indicating greater closeness with mothers in the African American than in the European American community.

Clearly, such types offer a tool for understanding families. So, let us keep these types in mind as we look at parenting in different contexts.

PARENTING DURING THE TRANSITION TO ADULTHOOD

There are numerous paths to adulthood, each with its own particular stresses and strains. Parenting strategies must therefore differ somewhat to provide children the support they need.

Supporting Growth and Development

Parenting in this period involves continuing the strategies of later adolescence—conveying acceptance and support of children, as well as recognizing their increasing capacity to care for themselves and to make appropriate decisions. Parents use problem-solving strategies that give children an increasing share of authority in determining solutions.

Yet as Bowlby has pointed out, attachment figures also serve as potential helpers and nurturers as needed. This support takes many forms. Financial or economic support can take the form of paying for further education or paying children's living expenses while they get further training.[18] Parents can offer loans or gifts for cars, deposits for apartments, down payments for homes. The amount of financial help depends on parents' resources and their willingness to use them for increasingly independent children.

A recent study reveals significant differences between mothers' and children's expectations regarding the support that mothers would give children in young adulthood.[19] Few mothers expect to provide the support that many children assume will be there. Young men expect more support than do young women, and they expect more support than mothers expect to give.

What mothers will support varies widely. Although most will help with attending college or getting further education, beyond that, there is much less agreement on helping single versus married young adults, or helping children who live at home versus those who live away from home. So, each family has to negotiate acceptable solutions.

Social support is divided into emotional, instrumental, and informational benefits.[20] Emotional benefits include feeling cared for, valued, encouraged, understood, and validated as a person. Instrumental benefits include help with certain tasks such as child care or repairing cars. Informational benefits include advice about school, referral to resources, or guidance about tasks.

The Steep Climb to Adulthood
When Resources Are Scarce

Adolescents sometimes suddenly enter adulthood by taking on the roles of parent and worker. When families support this transition, they often reflect a closeness in which the adolescent contributes to the family's well-being.

The Role of Parent   After their babies are born, teen mothers usually continue to live with parents, sharing resources with parents in a mutual exchange of help. They may work while mothers care for their babies, or they may baby-sit younger siblings while they care for their own babies and the mothers work. In Chapter 14, we look at the effects of these living arrangements on children; here, we focus on the parent and "teen-adult" relationship. These families fall into what Bengtson calls tight knit families. They involve closeness, frequent contact and proximity, and exchange of help. When parents and children agree on issues, they meet all the criteria for tight knit families.

Early parenthood forces teen mothers, and fathers if involved, to become mature—to focus on others beside themselves, the usual focus of adolescent attention.

> For many poor adolescent girls, early motherhood promises to resolve salient developmental issues of identity, intimacy, and achievement. In the absence of other pathways to proficiency, childbearing represents a tangible achievement providing a new opportunity for mastery, and a new arena for experiencing oneself as competent. Some adolescents actually do succeed in realizing the goals that first led them to become parents. Among these young women, motherhood seems to serve as a psychological catalyst for these adolescents, a way to stop them from really destroying their lives—a sort of self-administered slap in the face. As one adolescent mother observed, "That's how I straightened myself out, by getting pregnant. After all the places that tried to help me, I ended up doing it myself. . . . I never went back to my old ways."[21]

The teens who succeed in achieving the adult roles of mother, partner, and student-worker are those who have emotional and practical support from their families, who participate in a good intervention program, and who receive further schooling and training for occupational success.

The Role of Worker   In inner city areas, many families depend on young teens to support themselves and meet their own needs for clothing and entertainment through low-wage jobs. As high school ends, parents depend on children's working longer hours and contributing their earnings to the family. These families are tight knit when they agree on issues.

Katherine Newman has followed the careers of low-wage, teen, and young adult workers in New York City over a nine-month period. She described the positive growth in identity and self-esteem that teens and young adults in inner cities feel as they take on the role of responsible worker and learn disciplined work habits. While teen employment in low-wage jobs has been found to interfere with school and positive adjustment in middle-class samples, in inner cities, work appears to teach teens the importance of planning and further schooling. Teens learn that without good school performance and more training, they will not be able to leave low-wage work.[22]

Even though teen jobs offer little prestige, and peers make fun of the low-paying work, young men and women can still gain a sense of autonomy and self-control from work. "I'm independent and I don't have to ask anyone for anything. You know, I can get things on my own, do things on my own, you know."[23]

Another benefit of work is feeling part of contemporary teen culture. Youth can buy some of the clothes and CDs that wealthier teens buy. They can make plans for future spending and enjoy achieving their goals. In working, they also join a social network that supports responsible behavior. They meet young people with a similar work ethic and avoid the street culture that encourages living in the present, hanging out, and dropping out of school. Employers sometimes serve as mentors; they reward positive work habits and encourage post–high school education.

Low-wage jobs will never enable a worker to move away from the family and live independently, but they will provide enough cash to pursue further training to climb the occupational ladder. When parents have sufficient resources and can allow children to keep some of their earnings, then young adults can live at home and attend technical schools or local colleges. As Newman concludes,

> Even in some of the poorest parts of New York City, a city with over 1 million people on welfare, adolescents are working in large numbers in low-wage jobs in order to escape the pressures of the streets, assist their parents in supporting the household, take responsibility for their own cash needs, and amass the capital it takes to invest in in post-high-school training and educational opportunities. In the course of their work experience, an involvement that typically begins between 13 and 15 years of age, they acquire a set of values that place a high premium on personal responsibility as well as a set of personal contacts that, over time, become central to their social lives. . . . Engagement in the work world confers dignity, enhances a sense of independence and personal responsibility, and makes it possible for young people to make meaningful contributions to their households and the well-being of their own children.[24]

We do not know the level of agreement in these close families, nor do we know how parent and child are interacting with each other. We can nonetheless see that at a time when many young adults are leaving home for college and becoming more distant from families, these youth remain close and involved with family members as equal contributors to family well-being.

A More Gradual Path to Adulthood

When the family has financial resources or when students earn scholarships and grants that enable them to go away to school, youth can enjoy certain areas of independence while still receiving parents' financial help and other support as needed. They are out of the home and making some decisions, but they have not taken on the adult roles of sustaining worker or parent.

College students who emphasize self-governance as a defining characteristic of becoming adult have high self-esteem and feel connected to others.[25] Boys who emphasize emotional detachment as a defining characteristic of adulthood, compared with boys who do not, report greater loneliness and lower self-esteem. In contrast, girls who emphasize emotional detachment this way feel higher self-esteem, greater life satisfaction, and less loneliness, compared with peers who do not emphasize detachment.

The quality of the parent-child relationship can ease or complicate children's entrance into adulthood. Parental values and encouragement of autonomy within the context of positive parent-child relationships promote young adults' success and well-being as they complete college and enter adulthood in their twenties.[26] College students also bring the effects of past family experiences into adulthood with them. A multinational survey of life satisfaction and positive moods in college students in thirty-nine countries found that young adults enter adulthood in good spirits when they come from families where parents have marriages with good or average agreement between partners.[27] When parents are married and argue or when they divorce and remarry and argue, young adults have lower life satisfaction and more negative moods. When parents argue and divorce, and children grow up in homes with no arguing, their level of life satisfaction and positive moods resembles that of youth from average marriages.

Children who emphasize self-governance as a defining characteristic of becoming an adult have high self-esteem and feel connected to others.

Problems Encountered in the College Years

Although the college years are supposed to be happy times of fun and learning, several universities document increases in the number of students reporting depression, anxiety, learning disabilities, and attention problems.[28] Columbia University reported a 40 percent increase in the number of students coming to the Counseling Center between 1994 and 2002. In addition, alcohol and drug use have increased,[29] with 1,400 college students' dying each year from alcohol-related accidents that include alcohol poisoning and car accidents. As in late adolescence, parents provide role models of healthy lifestyle and help college students get professional assistance as needed.

The Path to Adulthood for Adolescents with Chronic Physical Health Problems

Data from the National Longitudinal Survey of Youth (NLSY) has enabled researchers to track the paths of a nationally representative sample of 251 adolescents with chronic health problems such as asthma, diabetes, arthritis, and cerebral palsy as they become adults.[30] David Gortmaker and his colleagues first speculated that poor health might interfere with success in being a worker and marital partner. However, when they compared the adult status of those 251 youth with the rest of the sample on measures of work and career histories, family income, marital status, and self-esteem, they found few differences.

When assessed in their twenties, the two groups "attain levels of education, income, marriage, and self-esteem that are average for their age group."[31] They show differences in rate of employment, with 73 percent of the healthy group and 67 percent of the group with chronic conditions working, as well as a difference of $1,700 in annual income. On years of education, marital status, and self-esteem, no significant differences between the groups appear.

This does not mean that youth with severe physical health conditions, such as youth who are technology dependent on wheelchairs or other equipment, face no obstacles to achieving adult status. Nonetheless, while they or others with severe conditions have added problems, the majority of teens with chronic physical health problems achieve adult status that is comparable to their age group.

General Parenting Strategies for the Transition Period

While theory and research have traditionally focused on the importance of separation from the family, current work indicates that whatever the path to adulthood, positive attachments to parents and parents' support ease the way.[32] At work and at college, mentors also play a role similar to that of parents. Positive attachments to these figures improve the youths' adjustment in young adulthood.

PARENTING INDEPENDENT ADULT CHILDREN

There are many contexts for parenting independent adult children, and each shapes parents' behavior. Some independent adult children are single and live away from home with their own friends and activities, seeing the family at intervals. Other independent single adult children continue to live with the family or nearby and remain part of all family activities. Other independent adult children have established their own families and taken on the major life role of parent. Whether close by or far away, they relate to parents as colleagues.

Ongoing Nurturing

During this period children are expected to be self-supporting, independent, and responsible. They need love and emotional support and sometimes information and instrumental support. As noted earlier, demographic changes in economic and family stability have resulted in independent adult children's often requiring more material assistance from parents than did young adults in the past.[33]

The majority of parents give some form of help, most often in the form of advice and child care. In one study, though, 25 percent of adult children reported receiving $500 or more from parents in the last year. As we shall see, this is significantly more money than parents receive from adult children. See Table 12-2 for a summary of who gives and, in older years, who receives help.

■ **TABLE 12-2**
GIVING AND RECEIVING IN THE FAMILY

Adult parents give to adult children when

- Parents have the resources to do so
- Parents and children are geographically close
- There is a good relationship between parents and child
- A grandchild arrives
- Grandchildren are young
- Women are the parents

Older parents who are more likely to receive help from children are

- Women who have many children
- Women who have been caregivers
- Widows

Adapted from Steven H. Zarit and David J. Eggebeen, "Parent-Child Relationships in Adulthood and Later Years," in *Handbook of Parenting,* 2nd ed., ed. Marc H. Bornstein, vol. 1: *Children and Parenting* (Mahwah, NJ: Erlbaum, 2002).

Generational Closeness

From the description of Bengtson's five types of families, recall that three of the five types or about 60 percent of the sample reported closeness between the two generations, and three of the five types also described joint activities. The birth of grandchildren increases this closeness between generations. As noted earlier, parents are more likely to be giving when a grandchild arrives, as there is more for them to do. They have information about child rearing and information about the new parent as a baby and growing child that is of interest to the new parent as he or she sees the new baby develop. Parents can also provide instrumental help in the form of household help, child care, and general support.

As grandparents, they also have the marvelous opportunity to reexperience the joys of childhood without the responsibilities, unless they become the primary caregivers. As Gail Sheehy writes, "At this stage of our lives, we can let a grandchild take us back to one of the biggest delights of childhood—becoming so absorbed in playing a game or flying a kite or blowing bubbles that time passes and we don't even notice it."[34]

Grandparents serve their grandchildren as storytellers, family historians, playmates, and patient coaches in life.[35] This greatly benefits the grandchildren (see Chapter 4), but it also serves grandparents. Grandchildren give grandparents a sense of purpose in life, opportunities to pass on values, and sometimes a chance to redo or undo some of the parenting mistakes of the past. Specifically, grandparenting can sometimes help the relationship between parents and adult child and heal

INTERVIEW
with Julie and Leon

Julie and Leon are a married couple in their late sixties. They have four children—two sons, forty-four and forty-three, and two daughters, thirty-eight and thirty-six. All are currently married with children, and one has had a previous divorce. Each family has three children, ranging in age from newborn to eighteen. One daughter lives fifteen minutes from her parents, the sons live about an hour away, and one daughter lives about three hours away. They are a tight-knit family, spending holidays, vacations, and weekend recreational time together. Family members exchange help, with Julie and Leon providing baby-sitting and emotional support for grandchildren, and the children giving them special recreational opportunities such as an extended two-week vacation. Not only are the children close to the parents, but the children are close to each other and spend time together without the parents.

Julie and Leon became parents in the late 1950s when families were larger than they are now and when mothers stayed at home. Julie returned to work when her girls were ten and twelve, but she had a flexible job that enabled her to be home by three. She continued to work until her retirement two years ago. Leon retired the year before.

What do you think accounts for the fact that you have such a close-knit family and that your children get along with each other so well?

Julie: One of the secrets is, "Keep your mouth shut because so much is different now." Many of the things that we did in raising our children, especially in the first five years, are passé now.

Leon: For example, our children went to bed and stayed in their own beds all night. They could come in early in the morning, but they did not sleep with us at night. It's not right or wrong, but you adjust to differences.

We made sure our kids were active in sports, and when I came home from work, I played with them, practicing kicking for soccer or throwing for baseball. When the boys were in baseball, I was president of the Little League and scheduled all the games for a thousand kids in the league. We were just as active in the girls' sports. We made sure that, when possible, each of the kids attended the other kids' games or tournaments. The girls went to the boys' events, and even when the boys were in college, they attended the girls' games and competitions when they could.

I took time off from work to go to the games, in contrast to my father, who never came to see me play even if he was off work. He said it put too much pressure on me.

Julie: Having come from a divorced family, being involved with the children, being at home for them and not getting divorced were very important to me.

---

wounds from the past. The parent can also be more giving and understanding of the adult child, and the adult child can enjoy and benefit from the greater closeness and understanding of the parent. (See the interview with Julie and Leon.)

Sheehy sums it up, "Grandchildren soften our hearts. They loosen the sludge of old resentments and regrets. It's a chance for reconciliation between ourselves and our children."[36] The best gift of all is having the love you feel recognized in your grandchild's smiling response to you.

Leon: I wanted our home to be a place where the kids could bring their friends and play. My mother wouldn't let my friends in the house, and if she did, she criticized them so much afterwards that I never wanted her to see them. So I was determined to have the kids and their friends around and to spend a lot of time with them because I enjoyed it. I could relate to them, and it was easier than work. My sons are not having as much time to play with their children as I did.

Julie: We try not to talk about one child to the other. I did not like it when my grandmother came to visit, and she talked about one uncle to us, and then went and talked to another about us. If you do, later you can be quoted.

Leon: The kids like to include us in activities because they know we don't make comments, and they can be relaxed around us. I like all my sons- and daughters-in-law. They are all different, and each brings a new dimension to the family. If you don't like them, it comes through, and they don't like you. My sons-in-law are more comfortable around Julie because I am unpredictable, and they don't know what I might say.

Julie: We tried to teach the children to be happy for each other's successes. Sometimes kids are jealous, and they almost don't like to see the other succeed. We tried to say that your successes will come, too, so be happy for this one.

Leon: The kids appreciate each others' strengths and faults. If I ever detect little jealous criticisms in conversations, I put a stop to it right away.

I like to see all the cousins get along with each other. I was disappointed not to be closer to my nieces and nephews and not to have them close with my children, so I was determined that would not happen with my grandchildren. We have activities where all the cousins can be together and have fun.

It is so important that children know you love them. You don't just say it, but you are thoughtful about them and interested in them and ask them questions about what they are doing. Our granddaughter [eighteen] has called Julie a lifesaver. Julie has always been there for her when her divorced parents didn't get along. She came to live with us the last few months of high school and the summer after graduation because her father lived so far away from her friends, and she and her mother were not getting along. My parents were there for me. I could always call my father, get advice. He wrote me insightful letters, and I have continued that with my children. When I became an adult, I felt secure, knowing people cared for me and were cheering for me. We try to do that for our children and our grandchildren.

Sheehy's rules for effective grandparenting include the following: (1) provide support to your children, not advice; (2) learn to wait your turn for time with grandchildren; and (3) have close relationships by modern means of communication—e-mail, video conferencing by means of a software package, or sending photos from a digital camera.

Generational closeness decreases when parents divorce and even more when divorced parents remarry.[37] Divorce appears to have a ripple effect across the generations, affecting the relationships between parents and adult children and between grandparents and grandchildren. Grandparents who divorce are more likely to live farther away from children and grandchildren, see them less often, and have weaker ties with grandchildren. The effects of divorce are more pronounced for grandfathers and for paternal grandparents and less pronounced for maternal grandmothers and their grandchildren.

Conflicts between Parents and Adult Children

When parents and adult children in the Longitudinal Study of Generations (LSOG) were asked to describe areas of conflict, about one-third could not list any conflict, and many made explicit statements about the satisfactory nature of the relationship.[38] About two-thirds described an average of one area of conflict. The two most frequent areas accounting for the majority of problems were similar for the two generations—communication/interaction style and lifestyle habits/personal choices—with about a third of the complaints falling into each category. A third prominent area, accounting for about 16 percent of complaints, concerned conflicts about child-rearing values and practices.

Complaints about communication include being critical, deceptive, indirect, and verbally abusive. Both generations complained about feeling rejected and abandoned because the other family member interacted little with them. Some disagreements here related to divorce and centered on the treatment of one spouse by the other. Conflicts over lifestyles included conflicts regarding living with partners, financial spending habits, style of dress, alcohol use, and choice of friends.

Child-rearing conflicts centered on the spacing of children, level of permissiveness or control, and the level of acceptance and approval of grandchildren. Other areas of conflict included conflicts over values, religion, and politics (12 percent), conflicts over work habits (6 percent), and conflicts over household standards/ maintenance (2 percent).

An underlying theme of the verbal comments is that both parents and children want to feel close and get along, and both feel disappointed when this does not happen. There may be empty nests, but neither generation wants empty spaces in their hearts.

Promoting Positive Relationships between Parents and Adult Children

From working with adults and from experiences in his own family with his wife and nine children, Stephen Covey has developed the seven habits of highly effective families. These habits emphasize positive communication, understanding others' points of view, making plans to improve relationships and taking action to create the kinds of relationships one wants, and doing enjoyable activities with family members, including extended family members.

Covey has always valued intergenerational relationships and activities and has emphasized them in his family life. He believes that such activities provide support to all members. To illustrate the point with his children, he showed them they can easily break one Popsicle stick, but five Popsicle sticks stacked on top of each other are impossible to break. Similarly, family members together are stronger than anyone alone, and joint activities among family members provide energy and strength for all.

Covey's principles provide individuals ways to change themselves from the inside out. Over time, others will likely change in response, and change will be faster if all family members are following the same program. In parenting adult children, one person alone may want the changes but can promote change in others by taking the first step.

PARENTING DEPENDENT ADULTS

Some parents will always have parenting responsibilities in some form, because their children have significant disabilities that require active help. Adult children may suffer from mental retardation, congenital or birth injury, developmental problems such as autism, or serious psychological disorders that have limited their capacity for independence. Many forms of disability require ongoing parenting.

In the last three decades, many changes have increased the numbers of disabled children living with parents—the closing of institutions that formerly provided residential care for many disabled people, changes in medications that control behaviors, improved care and education of disabled people so there is less need of institutionalization, increased number of community programs providing work and activities, and increased community and government services.[40] All these changes have created a larger role for parents as the ongoing caregiver and advocate for the child.

The new parental responsibilities for lifespan care of children create stress and the need for coping strategies to maintain parents' own well-being. Disabilities can be so different, and parents' resources in meeting them so varied, that one can only paint a very broad picture of parenting adult dependent children. The adult parent-child relationship is shaped by cultural context, type of family, form of disability, resources of the family, and services the family obtains from outside agencies.[41]

Studies of family caregiving of mentally retarded and mentally ill adults reveal that in many ways the nature of the disability affects caregiving. Mental retardation, for example, appears to involve less stress for caregivers than does mental illness. Diagnosed early in life, mental retardation proceeds in generally predictable fashion. It has less stigma attached to it than do psychological problems, as it is no one's "fault." Caregivers often receive sympathy and admiration for providing in-home care.

In contrast, mental illness often is diagnosed in late adolescence or early adulthood after decades of competent development.[42] Caregivers go through a period of mourning for the time of normal development. Mental illness takes an unpredictable course, and symptoms may appear suddenly. In the minds of many, mental illness is the "fault" of parents or family members, and so they feel some shame. As a result, caregivers of mentally ill children have a small support network that usually includes someone who also has a mentally ill child.

Providing care for dependent adult children places demands on parents and family, but also gives them satisfaction as well.

Siblings are affected differently by the two disorders. Adults who have siblings with mental illness are more affected, in part because they wonder if this could happen to them or their children.[43] Some decide not to have children for fear of the risk of mental illness.

African American caregivers, and in some studies Latino caregivers, cope better with such stresses and consequently feel less burdened. The mutual-aid system that African Americans emphasize reduces stress even when they have fewer objective resources to help than do wealthier European Americans with a more extensive support system. Women of all ages are more likely to be caregivers than are men, who provide less help and experience less strain.[44]

Rachel Simon describes the satisfaction and insights she received from her relationship with her sister, Beth, who was mentally retarded and lived in a group home.[45] Rachel began to become a part of Beth's world when she took time to ride the buses with her. Laid off from her job, Beth spent her time riding the buses in Philadelphia from morning to night. She became friends with the drivers, the dispatcher, and the regular riders. On the other hand, Rachel was a hard-driving professional person who was devoted to work. She let friendships lapse and could not make a commitment to a long-term boyfriend when he asked her to marry him.

When Beth had to undergo eye surgery and became very nervous about the surgery and the recovery that would have to follow, Beth drew on her network of friends, who came to the hospital with her, took her into their homes following the surgery, and cared for her until she recovered. Witnessing the strong, caring bonds Beth had formed with other people changed Rachel, who said,

> I came to want a different life for myself than the one I'd had. And a few months after that, I phoned Sam [the boyfriend to whom she could not make a commitment]. We talked for a long time, and I was no longer scared. From there we began a surprising and wonderful courtship that resulted in our wedding in May 2001.[46]

So, Beth changed Rachel and helped her achieve a major life goal.

At some point in the course of caring for a dependent adult child, the question of placement occurs, such as in a group home. Parents may involve siblings in the plans and in the ongoing care that will have to continue when parents die. The move to some form of care may occur naturally as a part of general plans for the dependent adult, either because the parent cannot continue the caregiving or because the dependent adult is too difficult or erratic or even violent to maintain. Professionals and support group members can give guidelines and emotional support, but only parents can make the painful and saddening decisions required of them.

PRACTICAL QUESTION: WHAT IF ADULT CHILDREN VACILLATE BETWEEN DEPENDENCE AND INDEPENDENCE?

As we saw in parenting adult dependent children, it is stressful when adult children have sporadically increasing needs parents must meet. This happens with children who have some forms of mental illness, such as manic depression, criminal behavior or some forms of substance abuse. How can parents manage?

Depending on the particular circumstance, professional consultations can give guidance and direction for the most helpful behaviors. George McGovern, a former U.S. senator from South Dakota and a presidential nominee in 1972, wrote a poignant book about parenting his daughter, who died of alcoholism at age forty-five. He and his wife had paid for many therapy programs and tried to help in various ways, but professionals advised that they keep a little more distance from her.[47]

> As I have . . . reflected on what I would do differently with the benefit of hindsight, several thoughts have emerged. I would make a greater effort to share in her life and development from the beginning. I would watch over her more carefully—especially in the

adolescent high school years. I would, if I detected signs of alcoholism, inform myself thoroughly about this disease and do everything in my power to get her into a sound recovery program as quickly as possible. . . .

Once the disease had fastened on to her, I would stay in close communication with her, expressing my love and concern for her at all times. I would call her every few days in a nonjudgmental manner, just to let her know I shared and understood her pain.

I regret more than I can describe the decision Eleanor and I made under professional counsel to distance ourselves from Terry in what proved to be the last six months of her life. . . .

But if I could recapture Terry's life, I would never again distance myself from her no matter how many times I had tried and failed to help her. Better to keep trying and failing than to back away and not know what is going on. If she had died despite my best efforts and my close involvement with her life up to the end, at least she would have died with my arms around her, and she would have heard me say one more time: "I love you, Terry."[48]

PARENTING ONE'S OWN PARENT

Parenting one's own parent is a gradual process that actually begins when one is young. The preschooler who points out the location of an item the parent is searching for, the older child who sympathizes with a parent's difficult workload, the college student who gives the parents valuable insight on a problem all involve supporting and caring for the parent.

Parents today not only have longer lifespans, but they are healthier and wealthier than previous generations as they age. As such, some adult children may only parent their parent by giving advice on certain topics such as investment strategies or giving care for a brief period when a parent has an acute illness. Nonetheless, many adult children will become their parent's parent during these years for a variety of reasons. Increasing divorce means many aging parents do not have care from a spouse and have reduced economic resources as well.[49] Young adult children, however, must often work full-time and answer their own children's needs; they are often not geographically available to give care. Further, today's smaller families mean there are fewer children to share the caregiving.

There are many similarities between parenting adult dependent children and parenting an aging parent. Wives and daughters do the primary caregiving, husbands do less, and sons the least.[50]

While they are healthy and well-functioning, parents tend to give rather than receive help. When needs arise, though, children do step in to meet parents' needs, especially when relationships are good.[51] Children are most likely to give advice and help with home chores, repairs, shopping, and errands. Financial help is rarer; in one survey, only 3 percent of parents reported receiving $200 or more in five years. The more children one has, the more likely one is to receive help, so having many children continues to ensure help in older age. Those women who have been caregivers for so many years are more likely to receive aid than are men.

As noted earlier, divorce affects relationships through the generations. Parental divorce, which is becoming more frequent, reduces contact between parents and

INTERVIEW
It's Never Too Late

Knowing my interest in parenting, Harry Sirota, a Chicago optometrist, shared these anec-dotes from his own life.

Harry said to me, "It's never too late to learn and to change. And you can even be a par-ent to your parent. When my father was eighty-nine, he had a big birthday party, and I went home for it. There were lots of guests, but my father was sitting off to the side of the garden. He motioned me over to him and said, 'Sit down, I want to talk to you. I want to apologize for all the things I did when you were growing up. I wish I had been a different father.'"

"What did you do?" Harry asked his father.

"You know what I did. Why are you hurting me by making me tell you now?"

"I know that I know, but I want to know what you're apologizing for."

His father stopped, thought, then talked for half an hour about all the things he did. When he was through, he concluded, "I didn't mean to hurt you. I love you."

Harry replied, "I hated you for doing those things, but I want to thank you for apol-ogizing to me. If I had to do it to my children, I would find it very difficult."

His father said, "I want you to know I loved you then, I love you now, and I always will love you."

"Why are you telling me these things now?" Harry asked.

His father explained, "I'm sitting here looking at all these children and how parents behave with them, and I realize I made some terrible mistakes with you."

Harry said to me, "There was a great release from the anger I carried all those years." His father died a year later.

Harry went on to tell me how he had changed his mother's behavior. "In all my child-hood she never told me she loved me. So when she was about ninety, I thought I would give her what she couldn't give to me. I called every week, and it was usually a superfi-cial conversation, "How are you?" What are you doing?" At the end of one phone con-versation, I took a deep breath, and said, 'I . . .' It was so hard to say, I almost gave up, but I gritted my teeth and blurted out, 'I love you, Mom.' And she replied she loved me. Each week it was a little easier.

"Then about the sixth week, no sooner had I got into the conversation, she said, 'You know, son, I really love you.'"

"Giving them what they could not give to me has been healing for them and healing for me."

children and decreases the quality of their relationship, so that there is less mutual help between generations.[52] Interestingly, elderly widows receive more assistance than do married parents, perhaps because they have fewer resources.

Most cultures emphasize care of older parents. Both generations prefer parents to live independently when they are healthy and well functioning, but this does not always happen. A major transition occurs when a parent can no longer live alone. This decision is usually made by children, the parents, and the physician. A variety of alternatives exist. Parents may hire live-in help, but the most common arrange-ment is that the parent comes to live with the child; if needed, hired caregivers can come to the home or live in. Parents may also go to some form of residential living that involves levels of care—independent living, assisted living, and nursing care. There are also nursing homes and board and care homes. Even then, children will be involved in visiting, overseeing care, paying bills, and doing other necessary chores for parents. Making the decision for a parent to go into residential care is difficult for children. Parents sometimes spare children this task when they move into places with graded levels of care when healthy and simply move to the next level of care as needed.

Caregivers experience stress from many sources. They become depressed and isolated from others.[53] Conflict with noncaregiving brothers and sisters increases the stress, as does the decision to leave work to meet parents' needs. Caregiving can so take over caregivers' lives that they feel they have lost their personal identities. Social support from friends, siblings, and spouses reduces this stress. Married caregivers feel less strain than do single or divorced caregivers. Sibling support reduces strain as well. Caregivers who are active problem solvers manage the stress most effectively. Formal support, like day care programs, can reduce stress as well. Too many do not have access to them.

PARENTS' EXPERIENCES IN FACING TRANSITIONS

We have seen throughout this chapter the full span of parenting adults, which began when children first left home to be adults. "Empty nest" refers to the sad, empty feelings many parents have as children leave home and make their own lives. Even when children still live at home, parents' roles as caregiver and as primary authority decrease. Although parents welcome children's growing independence and competence, many long nostalgically for the days when everyone was together and all activities outside of work were family activities. Others, however, see these years as times of possibility for themselves.

Barbara Unell and Jerry Wyckoff describe this stage of parenthood as the family remodeling stage.[54] The home is no longer occupied as it once was. Children come and go during the college years or are out and working, so the home needs psychological "remodeling."

With more time and possibly more resources for their needs, parents often look at what they want to do with the rest of their lives. For example, Jane Pauley, an anchorwoman at NBC for about thirty years, decided to leave that job when her twins started college. She wanted time to figure out what she was going to do with the rest of her life. So, while children's leaving brings sadness, it can also spark excitement and renewed energy for the possibilities that greater freedom brings to adults.

The next stage of parenting is the plateau period. Children are grown and independent. Parents have created a satisfying lifestyle and are ready to enjoy grandparenting. Plateau parents have a sense of the circle of life and their role in it themselves. As their children become parents and they grandparents, they move on to mentor another generation. Plateau parents sometimes have to make choices about nurturing and giving, as they are part of the sandwich generation that nurtures aging parents as well as adult children.

Unell and Wychoff describe the final years of parenthood as the rebounding years, when aging parents bounce back from the stresses of illness or other crises and also respond to the overtures of other family members for contact and help. They seek attention and are waiting for family members to interact with them and help as needed. Unell and Wychoff identify three types of rebounders—the proud independents, the humble submissives, and the aged sages. Proud independents, as the name suggests, want to retain their autonomy as long as possible. They reject any offer of help and worry their children with their independent behaviors. Humble submissives feel apologetic at inconveniencing their children and rarely ask for help directly. As a result, they often do not get the help they want and do not recognize the help that is offered. They tend to feel rejected and complain about their life circumstances. Aged sages try to maintain independence but request help as they need it and express their appreciation for what others do for them. They enjoy others' company and do whatever they can to reciprocate the help they receive:

> When I stopped complaining that my daughter never called or my sons never came to see me, I suddenly became more popular. I had to learn not to push my grandchildren into taking care of me. Instead I asked them about their lives and didn't complain about mine. Like magic, they then started coming to family night at the retirement center where I live, showing off their children's report cards and pictures of their latest vacation. They even remembered to include me on the invitation list for my grandchildren's and great-grandchildren's birthday parties.[55]

Rebounders are in the stage of arriving at what Erik Erickson termed a sense of integrity (see Chapter 2), which involves feeling satisfied with one's life and accomplishments.

While parents usually have a greater emotional stake in children than children have in parents, still many adult children treasure their connection with their aging parent. They rely on being parented with advice and support even when they themselves are giving significant help to their parents.

Reviewing this chapter, we can see that acceptance, availability, nurturance, positive support, and problem solving are the basic strategies of parenting in the adult years, as in all the preceding years.

SUPPORT FOR PARENTS

Support groups provide services for parents across the lifespan.[56] They are available for parents of young children to help them cope with the diagnosis and the needs for extra stimulation and special services. Support groups also help parents cope with marital and personal issues that arise from dealing with a disabled child. As noted, such groups are especially important to help caregivers cope with mental illness, as caregivers often feel that only someone who has been in their shoes can understand their situation and feelings. Support groups are equally important for those parenting aging parents.

In addition to receiving emotional support, people who attend support groups get information on new treatments, resources in the community and how to access them, and coping strategies that work, as well as establishing a personal network they can rely upon for help.

Certainly, services need to be available for disabled adult children and their caregivers. Such programs need to be designed to counteract some families' tendencies to want to hide the disabled person and to counteract cultural beliefs that caring relatives should not rely on social programs to care for family members.[57]

Although we have focused on the demands of caregiving, benefits exist also. Many parents gain satisfaction from providing care for the adult child who lives with them. As parents' age, the adult dependent child with mental illness can sometimes care for the parent. Living with one's own aging parent can bring the joys of intergenerational closeness discussed earlier.

MAIN POINTS

Criteria for adulthood include being
- over eighteen
- financially and psychologically self-sustaining
- taking on adult roles of parent and worker

Theoretical perspectives include
- Erikson's life-span theory
- Attachment theory, emphasizing communication, availability, and nurturance from attachment figure
- Life-course theory, detailing the influence of historical times

Families
- differ in closeness, agreement, proximity, contact, and amount of help exchanged
- fall into five typologies—tight-knit, sociable, intimate but distant, obligatory, and detached, with women more likely to be in tight-knit families and men in sociable and obligatory family relationships
- give several types of support—financial, emotional, instrumental, and informational
- are most likely to give help when members are close, see each other frequently, and grandchildren are involved

When adolescents take on adult roles of parent and worker, they
- look to parental support to live at home
- contribute their labor and earnings to help their families
- can gain responsibility and independence

College youth
- who emphasize self-governance as a definer of adulthood have high self-esteem and feel connected to others

- enter adulthood influenced by childhood events such as parents' divorce
- suffer an increasing number of psychological and substance abuse problems

Adolescents with chronic physical health problems

- attain levels of education, income, marriage, and self-esteem comparable to youth with no physical problems
- have added problems when they must depend on technology

Conflicts with adult children center on

- communication/interaction style
- lifestyle habits and personal choices
- child-rearing values and practices

Positive relationships are promoted

- when grandparents and grandchildren enjoy the grandchildren's childhood together
- when parents emphasize positive communications, win-win solutions, and doing enjoyable activities together to increase family solidarity

Parenting dependent adults and older parents

- involves caregiving and seeking support
- can be enriching psychologically and emotionally
- often involves looking for some form of placement outside the home

The stages parents experience as children go through adulthood include

- the family remodeling stage
- the plateau state
- the rebounding stage

As in other phases of life, parenting in the adult years of life involves

- acceptance, availability, nurturance
- positive support and problem-solving help

EXERCISES

1. If you were a parent of two teenage children, what actions would you take so that your children would have a smooth transition to adulthood?
2. If you were an aging parent, what actions would you take to promote positive relationships with your children and grandchildren?
3. Have the class divide into small groups and discuss reasons for the growing number of psychological problems experienced by students in the college years. Also discuss what college administrations can do to reduce the problems students experience.
4. Imagine that you are the parent of a dependent adult child with mental retardation. Look in the community for the kinds of out-of-home living arrangements

possible for such individuals. What is the cost of such arrangements? Would the average person be able to afford them?

5. Imagine that you are the child of an aging parent who could not live alone. What living arrangements are possible for such a parent in the community? What is the cost of such arrangements?

ADDITIONAL READINGS

Covey, Stephen R. *The Seven Habits of Highly Effective Families*. New York: Golden Books, 1997.

Epstein, Joel. *Sex, Drugs, and Flunking Out*. Center City, MN: Hazelden, 2001.

Kastner, Laura S., and Wyatt, Jennifer. *The Launching Years*. New York: Three Rivers Press, 2002.

Koplewicz, Harold S. *More Than Moody*. New York: Putnam, 2002.

Unell, Barbara C., and Wyckoff, Jerry L. *The Eight Seasons of Parenthood*. New York: Times Books, 2000.

III

Parenting in Varying Life Circumstances

13

Parenting and Working

IN THE NEWS

New York Times, July 17, 2002
Mothers' working during their child's first nine months, especially working more than thirty hours per week, was associated with children's lower scores on school readiness test at age three. See page 404 for details.

 Go to PowerWeb at: www.dushkin.com/ powerweb to read articles and newsfeeds on **work and family** and other topics related to this chapter.

Combining working and parenting is a major challenge for today's men and women. The majority of mothers work from the time their children are infants, and more fathers than ever before are involved in child care. How do parents solve the problems that arise in integrating work and family lives? How do they find child care that promotes children's development? How do they adjust routines to enhance the quality of time they spend with children? How do they adapt to their many responsibilities yet maintain a sense of well-being?

This chapter examines the impact of working on parents, on their parenting, and on their children. In Chapter 1, Urie Bronfenbrenner described parents' work as part of the exosystem that exerts a major influence on children's development.[1] Our understanding of the relationship between parents' work and family life is limited for many reasons. First, parents' work varies in many ways from parent to parent— number of hours worked, level of job satisfaction, amount of stress. So, conclusions regarding parenting and work have to be generalized cautiously, because they may apply to only subgroups of parents. Second, families may experience several work and child-care patterns over even a short time in response to the family's economic and child-care needs, so it is difficult to identify one pattern that can be related to parents' and children's functioning. Third, research suggests that parents' work may have different effects on different children in the family, depending on birth order and personal characteristics.[2] Fourth, the relationship between parents' work and family life may change as the nature of work itself changes and society makes further adaptations to parents' work.

In our present society, most parents work. In 2001, both parents were employed in 63 percent of two-parent families with children under eighteen; only fathers were employed in 30 percent; only mothers were employed in 4 percent; and neither parent was employed in 3 percent. In families maintained by women, 74 percent of women were employed; in families maintained by men, 85 percent of men were employed.[3]

In this chapter, we look at how men and women integrate working and parenting, the day-care options available when neither parent can care for the child, the impact of day care on children, and ways parents care for themselves as they rise to the challenges of working and parenting.

DIMENSIONS OF PARTICIPATION IN WORK AND FAMILY LIFE

Graeme Russell describes six domains of parental involvement in family life and two levels of activity—involvement and responsibility.[4] The six domains that apply to either mothers' or fathers' participation are

1. Employment and financial support
2. Day-to-day care and interaction with children (physical and psychological availability to the child)
3. Child management and socialization (looking after basic needs for health care, social experience, emotional connections, cognitive stimulation)
4. Household work (cleaning, shopping, preparing meals)
5. Maintaining relationships between caregivers (exchange of information about the child, raising and resolving areas of conflict)
6. Parental commitment and investment (amount of time spent with the child relative to paid work and leisure time and the degree to which the child's needs have priority over parents' needs)

The roles in each of these areas will differ for each parent, depending on whether the person is involved or takes primary responsibility for the area. Men may care for children for a specified number of hours, but this differs from taking responsibility for the child's well-being—arranging doctor visits, social activities. Similarly, women may work and provide income but not feel the responsibility of being the financial provider for the family.

In 1960, fathers were the primary financial providers and put in 1 hour of work at home for every 4 hours worked by mothers who cared for the children and the house. In 1996, women spent about 3.7 hours per day on household chores and childcare, and men spent about 3 hours per day.[5] Men, however, worked an average of 48 hours per week at full-time jobs, and women worked 42. So, women did about 55 percent of the work at home, and men worked longer hours at a job. Although fathers in dual-earner families participate more than fathers in single-earner families, mothers in both families perform more child care.

Types of Families

There is no one way for parents to meet work and family needs. One study identified three family types in terms of work and parenting characteristics.[6] In *high-status families,* both parents had high levels of education and occupational status, were highly involved in their work, and earned more money than did the other two groups of families. In addition, the couples held less traditional ideologies on sex-role activities and shared tasks equally. They experienced a great deal of work overload and stress, however, and as a result had more marital conflict, less marital satisfaction, and less love between the spouses than did the other two groups. Parents confined tension to the marital relationship, and children in the families were not aware of the marital problems because the stress did not affect the ways parents treated the children.

In *low-stress families,* both parents reported low levels of work overload, high levels of marital satisfaction and love between the spouses, and low levels of conflict. Parents were available to take an active role in monitoring children, and such monitoring improved children's functioning.

In *main-secondary families,* fathers were the primary financial providers, and mothers provided a small supplementary income, frequently through employment in lower-status occupations. These families had the lowest incomes of the three types of families and the most traditional ways of organizing family activities. Girls in main-secondary families were more likely to engage in feminine tasks than were girls in other families. Marital satisfaction fell between that of the other two groups, as did their level of conflict.

After interviewing 150 families, Francine Deutsch identified four patterns of working and parenting, which she termed *equal sharers, 60–40 couples, 75–25 couples,* and *alternating shifters.*[7] She found that families sometimes moved among these patterns. When children were infants, some families were unequal sharers, becoming equal sharers after children were older. Even within the types of families, there were many variations. Equal sharers could be providing all the day care with flexible work hours, or they could have child care and work the same hours outside the home. Alternating shifters tended to have working-class occupations, as it is these types of occupations that offer daytime and evening shifts. Women's income in alternating-shift families was often very important, and women felt they had power and received appreciation for their contributions.

Deutsch found that these patterns of work influenced parents' ways of being with children but not the total amount of time they spent with children. Equal-sharing couples spent the same amount of time with children as did the other three groups of couples, but equal-sharing mothers were alone with children less frequently than were the other mothers. Equal-sharing fathers compensated for this, as they were alone with children more often than were fathers of the other groups. Further, equal-sharing parents were more often together with children than were parents of the other groups.

Deutsch found that the couples in the four groups did not differ markedly in politics, education, or class, but they did vary in how they negotiated the everyday issues of child care and household tasks. Couples who wanted equal sharing of parenting and working made every effort to distribute both kinds of tasks equally and to find friends who supported their decisions.

An interview study of middle-class men and women in dual-earner families looked at families at different points in the life cycle—some before or after having children but most in the childrearing stages of life.[8] This study focused on middle managers and professionals, as these people not only determine their own fates but also tend to shape the work lives of people they supervise. Sampling couples from upstate New York rather than those from an urban area may have resulted in an overrepresentation of families who have scaled back working demands, however.

In this sample, few participants had dual-career families in which both parents were highly involved in work and both were single-mindedly pursuing work goals. Dual-career couples usually had no children at home, or they hired help to meet many of the family demands. The vast majority of couples relied on one of three strategies for scaling back work demands to carve out time for the family. Although most couples had an egalitarian gender ideology, choices in day-to-day behaviors often resulted in traditionally gendered roles for men and women.

The three work-family strategies were termed *placing limits, job-versus-career,* and *trading-off.* Couples who placed limits (about 30 percent) turned down jobs or promotions that required relocation or traveling, refused overtime hours, and limited the number of hours worked. Women often did this when a child was born, and men sometimes did this when careers became established and parenting involvement grew. Job-versus-career strategies (relied on by about 40 percent) involved one parent's having an absorbing career and the other parent's having a job that produced income but was subordinated to the needs of the family and the parent with the career. In about two-thirds of these families, men had the career and women had the job, but in one-third, the wife had the career and the man the job. Often, chance or early advancement or opportunity determined which parent had the career. In the trading-off group, parents shifted back and forth between jobs and careers, depending on family needs and career opportunities.

The researchers were concerned that couples' scaling-back strategies appeared to be private solutions to public workplace problems. They believe that private solutions do not challenge the underlying assumptions that work can make demands on parents—such as 60-hour weeks—while doing little to help them meet family and work needs. The couples appeared to make few demands for formal policies of flex-time, job-sharing, or on-site day care and instead sought informal arrangements to meet family needs. Unfortunately, workers at lower levels in the employment hierarchy might not get such benefits without formal policies.

One can see that there are many ways to meet work and family needs and that families use more than one strategy to meet these needs over time. In a later section, we discuss ways parents can minimize stress in using these strategies.

Children's Ratings of Parents

Regardless of the strategies used by parents to meet their family and work responsibilities, children give their parents high marks. Ellen Galinsky, the president of the Families and Work Institute, has expressed concern that children's opinions have not been included in the discussions of the effects of parents' work on children and family life. In 1998, Galinsky interviewed a representative sample of 605 employed parents with children under eighteen and surveyed a representative sample of 1,023 third- to twelfth-grade children.[9] The sample of children varied with respect to the parents' work status—employed or nonemployed—and number of hours worked. Children's attitude toward their mother and their assessment of the parent-child relationship did not depend on the work status of the mother or the number of hours the mother worked. Nonemployed fathers were rated lower than were employed fathers in the areas of (1) making their children feel important and loved and (2) participating in important events in their children's lives. Children tended to give parents higher grades when the family was seen as financially secure. We discuss the influence of economic factors on parenting in greater detail in a later section.

Seventy-four percent of children felt mothers were very successful in managing work and family life, and 67 percent of children felt fathers were very successful. As shown in Table 13-1 (page 386), parents received high marks for making children feel important and loved, being understanding, appreciating children, and being there for conversation. Although mothers were overwhelmingly seen as the parent who was there for children at times of sickness, more frequently involved than fathers in school matters, and someone children could go to when upset, the ratings for fathers on other qualities were similar to those given to mothers. Fathers were seen as being appreciative of who the child really was, as spending time in conversation, and as controlling their temper with the child as well as the mother.

Parents gave themselves equally high marks in these areas. Children's ratings of parents were higher when they spent more time with parents and when the time with parents was not rushed. About 40 percent of mothers and children and 32 percent of fathers, however, felt that their time together was somewhat or very rushed.

■ **TABLE 13-1**
STUDENTS'* LETTER GRADES FOR PARENTS' BEHAVIORS

Letter Grade	A		B		C		D		E	
Parents' Behavior	M†	F‡	M	F	M	F	M	F	M	F
Being there for me when I'm sick	85	58	8	20	4	12	2	7	1	3
Appreciating me for who I am	72	69	15	16	6	8	4	5	3	2
Making me feel loved for who I am	72	66	16	18	8	9	4	4	1	2
Attending important events in my life	69	60	18	20	7	12	3	4	3	5
Being someone I can go to when I'm upset	57	48	18	19	11	14	6	8	8	10
Being involved in what's happening to me at school	55	45	22	24	11	15	7	10	5	6
Spending time talking to me	48	47	31	25	12	16	5	8	4	4
Controlling their temper when I do something wrong	28	31	31	28	19	18	11	11	11	12

*Students in third through twelfth grades
†M indicates percentage of students giving mother that grade
‡F indicates percentage of students giving father that grade
From Ellen Galinsky, *Ask the Children: What America's Children Really Think about Working Parents* (New York: Morrow, 1999).

Divergent Realities

Mothers, fathers, and children do not always share the same views of experiences. We therefore need to understand these divergences in order to avoid false assumptions about the meanings of events.

Divergences in Men's and Women's Perceptions   Recall the study in Chapter 10 in which mothers, fathers, and early adolescents carried pagers for a week. When beeped, family members wrote down their activities and their feelings. That study found that men and women experienced different levels of stress at work and at home.[10]

Though some were teachers and nurses, mothers who worked were usually low-paid office and service workers who worked longer hours than did husbands and had as much stress and conflict. Still, their average emotional rating at work was higher than that of men and of nonemployed women because of the social rewards with coworkers and feelings of having their work appreciated.

At home, however, they felt overwhelmed by household tasks and the responsibilities of caring for family members, and their emotional well-being was only slightly higher than that of nonemployed women. When work created extra stress, their emotional well-being fell below that of nonworking mothers. Nonworking mothers lacked the stimulation and the stress of work, and their overall mood ratings were only slightly lower than those of working women with minimal stress.

Regardless of the nature of their job, men were focused and absorbed at work. They felt alert, competent, and highly involved, as they felt primarily responsible for the family's financial well-being. They experienced frustration at work and saw the home as their place to unwind, rest, and relax. They did household chores, but at a relaxed, self-determined pace.

So, work appears more socially and emotionally rewarding for mothers than for fathers, though both are highly involved in it, and home appears more relaxing for fathers than for mothers. Thus, fathers and mothers feel more relaxed in the area traditionally assigned to the opposite sex.

Divergences in Parents' and Children's Perceptions   The survey responses Galinsky obtained from children revealed discrepancies between parents' and children's perceptions.[11] Children were more satisfied with the amount of time parents spent with them than were parents. About 44 percent of mothers and 56 percent of fathers felt they spent too little time with their children, whereas only 28 percent of children felt mothers spent too little time, and 35 percent of children felt fathers spent too little time. The survey asked children to name one wish that would change how parents' working affected the family. Parents expected children to say they wanted more time with parents. Children, however, had three more-important wishes. They wished that parents could earn more money, that they could return from work less stressed, and that they felt less tired. Also, when asked if they worried about their parents, approximately one-third of children aged eight to eighteen said that they often or very often worried about their parents, and another third said they sometimes worried. So, about two-thirds of children worry about parents at least some of the time. Children said they worried because they were part of a caring family, but they also worried because they felt their parents had a lot of stress from work. Thirty percent of children aged twelve to eighteen said the worst thing about having working parents was that they were stressed out from work. Given their concern about parents' stress level, one suspects that children wanted them to make more money so they would feel less stressed.

Further, children saw their parents as less emotionally available to them than parents believed they were, and children were more concerned about parents' anger than parents were. Ninety-six percent of mothers and 90 percent of fathers gave themselves As and Bs for being emotionally available when their children were upset, but only 75 percent of children gave mothers As and Bs, and 67 percent gave fathers As and Bs. Only 4 percent of mothers and 5.5 percent of fathers gave themselves Ds and Fs for controlling their tempers, whereas 22 percent of children gave mothers Ds and Fs, and 23 percent gave fathers Ds and Fs.

So, parents are sometimes not aware of children's wishes and priorities. Children want parents to be happier and less stressed and available for them emotionally without being angry.

THE FLOW OF WORK AND FAMILY LIFE

Galinsky believes that words such as *balancing, integrating,* and *combining* do not describe how parents deal with working and family life, as they imply that these two spheres of activity are separate. From her research and interviews, she believes work and family life flow together to form a stream of experience that adults navigate rather than balance or combine, as illustrated in Figure 13-1. Experiences at home carry over to work, and experiences at work spill over to feelings at home.

> Let's think of ourselves as navigating the stream. To steer through these waters, we need to understand the many outside forces affecting our passage—some of which are beyond our control; others of which are not. And we need to know ourselves: our life priorities and where we really want to go. We are at the helm, with at least some control over the course of our voyage.[12]

■ **FIGURE 13-1**
  A MODEL OF WORK AND FAMILY LIFE

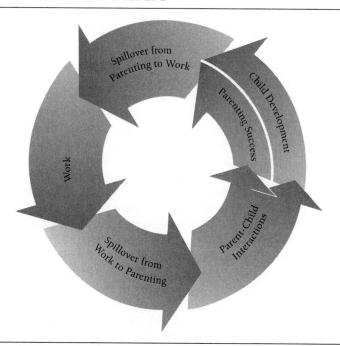

Ellen Galinsky, *Ask the Children: What America's Children Really Think about Working Parents* (New York: Morrow, 1999), 205. Copyright © 1999 by Ellen Galinsky. Reprinted by permission of Harper-Collins Publishers, Inc., William Morrow.

Parent-Child Interactions

Meeting children's basic psychological and physical needs absorbs parents' time at home. Galinsky describes eight basic needs children have that parents must meet—loving the child, responding to the child's cues, appreciating the child's individuality while also expecting success, providing values, providing constructive discipline, establishing structure and routine, helping with the child's education, and being emotionally available to the child. Parents meet children's needs in many ways.

Focusing on Children's Needs   A major strategy for employed parents is to focus their energy on meeting children's needs, especially their needs for relationships with parents. Fathers who engage in much child care when children are little maintain strong involvements in daily activities with children across the childhood years and into adolescence.[13] Such fathers play more games and share educational activities during the week, spending equal time with sons and daughters. The children of involved fathers are more socially mature at age six and more academically successful at age seven than are children of uninvolved fathers.

Employed mothers who work more than twenty hours a week spend less time with their infants and preschoolers than do nonemployed mothers. Mothers with a higher education compensate for time at work by spending more time with children in the evenings and on weekends. Children appear to become willing partners in this arrangement. They sleep more during the day-care hours and remain awake and play for longer periods in the evening. In single-earner families, evening time is reserved for fathers, but in dual-earner families, mothers use this time to relate to children, giving them verbal stimulation. Although fathers are "crowded out" in these early family interactions, they have their own time alone with children and, in fact, spend more time with their children than do fathers in single-earner families.[14]

Although employed mothers spend less time with their infants, they are as sensitive and responsive as nonemployed mothers.[15] Mothers who are satisfied with their work and feel they get support are more responsive with their toddlers than are unemployed mothers; they give more guidance and use lower power-assertive techniques.[16]

Once children reach school age, mothers spend more time in single activities[17] with children than do fathers (90 minutes versus 60 minutes per week). Although no significant differences exist between single- and dual-earner fathers in the amount of time spent with children, they allot the time differently. (See the interview with Susan McHale.)

Time with children fluctuates seasonally for some mothers, with nonemployed and seasonally employed mothers spending more time in activities with children in the summer than in the winter.[18] Mothers who are employed the same number of hours throughout the year do not show this seasonal variation. Parenting of seasonally employed mothers becomes more traditional in the summer, as they have more involvement with children at that time than do fathers. Parenting becomes more egalitarian when mothers return to work.

Maintaining mother-child activities is important because such activities may buffer the child against possible negative effects from maternal absence.[19] When

INTERVIEW
with Susan McHale

Susan McHale is an associate professor of human development at Pennsylvania State University and a codirector of the Pennsylvania State University Family Relations Project.

From your experience in studying dual-earner families, what kinds of things make it easiest for parents when both work?

We look at how the whole family system changes when mothers work, and we have found very interesting changes in how fathers relate to children between nine and twelve years old when their wives are employed. We collect a measure of "exclusive" or dyadic time—how much time the father spends alone with the child doing some fun activity like attending a concert or school activity. In single-earner families, fathers spend about 90 minutes a week with boys in "exclusive" (dyadic) activities and about 30 minutes with girls, so there is quite a sex distinction in these families. In dual-earner families, fathers spend equal amounts of "exclusive" time with boys and girls—about 60 minutes per week—so mother's working may enhance the relationship between *father* and daughter and decrease involvement between father and son.

We do not get any straightforward sex differences in the effects of mother's working—that is, boys do not necessarily do less well—unless these are mediated by some other process. For example, we have just finished a paper on parental monitoring of children's activities. To collect data on monitoring, we telephone both the parent and the child and ask specific questions about what has happened that day: Did the child do his homework? Did he have a special success at school that day? Our measure of monitoring is the discrepancy between the children's report and the parent's report. (We presume the children are right.) We thought that monitoring might be related to children's adjustment. We do find that in families where the child is less well monitored, boys are a little bit more at risk for problems in conduct and school achievement. This is independent of who does the monitoring; as long as you have at least one parent who is a good monitor, you do not get these effects.

mothers with full-time employment or an increase in work hours maintain their time in shared activities with their children, the children show no decrease in social and cognitive functioning, as compared with children of nonemployed mothers. When mothers' hours of employment decrease and activities shared with the children increase, the children's functioning improves; if activities do not increase when work hours decrease, there is no improvement.

In the early adolescent years, the overall amount of time children spend with parents does not differ in single- and dual-earner families, but again, the difference is in *how* the time is spent. Full-time employed mothers spend more time doing homework with children and less time in leisure activities.[20] Children of mothers employed part-time report more time spent playing sports with parents.

Monitoring   A major task of parenting is monitoring and supervising children's activities. Although working parents are often not home after school, they can mon-

When we look at what helps families function well when parents work, we find one factor is the agreement between *values* and *attitudes* on the one hand and the *actual roles* family members assume in daily life. This finding applies to adults and children. I am talking about sex-role attitudes. When parents have young children, we found the incongruencies between sex-role attitudes and behavior are related to problems in the marital relation. Specifically, when husbands and wives have traditional sex-role attitudes but the organization of daily life is egalitarian, couples were much more likely to fight, to have lower scores on a measure of love, and to find the relationship less satisfying.

When we looked at children's involvement in household chores, we found additional evidence of the importance of congruence between attitudes and family roles. For example, the more chores boys in dual-earner families perform, the better their adjustment; the reverse was true for boys in single-earner families, however. The mediating factor seems to be the father's sex-role attitudes. In single-earner families, fathers are more traditional and less involved in tasks themselves. Therefore, when sons do a lot of housework, their behavior is out of concordance with their fathers' values. In both kinds of families, dual and single earners, boys whose roles are incongruent with their fathers' values feel less competent and more stressed, and they report less positive relationships with their parents.

The congruence between values and beliefs and the kinds of family roles children and adults assume is what predicts better adjustment. Whether you can change people's attitudes and beliefs or whether it is easier to change family roles is hard to say. Part of the problem is that the work demands in dual-earner families require that family roles change before people feel really comfortable with that.

itor what school-age children do and make certain children engage in approved activities. Studies have found that parents in dual-earner families monitor as carefully as parents in single-earner families.[21] This is important because less well monitored boys have lower school grades and less skill in school-related activities, regardless of whether mothers are employed. Studies have not found girls' behavior as clearly related as boys' behavior to monitoring.

In a recent study of after-school experiences and social adjustment of early adolescent boys and girls, Gregory Pettit found that parents' careful monitoring of their early adolescents was related to a lack of externalizing problems such as disobeying and fighting.[22] Careful monitoring counterbalanced the effects of living in an unsafe neighborhood and having a lot of unsupervised activities with peers, two other predictors of externalizing problems. As children progress through adolescence, parents' lack of monitoring is also associated with both boys' and girls' engaging in disapproved activities such as drinking.[23]

Intentional Parenting   Galinsky uses the term *intentional parenting* to refer to the time, energy, and focus that working parents must bring to the process of meeting children's needs.[24] Parents feel good about their parenting when they spend time eating meals together and engaging in such activities as exercising, having fun together, or doing homework. They feel successful as parents and less stressed. Having supportive family and friends, having good day care, and having confidence that they are raising their child the way they want to also contribute to parents' feelings of success.

Despite the many demands these family activities make on parents, parents feel much less stress in caring for children than they do at work. Only 6 percent of parents say they feel a great deal of stress in caring for children, and an additional 36 percent say they feel a moderate amount of stress. By comparison, 24 percent experience a large amount of stress at work, and 45 percent experience a moderate amount.

To feel successful, though, parents have to maximize time with family members. Family time need not be considered only as time for leisure or relaxation but also as time for accomplishing tasks. When families work together, parents not only spend time with children, but they create more time for other activities as household work decreases for parents.

Encouraging Family Cooperation in Household Work   Although women usually retain primary responsibility for household management, men's participation in traditionally female household chores serves as a positive example for boys and girls, who do less stereotyping when fathers perform such chores.[25] Further, children who participate routinely in chores that benefit the family tend to show concern for others' welfare.[26]

Although women have traditionally borne the major responsibility for meeting the household needs, they are shifting the responsibility to the family as a whole. Jacqueline Goodnow and Jennifer Bowes's interviews with parents and children concerning the distribution of household work reveal that the meanings people attach to particular jobs (men's/women's work, Dad's/Mom's responsibility), the feelings they have about the jobs (like/dislike, feel competence/incompetence), and underlying principles of fairness shape how families distribute work.[27]

Several recommendations emerge from the discussion with families. First, a problem-solving approach that focuses on the specific question of "Who does this particular job?" is useful. Second, families must negotiate chores in an atmosphere of fairness, respect, and open-mindedness. When chores are assigned, people's preferences are respected and considered. Principles of fairness operate. Families naturally divide household chores into two categories: (1) self-care (making one's bed, picking up clothes or toys) and (2) family care (setting the table, taking out the garbage). Most families assign self-care responsibilities to children as the children become able to do them. Performing self-care chores gives children feelings of independence and competence, because they can care for themselves. As family chores are distributed among family members, children receive their share to promote feelings of being important participants in family life.

Parents who share the workload at home have more time to meet children's needs.

With a changing society expressing such varying opinions about family members' household responsibilities, families often feel dissatisfied with what they are doing and want to alter their patterns. Table 13-2 (page 394) contains suggestions for handling work responsibilities by maintaining respect and caring for each family member, staying flexible, and focusing on the positive benefits of all members' contributing to family life.

In brief, parents feel more satisfied with their family life and with their relationships with children when they have more time, do not feel rushed, and can focus on their children.[28] When they feel they have support from family and friends and can raise their children as they want, parents feel more successful. The same qualities related to parents' feelings of satisfaction and success are also associated with parents' reporting that their children have fewer problems with anxiety, depression, and inattention.

Spillover from Home to Work

About 70 percent of parents with children under eighteen say that their positive feelings about their children often or very often carry over to work, and about one-third say they often or very often have more energy on the job because of their children.[29] The parents who are more likely to have positive spillover from home to work are those who (1) are fathers, (2) put a higher priority on family life, (3) feel they have

■ **T A B L E   13-2**
MOVING TO NEW PATTERNS OF HOUSEHOLD WORK

1. *Take a look at what bothers you.* Ask yourself why you are doing this chore. What specifically bothers you about the chore? What is the worst part of the chore for you?

2. *List the alternatives.* Jobs can be changed in many ways—eliminated, reassigned to someone else in the family, reduced (e.g., iron only some things but not everything), moved outside the family.

3. *Look carefully at the way you frame the problem and at the way you talk and negotiate.* Explain what you want, stick to the point in discussing the problem, and frame the issues in terms of practicality, logic, or benefits to all family members. Avoid name-calling.

4. *Be prepared for difficulties.* The greatest difficulty is dealing with family members' having different standards for completing chores. Children often do not want to do chores, because of criticism. Focus on the effort each person puts in and do not insist on perfect completion.

5. *Remember that there is more than one way to express caring and affection in a family.* Men and women have to give up old beliefs that caring must be shown by being a "good provider" or a "good homemaker." Caring for a family is more than doing housework.

6. *Keep in mind the gains as well as the costs.* Although all family members give up time to do household chores, everyone gains. All family members gain in doing chores and contributing to family functioning. They gain self-respect, skills, and the primary benefit of greater closeness to other family members.

Jacqueline J. Goodnow and Jennifer M. Bowes, *Men, Women and Household Work* (Melbourne, Australia: Oxford University Press, 1994), 197–201.

support for doing their work—they have day care they trust and parental support at times of difficulty, (4) work more days per week but feel fewer stresses and strains at work, (5) have better-quality jobs with more autonomy and learning opportunities, and (6) have more workplace support from coworkers. The fact that fathers more often experience positive feelings at home is similar to the finding of Larson and Richards that fathers have more positive moods at home than do mothers.

When mothers want to work, when they feel that their children do not suffer from their working, and when they have husbands' support, they feel increased satisfaction with themselves and with life.[30] Even if they work when they would prefer to be at home, they do not experience depression or decreased well-being, provided they think that what they are doing is important for the family. Women who want to work but who stay at home for fear of adverse effects on their children become depressed.[31] Further, their children do not function as well as those whose mothers are satisfied with their choice. One study found that academic and social performance of kindergartners was related to mothers' satisfaction with their work status.[32] Children of mothers who stayed at home when they wanted to work or thought they should work had lower levels of performance than did their peers whose mothers either worked and enjoyed it or stayed home and enjoyed that.

Men have high self-esteem and morale when their wives work, provided that these men have nontraditional attitudes about working. When men have traditional beliefs that wives' working reflects negatively on their ability as a provider, then they show decreased morale.[33] Like mothers, fathers also experience a drop in morale when they are concerned about child care and children's adjustment to mothers' working.[34]

Spillover from Work to Home

Whether one or two parents are employed, parents' work shapes family life in many ways. Parents' job classification—professional, business, skilled or unskilled labor—is the main determiner of the family's social status. The family's social status, in turn, influences its social attitudes and child-rearing practices. Middle-class parents value self-reliance and independence in children. To encourage these qualities, such parents tend to explain what they want to their children to motivate them to do what is necessary on their own. Working-class parents value obedience and conformity in children and tend to use power-assertive techniques to force compliance. They use physical punishment more than do middle-class parents; they refuse to give explanations, simply stating, "Because I said so." They are less interested in explanations, saying, "Do it now."[35]

Social status also determines the effects of mothers' employment. In a broad range of middle-class children, followed from age one through adolescence, mothers' work status per se had little effect on children's development. The children of employed and nonemployed mothers were equivalent on cognitive, academic, social-emotional, and behavioral development. The quality of the homes and parent-child relationships, regardless of mothers' work status, determined children's growth. In lower-status African American families, however, mothers' employment was related to children's language and achievement.[36]

In another study, children of single working mothers had higher self-esteem and greater academic achievement and academic self-esteem, and they reported greater family cohesiveness, than did children whose mothers received aid to dependent children. In families with fewer resources, added income may be the main factor, but the influence of an achieving parent may be what contributes to the difference.

In addition to providing income for basic support and forming a pattern of family life, work also brings many psychological benefits in terms of advancing parents' social, cognitive, and emotional development.[37] Work helps parents develop a sense of competence and self-esteem. Mothers who worked as volunteers in Head Start programs, for example, became more confident and motivated to go on in school. One of the benefits of this child-centered program has been to empower the parents who have worked there.[38]

Work often helps parents develop interpersonal skills that they then use at home. Workers in a manufacturing plant described how they used democratic work practices in solving problems at home. One man told how he started holding team meetings with his family: "After all, a family is kind of a team."[39] A mother commented to a psychologist, "Well, my daughter was having trouble going to sleep so I decided to handle the problem like we would at work. I asked her what she thought would solve the problem, and she said 'Reading two stories to me.' I did that, and she went to sleep. That cured the problem."[40]

Work also offers a range of friendships and supports. When asked to describe how she handled stress at home, a mother said, "I go to work. At work we are like a family. Friends listen to me, and we have fun even though there is a lot of work."[41] Supervisors also offer support and help at times of trouble. When one father was severely ill, his supervisor organized coworkers to donate vacation hours so he could keep his benefits as long as possible.

About 77 percent of parents report that they often or very often feel successful at work.[42] Success is related to having time to get work done but more importantly to being able to focus on work without interruptions, being able to complete a task without getting job after job. Having a say in how the work is done, positive relationships with coworkers, and feeling the job is meaningful also contribute to feeling successful.

Nevertheless, a sizeable proportion of parents also report stress and frustration from work. Sixty-nine percent of parents report that they feel a moderate or large amount of stress, and 55 percent say they feel a moderate or large amount of frustration.[43] Stress appears to be related to job demands—working more hours per day and more days per week, having to take work home, having to travel more, feeling pressured to complete work in short periods of time with little control of how it is done, and feeling that the job is meaningless. Frustration has similar origins but is more related to the daily work schedule than to the total amount of time worked. Inability to focus, feeling unable to make decisions, feeling that the job entails no learning also increase frustration.

Galinsky's study revealed that the parents who were most likely to experience negative spillover from work to home were those who (1) put a higher priority on work than family, (2) were more likely to be managers or professionals with relatively large responsibilities at work, (3) had demanding jobs that were difficult to complete on time, (4) had jobs that were too stimulating or not stimulating enough, and (5) had less parenting support than did those who did not feel stress.[44]

Couples' diaries concerning work stress and home activities revealed that fathers with work overload were less active, less communicative, and more withdrawn.[45] Mothers compensated and did household chores, but fathers were not likely to reciprocate when mothers experienced overload. When parents had conflicts with supervisors or coworkers, they tended to argue more than before with spouses about home responsibilities. They confined arguments to spouses and did not include children.

A study of mothers and preschool children found that when mothers had stressful workdays, they were more withdrawn and less attentive, caring, and loving with their children.[46] Children tried to please mothers and engage them in activity but sometimes seemed less happy. Job stress was most upsetting to women who already had feelings of anxiety and depression.

Parents who felt positive spillover from work to home (about a third of the parents participating in Galinsky's study) were those who (1) were married, (2) had jobs that demanded more days per week, (3) experienced less stress and more autonomy at work, (4) had more supportive supervisors and coworkers, (5) had more parental support from family and friends, and (6) felt they were raising their children as they wanted.[47]

STRATEGIES FOR NAVIGATING WORK AND FAMILY LIFE

We have moved through the circular flow of work and family life and have seen common threads in feelings of success or stress in both places and in the process of making transitions between the two. Parents feel most successful and least stressed when they have time—time just to be with children and family without feeling rushed, time to engage in activities with them, and time to accomplish tasks at work. They feel successful when they have control of how they raise their children and how they do their work. They feel successful when they have support from family, friends, and coworkers and the work culture and when they can rely on trustworthy day care.[48]

Galinsky makes various specific suggestions for increasing positive feelings and reducing stress.[49] Navigating work consists of keeping job demands reasonable by seeking flextime, prioritizing work, and using problem-solving techniques. Parents improve their focus at work by finding ways to work without interruptions. They improve the quality of their jobs by learning new skills and gaining meaning from their work. They encourage positive relationships with supervisors and coworkers by appreciating support when given and making requests for reasonable modifications to the work environment to meet family needs.

Parents minimize difficulties in making transitions from work to home and from home to work in several ways. Parents do best in making the transition from work to home when they have some act or ritual that separates work from their home life— some do breathing exercises, some listen to music or books on tape or read on the way home. Parents also develop rituals that allow time with children to meet their needs when they first get home and then time to prepare dinner and do other household tasks. If parents have had a bad day at work, they are advised to tell their children and take extra time to reduce their stress. In making the transition from home to work, parents reduce stress by preparing for the next day (laying out clothes, making lunches) and allowing enough time in the morning to avoid rushing.

To navigate family life, Galinsky believes, parents need to reconsider the way they think about the time they spend with children. Children do not necessarily want more hours with parents. Children want stress-free, focused time with parents. They want parents to be calm and emotionally available to them. Galinsky recommends that parents spend time with children by hanging around and being available for conversation and supporting children's interests and activities. Because children

Parents have to make stress-free, fun times with children a major priority of family life.

are concerned about parents' control of anger, parents can improve relationships by communicating feelings in ways that encourage children to listen. Summarizing what she learned about promoting positive family life, Galinsky quotes a twelve-year-old:

> Listen. Listen to what your kids say, because you know, sometimes it's very important. And sometimes a kid can have a great idea and it could even affect you. Because, you know, kids are people. Kids have great ideas, as great as you, as great as ideas that adults have.[50]

Galinsky also recommends that parents talk about their work. Children hear little about work, especially from fathers. They often do not understand the positive aspects of their parents' work, and so they have a limited view of the meaning of work in people's lives. One of the reasons children are so concerned about parents' stress is that they hear mostly negative things about parents' work. Parents need to discuss what they do and the importance of their work. Children learn many indirect lessons about work from the way parents discuss coworkers and strategies for getting along.

On the basis of her interviews with parents, Deutsch also recommends that parents be proactive in making daily choices that enable both parents to have careers and be parents.[51] Couples committed to equal careers and parenting make choices at home and at work that support equality. That means scaling back work—limiting work hours per day, workdays per week, travel, overtime—and "allowing family obligations to intrude on work as a significant part of identity."[52] When both parents make adjustments, neither one has the traditional career.

Mothers also have to be willing to relinquish their identity as primary caregivers and let fathers assume major responsibility for child care and decisions about children. They have to recognize that children benefit when fathers are equal parents, because children can develop closer relationships with them. Marriages benefit as well, because couples share the responsibilities of parenting and work and neither partner feels overburdened.

DAY CARE

Types of Day Care

Parents seek child care in many places. Recent data concerning child care for children under five with employed mothers reveal that 47 percent were cared for by parents or other relatives, 30 percent in center-based programs, 17 percent in family day care homes, and 5 percent by a sitter at home.[53]

The most important factor in selecting day care, particularly for a child in the first year, is the quality of the caregiver. For toddlers and preschoolers as well, having a secure attachment with a sensitive caregiver promotes social competence. Once parents have a reliable, sensitive caregiver, they can focus on the opportunities available for the child to socialize with others and to be involved in stimulating activities.[54] The child's needs will depend somewhat on his or her age and temperament.

Each form of care has certain advantages and possible drawbacks. Care by parents and relatives has the advantage that children know these people and have special ties to them. Although parental care is usually of high quality, a parent may need to sleep after working a shift or may provide child care to other children. Thus, the quality of parental care can vary.[55]

Substitute care at home is expensive but requires that the child adjust to only the new person; and has the advantage of being available when the child is sick. As children get older, home care is often supplemented with nursery school attendance or other group activities so the child can be with peers.

Family day care—that is, care in the home of another family with other children—is cheaper than home care and has some advantages. A family day care setting provides an environment where children can engage in many of the same activities of home care with a mother or father figure.[56]

Because there are fewer children, family day care is sometimes more flexible than a center in meeting children's individual needs. Family day care homes are licensed; some are part of a larger umbrella organization that supplies toys and training to home caregivers. Caregivers who are part of such a network can give higher-quality care than can untrained caregivers. Guidelines for making a choice of a family day care home are similar to those for choosing a day care program. Parents should make one visit with the child and one visit alone when gathering information.

Day care centers provide care for children from infancy and may provide after-school care for children in the elementary grades. In most states, such centers must meet specific standards intended to ensure the health and safety of the children. The parent whose child goes to a day care center is sure of having child care available every day—at some centers from 7 A.M. until 7 P.M. Many centers have credentialed personnel who have been trained to work with children, and many centers have play equipment and supplies not found in most home-care situations. All centers provide opportunities for contact with same-age children.

When children start elementary school, they receive care there for three to six hours per day and require special provision only before or after school and over holidays. Approximately two to ten million children aged six to eleven are unsupervised after school.[57] Diaries of 1,500 children in 1997 indicate that about 12 to 14 percent of American children aged five to twelve are home alone for, on average, an hour after school.[58] The older the child, the larger the percentage in self-care—1 percent of children five to seven, 8 percent of children eight to ten, and 23 percent of children eleven to twelve.

Older, better-educated mothers are more likely to have children in self-care, perhaps because they are more available by phone than are less-educated mothers, who may have jobs where phone access is limited. Quiet children who are not aggressive and children living in stable neighborhoods are likely to be in self-care. Children from higher-income families are more likely to be involved in sports and other activities after school than are children from lower-income families. Although problems can arise with self-care, some children describe benefits such as increased independence, responsibility, and time to think and to develop hobbies.

Availability, Affordability, and Quality of Day Care

We have described the kinds of care possible, but how available and affordable are they? The average cost of care can vary from $4,000 to $10,000 per year, with the cost higher for infants and preschoolers.[59] Child care takes about 10 percent of an average family's income but about 22 to 25 percent of a poor family's income.[60]

Families receive little governmental support in arranging child care. A tax credit depending on the amount spent for child care does not cover the full cost of the care and helps primarily middle-class and upper-middle-class families. Single parents and lower-income parents do not pay sufficient taxes to benefit much from the credit. Although federal subsidies provide some block support for child-care expenses of poorer families, only about 10 to 15 percent of those eligible receive such benefits.

Quality of Care during Infancy and Early Childhood   Quality of care is a major determiner of the effects of nonparental child care on children. There are two kinds of indexes of quality of care—process measures and structural measures.[61] *Process measures* examine appropriate caregiving for children—that is, sensitive, responsive interactions and appropriate activities in a safe, stimulating setting. *Structural measures* look at the amount of teacher or caregiver training/experience, staff turnover, and recommended staff ratios of 1:4 for infants and 1:7 for preschoolers. In both center care and family day care, the quality of the interactions with the caregiver—the positive, sensitive responsiveness of the caregiver—is the best measure of the quality of the care.[62] Caregivers' salaries are good measures of caregiver stability; when salaries are high, caregivers stay.

In high-quality day care settings, children build secure attachments to teachers and develop the many positive social qualities associated with early secure attachment to parents.[63] Clearly, secure attachment to a teacher requires the same qualities in the teacher as those qualities in parents that promote attachment. This adult must be an available, stable, sensitive, responsive caregiver who provides stimulating activities and monitors the child's behavior to increase self-regulation. The child uses this figure as a safe base for exploring the world, just as he or she uses the secure attachment with the mother or father. In the child's first thirty months, it is important for the teacher to remain the same; otherwise, the child-teacher relationship becomes unstable. After thirty months, however, the teacher can change and the child-teacher relationship will still remain stable.[64]

Secure teacher attachment in the first year has a powerful impact on a child's development. Teacher attachment and day care qualities, not family socialization practices, are what predict later childhood competence for children entering day care in the first year.[65] For children entering day care at later ages, the family socialization in the first year and the child's characteristics are what predict later childhood competence.

There are, of course, confounding factors. Highly motivated, stable parents seek out high-quality care for children.[66] Those infants who go into low-quality care often have parents who are less organized and use less appropriate socialization practices. A vicious cycle may develop for the infant in low-quality care. Highly stressed families give less attention to the child, and the child goes into a day care setting with few adults to interact with and little to do. These children have less contact with adults and receive less stimulation both at home and in day care than do children of motivated parents. Thus, they have cumulative risks for problems in development.

Availability of Quality Care   Most experts agree that shortages exist in services for infants and school-age children. Recent studies have found that, even when available, day care is most often of mediocre quality.[67] Observations of care in centers and family day care found that in centers, 14 percent were of sufficiently high quality to promote development, 74 percent were of mediocre quality, and 12 percent were of such low quality as to be unstimulating and unable to fully meet children's health and safety needs. Forty percent of care for infants and toddlers was described as low quality. In family day care homes, 9 percent were found to be of good quality, 56 percent of adequate or custodial quality, and 35 percent of inadequate quality. The average family day care provider was described as "nonresponsive or inappropriate in interactions with children close to half the time."[68]

While good quality care is expensive to provide because it requires recommended staffing ratios, as well as educated and trained staff members who stay, still the fees charged to parents for good quality care are not that different from those for mediocre care. Parents need training and awareness to identify quality care. When

INTERVIEW
with Jay Belsky

Jay Belsky is a professor of human development at Pennsylvania State University in University Park. He is the initiator and director of the Pennsylvania Infant and Family Development Project, an ongoing study of 250 firstborn children whose parents were enrolled for study when the mothers were pregnant in 1981. He has done systematic research on the effects of day care.

What advice would you give to parents about day care in the first two years?
For working parents I say again and again that nothing matters as much as the person who cares for your baby. All too often parents don't look "under the hood" of the child care situation. They walk in, the walls are painted nicely, the toys are bright, the lunches are nutritious. Especially with a baby, once the minimal safety standards are met, what matters more than anything else psychologically is to find out about this person who'll care for the baby. So, who is this person, and what is his or her capacity to give individualized care? Because babies need individualized care, this issue matters above all else.

The second thing to consider is whether the caregiver and parent can talk together easily. Each person spends less than full time with the baby. The time factor is not necessarily handicapping them, but it can if information is not being communicated back and forth. So the trick then is, "If the caregiver gets to know my baby during the day, what can she tell me in the afternoon, and if I have the baby in the evening and the morning, what can I tell her when I drop the baby off?" There has to be an effective two-way flow of information.

The third thing to consider in selecting care is that the arrangement has to last a decent interval of time. That doesn't mean that you must take the child to the same center for a year's time; it means that the same *persons* take care of him or her for a year or so. If you find a great person who treats the child as an individual and communicates well with the parent but stays for only a few months, you are not buying yourself a lot. In a baby's life, changing caregivers more than once a year will be stressful. If a baby goes through three or four changes in a year, it may not matter what kind of caregiver he or she gets. Even though the caregivers may get to know the child, the child won't know them. Each has to know the other.

they compared parents' ratings of quality to their own, researchers found that parents identified as good quality what researchers described as mediocre.[69] See the interview with Jay Belsky on this topic.

Impact of Nonparental Care on Children

Reviewing studies on the effects of day care on children, the psychologist Michael Lamb writes,

> Exclusive maternal care through adulthood was seldom an option in any phase of human society; it emerged as a possibility for a small elite segment of society during one small portion of human history.[70]

In evaluating research, we must keep in mind first that a selection process related to mothers' education, personality, and interests determines who, in fact, chooses to return to work once children are born.[71] Second, the meaning of maternal employment in a child's life depends on (1) the child's characteristics (age, sex, temperament), (2) family characteristics (education and socioeconomic level, father's involvement in the home, mother's satisfaction with working), (3) work characteristics (the number of hours the mother works, the level of her stress at work), and, perhaps most important, (4) the nature of the child's substitute care. Because researchers cannot control all these factors, we have to interpret findings from several studies and draw our own conclusions. In discussing the research, we focus on children's social-emotional and cognitive functioning.

We know that early and continuing intervention programs that stimulate cognitive development, promote intellectual growth during the school years[72] and reduce grade retention and the need for special programs in the elementary school years. These programs stimulate intellectual growth in children from economically disadvantaged families. However, even controlling for effects of social class and family background, high-quality care in infancy is related to academic performance and verbal skills at age eleven.

Early research raised concerns that early and extensive day care could have negative effects on attachment and children's social-emotional and cognitive functioning. In the early 1990s, the National Institute of Child Health and Human Development (NICHD) initiated studies of 1,281 children from birth to age seven at ten sites around the country. The studies have looked at several questions and begun to provide answers.

1. *Does early and extensive child care affect the child's attachment with the mother?* The studies found that the mother's qualities of warmth, sensitivity, and responsiveness determined the child's attachment to the mother. "Child care by itself constitutes neither a risk nor benefit for the development of the infant-mother attachment relationship."[73] When mothers were low in responsiveness and sensitivity, then poor-quality care, unstable care, or extensive amounts of child care added to the risk of insecure attachment. High-quality child care seemed to compensate for effects of low maternal sensitivity and reduce the risk of insecure attachment to the mother.

2. *What are the most important predictors of children's cognitive and social-emotional functioning at twenty-four and thirty-six months?*[74] When measures of child care (quality, stability, type, and age of entry) and measures of family background and parenting were used to predict toddlers' cognitive and social competence, qualities of mothering were stronger and more consistent predictors of outcome than were child care measures. Of all child care measures, quality of care was the most consistent predictor.

3. *Are family factors less predictive of childhood outcomes for children in full-time child care since four months of age than for children in full-time maternal care?*[75] The answer was generally no. Family characteristics predicted social-emotional and cognitive functioning assessed at twenty-four and thirty-six

months for children in child care as well as they did for children in maternal care. For both samples, mothers' sensitivity, nonauthoritarian child rearing, and lack of depression predicted social and intellectual competence. There was a slight tendency for mothers' characteristics such as single-parent status to predict certain childhood behaviors more effectively when children were in full-time maternal care. In line with previous research, agreement between mothers' attitudes about working and their actual work status was a significant factor. Children whose mothers were employed and believed working was beneficial for children had fewer problems than children whose mothers worked but did not consider it beneficial. Children whose mothers did not work and thought not working was beneficial for children had fewer problems than did children whose mothers stayed home but did not consider it beneficial.

4. *How is the quality of care in the first three years related to cognitive and language development?* Whether children are at home or in some form of day care, the quality of that care—as judged by the sensitivity, responsiveness, appropriateness, and stimulation of the caregiver—was related to cognitive and language skills at age three. The more verbally stimulating and the more supportive the environment, the better the child performed on the measures.[76]

5. *What is the relationship between mothers' working in the first year of life and the child's performance on a measure of school readiness at age three?* When mothers worked in the first year, especially when they worked more than thirty hours per week, their children scored lower on a measure of school readiness test at age three than did children whose mothers did not work in the first year.[77] The effects were more marked for boys, for children with insensitive mothers, and for children with married parents. The findings with respect to children of married parents may reflect the fact that in two-parent families, the income from mothers' working many hours in the first year of life does not offset the negative aspects of extensive early maternal employment as it does in single-parent families.

The data indicated that children whose mothers worked extensive hours in the first year experienced poorer quality day care for the ensuing three years than did those children whose mothers did not work at that time. It is not quite clear why that should have been, but the poor quality of day care these children experienced may be a major factor in their poor performance. American[78] and European[79] studies in the past have shown that entering high-quality day care in the first year is associated with social and cognitive competence later. According to this data, however, even when quality of day care and the home environment were controlled for, children whose mothers worked in the first year had lower school readiness scores. These findings applied only to European American children in the sample. There were too few African American and Latino families to permit similar breakdowns.

Longitudinal data from the National Longitudinal Survey of Youth revealed similar findings. Maternal employment in the first year, especially early in the first year, was related to poorer cognitive and behavioral functioning in European American children at ages three and four and continuing on to ages seven or eight. A sensitive, nurturing home environment appears to buffer children from the effects of early employment. African American children's functioning did not decrease when mothers worked in the first year.[80]

These studies suggest that enabling mothers to remain at home longer and providing high-quality day care would promote the development of young children.

Nonparental Care during Later Childhood and Adolescence Extensive poor-quality care in the first year of life is related to hitting, kicking, and conflictful interactions in the first three years of elementary school.[81] Contemporaneous after-school day care that is not high quality is also related to children's being rated as noncompliant by teachers and less well liked by peers.[82] As in the early years, quality after-school care is related to effective functioning.[83]

Research suggests that low-income third-graders in formal after-school programs receive better grades in math, reading, and conduct than do children with other forms of care, including maternal care. From about the fifth grade on, children in self-care behave and perform similarly whether an adult is present or not.[84] Nevertheless, lack of supervision and monitoring of early adolescents is related to increased use of alcohol, cigarettes, and marijuana.[85] Eighth-graders in self-care for more than eleven hours a week—whether from dual- or single-earner families, from high- or low-income families, with good or poor grades, or active or nonactive in sports—were more likely than those not in self-care to use these substances. Self-care leads to feelings of greater autonomy and puts early teens at risk of being influenced by peers who are substance abusers.

In adolescence, however, maternal employment is also associated with self-confidence and independence. The benefits are more pronounced for girls who obtain good grades and think of careers for themselves, most likely because their mothers serve as role models of competence.[86]

Boys of employed mothers may not do as well in school, but that has not been a consistent finding in recent research.[87] Because fathers' involvement in the home is found to stimulate cognitive performance, it may be that fathers' increasing participation reduces that problem.

Gender Differences in Response to Nonparental Care In several studies, boys were found to be more vulnerable than girls when their mothers worked during the boys' early childhood. It is not clear whether boys require more attention, nurturance, and supervision; whether they are more sensitive to deficiencies in childcare settings; or whether they make more demands on parents who are stressed from working, have less patience with them, and see them more negatively.

Lois Hoffman concludes that boys may have a more difficult time in dual-earner families, and girls more problems in single-earner families.[88] In single-earner families, girls are more at risk for insecure attachments, their behavior is viewed more negatively by mothers, they have less time with fathers, and they receive less encouragement for independence. So, girls profit from living in dual-earner families (that is, having more time with fathers), but boys may not. It is possible, however, to combine the best of both forms of family life so boys and girls get an optimal balance of nurturance, attention, supervision, and independence.

PRACTICAL QUESTION: HOW DO WORKING PARENTS TAKE CARE OF THEMSELVES?

In the excitement and busyness of working, parents forget that the family started with the primacy of the couple. Further, the satisfaction that the couple have with each other and their ways of doing things make solutions effective. The continuance of a strong, loving bond between parents is a primary factor in the successful combining of work and parenting.

Further, more than anything else in the world, children want the family to stay together. To do this, parents need a strong relationship. Their relationship, however, usually gets put aside during child rearing, especially in the earliest years.

James Levine and Todd Pittinsky suggest that parents make a weekly date to do something without the children.[89] If money is a problem, they can set aside some special time at home—rent a video, have a special dinner. Baby-sitting, an expensive item, can be exchanged in baby-sitting cooperatives. The date should be exclusive time with the spouse to reconnect and share what is happening. Parents can organize daily rituals that give them special time together—reading the paper together, sitting close to each other while listening to music, talking after dinner, or just being physically close together watching TV. Telephone calls during the day also help parents stay connected.

Working parents who take care of themselves can take better care of their children and each other. Couples who exercise regularly, eat a balanced diet, and make sure they have private time for thinking and pursuing interests are less likely to be tense and tired and more likely to enjoy their job and family. Gloria Norris and JoAnn Miller suggest the following ways for parents to be good to themselves:[90]

1. Keep up friendships—exercising with a friend several times a week is ideal.
2. Develop ways of easing the transition from office to home—walk the last block or two, take a quick shower before dinner, rest for ten minutes after arriving home.
3. Learn personal signs of stress and do not ignore them; get rest and spend time relaxing.
4. Discover the most stressful times of the day and find ways of relieving tension; a different morning or evening routine can reduce stress.
5. Develop a quick tension reliever, like yoga exercises, deep breathing, or meditation.

The life of the working parent is challenging and demanding. Yet most working parents find the challenges worth the efforts required, as work makes life richer and more exciting for the whole family.

MAIN POINTS

Work

- influences social values in child rearing and the social life and status of families
- develops adults' skills and provides many supports
- creates stress that disrupts parenting skills

Among the many strategies they use to navigate the flow of work and family, parents

- place primary importance on spending time with children to meet their needs
- create time for children and family by sharing the workload at home
- maintain control of work demands through problem-solving methods
- build support systems at work and use high-quality child care

Nonparental care of children

- must meet established criteria to be considered quality care—specified child-staff ratios that vary according to the age of the child, staff training, safety, structure, organized activities programs
- does not interfere with secure mother-infant attachments unless mothers are low in sensitivity and responsiveness; in that case, poor-quality care, unstable care, or extensive amounts of care add to the risk of insecure attachments
- when of high quality, can compensate for the effects of low maternal sensitivity and responsiveness
- is not as predictive of children's development at twenty-four and thirty-six months as are parental qualities
- in early childhood promotes competence when children have secure attachments to sensitive teachers who provide stimulating activities and monitor them
- in the elementary school years and adolescence is associated with social and intellectual competence if children are supervised
- sometimes includes self-care by older children who enjoy independence but also require some form of monitoring

Effectively combining working and parenting

- requires that parents make daily decisions to share the workload at home
- involves parents' devoting time to sustaining their relationship

EXERCISES

1. Break into small groups and discuss the research finding that the effect of mothers' working seems to depend on the sex of the child. Discuss the finding that boys may experience more negative effects because they need more monitoring. How can parents take action to optimize effects for both boys and girls?

2. Imagine you had a child under age five—infant, toddler, or preschooler. Investigate day care options in the community for a child of that age. You might form groups to investigate care for a child of a particular age, with each student visiting at least one center to get information and summarize impressions. One group might investigate family day care in the area and compare the quality and the cost of care with that available in a center.

3. Design an ideal day care program for infants or toddlers, specifying the number of caregivers, their qualities, the physical facilities, and the daily routine.

4. Imagine what your family and work life will be like in ten years. Write diary entries for a day during the week and for a day on the weekend about your life at home and at work.

5. Write a short paper containing advice you could give to a parent of the same sex as you who feels frustrated and pressured trying to incorporate an infant and the care of the infant into his or her work life.

ADDITIONAL READINGS

Deutsch, Francine M. *Halving It All: How Equally Shared Parenting Works*. Cambridge, MA: Harvard University Press, 1999.

Galinsky, Ellen. *Ask the Children: What America's Children Really Think about Working Parents*. New York: Morrow, 1999.

Goodnow, Jacqueline J., and Bowes, Jennifer M. *Men, Women, and Household Work*. Melbourne, Australia: Oxford University Press, 1994.

Levine, James A., and Pittinsky, Todd L. *Working Fathers: New Strategies for Balancing Work and Family*. Reading, MA: Addison-Wesley, 1997.

Mason, Linda. *The Working Mother's Guide to Life*. New York: Three Rivers Press, 2002.

CHAPTER

14

Parenting in Diverse Family Structures

CHAPTER TOPICS

In this chapter you will learn about:

- Experiences of unmarried mothers and their children

- The process of divorce and whether parents should stay together for their children's sake

- Fathers' roles in children's lives

- The challenges of stepfamilies

- How lesbian/gay families function

IN THE NEWS

San Francisco Chronicle, January 24, 2003
Children growing up in single-parent families have twice the risk of developing serious psychological problems such as depression and alcohol-related problems as do children growing up in two-parent families. See page 411 for details.

> **Go to PowerWeb at:**
> www.dushkin.com/powerweb
> to read articles and newsfeeds
> on **family** and other topics related to this chapter.

Biologically speaking, it takes two parents to create a new life. In our society, family has traditionally meant a mother and father and their biological children. But now, more children are born to single mothers, and a sizeable number of children experience the divorce of their parents or the death of a parent with subsequent remarriage. How is life different for children in single-parent households? In households with gay or lesbian parents? How does life change when parents remarry? How can parents help children cope with all the special circumstances of living in a nontraditional family?

As noted in Chapter 3, 74 percent of children in the United States live with two parents, one of whom may be a stepparent, 22 percent live in households headed by women, and 4 percent live in households headed by men.[1] Single women raising children may be widowed, divorced, or separated from husbands, but a sizeable number are never-married mothers. The rate of births to unmarried women has been increasing in recent years, and in 1998, 33 percent of babies were born to unmarried mothers.[2]

Fifty percent of all children will experience the divorce of their parents and spend an average of five years in a single-parent family. Because one-third of children are born to unmarried mothers and because half of those children living with married parents will live in single-parent families as a result of divorce, living in a single-parent family has become normative, that is, experienced by the majority of children. About 75 percent of divorced mothers and 80 percent of divorced fathers marry again, so a sizeable number of children will live in stepfamilies. Many experience a second divorce, as approximately 50 percent of remarriages end in divorce.[3] This chapter describes the challenges parents and children face as they experience such changes.

Both numbers and proportions of single-parent families have increased in all Western countries and in all ethnic groups in the United States. African American families have a somewhat higher rate of single-parent families than do other groups; this does not appear to be the result of increased sexual activity among young women but rather of the fact that birthrates have remained the same in this group while rates of marriage have dropped. Thus, more children are born to unmarried mothers.[4]

Single-parent families not only have grown—from 9 percent of families in 1960 to 26 percent of families in 2001—they have also become more diverse in form.[5] In 1970, 73 percent of children in single-parent families lived with a separated or divorced parent, 20 percent with a widowed parent, and only 7 percent with a never-married parent. In 1990, 31 percent lived with a never-married parent, 62 percent with a separated or divorced parent, and only 7 percent with a widowed parent. Further, never-married parents have a variety of lifestyles, as we shall see.

Because the child's experience depends on the specific conditions in his or her family, it is difficult to generalize about the effects of being reared in a single-parent family. Many studies suggest that children in single-parent families are at greater risk for developing emotional and academic problems.[6] This should not be surprising, as it is more difficult for one parent to provide as much nurturance, monitoring, and supervision as two parents, who have the additional benefits of greater resources and support from each other.

A major reason for the difficulties of single-parent families may be the increased rate of poverty. In 2000, the average income of female heads of household was $25,794; for male heads of household, $37,529; and for married-couple families, $59,184.[7] Half of all single parents are poor, and "no other major demographic group is so poor and stays poor for so long."[8] As noted in Chapter 3, economic hardship and poverty bring stress, which decreases parents' abilities to be nurturant and effective in setting limits.

However, economic factors are not the only difficulties these families face. A longitudinal study following one million Swedish children for a ten-year period found that children living with a single parent for five years or more, compared with children living with two parents, faced twice the risk for serious psychological problems such as depression, suicide or attempts at suicide, and alcohol-related problems.[9] Researchers doubted the contribution of economic factors, as the standard of living for single parents is higher than it is in other countries, yet the children of single parents have as many problems as do the children of single parents in Britain and the United States. These researchers pointed to decreased parenting effectiveness of single parents. Researchers at the Oregon Social Learning Institute trained the single mothers of young boys, aged six to ten, to use positive parenting techniques to replace the coercive, negative methods they had been using.[10] (See Chapter 8 and the description of Gerald Patterson's work for a fuller description of the parenting behaviors.) Training took place over a fourteen-week period in one-and-a-half-hour weekly parenting groups. Dinner, child care, and transportation were provided, and there were telephone checks during the week. There was no training or intervention for children. Families were followed for thirty months. Teachers' ratings and test scores revealed that children of trained mothers decreased in aggressiveness and increased in adaptability and productiveness at school. They also became better readers. Children themselves reported they got along better with their peers, and they felt less depressed. Mothers also reported less depression.

Another factor is lack of support in dealing with increased stress. In studies of single mothers committed to raising their children alone, single mothers reported more stress than did mothers in two-parent families, even when families were matched on education, income, and area of residence.[11] The single mothers had to work longer hours and were more worried about finances than were their married counterparts. The greatest difference between these two groups of mothers, however, was that single mothers had fewer social and emotional supports when their children were young. It was precisely this kind of support that predicted optimal parent-child interactions in both single- and two-parent families. When single mothers had social-emotional support, their children's behavior was similar to that of children in two-parent families. Stressful life events such as poverty, which occurs more frequently in single-parent families, reduced overall parent effectiveness. Mobilizing both economic and social-emotional resources can help single-parent families function as effectively as two-parent families.

THE EXPERIENCES OF UNMARRIED MOTHERS AND THEIR CHILDREN

Recall the information in Chapter 6 on the characteristics of unmarried mothers prior to the birth. Approximately one-third of babies are born to never-married mothers living alone, with the child's father, or with a same-sex partner. Here we look at what happens to them and their children and focus on the unmarried mothers in the years following the birth and beyond.

Unmarried Mothers in the Years following the Birth

Those women who marry following their child's birth have family incomes that parallel those of children born to married parents. "This pattern suggests that the order of these two events—birth and marriage—[is] not as critical for demographic and economic outcomes as whether both events do occur."[12]

One study found that other actions mothers took after birth also had an impact on their economic self-sufficiency when the child was aged five to seven.[13] Those mothers who shared housing with relatives and got more education were more likely to be economically self-sufficient than were those who received welfare after the birth. Those who got valuable work experience and those who postponed an additional birth increased their chances of economic self-sufficiency.

As noted, living arrangements for children born to never-married mothers vary. In one sample, about two-thirds of children born to unmarried mothers started out in a single-mother family, and about one-third reported not living in a single-parent family in the first year.[14] Many of this latter group of children were formally adopted or informally adopted by another family member, lived with their biological mother and father, or lived in a three-generation family (that is, with their mother and her parent or parents). Nearly half the sample lived with grandparents at some point during their childhood, often with but sometimes without the mother. Only 20 percent lived exclusively in a single-parent home through the first fifteen years.

Outcomes of Children Born to Unmarried Mothers

Children born to unmarried mothers take many paths to adulthood; no one outcome characterizes them all. One study found that living with two legal parents through adoption had a positive impact on children's high school completion, which in turn predicted their economic self-sufficiency in adulthood.[15] Living in a stepfamily with two parents did not produce such positive benefits and was associated with lower educational attainment and leaving home early. Living in a stable single-parent family, however, seemed to provide a secure base for children, who as adults did as well as or better than children living in other arrangements. They had more education and slower transitions to independence. The stability of legally adopted children and the consistency children experienced in a stable single-parent home may have reduced the stress experienced by children in stepfamilies, who had many transitions to make.

Living with grandparents without the mother was related to lower educational attainment and to a higher probability of leaving home by age eighteen. Children who lived with their grandparents and mother in a three-generation family, by contrast, appeared to experience greater stability and achieve higher education than did those who lived with their grandparents alone.

Protective factors in the child, the mother, the parent-child relationship, and the larger social context buttress children from stress and predict positive outcomes for them.[16] In one study, eight protective factors were divided into four categories: the child's characteristics (positive sociability and attentiveness), maternal qualities (efficacy and low risk of depression), parenting qualities (positive parent-child rela-

When single mothers provide stable living arrangements and rely on positive, supportive parenting strategies, their children function effectively.

tionship and the father's involvement), and qualities of the larger social context (social support and few difficult life experiences). In a sample of disadvantaged mothers, 95 percent of whom were never married, families averaged three out of the eight protective factors, and 20 percent of families had five or more protective factors.

Protective factors assessed when children were eighteen and twenty-one months of age predicted measures of cognitive and social functioning at forty-two months of age. All protective factors except the father's involvement predicted competent psychological functioning, as measured by low scores on a behavior problem index covering aggressive, anxious, depressed, hyperactive, dependent, and withdrawn behaviors. Only the child's characteristics and positive parent-child relationship predicted cognitive competence, as measured by higher scores on a school-readiness test. The most important aspect of the parent-child relationship for later well-being was the absence of harsh discipline. Economic disadvantage may have its greatest impact on families by intensifying maternal distress that leads to harsh discipline. The more protective factors in the child's family, the better the child functioned. Nevertheless, even the children with the greatest number of protective factors scored below average, at the thirty-second percentile, on the measure of school readiness.

The evidence from many studies, then, suggests that there is not a single outcome for children of never-married mothers. When children (1) have stable living arrangements through legal adoption, living in a three-generation family, or living with a stable single mother and (2) experience positive parenting, they have greater social and cognitive competence. As we can see, the same qualities that predict effective functioning in children in two-parent households predict positive outcomes for children of never-married mothers.

MARITAL OR PARTNER CONFLICT

We have seen in earlier chapters that marital or partner satisfaction and intimacy contribute to parents' sense of well-being, their confidence, and their skills as parents. Nonetheless, even when parents are happily married, they argue. As noted in Chapter 4, parents' disagreements need not distress children. When parents argue in moderate emotional tones and resolve their conflicts in mutually agreeable ways, children respond in the same way they do to friendly interactions. In fact, children can learn valuable negotiating skills. Even when anger is unresolved, children feel no ill effects if parents encapsulate the anger and confine it to the marital or partner relationship and refuse to allow it to spill over to the parent-child relationship.[17]

Unresolved conflicts affect children in two ways. Observed anger that goes unresolved directly affects children's physiological and social functioning in negative ways, as noted in Chapter 4. Second, marital conflict affects children indirectly by impairing parents' skills and behavior with children. When parents are unhappy with each other, they experience more anger, sadness, and guilt and frequently express these emotions in the family, becoming more negative and intrusive with children.[18]

Other aspects of conflict determine its effects on children as well. When conflicts are intense, center on child-related issues, and imply that the child is to blame, the child feels more upset. If parents directly explain to the child that he or she is not at fault in the argument, the child feels less distress, even when the conflict is intense and is associated with child-rearing issues.[19]

In a negative atmosphere, children develop behavior problems. Children from high-conflict homes are at risk for developing (1) externalizing problems such as increased aggressiveness, noncompliance, and unacceptable conduct; (2) internalizing problems such as depression, anxiety, and social withdrawal; (3) problems in school such as poor grades; and (4) an angry, negative view of themselves and the world.[20] These problems persist, and in adolescence, both boys and girls who experienced parental disagreements in the preschool years are poorly controlled and interpersonally challenged.[21] Boys also show difficulties in intellectual functioning. So, boys whose parents later divorce are already impulsive and poorly controlled ten years before a divorce.[22]

Again, the keys to minimizing the impact of conflict on children are to resolve the conflicts in mutually agreeable ways and to remove any feelings of self-blame the child may have about the conflict.

THE PROCESS OF DIVORCE

When parents cannot resolve their conflicts, they often seek a divorce. Mavis Hetherington, who has carried out longitudinal studies of intact, divorced, and remarried families, describes four considerations that underlie all her research: (1) divorce is not a single event but an event that triggers many changes for children and parents over time; (2) changes associated with marital transitions have to be viewed as changes in the entire family system; (3) the entire social milieu—peer group, neighborhood, school, friendship network—influence an individual's response to the transition; and (4) there is great diversity in the ways children and parents respond to marital transitions.[23] Most studies of families in transition focus on European American middle-class families, and we do not know how widely we can generalize these findings.

Hetherington and Kathleen Camara emphasize that divorce is a parental solution to parental problems.[24] Children often view divorce as the cause of all their problems. For both parent and child, however, divorce brings many related stresses. Financial problems arise; there is no way two families can live as cheaply as one. Often, mothers must go to work or increase their hours at work; as a result, children may see not only much less of their father, who is no longer living with them, but also less of their mother, who must work more. Reduced income means many families must move, so the child has a new neighborhood, new school, and new friends. As resources grow more limited, parents may become more irritable, discouraged, and impatient with children.

As the divorce rate has risen, society has begun to accommodate the needs of divorcing families. The legal system has changed, making it easier for both parents to continue to be involved in the care of children. With joint legal custody, divorced mothers and fathers continue to make decisions about children, with each parent taking an equal part. Some have joint physical custody, in which children spend significant amounts of time with both parents. When parents have difficulty coming to agreement about custody issues, many states now provide court mediation services. Professional counselors help parents explore children's and parents' needs and reach agreement on reasonable living arrangements.

Further, laws have been passed to make it easier for single mothers to obtain child support payments decreed by the court. This is imperative because, as noted, mothers who are single heads of household have incomes far below those of other family units.

Telling Children about Divorce

When a couple decide to divorce, it is best if both parents together tell the children about the divorce before one parent leaves the home. Judith Wallerstein suggests wording like this: "We married fully hoping and expecting to love each other forever, but we have discovered that one (or both) of us is unhappy. One (or both) does not love the other anymore. We fight with each other. The divorce is going to stop the fighting and restore peace."[25] Parents present the decision as rational but sad:

> The goal is to present the child with models of parents who admit they made a serious mistake, tried to rectify the mistake, and are now embarking on a moral, socially acceptable remedy. The parents are responsible people who remain committed to the family and to the children even though they have decided to go their separate ways.[26]

When parents express their sadness at the solution, then children have permission to mourn without hiding their feelings from adults. It is also important to express reluctance at the solution, because children need to hear that parents know how upsetting this will be for them: "Put simply, parents should tell the children they are sorry for all the hurt they are causing."[27]

There are many things, however, divorcing parents should *not* say. First, they should not burden their children with their own negative views of each other. Second, they should not blame the other parent for all the problems. Third, they should not ask children to take sides—children usually need and want to be loyal to both parents.

Wallerstein comments on how little support most children get as they go through the initial turmoil of divorce. Often, no one talks to them, no one listens to them talk about their feelings or answers their questions, and few relatives give added help and support. Children frequently are left on their own to manage as best they can.

To keep communication going, each parent should permit children to express their feelings and should guide the children into acceptable forms of behavior that remedy what can be changed. Parents need to hear if children are angry at them or the other parent. Using active listening and sending I-messages are appropriate ways to keep channels of communication open.

Children's Reactions to Divorce

Emotional reactions to divorce, common to children of all ages, include sadness, fear, depression, anger, confusion, and sometimes relief; the predominant emotions vary with the child's age and require somewhat different reactions from parents.[28] In the preschool years, children often feel abandoned and overwhelmed; they worry that they may have caused the divorce. Although they usually try hard to handle their feelings with denial, they need parents who will talk to them and explain what is happening, not once but many times. Children may regress, begin wetting their bed, have temper tantrums, and develop fears. Parents can help most by providing emotional support. Outside interventions are not as useful as interventions by parents. Parents are urged to (1) communicate with the child about the divorce and the

When a couple decide to divorce, it is best if both parents tell the child before a parent leaves the home, even though doing so is difficult and painful.

new adjustments, explaining in simple language the reasons for each change that occurs, and (2) reduce the child's suffering, where possible, by giving reassurance that the child's needs will be met and by taking actions such as arranging visits with the absent parent.

Preschool children are often protected initially by their ability to deny what is happening. Five- to seven-year-olds are vulnerable because they understand more but do not have the maturity to cope with what they see and hear. The most common reaction of a child this age is sadness and grief. The child is not yet old enough or independent enough to arrange activities that will bring pleasure and some relief from the worry. The divorce dominates the thoughts of a child this age. One little girl, whose parents had just divorced, was asked what she would like if she could have just three wishes. Her reply: "First, that my daddy would come home. Second, that my parents would get back together. And third, that they would never, ever divorce again."[29]

Fear is another frequent response. Children worry that no one will love them or care for them. Their world has fallen apart and is no longer safe. Many children feel that only a father can maintain discipline in the family.

Children aged five and older may find outside intervention useful, and several weeks of counseling can help them sort out their feelings about the divorce, custody, and visitation. Counseling provides a neutral third party to validate children's feelings. When children are depressed, angry, and worried, it is reassuring for them to hear a professional person say, "Yes, this is a very difficult time, and it is understandable that you feel upset and sad." Children can then accept their feelings more easily.

In helping older children handle divorce, parents need to keep in mind that these children may feel responsible—they may believe they have done something that has brought about the divorce or that they could have fixed the marital difficulties. Parents need to say clearly and often, when opportunities arise, that the divorce was *not* caused by the children but was caused by difficulties between the parents. In addition, parents need to remember that children worry about them and how they are doing. Parents cannot always confine their grief and distress to times when the children are not there, but parents can help children by trying to do so.

The children of a divorcing or divorced couple need, perhaps more than anything else, to be able to talk with their parents about what is happening. Parents can encourage children to ask questions and to express their feelings. They should also respond to questions with clear statements. Children need to know the practical arrangements—where they will be living and with whom—and to know that their parents will continue to care about their welfare and about their feelings.

Thus far, we have seen the reactions of children who regret their parents' divorce, but about 10 percent of children feel relieved when their parents divorce.[30] Often, these are older children who have witnessed violence or severe psychological suffering on the part of a parent or other family member. These children feel that dissolution of the marriage is the best solution, and progressing from a conflict-ridden home to a more stable environment with one parent helps these children's overall level of adjustment and functioning.

From a follow-up of children fifteen years after divorce, Wallerstein and Sandra Blakeslee conclude that it is very difficult to determine the long-term adjustment of the child based on the child's reactions at the time of the divorce.[31] Some of the children who had strong, disorganizing reactions were doing well many years later, whereas some others who made a good initial adjustment had long-standing problems.

Parents' Reactions to Divorce

Parents react to divorce in many and varied ways, almost all intense. They often suffer many symptoms—headaches, rapid heartbeat, fatigue, dizziness.[32] Their moods and behavior change at the time of the divorce, and these mood changes may be one of the most upsetting aspects of the divorce process for their children. Each parent may respond differently at different times, and both may show similar behavior only when they are angry with each other. Children are helpless in the face of their parents' extreme moods. One parent may be sad, depressed, and lacking in energy; the other may be busy, agitated, and preoccupied with his or her concerns. Both often lack self-esteem and seek out people or experiences to make them feel good again.

Divorced men and women both start dating again, though men date in larger numbers and older women tend to remain isolated and alone. Heterosexual relationships now become a source of anxiety and tension. Women wonder how to respond to sexual advances, and men worry about sexual performance. Nevertheless, new intimate relationships after divorce tend to boost parents' self-esteem.

Parents must deal with the intense feelings that arise during the divorce process, even if those feelings were not there in the beginning. They feel sad at the end of their marriage, even if the dissolution was necessary. They feel pain as the divorce becomes real—material possessions are divided, money is dispersed, and custody and visiting rights are arranged. Anger keeps the relationship alive for a time, but gradually detachment and distance signal that the marital relationship has truly ended. The loss is real.

Long-term emotional reactions to the divorce are diverse. Seventy-five percent of divorced custodial mothers report that at the end of two years, they feel happier than they did in the last year of the marriage. Many of these women go on to develop independent lives and careers that increase their self-esteem. Some divorced women, however, report depression, loneliness, and health problems six to eleven years after the divorce. Still, they do not have as many problems as do nondivorced women in high-conflict marriages, who are more depressed and anxious and have more physical problems.[33]

Factors Affecting Adjustment to Divorce

Several factors influence how well a family adapts to divorce:[34] (1) the amount of conflict among family members, (2) the availability of both parents to their children, (3) the nature of the relationship changes in the family, (4) the responsibilities family members take, and (5) the defensibility of the divorce from the child's point of view.[35]

Moving from a household with two parents always in conflict to a stable household with one parent can lead to better adjustment for children.[36] Parents often continue the fighting when they live separately, however, and this is harmful to children; boys tend to react with undercontrolled behavior and girls with overcontrolled behavior.[37] The increased conflict children witness during divorce, not the divorce itself, may be what leads to their poorer adjustment. Increased conflicts can also occur between parents and children in a one-parent household in which the second parent is not available as a buffering agent. In addition, a parent may find the child a convenient target for feelings aroused by the other parent. In the midst of this raging conflict, the child feels quite alone. Minimizing the fighting in all arenas aids everyone's adjustment.

Parents can help insulate their children from the conflict that accompanies a divorce. Table 14-1 (page 420) lists some behavior characteristics of parents who work to protect their children from the parents' own conflicts.

When children have continuing relationships with both parents, they are more likely to adjust well following the divorce process.[38] It is impossible to predict how fathers, who are usually the ones to move out of the home, will respond after the divorce. Some previously devoted fathers find not living with their children so painful that they withdraw and see less of the children. Some previously uninvolved fathers discover that caring for children alone on visits deepens their attachment,

■ **TABLE 14-1**

OUT OF HARM'S WAY: PROTECTING CHILDREN FROM PARENTAL CONFLICT

Children can continue to grow and thrive even through a divorce if their parents insulate them from intense or prolonged hostilities. Parents who can accomplish this share some important qualities:

1. They make it clear that they value their child's relationship and time with them *and* with the other parent.
2. They work out a fair and practical time-sharing schedule, either temporary or long-term, as soon as possible.
3. Once that agreement is reached, they make every effort to live up to its terms.
4. They tell each other in advance about necessary changes in plans.
5. They are reasonably flexible in "trading off" to accommodate the other parent's needs.
6. They prepare the child, in a positive way, for each upcoming stay with the other parent.
7. They *do not* conduct adult business when they meet to transfer the child.
8. They refrain from using the child as a confidant, messenger, bill collector, or spy.
9. They listen caringly but encourage their child to work out problems with the other parent directly.
10. They work on their problems with each other in private.

Robert Adler, *Sharing the Children* (New York: Adler & Adler, 1988). Used with permission of the author.

and so they increase their contact with their children. Fathers are more likely to maintain relationships with their sons than with their daughters. In fact, many mothers relinquish custody of older sons to fathers because they feel sons need a male role model.

Not only do children need relationships with both parents; they also need to be able to relate to each separately as a parent.[39] Recently divorced parents, however, often find it difficult to direct their energy to parenting. Thus, at this time of great need in the first year following divorce, when they actually need *more* attention, children receive less. Frequently, children's behavior goes unmonitored, and rules are not enforced. The parent outside the home often becomes highly indulgent and permissive with children; seeing so little of them, he or she hates to spend precious time disciplining them. As in the past, however, children function most effectively when both parents take time to monitor their behavior and enforce the usual rules.

In the family with two households and both parents working, the need for children to take on more responsibilities increases.[40] When demands are not excessive and are tailored to the abilities of children, then children may feel pleased by contributing to the family and developing greater competence. When the demands are too great, however—when they are given too much responsibility for caring for younger children or doing chores—then children become resentful, feeling they are being robbed of their childhood. Realistic demands for responsibility can help children grow in this situation.

Children seem better able to cope with divorce and its aftermath when the divorce is a carefully thought out, reasonable response to a specific problem.[41] When the problem improves after the divorce, children are better able to accept it. They are less able to deal with the impulsive divorce that may have had little to do with the marriage but was related to other problems in the parents' life. For example, one woman divorced her husband following the death of her mother. She later regretted the decision but could not undo what had hurt four people.

Protective Factors for Children

Protective factors for children as they adjust to divorce include qualities of the child, supportive aspects of the family system, and external social supports.[42] The child's age, sex, and intelligence serve as protection. Younger children appear less affected than elementary school children or early adolescents at the time of the divorce or remarriage. Because they are becoming increasingly independent of the family, late adolescents seem less affected than younger children. Boys appear to suffer more difficulties at the time of the divorce, and girls appear to have more problems at the time of the mother's remarriage. Intelligence can help children cope with the stress.

The child's temperament also influences the process of divorce. An easy, adaptable temperament is a protective factor. In contrast, children with a difficult temperament are more sensitive and less adaptable to change; they can become a focal point for parental anger. In part, they elicit the anger with their reactive behavior; in part, they provide a convenient target for parental anger that may belong elsewhere.

For difficult children, the more stress they experience, the more problems they have. Easy children who face moderate amounts of stress actually develop increased coping skills and become more competent than when stress is either low or high.

We have already touched on some forms of family interaction that are protective—reduced conflict between the parents, structure and organization in daily life, and reasonable assignment of responsibilities within the family. Mothers must be especially firm and fair in establishing limits with boys, as their tendency is to develop a vicious repetitive cycle of complaining and fighting.

Researchers point to siblings and grandparents as potential supports.[43] When family life is harmonious after divorce, then sibling relationships resemble those in intact families.[44] When conflict between parents arises, siblings fight, with the greatest difficulty occurring between older brothers and younger sisters.

Grandparents can support grandchildren directly with time, attention, and special outings and privileges that help ease the pain of the divorce. As one girl said, "If it weren't for my grandparents, I don't think I could have made it past sixteen."[45] Grandparents provide support indirectly by helping one of the parents. In fact, returning to live in the home of one's parents is a solution many young parents choose when they do not have the res1ources to live on their own. Grandparents can be loving, stable baby-sitters who enrich children's lives in ways that no one else can. The mother can work and carry on a social life, knowing that her child is well cared for in her absence. This arrangement also usually reduces living expenses. When the mother and grandparents agree on child-rearing techniques and the mother is respected in the household as a mature adult, this solution may be attractive.

Such an arrangement, however, can reflect the neurotic needs of both the mother and the grandparents and thus create additional problems for the child. If the grandmother was a protective mother who refused to allow the daughter to become independent, that relationship may continue. The daughter may have tried to escape into a marriage that did not last. If the daughter returns to her parents' home, she may have to start again to develop her independence. She will have to establish new supports that will enable her to become more independent and to continue her growth as an individual.

School is another major source of support for children. Authoritative, kind teachers and peer friendships give pleasure and a sense of esteem to children. Educational and athletic accomplishments contribute to feelings of competence that stimulate resilience.

Some protective factors lie beyond a parent's control, including the age, sex, and temperament of the child, but many lie within it, such as setting aside anger, establishing structure, monitoring behavior, and seeking out external supports for children.

Family Changes over Time

Right after a divorce, custodial mothers are under pressure because of all the changes occurring in their lives.[46] Many of these women become more negative with their children than they were earlier, particularly with boys, and less involved in monitoring their behavior; a small group of these mothers, however, become too lenient and permissive. In response, both boys and girls become more anxious, demanding, aggressive, and noncompliant with peers and adults. As time passes, however, custodial mothers adjust and become more nurturant and more consistent in behavior management. Girls' behavior improves, and mothers and daughters often grow very close. Relationships with boys improve somewhat, but many boys continue to have some behavior problems.

Custodial fathers initially complain of feeling overwhelmed, angry, confused, and isolated, but after two years, they report better adjustment, perhaps because they generally have greater financial resources and better support than do mothers or because they typically get custody of older children.[47]

After the divorce, noncustodial fathers tend to become either permissive and indulgent or disengaged. They are less likely to be disciplinarians and more likely to play the role of recreational companion than are custodial mothers.[48] Many times, however, noncustodial fathers do not stay involved. One study reported that two years after the divorce, 25 percent of children had not seen their fathers in the past year; eleven years after the divorce, the number rose to 50 percent.[49] More recent work indicates, however, that three and a half years after the divorce, two-thirds of adolescents still have contact with their fathers, even if only at holidays and over summer vacation.[50] Noncustodial fathers are most likely to stay involved when they feel they play an important role in their children's lives and their long-term development.

Noncustodial mothers of adolescents are more likely to stay involved than are noncustodial fathers. Noncustodial mothers are more active and involved with and supportive of children than are noncustodial fathers, who often continue their role of recreational companion.[51]

Children's Behavior over Time

Children's behavior problems do improve over the first two years, but boys continue to have some difficulties six to eleven years after the divorce. Beginning at age ten, girls, especially early-maturing girls, show behavior problems as well. Both boys and girls are less competent in school, more defiant and noncompliant with rules, and more negative in mood—anxious, depressed, sometimes suicidal—compared with children of nondivorced parents.[52]

Early adolescents' rule breaking and resistance to custodial parents' authority may result from the early autonomy and independence many experienced during the family adjustment period immediately after the divorce. They have been joint decision makers with their custodial parents, and parents have been less insistent and demanding that children meet family rules. Therefore, they feel entitled to pursue their own ends.[53]

In intact families, parents exert more constraint on early adolescents. They insist that teens do chores and follow the rules. These parents monitor carefully; there are more arguments and less harmony in intact families than in divorced families. Divorced custodial mothers, however, become careful monitors in mid-adolescence, especially with daughters. So, at a time when parents in intact families are disengaging and trusting children's judgment in mid-adolescence (age fifteen), divorced mothers are often becoming more authoritative.[54]

Children in divorced families resist custodial mothers' authority; these mothers are more successful and the children have fewer problems when another adult (such as a grandparent, *not* a stepparent) lives in the home and reinforces the mother's authority.[55]

Feeling caught between divorced parents who are in conflict intensifies adolescents' anxiety, depression, and poor adjustment.[56] Even when parents have high conflict with each other, adolescents can do well, provided parents do not put them in the middle. The feeling of being caught between parents contributes to these children's problems.

Again, we find great diversity in children's adjustment.[57] Although many children of divorce show aggressive and insecure behaviors in adolescence, others are caring, competent teenagers who cooperate with divorced parents and make significant contributions to family functioning. Still others are caring, responsible teenagers whose autonomy and maturity are accompanied by feelings of depression and low self-esteem. They appear to worry that they will be unable to meet the demands placed on them. Those children who have the most difficulty with externalizing behaviors do not have a single caring adult in their lives. Their parents are neglectful, disengaged, and authoritarian, and the children cannot find support outside the family.

Hetherington and her coworkers found in their studies of children in remarriages that one of the biggest stresses in the remarriage was children's experiences during the divorce.[58] Divorce, with all its changes and losses—changes in economic resources, schools, friends, neighborhoods, and the exposure to parental fighting—affects children in fundamental ways. "Witnessing parents demean and criticize one another in an environment of hostility may diminish the capacity of parents in two ways, as effective role models for and as socializers of their children."[59] The fighting may well destroy trust in the hierarchy of rational authority that two parents working together creates for children.

Paul Amato and Brian Keith reviewed ninety-two studies to determine the degree of difficulty children of divorce experience.[60] They concluded that divorce is associated with increased risk for problems in cognitive and social competence. However, recent, better-controlled studies reveal that the differences between children of divorce and children in intact families are small and that there is much overlap in the functioning of the two groups.

Amato and Keith examined three possible sources of increased difficulties for children: parental loss, economic deprivation, and family conflict. Parental loss—whether as a result of divorce or the death of a parent—is a significant contributor to problems. Children who lose a parent through death experience difficulties similar to those of children whose parents divorce—shown by lower levels of well-being, poorer academic achievement, and conduct problems, compared with children in intact families—however, they do score significantly higher on measures of well-being, academic achievement, and conduct than do children in divorced families. Further, when custodial parents remarry, the children's behavior and functioning generally do not improve. Finally, involvement of the noncustodial parent brings only modest improvement. So, although parental loss is an important factor, it is not the only cause of difficulties in children of divorce.

Similar findings occur with economic disadvantage. When studies control for income, children of divorce still appear to have more problems than do children in intact families, and when parents remarry and income increases, children's behavior problems continue.

The third factor, family conflict, appears to be the main contributor to children's difficulties. Children in high-conflict, intact marriages have greater difficulties in self-esteem and adjustment than do children in divorced families in which such conflict is reduced. The level of family conflict and family conflict resolution styles are more powerful predictors of children's overall adjustment status than is family status (intact, divorced, or remarried). Further, longitudinal studies indicate that as time passes after the divorce and, presumably, the conflict, the children's adjustment improves (except when a developmental stage such as adolescence increases problems for all families). Finally, when postdivorce conflict is low, children function more effectively than when it is high. Thus, living in conflict—whether in an intact or a divorced family—appears to be the most powerful contributor to children's adjustment problems.

We now find that the effects of divorce do not necessarily end with childhood.[61] Young adults whose parents divorced when they were children (1) have lower educational attainment than do adults from intact families, (2) earn less money, (3) are more likely to have a child out of wedlock, (4) are more likely to get divorced, and (5) are more likely to be alienated from one parent. Again, outcomes vary. Most adult children of divorce function well within the normal range on most measures of adjustment. The only exception is in having poor relations with the father. Later in the chapter, we examine general guidelines for parenting at times of marital transitions.

SHOULD PARENTS STAY TOGETHER FOR THE SAKE OF THE CHILDREN?

Hetherington has conducted studies on divorce and remarriage and seeks to provide an answer to the often asked question, "Should parents stay together for the sake of the children?"[62] The answer depends on the nature of the conflict in the marriage, the various changes that follow the divorce, the quality of the postdivorce family relationships, and the degree to which the custodial parent relies on authoritative parenting.

Before the Divorce

Research comparing children in low-conflict nondivorced families with children in high-conflict nondivorced families and with children whose parents later divorce indicates that (1) children in low-conflict nondivorced families are the most socially and psychologically competent children and have the fewest problems and (2) children whose parents later divorce fall between children from low-conflict and high-conflict nondivorced families and are not significantly different from either group with the exception that they score higher than children in low-conflict nondivorced families on measures of aggressiveness and lower than that group on cognitive agency. So, children are more disadvantaged in a highly conflictual family atmosphere than in one in which parents will later divorce. The reason may be that in high-conflict nondivorced families, parenting is less effective than in low-conflict nondivorced families. Parents are less positive and more negative. There is more conflict between parent and child and less effective monitoring of the child's behavior. Again, parents who will later divorce fall between the two groups, with only slight differences between the low-conflict nondivorced mothers and later-divorcing mothers. Later-divorcing mothers are more negative and less effective in control before the divorce. Hetherington concludes, "Before the divorce the family dynamics leading to divorce are less deleterious than those associated with extremely high levels of overt marital conflict."[63]

Wallerstein would add another criterion for parents to consider in their deciding whether to stay together.[64] She believes that if parents can live together and parent together, they should stay together, as children benefit enormously from having two adults help them through childhood. She does not believe in continuing abusive or violent marriages, but she says that sometimes parents divorce not because the marriage is bad but because they want more stimulating, satisfying lives. In these situations, she recommends staying together to rear the children. Two parents together, she says, place children's needs at the forefront of family life. Parents talk about how to help children change behaviors; they work together to provide stimulating activities and relaxing time together. Children feel increased security in this atmosphere of support. They can pursue their own activities, maintain their friendships, and focus on their own lives. Feelings of stability increase because important relationships endure. In divorce, the focus unfortunately often centers on meeting parents' needs for visitation and support. Wallerstein acknowledges that some single parents can maintain children-focused families, but it is not easy or frequent in her experience.

After the Divorce

In the first two years following divorce, a greater number of girls in both high-conflict and low-conflict divorced families scored in the range of clinical problems on a child behavior checklist than did girls in high-conflict and low-conflict nondivorcing families. A greater number of boys in high-conflict divorced families and a smaller number of boys in low-conflict divorced families scored in the range of clinical problems on the same checklist than did boys from low-conflict nondivorcing families. Boys in low-conflict divorced families and boys from high-conflict nondivorcing families did not differ from each other. Boys from low-conflict nondivorcing families had the smallest percentage of boys scoring in the clinical range.

Two years after the divorce, children from high-conflict families—whether divorced or nondivorced—had the greatest number scoring in the range of clinical problems. Low-conflict families—whether divorced or nondivorced—had small numbers of girls scoring in the range of clinical problems. Although more boys in low-conflict divorced families than boys in low-conflict nondivorced families had clinical problems, the number was well below that of the number of boys from high-conflict families—whether divorced or nondivorced.

So, if conflict continues after the divorce, children might as well remain in a high-conflict nondivorced family and avoid all the trauma and changes of divorce. If, however, the divorce leads to a harmonious divorced family, then both boys and girls benefit, though girls appear to benefit more.

> The answer to our question about staying together for the sake of the children appears to be that if the stresses and disruptions in family processes, associated with an unhappy conflictual marriage and that erode the well being of children, are reduced by the move to a divorced single-parent family, divorce may be advantageous. If the diminished resources and increased risks associated with divorce also are accompanied by inept parenting and sustained or increased conflict, not only between the divorced couple but also between parents and children and siblings, it is better for children if parents remain in an unhappy marriage. Unfortunately, these "ifs" are difficult to determine when parents are considering divorce.[65]

FATHERS' ROLE IN CHILDREN'S LIVES

We saw in Chapter 13 that fathers' increased role in dual-earner families benefits children as well as mothers who are both working and rearing children. How, then, does the father's diminished role in the families of single mothers affect children?

Fathers' Absence

Using data from several national longitudinal samples, Sara McLanahan and Julien Teitler report the consequences of father absence for children's development and the factors underlying the consequences.[66] They report that in comparison with children growing up in two-parent families, children growing up apart from their biological fathers had lower grades, achieved less education, were more likely to drop out of school, and were less likely to get and keep a job. Adolescent girls in father-absent homes were far more likely to initiate sexual activity at an early age and to have a teen birth or a birth outside of marriage. In one study, 11 percent of adolescent girls in two-parent families had a teen birth, compared with 27 percent of girls in father-absent families.

Youth in one-parent homes were also less likely to make an easy transition from school to work, and 12 to 25 percent were considered idle because they were neither in school nor at work. Even when ability levels were controlled for, family structure significantly affected the transition.

The effects of father absence on educational attainment did not vary as a result of gender or racial or ethnic status of the family. Boys and girls of all ethnic groups had reduced educational attainment when fathers were absent. Boys from families with higher educational levels had higher dropout rates when families were disrupted than did boys from families with less education. Father absence had a greater effect on the risk for teen births for European American and Hispanic teens than for African American teens.

It did not seem to matter when father absence occurred or how long it lasted. Nor did it matter what family structure the child lived in, with one exception; children in homes with widowed mothers did nearly as well as children in two-parent families. Being born into a never-married family with more years of father absence did not increase the risk of problem behaviors, but the number of years living in a stepfamily without contact with the biological father had a negative effect and seemed to offset the benefits of marriage. In general, father absence matters more than the circumstances causing it, except in the case of widowhood.

Fathers' Contributions to Children's Lives

McLanahan and Teitler looked at fathers' contributions in three ways but cautioned that these three features—financial, social, and community—may be the result of another, as yet unidentified, factor. They point to fathers' financial contribution, which improves the resources available for child rearing. Without the additional resources, families may not have services such as health care and may live in poorer neighborhoods with poorer schools and fewer community services. They estimate that reduced income accounts for approximately 50 percent of the effects of father absence.

These researchers estimate that about half the disadvantage of father-absent homes results from poorer parent-child relationships, poorer relationships with adults, and a loss of resources in the community. As noted, it is extremely difficult for one parent to provide as much time, attention, and balance in parenting as two parents; nevertheless, some single-parent mothers do establish low-conflict homes in which children's functioning improves.

In contrast to McLanahan and Teitler, who have used large sociological surveys to support their views, Paul Amato has conducted new analyses of data to determine fathers' contributions to children's lives.[67] He looks at both mothers' and fathers' contributions in terms of human, financial, and social capital. *Human capital* refers to parents' skills, abilities, and knowledge that contribute to achievement in our culture. A useful measure of human capital is parent's education. *Financial capital* refers to the economic resources available to the family to purchase needed goods and services. *Social capital* refers to family and social relationships available to promote children's development.

Amato distinguishes between the benefits of the coparental relationship and those of the parent-child relationship. In a positive coparental relationship, the child views a model of how two people relate, cooperate, negotiate, and compromise. Children who learn these skills tend to get along better with peers and later partners. In providing a unified authority structure to children, two parents teach that authority is consistent and rational. Amato writes,

> Social closure between parents helps children to learn and internalize social norms and moral values. Also, a respect for hierarchical authority, first learned in the family, makes it easier for young people to adjust to social institutions that are hierarchically organized, such as schools and the workplace.[68]

Looking at many studies, Amato demonstrates that children's well-being is positively associated with (1) the father's education, (2) the father's income, (3) the quality of the coparental relationship, and (4) the quality of the parent-child relationship. These relationships hold in two-parent and one-parent families as well, even in studies where mothers' contributions are controlled for.

In his own longitudinal study, Amato interviewed individuals originally studied as children and followed up to early adulthood. He has found that fathers' education and income are related to children's education and that children's education has positive implications for such areas as friendships, self-esteem, and life satisfaction. Fathers' characteristics appear to account for more variance in children's education, self-esteem, and lack of psychological distress than do mothers' characteristics. Mothers' characteristics account for more variance in children's developing kin ties and close friends than do fathers' characteristics. Fathers' and mothers' characteristics account for equal amounts of variance in life satisfaction. Amato summarizes,

> Current research suggests that fathers continue to be important for their contributions of human and financial capital. Current research also suggests, however, that children benefit when fathers are involved in socioemotional aspects of family life . . . the current trend for fathers to be less involved in their children's lives (due to shifts in family structure) represents a net decline in the level of resources available for children.[69]

Studies show that nonresidential fathers who confine their activities with children to fun outings play a minimal role in children's development. Amato concludes that fathers matter "to the extent that they are able to provide appropriate support, guidance, and monitoring—especially if this occurs in the context of cooperation between the parents."[70]

Encouraging Fathers' Participation

James Levine, the founder of the Fatherhood Project in 1981, has written extensively on the advantages for children and fathers of fathers' increased involvement regardless of whether fathers are married to mothers.[71] He identifies three lessons he has learned over the years.

The first important ingredient in successfully involving fathers is the recognition that fathers want to be involved and can be effective parents with preparation and help. Second, single fathers need a support network that guides their behavior. Third, women play a key role in supporting men as fathers.

Figure 14-1 describes the "on-ramps" that facilitate men's connections with their children and families. Such on-ramps come from those in the community who interact with fathers—at the hospital, at doctors' visits, at schools. Levine writes,

> Our model does not absolve any man from primary responsibility; indeed, it holds that all fathers—whether unmarried, married, or divorced—are responsible for establishing and maintaining connection to their children. But it broadens that responsibility so it is also shared appropriately by all those in the community who, in their everyday work, have the

■ **FIGURE 14-1**
CONNECTION: A SHARED RESPONSIBILITY

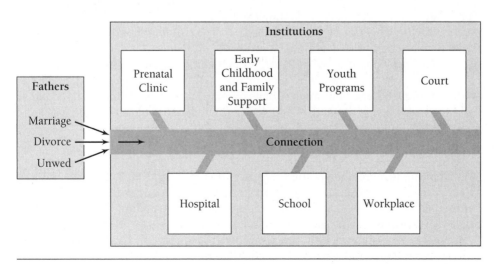

James A. Levine with Edward W. Pitt, *New Expectations: Community Strategies for Responsible Fatherhood* (New York: Families and Work Institute, 1995), 41. Reprinted with permission of the author.

opportunity and the capacity to build—or influence the building of—the on-ramps to connection.[72]

As Levine mentioned in his interview in Chapter 6, the context of interactions with fathers can help involve them. One example is the Hospital Paternity Establishment Program in West Virginia, which has increased the number of unwed fathers who establish paternity from 600 per year to 3,000 per year. Recall that changing expectations emphasize that new fathers need education about establishing paternity and that they need to be approached in terms of the benefits to the father and the child rather than to the state. Hospital staff were educated to involve fathers when they visited their newborns. Fathers then met with professionals, such as a child psychologist, who could explain the psychological importance of the father to the child; a doctor, who could explain the medical importance; and a lawyer, who could discuss the legal benefits to the child of having a father who is known. "Public education is the key," says Gary Kreps, who designed the program. "We need to start educating both moms and dads about the importance of fathers. And we need to educate teachers, counselors, coaches, the clergy, parents, and anybody who works with kids. And we need to educate our politicians."[73]

REMARRIAGE

As many as 35 percent of children, 54 percent of women, and 60 percent of men live in second marriages.[74] Remarriage provides many benefits to parents. First, it provides emotional closeness, intimacy, and sexual satisfaction. In caring relationships, parents feel greater self-esteem, contentment, and happiness. Second, parents have someone with whom they can share both the financial and caregiving responsibilities. Wallerstein and Blakeslee find that many parents do not repeat the mistakes of the first marriage.[75] Although remarried parents report feelings of stress and depression related to the many demands they experience, the marriages still are as happy as those in non-divorced families, perhaps because the couples are more pragmatic in their expectations and in seeking solutions to problems.[76]

We know most about remarried families that consist of the custodial mother, her children, and the stepfather, who may or may not have children. There are fewer studies of stepmothers. Few studies focus on marriages of single mothers who have children, even though these may have many characteristics of stepfamilies.

Challenges of Stepfamilies

Stepparenting is more demanding than parenting in intact families for several reasons.[77] First, a stepparent does not have long-standing emotional bonds with the children to help all of them overcome the feelings of frustration and stress that occur as a result of remarriage.

Second, a stepfamily includes more people than does a nuclear family, so it has different needs and interests to consider. There are husbands and wives, their biological children, ex-spouses, stepbrothers and stepsisters, half-brothers and half-sisters, and stepgrandparents. Parents have the multiple tasks of solidifying and maintaining marital ties while sustaining relationships with their biological children and promoting positive sibling relationships.

Third, members of stepfamilies may have deep feelings of jealousy and ambivalence. Because so many more people are involved and the newly married parents want to devote time to their relationship, stepparents may have less time to give to individual children. Children may feel that the new marriage is depriving them of their parent. Parents must accept those feelings as realistic—there *is* less time for each child. Conversely, the parents may feel that the children are intruding on the marriage.

Fourth, both parents and children are haunted by the earlier marriage. Stepparents may feel insecure, as they live with children who are constant proof that the spouse loved another person. Further, the biological parent usually continues to have contact with the former spouse because of the children.

Fifth, former spouses may use the children and their needs to attack the biological parent and the stepparent. One father and stepmother reported that the mother never bought the children clothes, and when the father did this in addition to making the monthly child support payment, the mother would not launder them. Conversely, one mother reported that the father and stepmother, rather than providing money for clothes for the children, instead bought the children fancy clothes that were appropriate for the lifestyle of the father and stepmother but not for the children's needs at school and play.

Sixth, there are no clear guidelines for being a stepparent. There are few enough for biological parents, but the role of stepparent remains even more vague. The stepparent must create his or her role according to his or her individual personality, the ages and sexes of the children, and the family's living arrangements. Stepparents who are forewarned about the problems of stepparenting and who think and talk in advance about how to cope with these problems can find their new roles rewarding and exciting.

Family Changes over Time

Just as parents' behavior changes after a divorce, remarried custodial mothers' behavior changes as well at the time of the remarriage.[78] These mothers become more negative and less controlling, and there is much conflict between mother and children, particularly daughters. If children are eight or younger when parents remarry, improvements occur with time. When children are nine or older, there are slight improvements, but monitoring and control stabilize at lower levels than in intact families. Regardless of the child's age at remarriage, conflicts increase in early adolescence and relationships are more conflictual than in intact families. Even in mid-adolescence, children remain more distant from their custodial, remarried mothers.

When children live with remarried custodial fathers, girls again are the ones who have greater difficulty.[79] Frequent contact with their biological mothers seems to increase the difficulty, but this unusual finding may be the result of biological mothers' having special problems that argued against their having custody. However, the

INTERVIEW
with Emily Visher and John Visher

Emily Visher, a clinical psychologist, and John Visher, a psychiatrist, are founders of the Step-family Association and authors of such books as Stepfamilies: Myths and Realities *and* Old Loyalties, New Ties: Therapeutic Strategies with Stepfamilies.

You have worked with stepparents and stepfamilies for many years, so I want to talk to you about what you feel are the important things for parents to do in order to ease the difficulties that can arise in stepfamilies.

E. Visher: We talk about a parenting coalition that is the coalition between all the adults in the child's life. For example, you see, there could be three or four parenting adults—if both parents have remarried, there will be four. If those adults can somehow develop a working relationship around raising the children, the loyalty conflicts of the children will be much less. The adults will get a lot out of it, too, because there is less tension, and better relationships develop between stepparent and stepchild.

We chose the word *coalition* because it means a temporary alliance of separate entities for accomplishing a task. The households and couples are separate, and it is a temporary alliance among all the adults. The task they are working on together is raising the children.

Families can flounder on the basis of the stepparent's trying to be a parent and the children saying basically, "I've got a mother or a father." We have moderated panels of teenagers in stepfamilies, and we always ask them, "What do you want your stepparents to be? What is their role?" I don't think we have ever heard anyone say anything other than "a friend." The difficulty is that by "friend," they mean something very different. They don't mean a pal; it's closer than that.

They are able to talk to the stepparent in a meaningful way that is different from the way they would talk to a parent. They are freer to talk to a stepparent because they are not so involved. One teenager on a panel said she wanted her stepfather to be her friend, and then later she said, "I love my stepfather, and I've never told him." She's saying she wants a friend, but she has very deep feelings for him. He was in the back of the room and heard her.

It is important to take a role that is satisfying to the adult and to the child, and that may be different for children living in the same household and for children in different households. The relationship is different depending on the age of the child—a six-year-old needs something different from a sixteen-year-old. For the young child, the stepparent may well become a parent.

J. Visher: The only power the stepparent has as a parent is delegated from the remarried parent.

E. Visher: The adults need to be supportive of one another. Together they need to decide what the house rules are, and the parent of the children takes care of enforcing the rules until a relationship is set up.

J. Visher: Another major tip is to develop realistic expectations about what it is going to take to make everything work. So many people feel that they have failed after a few weeks or months, that the remarriage has faltered because things are chaotic. It takes four or five years for things to settle down and for people really to get satisfaction out of the whole family relationship.

One of the keys is for people to inform themselves by reading or talking to other people who also are in stepfamilies. They learn that making the stepfamily work takes time and that you shouldn't expect close family relationships quickly.

The most common pattern now is for children to move back and forth and feel part of two households. If all the adults form a parenting coalition, then children are most likely to feel they belong in both places.

Working out the parenting coalition so that it is at least civil makes an enormous difference to everybody. The children can go through the remarriage smoothly if there is not constant warfare. Sometimes parents who divorce or separate are tied together in bonds of anger. The anger can reflect an inadequate separation between the biological parents. They keep together by fighting.

E. Visher: Truman Capote said, "It's easy to lose a good friend, but it's hard to lose a good enemy." The anger ties you together. Hostility eats you up, and you are not free to go on.

J. Visher: Most people don't understand how much damage they are doing to themselves and to the children. Sometimes people say, "How can I work with that S.O.B. when I couldn't even stay married to him?" We say maybe you can split off the part that does not want to be married to him and share the parenting experience.

E. Visher: What the children need from that parent is different from what the spouse needed.

What can you do to decrease the hostility?
J. Visher: One thing is to trade assurances between the households that you are not trying to take the child away from them or trying to get the child to like you better. Often, in a single-parent household, the parent is afraid of further loss, afraid that the ex-spouse and his or her new spouse will encourage the child to stay there and the child will want to because it is a more attractive place or there is more money. This fear fuels the anger and makes the parent cling to the child more and try to influence the child to turn against the other parent.

E. Visher: So we think that sometimes the anger is not left over from the former marriage but has to do with the fear that builds up between the two households, the fear of more loss. The other household becomes a threat, and the ex-spouses become like enemies rather than like people trying to raise a child. The parents are afraid of each other, and they are not aware that the anger substitutes for fear. If they are more aware of it, they can deal with it.

Also important is the guilt the remarried parent feels. He or she feels guilty that the children have been unhappy through the death or divorce and then the remarriage. That parent has a real investment in its being a big, happy family right away. Yet they have difficulty setting limits for the children who live there or visit there. The stepparent goes up the wall.

Sometimes they feel that to form a good couple relationship and make that primary is a betrayal of their relationship with their child. The parent-child relationship is different from the relationship with the spouse.

(continued)

INTERVIEW

with Emily Visher and John Visher *(continued)*

J. Visher: There may be an unusually strong bond between parent and child; perhaps it has lasted for many years, and the new spouse is a rival. It becomes a power struggle between spouse and child for the loyalty of the biological parent. The child is sometimes suddenly out of a job as confidant.

E. Visher: I don't think people realize the change for the children, that now they have to share. One mother described that she and her daughter had lived together for five years. When she came home from work, she talked to her daughter. Now that she is remarried, she talks to her husband. That one little thing is not so little, as the daughter has to share her mother.

If people are aware of the losses for the children in the new structure, they can acknowledge those changes with the children and do things differently—sit down with the children alone and talk. When children sense their feelings are accepted, they will talk about them. One stepmother commented to her stepson that when the father talked to the son, she felt left out, and she wondered if he felt left out when the father talked to her. He agreed he did, and they talked about it. There was not a lot they could change, but after they had the talk, they got along better.

J. Visher: We hope that as people are more informed, they will be able to deal more effectively with the situation.

longer girls live in such families, the more positive the relationship grows between the daughter and the stepmother.

There are no differences in how biological parents parent their own children in nondivorced and remarried families. Regardless of family status, mothers and fathers are warmer, more supportive, and closer to their biological children than to their stepchildren, and their children are more often closer to them.[80]

No matter what the age of a child at a parent's remarriage, stepfathers initially feel less close to their stepchildren than to their biological children, and they do not monitor behavior as well as fathers do in intact families. When children are relatively young at the time of the remarriage, stepfathers may be able to build relationships with stepchildren by taking on the role of a warm and supportive figure and forgoing the role of disciplinarian until a relationship is established. Preadolescent boys may settle down in a relationship with a stepfather, but preadolescent girls usually resist stepfathers' overtures and direct angry, negative behavior to the custodial mother.[81]

When children are early adolescents at the time of the remarriage, there appears to be little adaptation to the new family over a two-year period.[82] Children are negative and resistant even when stepfathers attempt to spend time with them and establish a relationship. As a result, stepfathers remain disengaged, critical, and distanced from the day-to-day monitoring of children. The negative behavior of the children shapes stepparents' behavior more than stepparents shape children's behavior. When, however, stepparents can be authoritative parenting figures—warm, positive, appropriate in monitoring—then children's adjustment improves. With adolescents, stepparents fare better when they are authoritative from the start.

Adolescents at the time of the remarriage are often resistant, withdrawn, and unwilling to become involved with stepparents. They frequently retreat from the families and establish strong relationships with families of friends. At the same time, they become more argumentative with the biological parents, both custodial and noncustodial. Their emotional attachment to parents appears in a negative rather than a positive way. As noted, adolescents feel closer to noncustodial mothers than to noncustodial fathers.[83]

In stepfamilies, marital happiness has a different relation to children's behavior than it has in intact families.[84] In nondivorced families, marital happiness is related to children's competent functioning and positive relationships with parents. In stepfamilies, marital happiness is related to children's negative and resistant behavior with parents. Girls may especially resent the loss of the close relationship with their custodial mother. Boys, having less to lose, may settle more easily into a relationship with a stepfather. Nevertheless, adolescent daughters respond positively to the satisfying marital relationship, perhaps because it serves as a protective buffer to an inappropriate relationship between stepfather and stepdaughter.

Relationships with siblings are less positive and more negative in remarried families than in nondivorced families.[85] Although girls tend to be warmer and more empathetic than boys, they are almost equally aggressive. As siblings become adolescents, they become more separated from each other. Interestingly, relationships with their stepsiblings appear less negative than relationships with their own siblings.

Children's Behavior over Time

Children's adjustment in stepfamilies varies. Often, initial declines in cognitive and social competence follow the remarriage, but when boys are young and stepparents are warm and authoritative, problem behaviors improve, and boys in these stepfamilies show levels of adjustment similar to those of boys in nondivorced families. Young girls continue to have more acting-out and defiant behavior problems than do girls in intact or divorced families.[86]

Most gender differences in adjustment disappear at early adolescence, when both boys and girls have more problems. At all ages, children in remarried families, like children in divorced families, have poorer school performance, problems in social responsibility, and more rule-breaking behaviors than do children in intact families. Parenting by the same-sex parent, whether custodial or noncustodial, is positively related to the child's adjustment.[87]

Although some children in remarried families have adjustment problems, the majority do well. Between two-thirds and three-quarters score within the average range on assessment instruments. Although this falls below the comparable figure of 90 percent for children of nondivorced parents, it indicates that most children in remarried families are doing well.[88]

As with children of divorced families, children of remarried families are at a disadvantage in early adulthood.[89] Compared with children of nondivorced parents, they are more likely to leave home at an early age, less likely to continue in school, and more likely to leave home as a result of conflict. As adults, they feel they can rely less on their families. Still, responses vary, and many of these children feel close to and supported in stepfamilies.

Many of the difficulties stepfamilies encounter can be avoided or lessened if they are anticipated and prepared for. Stepfamilies can strengthen their ties in many ways, such as nurturing relationships, finding personal space and time, and building family trust.[90]

Types of Stepfamilies

From his ten-year study of 100 stepfamilies made up of custodial mothers, stepfathers, and young children and a controlled sample of 100 nondivorcing families, James Bray has provided a basic understanding of developmental issues facing stepfamilies.[91] His major findings include the following:

1. A stepfamily has a natural cycle of changes and transition points.

2. A stepfamily takes many years to form a basic family unit.

3. The greatest risk to the stepfamily occurs in the first two years, when about 25 percent of remarriages fail.

4. In a stepfamily, there is no honeymoon period of high satisfaction followed by a gradual decrease, as there is in a first marriage; in a stepfamily, marital satisfaction starts at a moderate level and builds up from there or decreases to the point of divorce.

5. A stepfamily has four basic tasks to achieve cohesion:

    a. Integrating the stepfather into the family

    b. Creating a satisfying second marriage

    c. Separating from the ghosts of the past

    d. Managing all the changes

6. A stepfamily eventually takes one of three forms: *neotraditional, matriarchal,* or *romantic*. Neotraditionals almost always succeed, matriarchals succeed much of the time, and romantics face great risk of divorce.

The neotraditional family is described as a "contemporary version of the 1950s, white-picket fence; it is close-knit, loving, and works very well for a couple with compatible values."[92] The matriarchal family is one in which the wife-mother is a highly competent woman who directs and manages all the family activities. The romantic family seeks everything the neotraditional family does but wants it all immediately, as soon as the marriage occurs. The romantic family is at great risk for not surviving the conflicts and changes of the first two years. The three types of families do not differ in the crises and turning points they face, but they do differ in their expectations and their willingness to change their expectations and their behaviors to solve the problems they confront.

The first cycle of change that stepfamilies experience in the process of their formation occurs in the first two years of the remarriage. In this stressful period, all members of the family try to find ways to live together, deal with ex-spouses and noncustodial parents, and form a stable unit that brings everyone happiness. Parents' adjustments are often complicated by their unrealistic expectations about how well everyone will get along and how quickly love will form among family members. Such expectations are natural, but they have to be revised in the light of experience.

By the end of two years, the second cycle begins; family members find mutually satisfying ways of getting along, and a family unit is established. Tensions are reduced, and happy stepfamilies resemble nondivorced families. A third cycle of change occurs when children move into adolescence, become more insistent on independence and individuality, and often seek new relationships with noncustodial parents, stepparents, and custodial parents.

Neotraditional families successfully navigate the changes because they give up unrealistic expectations and because they communicate feelings and solve problems. Bray describes the neotraditional family as having the ability to (1) identify and express feelings clearly, (2) identify and understand other family members' thoughts, feelings, and values so differences are bridged, (3) resolve conflicts, (4) state a complaint so the other person feels empathy for the complaint, (5) establish new rituals that help define the family as a unit, and (6) accept other family members.

In matriarchal families, the mother is the leading decision maker. If the spouse or children resist at any point, then difficulties occur. These women are highly resourceful and competent; they often recognize when they themselves must change to meet the demands of the situation.

Romantic families seek the same cohesiveness and close ties that neotraditional families do, but they find it very difficult to give up unrealistic expectations and solve the problems at hand. They deny that stepfamilies face special difficulties, and they expect everyone to behave as they would in a first marriage. For example, they are unprepared for the divided loyalties children feel and their attachments to noncustodial parents, and they feel hurt when children do not transfer all their affections to the stepfamily. They get stuck in their hopes and desires and do not develop strategies to deal with the realities of everyone's feelings. Thus, in the second cycle, when other families feel less stress, these families are rehashing the unresolved issues of the first cycle.

Bray reports that despite the crises and difficulties of remarriage, many stepfamilies succeed and form stable, cohesive family units that give all members a sense of warmth and accomplishment. A significant number of stepfamilies do not succeed, however, and dissolve the marriages because the parents do not have the commitment to work through the problems to reach a joint resolution. Because these parents have already survived the unhappiness of one divorce, they know they can survive another and may be quicker to seek it in order to end the stress of the remarriage. A third group of families stay together and seem happy enough, but they lack a sense of vitality and seem to "just get by." These families do not want open communication or to really understand each other and instead choose habitual ways of relating to each other.

Bray asked successful families what got them through all the stressful periods. "The consistent answer was commitment. Commitment to a life together, not just getting by but living and loving fully, communicating about issues, building a stable family, and enjoying a good life together."[93]

LESBIAN AND GAY PARENTS

Lesbian and gay parents are a heterogeneous group.[94] The majority of lesbian and gay parents have children in the context of heterosexual marriages and later divorce, adopt a lesbian or gay identity, and rear children with partners of the same sex. These families face not only all the stresses of remarried families but also the pressure of prejudice against lesbian and gay parents. Much of the initial research done on lesbian and gay parents and their children has been conducted in order to prevent their being denied custody of and visitation with their children.

More and more lesbian and gay parents are choosing parenthood after proclaiming a lesbian or gay identity. They are usually living with partners and choose to have a child through assisted reproductive technology or surrogate parenthood. The child may have a biological relationship with one parent, with the other parent becoming a coparent through legal adoption of the child, or the child may have no biological relationship with either parent. A single lesbian or gay person may have a child in the same way.

Divorced Lesbian and Gay Parents

The largest group studied has been divorced lesbian mothers. Concerns have focused on their mental health and on their sex-role behavior and its effects on children. Most studies have compared lesbian and heterosexual mothers and find no differences between them on self-concept, overall psychological adjustment, psychiatric status, sex-role behavior, or interest in children and child rearing. Divorced lesbian mothers are more worried about custody issues than are divorced heterosexual mothers. They are more likely to be living with partners. Studies reveal no differences between the biological fathers of children of lesbian mothers and fathers divorced from heterosexual mothers in terms of paying child support, but fathers in the former group are more likely to have frequent visitation.

Research is just beginning on such topics as when and how lesbian mothers should reveal their sexual identity to children. Although there is no firm agreement, it is thought best to avoid doing this during the child's adolescence so that the child's own sexual identity and identity formation can occur without distraction.

Much less is known about divorced gay fathers. There is no research comparing the psychological stability of gay and heterosexual divorced fathers, perhaps because men do not often seek physical custody. Research comparing their parenting behaviors suggests that gay fathers are more responsive, more careful about monitoring, and more likely to rely on authoritative parenting strategies than are heterosexual divorced fathers. Studies of the family lives of gay fathers, teen sons, and fathers' partners indicate greater family happiness when the partner has a good relationship with the adolescent boy. Comparisons of divorced lesbian mothers and gay divorced fathers reveal that gay fathers report more income and more frequent sex-stereotypic toy play by their children.

Lesbian and Gay Couples' Transition to Parenthood

In the 1990s, many lesbian and gay individuals in committed partnerships chose to have children either through assisted reproductive technology or through adoption, but such couples often faced prejudice in a situation that is stressful enough. Little research has addressed the questions of how and when lesbian and gay couples decide to have children. Research has focused instead on how lesbian and gay couples make the transition to parenthood and divide the responsibilities of child care and household work.

In lesbian partnerships, the biological mother takes primary care of the child in the earliest months, but nonbiological parents often report an immediate attachment to the child and take a larger role when the child is twelve months or older. There was more equal sharing of child care and household work in lesbian partnerships than in heterosexual marriages. Lesbian partners also report a high level of relationship satisfaction and greater satisfaction with the division of labor. Nonbiological mothers were seen as more knowledgeable about child care and more willing to assume equal care of the child than were heterosexual fathers.

A study comparing single and coupled lesbian mothers with single and coupled heterosexual mothers found that (1) single heterosexual and lesbian mothers were warmer and more positive with their children than were coupled heterosexual-mothers, and all lesbian mothers were more interactive with their children than were single heterosexual mothers, and (2) single heterosexual and lesbian mothers reported more serious, though not more frequent, disputes with children than did coupled heterosexual mothers.

In a study of gay fathers choosing parenthood, gay fathers reported higher self-esteem and fewer negative attitudes about homosexuality than did gay men who elected not to become fathers.[95] There are few other differences between the two groups of men, and the author speculates that higher self-esteem may result from parenthood rather than be a determiner of it.

Children of Lesbian and Gay Parents

A major question of research has been whether lesbian and gay parents influence the gender identity of their children in the direction of lesbian/gay gender identity and same-sex sexual orientation (choice of partner). There is no evidence that children of lesbian and gay parents have an increased likelihood of having a lesbian/gay gender identity or same-sex sexual orientation. Nor is there evidence that they are at increased risk of sexual abuse in lesbian or gay homes.

Children living with lesbian and gay parents are as well adjusted and socially competent as children living with heterosexual parents. Children of lesbian parents show no special problems with self-concept, gender identity, or sexual orientation. The results of research on lesbian and gay parents and their children indicate that the sexual adjustment of the parent does not predict the child's adjustment and that family process variables operate in much the same way in lesbian and gay families as in heterosexual families—that is, when parents are warm and involved, as many lesbian and gay parents are, their children do well.

PRACTICAL QUESTION: WHAT SHOULD PARENTS DO AT TIMES OF MARITAL AND PARTNER TRANSITIONS?

Research suggests several things parents going through family breakups or transitions can do. First, these parents should maintain positive emotional relationships with children. Even if there is pronounced conflict between parents, parent-child relationships can be satisfying if parents make a special effort to keep children out of the conflict. Parents need to make time for the open communication of feelings, for asking and answering questions, and for sharing enjoyable activities. These same rules apply to relationships with stepchildren.

Second, parents must learn effective ways of resolving conflicts, regardless of who is involved. (See Table 14-1, which lists suggestions for minimizing harm from conflict between parents, and Chapter 4 for a discussion on effective ways of dealing with anger between parents and children.) According to Amato, the most important thing society can do to promote safe and secure environments for children is to encourage parents to learn ways to resolve conflicts within marriages and to settle disputes if they get divorced so children are not put in the middle.[96] Children's feelings of self-blame, whether parents are married or divorced, are one of the contributors to children's poor adjustment to life.

Third, parents need to model and encourage positive relationships with all family members—siblings, grandparents, and all the relatives involved in stepfamilies.

Fourth, parents need to help children seek positive experiences in their own social milieu—with friends, relatives, schoolmates, and teachers. These supports help children cope in times of change.

Finally, parents need to recall that, at times of marital transition, they need to do all the things that are beneficial in nondivorced families, but they need to do more of them to buffer children from the stress of change. It is harder to do these things when parents themselves are under stress. Still, parents promote children's growth and competence in all times of change when they foster close, positive emotional relationships with children and monitor their behavior carefully to ensure that it falls within appropriate limits.

THE POWER OF AUTHORITATIVE PARENTING

Hetherington's work,[97] as well as that of other researchers,[98] reveals that regardless of family structure (one or two parents, biological parent or stepparent, lesbian or gay parents), regardless of ethnic background or age or gender, children do well with authoritative parenting. When parents can respond to children's needs and individuality and also monitor and control behavior, children function well. Similarly, regardless of family structure, children do poorly with authoritarian and harsh, demanding parenting. Authoritative parenting not only contributes to positive parent-child relationships but also builds positive sibling relationships, which increase child competence.

MAIN POINTS

Single parents are

- a heterogeneous group made up of never-married, separated or divorced, and widowed adults with children
- more frequently women than men, with 22 percent of families with children headed by women and 4 percent headed by men
- most effective when they organize stable living environments and use authoritative parenting

The process of divorce

- is often preceded by marital conflict, which upsets children and arouses their feelings of self-blame
- is a major disruption for all family members
- involves many changes that can include fewer economic resources as well as a new neighborhood, a new school, and new friends
- places stress on children and parents, which can be reversed if parents establish low-conflict divorced homes

Protective factors for children at the time of divorce include

- a child's age, sex, intelligence, and temperament
- manageable amounts of stress and appropriate support from grandparents and other relatives
- educational and athletic accomplishments that contribute to children's feelings of competence and stimulate resilience

Children's behavior

- becomes more problematic at the time of divorce but improves as time passes
- is less carefully monitored in single-parent than in dual-parent homes in early adolescence
- improves when parents resolve their anger and use authoritative parenting

Men make positive contributions to children's development when

- they provide their human, financial, and social capital to the family
- the social context encourages their involvement

When parents remarry, they

- experience many emotional benefits such as closeness, intimacy, and sexual satisfaction
- do not necessarily repeat the mistakes of the first marriage
- experience stress as they integrate everyone into a new family with few guidelines

When parents remarry, children

- differ in their reactions, with girls having more difficulty in adjusting to parents' remarriage than do boys
- show initial declines in social and cognitive competence
- show improvements in behavior, following an initial decline, when parenting figures are warm and authoritative

Stepfamilies

- often have unrealistic expectations about how quickly closeness and cohesiveness of family members develop
- need empathy and communication skills to work through the crises and conflicts that occur in the first two years

Lesbian and gay parents

- are as effective as parents in heterosexual marriages
- have children who function as well as children of heterosexual parents
- share child care and household work more equally than heterosexual parents

Parenting tasks at times of partner and marital transition include

- maintaining positive emotional relationships with children
- learning effective conflict resolution skills
- relying on authoritative parenting strategies
- modeling positive relationships with the extended family
- encouraging children to have positive experiences in their own social world

EXERCISES

1. Suppose your friend's parents divorced when he or she was a small child and now your friend fears intimacy and commitment. What could you do to help him or her be less fearful? What advice could you offer your friend to lessen such fears? In a class discussion, share your ideas on how to advise your friend.

2. Imagine that your married brother, sister, or friend came to you and said he or she was getting a divorce and wanted help in making arrangements so his or her eight-year-old daughter and six-year-old son would experience the fewest negative effects. What guidelines would you give your relative or friend?

3. Pair off with a classmate, preferably of the same sex. Imagine one of you is eight and the other fifteen years old. One of your parents has just married your

partner's parent; you are now stepbrothers or stepsisters. Discuss how you feel now that you are going to be living intimately with each other—perhaps sharing a room, having your time with your biological parent reduced so the parent can spend time with this stranger, having the amount of money available to you dependent on the needs of these new people. Would being older or younger make a difference in your reactions? Describe what your parents could do to ease the adjustment process.

4. Attend divorce court for a morning and summarize the cases presented there. What issues do parents argue about? What issues about children arise? Describe whether you agree with the judge's ruling, and state why.

5. Write a script for what a mother and stepfather might say to the mother's two children (aged nine and thirteen) and the stepfather's two children (aged six and nine, who visit every other weekend), about their expectations of how they hope the children will get along and how the parents will handle arguments as they arise. What rules can parents set for children of these ages? What will the stepfather's role be?

ADDITIONAL READINGS

Bray, James H., and Kelly, John. *Stepfamilies: Love, Marriage, and Parenting in the First Decade.* New York: Broadway Books, 1998.

Hetherington, E. Mavis, and Kelly, John. *For Better or Worse: Divorce Reconsidered.* New York: Norton, 2002.

Lamb, Michael E., ed. *Parenting and Child Development in Nontraditional Families.* Mahwah, NJ: Erlbaum, 1999.

Levine, James A., and Pitt, Edward W. *New Expectations: Community Strategies for Responsible Fatherhood.* New York: Families and Work Institute, 1995.

Martin, April. *The Lesbian and Gay Parenting Handbook.* New York: HarperCollins, 1993.

Wallerstein, Judith S., Lewis, Julia M., and Blakeslee, Sandra. *The Unexpected Legacy of Divorce.* New York: Hyperion, 2000.

15

Parenting in Times of Trauma

IN THE NEWS

San Francisco Chronicle, March 19, 2003
Bay area parents seek guidelines for helping their children cope with the anxieties aroused by the war in Iraq. See page 466 for details.

Go to PowerWeb at:
www.dushkin.com/powerweb
to read articles and newsfeeds
on **child abuse**, **parenting**, **violence**,
and other topics related to this chapter.

When traumatic events occur, parents face enormous challenges. What reactions can parents expect from children? What can parents do to help children cope? Which children are most likely to suffer long-term effects from traumatic events? What can parents do to protect children from violence and enable them to feel secure in a world that is sometimes unsafe?

This chapter focuses on various forms of violence and maltreatment children can experience: exposure to family violence, sexual abuse, physical abuse, neglect, and violence in the community. We look at definitions and the incidence and prevalence of such behaviors. We also examine the ways children react to such experiences, and discuss ways to help children deal with them. We finally focus on how parents can help children minimize their risk of violent encounters.

VICTIMIZATION OF CHILDREN

Children are more prone to victimization than are adults. Throughout childhood, they are more often subject to family violence, and adults report beating them harder than they beat spouses. Children also face a greater risk of sexual abuse. Teenagers are more subject than adults to all the crimes reported by adults, and both children and teenagers experience forms of assault that adults do not, such as sibling assault.

Highlighting the many dangers with which children live, Figure 15-1 (page 446) shows the rates per 1,000 children of various kinds of violence and abuse. David Finkelhor and Jennifer Dziuba-Leatherman group forms of victimization into three categories: (1) the *pandemic* (frequent events affecting most children, such as sibling fights), (2) the *acute* (events that affect a small but significant percentage of children, such as neglect and sexual and physical abuse), and (3) the *extraordinary* (events such as kidnapping and homicide). The most frequent events, experienced by five to eight of every ten children, are sibling assault, physical punishment (usually by parents), and theft. These events are rarely studied, but they should be because so many children experience them and report fears about them.

Children are more at risk for victimization than are adults, for several reasons. First, children depend more on others for care. The concept of neglect, for example, has no meaning in regard to independent adults. Second, because children are small and less cognitively mature, they cannot easily protect themselves from older children and adults. Third, children have less choice about their surroundings and associates than do adults. They have to live at home and go to school, where they are sometimes forced into contact with abusive people. They cannot leave.

Besides being potentially unwise, separating the various kinds of abuse is difficult because the different types overlap considerably. In one sample, all 70 children experienced more than one form of abuse; in another, 90 percent of 160 children experienced more than one form.[1] Maltreatment of a single kind may be quite rare in reality.

A major conclusion from studies of both physical and sexual abuse is that there is no one path, no one set of risk factors, and no definite set of characteristics that qualify as "the effects" of abuse.[2] Jay Belsky wrote in 1993, "All too sadly, there are many pathways to child abuse and neglect."[3] We can add that there are many effects triggered by the abuse. In the following section, we examine a model that describes the many factors that lead to abuse and violence and their potential consequences, but first let us look at the criteria of violence.

■ **FIGURE 15-1**
TYPOLOGY OF CHILD VICTIMIZATION

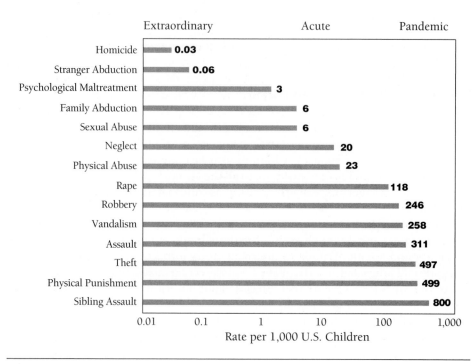

David Finkelhor and Jennifer Dziuba-Leatherman, "Victimization of Children," *American Psychologist* 49 (1994): 176. © 1994 American Psychological Association. Used with permission.

In 1994, approximately three million children were reported to Children's Protective Services (CPS) for suspected abuse. About a third—one million cases—were substantiated.[4] Of this million, 54 percent were cases of neglect, many of which may have been associated with poverty. About one-quarter involved physical abuse, 11 percent were primarily sexual abuse, 3 percent were emotional neglect, and 6 percent fell outside of these categories.

Population surveys result in higher figures.[5] A Gallup poll of a representative sample of one thousand U.S. families reported in 1995 that 5 percent of children met the criteria of physical abuse, and approximately 2 percent met the criteria for sexual abuse. These are ten to sixteen times higher than the rates reported to official agencies.

The criteria for establishing abuse must be specified. For example, because Finkelhor and Dziuba-Leatherman consider spanking as physically violent, they categorize far more children as being victimized than does Gallup's poll, which defines physical abuse as being hit with an object (reported for only 5 percent of the children).

Robert Emery and Lisa Laumann-Billings believe it might be useful to distinguish between family *maltreatment,* characterized by minimal physical, sexual, or psychological harm, and *family violence,* characterized by serious physical injury, sexual exploitation, or psychological trauma.[6] This distinction is made not to minimize the physical and psychological effects of maltreatment but to separate cases that need supportive services from those that require serious coercive intervention, such as the removal of the child from the home. At present, so many resources go into investigating cases and making sure violence exists that little remains for the larger number of families in which maltreatment is the problem. At present, these families receive little treatment, guidance, or support to help them learn to manage aggressive feelings more appropriately.

AN ECOLOGICAL/TRANSACTIONAL MODEL OF CHILD ABUSE AND COMMUNITY VIOLENCE

Dante Cicchetti and Michael Lynch propose an ecological/transactional model to describe how the child's environment interacts with the characteristics of the caregiver and the child to shape the child's level of risk and the child's development subsequent to abuse.[7] They also refer to risk factors that increase the possibility of negative outcomes and protective factors that buffer children from the impact of negative events.

Risk and protective factors exist at the cultural, community, family, and individual level of experience. Using Urie Bronfenbrenner's ecological model presented in Chapter 2, the researchers describe the macrosystemic cultural beliefs that contribute to abuse—for example, that physical force is an acceptable way to settle differences, that children are property and one can spank them if one wishes, that sexual gratification is a sign of manliness.

At the exosystemic level, community factors such as the absence of supervised play areas and recreational activities for children, and the social isolation of poor neighborhoods, contribute to increased risk for abuse. Community factors interact with individual characteristics to increase risk.

Factors at the community level can interact with factors at the family level. For example, a neighborhood with high unemployment and drug addiction may have a higher rate of violent crime than would a less-stressed community; the prevalence of violent crime can in turn add to the distress of an unemployed father, who then becomes more physically punishing with his son. Unemployed parents lack the resources needed to move out of such neighborhoods and must deal with the ongoing frustrations that interfere with their parenting.

Children also experience violence at the *microsystemic level* in daily interactions with siblings, parents, peers, and teachers. Both parents and children bring their individual characteristics to these interactions. Parents who maltreat children, compared with those who do not, are more likely to have experienced abuse in their own childhood. Still, the majority of adults who have been abused do not abuse their children. Abusive parents tend to form unstable, conflicted adult-adult relationships,[8] and they interact with children in many negative ways besides the actual abuse. They are less satisfied with their children and use more disciplinary techniques than do nonmaltreating parents. They want their children to be independent but insist that they meet unrealistically high standards. Abusive parents quite often reverse roles and expect children to act as their caregivers.

Children's individual characteristics also can influence the likelihood of abuse. There is the child's sex; in several studies, boys were found to be more likely to experience physical abuse[9] and girls more likely to experience sexual abuse.[10] The child's age is a factor; the median age for sexual abuse is about eight,[11] but approximately one-third of sexually abused children are under six.[12] Physical abuse peaks between the ages of three and eight. Although children appear to face less risk after age eight, recent data show that adolescents are subject to significant abuse as well.[13] This finding may be a function of more careful reporting of adolescent injuries. Children who are physically abused may be noncompliant and difficult to care for, but this behavior most likely results from rather than causes negative caregiving.

Finally, children experience violence at the *ontogenic level*—that is, in how they develop as an individual. Cicchetti and Lynch identify five areas that may be problematic for children's development following abuse: the attachment relationship with the parent, regulation of emotion, self-concept, peer relationships, and adaptation to school and learning.

The model developed by Cicchetti and Lynch also has implications for interventions. First, there are interventions at the microsystemic level, with the individual and the family—helping them deal with the situation, the feelings that arise from it, and the problems that ensue.

Then there are interventions at the exosystemic level—helping parents and children reach out to social agencies and social structures such as schools and community organizations to get support to enable the family to cope. Community and state agencies offer a variety of programs to train parents in anger management, stress reduction, and effective disciplinary techniques. Comprehensive programs seek to preserve the family by meeting its many needs for such services as financial and household management, help in finding employment, and alcohol abuse treatment. They provide broad-based services while the family stabilizes and becomes involved in a network of agencies that can continue to meet such needs.[14] These services reduce the need for social agencies to provide out-of-home living arrangements for abused children.

Community agencies also identify high-risk parents who, because of their own characteristics (for example, substance abuse) or characteristics of their children (physical injuries or conditions that make care difficult), need special services to prevent possible abuse.[15] These agencies provide, often in the home, training and modeling in appropriate caregiving and help parents adopt effective problem-solving skills.

Finally, there are interventions at the macrosystemic level—changing the societal views of violence and sexuality that permit victimization of children. Although this is a complicated process, giving all parents training in effective caregiving and childrearing strategies makes abuse less likely.[16] Requiring parent training as part of a junior high or high school education not only provides needed skills but also sends a strong social message about the importance of parenting skills. Abuse of children affects our entire society; we all must live and interact with those who are hurt by abuse and must provide services to deal with the hurt.

Currently, research on the most effective forms of intervention is limited. However, all levels of intervention appear necessary to help children and prevent the recurrence of abuse.[17]

DEALING WITH CHILD ABUSE AND VIOLENCE

As noted by Finkelhor and Dziuba-Leatherman, children in U.S. society are at risk for a variety of traumatic experiences. Among them are exposure to family violence, sexual abuse, physical abuse, neglect, and community violence. Because all have the potential to cause lasting physical and psychological harm, parents must handle such situations with care.

Exposure to Family Violence

Although concerns about family violence between intimate partners have increased over the past three decades, children's exposure to family violence was not discussed in the research literature until the 1980s, and even now, the body of knowledge in this area is limited.[18] The term *domestic violence* encompasses many behaviors and can vary in meaning depending on who uses the term. Legal definitions emphasize acts of physical harm (including forced sexual acts and threats of harm) carried out against intimate partners. Clinical definitions are broader; in addition to physical and sexual attacks, they include economic coercion and psychological attacks against intimate partners. The term *exposure* (to domestic or family violence) is used rather than *witness* to include children who hear the violence, see the effects of the violence, or are involved in interrupting the violence by calling the police. Although exposure to family violence refers to violence between adults, one suspects that children who are exposed to parent-child abuse of a sibling suffer many of the same problems.

Most studies focus on male abusers and female victims, yet a review of several studies suggests that men and women are equally likely to be victimized. Nonetheless, women sustain the more serious injuries. Domestic violence occurs in many different kinds of families.[19] One study identified five different patterns: (1) ongoing/episodic male battering, (2) female-initiated violence, (3) male-controlling violence, (4) separation/divorce violence, and (5) psychotic/paranoid violence.

Children are involved in domestic violence in various ways. In one study, children were involved in the onset of the violence in 20 percent of the incidents.[20] They were involved in making 10 percent of the 911 calls. In a review of several studies, 40 to70 percent of children from violent homes were also physically abused, and 40 percent of physically abused children came from violent homes.

Prevalence   There are no reliable national statistics on the prevalence of domestic violence, though it is estimated that three to ten million children are exposed to it.[21]

Such exposure begins in utero, as attested by the fact that 16 percent of women questioned in prenatal clinics reported spousal abuse, and half of them reported several incidents.[22] Severe abuse during pregnancy was also correlated with drug and alcohol use, smoking, low maternal weight gain, and delay in getting prenatal care. An intensive, five-city research project found that children, particularly young children, were more likely than older children to be in homes with domestic violence.[23] Homes with domestic violence also included other risk factors such as poverty, substance abuse, single-female heads of household, and heads of household with limited education.

Effects on Children   Children show a range of reactions to domestic violence, depending on their age and temperament, the specific nature of the violence, its severity and chronicity, and their involvement in it.[24] Children's emotional responses to the events include terror, fear of death, and fear of loss of the parent. As a result of the violence, children may experience the world as a hostile, unpredictable place, where disaster may strike suddenly. There is growing evidence that young children who witness extensive partner conflict and violence are at risk for neurobiological changes in brain structure, which in turn affect later neurological development.[25] The nature of the violent arguing determines how the brain will internalize the experience. If the child is terrified, the brain may be in a constant state of hyperarousal, which will make it difficult for the child to absorb cognitive stimulation and information.

Children suffer a variety of symptoms. Compared with children from nonviolent homes, children exposed to domestic violence are at higher risk for physical symptoms of insomnia, nightmares, tics, and bed-wetting.[26] They are more likely to have increased externalizing behavior problems (aggressiveness, temper tantrums, fighting with peers) and increased internalizing problems (anxiety, fear, depression, loss of self-esteem). They also score lower on measures of verbal, motor, and cognitive skills and have poorer concentration and attention for schoolwork.

Interventions   The first form of intervention is to help the nonviolent parent establish a safe and stable home.[27] Parents who live with domestic violence sometimes develop *posttraumatic stress disorder* (psychological symptoms in response to an unusual, dramatic event); as part of this disorder, they may become desensitized to violence in the home and minimize the events and thus fail to protect the child as the situation would warrant. Feeling hopeless, helpless, and depressed, the victimized parent may not be available to the child as a caregiver or as a source of help in coping with the events. Thus, outside help to the family is first directed to the parent and to efforts to stabilize the home so that the parent can serve as the primary source of help for the child.

Second, the child needs an explanation of the violent events and an opportunity to express the feelings triggered by the violence. Third, parents provide honest answers to their child's fears and worries and offer as much reassurance as is possible and realistic given the circumstances.

Crisis counseling in homes or in shelters can help children adapt to what has happened.[28] Group therapy programs give children an opportunity to talk about the violence, improve their self-esteem as they realize this happens to other children, reduce their feelings of guilt, and develop safety skills.

In addition to services provided to the child and family, there are community interventions such as educating teachers to help children cope with violence. Sometimes young children spontaneously talk about domestic violence or write about it. Teachers must be prepared to deal with these situations sensitively and effectively so that problems do not continue. Community interventions also educate health-care, legal, and law enforcement professionals on ways to respond to victims of domestic violence in sensitive and effective ways. Broader community action includes preventive programs designed by health-care and educational systems to make the public aware of the need to reduce domestic violence.[29] A major stumbling block, however, is the cultural belief that domestic violence is not wrong or harmful but a personal matter between two adults. Educating the public as to the negative effects of such violence on adults and children and providing opportunities for learning better ways of solving conflict are the primary tasks of prevention.

> Although evaluative data are limited, early results point to promising strategies and theories that can be applied to the prevention of domestic violence. They include: home visitation, collaborative efforts among child protection agency personnel and domestic violence service providers, prevention efforts that address violence both in homes and in communities, school-based programs, and public education programs and public education campaigns tailored to address the unique perspectives of specific segments of the population.[30]

Sexual Abuse

The National Center on Child Abuse and Neglect defines child sexual abuse as

> contacts or interactions between a child and an adult when the child is being used for the sexual stimulation of the perpetrator or another person. Sexual abuse may also be committed by a person under the age of 18 when the person is either significantly older [five years or more] than the abuse victim or when the perpetrator is in a position of power or control over another child.[31]

Abusive experiences can range from intercourse to touching to viewing an exhibitionist. Abuse can occur within the family (incest or intrafamilial) or outside the family (extrafamilial). Although much of the research on abuse has focused on girls, we are increasingly aware of abuse perpetrated on boys.

Prevalence   Determining the incidence and prevalence of sexual abuse in childhood is extremely difficult, as the acts are taboo and most are not reported. In a sample of 1,800 college students, one-third of both men and women reported experiencing sexual abuse in childhood. Only half of the women and a tenth of the men had reported the incident to an adult. Estimates are that one in four girls and one in six boys has experienced some form of sexual abuse by age eighteen.[32]

Diana Russell interviewed a random sample of San Francisco women concerning childhood sexual abuse.[33] Her definition of abuse included only actual sexual contact, not exhibitionism. She found that by the age of eighteen, 16 percent of women had been abused by a family member and 31 percent by a person outside the family. When intrafamilial and extrafamilial abuse were combined, 38 percent of 930 women reported at least one experience of abuse by age eighteen and 28 percent by age fourteen. Only 2 percent of intrafamilial abuse and 6 percent of extrafamilial abuse were ever reported to police.

In intrafamilial abuse, 38 percent of the abusers were members of the nuclear family (parents or siblings). Other relatives identified as abusers were most frequently uncles, male first cousins, and grandfathers. Of extrafamilial abusers, only 15 percent were strangers; 42 percent were acquaintances, and 43 percent were friends of the victim or family.

Karen Meiselman describes the family at high risk for incest as having one or more of the following components: (1) an alcoholic and violent father; (2) a mother who is away from home, physically ill, depressed, or passive; (3) an older daughter who has had to act as a surrogate mother (doing most of the chores, caring for younger siblings or for her father); (4) parents who have failed to establish a satisfying sexual relationship; (5) fathers and daughters who spend much time alone with each other; (6) any condition, such as psychosis or below-average intelligence, that reduces an individual's capacity for self-control; (7) previous incest in a parent's family; and (8) a romantic attachment with an unusual amount of physical affection between adult and child.[34]

Effects on Children   The impact of sexual abuse depends very much on the child and the specific circumstances of the abuse—the nature, duration, and frequency of the physical contact and the identity of the perpetrator. Further, it is difficult to disentangle the effects of the family conflict prior to the abuse, the abuse itself, and the events around the disclosure of the abuse. A broad review of studies[35] suggests that sexual abuse that is likely to produce a greater number of symptoms involves (1) a close relationship with the perpetrator; (2) sexual acts of oral, anal, or vaginal penetration; (3) frequent occurrences; (4) a long duration; and (5) lack of maternal support at the time of disclosure. These separate aspects of abuse, however, are related to one another. A close family member often has greater opportunity for frequent contact with the victim over a long period of time.

Sexually abused children report many different symptoms following the abuse; no one symptom characterizes the majority of sexually abused children.[36] The most frequently reported symptoms are fears, nightmares, sexualized behaviors (sexualized play with dolls or toys, putting things in the vagina or anus, public or inappropriate masturbation) that suggest sexual stimulation from adults or peers, depression, aggression, withdrawal, school problems, poor self-esteem, acting out, regression of behavior, and symptoms of posttraumatic stress (reliving the experience, dread of dire consequences to the victim). These symptoms generally follow the patterns of difficulties that Cicchetti and Lynch proposed in their transactional/ecological model of maltreatment: difficulties in attachment, regulation of emotion, self-concept, peer relationships, and school performance. Although there is no clear-cut evidence of insecure attachment relationships, the symptoms reported reflect all the other difficulties in development.

Preschoolers most often report fears, nightmares, sexualized behaviors, withdrawal, and aggressive and uncontrolled behaviors. School-age children report all these symptoms, as well as school problems, hyperactivity, and regressive behaviors. Adolescents most often report depression, suicidal acting out, anger, running away, and antisocial behavior. Depression is the most commonly reported symptom in adults who have been sexually abused.

Between a third and a half of children who have been sexually abused report no symptoms initially.[37] These may be the children who experienced the least-damaging abuse or received the most supportive response at the time of disclosure, and they may be the most resilient children. It is possible, however, that they have suppressed their feelings and may experience difficulties later. Evidence from longitudinal work suggests that between 10 and 24 percent of children report an increasing number of symptoms over a two-year period. In most cases, though, symptoms decrease over an eighteen-month period, with fears, nightmares, and anxiety disappearing first and anger and aggressiveness with peers and siblings tending to remain longer. Follow-up one to five years later reveals that a small percentage of children—6 to 19 percent—are abused again. This is lower than the reabuse rate for physical abuse and neglect.

Four mechanisms are believed to account for the variety of symptoms sexually abused children experience:[38] (1) traumatic sexualization (the child's learning inappropriate sexual responses as well as faulty beliefs and ideas about sexual behavior), (2) betrayal, (3) stigmatization, and (4) powerlessness. "Traumatic sexualization is the process by which a child's sexuality is shaped in developmentally inappropriate and interpersonally dysfunctional ways."[39] The child learns sexually inappropriate responses through rewards of attention and affection, or the child's anatomy is fetishized, or the child associates pain and fear with sexual activity. A child too young to understand the sexual implications of the activity may be less traumatized.

Children may experience the pain of betrayal, the feeling that someone they trusted or depended on has harmed them. Feelings of betrayal may come from the abuse itself or from the way the family responds to the abuse. When the adult is a trusted family member or when a family member knows about the abuse but does not act to protect the child, the child feels betrayed. The family's response to disclosure can also trigger a sense of betrayal. If the focus of concern is on the perpetrator or on the consequences to other family members, or if the child is blamed or rejected, then the abused child may feel betrayed.

Children also feel powerless and helpless when someone has completely disregarded their feelings and forced them to perform or experience unwanted acts. If the child is threatened or feels trapped or is not believed or supported at the time of disclosure, then the child experiences powerlessness. If the child can act to end the abuse and is supported, these feelings decrease.

When a child is stigmatized for the sexual activity, the experience of abuse then may become part of the child's self-image. Sometimes, the abuser blames the child or makes the child feel shameful for the activity. Others in the family or community may blame the child or feel the child is now "damaged goods" because he or she has

INTERVIEW
with Jill Waterman

Jill Waterman is an adjunct professor of psychology at the University of California in Los Angeles. She has coauthored Sexual Abuse of Young Children: Evaluation and Treatment *and* Behind the Playground Wall: Sexual Abuse in Preschools.

Parents worry that their children may be sexually abused. Do you think there is a greater risk for children, or is the increase in reports of child abuse a function of greater sensitivity to the problem?

I think the increase in the number of reports is due to the awareness of the problem and breaking the taboos about telling. There is more support for children who do tell.

Some parents fear sending their children to preschool because of the possibility of abuse there. Is this a valid concern?

For preschoolers, the likelihood of being abused in day care, including preschool, is less than the risk of being abused at home. Currently, 5.5 children per 10,000 are abused at day care, whereas 8.9 per 10,000 are abused at home. To reduce the risk at preschool, parents need to be sure that (1) they are welcome at the school at any time (there should be no time when they are barred from the school), (2) the school is an open environment where all personnel are easily observed (avoid schools with isolated areas or classrooms), (3) they can observe and feel confident about the way the adults in the school interact with children.

In the past, girls were more at risk for abuse than boys. Now, however, at the preschool level, the risk is about equal for boys and girls. Boys' experiences were underreported, perhaps because boys worried about being victims or being seen as wimpy, but now there is an increase in reporting of boys being abused. Still, in the latency and adolescent years, more girls than boys are abused.

There is more awareness now that women may also be molesters. When women are molesters, they are more likely to be part of a team with a man rather than be a solo molester—an aunt and an uncle, for example. Still the great majority of molesters are males.

There is a real increase in those identified as juvenile offenders or older children who molest other children. In almost all cases, they are repeating abuse done to them by adults.

How can a parent minimize the likelihood that the child will be abused?

First, teach children that their bodies are their own and no one has the right to touch them. Children have a right to stop whoever does touch or tries to touch their bodies. Second, teach children the concept of private parts of the body—that area that is covered by a bathing suit—and teach the concept of good touch and bad touch. When parents are comfortable with affection and have children who feel comfortable with giving and receiving affection, then children have a sense of what feels good and is good touch. Those children are more likely to identify bad touches quickly. Third, help children identify an adult they can go to if bad touching occurs. Teach them which adults can help—teachers, principals, group leaders. Role-play with them how they would tell someone.

Whom are children most likely to tell about abuse?

Whether the abuse is inside or outside the home, the child is most likely to tell the mother. An adolescent may tell a friend, who then tells her mother, who then reports. Most molesters never admit what they have done. Often, there is no way to prove it, because much abuse does not involve penile intercourse. Touching and oral sex may leave no evidence at all.

In the event a child does not tell a parent, what are signs by which a parent might tell whether a child has been sexually abused?

In most cases, there are no blatant behavioral indicators of sexual abuse. Rarely, the child may have genital bruising or bleeding. If the child begins sexual play with other children repeatedly, I would be concerned. If a child becomes preoccupied by masturbation to the extent of preferring to masturbate rather than interact with family or other children, I would also be concerned. More commonly, a sexually abused child may shows signs of distress that could be due to a variety of causes, not just abuse. Some of these distress signs are nightmares, sudden fears, withdrawal, or depression. However, these signs would alert a parent only to distress in a child, not necessarily sexual abuse.

If a child has been abused, how can parents act to minimize the impact of the event on the child?

The most important factor is how the parents respond. When parents believe the child and act to protect the child from the molester and get therapy and help for the child, then the child is best able to handle what has happened. When parents do not believe the child or support the perpetrator, the child does least well. This may seem counter to what you would expect, but mothers are more likely to believe a daughter if she is reporting the biological father than if she reports a stepfather. The explanation may be that the mothers have a greater stake in a relationship with a boyfriend or stepfather—it is a newer relationship—than with the biological father and are therefore more likely to support the newer man in their life.

A mother may not support her daughter because she has been abused herself and has not yet resolved that issue in her mind. To support her daughter, she would have to face what has happened to herself as well. Or the mother may have blocked from her mind the experience of her own abuse with only occasional flashbacks. Since these trigger a lot of internal conflict, she needs to deny her child's abuse.

The worst outcomes for abused children occur when a close family member has abused the child, so the child has difficulty developing trust in other relationships. There is mixed evidence concerning how much the severity (frequency, length of time, types of acts) of the abuse affects the outcome for the child. Sometimes, the severity

(continued)

INTERVIEW
with Jill Waterman *(continued)*

seems to have great impact, sometimes not. Still, the response of the parents is the most important determiner.

Research shows that sexual abuse of a child is a family trauma and has a major impact on parents. In a study of children abused outside the home, many couples found it difficult to have sex in the first nine months. The parents got images of the child in a sexual situation and could not continue. A small but significant number of couples developed alcohol and drug problems, and a significant number of parents reported they were depressed. They had a decreased trust in all societal institutions—the law, religions, schools, police, media. They lost their belief in a fair, just world.

In another follow-up study we did of children, 46 percent of abused children had scores in the clinical range on behavior problem checklists at the time of the disclosure. Five years later, only 17 percent had scores in that range. Remember, though, that only 2½ percent of a representative sample score in that range. All the abused children received treatment, but many still experienced internal distress several years later. These children are more likely to have symptoms of anxiety and somatic concerns than acting-out, aggressive problems.

What kinds of therapy are most helpful for children who have been abused?

Well, everyone in the family needs some form of individual therapy. Each member needs someone to talk to, to explain what the experience is like for them and to express his or her feelings. Groups are helpful for children of all ages, even for little children. Linda Damon of the San Fernando Valley Child Guidance Clinic developed parallel groups for mothers and children in therapy. Some therapists work with the mothers on a series of topics, and other therapists work with the children on the same topics. The therapists talk to the mothers about what to expect from the children on that week's topic. For example, on the topic that it is okay to say "No," the therapists tell mothers that this week they might expect the children to say a lot of no's. Moms, instead of getting angry at them, should help children see the situations in which it is appropriate to say "No" and those in which, like going to bed, you have to do it anyhow.

Groups for all children over age four have the advantage of reducing children's feelings of being weird. They don't feel like "damaged goods," because they see other children who have gone through the same thing and are doing well. So, the group helps to take the stigma away from being abused.

Family therapy has a place down the road, I think, only when the perpetrator admits what he has done and the family has made a decision to stay together. Then you really need family therapy.

How long does it take for the child to come to terms with the abuse?

It depends on what happened as well as the age of the child. Some people argue that if the child is really young, he or she does not truly understand the meaning of the events and is less likely to experience negative outcomes. The research data are mixed about the age at which children are most or least affected. As children get older—in midlatency—they may feel they are responsible for what happened, that it is their fault. Adolescents may feel guilty as well. Treatment helps them to deal with these feelings.

had such experiences. Keeping the abuse a secret may heighten the child's sense of shame. When a child learns that abuse happens to other children and that the children are not at fault, he or she may feel less stigmatized.

Traumatic sexualization can account for the increased sexualized behavior some children show. Stigmatization may account for depression and poor self-esteem. Powerlessness can be related to fears, feelings of dread, and a sense of imminent disaster; feelings of betrayal may account for the anger, aggressiveness, and antisocial acting out that abused children display.

An agreed-on finding is that the family plays a powerful role in helping the child deal with the effects of abuse.[40] Family support, particularly from the mother, is the key to the child's improvement. When mothers believe the child and take action to protect him or her, the child has the fewest symptoms over time. Conversely, a maltreating, dysfunctional family, unable to focus on the needs of the child, no doubt contributes to the impact of the abuse.

Court involvement may slow a child's recovery.[41] If the child has to make numerous court appearances, if the legal process extends over time, and if the child is afraid of the perpetrator, then negative effects and symptoms of the abuse may be prolonged. If the case is settled quickly and if the child has to testify only once and can testify by closed-circuit television, then risks to his or her recovery are reduced.

Recent studies of school-age children including adolescents suggest that abuse may push such children's development along distinctive pathways that can create additional problems.[42] Sexual abuse in childhood may result in reduced learning and in poorer social competence at school, in poorer overall academic performance, and in school avoidance. These behaviors have profound consequences for later occupational success. Similarly, problems with a negative self-image and self-concept can lead to a broad spectrum of problems for these children in schoolwork and with peers.

Interventions   What should be done when sexual abuse has occurred and has been reported? First, the security of the child should immediately be arranged. Second, the child should have the opportunity to vent with a therapist feelings of anger, fear, guilt, and shame about the act. Although some children may initially resist, an experienced therapist can encourage the child to talk and can offer reassurances that help the child deal with the feelings of betrayal and powerlessness. In play, the child regains feelings of personal power and confidence. Support of these feelings helps the child rebuild trust. The child learns to control his or her world again, and healing and growth proceed.[43]

Group therapy for children helps them deal with the experience of abuse, and participation in such a group may do even more than a therapist can to help children talk about and handle what has occurred and what they are feeling. For example, when a young girl hears that others have had a similar experience, when she realizes that she has not been singled out for some inexplicable reason, she may find it easier to accept her own victimization.

Family therapy helps all members cope with their reactions to the abuse. Parents and siblings may have strong feelings of sadness, anger, and guilt. They, too, need help in coming to terms with what has happened.

Physical Abuse

There is no commonly agreed-on definition of physical child abuse. In defining an act as physically abusive, consideration is given to the nature of the act, its intensity and frequency, its impact on the victim, the intent of the perpetrator, and community standards. Some acts are so clearly abusive that everyone would label them as such (for example, physical discipline that resulted in a broken bone or severe injury), and some acts are clearly not abusive (for example, talking to a child calmly and respectfully about a misdeed). Between the two extremes, abuse becomes a matter of interpretation. Some define abuse as any physical act that the recipient does not want; others, as extreme yelling and pushing; others, as any spanking; and still others, as any spanking that results in a bruise or injury. Robert Emery suggests that the same standards of violence that apply to acts between strangers in public be used to define violence in the home with family members.[44]

The question arises as to whether violence toward children is a single continuum, varying from no physical punishment at the low end, through varying degrees of abuse, to homicide at the high end.[45] If one believes in a single continuum, one would search for mechanisms that underlie all aspects of violence. Another theory is that physical punishment, mild abuse, severe abuse, and homicide represent different categories of behavior. The search, then, is for mechanisms that underlie each category and that may differ from category to category. Evidence from the Second National Family Violence Survey supports a distinction between physical punishment and severe abuse, because the predictors are somewhat different.[46]

Prevalence   Depending on their source, statistics on abuse vary. In a 1985 national telephone survey, the caregivers for 60 percent of children reported that they used physical punishment and minor violence (pushing, grabbing, shoving, and slapping) with children. The caregivers for 10 percent of children reported one or more instances of physical abuse or severe violence, consisting of kicking, biting, hitting with a fist or object, or burning.[47]

These were self-reports of punishment and abuse. In 1994, three million agency reports of suspected child abuse were made.[48] The number of reports of abuse to social agencies falls far below the self-report rate of 10 percent. Had caregivers for 10 percent of all children been reported as abusers, the number of reports would have been about six million. Between 1,200 and 5,000 children die from abuse each year.[49]

Certain characteristics of parent, child, and living setting are related to physical abuse. In the National Family Violence Survey, female caregivers most frequently reported physical punishment and minor violence, but there were no sex differences in reported physical abuse or severe violence.[50] Younger parents with many children were more likely than others to be abusive. Although abuse occurs at all socioeconomic levels, it was most frequently reported when fathers were unemployed or underemployed and when families lived below the poverty line. Abusive parents also were more likely to report drug use. For example, state agencies reported in a survey that substance abuse was the major issue in 68 percent of child protection cases being followed.[51]

Sibling violence is the most common form of victimization experienced by children.

Other studies have shown that 30 percent of parents who have been abused abuse children, but still, the majority who experienced abuse do not repeat it.[52] Compared with nonabusive parents, abusive parents are nonetheless more likely to form families in which spousal abuse and domestic violence occur.[53] More demanding and more negative with children, these parents tend to view child rearing as a burden. They believe in strict, firm, physical discipline. Although people have talked about the "abusive personality," research has not identified it. A maltreating individual is associated with being especially reactive to negative events and with having low self-esteem, poor impulse control, and impaired capacity for empathy.

Characteristics of the physically abused child include (1) age—most are between three and eight years of age, although an increasing number of teenagers are being reported as abused—and (2) sex, with boys being more often physically abused.[54] Any negative qualities of abused children prior to the abuse are thought to result from parents' generally negative child-rearing behaviors.

Abused parents who do not abuse their children have higher IQs, greater emotional stability, and less anxiety and depression than do abused parents who abuse their children. They are also more likely to have a supportive partner.[55]

Glenn Wolfner and Richard Gelles, who have studied family violence extensively, believe that violence to children is the result of parents' predispositions to violence in combination with stressful life conditions.[56] The potential for violence is present in everyone in varying degrees as a result of social learning. Those individuals who have learned to respond to stress with violence are those most likely to abuse children when they experience stressors such as job loss or financial problems.

Effects on Children   Children react to physical abuse in many ways. As we saw in discussing Cicchetti and Lynch's transactional/ecological model, five main areas of development are affected: attachment relationships, regulation of emotion, self-concept, peer relationships, and school adjustment.[57]

When children are maltreated in infancy and early childhood, they often develop insecure or disorganized/disoriented attachments. In one study, 80 percent of maltreated infants were classified as disorganized/disoriented in their attachments to their mother, compared with 20 percent of nonmaltreated infants. Further, these disorganized attachments were stable, as 90 percent of these infants were classified in the same way a year later. When children are between ages seven and thirteen at the time of abuse, about 30 percent report confused patterns of relationships to their mother, so age appears to reduce the impact on this attachment.

Abused children's internal working models of relationships based on experiences with abusive parents may generalize to other relationships, leading these children to have negative views of how others will treat them and how reliable and predictable others are. Thus, not surprisingly, abused children often have problems with peers. Some abused children are fearful and insecure with peers, often withdrawing from or avoiding them. Others are physically and verbally aggressive and find it difficult to be positive and considerate.

Children's ability to regulate their feelings affects all aspects of their functioning. Abused children have difficulty controlling their emotions, in part because these emotions are so intense. The children are likely to feel chronic stress, anxiety, depression, and helplessness. They tend to be inflexible and inappropriate in expressing their feelings. They also have difficulty in communicating their feelings verbally and in identifying the feelings of others. They lack the cognitive control of feelings that children their age usually have. Peer difficulties result as well, because peers find it hard to be with children who lack control of their feelings.

In view of their poor attachment relationships and intense amounts of uncontrolled feelings, it is not surprising that abused children often have unrealistic self-concepts. When young, they may inflate their sense of competence, feeling overly confident, but as they get older, they describe themselves as less able than and less accepted by others.

Emery states that it is not clear whether the many symptoms come from the abuse itself or from family interactions leading up to the abuse.[58] He notes that angry episodes, even those not involving the child, distress the child (see Chapter 4). Children's distress motivates them to get involved in parental conflicts in order to end them. Because their misbehavior distracts parents from their quarrels, children tend to repeat misbehavior to stop conflicts even if doing so causes them to become victims.

Despite the abuse they experience, a sizeable number of maltreated children develop competence and caring and are resilient and resourceful in surmounting problems. The most competent and best-functioning children are those who have developed ego control, ego resilience, and self-esteem.[59] The capacity for a more reserved, controlled, and rational way of interacting with others predicts overall competence in maltreated children. This factor does not predict competence in non-maltreated children, perhaps because control is not as central to competence in nonmaltreated children.

Interventions   Just as with child sexual abuse, there are two forms of intervention for physical abuse: (1) providing security and safety for the child and (2) getting psychological services. There is some indication that, at least with spousal abuse, having the perpetrator arrested prevents recurrence more effectively than mediating the dispute informally or having the perpetrator leave the property for forty-eight hours. In child abuse cases, children deserve at least as much physical protection as they would get if a stranger attacked them. Gelles believes some parents are so abusive on a single occasion that family reunification should never be considered.[60]

Physically abused children need the same form of therapy that sexually abused children do. They need the opportunity to vent and understand their intense feelings, to learn to express them appropriately, and to control them when they are intense. They need help forming positive, trusting relationships with both adults and peers, and they need help in developing the self-esteem that will enable them to explore their world actively.

Interventions are also directed toward the abusing parent. When appropriate, perpetrators are referred to abuse treatment programs. They are taught parenting skills and other ways to manage their anger. Sometimes, home visitors are sent to teach and monitor parenting skills. In a sense, these interventions help provide the community resources that parents had earlier failed to to access.

Neglect

Although families are charged with caring for and protecting children, some do not perform these tasks. Neglect is defined as a parent's or caregiver's act of omission that involves refusal or delay in meeting health needs; needs for food, clothing, and shelter; psychological needs for affection, attention, and supervision; and educational needs.[61]

Prevalence   The National Incidence Study of 1994 found that neglect was the most frequent form of child maltreatment and estimated that 879,000 children were victims of neglect in that year.[62] Although prevalent, neglect is less often studied than are other forms of abuse. As such, less is known about neglect and the children who experience it than is known about physical and sexual abuse.

Child neglect occurs most frequently in the context of poverty, even after taking into account the fact that inadequate care due to limited resources is not considered neglect.[63] When families are poor, they lack health-care benefits and face increased hazards such as lead exposure and dangerous neighborhoods, as well as poor educational facilities. Nevertheless, most poor families do not neglect their children. Neglect is not associated with any racial group when socioeconomic status is controlled for, but it is associated with the stress of unemployment, illness, and frequent moves.

A second major family risk factor for neglect is parental substance abuse.[64] In one review of studies, substance and alcohol abuse figured in 80 to 90 percent of the cases of physical abuse and neglect. A question has been raised as to whether mothers should be cited as physically abusing or neglecting their babies when they engage in prenatal drug use.

Few child characteristics have been consistently associated with neglect. We do know, however, that neglect occurs primarily in young children. In one study, one-third of reports concerned children under four years of age.

Effects on Children   Neglected children have a greater likelihood of attachment problems, low self-esteem, increased dependency, and anger, compared with physically abused or nonmaltreated children.[65] Neglected children also have more language problems and slower academic and cognitive development. They are often passive and withdrawn in social behavior. Longitudinal follow-ups of neglected children indicate that they are at risk for delinquent behavior. Physical and medical problems are also associated with neglect; half of the fatalities in swimming pools and fires are attributed to lack of appropriate supervision.

Interventions   Interventions focus on two areas: prevention of neglect and care of the child once neglect has occurred.[66] Many of the interventions described here apply to the prevention and treatment of physical abuse as well. Prevention includes increased services to families at risk during infancy and early childhood to (1) provide information and access to additional sources of assistance such as home health nurses, (2) model appropriate care, and (3) connect families to community services. Community services include youth athletic programs and after-school and church programs that help children develop feelings of competence and self-esteem; community programs aimed at adults include parenting programs and parent support groups.

Once neglect has occurred, there must be provision of care for the child, either through increased services to the family in the home or through the removal of the child from the family. One study of suspected neglect found that one-third of children could be cared for in the home with increased money for food and housing.[67] When neglect occurs as a result of substance abuse, however, the child may have to be removed from the home.

Douglas Besharov, the first director of the National Center for Child Abuse and Neglect, has made several recommendations that center on two areas in need of reform: the reporting process and the child protective decision-making process.[68] He believes that, first, the child abuse laws need to be clarified to state specifically the parenting behaviors that require reporting. At present, the laws are so vague and so many reports are made that endless hours go into investigating cases that turn out not to involve abuse or neglect. Second, once laws are clarified, all professionals making such reports should be educated so that they can make accurate reports. Third, all the reports must be screened carefully so that all are acted on in appropriate ways. Finally, those individuals and agencies making reports need feedback about their accuracy. Although Besharov does not believe that better reporting and more realistic and long-term responses to neglect and abuse cases will eliminate child abuse deaths, he does believe that there will be no progress without these kinds of reforms.

Leroy Pelton, the director of the University of Nevada School of Social Work, strongly urges separating the investigative work from the preventive and supportive services of welfare agencies. This would enable parents to come for help and support in times of need without fearing that children will be removed from the home. Michael Weber has served as the associative director of the National Committee to Prevent Child Abuse and as president of the National Association of Public Child Welfare Administrators. He believes that no one agency can take responsibility for preventing and treating maltreatment. He recommends that partnership-oriented, community-based child protection networks be formed to focus on (1) the prevention of problems, (2) early intervention when trouble first starts, (3) the provision of treatment and services to families, and(4) sufficient treatment so children do not grow up to repeat the maltreatment.[69]

All these suggestions provide basic ways maltreatment can be prevented, more quickly identified, and treated. Both preventing maltreatment and providing services for maltreated children and their families require clear definitions and the resources and personnel of all the community agencies involved.

Other Forms of Personal Abuse

Emotional abuse includes terrorizing, exploiting, and missocializing children.[70] Defined as acts of omission or commission that damage the behavioral, cognitive, affective, and physical functioning of the child, emotional abuse is hard to prove. Emotional abuse is associated with a child's withdrawal, loss of self-esteem, aggressiveness, and failure to trust others.

Moral-legal-educational maltreatment involves failure to help the child develop appropriate social and moral values. Behaviors include such acts as exposing the child to illegal drugs or giving them to the child, involving the child in illegal activity, and failing to intervene when the child is involved in such activity.

Because the majority of abused children experience more than one form of abuse, pure subtypes of abuse rarely exist, but some differences among parents who commit different types of abuse are beginning to be identified.[71] For example, physically abusive parents may be more likely to have insecure adult attachments to their own parents so that they dismiss or deny painful experiences and so are less likely to appreciate their own child's pain. Neglectful parents appear to have insecure adult attachments in which they are preoccupied with feelings, making them less available to monitor and care for children.

Community Violence

We have seen that in any form, exposure to unresolved anger and aggression harms children, whether they witness it or experience it. Children do not face aggression only in their personal lives. Our society has become increasingly violent, with many children exposed to traumatic events. Although a large proportion of violence occurs in lower socioeconomic areas, people are exposed to violence in restaurants, schools, and middle-class communities. No child is immune to the effects of community violence. Even if it does not touch a child personally, he or she may be acquainted with someone who has had a family member die or experience harm from violence.

Prevalence   Children are more likely to witness violence outside the home than to experience it. In a study in a low-income, moderately violent neighborhood in Washington, D.C., 19 percent of children in grades one and two had been physically threatened, chased, mugged, or shot, and 61 percent had witnessed such acts as muggings, stabbings, and illegal drug use, not once but several times per year.[72] By grades five and six, 32 percent of children had been victims, and 72 percent had witnessed violence.

When questioned, older children reported that none of the victimizations took place at home. Nonetheless, 48 percent occurred near home, and 55 percent took place at or near school. Thus, the violence the children witnessed took place in their immediate environment. Although it occurred outside the home, children knew about two-thirds of the perpetrators; the rest were strangers to them.

Parents report that their children experience or witness less violence than the children report. However, children may not tell parents all they see. Anecdotal reports suggest that parents may discourage children from talking about the violence they see.[73] This is unfortunate in that it prevents children from dealing with their feelings and parents from helping their children cope with the violence.

Effects on Children   Exposure to community violence by itself does not predict personal problems and school difficulties. Even in combination with many other stressors, such as low income, many family moves, and the father's absence, it does not predict difficulty.[74] To have a negative effect, community violence must impact family life. When this violence erodes the safety and stability of the child's home, such as when drug dealing and guns are in the home, then the child is affected. Thus, the child experiences community violence at the level of the microsystem—in day-to-day interactions with his or her parents. When parents can somehow prevent the stressors from disrupting the stability of the home and not allow the violence in the community to influence parent-child relationships, children can then function successfully. John Richters and Pedro Martinez write,

> It seems reasonable to assume that family stability and safety are ultimately the products of choices made by children's caretakers about how they will cope with and/or react to the circumstances within which they find themselves. We have much to learn about how, why, and in what ways, such choices are made, but in advance of those answers it seems self-evident that these are factors over which caretakers have and must exercise control.[75]

Children exposed to community violence develop many of the symptoms of children who have been physically or sexually abused. They have difficulty sleeping, remembering, and concentrating, and they exhibit anxious attachment to parents (not wanting them to leave), aggressive play, severe limitation of activities and exploration, and regressive behavior.[76] Lenore Terr describes the denial and numbing children use to block out frightening reality.[77] Children also experience feelings of grief and loss when a significant loved one dies as a result of violence.

All these reactions make it hard for children to develop intellectually and socially. They come to expect violence and develop a sense of fatalism about their lives, a feeling that they have no future. They believe that planning is unimportant because they could be crippled or killed before their plans are fulfilled.

Even in adverse circumstances, a significant number of children function well at school and appear to have few behavior problems. Such children are active individuals who seek to surmount obstacles. The main agent for helping them is their family and the stability it provides.[78] A second source of help is their own internal sense that life can improve, that they can influence what happens to them and make life better in the future.[79] Children who live in difficult circumstances but still maintain positive expectations of the future are more successful later on. But again, the immediate family members do the most to help children build positive expectations about the future. James Garbarino and his colleagues summarize the parents' role and its dangers:

> If parents, or other significant caregivers, can sustain a strong attachment to their children, can maintain a positive sense of self, and can have access to basic resources, children will manage, although it may be at great cost to the psychic and physical welfare of those parents, who may be "used up" caring for their children.[80]

Coping Resources   Several factors influence how children cope with violence.[81] Intelligence, self-confidence, self-esteem, sociability, an easygoing attitude, and affectionate nature all increase children's coping ability. Such children demand little, yet they relate positively and happily to others and tend to receive support. Environmental factors include the presence of at least one stable emotional relationship with a caregiver who serves as a model of coping, as well as social relationships outside the family with relatives and family friends. The community can give support in many ways; friends, neighbors, teachers, and members of religious groups can provide support and encourage the competence of parents and children.

School is a major refuge for children who confront difficult experiences. After the family, school is the most important social institution in children's lives. Many resilient children find a source of self-esteem and competence in school activities. They make friends with and get support from schoolmates and from teachers who take an interest in them.

In *Children in Danger,* James Garbarino and his associates describe the schools as a major unit of intervention to counteract the community violence in children's lives.[82] He outlines a school-based intervention program in which teachers form close emotional attachments with students to promote their development. The researchers believe that these relationships serve as the basis for learning in all areas.

Teachers and programs provide structure and control for these children, who adopt the values, behavior, and attitudes of a significant other person.

In Garbarino's plan, day care centers can be included in programs to reach children below school age. An attachment teacher is assigned to every six or seven students, and a consistent substitute attachment and subgroup are assigned to each child. Children have an unvarying placement in small groups. Formal teaching programs stimulate the child's curiosity and level of development.

The organized school environment, with familiar teachers and programs, provides security and predictability in a changing world. By taking courses in child development and in understanding children's reactions to stress, violence, and loss, teachers are specially trained to work with these children. Teachers remain available to students who exhibit fluctuating or changing emotions and help the children deal with them.

Therapy can help children cope with their emotional reactions to trauma.[83] All major personality shifts resulting from trauma require treatment. Such personality changes occur in almost all physically and sexually abused children, as well as those who experience some form of trauma.

Parents should arrange for psychiatric treatment for a child as soon after a trauma as possible. If several children are involved, participants can be seen in a minimarathon group session with a highly trained professional. When each member shares his or her experiences, the possibility of anyone's denying the situation (and thus prolonging traumatization) is lessened. Schools serve as the familiar setting appropriate for such group sessions. If a family has been traumatized, then it can be treated as a unit. However, family therapy is not recommended when a parent has physically or sexually abused a child, because the child is not really free to express anger in the presence of the abuser.

Behavioral therapy is useful for children who have developed fears as a result of the trauma. Deconditioning can supplement individual treatment designed to deal with the emotional reactions, but behavioral therapy by itself is limited.

A person should begin treatment as soon as possible after the trauma. However, treatment is useful any time a person recognizes that he or she is suffering the effects of a trauma, even if therapy cannot reverse all the effects of the experience.

Parents want to know what to do to prevent violence and trauma in their children's lives. Nothing can completely prevent violence, but children who receive support are most likely to recover from the experience.

Managing Fears of National Violence   Since September 11, 2001, Americans have lived with the fears of possible terrorist killings through bombs, biochemical agents released in the air or in the mail, and shootings. These fears have been heightened as the nation has engaged in war overseas. At the national level, we are now experiencing the ongoing fears people in inner cities have experienced for years, and the research on handling fear and stress in that situation can be applied to our present national tragedy.

Parents want to know what to do to help their children in these scary times. Parents, as we have learned, are the most important figures in helping children cope. Here, as well as at the chapter's end, are suggestions parents can use.[84]

1. Examine and manage their own fears, because children model their responses on their parents' behavior.

2. Turn off the television and radio when their children are awake, to reduce the stress of repeated exposure to visual images and discussion of the tragedies.

3. Listen and observe children to determine their level of stress as reflected in eating, sleeping, and level of energy. Parents should respond to children's questions and concerns in a supportive way.

4. Give honest statements of reassurance—saying they and the government are working to keep children safe, not promising that nothing bad will happen.

5. Respond in age-appropriate ways when talking to children. Preschoolers do not need the level of information and discussion useful for older children.

6. Maintain daily activities and routines, as familiar patterns of behavior provide reassurance and feelings of security.

7. Have a friend's phone number outside the community whom all family members can call to report safety and whereabouts in the event of a community disaster.

8. Appreciate and comment on the good things in life today—for example, the family's being together, the closeness with friends. Feelings of enjoyment provide a reserve of strength to deal with stress when it comes.

9. Read stories about the country's history that inspire and give confidence that we can survive and flourish in the face of stuggle and adversity—getting to the Pacific coast from St. Louis, getting to the moon, surviving the battles of the Revolution and of the War of 1812, when the White House burned.

10. Volunteer with children in some activity to make a part of the world a better place. We cannot directly influence those who might wish to hurt us now, but we can increase the pleasure and joy some people get out of life.

Common Themes in Abuse and Violence

Several general themes emerge in the study of abuse and violence. First, no one set of circumstances leads inevitably to abuse and violence; rather, many risk factors increase the likelihood of abuse and violence and increase the traumatic effects on children.

Second, children respond in many ways to trauma, and several different kinds of trauma lead to similar problems in children. For example, all forms of abuse are associated with difficulties in emotional control, in relationships with adults and peers, in self-concept, and in school adjustment. Further, problems resemble those seen in children when their parents lose their jobs or suffer from prolonged unemployment, get divorced, or remarry and blend families. Sexualized behavior seems to be the one form of reaction that is most frequently linked with sexual abuse.

A question arises as to whether abuse and violence contribute significant difficulties beyond those related to low income or negative life stress. A recent study statistically disentangled the contributions of physical abuse, low income, and life stress.[85] Indeed, physical abuse made a significant contribution to children's behavior problems beyond that related to economic disadvantage and stress as a result of negative life events.

Physical abuse was associated with additional problems in relationships with peers, and peer problems occurred after physical abuse, regardless of the sex, socioeconomic status, or stress level of the abused person. The abusive experience in the family appears to lead to distortions in how people relate to each other and what is required to get along. As noted earlier, this is especially sad because children then lose a major source of support in coping with other problems. Other stressors such as low income and negative life events produce few changes in self-perceptions or behavior problems unless they are unusually severe. Therefore, other difficulties in life appear to produce less marked changes in children's moods and behaviors. Abuse and violence damage children's trust in their peers and decrease their capacity for positive relationships, thus removing an important resource for such children.

In all these difficult situations, the family remains the main source of support for children. Agencies and therapies can help, but it is individuals who are close and have a sense of the child's individuality who are truly helpful. If parents cannot do this, other relatives or family friends, teachers, or day care workers can step in.

Commitment to Provide Safety

In New York, New Jersey, Florida, and California, the tragic deaths, disappearances, and injuries of children in the care of state agencies after they have been removed from their families because of neglect or abuse have raised concerns about the ability of state agencies to step in and protect children, as is their mandate.

New York City Commissioner for the Administration for Children's Services, William C. Bell, described the changes the city made following the 1996 death of Elisa Izquierdo who, despite many reports to agencies and the involvement of welfare personnel, was beaten and abused for most of her six years and was finally killed by her mother. The city reorganized services to improve its care of children, but he wrote that there is no quick fix to solve problems: "Lasting results came only with deliberate measures."[86]

Reform required the cooperation of city government leaders, child welfare agencies, court services, and union leaders. The number and education of case workers increased. Training programs and merit-based pay raises were established. Close collaboration with police and legal agencies enabled case workers to deal quickly with fatalities and severe trauma from abuse. Close collaboration with neighborhood agencies and the foster care system made it possible for all individuals involved in a case to meet within seventy-two hours of the child's being taken into foster care. Parents received parenting training in their homes.

These changes have led to a reduction in cases from twenty-six per worker to eleven, and in the number of children in foster care from 41,000 in 1996 to about 26,000 in 2002.

Political will, competent leadership, level heads, and a clear plan of action were what were needed for sustained, lasting changes in children's services here in New York City. A commitment to engage in a long-term strategy—and not a knee-jerk response—is what can turn tragedies into the catalysts needed for successful change.[87]

PREVENTION OF VIOLENCE

In a chapter concerning the neurobiological effects of experiencing and witnessing trauma, Bruce Perry writes,

> The ultimate solution to the problems of violence, whether from the remorseless predator or the reactive, impulsive youth, is primary prevention. Our society is creating violent children and youth at a rate far faster than we could ever treat, rehabilitate, or even lock them away. No single intervention strategy will solvethese heterogeneous problems. No set of intervention strategies will solve these transgenerational problems. In order to solve the problems of violence, we need to transform our culture.[88]

Where can we start? Katherine Christoffel describes the necessity of viewing violence in the form of firearm injuries and deaths as a public health problem rather than a criminal one.[89] Once we do that, the main goal becomes decreasing injuries, and we can search for a variety of strategies to do this.

In describing how we reduced motor vehicle injury deaths, Christoffel illustrates how we might reduce violence. In the late 1960s, motor vehicle injury deaths were redefined as a public health problem, and a variety of actions were taken to decrease them. Car manufacturers improved the safety of cars, passenger restraints were developed, road construction improved, and changes in the driving laws to increase penalties for driving while intoxicated and failure to use seat belts were passed. The number of deaths dropped from 55,000 in 1968 to 45,000 per year in 1990, though the number of cars and drivers had increased.

Using a public health model, one can make the public aware of the risk we all face from firearms. While deaths from motor vehicles are dropping, deaths from firearms are rising. In 1995, 36,000 individuals died from injuries caused by firearms and 43,360 from injuries caused by automobile accidents.[90] It is estimated that in the near future, deaths from firearms will exceed deaths from car accidents.

By recognizing the lethality of guns and their risk to the general population, the public can shift the focus from crime, law enforcement, and civil liberties to a focus on preventing and reducing injuries and deaths from firearms. The emphasis is then placed on having handgun-free homes and neighborhoods, restricting handgun sales and ownership, and developing other self- and home-protection devices. For example, we can emphasize the safe storage of guns and ammunition in locked and separated areas, push for firearm manufacturers to install safety locks on guns, and urge state representatives to pass laws making owners responsible for others' use of their guns.

Although we have taken some action to regulate the purchase of guns, we have paid little attention to gun manufacturers and distributors. Licenses to distribute handguns are cheap and can be obtained through the mail. In 1990, there were more firearm licenses than gas stations in the United States. Many of these distributors, unknown to local officials, operate out of their homes. Thus, their compliance with existing laws may be minimal and could no doubt be improved if all distributors were known.

Another form of prevention is to encourage health professionals to advise and counsel all families on the danger of handguns and the need to have them locked away. They can track the number of injuries and deaths from handguns carefully and educate the public on the importance of reforms to control handgun use and storage.

We can also work to change the content of the media.[91] Research indicates that media violence contributes to violent behavior in three ways: (1) it increases aggressive behavior and willingness to use violence, (2) it desensitizes viewers so that they accept violence as a normal part of life, and (3) it creates a belief in a "mean world syndrome" that makes people more fearful of the world because they see it as dangerous.

John Murray suggests that families need to act in three ways to counteract media violence.[92] First, they need to change their behavior at home. So that children can become informed consumers of television fare, parents need to watch television with children and talk about what they see. Parents and children can learn from each other in these discussions. Second, parents can lobby for the inclusion of media literacy courses, so, again, children learn critical-viewing habits. Third, parents can begin to lobby the government and industries to make children's television less violent. For example, they might lobby the industry to reduce the amount of time allocated to violent programs during prime time. There are encouraging signs that the chairman of the Federal Communications Commission is ready to make changes. These are just a few of the actions that parents can pursue as they seek to make the world a safer place for children.

THE CHALLENGE MODEL

Therapy can help children deal with the effects of certain traumatic events and troubled family situations. Some therapists have become concerned, however, that certain forms of intervention so emphasize the pain and damaging effects of these difficulties that children and adults believe they are doomed to emotionally impoverished lives as a result of the trauma.

Steven Wolin and Sybil Wolin term this the *damage model* of human development, in that it focuses on the harmful effects produced by traumas; therapy in this model can only help individuals understand the damage and how it occurred. Drawing on clinical insights and on the research of such people as Ruth Smith and Emmy Werner (see the interview with Emmy Werner in Chapter 4), Wolin and Wolin have developed a *challenge model* of development.[93] Although adversity brings stress, harm, and vulnerability to the individual, Wolin and Wolin believe it also stimulates the person to branch out, to take measures to protect himself or herself and find other sources of strength that promote development. So, the individual

Children cope best with community disasters when family members are supportive.

experiences pain but develops resiliencies that can limit the pain and promote accomplishment and satisfaction.

In their book *The Resilient Self,* Wolin and Wolin identify seven resiliencies that help individuals rebound in the face of difficult circumstances:

1. *Insight*—[developing] the habit of asking tough questions and giving honest answers
2. *Independence*—drawing boundaries between yourself and your troubled parents; keeping emotional and physical distance while satisfying the demands of your conscience
3. *Relationships*—[building] intimate and fulfilling ties to other people that balance a mature regard for your own needs with empathy and the capacity to give to someone else.
4. *Initiative*—taking charge of problems; exerting control; [acquiring] a taste for stretching and testing yourself in demanding tasks
5. *Creativity*—imposing order, beauty, and purpose on the chaos of your troubling experiences and painful feelings
6. *Humor*—finding the comic in the tragic
7. *Morality*—[developing] an informed conscience that extends your wish for a good personal life to all of humankind[94]

Their book describes the many ways resiliencies grow in childhood, adolescence, and adulthood and offers an optimistic approach that encourages survivors of traumas and difficult childhood experiences to review their lives in terms of the strengths they have developed. As a result, people experience pride in their ability to overcome hardships—whether as a result of violence or abuse or natural disasters such as floods and earthquakes—and confidence in their capacity to make further changes as needed. In focusing on pain and the sources of pain in the past, the damage model tends to discourage individuals, because the past cannot be changed and the pain undone. In contrast, the challenge model asserts that life can be satisfying and productive even with the scars of the past.

PRACTICAL QUESTION: HOW CAN WE KEEP CHILDREN SAFE?

As children spend more time away from parents and home, going to and from school or to friends' homes, parents become concerned about their safety. They want to help children be independent and safe in the world, yet they do not want to frighten them and make them afraid of strangers and new experiences. Grace Hechinger, an education consultant, has interviewed police officials, school safety officials, individuals involved in neighborhood safety programs, and victims of crime and assaults.[95] From this research, she has organized information to help parents prepare their children to be safe as they spend more time on their own.

Fostering children's awareness of danger, sense of caution, and preparedness for unsafe situations does not mean making children live in fear. Children can learn that even though most people in the world are good and helpful and most situations are safe, some people and experiences are not, and everyone must learn to protect himself or herself from dangers that arise. Parents can help by putting this knowledge in perspective for children. Life has always involved danger of some sort, and many objects or experiences that are positive also have dangerous aspects. Cars are useful—they get us to work, to stores, to hospitals—but they can be dangerous if they hit us while we are crossing the street. The answer lies not in eliminating cars, because before we had cars, there were dangers from horses and horse-drawn vehicles. The solution is to take precautions to minimize the dangers and enjoy the benefits.

Families need to develop a set of instructions, to be discussed and revised as necessary, regarding certain dangerous situations. A one-time discussion is not enough; parents must periodically review instructions with children. Children can learn these safety rules gradually—for example, when and where they may go alone or what they should do if bothered by someone on the street or in a store, even when parents are nearby. Learning safety rules can become as natural to children as learning to brush their teeth. Parents emphasize teaching children the skills to deal with the environment, to make them competent and independent.

Although parents worry that talk of possible fearful events will damage the child, the risks that come with ignorance are much greater. Parents can begin with simple discussions of traffic safety—where, when, and how to cross the street. They can move from that topic to others of importance for the child. Television may prompt some discussion. Hechinger recommends playing the game "What If?" Parents ask a variety of questions and give children chances to develop solutions to difficult situ-

■ **TABLE 15-1**
SOME "WHAT IF?" QUESTIONS FOR YOUNG CHILDREN

Parents ask children what they would do if the following situations arose. If children give the wrong answers, parents can calmly tell them more practical alternative responses. What if:

1. We were separated in a shopping center, in the movies, at the beach?

2. You were lost in a department store, in the park, at a parade?

3. A stranger offered you candy or presents to leave the playground?

4. A stranger wanted you to get into his car?

5. A stranger started fussing with your clothing?

6. Your friends wanted to play with matches?

7. Someone you did not know asked [for] your name and phone number?

Grace Hechinger, *How to Raise a Street-Smart Child* (New York: Ballantine Books, 1984), 59.

ations. Parents should not be upset if their children's initial answers are impractical, because they can guide their children in learning more reasonable responses. Table 15-1 gives some sample "What If?" questions.

Parents should have clear safety rules on (1) behavior for a fire at home, (2) traffic behavior, whether on foot or on a bicycle, (3) boundaries within which the child can come and go freely and outside of which an adult or parent must be present, (4) behavior in public with strangers, (5) behavior at home if strangers telephone or come to the house, (6) behavior when the child is a victim or witness of muggings by peers or adults, and (7) behavior when sexual misconduct occurs.

If children are victimized—their bike is stolen, their money is taken, a stranger approaches them—parents' reactions can help speed the healing process. When parents listen to children's reactions and help children take constructive action, such as notifying the police, they help children cope. When parents' responses are exaggerated ("This is horrible!") or detached ("I cannot deal with this"), children get no help in coping with their feelings. If they cannot talk about how they feel, they will find it difficult to work out their feelings. Active listening and simple I-messages ("If that happened to me, I'd be really upset") give children a chance to say what the experience meant to them. Sometimes, children need to describe the event several times. Each time, more details emerge, as do more feelings. Gradually, after the incident, children regain their self-confidence. If a child's eating, sleeping, or play habits change or if marked changes in schoolwork or personality continue for some time, professional help should be sought.

An important step in promoting children's safety is working with people in the community. Developing community awareness and programs gives everyone a positive feeling of working together, which does much to banish fear. Promoting public safety programs with school and police officials and organizing block-parent programs to help children in the neighborhood are useful steps. In block-parent programs, one house in the neighborhood is designated as a house where children can come if they need help or reassurance when no one is home.

Family members grow stronger when they face problems and work together to deal with them. Sense of community grows when families and agencies cooperate to make the environment safe for children.

MAIN POINTS

Victimization

- can be classified as pandemic, acute, or extraordinary
- is more common for children than for adults
- occurs mainly because children are more dependent on adults, are less able to protect themselves, and have less control of associates and surroundings

An ecological/transactional model of community violence and child maltreatment

- focuses on risk and protective factors
- describes characteristics of the child, parent, and environment that increase the risk of violence
- describes violence at several ecological levels: the macrosystem, the exosystem, the microsystem, and the ontogenic, or personal, level
- emphasizes that factors at different levels interact to increase the likelihood of violence
- has implications for types of intervention at the various ecological levels

Exposure to family violence

- occurs in many different kinds of families
- affects a child's physical, psychological, and cognitive functioning
- requires interventions aimed at helping the nonabusing parent as well as the child
- requires organized community interventions to prevent family violence

Sexual abuse in childhood

- is experienced by one in four girls and one in six boys by the age of eighteen
- affects children in different ways, depending on the specific act, its duration, its frequency, and the identity of the perpetrator
- appears most traumatic when it involves someone close who frequently engages in forceful sexual acts of penetration over a long time period and when mothers provide little support
- results in behavior changes such as sexualized behavior and changes in emotional regulation, in attachment relations, in self-concept, in relations with peers, and in school adjustment
- does not always produce symptoms; about one-third to one-half of children show no symptoms at the time they are studied

Sexual child abuse victims
- require protection from the abuser
- can profit from individual, group, and family therapy

Physical child abuse
- is difficult to define precisely
- results from a variety of factors, including characteristics of the parents, the family, and the environment
- is learned in the context of the family
- results in a wide variety of symptoms relating to self-concept, emotional control, relations with peers and adults, and adjustment in school
- creates victims who can nevertheless be resourceful and surmount problems
- requires therapy for the victim, perpetrator, and family
- may be so severe on a single occasion that the child should not live with the abuser again

Neglect
- is a common but little-studied form of abuse
- occurs in families with other risk factors such as poverty and substance abuse
- can be prevented with increased services to children and families
- requires community-wide programs to prevent it and treat its victims

Community violence
- affects all children but mostly those in poor neighborhoods
- is more often witnessed than experienced
- has a negative impact when it erodes the safety and stability of family life
- results in many symptoms that hinder children's development
- requires interventions at the community level to decrease the violence and provide support for children who experience such violence
- creates effects that parents and individual, group, and family therapy can mitigate

The challenge model
- focuses on strengths people develop to cope with negative family experiences or other traumas
- identifies seven resiliencies: insight, independence, relationships, initiative, creativity, humor, and morality
- presents an optimistic view of people's capacity to create satisfying lives despite the scars of painful experiences

Keeping children safe
- requires that parents teach children about potential dangers and ways to minimize them

- requires that parents teach children coping techniques for dangerous situations
- means that parents and society as a whole have to work to provide a safer community for everyone

EXERCISES

1. Imagine that a close friend told you that her four-year-old had just showed her how a twenty-five-year-old male relative had touched her genitals. The daughter said he told her it was a secret between them, but she decided to tell her mother because they do not keep secrets from each other. How would you advise your friend to help her daughter after she has reported the event to the authorities? What would you advise her to do to help herself?

2. Divide into groups of four and describe the general information you would choose to include in an eight-session parenting course for men and women who have physically abused their children. Share your group's results with the entire class. What elements were chosen by only one or two groups? Combine the best information from all groups and come up with one eight-session program. If possible, compare it with a program offered in your area, such as Parental Stress.

3. Divide into groups of four and describe a parenting program for adolescent mothers and fathers to prevent physical child abuse. Is it identical to the program designed for those who have already committed abuse? In what ways does it differ?

4. Imagine that you had unlimited money to go into a low-income housing project in a high-crime area. What kinds of programs would you devise to help children cope with the violence they witness around them?

5. Think about what you most feared as a young child. What would you tell a nine-year-old brother or sister who was afraid of being kidnapped on the street? Of experiencing an earthquake or hurricane or flood? Of being shot?

ADDITIONAL READINGS

Adams, Caren, and Fay, Jennifer. *Helping Your Child Recover from Sexual Abuse.* Seattle: University of Washington Press, 1992.

Garbarino, James, Dubrow, Nancy, Kostelny, Kathleen, and Pardo, Carole. *Children in Danger.* San Francisco: Jossey-Bass, 1992.

Kraizer, Sherryll. *The Safe Child Book.* New York: Fireside, 1996.

Melton, Gary B., and Barry, Frank D., eds. *Protecting Children from Abuse and Neglect.* New York: Guilford Press, 1994.

Osofsky, Joy D., ed. *Children in a Violent Society.* New York: Guilford, 1997.

EPILOGUE

We have looked at parenting behaviors in many different circumstances. We have discussed parenting children of all ages living in families of diverse values and goals and in diverse family structures with one or two parents, who are sometimes of the same sex. We have looked at parenting in ordinary times and in times of special stress such as divorce or trauma. No matter what the age of the child; no matter whether the child is a biological or an adopted child, a child with special gifts or special needs, or a child with the usual gifts and needs; no matter whether parents are married, single, or remarried—three basic principles stand out. The first two tell parents what to do, and the third tells parents what not to do.

The principles are straightforward. First, give children positive attention. Second, provide positive support through modeling, guidance, and appropriate consequences. Third, deal with unresolved anger and hostility directed at the child or expressed to or about others in the child's presence. The persistence of such feelings destroys children's good feelings and their effectiveness in the world.

The three principles are much easier to state than to carry out. In the hustle and the hassles of everyday life, finding time to give children the positive attention that increases their self-confidence and good feelings is difficult. Positive attention does not mean accepting and approving all behaviors. It does mean that parents view children in terms of their special qualities and strengths, and that parents maintain their positive view of children at the same time that they help them make needed changes through modeling and active teaching.

We all know that anger and irritations are part of life, and by themselves are not damaging. In fact, they can stimulate positive action to resolve the situation that produced the feelings, and they provide needed energy for action when a person is attacked or threatened. But parents' unresolved anger at issues about children or in their own lives drains children's energy, joy in life, and ability to respond to the challenges in their own lives. So, parents must find ways to avoid, resolve, or detach from such feelings.

Relying on these three principles, parents can help children grow and realize their potential. No matter how strong the desire, parents can not guarantee children a problem-free life, especially in these historical times, but they can guarantee children a lifetime attachment that provides the support and help necessary to grow and to meet life's challenges.

Throughout the book, we have seen that parents benefit from support as they go about rearing the next generation. In our individualistic society, this support usually comes from individuals and voluntary organizations. Government programs do not give much help to the vast array of parents, though such programs are effective in providing services for limited periods—for example, home visiting programs for parents of infants or early childhood stimulation programs for children with special needs.

In most parents' lives, support comes primarily from marital partners, extended family members such as grandparents, friends, coworkers, and organizations like

CHADD (Children and Adults with Attention Deficit Disorder) designed to help special groups of parents and children. More recently, organizations like the National Parenting Association have addressed the broader needs of all parents. Further, parents themselves have followed the Youth Charter plan of William Damon to organize the entire community to address the needs of all youth. This is vitally important for all of us, because children are the future of our society.

If you are not a parent or grandparent, you may wonder what you can do to help parents. First, every one of us can give parents the respect and acknowledgment for their hard work and sacrifice that our society generally withholds from parents.

Second, with whatever your special skills, you may be able to take actions in your everyday life to support parents and parenting. A single individual has tremendous power, as the actions of Barbara Barlow illustrate.[1] A pediatric surgeon at Harlem Hospital in New York, she became concerned at the growing number of preventable injuries she was treating. Children fell from open windows, were hit by automobiles while playing in the street, and were victims of violence.

In 1988 she started Harlem Hospital's Injury Prevention Project (IPP) with a grant from the Robert Wood Johnson Foundation. With a staff of three, she worked to rebuild playgrounds and parks in the community, making them safe places to play. She photographed all the parks and playgrounds and took the information to the Parks Department and the Board of Education. The Parks Department has since made nearly all the parks in the area safe. Private funding was obtained, and with the suggestions of teachers and students, eight new parks were built.

The Injury Prevention Program has expanded to include activities that foster children's competence. For example, an in-hospital art program allows patients to express their feelings about illness and hospitalization. Children have exhibited and sold their work, with half of the profits going to the children and half to the art program. The IPP also sponsors baseball teams, a soccer team, a dance program serving 200 children, and a greening program in which children can grow vegetables and flowers.

Since the implementation of this program, major injuries to children in Harlem have decreased by 37 percent. Motor vehicle accidents have decreased by 50 percent, and fewer children fall from windows. In addition, dancers, athletes, artists, and gardeners have developed skills they would not have been able to develop without the programs.

An increase in violent injuries led Barlow to start the Anti-Violence Project, which contains several specific programs for (1) teaching children how to stay safe, (2) helping children deal with violence after they experience it, and (3) teaching the children, their parents, and educators, conflict resolution techniques and other ways to avoid violence.

Funding for all these programs comes from individuals, corporations, foundations, and fees from Barlow's speaking engagements. She concludes,

> You have to give to get in this world, and we give a lot. We put in lots of hard work, but it's immensely satisfying. There is no such thing as not being able to make things better. In any community, every individual can make a tremendous difference if they truly care, if they look around to see what needs to be done.[2]

NOTES

PREFACE

1. David Gutmann, "Parenthood: A Key to the Comparative Study of the Life Cycle," in *Life Span Developmental Psychology: Normative Life Crises,* ed. Nancy Daton and Leon H. Ginsberg (New York: Academic Press, 1975), 175.

CHAPTER 1

1. U.S. Bureau of the Census, *Statistical Abstract of the United States: 2002,* 122nd ed. (Washington, DC: U.S. Government Printing Office, 2001).
2. William Morris, ed., *The American Heritage Dictionary of the English Language* (Boston: American Heritage Publishing and Houghton Mifflin, 1969).
3. Ellen Goodman, "Why Jaycee Is Parentless," *San Francisco Chronicle,* 16 September 1997, p. A21.
4. Morris, *American Heritage Dictionary.*
5. Jay Belsky, "The Determinants of Parenting: A Process Model," *Child Development* 55 (1984): 83–96.
6. Urie Bronfenbrenner and Pamela A. Morris, "The Ecology of Developmental Processes," in *Handbook of Child Psychology,* 5th ed., ed. William Damon, vol. 1: *Theoretical Models of Human Development,* ed. Richard Lerner (New York: Wiley, 1998), 996, 1015.
7. Mary Jane Gandour, "Activity Level As a Dimension of Temperament in Toddlers: Its Relevance for the Organismic Specificity Hypothesis," *Child Development* 60 (1989): 1092–1098.
8. Belsky, "Determinants of Parenting."
9. Carolyn Pape Cowan and Philip A. Cowan, *When Partners Become Parents* (New York: Basic Books, 1992).
10. Mark Mellman, Edward Lazarus, and Allan Rivlin, "Family Time, Family Values," in *Rebuilding the Nest,* ed. David Blankenhorn, Steven Bayme, and Jean Bethke Elshtain (Milwaukee, WI: Family Service of America, 1990), 73–92.
11. Lois Wladis Hoffman and Jean Denby Manis, "The Values of Children in the United States: A New Approach to the Study of Fertility," *Journal of Marriage and the Family* 41 (1979): 583–596.
12. Bronfenbrenner and Morris, "Ecology of Developmental Processes," 1015.
13. *People,* 10 November 1997.
14. Arthur T. Jersild et al., *Joys and Problems of Child Rearing* (New York: Bureau of Publications, Teachers College, Columbia University, 1949).
15. U.S. Bureau of the Census, *Statistical Abstract of the United States: 2002.*
16. Ann Crittenden, *The Price of Motherhood* (New York: Holt, 2001).
17. Catherine E. Ross and Marieke Van Willigen, "Gender, Parenthood, and Anger," *Journal of Marriage and the Family* 58 (1996): 572–584.
18. Richard M. Lerner, Elizabeth E. Sparks, and Laurie D. McCubbin, "Family Diversity and Family Policy," in *Handbook of Family Diversity,* ed. David H. Demo, Katherine R. Allen, and Mark A. Fine (New York: Oxford University Press, 2000), 391.
19. Diana Baumrind and Ross A. Thompson, "The Ethics of Parenting," in *Handbook of Parenting,* 2nd ed., ed. Marc H. Bornstein, vol. 5: *Practical Issues in Parenting* (Mahwah, NJ: Erlbaum, 2002), 3–34.
20. Belsky, "Determinants of Parenting."
21. John Newson and Elizabeth Newson, "Cultural Aspects of Child Rearing in the English-Speaking World," in *Integration of a Child into a Social World,* ed. Martin M. P. Richards (Cambridge University Press, 1974), 53–82.
22. Herbert Ginsburg and Sylvia Opper, *Piaget's Theory of Intellectual Development* (Englewood Cliffs, NJ: Prentice-Hall, 1969).
23. David C. Rowe, *The Limits of Family Influence* (New York: Guilford, 1994).
24. Judith Rich Harris, *The Nurture Assumption: Why Children Turn out the Way They Do* (New York: Free Press, 1998).
25. Baumrind and Thompson, "Ethics of Parenting."
26. Matthew Purdy, Andrew Jacobs, and Richard Lezin Jones, "Life behind Basement Doors: Family and System Fail Boys," *New York Times,* 12 January 2003, p. A1.

27. David Kacieniewski, "State Admits Losing Track of Children," *New York Times,* 11 January 2003, p. A15.

28. Richard Lezin Jones and Leslie Kaufman, "Gaps in Children's Safety Net Are Seen in New Jersey Case," *New York Times,* 14 March 2003, p. A25.

29. Robin Meredith, "Parents Convicted for a Youth's Misconduct," *New York Times,* 10 May 1996.

30. Ross D. Parke and Raymond Buriel, "Socialization in the Family: Ethnic and Ecological Perspectives," in *Handbook of Child Psychology,* 5th ed., ed. William Damon, vol. 3: *Social, Emotional, and Personality Development,* ed. Nancy Eisenberg (New York: Wiley, 1998), 463–552.

31. Harriet Chiang, "Father Figure Wins Custody," *San Francisco Chronicle,* 7 June 2002, A1.

32. Michael Janofsky, "Custody Case in California Paves Way for 'Fathers.'" *New York Times,* 8 June 2002, p. A13.

33. Baumrind and Thompson, "Ethics of Parenting."

34. Ibid.

35. James Rainey and Dan Morrison, "Boy's Grim Life May Be Key to Attack on Baby," *San Francisco Chronicle,* 28 April 1996; Lori Olszewski, "Charges Suspended against Boy in Baby Beating Case," *San Francisco Chronicle,* 13 July 1996.

36. Edward Epstein and Michael Taylor, "How Law Treats Violent Kids: Big Change since 1971 Alba Case," *San Francisco Chronicle,* 6 May 1996.

37. Arnold J. Sameroff et al., "Family and Social Influences on the Development of Child Competence," in *Families, Risk, and Competence,* ed. Michael Lewis and Candice Feiring (Mahwah, NJ: Erlbaum, 1998), 161–185.

38. Ibid., pp. 178–179.

39. Arnold Sameroff, "Democratic and Republican Models of Development: Paradigms or Perspectives," *APA Division 7 Newsletter* (Fall 1996): 8.

40. Ronald Seifer et al., "Child and Family Factors That Ameliorate Risk between 4 and 13 Years of Age," *Journal of the American Academy of Child and Adolescent Psychiatry* 31 (1992): 893–903.

41. U.S. Bureau of the Census, *Statistical Abstract of the United States: 2002.*

42. Arab American Institute, available at www.aaiusa.org.demographics.htm.

43. Nicholas Kulish, "Snapshot of America 2000," *Wall Street Journal,* 6 August 2002, p. B1.

44. U.S. Bureau of the Census, *Statistical Abstract of the United States: 2002.*

45. Ibid.

46. Mellman, Lazarus, and Rivlin, "Family Time, Family Values."

47. John P. Robinson and Geoffrey Godbey, *Time for Life: The Surprising Ways Americans Use Their Time* (University Park: Pennsylvania State University Press, 1997).

48. Heidi Benson, "Divorcing the 'Other Parent,'" *San Francisco Chronicle,* 12 June 2002, p. D1.

49. Marc Miringoff and Marque-Luisa Miringoff, *The Social Health of the Nation* (New York: Oxford University Press, 1999).

50. Jack C. Westman, ed., *Parenthood in America: Undervalued, Underpaid and Under Seige* (Madison: University of Wisconsin Press, 2001).

51. Urie Bronfenbrenner, "Growing Chaos in the Lives of Children: How Can We Turn It Around?" in *Parenthood in America,* ed. Jack C. Westman (Madison: University of Wisconsin Press, 2001), 197–210.

52. James Garbarino, "Supporting Parents in a Socially Toxic Environment," in *Parenthood in America,* ed. Westman, pp. 220–231.

53. Jean M. Twenge, "The Age of Anxiety? Birth Cohort Change in Anxiety and Neuroticism, 1952–1993," *Journal of Personality and Social Psychology* 79 (2000): 1007–1021.

54. Harris, *Nurture Assumption,* p. 351.

55. Judith Rich Harris, "Socialization, Personality Development, and the Child's Environments: Comment on Vandell (2000)," *Developmental Psychology* 36 (2000): 711–723.

56. Ibid.

57. Harris, *Nurture Assumption.*

58. Harris, "Socialization, Personality Development, and the Child's Environments."

59. W. Andrew Collins et al., "Contemporary Research on Parenting: The Case for Nature and Nurture," *American Psychologist* 55 (2000): 218.

60. Lynn Singer et al., "Relationship of Prenatal Cocaine Exposure and Maternal Postpartum Psychological Distress to Child Development Outcome," *Development and Psychopathology* 9 (1997): 473–489.

61. Gurney Williams III, "Toxic Dads," *Parenting,* October 1998, p. 94.

62. Collins et al., "Contemporary Research on Parenting," p. 219.

63. Collins et al., "Contemporary Research on Parenting"; Eleanor E. Maccoby, "Parenting Effects: Issues and Controversies," in *Parenting and the Child's World: Influences in Academic, Intellectual, and Socio-Emotional Development,* ed. John G. Borkowski, Sharon Landesman Ramey, and Marie Bristol-Power (Mahwah, NJ: Erlbaum, 2002), 35–46.

64. Collins et al., "Contemporary Research on Parenting."

65. Eleanor E. Maccoby, "Parenting and Its Effects on Children: On Reading and Misreading Behavior Genetics," *Annual Review of Psychology* 51 (2000): 1–27.

66. C. Robert Cloninger et al., "Predisposition to Petty Criminality in Swedish Adoptees. II. Cross-Fostering Analysis of Gene-Environment Interaction," *Archives of General Psychiatry* 39 (1982): 1242–1247.

67. Jerome Kagan, Doreen Arcus, and Nancy Snidman, "The Idea of Temperament: Where Do We Go from Here?" In *Nature and Nurture in Psychology,* ed. Robert Plomin and Gerald E. McClearn (Washington, DC: American Psychological Association, 1993), 197–210.

68. Robert L. Nix et al., "The Relation between Mothers' Hostile Attribution Tendencies and Children's Externalizing Behavior Problems: The Mediating Role of Mothers' Harsh Discipline Practices," *Child Development* 70 (1999): 896–909.

69. Collins et al., "Contemporary Research on Parenting."

70. Stephen J. Suomi, "Attachment in Rhesus Monkeys," in *Handbook of Attachment: Theory, Research, and Clinical Applications,* ed. Jude Cassidy and Phillip R. Shaver (New York: Guilford, 1999), 181–197.

71. Stephen J. Suomi, "Parents, Peers, and the Process of Socialization in Primates," in *Parenting and the Child's World,* ed. Borkowski, Ramey, Bristol-Power, pp. 265–279.

72. Suomi, "Attachment in Rhesus Monkeys"; Suomi, "Parents, Peers, and the Process of Socialization in Primates."

73. L. Alan Sroufe, "From Infant Attachment to Promotion of Adolescent Autonomy: Perspective Longitudinal Data on the Role of Parents in Development," in *Parenting and the Child's World,* ed. Borkowski, Ramey, and Bristol-Power, p. 198.

74. Laraine Masters Glidden, "Parenting Children with Developmental Disabilities: A Ladder of Influence," in *Parenting and the Child's World,* ed. Borkowski, Ramey, and Bristol-Power, pp. 329–344.

75. Ibid., p. 336.

76. Benjamin S. Bloom, ed., *Developing Talent in Young People* (New York: Ballantine, 1985).

77. Philip A. Cowan and Carolyn Pape Cowan, "What an Intervention Design Reveals about How Parents Affect Their Children's Academic Achievement and Behavior Problems," in *Parenting and the Child's World,* ed. Borkowski, Ramey, and Bristol-Power, pp. 75–97.

78. Ibid., p. 87.

79. Anne Anastasi, "Heredity, Environment, and the Question 'How?'" *Psychological Review* 65 (1958): 197–208.

80. David T. Lykken, "Parental Licensure," *American Psychologist* 56 (2001): 885–886.

81. Sandra Scarr, "Toward Voluntary Parenthood," *Journal of Personality* 68 (2000): 615–623.

82. David T. Lykken, "The Causes and Costs of Crime and a Controversial Cure," *Journal of Personality* (2000): 598.

83. Urie Bronfenbrenner and Peter R. Neville, "America's Children and Families: An International Perspective," in *Putting Families First,* ed. Sharon L. Kagan and Bernice Weissbourd (San Francisco: Jossey-Bass, 1994), 3–27.

84. Elizabeth Olson, "U.N. Surveys Paid Leave for Mothers," *New York Times,* 16 February 1998, p. A5.

85. Jay Belsky and John Kelly, *The Transition to Parenthood* (New York: Delacorte, 1994), 23.

86. Steve Farkas et al., *Kids These Days: What Americans Really Think about the Next Generation* (New York: Public Agenda, 1997).

87. Sylvia Ann Hewlett and Cornel West, *War against Parents* (Boston: Houghton Mifflin, 1998).

88. E. J. Dionne, Jr., "New Efforts to Mend Tattered Health System," *San Francisco Chronicle,* 14 August 1999, p. A27.

CHAPTER 2

1. Robert B. Cairns, "The Making of Developmental Psychology," in *Handbook of Child Psychology,* 5th ed., ed. William Damon, vol. 1: *Theoretical Models of Human Development,* ed. Richard M. Lerner (New York: Wiley, 1998), 25–105.

2. Arnold Gesell, "Motivation and the Patterning of Behavior," in *A Handbook of Child Psychology,* 2nd ed., ed. Carl Murchison (Worcester, MA: Clark University Press, 1933), 158–203.

3. Gilbert Gottlieb, "Experiential Canalization of Behavioral Development: Theory," *Developmental Psychology* 27 (1991): 5.

4. Gilbert Gottlieb, Douglas Wahlsten, and Robert Lickliter, "The Significance of Biology for Human Development: A Developmental Psychobiological Systems View," in *Handbook of Child Psychology,* 5th ed., ed. Damon and Lerner, vol. 1, p. 260.

5. Gottlieb, "Experiential Canalization"; Gottlieb, Wahlsten, and Lickliter, "The Significance of Biology."

6. Ibid.

7. Ibid.

8. Ibid.

9. Arnold J. Sameroff et al., "Family and Social Influences on the Development of Child Competence," in *Families, Risk, and Competence,* ed. Michael Lewis and Candice Feiring (Mahwah, NJ: Erlbaum, 1998), 161–185.

10. David T. Lykken, "Parental Licensure," *American Psychologist* 56 (2001): 883–894.

11. Rima Shore, *Rethinking the Brain* (New York: Families and Work Institute, 1997), 15.

12. Daniel J. Siegel, *The Developing Mind* (New York: Guilford, 1999), 14.

13. David F. Bjorklund, Jennifer L. Yunger, and Anthony D. Pellegrini, "The Evolution of Parenting and Evolutionary Approaches to Childrearing," in *Handbook of Parenting,* 2nd ed., ed. Marc H. Bornstein, vol. 2: *Biology and Ecology of Parenting* (Mahwah, NJ: Erlbaum, 2002), 3–30.

14. David F. Bjorklund and Anthony D. Pellegrini, " *Child Development* 71 (2000): 1688.

15. Bjorklund, Yunger, and Pellegrini, "The Evolution of Parenting," p. 6.

16. Ibid.

17. Ibid.

18. Ibid.

19. Ibid., p. 22.

20. Peter Huttenlocher, *Neural Plasticity* (Cambridge, MA: Harvard University Press, 2002), 203.

21. Huttenlocher, *Neural Plasticity,* p. 189.

22. Bjorklund, Yunger, and Pellegrini, "The Evolution of Parenting," p. 25.

23. Richard M. Lerner et al., "Developmental Systems Perspective on Parenting," in *Handbook of Parenting,* 2nd ed., ed. Bornstein, vol. 2, pp. 315–344.

24. Urie Bronfenbrenner and Pamela A. Morris, "The Ecology of Developmental Processes," in *Handbook of Child Psychology.* 5th ed., ed. Damon and Lerner, vol. 1, pp. 993–1028.

25. Judith A. Schickedanz et al., *Understanding Children,* 2nd ed. (Mountain View, CA: Mayfield, 1993).

26. John B. Watson, *Psychological Care of Infant and Child* (New York: Norton, 1928), 81–82.

27. Daphne Blunt Bugental and Jacqueline J. Goodnow, "Socialization Processes," in *Handbook of Child Psychology*, 5th ed., ed. William Damon, vol. 3: *Social, Emotional, and Personality Development,* ed. Nancy Eisenberg (New York: Wiley, 1998), 389–462.

28. E. Mark Cummings and Jennifer S. Cummings, "Parenting and Attachment," in *Handbook of Parenting,* 2nd ed., ed. Marc H. Bornstein, vol. 5: *Practical Issues in Parenting,* (Mahwah, NJ: Erlbaum, 2002), 35–58.

29. Benjamin Spock, *Baby and Child Care* (New York: Pocket Books, 1946).

30. Calvin S. Hall and Gardner Lindzey, *Theories of Personality,* 2nd ed. (New York: Wiley, 1970).

31. Rudolf Dreikurs, *The Challenge of Parenthood,* rev. ed. (New York: Hawthorn, 1958).

32. Rudolf Dreikurs with Vicki Soltz, *Children: The Challenge* (New York: Hawthorn, 1964).

33. Don Dinkmeyer and Gary D. McKay, *STEP/TEEN: Systematic Training for Effective Parenting of Teens* (Circle Pines, MN: American Guidance Service, 1983).

34. Erik H. Erikson, *Childhood and Society,* 2nd ed. (New York: Norton, 1963).

35. Erik H. Erikson, "Human Strength and the Cycle of Generations," in *Insight and Responsibility,* ed. Erik H. Erikson (New York: Norton, 1964), 109–157.

36. Ross A. Thompson, "Early Sociopersonality Development," in *Handbook of Child Psychology,* 5th ed., ed. Damon and Eisenberg, vol. 3, p. 35.

37. Cummings and Cummings, "Parenting and Attachment."

38. Mary Main, "Epilogue: Attachment Theory," in *Handbook of Attachment Theory, Research, and Clinical Applications,* ed. Jude Cassidy and Phillip R. Shaver (New York: Guilford, 1999), 845–887.

39. Thompson, "Early Sociopersonality Development."

40. Ibid.

41. Karlen Lyons-Ruth et al., "Infants at Social Risk: Maternal Depression and Family Support Services as Moderators of Infant Development and Security of Attachment," *Child Development* 61 (1990): 85–98.

42. Thompson, "Early Sociopersonality Development."

43. Joy D. Osofsky, Della M. Hann, and Claire Peebles, "Adolescent Parenthood: Risks and Opportunities for Mothers and Infants," in *Handbook of Infant Mental Health,* ed. Charles H. Zeanah, Jr. (New York: Guilford, 1993), 106–119.

44. Lyons-Ruth et al., "Infants at Social Risk."

45. Jay Belsky et al., "Instability of Infant-Parent Attachment Security," *Developmental Psychology* 32 (1996): 921–924.

46. Thompson, "Early Sociopersonality Development."

47. Claire E. Hamilton, "Continuity and Discontinuity of Attachment from Infancy through Adolescence," *Child Development* 71 (2000): 690–694; Everett Waters et al., "Attachment Security in Infancy and Early Adulthood: A Twenty-Year Longitudinal Study," *Child Development* 71 (2000): 684–689.

48. Michael Lewis, Candice Feiring, and Saul Rosenthal, "Attachment over Time," *Child Development* 71 (2000): 707–720. Nancy S. Weinfield, L. Alan Sroufe, and Byron Egeland, "Attachment from Infancy to Early Adulthood in a High-Risk Sample: Continuity, Discontinuity, and Their Correlates," *Child Development* 71 (2000): 695–702.

49. Byron Egeland and Ellen A. Farber, "Infant-Mother Attachment Factors Related to Its Development and Changes over Time," *Child Development* 55 (1984): 753–771.

50. Thompson, "Early Sociopersonality Development."

51. Thomas G. R. Bower, *A Primer of Infant Development* (San Francisco: Freeman, 1977).

52. Thompson, "Early Sociopersonality Development."

53. Martha F. Erickson, L. Alan Sroufe, and Byron Egeland, "The Relationship between Quality of Attachment and Behavior Problems in Preschool in a High Risk Sample," in *Growing Points of Attachment Theory and Research,* ed. Inge Bretherton and Everett Waters, Monographs of the Society for Research and Development 50, Serial no. 109 (1985): 167–193.

54. Thompson, "Early Sociopersonality Development."

55. Abraham Sagi et al., "Sleeping out of Home in a Kibbutz Communal Arrangement: It Makes a Difference for Infant-Mother Attachment," *Child Development* 65 (1994): 992–1004.

56. Thompson, "Early Sociopersonality Development."

57. Ibid.

58. Ibid.

59. Nathan A. Fox, Nancy L. Kimmerly, and William D. Schafer, "Attachment to Mother/Attachment to Father: A Meta-Analysis," *Child Development* 62 (1991): 210–225.

60. Main, "Epilogue," p. 861.

61. Joan E. Grusec, Paul Hastings, and Norma Mammone, "Parenting Cognitions and Relationship Schemes," in *Beliefs about Parenting,* ed. Judith G. Smetana, New Directions for Child Development, no. 66 (San Francisco: Jossey-Bass, 1994), 5–19.

62. June Lichtenstein Phelps, Jay Belsky, and Keith Crnic, "Earned Security, Daily Stress, and Parenting: A Comparison of Five Alternative Models," *Development and Psychopathology* 10 (1998): 21–38.

63. Herbert Ginsburg and Sylvia Opper, *Piaget's Theory of Intellectual Development* (Englewood Cliffs, NJ: Prentice-Hall, 1969); Jean Piaget and Barbel Inhelder, *The Psychology of the Child* (New York: Basic Books, 1969).

64. John M. Belmont, "Cognitive Strategies and Strategic Learning," *American Psychologist* 44 (1989): 142–148; Laboratory of Comparative Human Cognition, "Culture and Cognitive Development," in *Handbook of Child Psychology,* 4th ed., ed. William Kessen, vol. 1: *History, Theory, and Methods* (New York: Wiley, 1982), 295–356; James V. Wertsch and Peeter Tulviste, "L. S. Vygotsky and Contemporary Developmental Psychology," *Developmental Psychology* 28 (1992): 548–557.

65. Ross D. Parke and Raymond Buriel, "Socialization in the Family: Ethnic and Ecological Perspectives," in *Handbook of Child Psychology,* ed. William Damon and Eisenberg, vol. 3, pp. 463–552.

66. Diana Baumrind, "The Development of Instrumental Competence through Socialization," in *Minnesota Symposia on Child Psychology,* ed. Ann D. Pick, vol. 7 (Minneapolis: University of Minnesota Press, 1973), pp. 3–46.

67. Eleanor E. Maccoby and John A. Martin, "Socialization in the Context of the Family: Parent-Child Interaction," in *Handbook of Child Psychology,* 4th ed., ed. Paul H. Mussen, vol. 4: *Socialization, Personality, and Social Development,* ed. E. Mavis Hetherington (New York: Wiley, 1983), 1–101.

68. Susie D. Lamborn et al., "Patterns of Competence and Adjustment among Adolescents from Authoritative, Authoritarian, Indulgent, and Neglectful Families," *Child Development* 62 (1991): 1049–1065; Laurence Steinberg et al., "Authoritative Parenting and Adolescent Adjustment: An Ecological Perspective," in *Examining Lives in Context,* ed. Phyllis Moen, Glen H. Elder, Jr., and Kurt Lusher (Washington, DC: American Psychological Association, 1995).

69. Anne C. Fletcher, Laurence Steinberg, and Elizabeth B. Sellers, "Adolescents' Well Being As a Function of Perceived Interparental Consistency," *Journal of Marriage and the Family* 61 (1999): 599–610.

70. Marjory R. Gray and Laurence Steinberg, "Unpacking Authoritative Parenting: Reassessing a Multidimensional Construct," *Journal of Marriage and the Family* 61 (1999): 574–587.

71. Ibid., p. 584.

72. Nancy Darling and Laurence Steinberg, "Parenting Style as Context: An Integrative Model," *Psychological Bulletin* 113 (1993): 487–496.

73. *Newsweek,* Spring–Summer 1997.

74. Tiffany Field, "The Effects of Mother's Physical and Emotional Unavailability on Emotion Regulation," in *The Development of Emotion Regulation,* ed. Nathan A. Fox, Monographs of the Society for Research in Child Development 59, serial no. 240 (1994): 208–227.

75. Urs A. Hunziker and Ronald G. Barr, "Increased Carrying Reduces Crying: A Randomized Controlled Trial," *Pediatrics* 77 (1986): 641–647.

76. Field, "Effects of Mother's Physical and Emotional Unavailability."

77. Jerome Kagan, Doreen Arcus, and Nancy Snidman, "The Idea of Temperament: Where Do We Go from Here?" in *Nature, Nurture, and Psychology,* ed. Robert Plomin and Gerald E. McClearn (Washington, DC: American Psychological Association, 1993), pp. 197–210.

78. Thompson, "Early Sociopersonality Development."

79. L. Alan Sroufe, Byron Egeland, and Terri Kreutzer, "The Fate of Early Experience following Developmental Change: Longitudinal Approaches to Individual Adaptation in Childhood," *Child Development* 61 (1990): 1363–1373.

80. Marjorie P. Honzik, "Environmental Correlates of Mental Growth: Prediction from the Family Setting at Twenty-one Months," *Child Development* 38 (1967): 337–364.

81. Geraldine Dawson et al., "Frontal Brain Electrical Activity in Infants of Depressed and Nondepressed Mothers: Relation to Variations in Infant Behavior," *Development and Psychopathology* 11 (1999): 589–605.

82. Siegel, *Developing Mind.*

83. Alison Gopnik, Andrew N. Meltzoff, and Patricia K. Kuhl, *The Scientist in the Crib* (New York: Morrow, 1999), 202.

84. John T. Bruer, *The Myth of the First Three Years* (New York: Free Press, 1999), 108–109.

85. Bruer, *Myth of the First Three Years.*

86. Sandra Blakeslee, "Old Brains Can Learn New Language Tricks," *New York Times,* 20 April 1999, p. D3.

87. Peter Marks, "Long Island Program Turns Around Troubled Students," *New York Times,* 14 April 1994.

88. Bruer, *Myth of the First Three Years.*

89. Dorothy H. Eichorn, Jane V. Hunt, and Marjorie P. Honzik, "Experience, Personality, and IQ: Adolescence to Middle Age," in *Present and Past in Middle Life,* ed. Dorothy H. Eichorn et al. (New York: Academic Press, 1981), 89–116.

90. Ibid., p. 116.

CHAPTER 3

1. William Morris, ed., *The American Heritage Dictionary of the English Language* (Boston: American Heritage Publishing and Houghton Mifflin, 1969).

2. Sara Harkness and Charles Super, "Culture and Parenting," in *Handbook of Parenting,* 2nd ed., ed. Marc H. Bornstein, vol. 2: *Biology and Ecology of Parenting* (Mahwah, NJ: Erlbaum, 2002), 253–280.

3. Velma McBride Murry, Emilie Phillips Smith, and Nancy E. Hill, "Race, Ethnicity, and Culture in Studies of Families in Context," *Journal of Marriage and Family* 63 (2001): 912.

4. Ross D. Parke and Raymond Buriel, "Socialization in the Family: Ethnic and Ecological Perspectives," in *Handbook of Child Psychology,* 5th ed., ed. William Damon, vol. 3, *Social and Emotional, and Personality Development,* ed. Nancy Eisenberg (New York, Wiley, 1998), 496.

5. Nicholas Wade, "Race Is Seen As Real Guide to Track the Roots of Disease," *New York Times,* 30 July 2002, p. D1.

6. Patricia M. Greenfield and Lalita K. Suzuki, "Culture and Human Development: Implications for Parenting, Education, Pediatrics, and Mental Health," in *Handbook of Child Psychology,* 5th ed., ed. William Damon, vol. 4: *Child Psychology in Practice,* ed. Irving E. Sigel and K. Ann Renninger (New York: Wiley, 1998), 1059–1109.

7. Jean L. Briggs, "Mazes of Meaning: How a Child and a Culture Create Each Other," in *Interpretive Approaches to Socialization,* ed. William A. Corsaro and Peggy J. Miller, New Directions for Child Development, no. 58 (San Francisco: Jossy Bass, 1992), 25.

8. James Youniss, "Rearing Children for Society," in *Beliefs about Parenting: Origins and Developmental Implications,* ed. Judith G. Smetana, New Directions for Child Development, no. 66 (San Francisco: Jossey Bass, 1994), 37–50.

9. Greenfield and Suzuki, "Culture and Human Development."

10. Rebecca I. New and Amy L. Richman, "Maternal Beliefs and Infant Care Practices in Italy and the United States," in *Parents' Cultural Belief Systems: Their Origins, Expressions, and Consequences,* ed. Sara Harkness and Charles M. Super (New York: Guilford, 1996), 385–404.

11. Nicholas Kulish, "Snapshot of America 2000," *Wall Street Journal,* 6 August 2001, p. B1.

12. Joseph E. Illick, *American Childhoods* (Philadelphia: University of Pennsylvania Press, 2002), 4.

13. Ibid, p. 5.

14. Samuel Eliot Morison, *The Oxford History of the American People* (New York: Oxford University Press, 1965).

15. Doris Y. Wilkinson, "American Families of African Descent," in *Families in Cultural Context: Strengths and Challenges in Diversity,* ed. Mary Kay DeGenova (Mountain View, CA: Mayfield, 1997), 35–59.

16. Morison, *Oxford History of the American People.*

17. Ibid.

18. Ibid.

19. Cynthia Garcia Coll and Lee M. Pachter, "Ethnic and Minority Parenting," in *Handbook of Parenting,* 2nd ed., ed. Marc H. Bornstein, vol. 4, *Social Conditions and Applied Parenting* (Mahwah, NJ: Erlbaum, 2002), 7.

20. Ibid.

21. Morison, *Oxford History of the American People.*

22. Cynthia Garcia Coll et al., "An Integration Model for the Study of Developmental Competencies in Minority Children," *Child Development* 67 (1996): 1891–1914.

23. Michael Novak, "Neither WASP nor Jew nor Black," in *Experiencing Race, Class, and Gender in the United States,* ed. Virginia Cyrus (Mountain View, CA: Mayfield, 1993), 32.

24. U.S. Bureau of the Census, *Statistical Abstract of the United States: 2001,* 121st ed. (Washington, DC: U.S. Government Printing Office, 2001).

25. Garcia Coll and Pachter, "Ethnic and Minority Parenting."

26. Vonnie C. McLoyd et al., "Marital Processes and Parental Socialization in Families of Color: A Decade Review of Research," *Journal of Marriage and the Family* 62 (2000): 1070–1093.

27. Parke and Buriel, "Socialization in the Family."

28. Morison, *Oxford History of the American People,* p. 3.

29. Ibid., p. 15.

30. Walter T. Kawamoto and Tamara C. Cheshire, "American Indian Families," in *Families in Cultural Context,* ed. De Genova, pp. 15–34; Morison; *Oxford History of the American People;* Parke and Buriel, "Socialization in the Family."

31. Ibid.

32. U.S. Bureau of the Census, *Statistical Abstract of the United States, 2001.*

33. Parke and Buriel, "Socialization in the Family."

34. Kawamoto and Cheshire, "American Indian Families," p. 21.

35. Ibid., p. 20.

36. Parke and Buriel, "Socialization in the Family."

37. U.S. Bureau of the Census, *Statistical Abstract of the United States, 2001.*

38. Garcia Coll and Pachter, "Ethnic and Minority Parenting."

39. Niara Sudarkasa, "Interpreting the Afro-American Family Organization," in *Black Families,* 2nd ed., ed Harriette Pipes McAdoo (Newbury Park, CA: Sage, 1988), 27–43.

40. Ibid.

41. John Hope Franklin, "A Historical Note on Black Families," in *Black Families,* 2nd ed., ed. McAdoo, pp. 23–26.

42. Ibid.

43. Morison, *Oxford History of the American People,* pp. 23–26.

44. Robert E. Martin, "Lynching," in *The Encyclopedia Americana,* vol. 17 (Danbury, CT: Grolier, 2000), 884–885.

45. Morison, *Oxford History of the American People.*

46. Andrew Billingsley, *Climbing Jacob's Ladder: The Enduring Legacy of African-American Families* (New York: Simon & Schuster, 1992); Franklin, "Historical Note on Black Families."

47. Billingsley, *Climbing Jacob's Ladder.*

48. Parke and Buriel, "Socialization in the Family."

49. Vonnie C. McLoyd, "The Impact of Economic Hardship on Black Families and Children: Psychological Distress, Parenting, and Socioemotional Development," *Child Development* 61 (1990): 311–346.

50. Ibid., p. 326.

51. Jacquelynne Faye Jackson, "Issues in Need of Initial Visitation: Race and Nation Specificity in the Study of Externalizing Behavior Problems and Discipline," *Psychological Inquiry* 8 (1997): 204–211.

52. Tom Luster and Harriette Pipes McAdoo, "Family and Child Influences on Educational Attainment," in *Black Children,* 2nd ed., ed Harriette Pipes McAdoo (Thousand Oaks, CA: Sage, 2002), 141–174.

53. Peter Irons, *Jim Crow's Children* (New York: Viking, 2002).

54. Billingsley, *Climbing Jacob's Ladder.*

55. David M. Halbfinger and Steven A. Holmes, "Military Mirrors a Working-Class America," *New York Times,* 30 March 2003, pp. A1, B12, B13.

56. Ibid., p. B12.

57. Billingsley, *Climbing Jacob's Ladder.*

58. Jim Herron Zamora, "Black Men Bring Hope to Bloody Streets," *San Francisco Chronicle,* 29 September 2002, p. A23.

59. Billingsley, *Climbing Jacob's Ladder,* p. 354.

60. U.S. Bureau of the Census, *Statistical Abstract of the United States: 2001.*

61. Parke and Buriel, "Socialization in the Family."

62. Morison, *Oxford History of the American People.*

63. Robin Harwood et al., "Parenting among Latino Families in the United States," in *Handbook of Parenting,* 2nd ed., ed. Bornstein, vol. 4, pp. 21–46.

64. Parke and Buriel, "Socialization in the Family."

65. Ibid., p. 509.

66. Harwood et al., "Parenting among Latino Families."

67. Robin L. Harwood et al., "Cultural Differences in Maternal Beliefs and Behaviors: A Study of Middle-Class Anglo and Puerto Rican Mother-Infant Pairs in Four Everyday Situations," *Child Development* 70 (1999): 1005–1016.

68. Andrew J. Fuligni, Vivian Tseng, and May Lam, "Attitudes toward Family Obligations among American Adolescents with Asian, Latin American, and European Backgrounds," *Child Development* 70 (1999): 1030–1044.

69. Harwood et al., "Parenting among Latino Families."

70. Diana Jean Schemo, "Education Study Finds Hispanics Both Gaining and Lagging," *New York Times,* 8 September 2002, p. A23.

71. Ibid.

72. Ruth Chao and Vivian Tseng, "Parenting of Asians," in *Handbook of Parenting,* 2nd ed., ed. Bornstein, vol. 4, pp. 59–93.

73. Ibid.

74. Parke and Buriel, "Socialization in the Family."

75. Ibid.

76. Ibid.

77. Chao and Tseng, "Parenting of Asians."

78. Parke and Buriel, "Socialization in the Family."

79. Chao and Tseng, "Parenting of Asians."

80. Fred Rothbaum et al., "Immigrant Chinese and Euro-American Parents' Physical Closeness with Young Children: Themes of Family Relatedness," *Journal of Family Psychology* 14 (2000): 334–348.

81. Chao and Tseng, "Parenting of Asians."

82. Ibid.

83. Mary Martini, "How Mothers in Four American Cultural Groups Shape Infant Learning During Mealtimes," *Zero to Three* 22 (February–March, 2002): 14–20.

84. Ibid., p. 20.

85. Arab American Institute Foundation, online at www.aaiusa.org/demographics.htm.

86. Barbara C. Aswad, "Arab American Families," in *Families in Cultural Context,* ed. DeGenova, pp. 213–237.

87. Helen Hatab Samhan, "Who Are Arab-Americans?" Arab American Institute Foundation, online at www.aaiusa.org.

88. Aswad, "Arab American Families," p. 231.

89. Ibid.

90. Ibid.

91. Samhan, "Who Are Arab-Americans?"
92. Arab American Institute Foundation, online at www.aaiusa.org.
93. Samhan, "Who Are Arab-Americans?"
94. Aswad, "Arab American Families."
95. Ibid., p. 225.
96. Jean M. Twenge and Jennifer Crocker, "Race and Self-Esteem: Meta-Analyses Comparing Whites, Blacks, Hispanics, Asians, and American Indians, and Comment on Gray-Little and Hafdahl (2000)," *Psychological Bulletin* 128 (2002): 371–408.
97. Paul R. Amato and Frieda Fowler, "Parenting Practices, Child Adjustment, and Family Diversity," *Journal of Marriage and Family* 64 (2002): 703–716.
98. Marjory R. Gray and Laurence Steinberg, "Unpacking Authoritative Parenting: Reassessing a Multidimensional Construct," *Journal of Marriage and the Family* 61 (1999): 574–587.
99. Vonnie C. McLoyd and Julia Smith, "Physical Discipline and Behavior Problems in African American, European American, and Hispanic Children: Emotional Support As a Moderator," *Journal of Marriage and Family* 64 (2002): 40–53.
100. Mary Kay DeGenova, "Introduction," in *Families in Cultural Context,* ed. DeGenova, p. 6.
101. Erika Hoff, Brett Laursen, and Twila Tardif, "Socioeconomic Status and Parenting," in *Handbook of Parenting,* 2nd ed., ed. Bornstein, vol. 2, pp. 231–252.
102. Betty Hart and Todd R. Risley, *Meaningful Differences in the Everyday Experiences of Young American Children* (Baltimore: Brookes, 1995).
103. Rand D. Conger et al., "Family Economic Stress and Adjustment of Early Adolescent Girls," *Developmental Psychology* 29 (1993): 206–219; Rand D. Conger et al., "A Family Process Model of Economic Hardship and Adjustment of Early Adolescent Boys," *Child Development* 63 (1992): 526–541; Constance A. Flanagan, "Change in Family Work Status: Effects on Parent-Adolescent Decision-Making," *Child Development* 61 (1990): 163–177; Constance A. Flanagan and Jacquelynne S. Eccles, "Changes in Parents' Work Status and Adolescents' Adjustment at School," *Child Development* 64 (1993): 246–257.
104. Leslie Morrison Gutman and Jacquelynne S. Eccles, "Financial Strain, Parenting Behaviors, and Adolescent Achievement: Testing Model Equivalence between African American and European American Single- and Two-Parent Families," *Child Development* 70 (1999): 1464–1476.
105. Ronald L. Simons et al., "Support from Spouse As Mediator and Moderator of the Disruptive Influence of Economic Strain on Parenting," *Child Development* 63 (1992): 1282–1301.
106. Ronald L. Simons et al., "Social Network and Marital Support As Mediators and Moderators of the Impact of Stress and Depression on Parental Behavior," *Developmental Psychology* 29 (1993): 368–381.
107. Vonnie C. McLoyd, "Children in Poverty: Development, Public Policy, and Practice," in *Handbook of Child Psychology,* 5th ed., ed. Damon, vol. 4, pp. 135–208.
108. Robert Pear, "Number of People Living in Poverty Increases in U.S.," *New York Times,* 25 September 2002, p. A1.
109. Mary E. Corcoran and Ajay Chaudry, "The Dynamics of Childhood Poverty," *Future of Children* 7, no. 2 (1997): 40–54.
110. McLoyd, "Children in Poverty."
111. U.S. Bureau of the Census (online): www.census.gov.
112. U.S. Bureau of the Census, *Statistical Abstract of the United States: 2001.*
113. Corcoran and Chaudry, "Dynamics of Childhood Poverty."
114. Ibid.
115. McLoyd, "Children in Poverty."
116. Corcoran and Chaudry, "Dynamics of Childhood Poverty."
117. McLoyd, "Children in Poverty."
118. Jeanne Brooks-Gunn and Greg J. Duncan, "The Effects of Poverty on Children," *Future of Children* 7, no. 2 (1997): 55–71.
119. Richard Rothstein, "Rx for Good Health and Good Grades," *New York Times,* 11 September 2002, p. A30.
120. Greg J. Duncan and Jeanne Brooks-Gunn, "Family Poverty, Welfare Reform, and Child Development," *Child Development* 71 (2000): 188–196.
121. Brooks-Gunn and Duncan, "Effects of Poverty on Children."
122. Katherine A. Magnuson and Greg J. Duncan, "Parents in Poverty," in *Handbook of Parenting,* 2nd ed., ed. Bornstein, vol. 4, pp. 95–121.
123. Duncan and Brooks-Gunn, "Family Poverty, Welfare Reform, and Child Development."
124. Pear, "Number of People Living in Poverty."

125. Nina Bernstein, "First Wave of New York Families Are Facing Lifetime Limit on Federal Welfare," *New York Times,* 30 November 2001, p. A21.

126. Duncan and Brooks-Gunn, "Family Poverty, Welfare Reform, and Child Development."

127. Richard Rothstein, "When Mothers on Welfare Go to Work," *New York Times,* 5 June 2002, p. A20.

128. Duncan and Brooks-Gunn, "Family Poverty, Welfare Reform, and Child Development," p. 193.

129. Ibid., p. 194.

130. Tammy L. Mann, "Findings from the Parent-Child Project and the Impact of Values on Parenting: Reflections in a 'Scientific' Age," *Zero to Three* 20 (December 1999–January 2000): 3–8.

131. Ibid., p. 8.

132. Ibid.

133. Vivian J. Carlson and Robin L. Harwood, "Understanding and Negotiating Cultural Differences Concerning Early Developmental Competence: The Six Raisin Solution," *Zero to Three* 20 (December 1999–January 2000): 19–24.

134. Ibid., p. 24.

CHAPTER 4

1. Lois Wladis Hoffman and Jean Denby Manis, "The Values of Children in the United States: A New Approach to the Study of Fertility," *Journal of Marriage and the Family* 41 (1979): 583–596.

2. Eleanor E. Maccoby and John A. Martin, "Socialization in the Context of the Family: Parent-Child Interaction," in *Handbook of Child Psychology,* 4th ed., ed. Paul H. Mussen and E. Mavis Hetherington, vol. 4: *Socialization, Personality, and Social Development* (New York: Wiley, 1983), 1–101.

3. J. Kirk Felsman and George E. Vaillant, "Resilient Children As Adults," in *The Invulnerable Child,* ed. E. James Anthony and Bertram J. Cohler (New York: Guilford Press, 1987), 298.

4. Charles R. Carlson and John C. Masters, "Inoculation by Emotion: Effects of Positive Emotional States on Children's Reactions to Social Comparison," *Developmental Psychology* 22 (1986): 760–765.

5. Jane B. Brooks and Doris M. Elliott, "Prediction of Psychological Adjustment at Age Thirty from Leisure Time Activities and Satis-

factions in Childhood," *Human Development* 14 (1971): 61–71.

6. Anita Weiner, Haggai Kuppermintz, and David Guttmann, "Video Home Training (The Orion Project): A Short-Term Preventive and Treatment Intervention for Families of Young Children," *Family Process* 33 (1994): 441–453.

7. Dorothy C. Briggs, *Your Child's Self-Esteem* (Garden City, NY: Doubleday, 1970), 61–62.

8. Ibid., p. 64.

9. Susan Engel, *The Stories Children Tell* (New York: Freeman, 1999, 184.

10. Ibid., p. 4.

11. Ibid.

12. Ibid.

13. Ibid.

14. Arnold J. Sameroff and Barbara H. Fiese, "Narrative Connections in the Family Context: Summary and Conclusions," in *The Stories Families Tell,* ed. Fiese et al., p. 122.

15. Steven J. Wolin and Linda A. Bennett, "Family Rituals," *Family Process* 23 (1984): 401–420.

16. Linda A. Bennett et al., "Couples at Risk for Transmission of Alcoholism: Protective Influences," *Family Process* 26 (1987): 111–129.

17. William J. Doherty, *The Intentional Family* (New York: Avon, 1997), 8.

18. Ibid., pp. 198–199.

19. Rudolf Dreikurs with Vicki Soltz, *Children: The Challenge* (New York: Hawthorn, 1964).

20. Ibid., p. 39.

21. Ibid., p. 108.

22. Gail D. Heyman, Carol S. Dweck, and Kathleen M. Cain, "Young Children's Vulnerability to Self-Blame and Helplessness: Relationship to Beliefs about Goodness," *Child Development* 63 (1992): 401–415; Martin E. P. Seligman, *Learned Optimism* (New York: Pocket Books, 1990).

23. Seligman, *Learned Optimism.*

24. Ibid., pp. 221–222.

25. Ibid., p. 222.

26. John M. Gottman, Lynn Fainsilber Katz, and Carole Hooven, "Parental Meta-Emotion Philosophy and the Emotional Life of Families: Theoretical Models and Preliminary Data," *Journal of Family Psychology* 10 (1996): 243–268.

27. John Gottman with Joan DeClaire, *The Heart of Parenting: Raising an Emotionally Intelligent Child* (New York: Simon & Schuster, 1997).

28. Ibid.

29. Nancy Eisenberg et al., "Parental Reactions to Children's Negative Emotions: Longitudinal Relations to Quality of Children's Social Functioning," *Child Development* 70 (1999): 513–534.

30. Thomas Gordon, *P.E.T.: Parent Effectiveness Training* (New York: New American Library, 1975); Thomas Gordon with Judith G. Sands, *P.E.T. in Action* (New York: Bantam Books, 1978); Thomas Gordon, *Teaching Children Self-Discipline* (New York: Random House, 1989).

31. Gordon with Sands, *P.E.T. in Action,* p. 47.

32. Judy Dunn, Jane Brown, and Lynn Beardsall, "Family Talk about Feeling States and Children's Later Understanding of Others' Emotions," *Developmental Psychology* 27 (1991): 448–455.

33. Adele Faber and Elaine Mazlish, *Liberated Parents/Liberated Children* (New York: Avon Books, 1975).

34. John A. Clausen, Paul H. Mussen, and Joseph Kuypers, "Involvement, Warmth, and Parent-Child Resemblance in Three Generations," in *Present and Past in Middle Life,* ed. Dorothy H. Eichorn et al. (New York: Academic Press, 1981), 299–319.

35. Brooks and Elliott, "Prediction of Psychological Adjustment."

36. Mark Mellman, Edward Lazarus, and Allan Rivlin, "Family Time, Family Values," in *Rebuilding the Nest,* ed. David Blankenhorn, Steven Bayme, and Jean Bethke Elshtain (Milwaukee: Family Service of America, 1990), 73–92.

37. John P. Robinson and Geoffrey Godbey, *Time for Life* (University Park: Pennsylvania State University Press, 1997).

38. Ibid., pp. 48–49.

39. Sandra L. Hofferth, "Changes in American Children's Time, 1981–1997," *Brown University Child and Adolescent Behavior Letter,* March 1999, p. 1.

40. Keith Crnic and Christine Low, "Everyday Stresses and Parenting," in *Handbook of Parenting,* 2nd ed., ed. Marc H. Bornstein, vol. 5: *Practical Issues in Parenting* (Mahwah, NJ: Erlbaum, 2002), 243–267; Theodore Dix, "The Affective Organization of Parenting: Adaptive and Maladaptive Processes," *Psychological Bulletin* 110 (1991): 3–25.

41. Ernest N. Jouriles, Christopher M. Murphy, and K. Daniel O'Leary, "Effects of Maternal Mood on Mother-Son Interaction Patterns," *Journal of Abnormal Child Psychology* 17 (1989): 513–525.

42. John U. Zussman, "Situational Determinants of Parenting Behavior: Effects of Competing Cognitive Activity," *Child Development* 51 (1980): 772–780.

43. Crnic and Low, "Everyday Stresses and Parenting."

44. Crnic and Low, "Everyday Stresses and Parenting"; Jay Belsky, Keith Crnic, and Sharon Woodworth, "Personality and Parenting: Exploring the Mediating Role of Transient Mood and Daily Hassles," *Journal of Personality* 63 (1995): 905–929.

45. Mona El-Sheikh, E. Mark Cummings, and Virginia Goetsch, "Coping with Adults' Angry Behavior: Behavioral, Physiological, and Verbal Responses in Preschoolers," *Developmental Psychology* 25 (1989): 490–498.

46. John M. Gottman and Lynn F. Katz, "Effects of Marital Discord on Young Children's Peer Interaction and Health," *Developmental Psychology* 25 (1989): 373–381.

47. E. Mark Cummings, "Coping with Background Anger in Early Childhood," *Child Development* 58 (1987): 976–984.

48. Jennifer S. Cummings et al., "Children's Responses to Adult Behavior As a Function of Marital Distress and History of Interparent Hostility," *Child Development* 60 (1989): 1035–1043.

49. John H. Grych and Frank D. Fincham, "Children's Appraisals of Marital Conflict: Initial Investigation of the Cognitive-Contextual Framework," *Child Development* 64 (1993): 215–230.

50. Katherine Covell and Brenda Miles, "Children's Beliefs about Strategies to Reduce Parental Anger," *Child Development* 63 (1992): 381–390.

51. E. Mark Cummings et al., "Resolution and Children's Responses to Interadult Anger," *Developmental Psychology* 27 (1991): 462–470.

52. Katherine Covell and Rona Abramovitch, "Understanding Emotion in the Family: Children's and Parents' Attributions of Happiness, Sadness, and Anger," *Child Development* 57 (1987): 985–991.

53. Robinson and Godbey, *Time for Life.*

54. Ibid., p. 295.

55. Ibid., p. 149.

56. Ibid., p. 316.

57. Carolyn Pape Cowan and Philip A. Cowan, *When Partners Become Parents* (New York: Basic Books, 1992).

58. Barbara J. Tinsley and Ross D. Parke, "Grandparents As Support and Socialization Agents," in *Beyond the Dyad,* ed. Michael Lewis (New York: Plenum, 1984), pp. 161–194.

59. Timothy F. J. Tolson and Melvin N. Wilson, "The Impact of Two- and Three-Generational Family Structure on Perceived Family Style," *Child Development* 61 (1990): 416–428.

60. Jane L. Pearson et al., "Black Grandmothers in Multigenerational Households: Diversity in Family Structures on Parenting in the Woodlawn Community," *Child Development* 61 (1990): 434–442.

61. Peter K. Smith and Linda M. Drew, "Grandparenthood," in *Handbook of Parenting,* 2nd ed., ed Marc H. Bornstein, vol. 3: *Being and Becoming a Parent* (Mahwah, NJ: Erlbaum, 2002), 141–172.

62. Ibid., p. 147.

63. Ibid.

64. Ibid.

65. Natalie Angier, "Weighing the Grandma Factor," *New York Times,* 5 November 2002, p. D1.

66. Ibid.

67. Smith and Drew, "Grandparenthood."

68. Crnic and Low, "Everyday Stresses and Parenting."

69. Ibid.

70. Nancy Samalin with Catherine Whitney, *Love and Anger: The Parental Dilemma* (New York: Penguin Books, 1992).

71. Jane Nelson, *Positive Discipline* (New York: Ballantine Books, 1981).

72. Dreikurs with Soltz, *Children,* pp. 55–56.

73. Arthur T. Jersild et al., *Joys and Problems of Child Rearing* (New York: Bureau of Publications, Teachers College, Columbia University, 1949), 1–2.

74. Ibid., p. 122.

75. Jay D. Schvaneveldt, Marguerite Fryer, and Renee Ostler, "Concepts of 'Badness' and 'Goodness' of Parents As Perceived by Nursery School Children," *The Family Coordinator* 19 (1970): 98–103.

76. John R. Weisz, "Autonomy, Control and Other Reasons Why 'Mom Is the Greatest': A Content Analysis of Children's Mother's Day Letters," *Child Development* 51 (1980): 801–807.

77. Personal communication.

CHAPTER 5

1. Patricia Chamberlain and Gerald R. Patterson, "Discipline and Child Compliance in Parenting," in *Handbook of Parenting,* ed. Marc H. Bornstein, vol. 4: *Applied and Practical Parenting* (Mahwah, NJ: Erlbaum, 1995), 205–225.

2. Diana Baumrind, "The Discipline Controversy Revisited," *Family Relations* 45 (1996): 405–414.

3. Eleanor E. Maccoby and John A. Martin, "Socialization in the Context of the Family: Parent-Child Interaction," in *Handbook of Child Psychology,* 4th ed., eds. Paul H. Mussen and E. Mavis Hetherington, vol. 4: *Socialization, Personality and Social Development* (New York: Wiley, 1983), 1–101.

4. Daphne Blunt Bugental and Jacqueline J. Goodnow, "Socialization Processes," in *Handbook of Child Psychology,* 5th ed., ed. William Damon, vol. 3: *Social, Emotional, and Personality Development,* ed. Nancy Eisenberg (New York: Wiley, 1998), 389–462.

5. Barbara Rogoff, "Cognition as Collaborative Process," in *Handbook of Child Psychology,* 5th ed., ed. William Damon, vol. 2: *Cognition, Perception, and Language,* ed. Deanna Kuhn and Robert S. Siegler (New York: Wiley, 1998), 679–744.

6. Jean V. Carew, *Experience and the Development of Intelligence in Young Children at Home and in Day Care,* Monographs of the Society for Research in Child Development 45, no. 187 (1980).

7. Joan E. Grusec and Jacqueline J. Goodnow, "Impact of Parental Discipline Methods on the Child's Internalization of Values: A Reconceptualization of Current Points of View," *Developmental Psychology* 30 (1994): 4–19.

8. Gerald R. Patterson and Philip A. Fisher, "Recent Developments in Our Understanding of Parenting: Bidirectional Effects, Causal Models, and the Search for Parsimony," in *Handbook of Parenting,* 2nd ed., ed. Marc H. Bornstein, vol. 5: *Practical Issues in Parenting* (Mahwah, NJ: Erlbaum, 2002), 59–88.

9. Maccoby and Martin, "Socialization in the Context of the Family," p. 65.

10. Charles R. Martinez, Jr., and Marion Forgatch, "Preventing Problems with Boys' Noncompliance: Effects of a Parent Training Intervention for Divorcing Mothers," *Journal of Consulting and Clinical Psychology* 69 (2001): 416–428; Patterson and Fisher,

"Recent Developments in Our Understanding of Parenting."

11. Martinez and Forgatch, "Preventing Problems with Boys' Noncompliance."

12. Joan E. Grusec, "Parental Socialization and Children's Acquisition of Values," in *Handbook of Parenting,* 2nd ed., ed. Bornstein, vol. 5, pp. 143–168.

13. Larry P. Nucci and Elliot Turiel, "Social Interactions and the Development of Social Concepts in Preschool Children," *Child Development* 49 (1978): 400–407.

14. Thomas Gordon, *P.E.T.: Parent Effectiveness Training* (New York: New American Library, 1975).

15. Rudolf Dreikurs with Vicki Soltz, *Children: The Challenge* (New York: Hawthorn, 1964).

16. Chamberlain and Patterson, "Discipline and Child Compliance in Parenting."

17. Elizabeth Thompson Gershoff, "Corporal Punishment by Parents and Associated Child Behaviors and Experiences: A Meta-Analysis and Theoretical Review," *Psychological Bulletin* 128 (2002): 539–579.

18. Ibid.

19. Diana Baumrind, "Necessary Distinctions," *Psychological Inquiry* 8 (1997): 176–182.

20. Vonnie C. McLoyd and Julia Smith, "Physical Discipline and Behavior Problems in African American, European American, and Hispanic Children: Emotional Support As Moderator," *Journal of Marriage and Family* 64 (2002): 40–53.

21. Gershoff, "Corporal Punishment"; Ray Guarendi with David Eich, *Back to the Family* (New York: Simon & Schuster, 1991).

22. Anthony M. Graziano, Jessica L. Hamblen, and Wendy A. Plante, "Subabusive Violence in Child-Rearing in Middle-Class Families," *Pediatrics* 98 (1996): 845–848.

23. Randal D. Day, Gary W. Peterson, and Coleen McCracken, "Predicting Spanking of Younger and Older Children by Mothers and Fathers," *Journal of Marriage and the Family* 60 (1998): 79–94; Jean Giles-Sims, Murray A. Straus, and David B. Sugarman, "Child, Maternal, and Family Characteristics Associated with Spanking," *Family Relations* 44 (1994): 170–176.

24. Glenn D. Wolfner and Richard J. Gelles, "A Profile of Violence toward Children: A National Study," *Child Abuse and Neglect* 17 (1993): 199–214.

25. Graziano, Hamblen, and Plante, "Subabusive Violence."

26. Day, Peterson, and McCracken, "Predicting Spanking."

27. Giles-Sims, Straus, and Sugarman, "Child, Maternal, and Family Characteristics."

28. Day, Peterson, and McCracken, "Predicting Spanking"; Gershoff, "Corporal Punishment"; Giles-Sims, Straus, and Sugarman, "Child, Maternal, and Family Characteristics."

29. Diana Baumrind, "The Development of Instrumental Competence through Socialization," in *Minnesota Symposium on Child Psychology,* vol. 7, ed. Ann D. Pick (Minneapolis: University of Minnesota Press, 1973), 3–46.

30. Day, Peterson, and McCracken, "Predicting Spanking."

31. McLoyd and Smith, "Physical Discipline and Behavior Problems."

32. Giles-Sims, Straus, and Sugarman, "Child, Maternal, and Family Characteristics."

33. Day, Peterson, and McCracken, "Predicting Spanking."

34. Giles-Sims, Straus, and Sugarman, "Child, Maternal, and Family Characteristics."

35. Ibid.

36. Day, Peterson, and McCracken, "Predicting Spanking."

37. Guarendi with Eich, *Back to the Family.*

38. Lawrence S. Wissow, "What Clinicians Want to Know about Teaching Families New Disciplinary Tools," *Pediatrics* 98 (1996): 816.

39. Thomas F. Caltron and John C. Masters, "Mothers' and Children's Conceptualizations of Corporal Punishment," *Child Development* 64 (1993): 1815–1828.

40. Baumrind, "Discipline Controversy Revisited."

41. McLoyd and Smith, "Physical Discipline and Behavior Problems."

42. Ibid., p. 50.

43. Robert E. Larzelere, "A Review of Outcomes of Parental Use of Nonabusive or Customary Physical Punishment," *Pediatrics* 98 (1996): 824–828.

44. Gershoff, "Corporal Punishment."

45. Diana Baumrind, Robert E. Larzelere, and Philip A. Cowan, "Ordinary Physical Punishment: Is It Harmful? Comment on Gershoff (2002)," *Psychological Bulletin* 128 (2002): 580–589.

46. Ibid., p. 585.

47. Patterson and Fisher, "Recent Developments."

48. Murray A. Straus, "Spanking and the Making of a Violent Society," *Pediatrics* 98 (1996): 837–844.

49. Diana Baumrind, "A Blanket Injunction against Disciplinary Use of Spanking Is Not Warranted by the Data," *Pediatrics* 98 (1996): 828–831.

50. Baumrind, "The Discipline Controversy Revisited," p. 413.

51. Robert W. Chamberlin, "'It Takes a Whole Village' Working with Community Coalitions to Promote Positive Parenting and Strengthen Families," *Pediatrics* 98 (1996): 805.

52. Baumrind, "The Discipline Controversy Revisited," p. 413.

53. Mary K. Rothbart and John E. Bates, "Temperament," in *Handbook of Child Psychology,* 5th ed., ed. Damon, vol. 3, p. 109.

54. Anneliese F. Korner, "Individual Differences at Birth: Implications for Early Experience and Later Development," *American Journal of Orthopsychiatry* 41 (1971): 608–619.

55. Rudolph Schaffer and Peggy E. Emerson, *The Development of Social Attachments in Infancy,* Monographs of the Society for Research in Child Development 29, whole no. 94 (1964).

56. Rothbart and Bates, "Temperament."

57. Anneliese F. Korner et al., "The Relation between Neonatal and Later Activity and Temperament," *Child Development* 56 (1985): 38–42.

58. Rothbart and Bates, "Temperament."

59. Carl E. Schwartz, Nancy Snidman, and Jerome Kagan, "Early Childhood Temperament As a Determinant of Externalizing Behavior," *Development and Psychopathology* 8 (1996): 527–537; Jerome Kagan, Doreen Arcus, and Nancy Snidman, "The Idea of Temperament: Where Do We Go from Here?" in *Nature and Nurture and Psychology,* ed. Robert Plomin and Gerald E. McClearn (Washington, DC: American Psychological Association, 1993), 197–210.

60. John E. Bates, Christine A. Maslin, and Karen H. Frankel, "Attachment Security, Mother-Child Interaction and Temperament As Predictors of Behavior Problem Ratings at Age Three Years," in *Growing Points of Attachment Theory and Research,* ed. Inge Bretherton and Everett Waters, Monographs of the Society for Research in Child Development 50, serial no. 109 (1985): 167–193.

61. Ann Sanson and Mary K. Rothbart, "Child Temperament and Parenting," in *Handbook of Parenting,* ed. Bornstein, vol. 4, pp. 299–321.

62. Avshalom Caspi and Phil A. Silva, "Temperamental Qualities at Age Three Predict Personality Traits in Young Adulthood: Longitudinal Evidence from a Birth Cohort," *Child Development* 66 (1995): 486–498.

63. Sanson and Rothbart, "Child Temperament and Parenting."

64. Kagan, Arcus, and Snidman, "The Idea of Temperament."

65. Sanson and Rothbart, "Child Temperament and Parenting."

66. Cynthia A. Stifter, Tracy L. Spinrad, and Julia M. Braungart-Rieker, "Toward a Developmental Model of Child Compliance: The Role of Emotion Regulation in Infancy," *Child Development* 70 (1999): 21–32.

67. Grazyna Kochanska, Terri L. Tjebkes, and David R. Forman, "Children's Emerging Regulation of Conduct: Restraint, Compliance, and Internalization from Infancy to the Second Year," *Child Development* 69 (1998): 1378–1389.

68. Sanson and Rothbart, "Child Temperament and Parenting."

69. Kagan, Arcus, and Snidman, "The Idea of Temperament."

70. Sybil Escalona, *The Roots of Individuality: Normal Patterns of Development in Infancy* (Chicago: Aldine, 1968).

71. Grusec, "Parental Socialization," p. 161.

72. Ibid.

73. Rosemary S. L. Mills and Kenneth H. Rubin, "Parental Beliefs about Problematic Social Behaviors in Early Childhood," *Child Development* 61 (1990): 138–151.

74. Ann V. McGillicuddy-De Lisi, "Parental Beliefs within the Family Context: Development of a Research Program," in *Methods of Family Research: Biographies of Research Projects,* ed. Irving E. Sigel and Gene H. Brody, vol. 1: *Normal Families* (Hillsdale, NJ: Erlbaum, 1990), 53–85.

75. Grazyna Kochanska, "Maternal Beliefs As Long-Term Predictors of Mother-Child Interactions and Report," *Child Development* 61 (1990): 1934–1943.

76. Jane Loevinger, "Patterns of Parenthood As Theories of Learning," *Journal of Abnormal and Social Psychology* 59 (1959): 148–150.

77. Ibid., p. 150.

78. Arnold Gesell and Frances L. Ilg, *The Child from Five to Ten* (New York: Harper & Row, 1946), p. 308.

CHAPTER 6

1. Lois Wladis Hoffman and Jean Denby Manis, "The Value of Children in the United States: A New Approach to the Study of Fertility,"

Journal of Marriage and the Family 41 (1979): 583–596.

2. Ibid.

3. Gerald Y. Michaels, "Motivational Factors in the Decision and Timing of Pregnancy," in *The Transition to Parenthood,* ed. Gerald Y. Michaels and Wendy A. Goldberg (New York: Cambridge University Press, 1988), 23–61.

4. Michaels, "Motivational Factors"; Ross D. Parke and Raymond Buriel, "Socialization in the Family: Ethnic and Ecological Perspectives," in *Handbook of Child Psychology,* 5th ed., ed. William Damon, vol. 3: *Social, Emotional, and Personality Development,* ed. Nancy Eisenberg (New York: Wiley, 1997), 463–552.

5. Michaels, "Motivational Factors."

6. Ibid.

7. Christoph Heinicke, "The Transition to Parenting," in *Handbook of Parenting,* 2nd ed., ed. Marc H. Bornstein, vol 3: *Being and Becoming a Parent* (Mahwah, NJ: Erlbaum, 2002), pp. 363–388.

8. Carolyn Pape Cowan and Philip A. Cowan, *When Partners Become Parents* (New York: Basic Books, 1992); Pamela Daniels and Kathy Weingarten, *Sooner or Later: The Timing of Parenthood in Adult Lives* (New York: Norton, 1983).

9. Ibid.

10. U.S. Bureau of the Census, *Statistical Abstract of the United States: 2002,* 122nd ed. (Washington, DC: U.S. Government Printing Office, 2001).

11. E. Michael Foster, Damon Jones, and Saul D. Hoffman, "The Economic Impact of Nonmarital Childbearing: How Are Older, Single Mothers Faring?" *Journal of Marriage and the Family* 60 (1998): 163–174.

12. Scott J. South, "Historical Change and Life Course Variation in the Determinants of Premarital Childbearing," *Journal of Marriage and the Family* 61 (1999): 752–763.

13. Foster, Jones, and Hoffman, "Economic Impact of Nonmarital Childbearing."

14. Wendy D. Manning, "The Implications of Cohabitation for Children's Well-Being," in *Just Living Together,* ed. Alan Booth and Ann C. Crouter (Mahwah, NJ: Erlbaum, 2002), 121–152.

15. Kelly Musick, "Planned and Unplanned Childbearing among Unmarried Women," *Journal of Marriage and Family* 64 (2002): 915–929.

16. Judith A. Seltzer, "Families Formed Outside of Marriage," *Journal of Marriage and the Family* 62 (2000): 1247–1268.

17. Charlotte J. Patterson, "Lesbian and Gay Parenthood," in *Handbook of Parenting,* 2nd ed., ed. Bornstein, vol. 3, pp. 317–338.

18. Ibid.

19. Lisa A. Serbin et al., "Intergenerational Transfer of Psychosocial Risk in Women with Childhood Histories of Aggression, Withdrawal, or Aggression and Withdrawal," *Developmental Psychology* 34 (1998): 1242–1262.

20. Lianne Woodward, David M. Fergusson, and L. John Horwood, "Risk Factors and Life Processes Associated with Teenage Pregnancy: Results of a Prospective Study from Birth to Twenty Years," *Journal of Marriage and Family* 63 (2001): 1170–1184.

21. Ibid.

22. Laura V. Scaramella et al., "Predicting Risk for Pregnancy by Late Adolescence: A Social Contextual Perspective," *Developmental Psychology* 34 (1998): 1233–1245.

23. Serbin et al., "Intergenerational Transfer of Psychosocial Risk."

24. Woodward, Fergusson, and Horwood, "Risk Factors and Life Processes."

25. Judith Musick, "The Special Role of Parenting in the Context of Poverty: The Case of Adolescent Motherhood," in *Threats to Optimal Development: Integrating Biological, Psychological and Social Risk Factors,* ed. Charles A. Nelson (Hillsdale, NJ: Erlbaum, 1994), 179–216.

26. Joy D. Osofsky, Della M. Hann, and Claire Peebles, "Adolescent Parenthood: Risks and Opportunities for Mothers and Infants," in *Handbook of Infant Mental Health,* ed. Charles H. Zeanah, Jr. (New York: Guilford Press, 1993), 106–119.

27. Woodward, Fergusson, and Horwood, "Risk Factors and Life Processes"; Serbin et al., "Intergenerational Transfer of Psychosocial Risk."

28. Osofsky, Hann, and Peebles, "Adolescent Parenthood."

29. Beverly I. Fagot et al., "Becoming an Adolescent Father: Precursors and Parenting," *Developmental Psychology* 34 (1998): 1209–1219.

30. Terrence P. Thornberry, Carolyn A. Smith, and Gregory J. Howard, "Risk Factors for Teenage Fatherhood," *Journal of Marriage and the Family* 59 (1997): 505–522.

31. Nancy J. Cobb, *Adolescence: Continuity, Change, and Diversity* (Mountain View, CA: Mayfield, 1992).

32. Brenda W. Donnelly and Patricia Voydanoff, "Factors Associated with Releasing for Adoption among Adolescent Mothers," *Family Relations* 40 (1990): 404–410.

33. Marsha Weinraub, Danille L. Horvath, and Marcy B. Gringlas, "Single Parenthood," in *Handbook of Parenting,* 2nd ed., ed. Bornstein, vol. 3, pp. 109–140.

34. Melissa Ludtke, *On Our Own: Unmarried Motherhood in America* (New York: Random House, 1997).

35. Jane Mattes, *Single Mothers by Choice,* 2nd ed. (New York: Times Books, 1997).

36. Marilyn Fabe and Norma Wikler, *Up against the Clock* (New York: Random House, 1979).

37. Cowan and Cowan, *When Partners Become Parents.*

38. Henry P. David, "Developmental Effects of Compulsory Pregnancy," *Child, Youth, and Family Services Quarterly,* Spring 1992.

39. James McCarthy and Janet Hardy, "Age at First Birth and Birth Outcomes," *Journal of Research on Adolescence* 3 (1993): 373–392.

40. Ibid.

41. U.S. Bureau of the Census, *Statistical Abstract of the United States: 2002.*

42. Carol Harkness, *The Infertility Book,* 2nd ed. (Berkeley, CA: Celestial Arts, 1992).

43. Emma Ross, "Patience for Parenthood," *San Francisco Chronicle,* 4 July 2002, p. A6.

44. Susan Golombok, "Parenting and Contemporary Reproductive Technologies," in *Handbook of Parenting,* 2nd ed., ed. Bornstein, vol. 3, pp. 339–360.

45. Christine A. Bachrach, Clifford C. Clogg, and Karen Carver, "Outcomes of Early Childbearing: Summary of a Conference," *Journal of Research on Adolescence* 3 (1993): 337–348.

46. Osofsky, Hann, and Peebles, "Adolescent Parenthood."

47. Nan Marie Astone, "Are Adolescent Mothers Just Single Mothers?" *Journal of Research on Adolescence* 3 (1993): 353–371.

48. Ibid.

49. Mignon R. Moore and Jeanne Brooks-Gunn, "Adolescent Parenthood," in *Handbook of Parenting,* 2nd ed., ed. Bornstein, vol. 3, pp. 173–214.

50. Lisa A. Serbin, Patricia L. Peters, and Alexander E. Schwartzman, "Longitudinal Study of Early Childhood Injuries and Acute Illnesses in the Offspring of Adolescent Mothers Who Were Aggressive, Withdrawn or Aggressive-Withdrawn in Childhood," *Journal of Abnormal Psychology* 105 (1996): 500–507.

51. Moore and Brooks-Gunn, "Adolescent Parenthood."

52. Janet B. Hardy et al., "Like Mother, Like Child: Intergenerational Patterns of Age at First Birth and Associations with Childhood and Adolescent Characteristics and Adult Outcomes in the Second Generation," *Developmental Psychology* 34 (1998): 1220–1232.

53. Sara Jaffee et al., "Why Are Children Born to Teen Mothers at Risk for Adverse Outcomes in Young Adultfood? Results from a 20-Year Longitudinal Study," *Development and Psychopathology* 13 (2001): 377–397.

54. Frank F. Furstenberg, J. Brooks-Gunn, and S. Philip Morgan, *Adolescent Mothers in Later Life* (Cambridge: Cambridge University Press, 1990), 145–146.

55. Andrew Yarrow, *Latecomers: Children of Parents over 35* (New York: Free Press, 1991).

56. David M. Brodzinsky and Ellen Pinderhughes, "Parenting and Child Development in Adoptive Families," in *Handbook of Parenting,* 2nd ed., ed. Marc H. Bornstein, vol. 1: *Children and Parenting* (Mahwah, NJ: Erlbaum, 2002), 279–311.

57. Leslie Granston, "A World of Possibilities: International Adoption," *Vassar,* Summer 2002, pp. 14–19.

58. Brodzinsky and Pinderhughes, "Parenting and Child Development in Adoptive Families."

59. Ibid.

60. Ibid.

61. Ibid.

62. Golombok, "Parenting and Contemporary Reproductive Technologies."

63. Brodzinsky and Pinderhughes, "Parenting and Child Development in Adoptive Families."

64. Gail S. Goodman, Robert E. Emery, and Jeffrey J. Haugaard, "Developmental Psychology and Law: Divorce, Child Maltreatment, Foster Care, and Adoption," in *Handbook of Child Psychology,* 5th ed., ed. William Damon, vol. 4: *Child Psychology in Practice,* ed. Irving E. Sigel and K. Ann Renninger (New York: Wiley, 1998), 775–874.

65. DiAnne Borders, Judith M. Penny, and Francie Portnoy, "Adult Adoptees and Their Friends: Current Functioning and Psychosocial Well-Being," *Family Relations* 49 (2000): 407–418.

66. Brodzinsky and Pinderhughes, "Parenting and Child Development in Adoptive Families."

67. C. Robert Cloninger et al., "Predisposition to Petty Criminality in Swedish Adoptees: II. Cross-Fostering Analysis of Gene-Environment Interaction," *Archives of General Psychiatry* 39 (1982): 1242–1247.

68. Brodzinsky and Pinderhughes, "Parenting and Child Development in Adoptive Families."

69. Golombok, "Parenting and Contemporary Reproductive Technologies."

70. Ibid.

71. Ibid.

72. Peggy Orenstein, "Looking for a Donor to Call Dad," *The New York Times Magazine,* 18 June 1995, p. 28.

73. Brodzinsky and Pinderhughes, "Parenting and Child Development in Adoptive Families."

74. Harkness, *Infertility Book,* p. 327.

75. Heinicke, "Transition to Parenting."

76. Eleanor E. Maccoby and John A. Martin, "Socialization in the Context of the Family: Parent-Child Interaction," in *Handbook of Child Psychology,* 4th ed., ed. Paul H. Mussen and E. Mavis Hetherington, vol. 4: *Socialization, Personality, and Social Development* (New York: Wiley, 1983), 1–101.

77. Jude Cassidy, "Emotion Regulation: Influences of Attachment Relationship," in *The Development of Emotion Regulation,* ed. Nathan A. Fox, Monographs of the Society for Research in Child Development 59, serial no. 240 (1994): 228–249.

78. Ross D. Parke and Barbara J. Tinsley, "Family Interaction in Infancy," in *Handbook of Infant Development,* 2nd ed., ed. Joy Doniger Osofsky (New York: Wiley, 1987), 579–641.

79. E. Mark Cummings and Patrick Davies, *Children and Marital Conflict: The Impact of Family Disputes and Resolution* (New York: Guilford Press, 1994).

80. Gretchen Owens et al., "The Prototype Hypothesis and the Origins of Attachment Working Models: Adult Relationships with Parents and Romantic Partners," in *Caregiving, Cultural, and Cognitive Perspectives in Secure-Base Behavior and Working Models,* ed. Everett Waters et al., Monographs of the Society for Research in Child Development 60, serial no. 244 (1995): 216–233.

81. Cowan and Cowan, *When Partners Become Parents.*

82. Jay Belsky and John Kelly, *The Transition to Parenthood* (New York: Delacorte Press, 1994).

83. Ellen Galinsky, *Between Generations: The Six Stages of Parenthood* (New York: Times Books, 1981).

84. Myra Leifer, "Psychological Changes Accompanying Pregnancy and Motherhood," *Genetic Psychology Monographs* 95 (1977): 55–96.

85. Cowan and Cowan, *When Partners Become Parents.*

86. Belsky and Kelly, *The Transition to Parenthood.*

87. Susan Goldberg and Barbara DiVitto, "Parenting Children Born Preterm," in *Handbook of Parenting,* 2nd ed., ed. Bornstein, vol. 1, pp. 329–354.

88. Ibid.

89. Galinsky, *Between Generations.*

90. Ibid., p. 317.

91. Kathryn E. Barnard, Colleen E. Morisset, and Susan Spieker, "Preventive Interventions: Enhancing Parent-Infant Relationships," in *Handbook of Infant Mental Health,* ed. Zeanah, pp. 386–401.

92. Amy Wolfson, Patricia Lacks, and Andrew Futterman, "Effects of Parent Training on Infant Sleeping Patterns, Parents' Stress, and Perceived Parental Competence," *Journal of Consulting and Clinical Psychology* 60 (1992): 41–48.

93. Cowan and Cowan, *When Partners Become Parents.*

CHAPTER 7

1. Thomas Anders, Beth Goodlin-Jones, and Avi Sadeh, "Sleep Disorders," in *Handbook of Infant Mental Health,* 2nd ed., ed. Charles H. Zeanah, Jr. (New York: Guilford, 2000), 326–328.

2. Marc Weissbluth, *Crybabies* (New York: Arbor House, 1984).

3. Ibid.

4. Daphne Blunt Bugental and Jacqueline J. Goodnow, "Socialization Processes," in *Handbook of Child Psychology,* 5th ed., ed. William Damon: vol. 3: *Social, Emotional, and Personality Development,* ed. Nancy Eisenberg (New York: Wiley, 1998), 1256–1297.

5. Andrew Meltzoff and M. Keith Moore, "Imitation of Facial and Manual Gestures by Human Neonates," *Science* 198 (1977): 75–78.

6. Tiffany Field, "The Effects of Mother's Physical and Emotional Availability on Emotion Regulation," in *Development of Emotional Regulation: Biological and Behavioral Considerations,* ed. Nathan A. Fox, Monographs of the Society for Research in Child Development 59, serial no. 240 (1994): 208–227.

7. Jayne Standley, "Music Therapy in the NICU: Promoting Growth and Development of Premature Infants," *Zero to Three* 23, no. 1 (2002): 23–30.

8. Colwyn Trevarthen and Stephen Malloch, "Musicality and Music before Three: Human Vitality and Invention Shared with Pride," *Zero to Three* 23, no.1 (2002): 10–18.

9. Carol Zander Malatesta and Jeannette M. Haviland, "Learning Display Rules: The Socialization of Emotion Expression in Infancy," *Child Development* 53 (1982): 991–1003.

10. Jeannette M. Haviland and Mary Lelwica, "The Induced-Affect Response: 10-Week-Old Infants' Responses to Three Emotion Expressions," *Developmental Psychology* 23 (1987): 97–104.

11. Carol Z. Malatesta et al., "Emotion Socialization and Expression Development in Preterm and Full Term Infants," *Child Development* 57 (1986): 316–330.

12. Ross A. Thompson, "Early Sociopersonality Development," in *Handbook of Child Psychology,* 5th ed., ed. Damon, vol. 3, pp. 25–104.

13. Ibid.

14. Ibid.

15. Robin Hornick, Nancy Risenhoover, and Megan Gunnar, "The Effects of Maternal Positive, Neutral, and Negative Affect Communication on Infant Responses to New Toys," *Child Development* 58 (1987): 936–944.

16. Susan Crockenberg and Esther Leerkes, "Infant Social and Emotional Development in Family Context," in *Handbook of Infant Mental Health,* 2nd ed., ed. Zeanah, pp. 60–90.

17. Gwen E. Gustafson, "Effects of the Ability to Locomote on Infants' Social and Exploratory Behaviors: An Experimental Study," *Developmental Psychology* 20 (1984): 397–405.

18. Herbert Ginsburg and Sylvia Opper, *Piaget's Theory of Intellectual Development* (Englewood Cliffs, NJ: Prentice-Hall, 1969); Jean Piaget and Barbel Inhelder, *The Psychology of the Child* (New York: Basic Books, 1969).

19. James V. Wertsch and Peeter Tulviste, "L. S. Vygotsky and Contemporary Developmental Psychology," *Developmental Psychology* 28 (1992): 548–557.

20. Lois Bloom, "Language Acquisition in Its Developmental Context," in *Handbook of Child Psychology,* 5th ed., ed. William Damon, vol. 2: *Cognition, Perception, and Language,* ed. Deanna Kuhn and Robert S. Siegler (New York: Wiley, 1998), 309–370.

21. Ibid.

22. Inge Bretherton et al., "Learning to Talk about Emotions: A Functionalist Perspective," *Child Development* 57 (1986): 529–548.

23. Ibid., p. 534.

24. Bloom, "Language Acquisition."

25. Malatesta and Haviland, "Learning Display Rules."

26. Ibid.

27. Eleanor J. Gibson and Richard D. Walk, "The Visual Cliff," *Scientific American* 202 (April 1960): 64–71.

28. Robin Hornick, Nancy Risenhoover, and Megan Gunnar, "The Effects of Maternal Positive, Neutral, and Negative Affect Communication on Infant Responses to New Toys," *Child Development* 58 (1987): 936–944.

29. Michael Lewis, "The Emergence of Emotions," in *Handbook of Emotions,* ed. Michael Lewis and Jeanette M. Haviland (New York: Guilford Press, 1993), 223–235.

30. Deborah Stipek, Susan Recchia, and Susan McClintic, *Self-Evaluation in Young Children,* Monographs of the Society for Research in Child Development 57, serial no. 226 (1992).

31. Pamela M. Cole, Karen Caplovitz-Barrett, and Carolyn Zahn-Waxler, "Emotion Displays in Two-Year-Olds during Mishaps," *Child Development* 63 (1992): 314–324; Deborah J. Stipek, J. Heidi Gralinski, and Claire B. Kopp, "Self-Concept Development in the Toddler Years," *Developmental Psychology* 26 (1990): 972–977.

32. Marion Radke-Yarrow et al., "Learning Concern for Others," *Developmental Psychology* 8 (1973): 240–260; Herbert Wray, *Emotions in the Lives of Young Children,* Department of Health, Education, and Welfare Publication no. 78-644 (Rockville, MD: 1978); Carolyn Zahn-Waxler et al., "Development of Concern for Others," *Developmental Psychology* 28 (1992): 126–136.

33. Florence L. Goodenough, *Anger in Young Children* (Minneapolis: University of Minnesota Press, 1931).

34. Ibid.

35. Claire B. Kopp, "Regulation of Distress and Negative Emotions: A Developmental View," *Developmental Psychology* 25 (1989): 343–354.

36. Ibid.

37. Harriet L. Rheingold, Kay V. Cook, and Vicki Kolowitz, "Commands Cultivate the Behavioral Pleasure of Two-Year-Old Children,"

Developmental Psychology 23 (1987): 146–151.

38. Susan Harter, "The Development of Self-Representations," in *Handbook of Child Psychology,* 5th ed., ed. Damon, vol. 3, pp. 553–617.

39. Claire B. Kopp, "Antecedents of Self-Regulation: A Developmental Perspective," *Developmental Psychology* 18 (1982): 199–214.

40. Donelda J. Stayton, Robert Hogan, and Mary D. Salter Ainsworth, "Infant Obedience and Maternal Behavior: The Origins of Socialization Reconsidered," *Child Development* 42 (1971): 1057–1069.

41. Kopp, "Antecedents of Self-Regulation."

42. Brian E. Vaughn et al., "Process Analysis of the Behavior of Very Young Children in Daily Tasks," *Developmental Psychology* 22 (1986): 752–759.

43. Marianne S. De Wolff and Marinus van IJzendoorn, "Sensitivity and Attachment: A Meta-Analysis on Parental Antecedents of Infant Attachment," *Child Development* 68 (1997) 571–591.

44. Mary Jane Gandour, "Activity Level As a Dimension of Temperament in Toddlers: Its Relevance for the Organismic Specificity Hypotheses," *Child Development* 60 (1989): 1092–1098.

45. Ross D. Parke, "Fathers and Families," in *Handbook of Parenting,* 2nd ed., ed. Marc H. Bornstein, vol. 3: *Being and Becoming a Parent* (Mahwah, NJ: Erlbaum, 2002), 27–73.

46. W. Jean Yeung et al., "Children's Time with Fathers in Intact Families," *Journal of Marriage and Family* 63 (2001): 136–154.

47. Ibid.

48. Parke, "Fathers and Families."

49. Kathryn E. Barnard and JoAnn E. Solchany, "Mothering," in *Handbook of Parenting,* 2nd ed., ed. Bornstein, vol. 3, pp. 3–25.

50. Parke, "Fathers and Families."

51. Jay Belsky, Bonnie Gilstrap, and Michael Rovine, "The Pennsylvania Infant and Family Development Project I: Stability and Change in Mother-Infant and Father-Infant Interaction in a Family Setting at One, Three, and Nine Months," *Child Development* 55 (1984): 692–705.

52. Marc H. Bornstein, "Parenting Infants," in *Handbook of Parenting,* 2nd ed., ed. Marc H. Bornstein, vol. 1: *Children and Parenting* (Mahwah, NJ: Erlbaum, 2002), 3–43.

53. T. Berry Brazelton and Stanley I. Greenspan, *The Irreducible Needs of Children* (Cambridge, MA: Perseus, 2000).

54. Patricia M. Greenfield and Lalita K. Suzuki, "Culture and Human Development: Implications for Parenting, Education, Pediatrics, and Mental Health," in *Handbook of Child Psychology,* 5th ed., ed. William Damon, vol. 4: *Child Psychology in Practice,* ed. Irving E. Sigel and K. Ann Renninger (New York: Wiley, 1998), 1059–1109.

55. Sylvia M. Bell and Mary D. Salter Ainsworth, "Infant Crying and Maternal Responsiveness," *Child Development* 43 (1972): 1171–1190.

56. Judy Dunn, *Distress and Comfort* (Cambridge, MA: Harvard University Press, 1977), 23.

57. Urs A. Hunziker and Ronald G. Barr, "Increased Carrying Reduces Crying: A Randomized Controlled Trial," *Pediatrics* 77 (1986): 641–647.

58. William A. H. Sammons, *The Self-Calmed Baby* (Boston: Little, Brown, 1989).

59. Gilda A. Morelli et al., "Cultural Variations in Infants' Sleeping Arrangements: Questions of Independence," *Developmental Psychology* 28 (1992): 604–613.

60. Klaus Minde, "The Sleep of Infants and Why Parents Matter," *Zero to Three* 19 (October–November 1998): 9–14.

61. Richard Ferber, *Solve Your Child's Sleep Problems* (New York: Simon & Schuster, 1985).

62. Athleen B. Godfrey and Anne Kilgore, "An Approach to Help Very Young Infants Sleep through the Night," *Zero to Three* 19 (October–November 1998): 15–18.

63. Morelli et al., "Cultural Variations in Infants' Sleeping Arrangements."

64. Suad Nakamura, "Adult Beds Are Unsafe Places for Children under Age Two to Sleep," American Medical Association media briefing on children's health, New York, 29 September 1999.

65. James J. McKenna, Sarah S. Mosko, and Christopher A. Richard, "Bedsharing Promotes Breastfeeding," *Pediatrics* 100 (1997): 214–219

66. Nakamura, "Adult Beds Are Unsafe."

67. John Seabrook, "Sleeping with the Baby," *New Yorker,* 8 November 1999.

68. James J. McKenna, "Cultural Influences on Infant and Childhood Sleep Biology, and the Science That Studies It: Toward a More Inclusive Paradigm," *Zero to Three* 20 (December 1999–January 2000): 17.

69. William Sears, introduction to *Attachment Parenting,* by Katie Allison Granju with Betsy Kennedy (New York: Pocket Books, 1999).

70. Katie Allison Granju with Betsy Kennedy, *Attachment Parenting* (New York: Pocket Books, 1999).

71. Ibid., p. 9.

72. Ibid., p. 10.

73. Kopp, "Antecedents of Self-Regulation."

74. Eleanor E. Maccoby and John A. Martin, "Socialization in the Context of the Family: Parent-Child Interaction," in *Handbook of Child Psychology,* 4th ed., ed. Paul H. Mussen and E. Mavis Hetherington, vol. 4: *Socialization, Personality, and Social Development* (New York: Wiley, 1983), 1–101.

75. Susan Crockenberg and Cindy Litman, "Autonomy As Competence in Two-Year-Olds: Maternal Correlates of Child Defiance, Compliance, and Self-Assertion," *Developmental Psychology* 26 (1990): 961–971.

76. George Holden, "Avoiding Conflicts: Mothers As Tacticians in the Supermarket," *Child Development* 54 (1983): 233–240; George W. Holden and Meredith J. West, "Proximate Regulation by Mothers: A Demonstration of How Differing Styles Affect Young Children's Behavior," *Child Development* 60 (1989): 64–69; Thomas G. Power and M. Lynne Chapieski, "Childrearing and Impulsive Control in Toddlers: A Naturalistic Investigation," *Developmental Psychology* 22 (1986): 271–275.

77. J. Heidi Gralinski and Claire B. Kopp, "Everyday Rules for Behavior: Mothers' Requests to Young Children," *Developmental Psychology* 29 (1993): 573–584.

78. Ibid.

79. Cheryl Minton, Jerome Kagan, and Janet A. Levine, "Maternal Control and Obedience in the Two-Year-Old," *Child Development* 42 (1971): 1873–1894.

80. Jeanne Brooks-Gunn and P. Lindsay Chase-Lansdale, "Adolescent Parenthood," in *Handbook of Parenting,* ed. Marc H. Bornstein, vol. 3: *Status and Social Conditions of Parenting* (Mahwah, NJ: Erlbaum, 1995), 113–149.

81. Joy D. Osofsky, Della M. Hann, and Claire Peebles, "Adolescent Parenthood: Risks and Opportunities for Mothers and Infants," in *Handbook of Infant Mental Health,* 2nd ed., ed. Zeanah, pp. 106–119.

82. Brooks-Gunn and Chase-Lansdale, "Adolescent Parenthood."

83. Ibid.

84. Sara Jaffee et al., "Why Are Children Born to Teen Mothers at Risk for Adverse Outcomes in Young Adulthood? Results from a 20-Year Study," *Development and Psychopathology* 13 (2001): 377–397; Judith Musick, "The Special Role of Parenting in the Context of Poverty: The Case of Adolescent Motherhood," in *Threats to Optimal Development: Integrating Biological, Psychological and Social Risk Factors,* ed. Charles A. Nelson (Hillsdale, NJ: Erlbaum, 1994), 179–216.

85. Musick, "The Special Role of Parenting."

86. Brooks-Gunn and Chase-Lansdale, "Adolescent Parenthood."

87. Frank F. Furstenberg, J. Brooks-Gunn, and S. Philip Morgan, *Adolescent Mothers in Later Life* (Cambridge, England: Cambridge University Press, 1990), 145–146.

88. Ross D. Parke and Raymond Buriel, "Socialization in the Family: Ethnic and Ecological Perspectives," in *Handbook of Child Psychology,* 5th ed., ed. Damon, vol. 3, pp. 463–552.

89. Ibid.

90. Beverly I. Fagot et al., "Becoming an Adolescent Father: Precursors and Parenting," *Developmental Psychology* 34 (1998): 1217.

91. Furstenberg, Brooks-Gunn, and Morgan, *Adolescent Mothers in Later Life.*

92. Al Santoli, "They Turn Young Men with Children into Fathers," *Parade Magazine,* 29 May 1994.

93. Ibid.

94. Tiffany Field, "Psychologically Depressed Parents," in *Handbook of Parenting,* ed. Marc H. Bornstein, vol. 4: *Applied and Practical Parenting* (Mahwah, NJ: Erlbaum, 1995), 85–99.

95. Ibid.

96. Linda C. Mayes and Sean D. Truman, "Substance Abuse and Parenting," in *Handbook of Parenting,* 2nd ed., ed. Marc H. Bornstein, vol 4: *Social Conditions and Applied Parenting* (Mahwah, NJ: Earlbaum, 2002), 329–359.

97. Ibid.

98. Ibid.

99. Rina Das Eiden, Felipa Chavez, and Kenneth E. Leonard, "Parent-Infant Interactions among Families with Alcoholic Fathers," *Development and Psychopathology* 11 (1999): 745–762.

100. Mayes and Truman, "Substance Abuse and Parenting."

101. Linda C. Mayes, "Developing Brain and In Utero Cocaine Exposure: Effects on Neural Ontogeny," *Development and Psychopathology* 11 (1999): 685–714.

102. Ibid., p. 706.

103. Carolyn Pape Cowan and Philip A. Cowan, *When Partners Become Parents* (New York: Basic Books, 1992), 142.

104. Ibid.

105. "Surge in Multiple Births Drives Premature Babies to Record," *New York Times*, 19 December 2002, p. A24.

106. Klaus Minde, "Prematurity and Serious Medical Conditions in Infancy: Implications for Development, Behavior, and Intervention," in *Handbook of Infant Mental Health*, 2nd ed., ed. Zeanah, pp. 176–194.

107. Susan Goldberg and Barbara DiVitto, "Parenting Children Born Preterm," in *Handbook of Parenting*, 2nd ed., ed. Bornstein, vol. 1, pp. 329–354.

108. Ibid.

109. Ibid., p. 339.

110. Ibid.

111. Mark T. Greenberg and Keith Crnic, "Longitudinal Predictors of Developmental Status and Social Interaction in Premature and Full-Term Infants at Age Two," *Child Development* 59 (1988): 544–553.

112. Goldberg and DiVitto, "Parenting Children Born Preterm."

113. Marilyn Stern and Katherine A. Hildebrandt, "Prematurity and Stereotyping: Effects on Mother-Infant Interaction," *Child Development* 57 (1986): 308–315.

114. Cynthia I. Zarling, Barton J. Hirsch, and Susan Landry, "Maternal Social Networks and Mother-Infant Interactions in Full-Term and Very Low Birthweight, Preterm Infants," *Child Development* 59 (1988): 178–185.

115. Glenn Affleck et al., "Effects of Formal Support on Mothers' Adaptation to the Hospital-to-Home Transition of High Risk Infants: The Benefits and Costs of Helping," *Child Development* 60 (1989): 488–501.

116. Leila Beckwith, "Prevention Science and Prevention Programs," in *Handbook of Infant Mental Health*, 2nd ed., ed. Zeanah, pp. 439–456.

117. Ellen Galinsky, *Between Generations: The Six Stages of Parenthood* (New York: Times Books, 1981).

118. Linda Mayes, "Harris Programs in Perinatal Mental Health at the Yale Child Study Center," *Zero to Three* 22, no. 6 (2002): 24–30.

119. Kathryn E. Barnard, Colleen E. Morisset, and Susan Spieker, "Preventive Interventions: Enhancing Parent-Infant Relationships," in *Handbook of Infant Mental Health*, ed. Charles H. Zeanah, Jr. (New York: Guilford Press, 1993), 386–401; Samuel J. Meisels, Margo Dichtemiller, and Fong-ruey Liaw, "A Multidimensional Analysis of Early Childhood Intervention Programs," in *Handbook of Infant Mental Health*, ed. Zeanah, pp. 361–385.

120. Dymphna C. van den Boom, "The Influence of Temperament and Mothering on Attachment and Exploration: An Experimental Manipulation of Sensitive Responsiveness among Lower-Class Mothers with Irritable Infants," *Child Development* 65 (1994): 1457–1477.

121. Marinus H. Van IJzendoorn, Femmie Juffer, and Marja G. C. Duyvesteyn, "Breaking the Intergenerational Cycle of Insecure Attachment: A Review of the Effects of Attachment-Based Interventions on Maternal Sensitivity and Infant Security," *Journal of Child Psychology and Psychiatry* 36 (1995): 225–248.

122. Mayes, "Harris Programs."

123. Patricia K. Coleman and Katherine H. Karraker, "Self-Efficacy and Parenting Quality: Findings and Future Applications," *Developmental Review* 18 (1997): 47–85.

CHAPTER 8

1. Allison Gopnick, Andrew N. Meltzoff, and Patricia K. Kuhl, *The Scientist in the Crib* (New York: Morrow, 1999).

2. Jean Piaget and Barbel Inhelder, *The Psychology of the Child* (New York: Basic Books, 1969).

3. Ross A. Thompson, "Early Sociopersonality Development," in *Handbook of Child Psychology*, 5th ed., ed. William Damon, vol. 3: *Social, Emotional, and Personality Development*, ed. Nancy Eisenberg (New York: Wiley, 1997), 25–104.

4. Lois Bloom, "Language Acquisition in Its Developmental Context," in *Handbook of Child Psychology*, 5th ed., ed. William Damon, vol. 2: *Cognition, Perception, and Language*, ed. Deanna Kuhn and Robert S. Siegler (New York: Wiley, 1997), 309–370.

5. Ibid.

6. Sally K. Donaldson and Michael A. Westerman, "Development of Children's Understanding of Ambivalent and Causal Theories of Emotions," *Developmental Psychology* 22 (1986): 655–662.

7. Richard A. Fabes et al., "Preschoolers' Attributions of the Situational Determinants of Others' Naturally Occurring Emotions,"

Developmental Psychology 24 (1988): 376–385.

8. Gertrude Nunner-Winkler and Beate Sodian, *"Children's Understanding of Moral Emotions,"* Child Development 59 (1988): 1323–1338.

9. Frank A. Zelko et al., "Adult Expectancies about Children's Emotional Responsiveness: Implications for the Development of Implicit Theories of Affect," *Developmental Psychology* 22 (1986): 109–114.

10. William Roberts and Janet Strayer, "Parents' Responses to the Emotional Distress of Their Children: Relations with Children's Competence," *Developmental Psychology* 23 (1987): 415–422.

11. Michael Lewis, Catherine Stanger, and Margaret Sullivan, "Deception in Three-Year Olds," *Developmental Psychology* 25 (1989): 439–443.

12. Pamela M. Cole, "Children's Spontaneous Control of Facial Expressions," *Child Development* 57 (1986): 1309–1321.

13. Kurt W. Fischer and Daniel Bullock, "Cognitive Development in School Age Children: Conclusions and New Directions," in *Development during Middle Childhood: The Years from Six to Twelve,* ed. W. Andrew Collins (Washington, DC: National Academy Press, 1984).

14. Nancy Eisenberg et al., "The Relations of Emotionality and Regulation to Children's Anger-Related Reactions," *Child Development* 65 (1994): 109–128.

15. E. Mark Cummings, "Coping with Background Anger in Early Childhood," *Child Development* 58 (1987): 976–984.

16. Jerome Kagan and Nancy Snidman, "Temperamental Factors in Human Development," *American Psychologist* 46 (1991): 856–862.

17. Anders Broberg, Michael E. Lamb, and Philip Hwang, "Inhibition: Its Stability and Correlates in Sixteen- to Forty-Month-Old Children," *Child Development* 61 (1990): 1153–1163.

18. Jerome Kagan and Howard A. Moss, *From Birth to Maturity* (New York: Wiley, 1962).

19. Fabes et al., "Preschoolers' Attributions."

20. David Matsumoto et al., "Preschoolers' Moral Actions and Emotions in Prisoner's Dilemma," *Developmental Psychology* 22 (1986): 663–670.

21. Marion Radke-Yarrow et al., "Learning Concern for Others," *Developmental Psychology* 8 (1973): 240–260; Herbert Wray, *Emotions in the Lives of Young Children* (Rockville, MD:

U.S. Department of Health, Education, and Welfare, 1978), publication no. 78–644.

22. Susan Harter, "The Development of Self-Representations," in *Handbook of Child Psychology,* 5th ed., ed. Damon, vol. 3, pp. 553–617.

23. Deborah J. Stipek, Theresa A. Roberts, and Mary E. Sanborn, "Preschool-Age Children's Performance Expectations of Themselves and Another Child As a Function of the Incentive Value of Success and the Salience of Past Performance," *Child Development* 55 (1984): 1983–1989.

24. Beverly I. Fagot, "Parenting Boys and Girls," in *Handbook of Parenting,* ed. Marc H. Bornstein, vol. 1: *Children and Parenting* (Mahwah, NJ: Erlbaum, 1995), 163–183.

25. Diane N. Ruble and Carol Lynn Martin, "Gender Development," in *Handbook of Child Psychology,* 5th ed., ed. Damon, vol. 3, pp. 933–1016.

26. Susan Golombok and Robyn Fivush, *Gender Development* (New York: Cambridge University Press, 1994).

27. Carolyn Pope Edwards and Wen-Li Liu, "Parenting Toddlers," in *Handbook of Parenting,* 2nd ed., ed. Marc H. Bornstein, vol. 1: *Children and Parenting* (Mahwah, NJ: Erlbaum, 2002), 45–71.

28. Golombok and Fivush, *Gender Development,* p. 111.

29. Ruble and Martin, "Gender Development."

30. Beverly I. Fagot and Mary D. Leinbach, "The Young Child's Gender Schema: Environmental Input, Internal Organization," *Child Development* 60 (1989): 663–672.

31. Patricia J. Bauer, "Memory for Gender-Consistent and Gender-Inconsistent Event Sequences by Twenty-five-Month-Old Children," *Child Development* 64 (1993): 285–297.

32. Ruble and Martin, "Gender Development."

33. Deanna Kuhn, Sharon Churnin Nash, and Laura Brucken, "Sex Role Concepts of Two- and Three-Year-Olds," *Child Development* 49 (1978): 445–451.

34. Campbell Leaper, "Parenting Boys and Girls," in *Handbook of Parenting,* 2nd ed., ed. Bornstein, vol. 1, pp. 189–225; Ruble and Martin, "Gender Development."

35. Carolyn Zahn-Waxler, "Warriors and Worriers: Gender and Psychopathology," *Development and Psychopathology* 5 (1993): 79–89.

36. Margaret Beale Spencer and Carol Markstrom-Adams, "Identity Processes

among Racial and Ethnic Minority Children in America," *Child Development* 61 (1990): 290–310.

37. Frances E. Aboud, "The Development of Ethnic Identification and Attitudes," in *Children's Ethnic Socialization,* ed. Jean S. Phinney and Mary Jane Rotheram (Beverly Hills, CA: Sage, 1987).

38. Claire B. Kopp, "Antecedents of Self-Regulation: A Developmental Perspective," *Developmental Psychology* 18 (1982): 199–214.

39. J. Heidi Gralinski and Claire B. Kopp, "Everyday Rules for Behavior: Mothers' Requests to Young Children," *Developmental Psychology* 29 (1993): 573–584.

40. Leon Kucynski and Grazyna Kochanska, "Development of Children's Noncompliance Strategies from Toddlerhood to Age 5," *Developmental Psychology* 26 (1990): 398–408.

41. Susan Crockenberg and Cindy Litman, "Autonomy As Competence in Two-Year-Olds: Maternal Correlates of Child Defiance, Compliance, and Self-Assertion," *Developmental Psychology* 26 (1990): 961–971; Eleanor E. Maccoby and John A. Martin, "Socialization in the Context of the Family: Parent-Child Interaction," in *Handbook of Child Psychology,* 4th ed., ed. Paul H. Mussen and E. Mavis Hetherington, vol. 4: *Socialization, Personality, and Social Development* (New York: Wiley, 1983), 1–101.

42. Sandra R. Kaler and Claire B. Kopp, "Compliance and Comprehension in Very Young Toddlers," *Child Development* 61 (1990): 1997–2003.

43. Keng-Ling Lay, Everett Waters, and Kathryn A. Park, "Maternal Responsiveness and Child Compliance: The Role of Mood As Mediator," *Child Development* 60 (1989): 1405–1411.

44. Ross D. Parke and Raymond Buriel, "Socialization in the Family: Ethnic and Ecological Perspectives," in *Handbook of Child Psychology,* 5th ed., ed. Damon, vol. 3, pp. 463–552.

45. Thompson, "Early Sociopersonality Development."

46. Leaper, "Parenting Boys and Girls"; Ruble and Martin, "Gender Development."

47. Campbell Leaper, "Gender Affiliation, Assertion, and the Interactive Context of Parent-Child Play," *Developmental Psychology* 36 (2000): 381–393.

48. Fagot, "Parenting Boys and Girls."

49. Leaper, "Parenting Boys and Girls."

50. Kay Bussey and Albert Bandura, "Self-Regulatory Mechanisms Governing Gender Development," *Child Development* 63 (1992): 1247.

51. Leaper, "Parenting Boys and Girls"; Ruble and Martin, "Gender Development."

52. Robert H. Bradley et al., "Home Environments of Children in the United States Part I: Variations by Age, Ethnicity, and Poverty Status," *Child Development* 72 (2001): 1844–1867.

53. Robert H. Bradley et al., "The Home Environments of Children in the United States Part II: Relations with Behavioral Development through Age Thirteen," *Child Development* 72 (2001): 1868–1886.

54. Catherine S. Tamis-LeMonda, Ina C. Uzgiris, and Marc H. Bornstein, "Play in Parent-Child Interaction" in *Handbook of Parenting,* 2nd ed., ed. Marc H. Bornstein, vol. 5, *Practical Issues in Parenting* (Mahwah, NJ: Erlbaum, 2002), 221–241.

55. Grazyna Kochanska, "Mutually Responsive Orientation between Mothers and Their Young Children: Implications for Early Socialization," *Child Development* 68 (1997): 94–112.

56. Jane B. Brooks, *The Process of Parenting,* 5th ed. (Mountain View, CA: Mayfield, 1999), 193.

57. Gerald R. Patterson, "The Early Development of the Coercive Family Process," in *Antisocial Behavior in Children and Adolescents,* ed. John B. Reid, Gerald R. Patterson, and James Snyder (Washington, DC: American Psychological Association, 2002), 25–44.

58. Jay Belsky, Sharon Woodworth, and Keith Crnic, "Troubled Family Interaction during Toddlerhood," *Development and Psychopathology* 8 (1996): 477–495.

59. Patricia M. Greenfield and Lalita K. Suzuki, "Culture and Human Development: Implications for Parenting, Education, Pediatrics, and Mental Health," in *Handbook of Child Psychology,* 5th ed., ed. William Damon, vol. 4: *Child Psychology in Practice,* ed. Irving E. Sigel and K. Ann Renninger (New York: Wiley, 1997), 1059–1109.

60. Ibid.

61. Ibid.

62. Robert B. Stewart et al., "The Firstborn's Adjustment to the Birth of a Sibling: A Longitudinal Assessment," *Child Development* 58 (1987): 341–355.

63. Wyndal Furman and Richard Lanthier, "Parenting Siblings," in *Handbook of Parenting,* 2nd ed., ed. Bornstein, vol. 1, pp. 165–188.

64. Radke-Yarrow et al., "Learning Concern for Others."

65. Gene H. Brody, Zolinda Stoneman, and Michelle Burke, "Child Temperaments, Maternal Differential Behavior, and Sibling Relationships," *Developmental Psychology* 23 (1987): 354–362; Robert B. Steuart et al., "The Firstborn's Adjustment to the Birth of a Sibling: A Longitudinal Assessment," *Child Development* 58 (1987), 341–355; Clare Stocker, Judy Dunn, and Robert Plomin, "Sibling Relationships: Links with Child Temperament, Maternal Behavior, and Family Structure," *Child Development* 60 (1989): 715–727.

66. Judith F. Dunn, Robert Plomin, and Denise Daniels, "Consistency and Change in Mothers' Behavior toward Young Siblings," *Child Development* 57 (1986): 348–356; Judith F. Dunn, Robert Plomin, and Margaret Nettles, "Consistency of Mothers' Behavior toward Infant Siblings," *Developmental Psychology* 21 (1985): 1188–1195.

67. Carollee Howes, *Peer Interaction of Young Children,* Monographs of the Society for Research in Child Development 53, serial no. 217 (1987).

68. Tiffany Field, Louis De Stefano, and John H. Koewler, III, "Fantasy Play of Toddlers and Preschoolers," *Developmental Psychology* 18 (1982): 503–508.

69. Donald S. Hayes, "Cognitive Bases for Liking and Disliking among Preschool Children," *Child Development* 49 (1978): 906–909.

70. Willard W. Hartup et al., "Conflict and the Friendship Relations of Young Children," *Child Development* 59 (1988): 1590–1600.

71. Michael P. Leiter, "A Study of Reciprocity in Preschool Play Groups," *Child Development* 48 (1977): 1288–1295.

72. Kenneth H. Rubin, William Bukowski, and Jeffrey G. Parker, "Peer Interactions, Relationships, and Groups," in *Handbook of Child Psychology,* 5th ed., ed. Damon, vol. 3, pp. 619–700.

73. Ibid.

74. Patty Rhule, "Sleep Trouble in School-Age Kids," *USA Weekend,* 15–17 November 2002, p. 16.

75. Alice M. Gregory and Thomas G. O'Connor, "Sleep Problems in Childhood: A Longitudinal Study of Developmental Change and Association with Behavioral Problems," *Journal of the American Academy of Child and Adolescent Psychiatry* 41 (2002): 964–971.

76. Rhule, "Sleep Trouble."

77. Richard Ferber, *Solve Your Child's Sleep Problems* (New York: Simon & Schuster, 1985).

78. Ibid., p. 49.

79. Adele Faber and Elaine Mazlish, *Liberated Parents/Liberated Children* (New York: Avon, 1975).

80. Thomas Gordon with Judith Gordon Sands, *P.E.T. in Action* (New York: Bantam Books, 1978).

81. Rudolf Dreikurs with Vicki Soltz, *Children: The Challenge* (New York: Hawthorn, 1964).

82. John D. Krumboltz and Helen B. Krumboltz, *Changing Children's Behavior* (Englewood Cliffs, NJ: Prentice-Hall, 1972).

83. Stanley Turecki and Leslie Tonner, *The Difficult Child* (New York: Bantam Books, 1985).

84. Faber and Mazlish, *Liberated Parents/Liberated Children.*

85. David M. Buss, Jeanne H. Block, and Jack Block, "Preschool Activity Level: Personality Correlates and Developmental Implications," *Child Development* 51 (1980): 401–408.

86. David M. Buss, "Predicting Parent-Child Interactions from Children's Activity Level," *Developmental Psychology* 17 (1981): 59–65.

87. Donald H. Meichenbaum and Joseph Goodman, "Training Impulsive Children to Talk to Themselves: A Means of Developing Self-Control," *Journal of Abnormal Psychology* 77 (1971): 115–126.

88. Robert Eimers and Robert Aitchison, *Effective Parents/Responsible Children* (New York: McGraw-Hill, 1977).

89. Kenneth H. Rubin and Kim B. Burgess, "Parents of Aggressive and Withdrawn Children," in *Handbook of Parenting,* 2nd ed., ed. Bornstein, vol. 1, pp. 383–418.

90. Patterson, "Early Development of the Coercive Family Process"; Gerald R. Patterson, "Future Extensions of the Model," in *Antisocial Behavior in Children and Adolescents,* ed. Reid, Patterson, and Snyder, pp. 273–283.

91. Paul D. Hastings et al., "The Development of Concern for Others in Children with Behavior Problems," *Developmental Psychology* 36 (2000): 531–546.

92. Rubin and Burgess, "Parents of Aggressive and Withdrawn Children."

93. Linda Gilkerson and Frances Stott, "Parent-Child Relationships in Early Intervention with Infants and Toddlers with Disabilities

and Their Families," in *Handbook of Infant Mental Health*, 2nd ed., ed. Charles H. Zeanah, Jr. (New York: Guilford, 2000), 457–471.

94. Ibid., p. 460.

95. Penny Hauser-Cram et al., *Children with Disabilities*, Monographs of the Society for Research in Child Development 66, serial no. 266 (2001).

96. Ellen Galinsky, *Between Generations: The Six Stages of Parenthood* (New York: Times Books, 1981).

97. Ibid., pp. 136–137.

98. Philip A. Cowan and Carolyn Pape Cowan, "What an Intervention Design Reveals about How Parents Affect Their Children's Academic Achievement and Behavior Problems," in *Parenting and the Child's World: Differences in Academic, Intellectual and Socio-Emotional Development*, ed. John G. Borkowski, Sharon Landesman Ramey, and Marie Bristol-Power (Mahwah, NJ: Erlbaum, 2002), 75–97.

CHAPTER 9

1. Kim Severson, "Politicians Prodded on Child Custody," *San Francisco Chronicle*, 12 December 2002, p. A1.

2. W. Andrew Collins, Stephanie D. Madsen, and Amy Susman-Stillman, "Parenting during Middle Childhood," in *Handbook of Parenting*, 2nd ed., ed. Marc H. Bornstein, vol. 1: *Children and Parenting* (Mahwah, NJ: Erlbaum, 2002), 73–101.

3. J. David Hawkins, "Academic Performance and School Success: Sources and Consequences," in *Enhancing Children's Wellness*, ed. Roger P. Weissberg et al. (Thousand Oaks, CA: Sage, 1997), 278–305.

4. Jacquelynne S. Eccles, Allan Wigfield, and Ulrich Schiefele, "Motivation to Succeed," in *Handbook of Child Psychology*, 5th ed., ed. William Damon, vol. 3: *Social, Emotional, and Personality Development*, ed. Nancy Eisenberg (New York: Wiley, 1998), pp. 1017–1095.

5. Ben Carson with Gregg Lewis, *The Big Picture* (Grand Rapids, MI: Zondervan, 1999).

6. Ibid., p. 50.

7. Deborah A. Phillips, "Socialization of Perceived Academic Competence among Highly Competent Children," *Child Development* 58 (1987): 1308–1320.

8. Peter Ernest Haiman, "How Children Manage Frustration Affects Ability to Focus and Learn," *Brown University Child and Adolescent Newsletter* 16 (February 2000): 1.

9. Sheppard G. Kellam et al., "The Effect of the Level of Aggression in the First Grade Classroom on the Course and Malleability of Aggressive Behavior in Middle School," *Development and Psychopathology* 10 (1998): 165–185.

10. Hawkins, "Academic Performance and School Success."

11. Karl L. Alexander and Doris R. Entwisle, *Achievement in the First Two Years of School: Patterns and Processes*, Monographs of the Society for Research in Child Development 53, serial no. 218 (1988).

12. Gary W. Ladd and Joseph M. Price, "Predicting Children's Social and School Adjustment Following the Transition from Preschool to Kindergarten," *Child Development* 58 (1987): 1168–1189.

13. Karin S. Frey and Diane Ruble, "What Children Say about Classroom Performance: Sex and Grade Differences in Perceived Competence," *Child Development* 58 (1987): 1066–1078.

14. Karen Klein Burhans and Carol S. Dweck, "Helplessness in Early Childhood: The Role of Contingent Worth," *Child Development* 66 (1995): 1719–1738.

15. Eccles, Wigfield, and Schiefele, "Motivation to Succeed."

16. Patricia M. Greenfield and Lalita K. Suzuki, "Culture and Human Development: Implications for Parenting, Education, Pediatrics, and Mental Health," in *Handbook of Child Psychology*, 5th ed., ed. William Damon, vol. 4: *Child Psychology in Practice*, ed. Irving E. Sigel and K. Anne Renninger (New York: Wiley, 1998), 1059–1109.

17. Harold W. Stevenson, Chuansheng Chen, and David H. Uttal, "Beliefs and Achievements: A Study of Black, White, and Hispanic Children," *Child Development* 61 (1990): 508–523.

18. Deborah J. Stipek and Karen M. DeCotis, "Children's Understanding of the Implications of Causal Attributions for Emotional Experiences," *Child Development* 59 (1988): 1601–1616.

19. Dayna Fuchs and Mark H. Thelen, "Children's Expected Interpersonal Consequences of Communicating Their Affective State and Reported Likelihood of Expression," *Child Development* 59 (1988): 1314–1322.

20. Nancy Eisenberg et al., "The Relations of Children's Dispositional Prosocial Behavior to Emotionality, Regulation, and Social

Functioning," *Child Development* 67 (1996): 974–992.

21. Charles L. McCoy and John C. Masters, "The Development of Children's Strategies for the Social Control of Emotion," *Child Development* 56 (1985): 1214–1222.

22. Nancy Eisenberg and Paul H. Mussen, *The Roots of Prosocial Behavior in Children* (Cambridge, England: Cambridge University Press, 1989).

23. Steven R. Asher et al., "Peer Rejection and Loneliness in Childhood," in *Peer Rejection in Childhood,* ed. Steven R. Asher and John D. Coie (Cambridge, England: Cambridge University Press, 1990), 253–273.

24. Michael Rutter, Jack Tizard, and Kingsley Whitmore, eds., *Education, Health and Behavior* (Huntington, NY: Kruger, 1981).

25. Kaoru Yamamoto et al., "Voices in Unison: Stressful Events in the Lives of Children in Six Countries," *Journal of Child Psychology and Psychiatry* 28 (1987): 855–864.

26. Elaine Shaw Sorensen, *Children's Stress and Coping* (New York: Guilford, 1993).

27. Jennifer L. Altshuler and Diane N. Ruble, "Developmental Changes in Children's Awareness of Strategies for Coping with Uncontrollable Stress," *Child Development* 60 (1989): 1337–1349.

28. Sorensen, *Children's Stress and Coping.*

29. Molly Reid et al., "My Family and Friends: Six- to Twelve-Year-Old Children's Perceptions of Social Support," *Child Development* 60 (1989): 907.

30. Mary J. Levitt, Nathalie Guacci-Franco, and Jerome L. Levitt, "Convoys of Social Support in Childhood and Early Adolescence," *Developmental Psychology* 29 (1993): 811–818.

31. Susan Harter, "The Development of Self-Representations," in *Handbook of Child Psychology,* 5th ed., ed. Damon, vol. 3, pp. 553–617.

32. David M. Brodzinsky and Ellen Pinderhughes, "Parenting and Child Development in Adoptive Families," in *Handbook of Parenting,* 2nd ed., ed. Bornstein, vol. 1, pp. 279–311.

33. Ibid., p. 290.

34. Phyllis A. Katz and Keith R. Ksansnak, "Developmental Aspects of Gender Role Flexibility and Traditionality in Middle Childhood and Adolescence," *Developmental Psychology* 30 (1994): 272–282.

35. Joel Szkrybalo and Diane N. Ruble, "God Made Me a Girl: Sex-Category Constancy Judgments and Explanations Revisited,"

Developmental Psychology 35 (1999): 392–402.

36. Lynn S. Liben and Rebecca S. Bigler, *The Developmental Course of Gender Differentiation,* Monographs of the Society for Research in Child Development 67, serial no. 269 (2002); Diane N. Ruble and Carol Lynn Martin, *Commentary: The Developmental Course of Gender Differentiation,* Monographs of the Society for Research in Child Development 67, serial no. 269 (2002).

37. Frances E. Aboud, "The Development of Ethnic Self-Identification and Attitudes," in *Children's Ethnic Socialization,* ed. Jean S. Phinney and Mary Jane Rotheram (Beverly Hills CA: Sage, 1987), 32–55.

38. Sandra L. Hofferth and John F. Sandberg, "How American Children Spend Their Time," *Journal of Marriage and Family* 63 (2001): 295–308.

39. Frances E. Aboud, "The Formation of In-Group Favoritism and Out-Group Prejudice in Young Children: Are They Distinct Attitudes?" *Developmental Psychology* 39 (2003): 48–60.

40. Susan Harter, "Causes, Correlates, and the Functional Role of Global Self-Worth: A Life-Span Perspective," in *Competence Considered,* ed. J. Kolligian and Robert Sternberg (New Haven, CT: Yale University Press, 1990), 67–97.

41. Ibid.

42. Jean M. Twenge and Jennifer Crocker, "Race and Self-Esteem: Meta-Analysis Comparing Whites, Blacks, Hispanics, Asians, and American Indians and Comment on Gray-Little and Hofdahl (2000)," *Psychological Bulletin* 128 (2002): 371–408.

43. Tamara J. Ferguson, Hedy Stegge, and Ilse Damhuis, "Children's Understanding of Guilt and Shame," *Child Development* 62 (1991): 827–839.

44. Hazel J. Markus and Paula S. Nurius, "Self-Understanding and Self-Regulation in Middle Childhood," in *Development during Middle Childhood,* ed. W. Andrew Collins (Washington, DC: National Academy Press, 1984), pp. 147–183.

45. Eliot Turiel, "The Development of Morality," in *Handbook of Child Psychology,* 5th ed., ed. Damon, vol. 3, pp. 863–932.

46. Melanie Killen et al., *How Children and Adolescents Evaluate Gender and Racial Exclusions,* Monographs of the Society for

Research in Child Development 67, serial no. 271 (2002).

47. Turiel, "Development of Morality."

48. Collins, Madsen, and Susman-Stillman, "Parenting during Middle Childhood."

49. Kenneth H. Rubin, William Bukowski, and Jeffrey G. Parker, "Peer Interactions, Relationships, and Groups," in *Handbook of Child Psychology,* 5th ed., ed. Damon, vol. 3, pp. 619–700.

50. Ronald Seifer et al., "Child and Family Factors That Ameliorate Risk between 4 and 13 Years of Age," *Journal of the American Academy of Child and Adolescent Psychiatry* 31 (1992): 893–903.

51. Robert L. Nix et al., "The Relation between Mothers' Hostile Attribution Tendencies and Children's Externalizing Problems: The Mediating Role of Mothers' Harsh Discipline Practices," *Child Development* 70 (1999): 896–909.

52. Thomas G. O'Connor et al., "Genotype-Environment Correlations in Late Childhood and Early Adolescence: Asocial Behavioral Problems and Coercive Parenting," *Developmental Psychology* 34 (1998): 970–981.

53. Collins, Madsen, and Susman-Stillman, "Parenting during Middle Childhood."

54. Judith G. Smetana, "Adolescents' and Parents' Reasoning about Actual Family Conflict," *Child Development* 60 (1989): 1052–1067.

55. Graeme Russell and Alan Russell, "Mother-Child and Father-Child in Middle Childhood," *Child Development* 58 (1987): 1573–1585.

56. Frances K. Grossman, William S. Pollack, and Ellen Golding, "Fathers and Children: Predicting the Quality and Quantity of Fathering," *Developmental Psychology* 24 (1988): 822–891.

57. Russell and Russell, "Mother-Child and Father-Child."

58. Molly Reid, Sharon Landesman Ramey, and Margaret Burchinal, "Dialogues with Children about Their Families," in *Children's Perspectives on the Family,* ed. Inge Bretherton and Malcolm W. Watson, New Directions for Child Development, no. 48 (San Francisco: Jossey-Bass, 1990), 5–28.

59. Eleanor E. Maccoby, "Middle Childhood in the context of the Family," in *Development during Middle Childhood,* ed. Collins. pp. 184–239.

60. Michael C. Thornton et al., "Sociodemographic and Environmental Correlates of Racial Socialization by Black Parents," *Child Development* 61 (1990): 401–409.

61. Ibid.

62. Algea O. Harrison et al., "Family Ecologies of Ethnic Minority Children," *Child Development* 61 (1990): 347–362; Carolyn Bennett Murray and Jelani Mandara, "Racial Identity Development in African American Children: Cognitive and Experiential Antecedents," in *Black Children,* 2nd ed., ed. Harriette Pipes McAdoo (Thousand Oaks, CA: Sage, 2002), 73–96; Margaret Beale Spencer and Carol Markstrom-Adams, "Identity Processes among Racial and Ethnic Minority Children in America," *Child Development* 61 (1990): 290–310.

63. Collins, Madsen, and Susman-Stillman, "Parenting during Middle Childhood;" Wyndol Furman and Richard Lanthier, "Parenting Siblings," in *Handbook of Parenting,* 2nd ed., ed. Bornstein, vol. 1, pp. 165–188.

64. Ibid.

65. Clare M. Stocker and Lise Youngblade, "Marital Conflict and Hostility Links with Children's Sibling and Peer Relationships," *Journal of Family Psychology* 13 (1999): 598–609.

66. Clare M. Stocker, Rebecca A. Burwell, and Megan L. Briggs, "Sibling Conflict in Middle Childhood Predicts Children's Adjustment in Early Adolescence," *Journal of Family Psychology* 16 (2002): 50–57.

67. Gene H. Brody et al., "Sibling Relationships in Rural African American Families," *Journal of Marriage and the Family* 61 (1999): 1046–1057.

68. Kenneth H. Rubin, William Bukowski, and Jeffrey G. Parker, "Peer Interactions, Relationships, and Groups," in *Handbook of Child Psychology,* 5th ed., ed. Damon, vol. 3, pp. 619–700.

69. Rubin, Bukowski, and Parker, "Peer Interactions, Relationships, and Groups."

70. Nicki R. Crick and Jennifer K. Grotpeter, "Relational Aggression, Gender, and Social-Psychological Adjustment," *Child Development* 66 (1995): 710–722.

71. Ibid.

72. John D. Coie and Gina Krehbiel Koeppl, "Adapting Intervention to the Problems of Aggressive and Disruptive Children," in *Peer Rejection in Childhood,* ed. Asher and Coie, pp. 309–337.

73. Dan Olweus, "Annotation: Bullying at School: Basic Facts and Effects of a School Based Intervention Program," *Journal of Child Psychology and Psychiatry* 35 (1994): 1171–1190.

74. Nicki R. Crick and Jennifer K. Grotpeter, "Children's Treatment of Peers: Victims of Relational and Overt Aggression," *Development and Psychopathology* 8 (1996): 367–380.

75. David Schwartz et al., "Peer Group Victimization As a Predictor of Children's Behavior Problems at Home and at School," *Development and Psychopathology* 10 (1998): 87–99.

76. Susan K. Egan and David G. Perry, "Does Low Self-Regard Invite Victimization?" *Developmental Psychology* 34 (1998): 299–309.

77. Avi Sadeh, Reut Gruber, and Amiram Raviv, "The Effects of Sleep Restriction and Extension in School-Age Children: What a Difference an Hour Makes," *Child Development* 74 (2003): 444–455.

78. Barbara H. Fiese et al., "A Review of 50 Years of Research on Naturally Occurring Family Routines and Rituals: Cause for Celebration?" *Journal of Family Psychology* 16 (2002): 381–390.

79. Kelly J. Kelleher, "Increasing Identification of Psychosocial Problems: 1979–1996," *Pediatrics* 105 (2000): 1313–1321.

80. Tim Murphy and Loriann Hoff Oberlin, *The Angry Child* (New York: Three Rivers Press, 2001).

81. Gerald R. Patterson, "The Early Development of the Coercive Family Process," in *Antisocial Behavior in Children and Adolescents,* ed. John B. Reid, Gerald R. Patterson, and James Snyder (Washington, DC: American Psychological Association, 2002), 25–44.

82. Martin E. P. Seligman, *The Optimistic Child* (Boston: Houghton Mifflin, 1995).

83. Philip G. Zimbardo and Shirley Radl, *The Shy Child* (Garden City, NY: Doubleday, 1982).

84. Sherri Oden and Steven R. Asher, "Coaching Children in Social Skills for Friendship Making," *Child Development* 48 (1977): 495–506.

85. Marlene Jacobs Sandstrom and John D. Coie, "A Developmental Perspective on Peer Rejection: Mechanisms of Stability and Change," *Child Development* 70 (1999): 955–966.

86. Olweus, "Annotation: Bullying at School."

87. Joyce L. Epstein and Mavis G. Sanders, "Family, School, and Community Partnerships," in *Handbook of Parenting,* ed. Marc H. Bornstein, vol. 5: *Practical Issues in Parenting* (Mahwah, NJ: Erlbaum, 2002), 407–437.

88. Aletha C. Huston and John C. Wright, "Mass Media and Children's Development," in *Handbook of Child Psychology,* 5th ed., ed. Damon, vol. 4, pp. 1042–1043.

89. Aimee Dorr, Beth E. Rabin, and Sandra Irlen, "Parenting in a Multimedia Society," in *Handbook of Parenting,* 2nd ed., ed. Marc H. Bornstein, vol. 5: *Practical Issues in Parenting* (Mahwah, NJ: Erlbaum, 2002), 349–373.

90. Huston and Wright, "Mass Media and Children's Development."

91. Donna L. Mumme and Anne Fernald, "The Infant As Onlooker: Learning from Emotional Reactions Observed in a Television Scenario," *Child Development* 74 (2003): 221–237.

92. Robert Kubey, "Media Implications for the Quality of Family Life," in *Media, Children and the Family: Social Scientific, Psychodynamic and Clinical Perspectives,* ed. Dolf Zillmann, Jennings Bryant, and Aletha C. Huston (Hillsdale, NJ: Erlbaum, 1994), pp. 61–69.

93. Huston and Wright, "Mass Media and Children's Development," p. 1043.

94. Marites F. Pinon, Aletha C. Huston, and John C. Wright, "Family Ecology and Child Characteristics That Predict Young Children's Educational Television Viewing," *Child Development* 60 (1989): 846–856.

95. Kubey, "Media Implications."

96. John D. Coie and Kenneth A. Dodge, "Aggression and Antisocial Behavior," in *Handbook of Child Psychology,* 5th ed., ed. Damon, vol. 3, p. 799.

97. Ibid.

98. Ulysses Torassa, "Kids Less Violent after Cutting Back on TV," *San Francisco Chronicle,* 15 June 2001, p. A1.

99. Aletha C. Huston, Dolf Zillmann, and Jennings Bryant, "Media Influence, Public Policy and the Family," in *Media, Children and the Family,* ed. Zillman, Bryant, and Huston, pp. 3–18.

100. Dorr, Rabin, and Irlen, "Parenting in a Multimedia Society."

101. Ellen Galinsky, *Between Generations: The Six Stages of Parenthood* (New York: Times Books, 1981).

102. Joan Beck, *Effective Parenting* (New York: Simon & Schuster, 1976).

103. Emmy E. Werner and Ruth S. Smith, *Overcoming the Odds* (Ithaca, NY: Cornell University Press, 1992), p. 177.

104. Robert Coles, *The Spiritual Life of Children* (Boston: Houghton Mifflin, 1990), 127.

CHAPTER 10

1. Jeanne Brooks-Gunn and Edward O. Reiter, "The Role of Pubertal Processes," in *At the Threshold: The Developing Adolescent,* ed. S. Shirley Feldman and Glen R. Elliott (Cambridge, MA: Harvard University Press, 1990), 16–53.

2. Ibid.

3. Bruce J. Ellis and Judy Garber, "Psychosocial Antecedents of Variation in Girls' Pubertal Timing: Maternal Depression, Stepfather Presence, and Marital and Family Stress," *Child Development* 71 (2000): 485–501.

4. Xiaojia Ge, Rand D. Conger, and Glen H. Elder, Jr., "Pubertal Transition, Stressful Life Events, and Emergence of Gender Differences in Adolescent Depressive Symptoms," *Developmental Psychology* 37 (2001): 404–417.

5. Grayson N. Holmbeck, Roberta L. Paikoff, and Jeanne Brooks-Gunn, "Parenting Adolescents," in *Handbook of Parenting,* ed. Marc H. Bornstein, vol. 1: *Children and Parenting* (Mahwah, NJ: Erlbaum, 1995), 91–118.

6. Christy Miller Buchanan, Jacquelynne S. Eccles, and Jill B. Becker, "Are Adolescents the Victims of Raging Hormones? Evidence for Activational Effects of Hormones on Mood and Behavior at Adolescence," *Psychological Bulletin* 3 (1992): 62–107.

7. Jacquelynne S. Eccles, Allan Wigfield, and Ulrich Schiefele, "Motivation to Succeed," in *Handbook of Child Psychology,* 5th ed., ed. William Damon, vol. 3: *Social, Emotional, and Personality Development,* ed. Nancy Eisenberg (New York: Wiley, 1998), 1017–1095.

8. Ge, Conger, and Elder, "Pubertal Transition."

9. Eric Stice, Katherine Presnell, and Sarah Kate Bearman, "Relation of Early Menarche to Depression, Eating Disorders, Substance Abuse, and Comorbid Psychopathology among Adolescent Girls," *Developmental Psychology* 37 (2001): 608–619.

10. Mary C. Jones and Nancy Bayley, "Physical Maturing among Boys Related to Behavior," *Journal of Educational Psychology* 41 (1950): 129–148.

11. Jane Norman and Myron Harris, *The Private Life of the American Teenager* (New York: Rawson Wade, 1981).

12. Herbert Ginsburg and Sylvia Opper, *Piaget's Theory of Intellectual Development* (Englewood Cliffs, NJ: Prentice-Hall, 1969); Jean Piaget and Barbel Inhelder, *The Psychology of the Child* (New York: Basic Books, 1969).

13. Eccles, Wigman, and Schiefele, "Motivation to Succeed."

14. Jacquelynne Eccles et al., "Development during Adolescence: The Impact of Stage-Environment Fit on Young Adolescents' Experiences in Schools and in Families," *American Psychologist* 48 (1993): 90–101.

15. Edward Seidman et al., "The Impact of School Transition in Early Adolescence on the Self System and Perceived Social Context of Poor Urban Youth," *Child Development* 65 (1994): 507–522.

16. James Patrick Connell, Margaret Beale Spencer, and J. Lawrence Aber, "Educational Risk and Resilience in African American Youth: Context, Self, Action, and Outcomes in School," *Child Development* 65 (1994): 493–506.

17. Seidman et al., "Impact of School Transition."

18. Gene H. Brody et al., "Financial Resources, Parent Psychological Functioning, Parent Co-Caregiving and Early Adolescent Competence in Rural Two-Parent African American Families," *Child Development* 65 (1994): 590–605.

19. Robert W. Roeser, Jacquelynne S. Eccles, and Arnold J. Sameroff, "Academic and Emotional Functioning in Early Adolescence: Longitudinal Relations, Patterns, and Prediction by Experience in Middle School," *Development and Psychopathology* 10 (1998): 321–352.

20. Reed Larson and Maryse H. Richards, *Divergent Realities: The Emotional Lives of Mothers, Fathers, and Adolescents* (New York: Basic Books, 1994).

21. Reed Larson and Mark Ham, "Stress and 'Storm Stress' in Early Adolescence: The Relationship of Negative Events and Dysphoric Affect," *Developmental Psychology* 29 (1993): 130–140.

22. Larson and Richards, *Divergent Realities.*

23. Buchanan, Eccles, and Becker, "Are Adolescents the Victims of Raging Hormones?"

24. David Elkind, *Children and Adolescents,* 2nd ed. (New York: Oxford University Press, 1974).

25. Larson and Ham, "Stress and 'Storm Stress' in Early Adolescence."

26. Reed W. Larson, "Toward a Psychology of Positive Youth Development," *American Psychologist* 55 (2000): 170–183.

27. Ibid., p. 170.

28. Anne C. Petersen et al., "Depression in Adolescence," *American Psychologist* 48 (1993): 155–168.

29. Roberta G. Simmons et al., "The Impact of Cumulative Changes in Early Adolescence," *Child Development* 58 (1987): 1220–1234.

30. Mary J. Levitt, Nathalie Guacci-Franco, and Jerome L. Levitt, "Convoys of Social Support in Childhood and Early Adolescence: Structure and Function," *Developmental Psychology* 29 (1993): 811–818.

31. Susan Harter, "The Development of Self-Representations," in *Handbook of Child Psychology*, 5th ed., ed. Damon, vol. 3, pp. 553–617.

32. Erik H. Erikson, *Childhood and Society*, 2nd ed. (New York: Norton, 1963).

33. James E. Marcia, "Identity in Adolescence," in *Handbook of Adolescent Psychology*, ed. Joseph Adelson (New York: Wiley, 1980), 159–187.

34. Harold D. Grotevant, "Adolescent Development in Family Contexts," in *Handbook of Child Psychology*, 5th ed., ed. Damon, vol. 3, pp. 1097–1149.

35. William E. Cross, Jr., "A Two-Factor Theory of Black Identity: Implications for the Study of Identity Development in Minority Children," in *Children's Ethnic Socialization: Pluralism and Development*, ed. Jean S. Phinney and Mary Jane Rotheram (Beverly Hills, CA: Sage, 1987), 117–133.

36. Nancy L. Galambos, David M. Almeida, and Anne C. Petersen, "Masculinity, Femininity, and Sex Role Attitudes in Early Adolescence: Exploring Gender Intensification," *Child Development* 61 (1990): 1905–1914.

37. Phyllis A. Katz and Keith R. Ksansnak, "Developmental Aspects of Gender Role Flexibility and Traditionality in Middle Childhood and Adolescence," *Developmental Psychology* 30 (1994): 272–282; Thalma E. Lobel et al., "The Role of Gender-Related Information and Self-Endorsement of Traits in Preadolescents' Inferences and Judgments," *Child Development* 64 (1993): 1285–1294.

38. Jean S. Phinney, "Stages of Ethnic Identity Development in Minority Group Adolescents," *Journal of Early Adolescence* 9 (1989): 34–49.

39. Margaret Beale Spencer and Carol Markstrom-Adams, "Identity Processes among Racial and Ethnic Minority Children in America," *Child Development* 61 (1990): 290–310; Michael C. Thornton et al., "Sociodemographic and Environmental Correlates of Racial Socialization by Black Parents," *Child Development* 61 (1990): 401–409.

40. Phinney, "Stages of Ethnic Identity Development."

41. Jane B. Brooks, "Social Maturity in Middle Age and Its Developmental Antecedents," in *Present and Past in Middle Life*, ed. Dorothy H. Eichorn et al. (New York: Academic Press, 1981), 243–265.

42. Jack Block with Norma Haan, *Lives through Time* (Berkeley, CA: Bancroft Books, 1971).

43. Reed Larson and Maryse H. Richards, "Daily Companionship in Late Childhood and Early Adolescence: Changing Developmental Contexts," *Child Development* 62 (1991): 284–300.

44. Larson and Richards, *Divergent Realities*, p. 189.

45. Judith G. Smetana, "Adolescents' and Parents' Reasoning about Actual Family Conflict," *Child Development* 60 (1989): 1052–1067; Judith G. Smetana, "Concepts of Self and Social Convention: Adolescents' and Parents' Reasoning about Hypothetical and Actual Family Conflicts," in *Development during the Transition to Adolescence: Minnesota Symposia on Child Psychology*, vol. 21, ed. Megan R. Gunnar and W. Andrew Collins (Hillsdale, NJ: Erlbaum, 1988), 79–122.

46. Smetana, "Concepts of Self and Social Convention."

47. Laurence Steinberg, "Impact of Puberty on Family Relations: Effects of Pubertal Status and Pubertal Timing," *Developmental Psychology* 23 (1987): 451–460.

48. Per F. Gjerde, "The Interpersonal Structure of Family Interaction Settings: Parent-Adolescent Relations in Dyads and Triads," *Developmental Psychology* 22 (1986): 297–304.

49. Andrew J. Fuligni and Jacquelynne S. Eccles, "Perceived Parent-Child Relationships and Early Adolescents' Orientation toward Peers," *Developmental Psychology* 29 (1993): 622–632.

50. Holmbeck, Paikoff, and Brooks-Gunn, "Parenting Adolescents."

51. Ibid.

52. Hakan Stattin and Margaret Kerr, "Parental Monitoring: A Reinterpretation," *Child Development* 71 (2000): 1072–1085; Margaret Kerr

and Hakan Stattin, "What Parents Know, How They Know It, and Several Forms of Adolescent Adjustment: Further Support for a Reinterpretation of Monitoring," *Developmental Psychology* 36 (2000): 366–380.

53. Eva S. Lefkowitz, Marian Sigman, and Terry Kit-fong Au, "Helping Mothers Discuss Sexuality and AIDS with Adolescents," *Child Development* 71 (2000): 1383–1394.

54. Martha A. Rueter and Rand D. Conger, "Reciprocal Influences between Parenting and Adolescent Problem-Solving Behavior," *Developmental Psychology* 34 (1998): 1470–1482.

55. Cynthia Garcia Coll and Lee M. Pachter, "Ethnic and Minority Parenting," in *Handbook of Parenting,* 2nd ed., ed. Marc H. Bornstein, vol. 4: *Social Conditions and Applied Parenting* (Mahwah, NJ: Erlbaum, 2002), 1–20.

56. Carolyn Bennett Murray and Jelani Mandara, "Racial Identity Development in African American Children: Cognitive and Experiential Antecedents," in *Black Children,* 2nd ed., ed. Harriette Pipes McAdoo (Thousand Oaks, CA: Sage, 2002), 73–96.

57. David Elkind, *The Hurried Child,* 3rd ed. (Cambridge, MA: Perseus Books, 2001).

58. Bruce E. Compas et al., "Parents and Child Stress Symptoms: An Integrative Analysis," *Developmental Psychology,* 25 (1989): 550–559.

59. Norman and Harris, *Private Life of the American Teenager.*

60. Ibid.

61. Kenneth H. Rubin, William Bukowski, and Jeffrey G. Parker, "Peer Interactions, Relationships, and Groups," in *Handbook of Child Psychology,* 5th ed., ed. Damon, vol. 3, pp. 619–700.

62. Lynne Zarbatany, Donald P. Hartmann, and D. Bruce Rankin, "The Psychological Functions of Preadolescent Peer Activities," *Child Development* 61 (1990): 1067–1080.

63. Maryse H. Richards et al., "Developmental Patterns and Gender Differences in the Experience of Peer Companionship during Adolescence," *Child Development* 69 (1998): 154–163.

64. Holmbeck, Paikoff, and Brooks-Gunn, "Parenting Adolescents," p. 95.

65. Don Dinkmeyer and Gary D. McKay, *STEP/TEEN Systematic Training for Effective Parenting of Teens* (Circle Pines, MN: American Guidance Service, 1983).

66. Adele Faber and Elaine Mazlish, *How to Talk So Kids Will Listen and Listen So Kids Will Talk* (New York: Rawson Wade, 1980), 165.

67. Myrna B. Shure with Roberta Israeloff, *Raising a Thinking Preteen* (New York: Henry Holt, 2000).

68. Larson, "Toward a Psychology of Positive Youth Development," p. 170.

69. Ibid., p. 177.

70. Ibid., p. 179.

71. Ibid.

72. Kathryn R. Wentzel and Cynthia A. Erdley, "Strategies for Making Friends: Relations to Social Behavior and Peer Acceptance in Early Adolescence," *Developmental Psychology* 29 (1993): 819–826.

73. Sandra Graham and Cynthia Hudley, "Attributions of Aggressive and Nonaggressive African-American Male Early Adolescents: A Study of Construct Accessibility," *Developmental Psychology* 30 (1994): 365–373; Sandra Graham, Cynthia Hudley, and Estella Williams, "Attributional and Emotional Determinants of Aggression among African-American and Latino Young Adolescents," *Developmental Psychology* 28 (1992): 731–740.

74. Wentzel and Erdley, "Strategies for Making Friends."

75. Philip Zimbardo and Shirley Radl, *The Shy Child* (Garden City, NY: Doubleday, 1982).

76. Haim G. Ginott, *Between Parent and Teenager* (New York: Avon, 1969).

77. Robert Eimers and Robert Aitchison, *Effective Parents/Responsible Children* (New York: McGraw-Hill, 1977).

78. Mary Pipher, *Reviving Ophelia* (New York: Ballantine Books, 1994), 283.

79. Ibid., p. 257.

80. William Pollack, *Real Boys* (New York: Henry Holt, 1998).

81. Ibid., p. xxiv.

82. Ibid., pp. 391 and 398, respectively.

83. Ellen Galinsky, *Between Generations: The Six Stages of Parenthood* (New York: Times Books, 1981).

84. William Damon, *The Youth Charter: How Communities Can Work Together to Raise Standards for All Our Children* (New York: Free Press, 1997).

85. Ibid., p. ix.

CHAPTER 11

1. Susan G. Millstein and Iris F. Litt, "Adolescent Health" in *At the Threshold: The*

Developing Adolescent, ed. S. Shirley Feldman and Glen R. Elliott (Cambridge, MA: Harvard University Press, 1990), 431–456.

2. Cathy Schoen et al., *The Commonwealth Fund Survey of the Health of Adolescent Girls* (New York: Commonwealth Fund, 1997).

3. Millstein and Litt, "Adolescent Health."

4. Schoen et al., *Commonwealth Fund Survey.*

5. Jerald G. Bachman et al., "Transition in Drug Use during Late Adolescence and Young Adulthood," in *Transitions through Adolescence: Interpersonal Domains and Context,* ed. Julie A. Graber, Jeanne Brooks-Gunn, and Anne C. Petersen (Mahwah, NJ: Erlbaum, 1996), 111–140.

6. Schoen et al., *Commonwealth Fund Survey.*

7. Herant Katchadourian, "Sexuality," in *At the Threshold,* ed. Feldman and Elliott, pp. 330–351.

8. Joseph Lee Rodgers, "Sexual Transitions in Adolescence," in *Transitions through Adolescence,* ed. Graber, Brooks-Gunn, and Petersen, pp. 85–110.

9. Roger P. Weissberg and Mark T. Greenfield, "School and Community Competence-Enhancement and Prevention Programs," in *Handbook of Child Psychology,* 5th ed., ed. William Damon, vol. 4: *Child Psychology in Practice,* ed. Irving E. Sigel and K. Ann Renninger (New York: Wiley, 1998), 877–954.

10. Nancy J. Cobb, *Adolescence: Continuity, Change, and Diversity* (Mountain View, CA: Mayfield, 1992).

11. Rodgers, "Sexual Transitions in Adolescence."

12. James Jaccard, Patricia J. Dittus, and Vivian V. Gordon, "Parent-Adolescent Congruency in Reports of Adolescent Sexual Behavior and in Communications about Sexual Behavior," *Child Development* 69 (1998): 247–261.

13. Katchadourian, "Sexuality."

14. Patricia Barthalow Koch, "Promoting Healthy Sexual Development during Early Adolescence," in *Early Adolescence: Perspectives on Research, Policy, and Intervention,* ed. Richard M. Lerner (Hillsdale, NJ: Erlbaum, 1993), 293–307.

15. Lisa J. Crockett, "Early Adolescent Family Formation," in *Early Adolescence,* ed. Lerner, pp. 93–110.

16. Ibid.

17. Katherine Fennelly, "Sexual Activity and Childbearing among Hispanic Adolescents in the United States," in *Early Adolescence,* ed. Lerner, pp. 335–352.

18. Jeanne Brooks-Gunn and Frank F. Furstenberg, "Adolescent Sexual Behavior," *American Psychologist* 44 (1989): 249–257.

19. Melvin Zelnick and John F. Kantner, "Sexual Activity, Contraceptive Use, and Pregnancy among Metropolitan-Area Teenagers 1971–1979," *Family Planning Perspectives* 12 (1980): 230–237.

20. Daniel P. Keating, "Adolescent Thinking," in *At the Threshold,* ed. Feldman and Elliott, pp. 54–89.

21. Karen Bartsch, "Adolescents' Theoretical Thinking," in *Early Adolescence,* ed. Lerner, pp. 143–157.

22. Jacquelynne S. Eccles, Allan Wigfield, and Ulrich Schiefele, "Motivation to Succeed," in *Handbook of Child Psychology,* 5th ed., ed. William Damon, vol. 3: *Social, Emotional, and Personality Development,* ed. Nancy Eisenberg (New York: Wiley, 1998), 1017–1095.

23. Ibid.

24. Sanford M. Dornbusch et al., "The Relation of Parenting Style to Adolescent School Performance," *Child Development* 58 (1987): 1244–1257.

25. Robert B. McCall, Cynthia Evahn, and Lynn Kratzer, *High School Underachievers* (Newbury Park, CA: Sage, 1992).

26. U.S. Bureau of the Census, *Statistical Abstract of the United States: 2002,* 122nd ed. (Washington, DC: U.S. Government Printing Office, 2001).

27. Frank F. Furstenberg, "The Sociology of Adolescence and Youth in the 1990s: A Critical Commentary," *Journal of Marriage and the Family* 62 (2000): 896–910.

28. Ellen Greenberger and Laurence D. Steinberg, "The Workplace As a Contest for the Socialization of Youth," *Journal of Youth and Adolescence* 10 (1981): 185–210; Laurence Steinberg and Ellen Greenberger, "The Part-Time Employment of High School Students: A Research Agenda," *Children and Youth Services Review* 2 (1980): 161–185.

29. Mihaly Csikszentmihalyi and Reed Larson, *Being Adolescent* (New York: Basic Books, 1984), 234.

30. Michael Windle, "A Longitudinal Study of Stress Buffering for Adolescent Problem Behaviors," *Developmental Psychology* 28 (1992): 522–530.

31. Suniya S. Luthar, "Vulnerability and Resilience: A Study of High Risk Adolescents," *Child Development* 62 (1991): 600–616.

32. Jeanne Brooks-Gunn and Michelle P. Warren, "Biological and Social Contributions to Negative Affect in Young Adolescent Girls," *Child Development* 60 (1989): 40–55.

33. Albert Bandura, *Self-Efficacy: The Exercise of Control* (New York: Freeman, 1997).

34. Susan Harter et al., "The Development of Multiple Role-Related Selves," in *Development and Psychopathology* 9 (1977): 835–853.

35. Jack Block and Richard W. Robins, "A Longitudinal Study of Consistency and Change in Self-Esteem from Early Adolescence to Early Adulthood," *Child Development* 64 (1993): 909–923.

36. Jack Block, "Some Relationships Regarding the Self from the Block and Block Longitudinal Study," paper presented at the Social Science Research Council Conference on Selfhood, Stanford, CA, October 1985.

37. Patricia Barthalow Koch, "Promoting Healthy Sexual Development during Early Adolescence," in *Early Adolescence,* ed. Lerner, pp. 293–307.

38. Katchadourian, "Sexuality."

39. Koch, "Promoting Healthy Sexual Development during Early Adolescence."

40. Jean S. Phinney and Victoria Chavira, "Ethnic Identity and Self-Esteem," *Journal of Adolescence* 15 (1992): 271–281.

41. Jean S. Phinney and Mona Devich-Navarro, "Variations in Bicultural Identification among African-American and Mexican-American Adolescents," *Journal of Research on Adolescence* 7 (1997): 3–32.

42. Nancy Eisenberg et al., "Prosocial Development in Adolescence: A Longitudinal Study," *Developmental Psychology* 27 (1991): 849–857.

43. Harold D. Grotevant, "Adolescent Development in Family Contexts," in *Handbook of Child Psychology,* 5th ed., ed. Damon, vol. 3, pp. 1097–1149.

44. Richard Jessor et al., "Protective Factors in Adolescent Problem Behavior: Moderator Effects and Developmental Change," *Developmental Psychology* 31 (1995): 923–933.

45. Bachman et al., "Transitions in Drug Use."

46. Diana Baumrind, "The Influence of Parenting Style on Adolescent Competence and Problem Behavior," paper presented at the American Psychological Association Meetings, New Orleans, LA, August 1989.

47. Ibid., p. 16.

48. Laurence Steinberg et al., "Authoritative Parenting and Adolescent Adjustment: An Ecological Perspective," in *Examining Lives in Context,* ed. Phyllis Moen, Glen H. Elder, Jr., and Kurt Lusher (Washington, DC: American Psychological Association, 1995), 423–466.

49. Ibid., p. 443.

50. Anne C. Fletcher, Laurence Steinberg, and Elizabeth B. Sellers, "Adolescents' Well Being As a Function of Interparental Consistency," *Journal of Marriage and the Family* 61 (1999): 599–610.

51. Brooks-Gunn and Furstenberg, "Adolescent Sexual Behavior."

52. Ibid.

53. Ellen Greenberger and Laurence Steinberg, *When Teenagers Work* (New York: Basic Books, 1986).

54. Judith G. Smetana, "Adolescents' and Parents' Reasoning about Actual Family Conflict," *Child Development* 60 (1989): 1052–1067; Judith G. Smetana, "Concepts of Self and Social Convention: Adolescents' and Parents' Reasoning about Hypothetical and Actual Family Conflicts," in *Development during the Transition to Adolescence,* Minnesota Symposia on Child Psychology, vol. 21, ed. Megan R. Gunnar and W. Andrew Collins (Hillsdale, NJ: Erlbaum, 1988), 79–122.

55. Joseph P. Allen et al., "Longitudinal Assessment of Autonomy and Relatedness in Adolescent-Family Interactions As Predictors of Adolescent Ego Development and Self-Esteem," *Child Development* 65 (1994): 1179–1194.

56. R. Rogers Kobak et al., "Attachment and Emotion Regulation during Mother-Teen Problem Solving: A Control Theory Analysis," *Child Development* 64 (1993): 231–245.

57. Duane Buhrmester and Wyndol Furman, "Perceptions of Sibling Relationships during Middle Childhood and Adolescence," *Child Development* 61 (1990): 1387–1398.

58. B. Bradford Brown, "Peer Groups and Peer Culture," in *At the Threshold,* ed. Feldman and Elliott, pp. 171–196.

59. Wyndol Furman, "Friends and Lovers: The Role of Peer Relationships in Adolescent Romantic Relationships," in *Relationships As Developmental Contexts: The 30th Minnesota Symposium on Child Development,* ed. W. Andrew Collins and Brett Laursen (Hillsdale, NJ: Erlbaum, 1999), 133–154.

60. Brown, "Peer Groups and Peer Culture."

61. Duane Buhrmester, "Intimacy and Friendship, Interpersonal Competence, and Adjustment during Preadolescence and

Adolescence," *Child Development* 61 (1990): 1101–1111.

62. Jane Norman and Myron Harris, *The Private Life of the American Teenager* (New York: Rawson Wade, 1981).

63. Brown, "Peer Groups and Peer Culture."

64. Brown, "Peer Groups and Peer Culture."

65. Ritch Savin-Williams and Thomas Berndt, "Friendships and Peer Relations," in *At the Threshhold,* ed. Feldman and Elliott, pp. 277–307.

66. Furman, "Friends and Lovers."

67. Candice Feiring, "Concepts of Romance in Fifteen-Year-Old Adolescents," *Journal of Research on Adolescence* 6 (1996): 181–200.

68. Ibid.

69. Furman, "Friends and Lovers."

70. Michael D. Resnick et al., "Protecting Adolescents from Harm," *Journal of the American Medical Association* 278 (1997): 823–832.

71. Barbara J. Tinsley and Nancy B. Lees, "Health Promotion for Parents," in *Handbook of Parenting,* ed. Marc H. Bornstein, vol. 4, *Applied and Practical Parenting* (Mahwah, NJ: Erlbaum, 1995), 187–204.

72. Judy A. Andrews, Hyman Hops, and Susan C. Duncan, "Adolescent Modeling of Parent Substance Use: The Moderating Effect of the Relationship with the Parent," *Journal of Family Psychology* 11 (1997): 259–270.

73. Baumrind, "Influence of Parenting Style"; Jonathan Shedler and Jack Block, "Adolescent Drug Use and Psychological Health: A Longitudinal Inquiry," *American Psychologist* 45 (1990): 612–630.

74. Resnick et al., "Protecting Adolescents from Harm."

75. Melissa R. Herman et al., "The Influence of Family Regulation, Connection, and Psychological Autonomy on Six Measures of Adolescent Functioning," *Journal of Adolescent Research* 12 (1997): 34–67.

76. Grace M. Barnes and Michael P. Farrell, "Parental Support and Control As Predictors of Adolescent Drinking, Delinquency, and Related Problem Behaviors," *Journal of Marriage and the Family* 54 (1992): 763–776; Grace M. Barnes et al., "The Effects of Parenting on the Development of Adolescent Alcohol Misuse: A Six-Wave Latent Growth Model," *Journal of Marriage and the Family* 62 (2000): 175–186.

77. Resnick et al., "Protecting Adolescents from Harm."

78. Richard Jessor et al., "Protective Factors in Adolescent Problem Behavior: Moderation Effects and Developmental Change," *Developmental Psychology* 31 (1995): 923–933.

79. Resnick et al., "Protecting Adolescents from Harm."

80. Marcia Herrin and Nancy Matsumoto, *The Parent's Guide to Childhood Eating Disorders* (New York: Holt, 2002).

81. Ibid.

82. Ibid.

83. Resnick et al., "Protecting Adolescents from Harm."

84. Ibid.

85. Ibid.

86. Karen Bogenschneider et al., "'Other Teens Drink, but Not My Kid': Does Parental Awareness of Adolescent Alcohol Use Protect Adolescents from Risky Consequences?" *Journal of Marriage and the Family* 60 (1998): 356–373.

87. Ibid.

88. Resnick et al., "Protecting Adolescents from Harm."

89. Beth Polson and Miller Newton, *Not My Kid: A Parent's Guide to Kids and Drugs* (New York: Avon, 1985).

90. Baumrind, "Influence of Parenting Style"; Shedler and Block, "Adolescent Drug Use."

91. Nikki Babbit, *Adolescent Drug and Alcohol Abuse: How to Spot It, Stop It, and Get Help for Your Family* (Sebastopol, CA: O'Reilly, 2000).

92. James Garbarino, *Lost Boys: Why Our Sons Turn Violent and How We Can Save Them* (New York: Free Press, 1999).

93. Ibid., p. 74.

94. Ibid., p. 75.

95. Ibid., p. 149.

96. Deborah M. Capaldi and Mike Stoolmiller, "Co-occurrence of Conduct Problems and Depressive Symptoms in Early Adolescent Boys: III. Prediction to Young-Adult Adjustment," *Development and Psychopathology* 11 (1999): 59–84.

97. Ibid., p. 78.

98. Alice W. Pope and Karen L. Bierman, "Predicting Adolescent Peer Problems and Antisocial Activities: The Relative Roles of Aggression and Dysregulation," *Developmental Psychology* 35 (1999): 335–346.

99. Capaldi and Stoolmiller, "Co-occurrence of Conduct Problems."

100. Dante Cicchetti and Sheree L. Toth, "The Development of Depression in Children and

Adolescents," *American Psychologist* 53 (1998): 221–241.

101. Ibid.

102. Donald H. McKnew, Leon Cytryn, and Herbert Yahraes, *Why Isn't Johnny Crying?* (New York: Norton, 1983).

103. Cicchetti and Toth, "Development of Depression."

104. Harold S. Koplewicz, *More Than Moody: Recognizing and Treating Adolescent Depression* (New York: Putnam, 2002).

105. Ibid.

106. Anne C. Petersen et al., "Depression in Adolescence," *American Psychologist* 48 (1993): 155–168.

107. Petersen et al., "Depression in Adolescence."

108. Ibid.

109. Koplewicz, *More Than Moody.*

110. Ibid.

111. Petersen et al., "Depression in Adolescence."

112. Koplewicz, *More Than Moody.*

113. Martin E. P. Seligman, *The Optimistic Child* (New York: Houghton Mifflin, 1995).

114. Susan Harter, "Visions of Self beyond the Me in the Mirror," university lecture, University of Denver, 1990, 16.

115. Andrew J. Fuligni and Jacquelynne S. Eccles, "Perceived Parent-Child Relationships and Early Adolescents' Orientation toward Peers," *Developmental Psychology* 29 (1993): 622–632.

116. W. Andrew Collins et al., "Conflict Processes and Transitions in Parent and Peer Relationships," *Journal of Adolescent Research* 12 (1997): 178–198.

117. McCall, Evahn, and Kratzer, *High School Underachievers.*

118. Fitzhugh Dodson, *How to Discipline with Love* (New York: Rawson, 1977), 410.

119. Ibid., pp. 410–411.

120. Herrin and Matsumoto, *Parent's Guide to Childhood Eating Disorders.*

121. Koplewicz, *More Than Moody.*

122. Harold S. Koplewicz, "More Than Moody: Recognizing and Treating Adolescent Depression," *Brown University Child and Adolescent Newsletter* 18 (December 2002): 7.

123. Jane E. Brody, "Adolescent Angst or a Deeper Disorder? Tips for Spotting Serious Symptoms," *New York Times,* 24 December 2002, p. D5.

124. Babbit, *Adolescent Drug and Alcohol Abuse.*

125. Laurence Steinberg with Wendy Steinberg, *Crossing Paths: How Your Child's Adolescence Triggers Your Own Crisis* (New York: Simon & Schuster, 1994).

126. Phyllis York, David York, and Ted Wachtel, *ToughLove* (Garden City, NY: Doubleday, 1982).

CHAPTER 12

1. Karen Bogenschneider, "Has Family Policy Come of Age? A Decade Review of the State of U.S. Family Policy in the 1990s," *Journal of Marriage and the Family* 62 (2000): 1136–1159.

2. Gail S. Goodman, Robert E. Emery, and Jeffrey J. Haugaard, "Developmental Psychology and Law: Divorce, Child Maltreatment, Foster Care, and Adoption," in *Handbook of Child Psychology, 5th* ed., ed. William Damon, vol. 4: *Child Psychology in Practice,* ed. Irving E. Sigel and Ann Renninger (New York: Wiley, 1998), 775–874.

3. Julia A. Graber, Jeanne Brooks-Gunn, and Anne C. Petersen, "Adolescent Transitions in Context," in *Transitions through Adolescence,* ed. Julia A. Graber, Jeanne Brooks-Gunn, and Anne C. Petersen (Mahwah, NJ: Erlbaum, 1996), 369–383.

4. DeWayne Moore, "Parent-Adolescent Separation: The Construction of Adulthood by Late Adolescents," *Developmental Psychology* 23 (1987): 298–307.

5. Erik H. Erikson, *Childhood and Society,* 2nd ed. (New York: Norton, 1963).

6. John Bowlby, *The Making and Breaking of Affectional Bonds* (London: Tavistock, 1979), 129.

7. Mary D. Salter Ainsworth, "Some Considerations Regarding Theory and Assessment Relevant to Attachments beyond Infancy," in *Attachment in the Preschool Years: Theory, Research, and Intervention,* ed. Mark T. Greenberg, Dante Cicchetti, and E. Mark Cummings (Chicago: University of Chicago Press, 1990), 474.

8. Ibid., pp. 463–488.

9. Glen H. Elder, Jr., "The Life Course in Human Development," in *Handbook of Child Psychology,* 5th ed., ed. William Damon, vol. 1: *Theoretical Models of Human Development,* ed. Richard M. Lerner (New York: Wiley, 1998), 961.

10. Vern Bengtson, "Beyond the Nuclear Family: The Increasing Importance of Multigenerational Bonds," *Journal of Marriage and Family* 63 (2001): 1–16.

11. Ibid., p. 3.

12. Ibid., p. 5.

13. Steven H. Zarit and David J. Eggebeen, "Parent-Child Relationships in Adulthood and Later Years," in *Handbook of Parenting*, 2nd ed., ed. Marc H. Bornstein, vol. 1: *Children and Parenting* (Mahwah, NJ: Erlbaum, 2002), 135–161.

14. Bengtson, "Beyond the Nuclear Family," p. 7.

15. Ibid.

16. Carol L. Gohm et al., "Culture, Parental Conflict, Parental Marital Status, and the Subjective Well Being of Young Adults," *Journal of Marriage and the Family* 60 (1998): 319–334.

17. Bengtson, "Beyond the Nuclear Family."

18. Moncrieff Cochran, "Parenting and Personal Social Networks," in *Parenting: An Ecological Perspective*, ed. Tom Luster and Lynn Okagaki (Hillsdale, NJ: Erlbaum, 1993), 149–178.

19. Frances K. Goldscheider, Arland Thornton, and Li-Shou Yang, "Helping out Kids: Expectations about Parental Support in Young Adulthood," *Journal of Marriage and Family* 63 (2001): 727–742.

20. Cochran, "Parenting and Personal Social Networks."

21. Bertram J. Cohler and Judith S. Musick, "Adolescent Parenthood and the Transition to Adulthood," in *Transitions through Adolescence*, ed. Graber, Brooks-Gunn, and Petersen, 214.

22. Katherine S. Newman, "Working Poor: Low-Wage Employment in the Lives of Harlem Youth," in *Transitions through Adolescence*, ed. Graber, Brooks-Gunn, and Petersen, pp. 323–343.

23. Ibid., p. 338.

24. Ibid., p. 341.

25. Moore, "Parent-Adolescent Separation."

26. Kathy Bell et al., "Family Factors and Young Adult Transitions: Educational Attainment and Occupational Prestige," in *Transitions through Adolescence*, ed. Graber, Brooks-Gunn, and Petersen, pp. 345–366.

27. Gohm et al., "Culture, Parental Conflict."

28. Erica Goode, "Students' Emotional Health Worsens," *San Francisco Chronicle*, 3 February 2003, p. A9.

29. Ray Delgado, "Report on College Drinking's Toll Shows Health Crisis, Experts Say," *San Francisco Chronicle*, 10 April 2002, p. A7.

30. David Gortmaker et al., "An Unexpected Success Story: Transition to Adulthood in Youth with Chronic Physical Health Conditions,"

Journal of Research on Adolescence 3 (1993): 317–336.

31. Ibid., p. 333.

32. Harold D. Grotevant, "Adolescent Development in Family Contexts," in *Handbook of Child Psychology*, 5th ed., ed. William Damon, vol. 3: *Social, Emotional, and Personality Development*, ed. Nancy Eisenberg (New York: Wiley, 1998), 1097–1149.

33. Zarit and Eggebeen, "Parent-Child Relationships."

34. Gail Sheehy, "It's about Pure Love," *Parade Magazine*, 12 May 2002, pp. 6–8.

35. Ibid., p. 8.

36. Ibid., p. 7.

37. Valerie King, "The Legacy of Grandparent's Divorce: Consequences for Ties between Grandparents and Grandchildren," *Journal of Marriage and Family* 65 (2003): 170–183.

38. Edward J. Clarke et al., "Types of Conflicts and Tensions between Older Parents and Adult Children," *Gerontologist* 39 (1999): 261–270.

39. Stephen R. Covey, *The Seven Habits of Highly Effective Families* (New York: Golden Books, 1997).

40. Marsha Mailick Seltzer and Tamar Heller, "Families and Caregiving across the Life Course: Research Advances on the Influence of Context," *Family Relations* 46 (1997): 321–323.

41. Ibid.

42. Jan S. Greenberg et al., "The Differential Effects of Social Support on the Psychological Well Being of Aging Mothers of Adults with Mental Illness or Mental Retardation," *Family Relations* 46 (1997): 383–394.

43. Marsha Mailick Seltzer et al., "Siblings of Adults with Mental Retardation or Mental Illness: Effects on Lifestyle and Psychological Well Being," *Family Relations* 46 (1997): 395–405.

44. Harriet P. Lefley, "Synthesizing the Family Caregiving Studies: Implications for Service Planning, Social Policy, and Further Research," *Family Relations* 46 (1997), 445–450.

45. Rachel Simon, "Riding the Bus with Beth," *Reader's Digest*, September 2002, pp. 140–145.

46. Ibid, p. 145.

47. George McGovern, *Terry: My Daughter's Life and Death Struggle with Alcoholism* (New York: Villard, 1996).

48. Ibid., pp. 189–190.

49. Zarit and Eggebeen, "Parent-Child Relationships."
50. Ibid.
51. Ibid.
52. Ibid.
53. Ibid.
54. Barbara G. Unell and Jerry L. Wyckoff, *The Eight Seasons of Parenthood* (New York: Times, 2000).
55. Ibid., p. 270.
56. Lefley, "Synthesizing."
57. Ibid.

CHAPTER 13

1. Urie Bronfenbrenner, "Ecology of the Family As a Context for Human Development," *Developmental Psychology* 22 (1986): 723–742.
2. Ann C. Crouter et al., "Conditions Underlying Parents' Knowledge about Children's Daily Lives in Middle Childhood: Between- and Within-Family Comparisons," *Child Development* 70 (1999): 246–259.
3. U.S. Bureau of the Census, *Statistical Abstract of the United States: 2002,* 121st ed. (Washington, DC: U.S. Government Printing Office, 2001).
4. Graeme Russell, "Primary Caregiving Fathers," in *Parenting and Child Development in Nontraditional Families*, ed. Michael E. Lamb (Mahwah, NJ: Erlbaum, 1999), 57–81.
5. James A. Levine and Todd L. Pittinsky, *Working Fathers: New Strategies for Balancing Work and Family* (Reading, MA: Addison-Wesley, 1997).
6. Ann C. Crouter and Beth Manke, "Development of a Typology of Dual-Earner Families: A Window into Differences between and within Families in Relationships, Roles, and Activities," *Journal of Family Psychology* 11 (1997): 62–75.
7. Francine M. Deutsch, *Halving It All: How Equally Shared Parenting Works* (Cambridge, MA: Harvard University Press, 1999).
8. Penny Edgell Becker and Phyllis Moen, "Scaling Back: Dual-Earner Couples' Working Family Strategies," *Journal of Marriage and the Family* 61 (1999): 995–1007.
9. Ellen Galinsky, *Ask the Children: What America's Children Really Think about Working Parents* (New York: Morrow, 1999).
10. Reed Larson and Maryse H. Richards, *Divergent Realities: The Emotional Lives of Mothers, Fathers, and Adolescents* (New York: Basic Books, 1994).
11. Galinsky, *Ask the Children.*
12. Ibid., p. 205.
13. Adele Eskeles Gottfried, Allen W. Gottfried, and Kay Bathurst, "Maternal and Dual-Earner Employment Status and Parenting," in *Handbook of Parenting,* ed. Marc H. Bornstein, vol. 2: *Biology and Ecology of Parenting* (Mahwah, NJ: Erlbaum, 1995), 139–160.
14. Ann C. Crouter and Susan M. McHale, "The Long Arm of the Job: Influences of Parental Work on Child Rearing," in *Parenting: An Ecological Perspective*, ed. Tom Luster and Lynn Okagaki (Hillsdale, NJ: Erlbaum, 1993), 179–202.
15. Cynthia A. Stifter, Colleen M. Coulehan, and Margaret Fish, "Linking Employment to Attachment: The Mediating Effects of Maternal Separation Anxiety and Interactive Behavior," *Child Development* 64 (1993): 1451–1460.
16. Cheryl D. Hayes, John L. Palmer, and Martha J. Zaslow, eds., *Who Cares for America's Children?* (Washington, DC: National Academy Press, 1990).
17. Crouter and McHale, "The Long Arm of the Job."
18. Ann C. Crouter and Susan M. McHale, "Temporal Rhythms in Family Life: Seasonal Variation in the Relation between Parental Work and Family Processes," *Developmental Psychology* 29 (1993): 198–205.
19. Martha J. Moorehouse, "Linking Maternal Employment Patterns to Mother-Child Activities and Children's School Competence," *Developmental Psychology* 27 (1991): 295–303.
20. Maryse H. Richards and Elena Duckett, "The Relationship of Maternal Employment to Early Adolescent Daily Experience with and without Parents," *Child Development* 65 (1994): 225–236.
21. Ann C. Crouter, "Processes Linking Families and Work: Implications for Behavior and Development in Both Settings," in *Exploring Family Relationships with Other Contexts,* ed. Ross D. Parke and Sheppard G. Kellam (Hillsdale, NJ: Erlbaum, 1994), 9–28.
22. Gregory Pettit, "After-School Experience and Social Adjustment in Early Adolescence: Individual, Family, and Neighborhood Risk Factors," paper presented at the Meetings of the Society for Research in Child Development, Washington, DC, April 11, 1997.
23. Jean L. Richardson et al., "Substance Use among Eighth-Grade Students Who Take

Care of Themselves after School," *Pediatrics* 84 (1989): 556–566.

24. Galinsky, *Ask the Children.*

25. Grace G. Baruch and Rosalind C. Barnett, "Fathers' Participation in Family Work and Children's Sex Role Attitudes," *Child Development* 57 (1986): 1210–1223.

26. Joan E. Grusec, Jacqueline J. Goodnow, and Lorenzo Cohen, "Household Work and the Development of Concern for Others," *Developmental Psychology* 32 (1996): 999–1007.

27. Jacqueline J. Goodnow and Jennifer M. Bowes, *Men, Women and Household Work* (Melbourne, Australia: Oxford University Press, 1994).

28. Galinsky, *Ask the Children.*

29. Ibid.

30. Ellen Greenberger and Robin O'Neil, "Parents' Concerns about Their Child's Development: Implications for Fathers' and Mothers' Well Being and Attitudes toward Work," *Journal of Marriage and the Family* 52 (1990): 621–635; Ellen Greenberger and Robin O'Neil, "Spouse, Parent, Worker: Role Commitments and Role-Related Experiences in the Construction of Adults' Well Being," *Developmental Psychology* 29 (1993): 181–197.

31. Ellen Hock and Debra K. DeMeis, "Depression in Mothers of Infants: The Role of Maternal Employment," *Developmental Psychology* 26 (1990): 285–291.

32. Anita M. Farel, "Effects of Preferred Maternal Roles, Maternal Employment and Sociodemographic Status on School Adjustment and Competence," *Child Development* 50 (1980): 1179–1186.

33. Lois Wladis Hoffman, "Effects of Maternal Employment in the Two-Parent Family," *American Psychologist* 44 (1989): 283–292.

34. Greenberger and O'Neil, "Parents' Concerns about Their Child's Development"; Greenberger and O'Neil, "Spouse, Parent, Worker."

35. Melvin L. Kohn, *Class and Conformity: A Study in Values* (Homewood, IL: Dorsey Press, 1969).

36. Crouter, "Processes Linking Families and Work."

37. Elizabeth Menaghan and Toby Parcel, "Parental Employment and Family Life: Research in the 1980s," *Journal of Marriage and the Family* 52 (1990): 1079–1098.

38. Crouter, "Processes Linking Families and Work."

39. Ibid., p. 21.

40. Personal communication to author.

41. Ibid.

42. Galinsky, *Ask the Children.*

43. Ibid.

44. Ibid.

45. Niall Bolger et al., "The Contagion of Stress across Multiple Roles," *Journal of Marriage and the Family* 51 (1989): 175–183.

46. Rena L. Repetti and Jennifer Wood, "Effects of Daily Stress at Work on Mothers' Interactions with Preschoolers," *Journal of Family Psychology* 11 (1997): 90–108.

47. Galinsky, *Ask the Children.*

48. Ibid.

49. Ibid.

50. Ibid., p. 330

51. Deutsch, *Halving It All.*

52. Ibid., p. 232.

53. Sandra L. Hofferth, "Child Care in the United States Today," *The Future of Children,* no. 2 (1996): 41–61.

54. Carollee Howes, Deborah A. Phillips, and Marcy Whitebook, "Thresholds of Quality: Implications for the Social Development of Children in Center-Based Child Care," *Child Development* 63 (1992): 449–460.

55. Harriet B. Presser, "Child Care Supply and Demand: What Do We Really Know?" in *Child Care in the 1990s: Trends and Consequences,* ed. Alan Booth (Hillsdale, NJ: Erlbaum, 1992), 26–32.

56. Sally Provence, Audrey Naylor, and June Patterson, *The Challenge of Daycare* (New Haven, CT: Yale University Press, 1977).

57. Edward F. Zigler and Mary E. Lang, *Child Care Choices* (New York: Free Press, 1991).

58. Leslie Berger, "What Children Do When Home and Alone," *New York Times,* 11 April 2000, p. D8.

59. Alice Sterling Honig, "Choosing Child Care for Young Children," in *Handbook of Parenting,* 2nd ed., ed. Marc H. Bornstein, vol. 5, *Practical Issues in Parenting* (Mahwah, NJ: Erlbaum, 2002), 375–405.

60. Hofferth, "Child Care in the United States."

61. Michael E. Lamb, "Nonparental Child Care: Context, Quality, Correlates," in *Handbook of Child Psychology,* 5th ed., ed. William Damon, vol. 4: *Child Psychology in Practice,* ed. Irving E. Sigel and K. Ann Renninger (New York: Wiley, 1998), 73–133.

62. NICHD Early Child Care Research Network, "Early Child Care and Self-Control, Compliance, and Problem Behavior at Twenty-Four

and Thirty-Six Months," *Child Development* 69 (1998): 1145–1170.

63. Hayes, Palmer, and Zaslow, *Who Cares for America's Children?*

64. Carollee Howes, Claire E. Hamilton, and Catherine C. Matheson, "Children's Relationships with Peers: Differential Associations with Aspects of the Teacher-Child Relationship," *Child Development* 65 (1994): 253–263.

65. Carollee Howes and Claire E. Hamilton, "Children's Relationships with Child Care Teachers: Stability and Concordance with Parental Attachments," *Child Development* 63 (1992): 867–878.

66. Carollee Howes, Catherine C. Matheson, and Claire E. Hamilton, "Maternal, Teacher, and Child Care History Correlates of Children's Relationships with Peers," *Child Development* 65 (1994): 264–273.

67. Suzanne W. Helburn and Carollee Howes, "Child Care Cost and Quality," *The Future of Children* 6, no. 2 (1996): 62–82.

68. Ibid., p. 69.

69. Ibid.

70. Michael E. Lamb, "Nonparental Child Care," in *Parenting and Child Development in Nontraditional Families,* ed. Lamb, p. 39.

71. Crouter, "Processes Linking Families and Work."

72. Lamb, "Nonparental Child Care," in *Handbook of Child Psychology,* 5th ed., ed. Damon, vol. 4.

73. NICHD Early Child Care Research Network, "The Effects of Infant Child Care on Infant-Mother Attachment Security: Results of the NICHD Study of Early Child Care," *Child Development* 68 (1997): 876.

74. NICHD, "Early Child Care and Self-Control."

75. NICHD Early Child Care Research Network, "Relations between Family Predictors and Child Outcomes: Are They Weaker for Children in Child Care?" *Developmental Psychology* 34 (1998): 1119–1128.

76. NICHD Early Childhood Care Research Network, "The Relation of Child Care to Cognitive and Language Development," *Child Development* 71 (2000): 960–980.

77. Jeanne Brooks-Gunn, Wen-Jui Han, and Jane Waldfogel, "Maternal Employment and Child Cognitive Outcomes in the First Three Years of Life: The NICHD Study of Early Child Care," *Child Development* 73 (2002): 1052–1072.

78. Tiffany Field, "Quality of Infant Day-Care and Grade School Behavior and Performance," *Child Development* 62 (1991): 863–870.

79. Bengst-Erik Andersson, "Effects of Day Care on Cognitive and Socioemotional Competence of Thirteen-Year-Old Swedish Schoolchildren," *Child Development* 63 (1992): 20–36.

80. Wen-Jui Han, Jane Waldfogel, and Jeanne Brooks-Gunn, "The Effects of Early Maternal Employment on Later Cognitive and Behavioral Outcomes," *Journal of Marriage and Family* 63 (2001): 336–354.

81. Ron Haskins, "Public School Aggression among Children with Varying Day-Care Experience," *Child Development* 56 (1985): 689–703.

82. Deborah Lowe Vandell and Mary Ann Corasaniti, "The Relation between Third-Graders' After-School Care and Social, Academic, and Emotional Functioning," *Child Development* 59 (1988): 868–875.

83. Hayes, Palmer, and Zaslow, *Who Cares for America's Children?*

84. Lamb, "Nonparental Child Care," in *Parenting and Child Development in Nontraditional Families,* ed. Lamb.

85. Richardson et al., "Substance Use among Eighth-Grade Students."

86. Hoffman, "Effects of Maternal Employment."

87. Ibid.

88. Ibid.

89. Levine and Pittinsky, *Working Fathers.*

90. Gloria Norris and JoAnn Miller, *The Working Mother's Complete Handbook* (New York: Dutton, 1979).

CHAPTER 14

1. U.S. Bureau of the Census, online at www.census.gov.

2. "Women in Their 20s Create a Baby Boomlet," *San Francisco Chronicle,* 27 March 2000, p. A8.

3. E. Mavis Hetherington and W. Glenn Clingempeel, *Coping with Marital Transitions: A Family Systems Perspective,* Monographs of the Society for Research in Child Development 57, serial no. 227 (1992): 2–3.

4. Marsha Weinraub, Danielle L. Horvath, and Marcy B. Gringlas, "Single Parenthood," in *Handbook of Parenting,* 2nd ed., ed. Marc H. Bornstein, vol. 3: *Being and Becoming a Parent* (Mahwah, NJ: Erlbaum, 2002), 109–140.

5. Ibid.

6. Ibid.

7. U.S. Bureau of the Census, *Statistical Abstract: 2002,* 121st ed. (Washington, DC: U.S. Government Printing Office, 2001).

8. Marsha Weinraub and Marcy B. Gringlas, "Single Parenting," in *Handbook of Parenting,* ed. Marc H. Bornstein, vol. 3: *Status and Social Conditions of Parenting* (Mahwah, NJ: Erlbaum, 1995), 66.

9. Emma Ross, "One Parent, Twice the Trouble," *San Francisco Chronicle,* 24 January 2003, p. A8.

10. Marion Forgatch and David DeGarmo, "Extending and Testing the Social Interaction Learning Model," in *Antisocial Behavior in Children and Adolescents,* ed. John B. Reid, Gerald R. Patterson, and James Snyder (Washington, DC: American Psychological Association, 2002), 235–276.

11. Weinraub and Gringlas, "Single Parenthood," p. 66.

12. Anne K. Driscoll et al., "Nonmarital Childbearing among Adult Women," *Journal of Marriage and the Family* 61 (1999): 186.

13. Jodi R. Sandfort and Martha S. Hill, "Assisting Young, Unmarried Mothers to Become Self-Sufficient: The Effects of Different Types of Early Economic Support," *Journal of Marriage and the Family* 58 (1996): 311–326.

14. William S. Aquilino, "The Life Course of Children Born to Unmarried Mothers: Child Living Arrangements and Young Adult Outcomes," *Journal of Marriage and the Family* 58 (1996): 293–310.

15. Ibid.

16. Martha J. Zaslow et al., "Protective Factors in the Development of Preschool-Age Children of Young Mothers Receiving Welfare," in *Coping with Divorce, Single Parenting, and Remarriage,* ed. E. Mavis Hetherington (Mahwah, NJ: Erlbaum, 1999), 193–223.

17. E. Mavis Hetherington, "Should We Stay Together for the Sake of the Children?" in *Coping with Divorce, Single Parenting, and Remarriage,* ed. Hetherington, pp. 93–116.

18. Robert Fauber et al., "A Mediational Model of the Impact of Marital Conflict on Adolescent Adjustment in Intact and Divorced Families: The Role of Disrupted Parenting," *Child Development* 61 (1990): 1112–1123.

19. John H. Grych and Frank D. Fincham, "Children's Appraisals of Marital Conflict: Initial Investigation of the Cognitive-Contextual Framework," *Child Development* 64 (1993): 215–230; John H. Grych, Michael Seid, and Frank D. Fincham, "Assessing Marital Conflict from the Child's Perspective," *Child Development* 63 (1992): 558–572.

20. E. Mark Cummings and Patrick Davies, *Children and Marital Conflict: The Impact of Family Disputes and Resolution* (New York: Guilford Press, 1994).

21. Brian E. Vaughn, Jeanne H. Block, and Jack Block, "Parenting Agreement on Child Rearing during Early Childhood and the Psychological Characteristics of Adolescents," *Child Development* 59 (1988): 1020–1033.

22. Jeanne H. Block, Jack Block, and Per F. Gjerde, "The Personality of Children prior to Divorce: A Prospective Study," *Child Development* 57 (1986): 827–840.

23. E. Mavis Hetherington, "An Overview of the Virginia Longitudinal Study of Divorce and Remarriage with a Focus on Early Adolescence," *Journal of Family Psychology* 1 (1993): 39–56.

24. E. Mavis Hetherington and Kathleen A. Camara, "Families in Transition: The Process of Dissolution and Reconstruction," in *A Review of Child Development Research,* vol. 7, ed. Ross D. Parke (Chicago: University of Chicago Press, 1984), pp. 398–439.

25. Judith S. Wallerstein and Sandra Blakeslee, *Second Chances* (New York: Ticknor & Fields, 1989), 286.

26. Ibid.

27. Ibid., p. 287.

28. Judith S. Wallerstein and Joan B. Kelly, *Surviving the Breakup* (New York: Basic Books, 1980).

29. Ibid., p. 66.

30. Ibid.

31. Wallerstein and Blakeslee, *Second Chances.*

32. M. Janice Hogan, Cheryl Buehler, and Beatrice Robinson, "Single Parenting: Transitioning Alone," in *Stress and the Family*, vol. 1: *Coping with Normative Transitions,* ed. Hamilton I. McCubbin and Charles R. Figley (New York: Brunner/Mazel, 1983), 116–132.

33. Hetherington, "Overview of the Virginia Longitudinal Study."

34. Hetherington and Camara, "Families in Transition."

35. Wallerstein and Kelly, *Surviving the Breakup.*

36. Ibid.

37. Hetherington and Camara, "Families in Transition."

38. Hetherington and Camara, "Families in Transition"; Wallerstein and Kelly, *Surviving the Breakup.*

39. Ibid.

40. Ibid.

41. Wallerstein and Kelly, *Surviving the Breakup*.

42. E. Mavis Hetherington, "Coping with Family Transitions: Winners, Losers, and Survivors," *Child Development* 60 (1989): 1–14.

43. Wallerstein and Blakeslee, *Second Chances*.

44. Carol E. MacKinnon, "An Observational Investigation of Sibling Interactions in Married and Divorced Families," *Developmental Psychology* 25 (1989): 36–44.

45. Wallerstein and Blakeslee, *Second Chances*, p. 110.

46. Hetherington, "Overview of the Virginia Longitudinal Study."

47. James H. Bray and E. Mavis Hetherington, "Families in Transition: Introduction and Overview," *Journal of Family Psychology* 7 (1993): 3–8.

48. Sanford L. Braver et al., "A Longitudinal Study of Noncustodial Parents: Parents without Children," *Journal of Family Psychology* 7 (1993): 9–23.

49. Hetherington, "Overview of the Virginia Longitudinal Study."

50. Eleanor E. Maccoby et al., "Postdivorce Roles of Mothers and Fathers in the Lives of Their Children," *Journal of Family Psychology* 7 (1993): 24–38.

51. E. Mavis Hetherington and Kathleen M. Jodl, "Stepfamilies As Settings for Child Development," in *Stepfamilies: Who Benefits? Who Does Not?* ed. Alan Booth and Judy Dunn (Hillsdale, NJ: Erlbaum, 1994), pp. 55–79.

52. Hetherington, "An Overview of the Virginia Longitudinal Study."

53. Sanford M. Dornbusch et al., "Single Parents, Extended Households and the Control of Adolescents," *Child Development* 56 (1985): 326–341; Judith G. Smetana et al., "Adolescent-Parent Conflict in Married and Divorced Families," *Developmental Psychology* 27 (1991): 1000–1010.

54. Hetherington and Clingempeel, *Coping with Marital Transitions*.

55. Dornbusch et al., "Single Parents."

56. Christy M. Buchanan, Eleanor E. Maccoby, and Sanford M. Dornbusch, "Caught between Parents: Adolescents' Experience in Divorced Homes," *Child Development* 62 (1991): 1008–1029.

57. Hetherington, "Overview of the Virginia Longitudinal Study."

58. Edward R. Anderson et al., "The Dynamics of Parental Remarriage: Adolescent, Parent, and Sibling Influences," in *Coping with Divorce, Single Parenting, and Remarriage*, ed. Hetherington, pp. 295–319.

59. Ibid., p. 316.

60. Paul R. Amato and Brian Keith, "Parental Divorce and the Well Being of Children: A Meta-Analysis," *Psychological Bulletin* 110 (1991): 26–46; Dornbusch et al., "Single Parents."

61. Nicholas Zill, Donna Ruane Morrison, and Mary Jo Coiro, "Long-Term Effects of Parental Divorce on Parent-Child Relationships, Adjustment, and Achievement in Young Adulthood," *Journal of Family Psychology* 7 (1993): 91–103.

62. Hetherington, "Should We Stay Together?"

63. Ibid., p. 101.

64. Judith S. Wallerstein, Julia M. Lewis, and Sandra Blakeslee, *The Unexpected Legacy of Divorce* (New York: Hyperion, 2000).

65. Hetherington, "Should We Stay Together?" p. 115.

66. Sara McLanahan and Julien Teitler, "The Consequence of Father Absence," in *Parenting and Child Development in Nontraditional Families*, ed. Michael E. Lamb (Mahwah, NJ: Erlbaum, 1999), 83–102.

67. Paul R. Amato, "More Than Money? Men's Contributions to Their Children's Lives," in *Men in Families: When Do They Get Involved? What Difference Does It Make?* ed. Alan Booth and Ann C. Crouter (Mahwah, NJ: Erlbaum, 1998), 241–278.

68. Ibid., p. 244.

69. Ibid., pp. 271–272.

70. Ibid., p. 257.

71. James A. Levine with Edward W. Pitt, *New Expectations: Community Strategies for Responsible Fatherhood* (New York: Families and Work Institute, 1995).

72. Ibid., p. 41.

73. Ibid., p. 108.

74. Monica McGoldrick and Betty Carter, "Forming a Remarried Family," in *The Changing Family Life Cycle,* 2nd ed., ed. Betty Carter and Monica McGoldrick (New York: Gardner Press, 1988), 399–429.

75. Wallerstein and Blakeslee, *Second Chances*.

76. Hetherington and Clingempeel, "Coping with Marital Transitions."

77. Fitzhugh Dodson, *How to Discipline with Love* (New York: Rawson Associates, 1977).

78. Hetherington and Jodl, "Stepfamilies As Settings for Child Development."

79. W. Glenn Clingempeel and Sion Segal, "Step-parent-Stepchild Relationships and the Psychological Adjustment of Children in Stepmother and Stepfather Families," *Child Development* 57 (1986): 474–484.

80. Hetherington and Jodl, "Stepfamilies As Settings for Child Development."

81. Ibid.

82. Hetherington, "Overview of the Virginia Longitudinal Study."

83. Hetherington and Clingempeel, "Coping with Marital Transitions."

84. Hetherington and Jodl, "Stepfamilies As Settings for Child Development."

85. Hetherington and Clingempeel, "Coping with Marital Transitions."

86. Hetherington and Jodl, "Stepfamilies As Settings for Child Development."

87. Ibid.

88. Ibid.

89. Lynn White, "Stepfamilies over the Life Course: Social Support," in *Stepfamilies,* ed. Booth and Dunn, pp. 109–137.

90. Emily Visher, "The Stepping Ahead Program," in *Stepfamilies Stepping Ahead,* ed. Mala Burt (Baltimore: Stepfamilies Press, 1989), 57–89.

91. James H. Bray and John Kelly, *Stepfamilies: Love, Marriage, and Parenting in the First Decade* (New York: Broadway Books, 1998).

92. Ibid., p. 16.

93. Ibid., p. 265.

94. Charlotte J. Patterson and Raymond W. Chan, "Families Headed by Lesbian and Gay Parents," in *Parenting and Child Development in Nontraditional Families,* ed. Lamb, pp. 191–219.

95. Ibid.

96. Paul R. Amato, "The Implications of Research Findings on Children in Stepfamilies," in *Stepfamilies,* ed. Booth and Dunn, pp. 81–87.

97. Hetherington, "Should We Stay Together for the Sake of the Children?"

98. Shelli Avenevoli, Frances M. Sessa, and Laurence Steinberg, "Family Structure, Parenting Practices, and Adolescent Adjustment: An Ecological Examination," in *Coping with Divorce, Single Parenting, and Remarriage,* pp. 65–90; Kirby Deater-Deckard and Judy Dunn, "Multiple Risks and Adjustment in Young Children Growing up in Different Settings," in *Coping with Divorce, Single Parenting, and Remarriage,* pp. 47–64.

CHAPTER 15

1. Jay Belsky, "Etiology of Child Maltreatment: A Developmental-Ecological Analysis," *Psychological Bulletin* 114 (1993): 413–434.

2. Kathleen A. Kendall-Tackett, Linda Meyer Williams, and David Finkelhor, "Impact of Sex Abuse on Children: A Review and Synthesis of Recent Empirical Studies," *Psychological Bulletin* 113 (1993): 164–180.

3. Belsky, "Etiology of Child Maltreatment," p. 413.

4. Robert E. Emery and Lisa Laumann-Billings, "An Overview of the Nature, Causes, and Consequences of Abusive Family Relationships: Toward Differentiating Maltreatment and Violence," *American Psychologist* 53 (1998): 121–135.

5. Ibid.

6. Ibid.

7. Dante Cicchetti and Michael Lynch, "Toward an Ecological/Transactional Model of Community Violence and Child Maltreatment: Consequences for Child Development," *Psychiatry* 56 (1993): 96–118.

8. Fred A. Rogosch et al., "Parenting Dysfunction in Child Maltreatment," in *Handbook of Parenting,* ed. Marc H. Bornstein, vol. 4: *Applied and Practical Parenting* (Mahwah, NJ: Erlbaum, 1995), 127–159.

9. Glenn D. Wolfner and Richard J. Gelles, "A Profile of Violence toward Children: A National Study," *Child Abuse and Neglect* 17 (1993): 199–214.

10. David Finkelhor and Jennifer Dziuba-Leatherman, "Victimization of Children," *American Psychologist* 49 (1994): 173–183.

11. Penelope K. Trickett, Catherine McBride-Chang, and Frank W. Putnam, "The Classroom Performance and Behavior of Sexually Abused Females," *Development and Psychopathology* 6 (1994): 183–194.

12. Patricia J. Mrazek, "Maltreatment and Infant Development," in *Handbook of Infant Development,* ed. Charles H. Zeanah, Jr. (New York: Guilford Press, 1993), 159–170.

13. Belsky, "Etiology of Child Maltreatment."

14. David A. Wolfe, "The Role of Intervention and Treatment Services in the Prevention of Child Abuse and Neglect," in *Protecting Children from Abuse and Neglect,* ed. Gary B. Melton and Frank D. Barry (New York: Guilford Press, 1994), 224–303.

15. Ibid.

16. Ibid.

17. Ibid.

18. John W. Fantuzzo and Wanda K. Mohr, "Prevalence and Effects of Child Exposure to Domestic Violence," *The Future of Children* 9, no. 3 (1999): 21–32.

19. Kathleen J. Sternberg and Michael E. Lamb, "Violent Families," in *Parenting and Child Development in Nontraditional Families,* ed. Michael E. Lamb (Mahwah, NJ: Erlbaum, 1999), 305–325.

20. Fantuzzo and Mohr, "Prevalence and Effects of Child Exposure to Domestic Violence."

21. Lucy Salcido Carter, Lois A. Weithorn, and Richard E. Behrman, "Domestic Violence and Children: Analysis and Recommendations," *The Future of Children* 9, no. 3 (1999): 4–20.

22. Sternberg and Lamb, "Violent Families."

23. Fantuzzo and Mohr, "Prevalence and Effects of Child Exposure to Domestic Violence."

24. Betsy McAlister Groves, "Mental Health Services for Children Who Witness Domestic Violence," *The Future of Children* 9, no. 3 (1999): 122–133.

25. Bruce D. Perry, "Incubated in Terror: Neurodevelopmental Factors in the 'Cycle of Violence,'" in *Children in a Violent Society,* ed. Joy D. Osofsky (New York: Guilford, 1997), 124–149.

26. Fantuzzo and Mohr, "Prevalence and Effects of Child Exposure to Domestic Violence."

27. Betsy McAlister Groves and Barry Zuckerman, "Interventions with Parents and Caregivers of Children Who Are Exposed to Violence," in *Children in a Violent Society,* ed. Osofsky, pp. 183–201.

28. Ibid.

29. David A. Wolfe and Peter G. Jaffe, "Emerging Strategies in the Prevention of Domestic Violence," *The Future of Children* 9, no. 3 (1999): 133–144.

30. Ibid., p. 141.

31. Sally Zierler, "Studies Confirm Long-Term Consequences of Childhood Sexual Abuse," *Brown University Child and Adolescent Behavior Newsletter* 8 (November 1992): 3.

32. Ibid.

33. Diana E. H. Russell, "The Incidence and Prevalence of Intrafamilial and Extrafamilial Sexual Abuse of Female Children," in *Handbook on Sexual Abuse of Children,* ed. Leonore E. Auerbach Walker (New York: Springer, 1988), 19–36.

34. Karin C. Meiselman, *Resolving the Trauma of Incest* (San Francisco: Jossey-Bass, 1990).

35. Kendall-Tackett, Williams, and Finkelhor, "Impact of Sex Abuse on Children."

36. Ibid.

37. Ibid.

38. David Finkelhor and Angela Browne, "Assessing the Long-Term Impact of Child Sexual Abuse: A Review and Conceptualization," in *Handbook on Sexual Abuse of Children,* ed. Walker, p. 62.

39. Ibid., pp. 62–63.

40. Kendall-Tackett, Williams, and Finkelhor, "Impact of Sex Abuse on Children."

41. Ibid.

42. Trickett, McBride-Chang, and Putnam, "Classroom Performance and Behavior of Sexually Abused Females."

43. Leonore E. A. Walker and Mary Ann Bolkovatz, "Play Therapy with Children Who Have Experienced Sexual Assault," in *Handbook on Sexual Abuse of Children,* ed. Walker, pp. 249–269.

44. Robert E. Emery, "Family Violence," *American Psychologist* 44 (1989): 321–328.

45. Richard J. Gelles, "Physical Violence, Child Abuse, and Child Homicide: A Continuum of Violence or Distinct Behaviors?" *Human Nature* 2 (1991): 59–72.

46. Wolfner and Gelles, "Profile of Violence toward Children."

47. Ibid.

48. Emery and Laumann-Billings, "Overview of the Nature, Causes, and Consequences of Abusive Family Relationships."

49. David A. Hamburg, *Today's Children* (New York: Times Books, 1992).

50. Wolfner and Gelles, "Profile of Violence toward Children."

51. Rogosch et al., "Parenting Dysfunction in Child Maltreatment."

52. Gail S. Goodman, Robert E. Emery, and Jeffrey J. Haugaard, "Developmental Psychology and Law: Divorce, Child Maltreatment, Foster Care, and Adoption," in *Handbook of Child Psychology,* 5th ed., ed. William Damon, vol. 4: *Child Psychology in Practice,* ed. Irving E. Sigel and K. Ann Renninger (New York: Wiley, 1998), 775–874.

53. Rogosch et al., "Parenting Dysfunction in Child Maltreatment."

54. Belsky, "Etiology of Child Maltreatment."

55. Goodman, Emery, and Haugaard, "Developmental Psychology and Law."

56. Wolfner and Gelles, "Profile of Violence toward Children."

57. Cicchetti and Lynch, "Toward an Ecological/Transactional Model."

58. Emery, "Family Violence."

59. Dante Cicchetti et al., "Resilience in Maltreated Children: Processes Leading to Adaptive Outcome," *Development and Psychopathology* 5 (1993): 629–647.

60. Richard J. Gelles, "Abandon Reunification Goal for Abusive Families and Replace with Child Protection," *Brown University Child and Adolescent Behavior Newsletter* 8 (June 1992): 1

61. Diana J. English, "The Extent and Consequences of Child Maltreatment," *The Future of Children* 8, no. 1 (1998): 39–53.

62. Ibid.

63. Howard J. Dubowitz, "The Families of Neglected Children," in *Parenting and Child Development in Nontraditional Families,* ed. Lamb, pp. 327–345.

64. Ibid.

65. Ibid.

66. Douglas J. Besharov et al., "Four Commentaries: How We Can Better Protect Children from Abuse and Neglect," *The Future of Children* 8, no. 1 (1998): 120–132.

67. Richard Wexler, "Beware the Pitfalls of Foster Care," *New York Times,* 21 January 1996.

68. Besharov, "Four Commentaries."

69. Ibid.

70. Goodman, Emery, and Haugaard, "Developmental Psychology and Law."

71. Rogosch et al., "Parenting Dysfunction in Child Maltreatment."

72. John E. Richters and Pedro Martinez, "The NIMH Community Violence Project: I. Children As Victims of and Witnesses to Violence," *Psychiatry* 56 (1993): 7–21.

73. Pedro Martinez and John E. Richters, "The NIMH Community Violence Project: II. Children's Distress Symptoms Associated with Violence Exposure," *Psychiatry* 56 (1993): 22–35.

74. John E. Richters and Pedro Martinez, "Violent Communities, Family Choices, and Children's Choices: An Algorithm for Improving the Odds," *Development and Psychopathology* 5 (1993): 609–627.

75. Ibid., pp. 622–623.

76. Ibid.

77. Lenore Terr, *Too Scared to Cry* (New York: Harper & Row, 1990).

78. James Garbarino et al., *Children in Danger* (San Francisco: Jossey-Bass, 1992).

79. Peter A. Wyman et al., "The Role of Children's Future Expectations in Self System Functioning and Adjustment to Life Stress: A Prospective Study of Urban At-Risk Children," *Development and Psychopathology* 5 (1993): 649–661.

80. Garbarino et al., *Children in Danger,* p. 110.

81. Ibid.

82. Ibid.

83. Terr, *Too Scared to Cry.*

84. Joshunda Sanders, "What to Tell Kids about War," *San Francisco Chronicle,* 19 March 2003, p. A21; www.savethechildren.org; www.nmha.org/reassurance/anniversary.

85. Alexandra Okun, Jeffrey G. Parker, and Alytia A. Levendosky, "Distinct and Interactive Contributions of Physical Abuse, Socioeconomic Disadvantage, and Negative Life Events to Children's Social, Cognitive and Affective Adjustment," *Development and Psychopathology* 6 (1994): 77–98.

86. William C. Bell, "Tough Lessons in Child Welfare Reform," *New York Times,* 21 January 2003, p. A23.

87. Ibid.

88. Perry, "Incubated in Terror," p. 144.

89. Katherine Kaufer Christoffel, "Firearm Injuries Affecting United States Children and Adolescents," in *Children in a Violent Society,* pp. 42–71.

90. U.S. Bureau of the Census, *Statistical Abstract of the United States: 1998,* 118th ed. (Washington, DC: U.S. Government Printing Office, 1998).

91. John P. Murray, "Media Violence and Youth," in *Children in a Violent Society,* ed. Osofsky, pp. 72–96.

92. Ibid.

93. Steven J. Wolin and Sybil Wolin, *The Resilient Self* (New York: Villard Books, 1993).

94. Ibid, pp. 5–6.

95. Grace Hechinger, *How to Raise a Street-Smart Child* (New York: Ballantine Books, 1984).

EPILOGUE

1. Amy Arner Sgarro, "A Surgeon and Her Community," *Vassar Quarterly,* Spring 1993, pp. 10–13.

2. Ibid, p. 13.

CREDITS

Text Credits

Table 1-2, Excerpt from Sylvia Ann Hewlett and Cornell West, *The War Against Parents.* Copyright © 1998 by Sylvia Ann Hewlett and Cornell West. Reprinted by permission of Houghton Mifflin Company. All rights reserved. **Figure 1-2,** From Marque-Lusia Miringoff, "The Social Health of the Nation," *Vassar,* Winter, 2001, p. 25. **Figure 1-3,** From Rudolf Dreikurs, M.D., and Vicki Soltz, R.N., *Children: The Challenge.* Copyright © 1964 by Rudolf Dreikurs, M.D. Used by permission of Dutton, a division of Penguin Group (USA) Inc. **Figure 2-1,** From Gilbert Gottlieb, *Individual Development and Evolution: The Genesis of Novel Behavior.* New York: Oxford University Press, 1992. **Table 3-1,** From William Damon, *Handbook of Child Psychology,* Fifth Edition, Vol. 4. Used by permission of John Wiley & Sons, Inc. **Table 3-3,** From Jeanne Brooke-Gunn and Greg J. Duncan, "The Effects of Poverty on Children," *The Future of Children,* 7 (2) (1997), pp. 58–59. Reprinted with the permission of the David and Lucile Packard Foundation. **Figure 10-1,** From "A Two-Factor Theory of Black Identity," *Children's Ethnic Socialization, Vol. 81.* **Figure 11-1,** From Cathy Schoen et al., *The Commonwealth Fund Survey of the Health of Adolescent Girls.* New York: The Commonwealth Fund, 1997, p. 25. **Figure 12-1 and Table 12-1,** From Vern L. Bengston, "Beyond the Nuclear Family: the Increasing Importance of Multigenerational Bonds," *Journal of Marriage and Family,* 63. Copyright © 2001 by the National Council on Family Relations, 3989 Central Ave. NE, Suite 550, Minneapolis, MN 55421. Reprinted by permission. **Figure 13-1,** From Ellen Galinsky, *Ask the Children.* Copyright ©1999 by Ellen Galinsky. Reprinted by permission of HarperCollins Publishers, Inc. **Figure 14-1,** From James Levine with Edward W. Pitt, *New Expectations: Community Strategies for Responsible Fatherhood.* New York: Families and Work Institute, 1995, p. 41. Reprinted by permission of the Families and Work Institute, www.familiesandwork.org.

Photo Credits

Page 15, © Ariel Skelley/CORBIS. Page 60, © Elizabeth Crews. Page 73, © Jose Carrillo/PhotoEdit. Page 114, © Joel Gordon. Page 124, © Michael Newman/PhotoEdit. Page 127, © Elizabeth Crews/Stock, Boston. Page 138, © Ulrike Welsch. Page 145, © Bob Daemmrich/The Image Works. Page 165, © Elizabeth Crews. Page 209, © Frank Siteman/Jeroboam Inc. Page 227, © Robert Brenner/PhotoEdit/PictureQuest. Page 260, © Robert Brenner/PhotoEdit. Page 295, © BAUMGARTNER OLIVIA/CORBIS SYGMA. Page 315, © Paul Barton/CORBIS. Page 334, © Elizabeth Crews. Page 363, © John Henley/CORBIS. Page 370, © Richard Hutchings /PhotoEdit. Page 393, © Lawrence Migdale/Photo Researchers, Inc. Page 398, © Nancy Sheehan/PhotoEdit. Page 413, © Joel Gordon 1994. Page 417, © Howard Grey/Getty Images. Page 459, © Catherine Ursillo/Photo Researchers, Inc. Page 471, © Okoniewski/The Image Works.

INDEX